MADELEINE CLARK WALLACE LIBRARY

WHEATON   COLLEGE

NORTON, MASSACHUSETTS

Ruth Stevens Berry
W 1925
Book Fund

Genesis as Dialogue

Genesis as Dialogue

A LITERARY,
HISTORICAL, &
THEOLOGICAL
COMMENTARY

Thomas L. Brodie

OXFORD
UNIVERSITY PRESS

2001

OXFORD
UNIVERSITY PRESS

Oxford   New York
Athens   Auckland   Bangkok   Bogotá   Buenos Aires   Cape Town
Chennai   Dar es Salaam   Delhi   Florence   Hong Kong   Istanbul   Karachi
Kolkata   Kuala Lumpur   Madrid   Melbourne   Mexico City   Mumbai   Nairobi
Paris   São Paulo   Shanghai   Singapore   Taipei   Tokyo   Toronto   Warsaw

and associated companies in
Berlin   Ibadan

Copyright © 2001 by Thomas L. Brodie

Published by Oxford University Press, Inc.
198 Madison Avenue, New York, New York 10016

Oxford is a registered trademark of Oxford University Press

All rights reserved. No part of this publication may be reproduced,
stored in a retrieval system, or transmitted, in any form or by any means,
electronic, mechanical, photocopying, recording, or otherwise,
without the prior permission of Oxford University Press.

Library of Congress Cataloging-in-Publication Data
Brodie, Thomas L.
Genesis as dialogue : a literary, historical, and theological commentary /
Thomas L. Brodie.
    p.   cm.
Includes bibliographical references and index.
ISBN 0-19-513836-8
1. Bible. O.T. Genesis—Commentaries.   I. Title.
BS1235.3 .B74 2001
222'.1107—dc21   00-036326

9 8 7 6 5 4 3 2 1

Printed in the United States of America
on acid-free paper

To the memory of
Theresa Gerard Zungu O.P., 1970–1995
who loved Genesis
Nkosi Sikelele iAfrika

and to the Clare hurlers
passion with a clear head
days better than dreams
Conocaimir an lá

It is not the literal past that rules us. . . . It is images of the past. These are often as highly structured and selective as myths. Images and symbolic constructs of the past are imprinted, almost in the manner of genetic information, on our sensibility. . . . A society requires antecedents. Where these are not naturally at hand, where a community is new or reassembled after a long interval of dispersal or subjection, a necessary past tense to the grammar of being is created by intellectual and emotional fiat.

George Steiner (1971, 13)

For the communities of faith that have valued the book of Genesis, it is finally a theological statement. The world and Israel belong to God, exist because of God's intention, and are called to live towards God's hope. Every scientific, historical, or literary analysis that misses this claim misunderstands the text.

Walter Brueggemann (1985, 338)

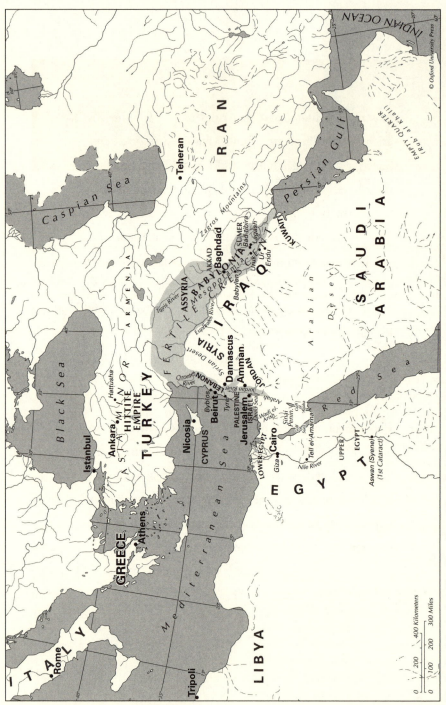

The lands of the Ancient Near East. From *The Oxford History of the Biblical World*, ed. Michael Coogan, copyright 1999 by Oxford University Press, Inc. Used by permission.

During the days of the vast Persian Empire (ca. 550–330 BCE)—when far-flung Greeks were accomplishing a luminous cultural revolution; when, through the interwoven power of Persians and Greeks, the known world from the Indus to Italy was united as never before; and when writing, already more than two thousand years old, was moving beyond epic poetry toward new sophisticated forms, especially toward Greek-language prose historiography—a group of Judeans assembled in one place, probably Jerusalem or Babylon, and took charge of the writing of their own history. This history echoed centuries, perhaps even millennia, but its focus was specific—Judea, especially Jerusalem. The resulting multivolume account—from creation to the fall of Jerusalem (Genesis-Kings, "the Primary History," spanning over 3,500 years)—did not just provide a history for the people of Judea; it transformed history-writing and became a landmark of world literature. Writing had reached a new level.

Such is one of this book's conclusions.

Other writers did likewise. Herodotus and Thucydides also wrote histories, and of comparable length. And other cities, not just Jerusalem, built other sweeping foundational narratives. Athens, by employing a well-established author, Hellanicus, assured the composing of its own ancient history. So in time did Babylon and Egypt—both relying on priest-writers. And so eventually did Rome.

But the Jerusalem-oriented history was far more than history, more than a variation on the Greeks. It had a unique resonance. Adapting Mesopotamian tradition, it hearkened all the way back to creation. And, having absorbed many of the prophets, it contained a great inner depth, a sense of reality as echoing. The center of Jerusalem was Zion, Mount Zion; and behind Zion (Sion) lay Sinai, Mount Sinai—one place of divine presence behind the other. The Jerusalem-oriented history was so constructed that Mount Sinai's incomparable mystique—God's great power and Moses' peerless leadership (Exodus-Deuteronomy)—hovered over the portrayal of Mount Zion, over the story of Jerusalem (Samuel-Kings). And between the two stories of Sinai and Zion, lending further perspective to both, was a centuries-long history of conquest, failure, and judgment (Joshua-Judges). Jerusalem, therefore, might look drab on a given day, might suffer misery, but it was no vacuous city. Filtered through it was an extraordinary presence which, whatever the vicissitudes of history, was ultimately liberating and ennobling.

The flagship for this multivolume historiography was the book of Genesis. Genesis is one of the world's great writings, but in modern times it has been fragmented and trivialized—often reduced to a badly edited collection of second-rate historical sources. The fragmentation is double—inside and outside: it has been separated within itself (broken into parts, into hypothetical sources); and, to a large extent, it has been separated from outside literature. Thus, it has been both maimed and exiled.

The fragmenting process knows much, but it also misses much, and so becomes destructive. It is like a wonderfully clever genderless visitor from Pluto, which, descending to Earth through a morning mist, sees a brother and sister walking together across the fields to school. Endowed with great perception, it quickly catalogues the differences between the two, deduces that they belong to different planets—one to Venus, the other to Mars—and with great effort and care dispatches them on separate rockets to their planets of origin.

Aspects of this analogy are overdrawn, but its essence—the destructive separating of things from one another and from their primary context—is depressingly true. The two creation texts (Genesis 1–2) are indeed very different, but in the context of ancient literature they are also deeply complementary: together they represent the two basic literary forms for depicting creation (Westermann, I, 22). As such, and in their content, these creation narratives form a unity. But much modern biblical criticism was virtually founded on the separating of these two texts (Genesis 1–2), and biblical studies as a whole became contaminated by the example of that foundational barbarism. Here the present writer also has been guilty.

"Barbarism" is used here in a precise sense. Though plausibly reasoned and nobly intended, the fragmenting of Genesis entailed the de facto destruction of a great work of art.

However, the barbaric moment may be seen as a necessary phase. Ultimately, modern research is not negative. On the contrary, it is now having a very positive effect. It has led, in recent years, to two major streams of development, and these have begun to bridge the two forms of fragmentation.

The first stream concerns the alleged fragmentation within—inside Genesis. Genesis may indeed appear confused or broken—it has many variations—but there has been an increasing appreciation that the variations have a positive role: they are part of Genesis's literary art, and so the text begins to emerge as a unity (e.g., Fokkelman, 1975; Alter, 1981; Sternberg, 1985; Brichto, 1998).

The second stream concerns the alleged fragmentation outside—the separation from other writings. Genesis is being connected increasingly with several major bodies of literature, especially with antiquarian historiography, epic, and prophecy. Antiquarian historiography (including Greek historiography; van Seters, 1992) accounts partly for Genesis's literary form or genre. Epic (mostly

Mesopotamian) provides much of the plot of Genesis 1–9. And Israelite prophecy accounts for further aspects of the Pentateuch, especially of Genesis (Schmid, 1976; van Seters, 1992, 1994). There is the possibility, therefore, as never before in modern times, of restoring Genesis both to its inner unity and to its place in world literature.

However, the two streams tend to operate in isolation. Those bridging the inner gap, tracing Genesis's artistry and unity, generally follow a method that is primarily literary. Those bridging the outer gap, linking Genesis with other literatures, use a method that is primarily historical. The two methodologies—literary and historical—often remain apart.

This volume brings the streams together. While avoiding undue historical speculation and undue literary theorizing, it seeks to synthesize what is best in both methods.

In making this synthesis, it is necessary to take account of a further new development. In the 1980s and especially in the 1990s, Genesis suddenly emerged as an arresting psychodrama. There was a flood of books on the psychological aspect, as well as a television series. This awareness of Genesis's psychological dimension is a positive development, provided the book is not thereby reduced to psychology—as it was previously reduced to history, and as it has sometimes been reduced to clever literary technique. Genesis is not small. It is indeed a form of history; and it is psychological; and it also uses literary technique. But it is much more.

Based on such developments, this study proposes three main ideas.

First, regarding content: Genesis is primarily about human existence. Among Genesis's three main levels of interest—concerning individuals, groups, and humans in general—it is the third level, regarding human existence in general, which is primary and which governs the overall work. Thus, Genesis is indeed a form of history; it serves as prologue to the Primary History and includes the literary form of antiquarian historiography. But it is more than history; under the mantle of antiquarian historiography it synthesizes several literary genres. Genesis is didactic and encyclopedic. Thus, it is concerned not only with antiquarian history but even more so with human existence. The Jacob narrative, for instance, is not an antiquarian curiosity. While full of historical echoes, it is primarily a sophisticated portrayal of the progress and pitfalls of human life. Jacob is indeed the founder of Israel, the father of the twelve, but he is also, at one level, an open-ended model for all humans. His is a primordial biography—the first in the Bible. And in that biography the sense of life is not negative. At the end, when, against all odds, the aged Jacob comes before the great Pharaoh, the patriarch's ironic words effectively summarize life—short and difficult, but surrounded by blessing (47:7–10).

Second, regarding structure: Genesis consists of twenty-six diptychs. Building on older insights that several Genesis texts occur in pairs and that Genesis is somehow binary or dialogical, this study makes a basic observation: The entire book is composed of diptychs—accounts which, like some paintings, consist of two parts or panels. There are, for instance, two panels of creation (1:1–2:24), two of primordial sin (2:25–4:16), two genealogies (4:17–chap. 5), two parts to the flood story (6:1–9:1:17), two complementary histories about Noah's sons (9:18–chap. 10), and so on—to a total of twenty-six diptychs (six in chaps. 1–11, seven in the Abraham story, six in the initial Jacob story, and seven in the Joseph story). Genesis then falls into fifty-two panels—a refinement of the medieval division into fifty chapters. The relationships between the matching panels vary. In some diptychs, the unity between the two panels is easy to see. Others require patience. Generally, they tend to go from easy to more difficult.

The overall purpose of these diverse variations within diptychs is artistic—to communicate at some level a sense of the depth of things. The two-part account of creation (Gen. 1:1–2:24), for instance, looks strained, even contradictory; as history it does not flow, but as literary art, art that is related to theology, it is a sophisticated unity.

This idea of a pervasive diptych structure allows for further detailed structures—such as those indicated by Fokkelman (1975)—but it places these other structures within the context of a scheme that is broader and in many ways simpler.

Detecting the division into diptychs is as important as recognizing how a play is divided into various acts and scenes. By identifying the unit to be interpreted, it provides an initial clue to interpretation. The medieval division into fifty chapters, while generally useful, is sometimes misleading.

In modern studies, the diptych arrangement has long been recognized in part; in particular, it has long been seen that the creation account is somehow twofold. But the partial nature of the recognition has caused confusion: along with other factors, it has contributed to the idea that Genesis is somehow based on a combining of at least two sources. Full recognition of the diptych structure helps to lessen this confusion, and so helps to clear the air for discussing the question of Genesis's sources.

Third, regarding sources: Genesis uses world literature. This study builds on an idea that has been developing slowly for more than a century: many of Genesis's sources, far from being lost—as was first presumed (from Astruc, 1753, to Wellhausen, 1876)—still exist, and, through patient comparative work, these sources can be identified and verified.

What emerges is that Genesis's status in world literature is no accident; it was built on such literature. The author of Genesis used a powerful formula: in shaping the Jerusalem-oriented history, he not only drew partly on Greek historiography but also enriched it with two classic ingredients—the world's greatest epic poetry; and Israel's greatest prophetic writings, including Ezekiel, Jeremiah, and Isaiah. From these, there was much to learn. Homer, too, had been didactic and encyclopedic (Havelock, 1963, 61–86).

Such classic ingredients of course did not remain in their original form. Poetry was rendered into prose. And the epics were refashioned in light of prophecy; they were Israelitized, radically. The governing spirit of Genesis is not Mesopotamian or Greek. It is a deepened understanding of Ezekiel, Jeremiah, and Isaiah.

Genesis, therefore, is not something isolated or adrift. It is a synthesis, firmly rooted in the world's leading literature, especially in historiography, epic, and prophecy.

As the connection of Genesis with known writings becomes clearer, the theory of hypothetical sources (J, E, D, and P) becomes increasingly unnecessary.

These three ideas—focus on human existence; binary/diptych structures; and the combining of existing documents (epic and prophecy)—are proposed here for a larger purpose, namely to clear the ground for commenting on the full text in its final form, the only form about which one may speak with assurance.

The commentary is orientational. It does not attempt to replace the detail of commentaries by authors such as Westermann, Wenham, and Sarna. Rather, it seeks, amid the mass of detail that is supplied both by these useful commentaries and by other studies and methods, to give an overall sense of direction.

Undue detail can obscure what is essential. So can undue preoccupation with sources; and for that reason the question of sources is largely relegated to the appendices. Ultimately, the issue of sources is secondary.

Formerly, it seemed otherwise.

When I first taught Genesis, in Tunapuna, at the regional seminary in Trinidad and Tobago in 1968, the emphasis was on form criticism and history, including sacred history (*Heilsgeschichte*). Since the nineteenth century, variations in the text had led to the widespread theory that the Pentateuch was composed of four main sources, and each of these sources seemed to open a path to the past. By following those paths one came to great historical events and traditions—events and traditions which were full of meaning. The teaching was not always easy—the paths sometimes appeared obscure, the journey backward uncertain—but the presuppositions seemed reasonable and the goal worthwhile. We all learned.

By 1976, however, when I began teaching in the United States, the foundations of Pentateuchal studies were moving. The movement would prove to be many-sided. It particularly concerned history, sources, and literary unity.

As regards history, Thompson (1974) and van Seters (1975) had undermined prevailing ideas about the historicity of the Genesis narratives. The origin of Genesis seemed to shift—away from the dusty villages of the second millennium and toward the time of the exile (587 BCE).

As regards sources, two studies converged: Rendtorff (1977) undermined many of the arguments for the theory of four sources; and Schmid (1976) indicated that part of the Pentateuch depends on texts from the prophets. The result, in principle, was a further shift away from the idea of four hypothetical sources and toward a relationship with known documents—the prophetic writings. This shift toward known documents was not altogether new. Already in the nineteenth century, Genesis had begun to be linked with surviving epics.

As regards literary unity, the shift was even greater. In the 1970s, a significant number of biblical scholars began to conclude that history and sources are not the primary issues. Rather, the biblical books—regardless of origin—have a certain literary unity, and the first task of the interpreter is to take that unity seriously. In 1975, Fokkelman's analysis of sample texts indicated that Genesis is in fact a unity, and in the same year Chouraqui added his unique voice. After years of painstaking translation, Chouraqui expressed his suspicion that, like other biblical texts, Genesis "was 'constructed' with the same exactness, the same precision, as is used today in assembling the elements of a computer or a rocket" (1975, 455). Later years, especially the 1990s, would produce further awareness of the writing genius behind Genesis. Rosenberg (1996, 1–22), for instance, despite gratuitous claims about Genesis's origin, communicated a powerful sense of the book's nature: it is masterful literary art, a model of writing.

But—returning to the 1970s—background still seemed indispensable. If Genesis could not be traced reliably to events, traditions, and hypothetical sources, then perhaps, as Schmid had indicated, it could be traced to actual prophetic writings. Accordingly, I wrote an article showing the similarities, as I saw them, between the return of Israel as described in Jeremiah 30–31 and the return of Jacob/Israel as narrated in Genesis 32–33. My thesis: the Genesis account depends on the poetry of Jeremiah; the Jacob story, to some degree, is historicized prophecy. Before submitting the article I sent it for criticism to Brevard Childs. He was sympathetic to the similarities, but added a telling question: How do you know the direction of dependence? Did Genesis use Jeremiah—or did Jeremiah use Genesis?

I rewrote the arguments and the article was published (*JSOT*, 1981), but the question of the direction of dependence seemed to burden the presentation of the similarities; and if I kept trying to publish in Pentateuchal studies, that burden would remain. It seemed better therefore while still teaching Old Testament, to concentrate on publishing in New Testament, particularly concerning the similarities between the Old Testament and the New (Brodie, 1979–1999). There at least, there would be no problem about the direction of dependence.

As the years passed, the literary emphasis, despite obscurantist growing pains, gradually gathered credibility. Whether in teaching the Old Testament or writing about the New, it slowly became clear to me that the primary path to meaning, and even to history and social background, is the finished text. The finished text is the number one artifact. Consequently, when the time came for publishing on the Gospel of John, the emphasis fell on the Gospel's final form (Brodie, 1993), and the question of background and sources took a secondary role (Brodie, 1993a). The conclusion was clear: the literary approach works; the question of sources does not have to dominate the interpretation of the text. In principle, the way was open for the return to writing on Genesis. The discussion of sources, whatever its importance, could be reserved for appendices.

In practice, the impetus to write came from other factors, partly from work circumstances in South Africa, partly from sheer love of the book—an old friend and number one choice if abandoned on a desert island—and partly from a conviction, gained over many years, that Genesis is composed of twofold scenes, diptychs. The investigation of the diptych phenomenon led to other questions, and increasingly Chouraqui's suspicion has come to be vindicated: Genesis was indeed composed with extraordinary complexity and precision.

ACKNOWLEDGMENTS

To acknowledge all that has helped me to understand Genesis is like trying to acknowledge all that has ever been done for me. The stories of Genesis seemed to come with life itself, and as I write I have in front of me the battered *Illustrated Bible History* ("Schuster") that my father used in our primary school and for our confirmation. Even now its simple illustrations seem like icons. They shaped the world and planted seeds of Genesis in our souls.

Those seeds were nurtured by later teachers in Ireland, Rome, and Jerusalem, and they were particularly developed by decades of students—in the West Indies, Florida, Berkeley, St. Louis, and Kwa-Zulu Natal—who accompanied me on repeated journeys through the soul-searching landscapes of Genesis.

During the final years of writing I have been helped by many others. The meetings of the Boston Theological Institute sharpened my sense of the problems. Richard Clifford S.J. and John Kselman S.S. of Weston Jesuit School of Theology provided various forms of encouragement and help. Reverend Michael Tunnicliffe of Luther King House, Manchester, United Kingdom, corrected some final details. Cynthia Read of Oxford University Press guided the process of publication. Philip McShane O.P. and Joe O'Brien O.P. rescued me from several computer crises. There seems to be no end to the patience of librarians, particularly those at Weston Jesuit School of Theology and at Harvard Divinity School. Gloria Korsman tracked down the illustration for the cover.

Others were patient in a different way. The Dominicans allowed me time and freedom. My family of origin, especially my surviving parent, my mother, did not complain. Relatives and friends tried to make allowances for a fascination with an old book.

To all, from the beginning until now, thanks indeed.

Centre for Biblical Teaching and Research   T. B.
Mary Immaculate College, University of Limerick
October 2000

CONTENTS

APPENDICES

A NOTE ON METHOD

Priority of the Literary Aspect—before History and Theology

The study of Genesis has generally involved two central disciplines—history and theology. It is tempting, therefore, in approaching the book, to begin with these. History would survey several centuries and suggest sources and forces that could cast light on the text and its historicity. Theology—perhaps after gleaning something from the historical inquiry—would move quickly to the ultimate questions of meaning.

However, priority in importance does not mean priority in the order of investigation. To some degree, the first thing to be clarified concerning Genesis is neither its (historical) origin nor its (theological) destination, but simply the text itself. The text, the finished writing, is the number one artifact, and no amount of historical background or theological acumen can substitute for taking that artifact seriously. Before asking "What was the historical background?" one must first ask "Historical background of what?" To do otherwise is like trying to figure out "who done it" without knowing what was done. It generates a situation where, in Sarason's words, "The historical question is posed prematurely" (1981, 61; cf. Moberly, 1992, 73).

As an artifact, an object, Genesis is literary, at least in the basic sense that it consists of writing—words and sentences on pages of some kind. And the first step in taking it seriously is to be sensitive to writing—to the full text and to the procedures normally involved in writing, in other words, to literary procedures. The literary aspect has "operational priority" (Polzin, 1980, 5–7, esp. 6). Literary procedures are like the foundations of a house: on their own they are unimpressive and almost useless, but to build without them is to invite disaster.[1]

---

1. If an investigation is not founded on an adequate treatment of the literary dimension, then other factors begin to determine the direction of the investigation. Whybray (1996, 72, 74) implies that some decisions about what is historical spring not from evidence but from two very diverse kinds of energy—faith or iconoclasm.

It could be objected that for many years Genesis research has almost always begun with an emphasis on the literary—with the theory of four sources (J, E, D, and P). But this theory is not fully literary; it is primarily historical. Historical reconstruction has given it its central energy and its endurance (see Appendix 4). Wellhausen was not primarily a littérateur; he was a historian. To place some form of the JEDP theory at the beginning of an investigation of Genesis is to put the historical before the literary, thus violating the first principle of method.

Attending to the literary dimension need not mean entering into obscure debates about literary theory. In literary matters, theory has frequently been unproductive (Alter, 1984). Niditch (12) summarizes: "Rather than beginning with assumptions about the historical reliability of a text and the date when it was written down, one should ask what sort of literature this is in terms of its style, structure, content and messages."

Among these literary questions, one of the most fundamental is the discernment of basic structures—such as discerning that a play is divided into so many acts and scenes. Letellier (1995, 30), when introducing his study of Genesis 18 and 19, clarifies the issue:

> The first concern in analyzing any biblical text is to ascertain its limits, where
> it begins as a literary unit and where it ends. J. Muilenberg has established

---

Other analyses are more complex. The canonical approach, for example, though necessary in its emphasis on the finished text and on theology, tends to be impatient with many of the trivial-looking details of the literary aspect.

History that is unduly self-preoccupied—impatient with full literary analysis—tends to endless circling and inconclusiveness (see Davies, 2001). The past, by its nature, is largely lost; and historical research sometimes develops into an effort to retrieve the unretrievable. If the past that is sought never existed, the futility of the quest, instead of generating a cessation of scholarship on that issue, sometimes generates increased efforts—and thus at times the increased circling and inconclusiveness.

The bypassing of adequate literary analysis may also be seen even in such fine scholars as van Seters and Halpern. Van Seters is a far-seeing pioneer on several fronts (historicity; dating; literary genre; relationship to the prophets and Greeks)—a pioneer to whom this writer is greatly indebted. Yet, perhaps because of the demands of his wide-ranging exploration and because his primary orientation is historical rather than literary, van Seters has never fully engaged the completed text of Genesis in all its unity and artistry. At some level the historical investigation (the historical component) has gained priority over the literary, to the detriment not only of the literary but also of the historical. This does not, of course, invalidate van Seters's pivotal contribution, but it limits it unnecessarily.

The work of Halpern (1988) is brilliant. Yet in constructing history Halpern uses parts of Judges as if they were separable blocks, each with its own history. In saying this he has not paused sufficiently to grasp the book's literary unity—a unity which is not only editorial, as Halpern observes, but pervasive, continuous. Halpern indicates (1988, 61) that Judges is not continuous in the same direct way as the Court History. This is true, but it is continuous nonetheless, though in a different, spiraling, way (see, for instance, Webb, 1987; Kim, 1993). Once the pervasive literary unity of Judges emerges, it is no longer possible to separate specific units and to use them as if they had independent histories.

this as a first principle of rhetorical criticism. . . . He asserts that the literary unit is "an indissoluble whole, an artistic and creative unity the contours of which must be perceived if the central preoccupation or dominant motif invariably stated at the beginning is to be resolved."

One of the theses of this commentary is that the basic literary units are the diptychs, blocks of about two chapters. Genesis 18–19, approximately, is such a diptych. (As will be seen later, the precise limits are 18:1–19:29.)

Accordingly, one of the first steps in this work will be to identify the limits of the various units or diptychs and to summarize what Muilenburg would call its central preoccupation or dominant motif. This twofold process—identifying the unit and summarizing its preoccupation—will be dealt with in diverse ways: initially, in the introduction, by outlining Genesis's units and concerns; and later, in the commentary proper, under the headings of "Introductory Aspects." These introductory aspects generally include the following:

The Basic Story Line

Literary Form

Complementarity of the Two Panels

Relationship to Preceding Chapters

Leading Elements

Structure

While structure is important—like knowing where the door is in a building—the arguments for discerning it are sometimes so detailed that many readers may prefer to skip them initially, especially in the sections headed "Structure." The discussion of artistic structure in Chapter 2 is quite extended, but, if one has the time to take it slowly, the artistry in question is fascinating. So is the issue of complementarity, especially in sections on "Complementarity of the Two Panels," but it often needs time and patience.

References normally contain both names and dates, but for the sake of greater simplicity commentators are generally cited by name only.

This book is intended not only for researchers but also for students, preachers, and general readers. This involves some anomalies, such as explaining terms already known to researchers, but, overall, it seems to be the best policy.

In accordance with the methodological priority of the literary aspect, the following introduction deals first with the text and its immediate context (chaps. 1–5), then with the historical background (chaps. 6–10), and finally with issues of meaning and theology (chaps. 11–15).

AB	Anchor Bible
ABD	*Anchor Bible Dictionary* (ed. D. N. Freedman; New York, 1992)
ABRL	Anchor Bible Reference Library
ACEBT	*Amsterdamse Cahiers voor Exegese en Bijbelse Theologie*
AnBib	Analecta biblica
ANET	*Ancient Near Eastern Texts* (ed. J. B. Pritchard; Princeton, 1978)
ANRW	*Aufstieg und Niedergang der Römischen Welt* (ed. W. Hase; Berlin, 1972–)
ATD	Das Alte Testament Deutsch
AThANT	Abhandlungen zur Theologie des Alten und Neuen Testaments
BA	*Biblical Archaeologist*
BETL	Bibliotheca ephemeridum theologicarum lovaniensium
BI	*Biblical Interpretation*
Bib	*Biblica*
BibRev	*Bible Review*
BIRS	Bibliographies and Indexes in Religious Studies
BIS	Biblical Interpretation Series
BLS	Bible and Literature Series
BZ	*Biblische Zeitschrift*
BZAW	Beihefte zur ZAW
CANE	*Civilizations of the Ancient Near East* (ed. J. M. Sasson; New York, 1995)

CBA	Catholic Biblical Association
CB OT	Conjectanea Biblica, Old Testament Series
CBQ	*Catholic Biblical Quarterly*
CBQMS	Catholic Biblical Quarterly Monograph Series
Ch(s)	Chapter(s)—exceptional abbreviation
Chap(s).	Chapter(s)—standard abbreviation
CMSM	Conference of Major Superiors of Men
CR: BS	*Currents in Research: Biblical Studies*
Crucial Bridge	*The Crucial Bridge: The Elijah-Elisha Narrative as an Interpretive Synthesis of Genesis-Kings and a Literary Model for the Gospels* (by T. L. Brodie)
DBS	*Dictionnaire de la Bible, Supplément* (Paris, 1928–)
EH	Europäische Hochschulschriften
EstBib	*Estudios Biblicos*
ExpT	*Expository Times*
Fr	French original
Ger	German original
HBC	*Harper's Bible Commentary* (ed. J. L. Mays; San Francisco, 1988)
HBD	*Harper's Bible Dictionary* (ed. P. A. Achtemeier; San Francisco, 1985)
Hebr	Hebrew original
HSM	Harvard Semitic Monographs
HSS	Harvard Semitic Studies
HTR	*Harvard Theological Review*
ICC	International Critical Commentary
IDB	*Interpreter's Dictionary of the Bible*
IDBSup	*Interpreter's Dictionary of the Bible, Supplement* (ed. K. Crim; Nashville, 1976)
Int	*Interpretation*
IrBibSt	*Irish Biblical Studies*
ITC	International Thelogical Commentary
JAAR	*Journal of the American Academy of Religion*
JAOS	*Journal of the American Oriental Society*

JBC	*Jerome Biblical Commentary* (ed. R. E. Brown et al.; Englewood Cliffs, NJ: 1968). Cited by article number and section.
JBL	*Journal of Biblical Literature*
JBQ	*Jewish Biblical Quarterly*
JETS	*Journal of the Evangelical Theological Society*
JHC	*Journal of Higher Criticism*
JR	*Journal of Religion*
JSNT	*Journal for the Study of the New Testament*
JSOT	*Journal for the Study of the Old Testament*
JSOTSup	Journal for the Study of the Old Testament, Supplement Series
NAB	*New American Bible*
NCE	*New Catholic Encyclopedia* (ed. M. R. P. McGuire; New York: 1967)
NIB	New Interpreter's Bible
NJBC	*New Jerome Biblical Commentary* (ed. R. E. Brown et al.; Englewood Cliffs, NJ: 1990). Cited by article number, or by article number and section.
NTS	*New Testament Studies*
OBO	Orbis biblicus et orientalis
OBT	Overtures to Biblical Theology
OCD	*Oxford Classical Dictionary*, 3d ed., 1996
OTA	*Old Testament Abstracts*
OTS	Outestamentishe Studiën
PCB	*Peake's Commentary on the Bible* (ed. M. Black and H. H. Rowley; London/Edinburgh: Nelson, 1962)
PIBA	*Proceedings of the Irish Biblical Association*
PWCJS	Proceedings of the World Congress of Jewish Studies
RB	*Revue biblique*
RSN	*Religious Studies News*
SANT	Studien zum Alten und Neuen Testament
SBL	Society of Biblical Literature
SBLDS	Society of Biblical Literature Dissertation Series
SBT	Studies in Biblical Theology
SCR	Studies in Comparative Religion

SJOT	*Scandindavian Journal of the Old Testament*
StBib	Stuttgarter Bibelstudien
TBT	*The Bible Today*
ThDig	*Theology Digest*
Them	*Themelios*
TRu	*Theologische Rundschau*
TynB	*Tyndale Bulletin*
VT	*Vetus Testamentum*
VTSup	Vetus Testamentum, Supplements
WMANT	Wissenschaftliche Monographien zum Alten und Neuen Testament
ZAW	*Zeitschrift für die alttestamentliche Wissenschaft*

INTRODUCTION

PART ONE

THE TEXT AND ITS IMMEDIATE CONTEXT (GENESIS-KINGS, "THE PRIMARY HISTORY")

The Case for Unity, Especially as Dialogical (Diptych-based)

These opening chapters (1–5) focus primarily not on history or theology but on the shape of the text—its structure. Structure is like anatomy. Knowledge of anatomy does not impart healing, but without such knowledge a doctor has little chance of detecting what is happening.

Chapter 1 determines whether the body in question (Genesis) is in fact just one body and not a jumble of bodies or a body that is broken or fractured. The conclusion is as follows: Despite the body's complexity and diversity, it is one. Genesis is a single unified text.

Chapter 2 looks more closely at the nature of that unity, at the diverse structures holding Genesis together. Among these structures the most basic is binary: Genesis often balances two texts or features against one another, thus giving a form of dialogue or diptych.

Chapter 3 investigates the theory or purpose behind such structures, especially behind the dialogue or diptych. The conclusion is that Genesis regards truth itself as in some way dialogical (not monological or simple).

Chapter 4 stands back as it were from the diptych arrangement and tries to reach a clearer sense of its role: Is the diptych arrangement essential or is it just packaging ("redaction")?

Chapter 5 sets Genesis in the context of the Primary History (Genesis-Kings). Just as there is increasing evidence that Genesis itself is a unity, so also evidence is emerging that the whole of the Primary History is a literary unity. Setting Genesis within Genesis-Kings is somewhat like setting a person within the context of his or her family. It provides a new way of understanding somebody.

Genesis's Unity

The Shift in the Evidence

Genesis is a book about origins—the origins of the universe, humanity, civilization, Israel—and as such has generally been regarded as a form of history. But "history" is too narrow a category or genre for Genesis—it is not tied to simple factual reporting—and so it is now more frequently reclassified as historiography, the ancient mode of writing which, while portraying the past, communicated something larger. Even "historiography" is inadequate. Like the larger body of the Primary History, Genesis contains a transforming and cross-fertilization of diverse genres (Damrosch, 1987, 41–47). Hence, while it is often permissible, for simplicity's sake, to classify Genesis as historiography, specifically antiquarian historiography (van Seters, 1992, 31, 34), it is necessary to allow that the full category or genre may be more complex.

At times this possible complexity is forgotten. Genesis is classified narrowly, as history or as some specific form of historiography, and as such the book lacks unity.

Arguments against Unity

The main problems highlighted by modern research, the main reasons for rejecting unity, are as follows:

1. *Variation in style and language.* The initial description of creation (Gen. 1:1–2:4a), for example, sounds solemn and repetitious; but the further picture of creation, in the Garden of Eden (2:4b–24), is more colorful and down-to-earth.

2. *Variation in the name for God.* Variation in the divine name occurs even within the opening chapters. Compare, for instance, "God" (Gen. 1:1–2:4a), "Yhwh God" (2:4b–chap. 3), and "Yhwh" (4:1–16).

3. *Variation in viewpoint or theology.* At first God seems elevated and distant (Gen. 1:1–2:4a), but then (2:4b–4:16) God is presented as anthropomorphic, close to humanity.

4. *Repetitions and doublets.* Some events are recounted not once but twice or even three times. For instance, Joseph seems to reveal himself twice (45:3–4), and an episode about an endangered wife occurs three times (12:10–20; chap. 20; 26:1–11).

5. *Internal contradictions.* Some contradictions seem slight, but others are glaring. The passers-by in the sale of Joseph, for instance, are de-

scribed first as Ishmaelites, then as Midianites (38:25–28, 36); the contradiction is "utterly irreconcilable" (R. E. Friedman, addressing the
Society of Biblical Literature, Philadelphia, Nov. 18, 1995; cf. Campbell and O'Brien, 1993, 225).

6. *The diversity of stories—in content and especially in form.* Gunkel detected an important feature: Genesis seems episodic. Rather than being
one continuous story, it is like a series of stories or episodes; the stories
are diverse in content, and even more so in form. Gunkel (1910, lvi–
lxxx; 1994, 63–92) concluded that this diversity, especially the diversity
of forms, is to be attributed to the dynamics of oral tradition. Genesis
therefore can be perceived as a disparate collection of orally transmitted
stories.

Gunkel did not abandon all elements of the unity of the finished book, but
the energy of his analysis tended toward tracing the diverse forms into the
recesses of history, and so the emphasis fell not on any unity but on the idea
of original diversity. Consequently, in the perception of many, Genesis appeared
radically splintered.

For all these reasons, then, Genesis appears confused.

Yet there is another view. Adar (1990, 9), for instance, sees a book that is
unified: "Even on the assumption that the Book of Genesis is composed of
different elements, it is clear that they have been blended into an integral whole.
The analytical approach of . . . scholars who fractionalize the Book . . . is diametrically opposed to that of the author of Genesis."

Adar's view is no longer exceptional. The number of those who favor a
literary or rhetorical approach to the Bible is now sufficient to have generated
at least three book-length bibliographies (Minor, 1992; Mark Powell, 1992; Watson and Hauser, 1994), and several authors have written specifically about the
unity of Genesis or parts of Genesis. Among them:

Genesis as a whole: Baker (1980), Cassuto (1973), Dahlberg (1976, 1982),
Fokkelman (1987), Fox (1989), Greenstein (1982), Sarna (1981)

Gen. 1–11: Clines (1976a), Kikawada and Quinn (1985), P. Miller (1978),
Combs and Post (1987)

Gen. 1–2: Bal (1986), Gordon (1978), Gros Louis (1974, 41–51)

Gen. 2–3: Walsh (1977)

Gen. 2:1–4:16: Hauser (1980)

Gen. 6–9: Wenham (1987), Kessler (1974, Gen. 7), Longacre (1979, 1985),
Niccacci (1994)

Gen. 11:1–9: Kikawada (1974), van Wolde (1994, 84–109)

Gen. 12: Kikawada (1973)

Gen. 20:1–22:19: Alexander (1997)

The Joseph story: McGuire (1981), Coats (1976), Longacre (1989), Rendsburg (1990), Savage (1980)

The Pentateuch: Clines (1976), Mann (1988)

Given these contributions—and there are others—it is necessary to try to summarize what has been happening.

In the literary studies published since the 1970s, biblical narrative has undergone a long, slow process of recognition: many of the confused-looking elements have been seen to be something else—expressions of literary art (for a survey see Trible, 1994, 73–87). This art is largely theology-oriented. The conclusion: Genesis, as well as being a form of history, has another dimension.

Literary criticism of Genesis is not new, but generally it has been practiced by historians and theologians—people whose primary competence was in their own field rather than in literary criticism. What was needed was an infusion of insight from those whose primary work was in appreciating literature—in recognizing literary art.

An example of such recognition occurs in Alter (1981). While examining the work of Culley—one of those who, following in the footsteps of Gunkel, regarded Genesis as largely the result of oral tradition—Alter encountered what claimed to be a detailed analysis of a specific case of oral tradition. He recalls the moment (1981, 50):

> As I stared at Culley's schematic tables, it gradually dawned on me that he had made a discovery without realizing it. For what his tables of parallels and variants actually reveal are the lineaments of a purposefully deployed literary convention [that is, a set scene or type-scene, with a series of standard elements]. The variations in the parallel episodes are not at all *random*, as a scrambling by oral transmission would imply.

The implications for Gunkel's work are far-reaching: what Gunkel had discovered, by and large, were not diverse oral forms but aspects of diverse literary conventions. Like Columbus, Gunkel made a great discovery, which he himself did not understand. The direction in which he pointed twentieth-century biblical research—through the jungles of oral tradition—was radically misleading. So also was his reading of Genesis.

There has been similar confusion about other features, including the apparent indicators of disunity. However, they have now begun to be recognized as features of literary art, art which encompasses theology.

1. *Variation in style and language.* Variation in style and language is relatively common in good writing. Examples vary from the deliberately childish style and language at the beginning of Joyce's *Portrait of the Artist* and of Alice Walker's *The Color Purple* to the variations suddenly introduced by the gravedigging scene in Shakespeare's *Hamlet* and by the cotton-picking scene in Steinbeck's *The Grapes of Wrath* (chap. 27). Beginnings tend to be particularly unusual—to be striking—whether in *Pilgrims' Progress* ("As I walked through the

wilderness of this world . . ."), *A Tale of Two Cities* ("It was the best of times, it was the worst of times . . ."), or the Gospel of John ("In the beginning was the Word . . ."). In the film *Apocalypse Now* the variation in light is a sign not of diverse producers nor of erratic electricity supplies but of a deliberate technique by which the diminishing of the light communicates a dark message. Variation is part of art. In Mozart's *Magic Flute* the "quite contrary styles are evidence of the highest possible playfulness and freedom, yet all of them are bound together . . . to form the most natural unity" (von Balthasar, 1992, 198). It is quite appropriate then that a great book like Genesis contain such variation.

2. *Variation in the name for God.* Variation of name—especially the names of people—is a common feature of human language. Someone who in her office, as a president, is "Madame President," or "Ms. Elizabeth R. Gomez," later in the day may become "Beth" or "Mommy." Diverse names capture diverse aspects. "Australia" can become "The Land of Oz"—a rich variation, but generally not to be used on solemn occasions. In the New Testament there is variation in the titles of Jesus, and also in the divine name—especially between "God" and "Father." John's prologue, for instance, begins with a heavy use of "God" (1:1–2, 6, 12–13), but the name tapers out and, after the word becomes flesh, is largely replaced by "Father" (1:14). The prologue's final verse uses both names, in effect combining and contrasting them: "No one has ever seen God; it is God the only Son, who is in the Father's bosom—he is the one who has made him known" (1:18). "God" tends to express the deity as distant; "Father," the deity as involved in human life.

A somewhat similar distinction applies to the change from "God" (Elohim, Gen. 1:1–2:4a) to "Yhwh God" (2:4b–chap. 3) to "Yhwh" (4:1–16). "God" is "the name expressive of greater distance" (Brichto, 1998, 104). One of the features of the opening chapters of Genesis (1:1–4:16) is that the distant "God" gradually comes closer—first, as "Yhwh God" in the Garden; and more so, simply as "Yhwh" in dealing with Cain. ("Yhwh" adapts the divine word to Cain's plea and places a sign on Cain, presumably by touching his body. "Yhwh" suggests the divinity as down-to-earth.)

In sum: Genesis begins with three stories that have an overall sense of descent—in creation, in the Garden, and in the field (with Cain)—stories that, because they are diverse, involve diverse aspects of God, and so, diverse names. This will be discussed in greater depth in the commentary.

3. *Variation in viewpoint or theology.* As implied in the preceding paragraphs, realities have diverse aspects and so of their nature are open to diverse viewpoints. Genesis is not small-minded or set at a fixed angle. It responds to the diversity of reality. Genesis moves, not only down through the generations and across the nations but also from one aspect of reality to another. In contrast to a theater, where the viewer is limited to a particular seat and so to a fixed view of the stage, the viewpoint of biblical narrative is like that of a film set—able to view the action from diverse perspectives (Berlin, 1983, 44–46).

The different views of God—first as distant (Gen. 1) and then as closely involved with humanity (Gen. 2)—are indications, not of disunity, but of basic complementarity, more neatly unified than the two basic components of an egg. Alter (1981, 141–147) analyzes Genesis 1–2 as an instance of "composite artistry" and concludes (146–147):

> God is both transcendent and immanent (to invoke a much later theological opposition). . . . The world is orderly . . . and at the same time there is a shifting tangle of resources. . . . The creation story might have been more "consistent" had it begun with Genesis 2:4b but it would have lost much of its complexity as a satisfying account of a bewilderingly complex reality that involves the elusive interaction of God, man and the natural world. It is of course possible, as scholars have tended to assume, that this complexity is the purely accidental result of some editor's pious compulsion to include disparate sources, but that is at least an ungenerous assumption, and, to my mind, an implausible one as well.

4. *Repetitions and doublets.* Repetition too is a common feature of art. Examples vary from songs' refrains to the practice in films of repeating a theme song or a phrase, such as "Play it, Sam," in *Casablanca*, or "Do Not Forsake Me" in *High Noon*. In some situations repetition is required—as in Joseph's need to repeat his stunning self-revelation (45:3–4; Alter, 1981, 175). In biblical narrative as a whole there is "an elaborately integrated system of repetitions, some dependent on . . . words . . . other[s] linked to . . . actions. The two kinds of repetition . . . are somewhat different in their effect, but they are often produced together . . . to produce a concerted whole" (Alter, 1981, 95; cf. Sternberg, 1985, 365–440). At times such concerted repetition is threefold; and the three actions may be consecutive or separated. In 2 Kings 1 they are consecutive: within a single chapter there are three repetitive encounters between Elijah and groups of soldiers. In the case of the endangered wife they are separate (12:10–20; chap. 20; 26:1–11), like three forms of a type-scene. An analogy to such repetition occurs in *Silverstreak*, a film about a train journey from Los Angeles to Chicago: the hero is removed from the train three times, in diverse circumstances. As Alexander (1992, 152) concludes on the basis of an independent analysis of the endangered-wife episodes: "It is now possible to view all three episodes as deriving from a single author, who . . . composed the later pericopes with a clear knowledge of what he had already written earlier."

5. *Internal contradictions.* In the sale of Joseph the overlap of two diverse groups—Ishmaelites and Midianites—is indeed glaring. But, *pace* Friedman, the two presences are not "utterly irreconcilable." On the contrary, they are an intimation of what will later be said clearly: in selling Joseph, there were two agents at work—human and divine. In Joseph's words (45:8), "It was not you who sent me here but God." The Ishmaelites encapsulate the human agency, the agency of the brothers (they are explicitly associated with them, 37:25–27); the Midianites, the agency of God.

The indication for this divine-human distinction lies in the detail of the way the two groups are described. First the Ishmaelites: "Then they sat down to eat bread. They lifted up their eyes, and saw, and behold a caravan of Ishmaelites coming from Gilead, their camels bearing gum and balm and myrrh, going along to bring them down to Egypt" (37:25–27). Everything about these Ishmaelites corresponds with the dimensions of tangible human actions. They are visible and calculable: they are seen from a distance, and there is clarity about their origin, their destination, and the contents of their caravan. In fact, at the level of the larger story, including the story of Ishmael (Gen. 16–17, 21, 25), "the only 'Ishmaelites' would be their first cousins" (Alter, 213). The Ishmaelites are like themselves.

The Midianites, in contrast, represent something unexplained. They come from nowhere and are not associated with the brothers: "And men passed by, Midianites, traders, and they drew Joseph up and they lifted him from the pit, and sold Joseph to the Ishmaelites. . . . The Midianites sold him in Egypt." Here there is no clear origin, destination, or caravan. All that is said is that they pass by and that they do the one thing that in the circumstances is necessary: they are merchants; they sell (37:28, 36). In comparison with the brothers and the Ishmaelites, they provide an alternative agency. In Isaiah (9:4) "the day of Midian" is associated with a dramatic divine intervention into a situation of oppression.

Thus there is a reasonable explanation. The two-sidedness of the narrative (Ishmaelites; Midianites) reflects the fact that, as Joseph himself will say explicitly (45:8), the original selling had two facets, two agencies.

The details of this explanation need further work. But such work is a mopping-up operation, the task of normal science. In the meantime the two-agencies explanation provides an alternative approach to the text, one that allows for unity.

This kind of correspondence—between events and another dimension—is close to allegory. Yet Genesis is not allegory. In a delicate balance, it stays within the literary genre of historiography, and the extra dimension, however central or focal, does not negate a basic rootedness in history.

This explanation may be reasonable, but it is not straightforward. The text uses reason but goes beyond it, shifting from the world of verifiable history into the world of art/poetry. It juxtaposes images in a way that breaks the observable sequence of events but that brings out the events' hidden dimension. It is easy to dismiss art/poetry—history is full of those who do so (from Plato to authoritarian rulers to technicians)—and it is easy also to disparage art/poetry that is theological (for instance, by referring to it condescendingly as "a sermon"), but, as more and more scholars are realizing, art and poetry are central to the Bible.

In the end, the overlap between the Ishmaelites and the Midianites leaves the reader with a choice: either the text is utterly bungled ("utterly irreconcilable") or it is coherent literary art with a theological purpose.

Conclusion: A Shift in the Weight of Evidence

The first issue is one of definition. If Genesis is defined essentially as history, even antiquarian history (van Seters, 1992), then it indeed lacks unity. But once allowance is made that the genre is more complex, that it uses history as a mantle for artistry—literary art that is theology-oriented—then it begins to emerge as unified.

The examples given here do not clinch the issue. And as the commentary proceeds, not all apparent signs of disunity will necessarily be accounted for. Problems will remain. But with each difficulty that is solved, the credibility of those remaining lessens. The Ishmaelites-Midianites puzzle has often been presented as a trump card, a clinching argument in favor of disunity. If this trump argument is open to a whole other interpretation, then further arguments seem less persuasive.

The result, as far as the unity of Genesis is concerned, is that the momentum is in the direction of unity. The weight of evidence has shifted.

---

2   Further Evidence of Genesis's Unity

Consistent Overlapping Structures—Chiasms, Spiraling Stories, and Double Dramas, Including Twenty-Six Diptychs

---

Having countered objections to Genesis's unity (see Chapter 1), it is now necessary to begin looking at that unity more closely. This chapter deals largely with some structures. The chapter's thesis is that the structures of Genesis are complex, but they are so consistent that they indicate unity.

Body-Like Complexity and Chiasms

Genesis is like the human body. The body is quite complex yet its various structures form a unity. One structure is binary: many parts of the body come in pairs. There may be important differences—one hand may be more able; one side of the brain may serve a different function; one leg may offer a better football kick—yet the two form a certain unity and they balance one another.

Another bodily structure may be called spiraling (or tapering): limbs vary in volume as they progress (the thigh is wider then the ankle, the upper arm is wider than the wrist). A further aspect of the body involves reversal: the breath goes in and out, in and out.

The easy unity of these three structures—binary, spiraling, and reversing—helps to illustrate the easy overlapping unity of the basic structures of Genesis. First, Genesis is binary: many of its structures involve balance between pairs (of texts). Second, Genesis also contains spiraling: the texts, instead of staying the same length, tend in general to spiral toward greater quantity (greater length and detail). And third, Genesis involves reversals: some stories, called chiasms, having given a certain sequence of elements, then reverse the sequence (ABCBA, or ABCDCBA, and so on). The story of the flood (6:1–9:17), for example, first builds up by several steps toward the complete covering of the earth, and then retraces its steps as it were. While the details of the chiastic structure of the flood story are debatable (cf. Anderson, 1978, 23–29; Clifford, 1990, 2:12), the basic coherence of the chiasm suggests the essential unity of the text.

There are several chiasms in Genesis, but this study does not emphasize them. In the present state of research they are often difficult to detect clearly, and for that reason, it is better not to build much on them. Accordingly this chapter concentrates on the two more basic kinds of structures: spiraling and binary.

It is important, however, before concentrating on just two kinds of structures, to emphasize that all three overlap. Just as the body integrates its many aspects, so too does Genesis. The presence of one does not exclude another. The presence of a chiastic structure in the flood story does not exclude features of pairing or spiraling. There is overlapping.

Spiraling Structures: Consistent Patterns of Expanding Episodes

At first sight the pattern of the stories in Genesis may seem erratic, disunified. The length of stories seems to vary unpredictably, and the stories themselves, at some levels, are not always clearly connected.

Amid the apparent confusion, two things are agreed. The beginning of Genesis is largely episodic; its diverse episodes seem loosely connected. Gunkel (1910, vii) calls it a collection. And Genesis's conclusion, especially the Joseph story, is largely the opposite—a single continuous narrative, like a short story or novella.

Both of these perceptions are true, yet they are but part of a single larger truth: *The whole book of Genesis moves systematically from episodes to continuous narrative*. The stories become more complex and unified. The shift from one mode to the other is not sudden; it is consistent and gradual, so gradual that, while the difference between the two ends is clear—like the difference between youth and old age—it is difficult to say when exactly the change occurs.

At first the amount of obvious continuity is very small. Within Genesis 1–11—a very disparate text—the only semi-continuous stories are those of Eden (barely two chapters, 2–3) and the flood (somewhat longer, 6:1–9:17). In the Abraham narrative (12:1–25:18) the first semi-continuous story is again barely two chapters (Abram's journey, chaps. 12–13), but the second, concerning Isaac's birth, is significantly longer (four chapters, chaps. 18–21). Furthermore, the Abraham account as a whole, while still quite episodic, is held together by a single figure.

The story of Rebekah (67 verses: chap. 24), though still part of the larger Abraham drama, moves the development of continuity a step further. This single chapter is so long and continuous that it prepares the way for the prolonged continuity that emerges first in the Jacob story and especially in the story of Joseph.

In Jacob's case (within 25:19–37:1) there is an almost continuous story of seven chapters (27–33), from the account of how Jacob stole Esau's blessing until his eventual return to meet Esau. And in the Joseph story continuity is almost pervasive; episodes are the exception.

This steady pattern of narrative expansion, from one end of Genesis to the other, is best pictured not as a straight line but as a spiral. The text tells a brief story—say, of two chapters—then circles around as it were before coming back to tell another, longer, story. Only at the end, in the Joseph narrative, does it give a single long story in full detail—a story that picks up the elements of the first story (Genesis 2–4) and uses them in a radically new way. It is no accident that, having begun with an account that opened the way for one brother to kill another, Genesis concludes with a long story about murderous brothers achieving reconciliation. Part of that reconciliation is seen already in Jacob's return to meet Esau, but only in the Joseph story does brotherly reconciliation reach completion.

What is true of story continuity—gradual expansion, like a spiral—is true also of several other features of Genesis: as the book develops there are a series of gradual changes. Characterization, for instance, appears slowly. There is only a minimum amount of characterization in chapters 1–11; Adam, Eve, and Noah are scarcely sketched. Abraham and Sarah, on the other hand, emerge more clearly. Then come striking portraits of Rebekah and Jacob; and finally, with full explicit characterization, Joseph.

It is likewise the case with the use of everyday details: at first they are scarce, but gradually they appear. Concerning appearance, for instance, nothing is said of Adam and Eve; Sarah and Rebekah, however, are described as beautiful (12:11, 14; 24:16); and, with yet greater detail, Rachel and Joseph are described as beautiful in both form and face (29:17; 39:7).

This same spiraling effect likewise occurs concerning the obvious intervention of God. At first (chaps. 1–11) God is the main actor on the stage, especially in the making of the world and in its remaking (the flood). In the Abraham narrative, God still intervenes regularly, but the spotlight has moved to Abraham and Sarah. At the end of the Abraham narrative, in the Rebekah story, there is an indication of what is to come: God, while still central to understanding what is happening, is essentially in the background, and there is a closer focus on the detail of human action. In the Jacob story God recedes farther than in the Abraham narrative; and in the Joseph story God scarcely ever intervenes visibly.

For Cohn (1996, 100, 102), "the diminishing divine role in events is . . . directly related to . . . the augmented role of human wisdom. . . . Genesis depicts the evolution of the divine-human relationship from the never-never land of Eden to the real world. . . ." The specific circumstances of the real world are debatable (Cohn, 102, suggests the exile), but what is important is the general idea—the move toward the real world. The motifs of Genesis 1–2, for instance, reappear in 8:1–9:29 but with a change of perspective—from "Golden Age" (idealistic) to historical (Kruger, 2001).

One of the features of the gradual expansion of the stories is a process of *dispersal:* instead of being confined to one episode, as sometimes happens in Genesis 1–11, basic elements tend, as Genesis advances, to be dispersed across several episodes or chapters. The flood, for instance, the great natural disaster of Genesis 1–11, is limited to one episode among many; but the famine, the great natural disaster of the Joseph story, is dispersed across seven chapters (Gen. 41–47).

Partly as a result of all these gradual changes, the development of history-like narrative is also gradual. At first, before the flood, the Genesis stories are mythical in the best sense; they have a quality that is virtually timeless; they happen in a world which, even when the years are counted, is far far away. However, with the flood and its aftermath (chaps. 6–11) there is a slight shift. The stories remain mythical, but particularly in the table of nations (chap. 10), there is some sense of the historical world.

In the case of the Abraham narrative (12:1–25:18), Abraham and Sarah are not mythical, but neither do they follow many of the basic patterns of history-like existence. Among other things, they have children at an extreme old age and they live respectively till the ages of 175 and 127.

Jacob, however, despite a long life (147 years) and some dramatic divine interventions, generally follows the patterns of ordinary history-like life; and Joseph even more so. Joseph dies at 110 (the ideal life span among Egyptians), and he uses human capacities to deal with history's practical problems. In Joseph's story, the narrative, as never before, comes down to earth; it achieves a new kind of clarity. Revelation happens in ordinary life.

Incidentally, given the gradualness of this shift from myth to history it is often better not to refer to Genesis 1–11 as "the primeval history." Genesis 1–11 is indeed primeval in some sense, but, even within Genesis 1–11, that sense varies, and there are primeval aspects also to some of the Abraham narrative. "Primeval history," when used of Genesis 1–11, tends, in practice, to set those chapters apart in a way that the book itself does not, and tends consequently to obscure the book's unity. It is better to refer to chapters 1–11 in some other way, perhaps simply as the Adam-Noah story.

Aspects of the same general shift—from initial episodes to later narrative which is more continuous—occurs in other texts also, for instance, in Judges, in the Elijah-Elisha narrative, and in the Gospels.

What is essential is that Genesis is not a collection of episodes that are loosely connected or poorly edited. Gunkel notwithstanding, it is not the result of some primitive process. Rather, it uses episodes and episodic technique as gradual steppingstones within a larger narrative development of moving from myth to history, from obscurity to clarity, from the fragmented world of expulsion and murder to a unified account of acceptance and reconciliation.

Double Dramas, Including Diptychs

The Four Major Dramas, Forming Two Double Dramas

Apart from containing stories that spiral and expand, Genesis also reflects a pattern that is much more regular and symmetrical. It contains four basic stories or dramas: Adam-Noah (chaps. 1–11), Abram-Abraham (12:1–chap. 25:18), Jacob (25:19–37:1), and Joseph (37:2–chap. 50). Aspects of these divisions are debated—how to name them, how to relate them to each other, and where to begin the Abraham story—but concerning the basic divisions there is general agreement.

The stories of Jacob and Joseph belong together in a special way: together they recount the life of Jacob, womb to tomb (25:19–chap. 50), and as such they form a complex unity, like a double drama, or like two sequential films. The double drama constitutes a single biography.

There is continuity also, but of a less obvious kind, between dramas one and two—between Adam-Noah and Abram-Abraham. The idea of covenant, for example, so central to Abraham (chaps. 15 and 17), is first emphasized with Noah (9:8–17). Further details will be seen later. So, again, but in a less obvious form, there is a kind of double drama (1:1–25:18).

Genesis therefore may be divided into two (1–25, and 25–50), each half containing a double drama. Accordingly, in the *New Jerome Biblical Commentary*, the task of commenting on Genesis is divided between two authors: Richard Clifford, 1–25, and Roland Murphy, 25–50.

Insofar as this arrangement is neatly symmetrical—two double dramas, the dramas being of comparable length (none excessively long or short)—the book as a whole has a basic unity. Yet, while this four-part structure is central, other structures, including the expanding stories, overlap it. Spread across the center of Genesis (12:1–37:1) is the single multifaceted story of the wanderings of Abraham, Isaac, and Jacob. In addition, the two ends (Gen. 1–11, and the Joseph story) balance each other in many ways: the earth, which sometimes seemed to be falling apart under the weight of sin in Genesis 1–11, is gathered together as it were under the wise rule of Joseph (Dahlberg, 1982). Further-

more, binding all together, from Adam to Joseph, is a series of carefully coordinated genealogies.

What is important is to allow the diverse structures to coexist; one does not
cancel the other. The neat division into four does not cancel the more varied
patterns, such as the genealogies, the spiraling stories, and the journeys of
Abraham, Isaac, and Joseph.

Within the Dramas, the Diptychs

The symmetry that is evident in the basic division of the book into four dramas
appears also *within* each drama: each drama consists of a series of paired texts—
like two-part paintings or diptychs. Within the Adam-Noah story (chaps. 1–
11), for example, there are six twos or pairings:

In chaps. 1–5

Two accounts of creation (1:1–2:4a, and 2:4b–24).

Two accounts of sin (2:25–chap. 3; and 4:1–16).

Two sets of genealogies (4:17–26; and chap. 5).

In chaps. 6–11

Two balancing parts of the flood story (chaps. 6–7; and 8:1–9:17).

Two texts based largely on Noah's sons (9:18–29; and chap. 10).

Two texts of human finiteness (Babel, the failed tower, 11:1–9; and
Shem's fading genealogy, 11:10–32).

The correspondence between the two parts of each diptych is sometimes easy
to see, sometimes difficult. Among the above six, the most difficult—the weakest
case—at least at first sight, is the last (in chap. 11); it needs careful analysis, and
needs comparison with the other diptychs, especially with 4:17–chap. 5.

This diptych structure overlaps with other structures. The Eden story, for
example—essentially chaps. 2–3—looks two ways. On the one hand, it has its
own internal unity, its own narrative coherence. On the other hand, it also
partakes in two other unities. Chapter 2, on creation, forms a pair with chapter
1; and chapter 3, involving sin, forms a pair with the sin of Cain (the details
will be seen later). Again, one structure, no matter how obvious, does not
exclude another; they overlap.

One of the central theses of this study is that, within Genesis, the basic unit
is the diptych. Binary organization, which to some degree has long been implicit
in the well-established division of the book into four, and sometimes into two,
goes further: it extends to the book's basic units.

Altogether there are twenty-six diptychs, each with two parts or panels—a
total of fifty-two panels. On average, the parts/panels are about the length of

Table 2.1. The Six Diptychs of Genesis 1–11

Act I (chaps. 1–5)	Act II (chaps. 6–11)
Twofold creation account	Twofold flood story
Creation—from God (1:1–2:4a)	Flood rises: creation undone (chs 6–7)
Creation—for humanity (2:4b–24)	Flood abates: creation remade (8:1–9:17)
Twofold sin account	Two stories of Noah's sons
Tree: undue eating, knowledge (2:25–ch 3)	Vine: undue drink, sight (9:18–29)
Sequence: two sons; murder (4:1–16)	Sequence: sons propagate nations (ch 10)
Two genealogies	Twofold fading
Genealogy; building (a city . . . ; 4:17–26)	Building (a city tower) fails (11:1–9)
Culminating genealogy (ch 5)	Culminating genealogy fades (11:10–32)

a conventional chapter. The division into fifty-two panels functions in practice as a refinement of the medieval division into fifty chapters.

The overall arrangement is simple yet challenging. Each of the four basic dramas (the Adam-Noah story, Abraham, Jacob, Joseph) consists essentially of six diptychs—two sets of three. As already seen, there are three in Genesis 1–5 and three in Genesis 6–11. Insofar as Genesis 1–11 may be called a *drama,* it is appropriate to speak also of *acts* and *scenes:* the drama of Genesis 1–11 consists of two acts (1–5 and 6–11), and each act contains three two-part scenes. In simplified terms, the three scenes of act 1 (chaps. 1–5) are grounded on Adam; those of act 2 (chaps. 6–11) on Noah. The relationship between the two acts is one of continuity and variation (see Table 2.1).

Details aside for the moment, some broad continuities may be noted. As many scholars have indicated, creation (1:1–2:24) is variously echoed in the flood (6:1–9:17). The two sin accounts (2:25–4:16, including Cain) are mirrored obscurely in the stories of Noah's sons (including Canaan, 9:18–chap. 10). In particular, the drama of the tree, nakedness, and the eyes (2:24–chap. 3), is partly reversed in the drama involving another strange tree (the vine) and the turning away of the eyes from nakedness (9:18–29). Finally, the powerful energy of the two genealogies (4:17–chap. 5) is largely reversed in the diverse but related episodes of the failed tower (11:1–9) and the fading genealogy (11:10–32; see commentary). The general impression, in the relationship between the various texts, is one of subtlety and precision.

The other dramas (Abraham, Jacob, Joseph) likewise have six diptychs (again two acts, each with three diptych scenes). But at two points, at the center and the end (24:1–25:18; and chaps. 49–50), there is a seventh—a diptych that is pattern-breaking and blessing-filled.

The diptychs may be outlined in diverse ways, highlighting diverse aspects. One way, already illustrated for Genesis 1–11, places the two acts—the two

Table 2.2. Genesis's Twenty-six Diptychs: An Outline

God's human world
The basic world and the world of Abraham (1:1–25:18)

1. Creation—from God (1:1–2:4a)
   Creation—for humanity (2:4b–24)
2. Sin: tree, undue eating, knowledge (2:25–ch 3)
   Sin (sequence): two sons; murder (4:1–16)
3. Genealogy; building (a city, etc.) (4:17–26)
   Culminating genealogy (ch 5)

---

4. Flood rises: creation undone (chs 6–7. WATER)
   Flood abates: creation remade (8:1–9:17)
5. Noah and sons: vine, undue drink, sight (9:18–29)
   Noah's sons (sequence): propagating nations (ch 10)
6. Building (a city tower) fails (11:1–9)
   Culminating genealogy fades (11:10–32)

---

7. The land; ambiguity of beauty (Sarai, 12:1–13:1)
   The land; ambiguity of wealth (Lot, 13:2–18)
8. War; covenant; Lot's people are brought back (14)
   Death; the people will be brought back; covenant (15)
9. Expelling the slave. Ishmael born (16)
   Covenant includes slaves. Ishmael circumcised (17)

---

10. Generous Abraham pleads for Sodom (Sarah; 18)
    Sodom destroyed (Lot; 19:1–29. FIRE)
11. Lot, Sarah, foreign children. Abimelech (19:30–ch 20)
    Abraham's child, and foreigners. Abimelech (21)
12. The offering (near-death) of Isaac (22)
    The death of Sarah (23)
13. Double betrothal: Abraham and Isaac (24)
    Double genealogy: Abraham and Ishmael (25:1–18)

---

main sections of each major drama—in parallel. However, it is probably better—closer to the flow of the story—to give priority to listing the various acts in sequence. Such is the basis of the more complete outline, Table 2.2.

Generally the acts tend to become longer (especially if one includes the extra scenes, 24:1–25:18, and chaps. 49–50). Genesis 6–11 is longer than 1–5. Genesis 18:1–25:18 is longer than 12–17. Then, starting over as it were, Genesis 31–36 is longer than 25:19–chapter 30; and Genesis 43–50 is longer than 37–42.

ACT 2: A SHIFT IN THE DRAMA

In each of Genesis's four major dramas the division between acts 1 and 2 is significant. The beginning of act 2 brings a specific turning point; the drama shifts. This occurs at the beginning of chapters 6, 18, 31, and 43. As already noted, in Genesis 1–11 the shift occurs with the introduction of Noah and the

Table 2.2. (*continued*)

The flow of a human life, from birth to death
The story of Jacob (25:19–50:26)

14. Isaac and his family (sons, wife; 25:19–26:11)
    Isaac and the outside world (contention; 26:12–33)
15. The blessing: Jacob deceives (26:34–27:45)
    The betrothal: Jacob is deceived (27:46–29:30)
16. The generating of Jacob's children (29:31–30:24)
    The generating of Jacob's flocks (30:25–43)

17. Jacob, fearful, faces Laban (31:1–32:2. ARMIES)
    Jacob, more fearful, faces Esau's 400 (32:3–ch 33)
18. Sex-related violence: Jacob's paralysis (34)
    Danger, death: Jacob's energy and hope (35:1–20)
19. Jacob's genealogy: incestuous, fading (35:21–29)
    Esau's genealogy: prosperous (36:1–37:1)

20. The selling of prophetic Joseph, led by Judah (37:2–36)
    Tamar and the initial conversion of Judah (38)
21. The testing of Joseph's character (39)
    The testing of Joseph's inner wisdom (40)
22. Remembered sin leads to Joseph's rise (41)
    Joseph's causes his brothers to remember sins (42)

23. Benjamin/Judah face (LORD) Joseph; meal (43)
    Benjamin/Judah face offended Joseph (44)
24. Joseph revealed, visionlike; embrace, journey (45)
    Jacob's journey, visions; embrace (46:1–47:11)
25. World famine; relationship to the land (47:12–28)
    Impending death: Jacob imparts blessing (47:29–chap. 48)
26. Jacob's blessing-filled death (49)
    Jacob's glorious burial (50)

flood (6:1–8). The Abraham account starts with people called Abram and Sarai (Gen. 12–17), but a new act begins when they receive new names and hear the announcement of the imminent birth of Isaac (Gen. 18–23). Likewise, Jacob's youth undergoes a radical shift when, having completed his development in Laban's household (Gen. 25:19–chap. 30), he sets off on a difficult journey home (Gen. 31–36). And Jacob's old age is divided partly on the basis of two pivotal losses—first of Joseph (Gen. 37–42), then of Benjamin (Gen. 43–48). Each of the four dramas, therefore, has a central shift between acts 1 and 2.

These four shifts have a certain continuity, and this continuity provides a glimpse into the larger kinds of continuities that exist between all four dramas. In each case the shift involves some form of confrontation with death. Noah has to deal with water (the flood, 6:1–9:17) and Abram with fire (at Sodom, 18:1–19:29). For Jacob, however, the pivotal engagement is not with flood or fire but with dangers that have a greater human involvement: first, in the great diptych concerning his meetings with Laban and Esau (chaps. 31–33), he faces the prospect of his own death, and he survives; and later, in the Benjamin-centered diptych, which turns the Joseph story around (chaps. 43–44), Jacob accepts the prospect of Benjamin's death, and Benjamin survives.

This is not the place to analyze the details of the Jacob story. What is important is to indicate briefly an example of the kind of continuity and variation that exists between the four great dramas of Genesis: at the center of each, the fourth diptych (the beginning of act 2) brings a turning point; and central to that turning point is an encounter with the threat of death. Yet in all four pivotal diptychs (flood, fire, Laban-Esau, and Benjamin) the emphasis falls not on death but on survival—on God's desire to save.

In each of the four dramas, the role of women is particularly noticeable in the opening diptychs: the woman/Eve; Sarai (and Hagar); Rebekah; and Tamar (and Potiphar's wife). This does not exclude women from later roles, but it is a striking feature. A similar phenomenon occurs in the Elijah-Elisha narrative. Each of its two main dramas contains an early emphasis on women: the widow (1 Kings 17); and the widow and the Shunammitess (2 Kings 4). (Something similar occurs in the Gospels: Matthew 1–2; Luke 1–2; John 2:1–11; 4:1–42.)

SEVENTH, BLESSING-FILLED, AND PATTERN-BREAKING

At the end of the stories of Abraham and Jacob, the end of each double drama, there is an extra diptych, seventh and blessing-filled, which does not fit the pattern of six. Thus the total of diptychs for each double drama is thirteen.

As already mentioned, these two pattern-breaking diptychs occur at the book's center and end. At the center there is the blessing-filled betrothal of Rebekah to Isaac, complemented by a picture of the marriage-related fertility and death of Abraham (24:1–25:18). At the end, there are the prophetic blessings of Jacob's testament, complemented by accounts of death and burial (Gen. 49–50).

These scenes, particularly the betrothal (chap. 24) and final testament (chap. 49), constitute highlights both of drama and meaning. In fact, the account of Rebekah, standing so gracefully at the center of all, is like a key to the meaning of the entire book.

Further Features of the Diptych

THE SHAPE OF THE DIPTYCH: MEASURES OF TWO OR THREE

The average size of each two-panel diptych is about two chapters (roughly a chapter per panel). Diptychs vary in size, as do the panels within individual diptychs. Sometimes the reasons for the variations are reasonably clear. It is probably not an accident, for instance, that within the twelve panels of Genesis 1–11, the shortest is that on Babel—the city that would reach the sky.

Carefulness of structure, already seen in the book as a whole, occurs also within each diptych. In the creation diptych, for example, each panel has its own unity—introduction, conclusion, and two or three main parts. The week of creation has just two main parts—but each part is divided into three (days 1–3 and 4–6). The picture of the Garden of Eden has three main parts—each divided into two (see Table 2.3).

The core of this structure—an introduction, two or three main parts, and a conclusion—occurs in virtually every panel of Genesis. Where the structure varies, the variation is generally understandable.

COMPLEMENTARITY

Between the panels of each diptych there are multiple connections. The overall relationship of the panels, however, is often neither direct sequence nor par-

Table 2.3 Creation (1:1–2:4a // 2:4b–24)

Creation from transcendence

Introduction: the formless waste (1:1–2)
Days 1–3, "Let there be light . . ."; finally dry land
    Day 1: light (1:3–5)
    Day 2: waters under, space above (1:6–8)
    Day 3: dry land (1:9–10)
         and plants (1:11–13)
Days 4–6, "Let there be lights . . ."; finally humankind
    Day 4: lights in the heavens (1:14–19)
    Day 5: fish under, birds above (1:20–23)
    Day 6: animals (1: 24–25)
         and humanity (1:26–31)
Conclusion: harmony: God rests (2:1–4a)

Creation as earthly

Introduction: the growthless earth (2:4b–5)
The man and the ground, stage one (2:6–9)
    The flow, and making the man from the ground (2:6–7)
    The garden and placing the man there (2:8–9)
The man and the ground, stage two (2:10–17)
    The fourfold river (2:10–14)
    Resting the man in the garden, and commanding him (2:15–17)
The man and the woman (2:18–23)
    The need for a corresponding person, not animals (2:18–20)
    Making the woman; joy (2:21–23)
Conclusion: harmony: the man in stable union with the woman (2:24)

allelism but complementarity. The time sequence of seven days, for instance (in 1:1–2:4a), is followed not by a further sequence of days, but by a panel that shifts the emphasis from time to space (to the fourfold river and the tree at the center, 2:4b–24).

Apart from a general complementarity, the relationship between the two panels is often like the relationship between photographs taken from two perspectives. The first, for instance, may be long-distance, and the second close-up. Often, the second takes an aspect of the first and expands it, like a map which, having taken one area or aspect of a more general map, develops it. Genesis 2, for instance, unpacks some of the focal points of Genesis 1. While Genesis 1 gradually builds up to the importance of (dry) land and humanity (days 3 and 6, respectively), Genesis 2 begins with these two realities (land/ ground, and humanity) and develops them.

THE DISTINCTNESS OF BEING THIRD

When the text contains three sections of any kind, the third is usually distinct. In some way or other it breaks away from the prevailing pattern. Within the creation week (1:1–2:4a), for instance, where each part has three days (days 1–3 and 4–6), those that are third (days 3 and 6) are distinct; they are climactic in content and twofold in structure.

Likewise, when the panel as a whole has three main parts the third part is distinct. In the Garden (Gen. 2:4b–24), for instance, parts one and two (2:6–9 and 2:10–17) focus on a person's primordial relationship to the ground, the soil; but the third part shifts the focus to a further primordial relationship—namely with another person (the man and the woman, 2:18–23).

This is likewise the case also within each act (each set of three diptychs). The three diptych scenes follow one another coherently, but the third is always somewhat apart—especially in time or space. In the opening act (Gen. 1–5), for instance, the first and second diptych scenes (creation, and sin; 1:1–4:16) are limited to the initial family. But in the third (the genealogies, 4:17–chap. 5), the action moves rapidly to another space and time. Similarly in act 2 (Gen. 6–11), the initial diptychs revolve in various ways around a foundational family (Noah and his sons; chaps. 6–10), but in the third diptych (the tower of Babel, and Shem's genealogy; chap. 11), there is a significant shift in space and time: people move east and generations flow by.

Other third diptychs—they begin in 16:1; 22:1; 29:31; 35:21; 41:1; 47:12— introduce further important changes: after ten years, the birth of Ishmael (16:3); after some time, in the land of Moriah, the offering of Isaac (22:1–3); the birth of eleven sons and a daughter (29:31–30:24); the departure to Migdal-Eder and Reuben's incest (35:21–22); after two years, Pharaoh's dream (41:1); and finally, the detailed account of the extending of Joseph's rule to all of Egypt (47:12–36).

The distinguishing of what is third, while practiced deliberately in composing Genesis, seems to build on an innate human tendency. In simple stories, for instance, including jokes, there are often three characters, and the third is frequently emphasized or different. Three involves manageable complexity, and as such is congenial.

Combining the Structures

Taking together the two main sets of structures—the expanding stories, and the diptychs—it is now possible to summarize the development of the narrative. Within the four major dramas, each act, each set of three diptychs, has one main story, and, as Genesis goes on, these stories tend both toward greater complexity, including length, and toward greater unity with one another.

In the Adam/Noah drama (Gen. 1–11) the two stories (Eden; the flood) are relatively short, and the unity between them seems minimal; the characters—scarcely sketched—are diverse, generations apart. However, close examination shows that in fact the two stories have several links (see commentary on the flood, chapter 19, especially under Relationship to Preceding chapters). The unity, while genuine, is not obvious at first.

Again in the Abram/Abraham drama (12:1–25:18) there seems to be little continuity between the two main stories (Abram's journey, chaps. 12–13; and the birth of Isaac, chaps. 18–21). But there are unifying characters (Abram/Abraham, Sarai/Sarah, Lot), and, unlike the Eden-flood relationship, one does not have to wait for commentary to see part of the link: there in one episode when the continuity is glaringly obvious—when Sarai/Sarah is endangered (12:10–13:1; chap. 20).

In the third drama (Jacob, 25:19–37:1) complexity and unity are even more obvious. There is one unifying character, described in considerable detail. And the two main stories, the outward journey (26:34–chap. 30) and the return (chaps. 31–33), almost blend into one.

In the Joseph drama (37:2–chap. 50) the blending is complete. The character of Joseph is filled out clearly and, apart from one digression—more apparent than real (Judah and Tamar)—the entire narrative flows into an all-encompassing complex unity. In the final chapters, when the complexity increases yet more (Westermann, III, 211), several diverse threads are drawn together. A similar literary phenomenon—unusual complexity—occurs at the end of the Gospel of John; there is an "interweaving of different threads" (Schnackenburg, 1982, 342; cf. Brodie, 1993, 575). Likewise, in T. S. Eliot's *Four Quartets:* "[T]he last lines of the last Quartet take up themes from all the preceding ones, thus linking the four together" (Bodelsen, 1966, 32).

The complexity at the end of Genesis, therefore, is best regarded not as something unwarranted or intrusive but as an appropriately artistic conclusion—

a culmination which draws all the threads into a unity. This is particularly true of the final sayings or blessings (chap. 49): they may seem different, even alien, but they contain an intense distillation of several basic threads of Genesis.

The variations in characterization—from Adam to Joseph—do not mean disunity. David's various wives, for instance, apart from being different in character, are described through at least three diverse modes of characterization: type or typical (someone barely sketched); agent or functional (someone who appears as a function of the plot or as part of the setting); and full-fledged (Berlin, 1983, 23–32). Such variation in the mode of characterization is not a reliable indicator that the David narrative lacks unity; and the same principle applies to Genesis. Genesis's characterizations, while diverse, reflect overall gradation, from minuscule to full.

The Spiraling Transition from Myth to History: A Closer Look

As already briefly mentioned, a central feature of Genesis is its gradual change from timeless symbol ("myth") to history-like narrative. "Myth," though notoriously controverted, may be taken to mean "an act of unlimited scope and import that occurred in a timeless age of the past" (Levenson, 1985, 103; cf. Childs, 1960, 20). Myth, understood positively, is a form of timeless symbol.

The story of Adam (Gen. 1–5) is best described as mythical; it is "the anthropological myth par excellence" (Ricoeur, 1967, 232). In its timeless symbolism it communicates more powerfully than history. Its timelessness also helps to account for its inclusion of people with lifespans of several centuries (chap. 5): within the context of timelessness, their long lives have a certain appropriateness; they suggest an era beyond the normal realm of time.

As Genesis goes on this timelessness gradually fades. Already, in the Noah story, there is a change, the beginning of a shift from timelessness to time. The shift is seen first in the introduction to the flood story (6:1–8): the text evokes a twilight world, distant, different, beyond normal human dimensions (sons of god marrying daughters of men, giants, in those days). Then, having evoked that twilight zone, the text takes leave of it, and begins to move toward a world where, in principle, life is limited to near-history-like proportions (one hundred and twenty years). The flood story proper begins to move toward a more normal sense of time: there is a new emphasis on days and dates, including the first impression of the passage of a year (7:7, 11; 8:13–14). The way of counting the days is repetitive and somewhat perplexing; it is as though, in some way, the flood story is evoking the initial stages of measuring ordinary time, of moving toward history. At the end of the Noah drama, in the Shem-Terah genealogy (11:10–32), the sense of moving toward history becomes stronger: the life spans are closer to being lifelike, and so are the conditions of Terah's household.

The Abraham story is a further step toward a history-like account, but it is only with the life of Jacob that there is a reasonably full portrayal of ordinary historical existence—from birth and youth to marriage, old age, and death (25:18–34).

In both cases—with Abraham and Jacob—the focus is on a specific family, and so the history in question may be called family history or family narrative. Yet the larger world is never forgotten. Abraham becomes involved with famine, war, and kings; and part of Jacob's old age is played out in the shadow of Egypt, Pharaoh, and a world famine.

The overall movement within Genesis—from myth to history—has been compared (by Kevin Burke, in conversation, Weston, School of Theology, Cambridge, MA, Oct. 11, 1996) with the sometimes slow transition from the deep dreams of night to the full awareness of day. The events that occur in dreams belong to a distinct realm: they do not follow historical sequence and constrictions, yet they are often deeply meaningful, symbols that provoke thought. On waking the dreamer begins to move to another level of awareness, and gradually there is a transition to the detail of daily life. The inner reality, which provoked the dream, is probably still present, but it is no longer obvious. At the end of Genesis, God no longer intervenes so obviously, but God is still at work.

Given the gradualness of the change, it is tempting to designate the whole book in a way that is vague, for instance, by calling it saga (Gunkel, 1910). But "myth" and "history," despite their difficulties, capture important aspects of the book. Genesis does not describe specific events as does a modern historian, but, on two grounds, Genesis may be described as historiographical: its *framework* of genealogies, while containing myth, is history-like; and as the book advances, *the nature of its narrative* too becomes increasingly history-like.

General Conclusion

The structures listed in this chapter—chiasms, spiraling stories, and double dramas, including diptychs—indicate in varying ways that the text of Genesis is a unity, not a collection of disparate episodes. Its several stories are built around a consistent pattern of spiraling expansion. And its four dramas consist of well-ordered diptychs. The persistent impression then is of a book that is a well-wrought unity—complex and sophisticated.

Such a view—complexity and sophistication—may seem to go against other aspects of Genesis. It is, after all, a very earthy book. But complex sophistication does not in fact exclude other features. The composition of the human body may be immensely sophisticated, but it can serve very down-to-earth purposes—to dig, to dance, to pray, or simply to journey onward. It is likewise with Genesis: its sophistication is all placed at the service of describing life's onward journey.

3   ## The Quest for the Theory behind the Diptychs

Truth as Dialogical (Binary/Diptych-Like)

The diptych arrangement has four features: the fact, the underlying reason, the origin, and the implication. In other words: Is it true? And if so, then Why? When? And so what?

The question of its truth—the establishing of the fact—was already discussed in chapter 2 and will be dealt with more fully on a case-by-case basis, particularly under the recurring heading "complementarity of the two panels."

The questions of its origins and its implications will be dealt with in subsequent chapters. Chapter 4 will discuss origins (whether original or redactional), and the commentary will deal with the implications, with the way diptych structure clarifies the text.

In the meantime, this chapter concentrates on *why*. Why diptychs? Why not recount the story in straight, linear fashion? What is the theory or rationale behind such an arrangement? It does not seem possible at the moment to give a definitive answer to this question, but there are clues.

The Complex Nature of Reality
(the Diptych as Mind-Opening)

Diptych structure may be due partly to the mind-set implicit in features of Hebrew poetry, particularly the way such poetry holds diverse elements in balance. The opening lines of Isaiah 40, for instance, "have a clear binary structure" (Fitzgerald, 1990, 12:8); and, in general, "the biblical line consists of two balanced cola" (12:11). Furthermore, balance occurs not only within lines but between lines: "The internal balance characteristic of the OT line does not exhaust the possibilities for balance in poetry. It is frequently extended to larger units . . . several lines or quite commonly two lines" (12:14). This basic phenomenon—balance—is sometimes described as parallelism (synonymous, antithetic, synthetic, Fitzgerald, 1968, 13:15–16). There is no clear limit to the ways in which one element may balance another (Fitzgerald, 1990, 12:11).

One form of balance or parallelism is particularly important, namely inversion: something already said is repeated or quoted, but in a form that is reversed or inverted (Bailey, 1996; Beentjes, 1996). This poetic phenomenon provides a clue to some of the relationships within the diptychs of Genesis. Sometimes within a diptych, the two panels show a form of inversion, like two sides of a coin.

A further part of the answer for the orderly diptych arrangement may have to do with the basic concept of order. Amid the confusion of history, religion brings reality into a certain order (Webb, 1981, 161–168, discussing philosopher Eric Voegelin). Genesis is history, but history set in extraordinary order. Such order may seem artificial, yet it accords with the larger order that, despite black holes, pervades the universe.

Yet another reason for using diptychs apparently has to do with the nature of reality. The perspective of modern rationalism, and especially of technical colleges, is essentially single, linear. Reality is weighed and measured. History is the facts. Such an approach is not to be neglected; it can be monumentally useful.

But reality is more complex, and so is the mind. Even for physics, reality is elusive, composed ultimately not of waves or particles but of wavicles, whatever these may be. Some of the most minute elements seem almost to flash in and out of existence. Genesis had no idea of modern physics, but at some level it knew that reality is not solid, that the mind and heart and soul need breathing space. And God is not solid—not a wooden idol—but can be viewed and experienced from diverse perspectives.

The twofold picture of creation, for instance, forms, as it were, a sense of space, a place in which the mind, instead of fastening, perhaps idolatrously, on one image, is teased to another viewing point. One mirror gives a single image; but two facing mirrors give processions of images, resonating energy and depth.

The diptych structure therefore, at least as applied to the presentation of creation, is one way both of evoking the richness and elusiveness of reality, and also of opening the mind, of giving it breathing space and freeing it from a form of spiritual and psychological fundamentalism. At a certain level the two-fold account is indeed perplexing, even contradictory. Yet at another level, as readers and hearers through the ages have experienced, there is something about the dual account that is deeply satisfying and that rings true.

The Complex Nature of Art (Based on Relationships, Not Absolutes)

Apart from the complexity of reality or nature there is the further complexity of perception and of art. Art imitates nature; complexity in one leads to complexity in the other. Understandably then art is not simple; it is inherently connected with relationships. This emphasis on relationship emerges strongly in two diverse literary critics, Kees Fens and Adele Berlin. According to Kees Fens:

All art owes its power and emotional force to friction or tension. Friction between possibilities and realities, ideal and real, creator and creation. Art is always the creation that never succeeds perfectly. . . . Every work of art articulates its denial. . . . To be and not to be at the same time; this is the essence of art. . . . These frictions may lead to sciences: literary, visual, rhetorical criticisms. These criticisms are dialectic in nature, reflecting the dialogue between work and reader, listener or observer. (quoted in van Wolde, 1994, 75)

For Berlin, perception itself is not simple. In art, for instance, there is

an important principle: our perception of what we see is based not on absolutes but on relationships. There is no correct size for painting a house or a flower. It depends on what else is in the picture, and where in the picture it is. . . . The size and color of objects to be represented are relative. They are successfully represented not if they match the size and color of the original, real-life model, but if they accurately represent certain relationships. These relationships then are clues to the interpretation of what is seen. . . . Biblical narrative sets up such relationships in a number of ways. (1983, 135)

One such way is the diptych. The two preceding quotations help to make the historical critic more patient with art and particularly with the tensions in Genesis. For Genesis, reality is never simple. There is a further aspect to things, an ambiguity; and, like an artist who wants to get beyond the surface of reality, Genesis seeks to hold reality in tension and to approach it from diverse angles. Combs and Post (1987, 33) speak of a comparative mode of thinking and of dialogue:

The composition of the text induces or rather forces the close reader of the text into a comparative mode of thinking and thus to understand the whole and its parts through and as a result of a dialogue between opposing or alternative views of the whole and its parts. . . . There are . . . two accounts of creation. . . . The redactor has not only not concealed their differences . . . but has taken pains to present the accounts as two distinct accounts . . . employ[ing] Elohim . . . [and] Yhwh. . . . After close study of the two accounts the reader asks: how do these accounts compare and what does the comparison teach? The close reader continues to observe that Genesis IV is to be compared to Genesis V. . . . Genesis I–XI calls for a comparative study within itself of its respective parts.

Aspects of the Combs-Post arrangement are questionable, but these two authors have an insightful sense of the text: it is meant to provoke some process of comparison or dialogue.

The idea that the texts of Genesis are involved in some form of dialogue is not new. Fokkelman's work (1975), in particular, though it does not use the specific image of the diptych, sees Genesis as "intensely dialogic . . . so that we can speak of dyads, such as Jacob-Rachel or Jacob-Laban" (Francis Landy, foreword to Fokkelman, 2d ed., 1991, xii); Genesis's theology is linked to "the duality of relationship" (xiv). In Alter's view (45) the contradiction between Genesis 10 and 11, concerning unity of language (10:31; 11:1), apparently reflects "a characteristically biblical way of playing dialectically with alternative possibilities;" and in the Joseph story "the doubling of the dream is a sign that what it portends will really happen, but it should also be observed that doublets are a recurrent principle of organization in the Joseph narrative, just as binary divisions are an organizing principle in the Jacob story . . ." (Alter, 210; cf. 178, 184). The dialogical aspect, therefore, is central.

Rainer Albertz (1992) has some similar ideas. Insofar as Albertz reconstructs history his work has been seen as "a tissue of hypotheses" (Murphy, 1993, 183). But Albertz has also made an important contribution: he has highlighted the extent to which Israelite religion is tension-filled and pluralistic.

The centrality of dialogue or dialectic is particularly clear in Walter Brueggemann (*Theology*, 1997). For him, the whole OT is like a a great juxtapositioning of testimony and countertestimony. The text is "dialogical-dialectic" (83), "polyphonic" (88), "pervasively disputatious" (317); there is "disjunction at the center" (269); biblical faith itself is "dialectical, resilient, disputatious" (400).

"Bakhtin, the Bible, and Dialogic Truth"

The dialogical element has received particular emphasis from Carol Newsom. Using the above title ("Bakhtin, the Bible, and Dialogic Truth," 1996), Newsom proposes an important thesis: truth itself is dialogical (or dialogic), and much of the Bible is dialogical in nature.

Newsom's emphasis on the concept of dialogical truth is inspired partly by the work of the Russian literary theorist and philosopher, Mikhail Bakhtin, who wrote mostly in the 1920s and 1930s, and died in 1975 (for further details, see Lechte, 1994, 7–12). In analyzing the works of Dostoevsky, Bakhtin noticed how the author did not impose an ideological unity on the characters; his accounts brought opposing elements of society together in fierce dialogue, but he allowed their diversity to stand, thus portraying ideas as dialogues that are open-ended (most authors, even if they portray very diverse characters, control them, ultimately bringing them within the authors' own viewpoints).

This led Bakhtin to a more general observation: ideas, of their nature, are dialogical. Even if I hold some idea fiercely, I do so in response to something already said and in anticipation of what may yet be said. "An utterance is always a reply" (Newsom, 1996, 302, quoting Bakhtin). An idea is like a conversation, or a polyphony.

The result of Bakhtin's investigations was the articulation of two concepts of truth—monologic and dialogic. Newsom summarizes:

The monologic conception of truth is fairly easy to grasp, because it is the conception of truth that has dominated modern thought for some time, characteristic not only of philosophy and theology but also of literature. There are three important features of the monologic sense of truth: First, the basic building block . . . —the "separate thought" [or] proposition. . . . Second . . . the tend[ency] to gravitate towards a system . . . [a] unity. . . . Third . . . that in principle [truth] can be comprehended by a single consciousness. . . . The proposition or system is structured in such a way that even if it is the product of many minds, it is represented as capable of being spoken by a single voice. (1996, 392)

Biblical criticism rightly noticed diverse voices in Scripture—for instance in Genesis 1 and 2—and proceeded to separate them. Yet, for various reasons, many scholars have felt uneasy with this process of separation. Newsom continues:

Driven by the "self-evident" claims of monologic truth . . . biblical criticism attempted to disentangle the various voices, so that one could identify the different monologic voices. . . . But what if a monologic conception of truth is not the only possibility? . . . The first and most important characteristic of dialogical truth is that . . . [in Bakhtin's words] it "requires a plurality of consciousnesses . . . [which] in principle cannot be fitted within the bounds of a single consciousness." A dialogic truth exists at the point of intersection of several unmerged voices. The paradigm, of course, is that of the conversation. One cannot have a genuine conversation with oneself. It requires at least two unmerged voices. (293–295)

Newsom goes on (294) to summarize three other features of dialogic truth:

- It is embodied (not abstract), rather as the participants in a dialogue or conversation are people, not propositions. (Bakhtin: "[T]he ultimate indivisible unit is not the assertion, but rather the integral point of view, the integral position of a personality.")
- Dialogic thought does not tend toward the systematic but toward "a concrete event made up of organized human orientations and voices" (Bakhtin). The result is not propositions but events. The truth can be grasped only by a plurality of consciousnesses.
- Dialogic truth is always open, an idea rendered into English as "unfinalizability." This also implies that people, and consequently ethics, are not finalizable.

For an author who has a concept of dialogical truth the purpose of writing therefore is not to propose a single vision, no matter how rich, but to present genuinely diverse consciousnesses. "Bakhtin . . . believed that it was possible to produce in a literary work something that approximated a genuine dialogue, a mode of writing he called polyphonic" (Newsom, 295).

Such a work leads to variations in roles and functions. The author, first of all, must, as it were, let go of the characters (a process Bakhtin compares with God allowing people to be free). The plot becomes less important, yielding place to the dialogic play of ideas. The reader, instead of simply observing—following the plot—is drawn into the play of ideas, thus becoming a participant. And the conclusion, instead of being closed, is open.

There is no question of attributing Bakhtin's precise idea of truth to the author of Genesis. "For Bakhtin, the polyphonic text is an intentional artistic representation of the dialogic nature of an idea. Whatever the Bible is, it is not that . . ." (Newsom, 297).

But Bakhtin's analysis helps to highlight a much more general concept, namely that in some basic way, truth is dialogical. Aspects of this larger truth occur, for instance, in fundamental observations about society and the church (Radcliffe, 1997, 23):

> According to Mary Douglas, a healthy society is one that has all sorts of counterbalancing structures and institutions that give a voice and authority to different groups so that no one way of being human dominates and no single map tells you how things are. . . . [And according to] Cardinal Newman . . . the church flourishes when we give recognition to different forms of authority. He names specifically tradition, reason and experience.

Such diversity is not to be taken for granted. Despite the growth of democracy, there has been a modern tendency, both in scientific disciplines and in politics, toward a simplified vision of truth. The twentieth century has seen unique examples of totalitarianism (in church and state), political correctness, and fundamentalism. As Newsom said (292), the monologic concept of truth has dominated modern thought.

Thus, quite apart from Bakhtin, there are two distinct ways of approaching human life and ideas—as monologic or, in some way, as dialogic.

Newsom maintains that the idea of dialogic truth helps to explain some of the most perplexing features of biblical composition (Levine, 1990, drawing partly on Bakhtin, speaks of "the dialogic discourse of Psalms"). In particular, Newsom has applied the idea of dialogic truth to Job (1996, 297–298; 1996a), and she sees it as applicable to the Primary History, especially Genesis 1–11 and the patriarchal narratives (1996, 298–304, esp. 299). She discusses Genesis's complex data, data sometimes accounted for by invoking two diverse sources:

> The Primary History presents one with . . . a "side-by-side" presentation of different textual voices. . . . Juxtaposition itself can produce a form of dialogism. Bakhtin uses the analogy of a painting in which the tone of a color is affected by the surrounding colors. . . . One of [the] implications is that the viewer (. . . or reader) may also play a role in bringing into dialogue colors/voices that are only juxtaposed in the painting/text. . . . The beginning of the narrative [Gen. 1–2] is particularly congenial to such an approach, since it presents us with . . . distinctive largely unmerged voices. . . .

Bakhtin's image, taken from painting, seems particularly expressive of the juxtapositioning in the diptychs.

Conclusion

Diptych structure is not something marginal in Genesis. It is at the center both of the book's structure and of its approach to meaning. As concerns structure, it provides the basic organizational unit. As concerns meaning, it ensures a plurality which guards against simplistic thinking, a warning about elevating any one image or idea to the level of an absolute. Its primary contribution to meaning, however, is not negative, is not a warning. It is a positive challenge to look further, a reminder that however noble one's view, there is another, there is more.

4   The Diptych Structure: Original or Redactional?

Does diptych structure belong to the entire fabric, or is it rather a form of stitch-work, knitting together the already formed parts of the text?

The answer is not simple. In the final edition the diptych structure appears at times to be pervasive, as though the various pieces were assembled with the express purpose of forming balancing pairs. The first obvious example of such pervasive complementarity consists of the two initial sin accounts (2:23–chap. 3; and 4:1–16). The simplest and most coherent explanation of the relationship between these two accounts is that they were composed as a unit. In other words, it is easier and more coherent to account for the two-part design by saying that the entire present text was planned as two-part, than to invoke a process which, as well as being more complicated, would also be more conjectural. In basic scientific methodology the advantage lies with the simplest explanation that accounts for the data, and the simplest explanation of Genesis 2:25–4:16 is that it was planned as a two-part unit. In that sense—at least in this case—the best working hypothesis is that the diptych structure is original; it belongs to the original plan.

However, while all twenty-six diptychs contain complementarity, there are instances when the complementarity does not appear to be pervasive. At first sight, it may seem, for instance, in the diptych that contains Dinah's rape (chap.

34) and Jacob's journey to Bethlehem (35:1–20), that the conjunction of the two parts is superficial, or, at most, very limited. It is plausible, then, in such a case, to say that the two parts first existed independently; they did not emerge originally from within a plan to build a diptych, but rather they were placed together and perhaps just retouched editorially.

Toward a Solution

For the moment the diptych proposal is a working hypothesis. It catches one aspect of Genesis, but the dimensions of that aspect's roots remain unclear. It is possible, in principle, that, even after extensive research, the accounts of Dinah's rape and Jacob's Bethlehem journey will remain like two islands, not clearly related to one another, and only poorly related to larger narrative strands.

To determine whether that is so, whether in many cases the two parts of the various diptychs are merely stitched together, research will need to examine several factors, particularly the following:

The full meaning of the individual texts or diptychs. The texts require scrutiny not only as straightforward history-like recounting, but also as art. The two accounts of creation, for instance, do not make coherent history, and therefore their relationship may seem to be superficial, redactional. But, at another level, their complementarity is deep, forming an artistic whole, and so there is a significant case that, whatever their background, they are integral parts of a single vision.

The immediate context of Genesis. The relationship between the two parts of a specific diptych will often be clarified by other diptychs or by Genesis as a whole. The balance, for instance, between the failed city-tower (Babel, 11:1–9) and the fading genealogy (Shem-Terah, 11:10–32), becomes clearer in light of the more obvious balance between the earlier genealogies (4:17–26, and chap. 5).

The further context of the Primary History. If within the Primary History the diptych phenomenon never again appears then the evidence for its presence is weakened. But if it does appear then there is support for its existence, and—of equal importance—there is a further opportunity to examine its nature. There is in fact at least one other major instance, namely in the Elijah-Elisha text (1 Kings 16:29–2 Kings 13), and the evidence in that case indicates that the narrative consists not of pre-existing patches which were stitched together but of a text which, from its inception, was woven so as to form a series of diptychs (*Crucial Bridge*, 2000, 1–79, esp. 1–27).

The larger context of the Bible as a whole. If biblical narrative as a whole is dialogical (Newsom, 1996), then diptych structure, instead of being a redactional afterthought, is more likely to belong to the essence of the text.

The context of diverse theories concerning sources. If Genesis is seen as a combining of parts of various lost documents (especially of J and P), then there is an initial plausibility to the idea that the diptych structure is in fact a redactional afterthought; it consists of pairing diverse parts of the hypothetical documents. Alternatively, if Genesis, instead of stitching parts of documents together, reworks its sources thoroughly and systematically (see Appendices 1–4, esp. 2–3), then the likelihood is greater that the relationship between the parts is deep-seated.

The issue—whether the diptych structure is original or redactional—is not minor. It has implications for the nature of the text. It is better then, even if one makes an initial judgment, to allow time so that the hypothesis can be tested.

Some will see the diptych structure as a secondary feature. Certainly within a number of diptychs the two parts are so diverse that the redactional hypothesis has an initial advantage.

For others the diptych structure will be primary, and seeing Genesis as diptych in nature will be comparable in its own small way to redefining the shape of the earth: the earth is not flat; it is round; and Genesis is not flat, not linear; it is diptych. Just as the earth's roundness is not an afterthought, but pertains to the nature of the planet, so the diptych nature of Genesis is not an afterthought; it pertains to the nature of the narrative.

General Conclusion to Chapters 1–4

The primary conclusion from Chapters 1–4 of this book is literary: There is significant evidence that Genesis is essentially a single work of art. Some of its variations and contradictions remain unexplained, but for several reasons, including awareness of diptych structure, the number of unexplained variations and contradictions is diminishing, and, accordingly, the hypothesis of artistic unity is becoming more plausible.

As for historical conclusions—especially concerning Genesis's date of origin—it is difficult at this early stage to be sure. Several writers have indicated, particularly since the work of Thompson (1974) and van Seters (1975), that many features of Genesis seem to belong not to the second millennium but to a time closer to the exile.

Still, the issue of Genesis's date has remained obscure and contentious, and it is better, rather than press for historical answers immediately, to stay with the leading artifact—the literary work.

As in many investigations a crucial clue comes from a connection. In this case the connection is not between people but between narratives—between

Genesis and the books that follow it (Exodus-Kings). Genesis, it emerges, cannot be considered alone; it is part of a larger work.

<table>
<tr><td>5</td><td>**Genesis as Part of a Larger Unity (the Primary History, Genesis-Kings)**

A Further Shift of Evidence</td></tr>
</table>

Having considered the text—Genesis itself—it is necessary, as a next step, to consider the immediate context. Context is a clue both to meaning and origin.

The purpose of this chapter is to indicate that the immediate literary context of Genesis consists of the entire Primary History (Genesis-Kings). Just as there has been a shift in the evidence concerning the unity of Genesis, so also concerning the unity of the Primary History. The evidence concerning the Primary History is not yet as strong as in the case of Genesis—the problem is literally bigger—but the shift is significant. More and more, Genesis-Kings is emerging as a unified corpus, with Genesis as its head.

The issue here is not sources, though it is often confused with that question (Genesis-Kings may have used hundreds of sources, some of them very old). Nor is the issue one of historicity—whether, for instance, Deuteronomy-Kings has little actual history (van Seters, 1983) or much (Halpern, 1988). The issue is whether the finished work, including Genesis, has a genuine literary unity.

At first sight it may seem that no such unity exists. The books from Genesis to Kings are immensely varied both in style and content. Just as Genesis has often been seen as an edited collection of diverse strata, so has the Primary History. It has been said that the Pentateuch consists largely of four diverse sources and that Deuteronomy-Kings has a complex editorial history (Römer and de Pury, 1996, 9–120, esp. pp. 50–58 on the Göttingen school).

Yet, as with Genesis, multiplicity of sources and complexity of structure need not mean lack of unity. This principle is also true, for instance, of great buildings or the human body: diversity of materials or food does not necessarily mean disunity, nor does complexity and variety of structure.

The arguments against the unity of the Primary History have a central weakness: *Supposed indications of disunity are essentially Genesis-like.* As stated, for instance, by A. Graeme Auld (addressing the SBL, New Orleans, Nov. 23, 1996), the many breaks and changes within the Primary History are largely of the same kind as the apparent breaks or changes in Genesis—the same, for example, as the apparent intrusion of the Judah-Tamar story in the Joseph narrative. But within Genesis such breaks and changes are gradually losing their force as indications of disunity (see Chapter 1). The Judah-Tamar story is integral to Genesis (see commentary on Gen. 37–38). And so such breaks and changes are also losing their force within the larger history.

By the same token, someone who rejects the unity of Genesis is more likely to reject the unity of the Primary History. Van Seters, for instance, despite making a lasting contribution, does not really engage the unity of Genesis, and so has little time for the unity of the Primary History. For him (1998, 7), the David story "could not possibly be understood as the culmination of the divine promise to Abraham" (1998, 7). This is partly true: there is tension between Abraham and David. But there is more to the culmination of the Primary History than David's aberrations.

It is always easy to highlight specific tensions within a complex body. The issue, however, is not whether there are tensions but whether, within the volume and nature of the larger body, the tensions have an understandable role. A government may consist of independent branches; and some branches, particularly the legislature, may be divided. But that does not mean the country lacks unity.

The case for the unity of the Primary History is still being forged. In the interim, while waiting for the process to develop, this chapter summarizes some preliminary evidence. The arguments may be grouped under three main headings: the emerging unity within specific books; the continuity *between* specific books; and the continuity within the Primary History as a whole.

The Unity within Specific Books

Genesis

Having once been the paradigm of dividedness, Genesis may now be seen differently: complex indeed—artistic and diptych-shaped—but essentially unified (see preceding chapters).

Exodus

Exodus may seem muddled (see Crüsemann, 1996, 28–31). Yet the covenant code (Exod 20:22–chap. 23), for instance, which is sometimes said to illustrate the disunity of Exodus, "has been found to be an artfully crafted unity . . . well integrated internally and in relation to the Pentateuch" (Sprinkle, 1994, 206).

In future research it seems useful to ask whether Exodus consists of ten diptychs, two of which—numbers five and ten—are expansive (somewhat as the flood diptych is expansive in Genesis 1–11, but more so). In tentative summary:

Initial Mission

1 A. Israel, threatened, seeks survival (chap. 1).
   B. The birth and survival of Moses (2:1–10).
2 A. Moses' betrothal (2:11–22).
   B. Moses' prophetic call (2:23–4:17).
3 A. The mission to confront Pharaoh; high hopes (4: 18–31).
   B. Confronting Pharaoh; hopes dashed (5:1–21).

Mission Renewed: Plagues and Passover

4 A. The call renewed (5:22–6:13).
   B. The call confirmed (6:14–7:7).
5 A. The plagues (7:8-chap. 11) (cf. the flood, Genesis 6–7, which un-
      does creation, Genesis 1).
   B. The Passover (12:1–13:16) (cf. exit from the ark, Gen 8:1–9:17,
      e.g., dates, worship, signs).
6 A. The crossing of the sea (13:17–chap. 14).
   B. The song of the sea (15:1–21).

Sinai: Covenant and Renewal

7 A. Water and remembered manna (15:22–chap. 16).
   B. Water and remembered battle (chap. 17).
8 A. Arrival at Horeb. Jethro proposes an administration to help Moses
      (chap. 18).
   B. Arrival at Sinai. God's revelation and the role of Moses (chap.
      19).
9 A. The Decalogue (20:1–21) (cf. Gen 1:1–2:4a).
   B. The covenant code (20:22–chap. 23) (cf. Gen 2:4b–4:16 and later
      parts of Genesis).
      (The relationship between the two codes echoes that between the
      two creation accounts).
10 A. The covenant ratified (chap. 24); and the ark commanded (chaps.
      25–31).
   B. The covenant renewed (chaps. 32–34); and the commands imple-
      mented (35–40). (The ark-related command-and-compliance
      echoes Genesis 1, the flood, and the plagues-and-Passover).

Leviticus

Here one may seem to be dealing with an odd collection of laws, yet when
Leviticus is read with certain poetical procedures in mind, particularly those of
parallelism and ring composition, it emerges as a unity: "We find an extremely

cerebral, closely argued theological statement based on a series of expanded analogies" (Douglas, 1995, 255; see also Douglas, 1999).

Numbers

The idea that Numbers lacks unity (see especially Noth, 1968, 4) has been strongly challenged, particularly by Douglas: "I . . . have advanced my rebuttal of the notion that Numbers lacks structure by finding thirteen well-demarcated units in alteration through the book" (1993, 83–123, esp. 113). She also speaks of "paired sections" (ibid.). It remains to be seen whether the thirteen units and paired sections have anything to do with the twenty-six diptychs of Genesis. Structure apart, Numbers does reflect Genesis; in effect, it comments on it (Douglas, 98–101).

Deuteronomy

The complexity and diversity of Deuteronomy have become proverbial, but again unity is not precluded. The pivotal introduction to the law (Deut. 4), for instance, has often been described as composite, even contradictory (God speaks from diverse places, from Horeb, v. 33, and from heaven, v. 36). But attention to the chapter's theology, especially to its balancing of God's transcendence and immanence, shows that the chapter is a unity (McConville and Millar, 1994, 133–137). It may also be worth asking whether the book as a whole consists of diptychs. These possible diptychs may be outlined tentatively as follows:

Background: Loss, and First Instructions (1:1–4:40)

1 A. Moses' words bring order to land and people (1:1–18).
   B. Rebellion against the word brings confusion and loss (1:19–46).
2 A. Repetition of simple instructions about walking with respect and restraint (2:1–23).
   B. More complex instructions about assertiveness in fighting and taking possession (2:24–chap. 3).
3 A. Initial instructions on Horeb, and on keeping God's word, laws, and rules (4:1–20).
   B. The consequences of failing to keep God's word. Specter of death and exile (4:21–40).

Learning and Relearning the Torah (4:41–chap. 11)

4 A. *Covenant:* The covenant of steadfast love; the ten words (4:41–5:22).
   B. *Shema:* Response: love in action; guarding the leading words (commandments) (5:23–chap. 6).

5　A. Costs and rewards of fidelity to the covenant: eliminations and blessings (chap. 7).

　　B. Cost and blessings: further/practical aspects (??) (chap. 8).

6　A. Sin: from a stiff neck to heart-based confidence. *Covenant renewed* (9:1–10:11).

　　B. No more stiff neck: a sense of God's acts and blessings. *Shema renewed* (10:12–chap. 11).

General Arrangement: Place, Time(s), and (Leading) People (Chaps. 12–18)

7　A. The establishment of true worship, in one place (12:1–28).

　　B. The abolition of false teaching (12:29–chap. 13).

8　A. Eating—as a holy and blessed people (14).

　　B. Releasing and celebrating, at set times—as a blessed people (15:1–16:17).

9　A. Truth-based justice: the judiciary (16:18–17:13).

　　B. Other key offices: king, priest, and prophet (17:14–chap. 18).

Life and Death; Man and Woman; Holiness and Kindness (Chaps. 19–26)

10　A. Accidents and false witnesses: coping with the threat of death (19).

　　B. Battles, sieges, and murder: death threatens more intensely (20:1–21:9).

11　A. Right relationships, especially between men and women (21:10–22:12).

　　B. Man-woman relationships: problems and crimes (22:13–30).

12　A. A people that remembers Egypt: kindness and holiness (23).

　　B. Kindness and individuals (24:1–25:4).

13　A. Pictures of death: the abandoned widow; and exploitation of the vulnerable (25:5–19).

　　B. Pictures of life: the grateful worshiper; and attention to duty (26).

Old Age and Death (Chaps. 27–34)

14　A. Woes: a covenant-related renewal, with curses/woes, and some blessings (27:1–28:46).

　　B. Woe intensified: war, exile, and siege-induced sickness (28:47–68).

15　A. A positive plea. The covenant renewed and deepened (chaps. 29–30).

　　B. Moses' imminent death. The covenant renewed, through writing and witness (chap. 31).

16　A. Song of witness to the Creator: infidelity, punishment, expiation (32:1–44).

    B. The song reflected in Moses' life; he is to go to the place of death
       (32:45–52).
17 A. Dying Moses pronounces blessing on the tribes (chap. 33).
    B. Moses' death, amid actual blessings (chap. 34).

Joshua

The book of Joshua contains complexity and gaps, yet while granting the presence of these features, Polzin indicates the book's unity: "Joshua [is] a sustained
meditation on what it means to interpret the word of God in general and the
book of the law in particular. . . . In the case of both law and land, gaps are
emphasized. The distance between the commands of the law and Joshua's (Israel's) fulfillment of them is the underlying theme of Joshua 1–12" (1980, 73–
145, esp. 144). Similar principles apply to the rest of the book (Polzin, 1980,
144–145).

Judges

Not only Polzin (1980, 146–204), but other writers also have indicated, sometimes in detail, the unity of Judges (see especially Exum, 1976, 1980, 1981;
Kim, 1993; Webb, 1987). An example of the care with which the book of Judges
has been assembled emerges in the Samson story, "a superb masterpiece of
Hebrew narrative art . . . structured at all the compositional levels with an almost architechtonic tightness" (Kim, 1993, 424). Kim's analysis of the Samson
story is akin to Chouraqui's sense (1975, 455) that Genesis has been composed
with the precision of a computer or rocket.

    One of the perplexing features of Judges—its double introduction (1:1–2:5;
2:6–3:6) and its double conclusion (chaps. 17–18; chaps. 19–21)—may be better
understood if the book is seen as following some form of the diptych arrangement that is central to Genesis.

Samuel (1 and 2)

Apart from the four-volume work of Fokkelman (1981–1993) and the more
readable two-volume study of Polzin (1989, 1993), evidence for the unity of the
books of Samuel or of major parts of them has been appearing from many
sources. Long (1989), for instance, discussing Saul, uses the subtitle, *A Case
for Literary and Theological Coherence*. Some of Long's conclusions may be
noted. Concerning Saul's early career, for example, there is a need for "a reassessment of the reputation of 1 Sam 9–11 as a *locus classicus* for source criticism
in Samuel" (236); and with regard to the larger body of 1 Sam. 5–15, there is
"a higher degree of narrative coherence and ideological consistency than has
commonly been recognized" (236). Gunn summarizes recent literary criticism
as "determined to show the extended nature of the 'Succession Narrative,' and

[to] reject the notion of shorter self-contained stories" (1991, 7). Eslinger concludes: "It is possible to read 1 Sam 1–12 as a unitary narrative, with a clear, logically progressive plot. Individual points of interpretation may be debated, modified, or rejected, but the fact that these chapters can be read as a unity is indisputable" (1985, 425).

Kings (1 and 2)

These books too sometimes seem confused, but again there is need for reassessment. The Elijah-Elisha narrative (1 Kings 16:29–2 Kings 13), for instance, consists of two bodies of material which to a significant degree repeat one another, thus giving rise to an argument that the narrative lacks unity, that it consists of two collections of diverse materials—two cycles. But these two major parts (2 Kings 16:29–2 Kings 2, and 2 Kings 3–13) have a precise complementarity: the first emphasizes transcendence; the second earthliness (*Crucial Bridge*, 2000, 6–7); and each part consists of four well-balanced diptychs (ibid., 8–27). Here, as in Genesis, the evidence for diptych structure is solid.

Overall, in assessing the various individual books, several problems remain. But these problems no longer seem as intractable as previously. The progress already made—for instance on Judges—promises well for further research.

Continuity between Books

Unity is found not only within books but also between them, particularly between those that are close to one another. It is useful first to summarize some of the main lines of this phenomenon:

Exodus has close echoes of Genesis.

Leviticus and Numbers elaborate on Exodus.

Numbers comments on Genesis.

Deuteronomy echoes/reshapes earlier books, especially Exodus and aspects of Genesis. (Apparently Deuteronomy also reflects Joshua-Kings.)

Joshua and his conquest resonate the memory of Moses.

Judges involves struggles, which constitute another form of conquest.

Samuel and Saul, their lives and struggles against the Philistines, have multiple echoes of the last great judge, Samson, including Samson's life and struggle against the Philistines (see preceding pages, on 1 and 2 Samuel).

The David/Solomon story grows out of that of Saul and also echoes Genesis.

A closer view of this phenomenon may be found, for instance, in 1 and 2 Samuel. In dealing with these books, Garsiel speaks not only of internal coherence but of continuity with Judges: "In the book of Samuel a closely wrought network of internal and external comparative structures has been built up. . . . Sometimes the comparisons extend beyond . . . the book of Samuel itself, for [some] structures . . . involve figures from the book of Judges as well. . . . For example . . . Saul . . . abounds in implied comparisons with . . . Gideon, Abimelech and Jepthath" (1985, 5). The continuities between Samuel and Genesis have been analyzed in considerable detail, especially by Brueggemann (1968, 1971, 1972, 1972a, 1973).

Continuity within the Primary History as a Whole

Apparently the continuity between individual books is but part of a yet larger phenomenon, namely the unity running through all of Genesis-Kings. This larger unity is indicated by several features or researchers:

David Noel Freedman

While arguing for an early date Freedman saw Genesis-Kings as a coherent history, what he called "the Primary History" (1963, 251): "We hold that the Law and the Former Prophets (which we designate the Primary History, i.e., . . . Genesis-Kings) comprise a literary unit which was compiled and published in its entirety by the middle of the sixth century B.C." Freedman's historical conclusion (the early dating) does not take due account of several factors, but his basic literary judgment is significant.

Richard Elliott Friedman

Friedman (1998) articulated important connections between the material usually attributed to one of the major Pentateuchal sources (J) and some of the contents of Joshua, Judges, Samuel, and Kings. In effect he indicated a series of close literary continuities running all the way from Genesis 2 to 1 Kings 5. Friedman's work has been obscured by sensationalism, by subservience to aspects of the Documentary Theory, and by claims to ninth-century authorship (1998, 51). Such claims mean that Friedman's conjectural masterpiece comes out of nowhere—a literary virgin birth. Yet his work has lasting value: he has clarified elements in the larger unity of Genesis-Kings.

Insofar as Friedman's contribution is positive it fits well into a larger body of research, which has been going on steadily for several years. Such research has indicated the following:

The Fundamental Unity of the Story/Plot

Very simply, the Primary History is a single story or history: "The Hebrew books from Genesis through Kings . . . fit together tightly. Where the Pentateuch leaves off, Joshua begins; where Joshua ends, Judges begins . . ." (Gordon, 1962, 282). Tight-fitting continuity is not an accident. It reflects some form of unity.

The Compactness of the Narrative

The Primary History's vastness—great vision, spanning millennia—may give the impression of a long process of collection. But in fact the entire work is essentially the same size as the most well-known single-author histories of Greek historiography, those of Herodotus and Thucydides. In other words, the Primary History is quite compact, easily conceivable as a single work, no bigger than a substantial paperback.

Unity of Overall Function

The Primary History is multifaceted but when taken as a whole, it achieves one central effect: it provides a form of founding myth or "a creation myth of Israel" (Ben Zvi, 1998, esp. 30). Unity in an effect (the building of a founding myth) is best explained by some corresponding unity in the cause (in the narrative). (Ben Zvi [1998, 26] affirms various aspects of the Primary History's unity, but in effect he excludes discussion of the possibility that it originated as a unity.)

The Essential Coherence of General Viewpoint

A further unifying factor is the basic underlying viewpoint. Whereas earlier scholarship tended to make a major ideological division between the Pentateuch and the subsequent history ("the deuteronomic history"), it is now becoming increasingly clear that, amid all this history's variations, there is a mainstream viewpoint, a viewpoint that is essentially deuteronomic (Whybray, 1987, 222–225). The term "deuteronomic history," as applied to Deuteronomy-Kings, tends to mislead. The entire Primary History is deuteronomic. This basic coherence does not exclude variation—there is variation even within Genesis 1–2—but the variation does not warrant literary division.

Continuity of Themes and Motifs

Within Genesis there are numerous themes and motifs that reappear in varied form in other parts of the Primary History. The Egyptian experience of Abraham and Sarah (Gen. 12–13), for instance—with its mixture of exploitation, well-being, suffering, plagues, and confrontation with Pharaoh—provides an intimation of the later Egyptian experience of Moses and the people. The importance of Hebron to Abraham (Gen. 13:18) provides a precedent for its importance in David's time (2 Sam. 2:1–5:5). In other ways, too, Genesis acts as an appropriate introduction to the whole Primary History (Abela, 2001; Sarna, xv).

Plausibility of the Project

The overall project—to write a city's history from the beginning—was not something unique. Other cities—and empires—were doing the same thing or would do so later: Athens (fifth century), Babylon (third century), Egypt (third century), Rome (several histories). Herodotus's fifth-century work, *Histories*, though not focused toward a single city, was wide-ranging in time and interest.

Plausibility of the Beginning and Ending

Two pivotal aspects of a writing are its beginning and end; they help to define the entire work. If the beginning or end does not function effectively in its respective role then one may reasonably doubt if it was originally intended for such a role. In the case of the Primary History the beginning and end (creation and the fall of Jerusalem) correspond to two of the most well-established precedents in ancient literature. The beginning reflected the literature of the East: "Mesopotamian literature was fond of taking many of its themes all the way back to Creation, sometimes even in matters of no great consequence" (Speiser, lvii). The end, recounting the fall of the city, corresponded to a great literary precedent from the Greeks—the fall of Troy, at the end of Homer's *Iliad* (Freedman, 1991, 9–10).

The Balance between the Beginning and the End

The beginning and end, apart from having an inherent literary plausibility, also have a certain balance—between the sin-and-exile story of Genesis 1–11 and the sin-and-exile story of Jerusalem's fall (Freedman, 1989; 1991, 8–9). In particular, there is a special correspondence between Genesis 11 (dispersal from Babel, and the fading genealogy) and 2 Kings 24–25 (fall of Jerusalem, exile to Babylon, and the end of the monarchy). Within the Primary History these are virtually the only chapters to use the word "Chaldeans" (Hebrew, *Kasidim;* Gen. 11:28,31; 2 Kings 24:2; 25:4–6, 10–13, 24–26).

Continuity of Sophisticated Structure

The sophistication of structure, which has already been noted in Genesis (in the preceding chapters), occurs again in parts of the Primary History. There are at least two major examples—the book of Judges (see Kim, 1993) and the Elijah-Elisha narrative (1 Kings 16:29–2 Kings 13; *Crucial Bridge*, 2000, 1–27). Further elements of Genesis-like structures occur elsewhere. The twofold account of creation (Gen. 1–2), for instance, finds an analogue in the two accountings of the people at the beginning of Numbers. Genesis 1–2 deals with seven-day creation, and then with *four-part Eden, around the tree;* Numbers 1–2 deals with the twelve-tribe nation, and then with a *four-part arrangement around the tabernacle.* Both the tree and the tabernacle evoke the sanctuary (cf. Wenham, 1994). Numbers 1–2 is like an echo of Genesis 1–2, but with a more specific focus—not on creation but on the people. It is better, however, at this point, not to press details. What matters is the larger continuity, involving significant structures, between Genesis and some later books.

Clines (1990, 85–98, esp. 93–98) indicates further "major structural aspects" (93) and consistent patterns, especially the pattern of decline or failure, meaning the pattern of hopes ending in apparent disappointment (93–98). Further patterns of unity and continuity emerge in Kissling's comparative study (1996) of Moses, Joshua, Elijah, and Elisha, and in Pleins's article, "Murderous Fathers, Manipulative Mothers, and Rivalrous Siblings: Rethinking the Architecture of Genesis-Kings" (1995).

Complementarity of the Two Sacred Mountains— Sinai and Sion/Zion

At first it may seem that the Primary History is divided against itself—focused first toward Sinai (in the Pentateuch) and later toward Jerusalem/Zion (in 2 Samuel and 1–2 Kings). But even in Genesis there are implicit reminders of Jerusalem (especially in Gen. 14, in the figure of Melchizedek of Salem) and in Exodus-Deuteronomy the tabernacle in the desert near Sinai has multiple suggestions of the Jerusalem temple on Mount Zion.

The result of having two sacred mountains is not to contradict but to create a sense of space and depth—a variation on the approach that uses diptychs in Genesis. Together the two form a certain unity (cf. Levenson, 1985, 18–21, 89–96, 187). Sinai on its own would be too distant (even the location was forgotten). Zion on its own would be shallow. Their strength lies precisely in their unity, and in the mystique that was thus imparted to Mount Zion—to Jerusalem. In the Mayan tradition—in Oaxaca, Mexico, for example—the primary emphasis is on the space *between* sacred buildings. Likewise with words; the spaces between the words often comunicate more than the words themselves. "Words and sentences are composed of silences more meaningful than the sounds" (Illich, 1973, 41).

Centered on the two geographical mountains there are, as it were, two literary mountains—Moses, and the Jerusalem kings—two extended dramas, which, by their importance and bulk, dominate the history.

The End: Exiled but Implicitly Hopeful

The end of Genesis, which looks forward to the return from Egypt ("God . . . will bring you from this land," says the dying Joseph, 50:24), provides a remarkable precedent for the ending of the entire Primary History—for the way it implicitly looks forward to the return from exile (2 Kings 25:27–30).

The Climactic Role of Judah

The most climactic speech in Genesis is not given by Abraham, Isaac, or Jacob, nor by Rebekah or Joseph; it is given by Judah. When Joseph wants to keep Benjamin, Judah intervenes dramatically, reviewing the painful history of the family and offering himself in Benjamin's place (44:18–34; the only longer speech in Genesis is that of Abraham's servant, at the center of the book, 24:34–49). Nor is Judah's speech an isolated feature; it is one of a series of integral passages which, during the Joseph story, gradually elevate Judah to prominence—prominence in both leadership and in conversion (37:26–27; chap. 38; 43:1–10; 44:18–34; 49:8–12). The story of Judah and Tamar (Gen. 38), far from being an intrusion in Genesis, is an indication of that future role. When the dust settles on Genesis, the front-rank leaders—Abraham, Isaac, Jacob, and Joseph—are all dead, and the person whose star is still rising is Judah. It was he, more than anyone except the dead Joseph, who received the lion's share of the blessings (49:8–12). Thus, the scene is set for a long history that will lead eventually to the conversion and prominence of Judah—and implicitly of Judea. The ultimate goal of the entire Primary History—Judah's return from exile and conversion—is already built into the very fabric of Genesis.

The Elijah-Elisha Narrative's Mirroring of the Rest of Genesis-Kings

The Elijah-Elisha narrative treats the rest of the Primary History as a unity. Beginning with Genesis, it reflects all the books or great characters of the Primary History (except perhaps Mosaic law); and it does so in the same order and in a way that constitutes an interpretive synthesis (*Crucial Bridge*, 2000, 29–78). It begins, for example, by inverting the great flood (Gen. 6:1–9:17) into a great drought (1 Kings 16:29–chap. 18) and by using that drought to reflect or refract other aspects of Genesis. Then it continues systematically: it distills the life of Moses (from part of Exodus-Deuteronomy), then the book of Joshua, then the stories of the Judges, and so on. Thus, it provides testimony, from within the History, that the History is to be taken as a whole, from start to finish. Unity is not something imposed afterward. Already, even before the History was finished, an integral part of the History regarded the whole of Genesis-Kings as belonging together.

*Mosaic Law's Mirroring of the Rest of the Primary
History, Including the Elijah-Elisha Narrative*

There is a significant claim that what happens in the Elijah-Elisha narrative—systematic distillation of the broader narrative—occurs also in the writing of Mosaic law (Carmichael, 1974, 1979, 1985, 1996). In other words, while the writer of the Elijah-Elisha narrative treated the overall narrative in one way—by reworking it all into a prophetic idiom—the formulator of Mosaic law also treated it all, including the Elijah-Elisha narrative, in another way, namely by reworking it into legal idiom and integrating it into the formulation of Mosaic law. Whatever the criticism of this claim (see Levinson, 1990), there are instances—for example, between Deuteronomy and Genesis—when Carmichael's evidence (1979) is strong. The essential point here is Carmichael's implication that at some level the formulator(s) of Mosaic law treated the rest of the Primary History as a unity.

Overall, in discussing the many continuities that run through Genesis-Kings, there obviously is room for greater clarity and precision. Yet the evidence already available is significant.

Ways of Visualizing the Unity of Genesis-Kings

The most obvious way of describing Genesis-Kings is to call it a great history, or in Freedman's phrase, "the Primary History." The category of "history" is inadequate but convenient (as mentioned earlier, the text involves a synthesis of genres; Damrosch, 1987, 41–47). The entire corpus constitutes a story, which runs from creation to a death-like fall—that of Jerusalem. It may also be seen as a pyramid centered on Deuteronomy (Freedman, 1991, 11), as follows:

$$
\begin{array}{ccc}
 & \text{Deuteronomy} & \\
\text{Numbers} & & \text{Joshua} \\
\text{Leviticus} & & \text{Judges} \\
\text{Exodus} & & \text{Samuel} \\
\text{Genesis} & & \text{Kings}
\end{array}
$$

This arrangement "has brought the covenant with its commandments to the center and heart of the total work, reinforcing its meaning and power, while at the same time keeping it where it belongs in the narrative sequence" (Freedman, 1991, 11). Freedman's further thesis (the closeness of the relationship of the Primary History to the commandments, 1991, 12–39) seems fragile, but his basic observation is valid: in some sense, Deuteronomy is at the center of the entire edifice. Even in quantity of text, Deuteronomy is central: the mid-point of the Primary History is the closing part of Deuteronomy. It is probably significant that in ancient compositions a major focus was not only on the end but also on the center (on Virgil, see Bonz, 2000, 41, 51; on Mark, see Stock, 1982, 47–53; 1989, 25; Standaert, 1978, 34–37, 174–261; cf. Robbins, 1996, 50–53).

To some degree, the centrality of Deuteronomy was acknowledged by very diverse sources—by scholarship, by Jewish tradition, and by Jesus. Scholarship indicated that Deuteronomy is both the conclusion of the Pentateuch and the foundation of Joshua-Kings. In Jewish tradition Deuteronomy contained two of the three texts, including the *Shema* (Deut. 6:4–9), which were sometimes worn on the body (in phylacteries). And Deuteronomy is the book most quoted by Jesus.

What is important is that the central role of Deuteronomy in scholarship and tradition accords with Freedman's contention that Deuteronomy has a special status from a strictly literary viewpoint, that it stands literally at the center of the Primary History. If a unified history requires a strong center, then the Primary History is well equipped. Like the keystone of a bridge, Deuteronomy is a sign of a larger unity.

General Conclusion to Chapters 1–5

The first conclusion is literary. There is significant evidence not only that Genesis is unified but that the same is true of the larger body of the Primary History. Many problems within the Primary History remain unresolved but, as with Genesis, the weight of evidence is shifting, and the idea of literary unity is gaining plausibility. It is the simplest hypothesis that accounts for the data.

The hypothesis that the Primary History is a collection is doubly inadequate. It is unnecessarily complex: it implies not just one writing process but several, plus an ill-defined procedure of gathering and editing. And it does not account for the data, for the deep-rooted continuity between the books. The simpler, adequate, hypothesis is that of literary unity.

This larger unity encompasses Genesis. Genesis may indeed be distinguished from Exodus-Kings, as may the hood of a garment from the rest of it. And like a hood, it may be the object of special attention. But in its fabric and design it is of a piece with the larger garment.

It is not appropriate then to separate the interpretation of Genesis from the larger corpus. There is a special relationship, for instance, between Genesis and the Elijah-Elisha narrative. Both texts—Genesis and the Elijah-Elisha narrative—have major interpretive roles. Genesis intimates all that is to come;[1] and

---

1. Genesis has been described as "the Old Testament of the Old Testament" (Moberly, 1992), as though Genesis belonged theologically to an older divine dispensation than the rest of the Pentateuch and of the Old Testament. The formulation ("OT of the OT") seems overdrawn but Moberly has a point: Genesis, the book of origins, portrays a unique time; and, correspondingly, Genesis has a unique status. Genesis has been also been described as "an introduction to the biblical world" (Adar, 1990), and this too captures an aspect of its role.

the Elijah-Elisha narrative reflects the completed work. Together they function respectively as prologue and interpretive interlude, and as such together they form a unity. They are like complementary aspects of the word—the word that is promised (Genesis), and the word that is fulfilled (Elijah-Elisha, with its emphasis on prophetic fulfillment).

The reflection of Genesis that occurs in the Elijah-Elisha narrative (especially in 1 Kings 16:29–chap. 18; *Crucial Bridge*, 2000, 42–46) serves not only to indicate the overall unity of the Primary History but also to clarify the meaning of Genesis itself. For instance, the pivotal image near the end of these chapters, that of fire coming down from heaven (1 Kings 18:20–39, esp. 20:38) is both an echo of the fire that consumed Sodom—the Genesis accounts of flood and fire are inherently connected—and a preparation for the images of heavenly fire that dominate the center of the narrative, namely the fire that came down from heaven and destroyed the fifty soldiers (2 Kings 1), and the subsequent fire, the fiery chariot, which, virtually in the sight of fifty prophets, took Elijah up to heaven (2 Kings 2). Genesis and its imagery may be at the other end of the Primary History but they are not forgotten. Genesis introduces the Primary History; the Elijah-Elisha narrative crystalizes it. The introduction and the crystallization mirror each other.

So when, for instance, it is said, most perplexingly, that Enoch "walked" with God and that God "took" him (Gen. 5:21–24) it is appropriate to look at the account of Elijah who, as he was walking along, was taken up to heaven (2 Kings 2:1–11). The account of Elijah's assumption has its own puzzles but the basic picture is clear. The intimation of life after death, which in the Enoch story is so faint that it could be missed or dismissed, becomes obvious in the case of Elijah. The same applies to other intimations in Genesis of life beyond death. It applies, for instance, to the tree of life, the burial of Sarah, and the story of Joseph. Such intimations are not to be dismissed.

The second conclusion is historical. Whatever the hesitations about dating Genesis to the exile or later, there are no such hesitations about the Primary History as a whole. The Primary History explicitly recounts the exile, and, at its conclusion—when the king of Judea is pardoned, released, and treated kindly (2 Kings 25:27–30)—there is an intimation of some form of recovery.

Given this literary unity and this suggestion of recovery, it is reasonable, as a working hypothesis, to ask whether the composition of the Primary History, including Genesis, occurred primarily during the time when the recovery actually took place—after the exile. This would make sense. The Primary History is a major work of interpretation. It meant standing back from a time of suffering and seeing it in a way that was comprehensive and essentially positive. Such an interpretive task is generally not undertaken quickly, amid shock and dislocation. It is necessary to allow some time.

Furthermore, from the pivotal role of Judah in Genesis, and the leading role of Levites (Moses and Aaron) in Exodus-Deuteronomy, to the climactic emphasis of the Elijah-Elisha narrative on the priests' role in reforming and repairing the temple (2 Kings 11–12), the entire history provides a rich and appropriate background for a postexilic Judea where priests and Levites are leaders. (For some scholars [especially, Ska, 2001] even the image of faithful Abraham fits best with the postexilic situation.)

Consequently, in seeking the historical background to the composition of the Primary History, including Genesis, and in trying to describe the compositional process itself, it is appropriate to ask whether the postexilic situation—the Persian empire (ca. 550–330 BCE)—provides the most credible setting.

The time has come, then, to shift the emphasis of this study from the text to its background—from the literary aspect to the historical. First, the history of the Persian empire.

PART TWO

HISTORICAL BACKGROUND

The Greco-Persian World and Its Impact on Questions of Sources and Composition

Now the discussion moves from the finished text to its background. Given the initial indications that the Primary History, including Genesis, was written in a world overshadowed by the diverse achievements of the Persians and the Greeks, it is appropriate first to summarize some general aspects of the Greco-Persian world in Chapter 6. The newness of this Persian period provides part of the matrix for the newness of Genesis and the Primary History.

Chapter 7 moves the focus in on some specific aspects of the Greco-Persian world: the spirit of theological inquiry; the codification of law, particularly as promoted by the long-reigning Darius (522–486 BCE); and, especially, the development of historiography among the Greeks of western Asia. It is this latter development, Greek historiography, which provides an appropriate cultural background for understanding the emergence of a narrative like the Primary History.

The role of Greek historiography as a background to the Primary History opens the way for a reconsideration of Genesis's sources in Chapter 8. These sources are of four main kinds—historiography, epic, prophecy, and law—but allowance must also be made for sources of other kinds.

Awareness of background and sources clarifies the question of composition in Chapter 9. And then, having come through many preliminary issues, it is finally appropriate to summarize the questions of date, people, and place in Chapter 10.

The Persian Empire

The era that saw the composition of the Primary History (Genesis-Kings) was that of the Persian empire.[1] The main rulers of the imperial dynasty (the Achaemenids) were as follows (with dates of accession; the date for Cyrus is that of defeating the Medes):

Cyrus (550) and Cambyses (529)

Darius (522)

Xerxes (486) and Artaxerxes (465)

Darius II (423); Artaxerxes II and III (404; 358); and Darius III (336)

The Persians were exceptional. Founded by the magnanimous Cyrus the Great, and marked by his spirit, the Persian empire brought a significant change. Of all the kingdoms and empires that the world had ever known—from third-millennium Sumer, Akkad, and Egypt to first-millennium Assyria and Babylonia—the Persian empire was greatest in its combination of size, coordination, and humaneness.

Its size was vast—from the western part of ancient India to northern Greece, and down, beyond Phoenicia, Damascus, and Jerusalem, to Egypt and Libya (for details, see Cook, 1983, 183–207). Apart from the Tigris and Euphrates, its rivers included the Nile and the Indus. And the seas on its borders included much of Aegean Sea, the Black Sea, the Caspian Sea, the Aral Sea, the Arabian Sea, the Persian Gulf, and the various coasts of the eastern Mediterranean. Thus, it included and surpassed all the territories of all the preceding empires in that part of the world. It was the largest political formation the world had ever seen.

As well as being vast, the empire was well coordinated. Its administration used one official language—Aramaic (Greenfield, 1985). There was a standardization of weights, measures, and money; money standardization was linked to the acquiring of Indian gold (Irving, 1979, 40). However, far from being a frozen bureaucracy, the empire was decentralized—divided into twenty states ("satra-

---

1. On Persian history, 550–330 BCE, see esp. Olmstead, 1948; Cook, 1983; Frye, 1984; Gershevitch, ed. 1985; *Achaemenid History*, Proceedings of the Achaemenid History Workshop, 8 vols., eds. H. Sancisi-Weerdenburg et al., Leiden, 1987–1994; Brentjes, 1995; Sancisi-Weerdenburg, 1995. On Judaism and the Persian empire, see esp. Grabbe, 1994, 119–145; Berquist, 1995.

pies"), which in turn were subdivided into provinces (the fifth satrapy contained several provinces, one of which was Yehud, a restricted form of Judea). Within this fluid administration was an efficient system of communications—a widespread road network combined with a form of regular postal service. The total mileage of imperial highways was about eight thousand miles (Graf, 1994, 188; cf. Mallowan, 1985, 402). Much of the road system had already been in place, but the Persians greatly improved it and did not hesitate to expand it. When the imperial army crossed to Europe and cut its way through the forests of northern Greece, it has been said that "the Tracians gaped at the new road with awe" (Burn, 1985, 320). The road network included extensions, which went up to the Black Sea and down to the Mediterranean, Damascus, Jerusalem, and Egypt, but the backbone of the network was an ancient highway, which effectively connected the capital, Susa, near the Persian Gulf, with Greek-speaking Ionia and with the Aegean Sea. Known as the Royal Persian Road ("the earliest long-distance road," Benson, 1981, 892–893), this highway was over fifteen hundred miles long, and it was rendered manageable by a system of hostels and some 111 intermediate stages. It took three months on foot, but the trained couriers—the form of postal service—could traverse it in just nine days (Beitzel, 1992, 781). This efficient system of travel and transport facilitated trade and cultural exchange. It also facilitated effective administration: "The King's writ ran from the Punjab to the Aegean" (Burn, 1985, 298).

Even at sea the Persians were sometimes innovative. Long before the Suez Canal, they opened a sea route from the East to the Mediterranean: they developed a canal from the Red Sea *to the Nile*—and thence to the Mediterranean (Irving, 1979, 38; Tuplin, 1991).

The empire, by and large, was also humane. "Few great leaders have left so good an impression with posterity as Cyrus. . . . Achaemenid rule gave Western Asia 200 years of peace" (Cook, 1983, 42, 229). When Babylon fell to Cyrus in the autumn of 539—an event as dramatic and peaceful as the 1989 fall of the Berlin Wall—he entered the vanquished city not as a strutting conqueror but, in his own words, "as a friend" (Negenman, 1969, 107). When he arrived at the statue of the Babylonian god Marduk, he respectfully took it by the hand (Young, 1981, 833; cf. Luckenbill, 1926, II, 35). In fact, his arrival in Babylon apparently brought a sigh of relief not only to the outside world but to the Babylonians themselves:

> When I entered Babylon as a friend and amid jubilation and rejoicing took my seat upon the throne . . . in the royal palace, then Marduk, the mighty lord, caused the magnanimous inhabitants of Babylon to take me to their hearts. And I daily bestirred myself to do him worship. The kings of the whole world, from the Upper Sea to the Lower Sea [= from the Mediterranean to the Persian Gulf], . . . all brought me rich tribute and kissed my feet in Babylon. . . . To the sacred cities on the other side of the Tigris, to the holy places which had long been in ruins, I caused to be returned the images that belonged to them, and I had permanent sanctuaries built for them.

I also gathered all the inhabitants and had them return to their dwelling-places. (From the Cylinder of Cyrus, cf. Negenman, 1969, 107)

Among those who were in Babylon on those memorable days, and among those whom Cyrus caused to return to their original dwelling-places, there were Judean exiles who, directly or indirectly, contributed to the composition of the Primary History, including the book of Genesis.

The Greek Expansion

Precisely during the years of the Persian empire something happened the like of which has scarcely ever been equaled. There was an extraordinary cultural flourishing. This development occurred especially among Greeks, but it was not something narrow or local. Its roots reached back into the art and literature of the ancient Near East, and its branches would eventually spread through later cultures. There has never been a single cultural expansion that was so innovative, diverse, and formative. A whole series of disciplines suddenly blossomed: travel books, cartography, historiography, drama (tragic and comic), lyric poetry, science, medicine, philosophy, democracy, rhetoric, politics, painting, sculpture, architecture. The names are exceptional: Anaximander, Hellanicus, Hecataeus, Archemides, Hippocrates (whence the oath), Thales, Pythagoras, Heracleitus, Herodotus, Thucydides, Xenophon, Demosthenes, Sappho, Aeschylus, Sophocles, Euripides, Aristophanes, Isocrates, Socrates, Plato, Aristotle. Even when the names were generally forgotten, as in painting, sculpture, and architecture, the influence lived on: "Throughout subsequent periods of the ancient world, the fifth century B.C. was known as the classical age when all the canons of style and dimensions were established" (Cheilik, 1991, 103).

This cultural blossoming was not hidden in some discreet academy in Athens. Several of the cultural leaders were also leaders in public life. Besides, the Greeks were scattered: due to frequent pressure from the north, they had poured down as it were through the Greek mainland, and, treating the sea as a congenial highway, had established themselves along the coasts of the Mediterranean, the Aegean, and the Black Sea (Boardman, 1980; Cheilik, 1991, 63; Livermore, 1966, 12; Bury and Meiggs, 1975, 68–80). In modern terms, they were spread—among other places—from Spain, France, and southern Italy to Egypt, Russia, and, crucially, western Asia (Turkey/"Asia Minor"/"Anatolia"). And with Greeks went their culture: "Wherever the Greek went, he retained his customs and language, and made a Greek 'polis.' It was as if a bit of Greece were set down on the remote shores of the [Black Sea] or Iberia" (Bury and Meiggs, 1975, 71).

During this time (550–330), therefore, the known world consisted of two main forces—the mighty Persian empire and the dazzling seafaring Greeks. Between them they stretched from the Indus to Italy, sometimes to Spain.

The Interweaving of Greeks and Persians

Theoretically two great forces may live apart, separated perhaps by an ocean or an iron curtain. But the Persian empire was no cocoon. It was acutely aware of cultural diversity and of what lay beyond its borders. It was "not only the first great empire of recorded history but [also] the first world civilization. It was not one culture imposed on another but a bringing together of diverse nations under one canopy" (Armajani, 1972, 27). To the east, Cyrus himself had been forced to protect the frontier, and one of the recurrent themes of subsequent Persian history was "the threat of peoples from the east" (Young, 1981, 833). There was significant awareness of India (Vogelsang, 1990; cf. Puri, 1963).

Above all, there was awareness of the Greeks, for several reasons. The Greek intellectual hub, the original center of Greek development, was not across the sea in Athens. It was within the Persian empire—in western Asia, Anatolia, especially in Ionia (biblical "Javan"). It was Ionia, rather than Athens, which first set the disciplines blossoming. Anatolia had also been, in previous centuries, the home of the Greeks' primordial poet and storyteller—Homer (ca. 700 BCE).

The reason for Anatolia's leadership is not far to find. As part of Asia it was closest to the great ancient heritage of Mesopotamia; "the Ionian islands and coast were in constant touch with the older civilizations of Asia" (Cheilik, 1991, 76). Contrary to the idea of a self-made classical Greek world, the Greeks were massively influenced by the East (for a summary of the evidence, see esp. Burkert, 1992), and much of this influence was filtered through Anatolia.

The Persians lost no time in absorbing this cultural crossroads. In fact, they conquered the Greek cities on the Aegean coast even before they captured Babylon. But the conquest ran in two directions: "Despite nominal Persian rule, many parts of Anatolia, especially those on the west and south coast, were increasingly hellenized" (Macqueen, 1995; cf. Yamauchi, 1996, 382).

And so from Ionia and the land of Homer communications were open in two opposite directions—across the sea to the lands and colonies of the Greeks, and along the Royal Road, which opened to the whole empire. Cultural exchange was easy. The average day's travel—about twenty miles—may seem little, but it was equal to average travel speed in the west until modern times (Beitzel 1992a, VI: 646–647). Even before the Persian empire there had been significant cultural communication between Greeks and the East. Not only Homer, but also his near contemporary Hesiod, who lived on mainland Greece, in Boetia, drew on the traditions of the Near East (Feldman, 1996, 19; Burkert, 1992, 5; cf. Vernant, 1982, 135). Already in the eighth century there was "a continuum of written culture . . . from the Euphrates to Italy" (Burkert, 1992, 31; cf. Müller, 1997).

What was true of culture was true also of trade. As never before the way was open for widespread exchange of goods and services. Merchants from eastern Iran were trading in upper Egypt (Armajani, 1972, 28). By the early sixth century, "Greek adventurers had served as mercenaries from the Egyptian cataracts to Babylon" (Drews, 1973, 4). In fact, both mercenaries and craftsmen moved freely (Burkert, 1992, 9–24).

Most dramatically, there was a major military and political involvement. Persia became involved in wars with the Greeks—wars against a revolt in Ionia, and wars that led to the gates of Athens (hence the battles of Thermopylae, Salamis, and Marathon). The wounds of these Greco-Persian wars soon healed. By 481 Greek-speaking Ionians were joining the Persian army (Young, 1981, 835), and in 449 Persia and Athens made peace (Garraty and Gay, 1972, 164). There was "a two-way process of acculturation and mutual influence" (Kuhrt and Sancisi-Weerdenburg, 1991, xiii). Eventually, around 330, the Greeks would conquer the Persians militarily, but long before that date the Greeks had made a huge impact.

In some ways the relationship between Greeks and Persians was quite complex. The most extensive sources for the history of the Persian empire were written by Greeks. Persia became involved in the internal quarrels of the Greeks, and a famous Greek expedition, chronicled by Xenophon, took sides in a quarrel among the Persians (405). When Themistocles, who had helped defeat the Persians, was banished from Athens, he fled to Persia and there, on an estate granted him by Artaxerxes I, lived like a landed gentleman, speaking Persian (Cook, 1963, 127). Other Greeks also received big estates (Cook, 1963, 128). Altogether there is evidence of "some three hundred Greeks who came to or lived at the Persian court in the period between Cyrus and Alexander" (Yamauchi, 1996, 383). Alcibiades, an Athenian leader and a disciple of Socrates, likewise took refuge in Persia before eventually returning to Athens (Cheilik, 1991, 97). The Persians at different times burned Athens (480 BCE) and financed the Spartans' fight against Athens (458, and again in 410); but later, fearing Sparta (ca. 394), they sent money to Athens to rebuild its walls (Cheilik, 1991, 86, 97 108; cf. Berquist, 1995, 107; Yamauchi, 1996, 379–394).

Apart from the general links between Greeks and the Persian empire as a whole, there was also the Greeks' apparent early connection with one specific area—the former Canaan and Judea, the area that was to fall within the empire's fifth state or satrapy. The words "Canaan" and "Israel" may seem far from the world of the Greeks, but this separation does not correspond to the reality of the first millennium BCE. "The geography of Palestine obliges us to consider the land a Mediterranean country. While the maps of course do justice to this fact, the OT histories as a rule do not. . . . Standard books such as *ANET* completely omit the Mediterranean factor" (Gordon, 1963, 19, 31).

Apart from geography, there was also a fundamental historical connection. The most obvious feature is the arrival of the Philistines—an Aegean people. The connection, however, is broader. According to Gordon, "The basic scheme of things is thus: Historic Greece and Israel sprang from a basically semitic Minoan-Canaanite culture of the second millennium; later they developed their distinctive classical cultures during the first two-thirds of the first millennium.

. . . [It has been] demonstrated that contacts were constant ever since 1000 BCE" (1963, 20, 21). The link between Canaan and the Aegean has been further indicated by the discovery of Ugarit (Gordon, 1962, 128–205). Ugarit in its time was a center of trade and influence, with trade routes equally to Greece and to diverse parts of the Near East, including Canaan (Pritchard, 1987, 44–45).

Well north of Ugarit, but still on the eastern coast of the Mediterranean, lie the archaeological remains of Al Mina, at the mouth of the Orontes. Here, in a particularly visible way, the Greeks left their mark—the result of living there and trading for centuries, particularly around 800–600 BCE (Boardman, 1980, 38–51). From Al Mina the way was open to Syria and thus to all those who dealt with Syria (Cook, 1963, 64; Burkert, 1992, 11). The Greeks had a special link with the Phoenicians, the people from whom they got their alphabet and with whom, in a special way, they shared the sea-lanes of the Mediterranean (Burkert, 1992, 21–30; Boardman, 1980, 210–216).

The interweaving of Greeks with Phoenicians, and thereby with the Fertile Crescent, is particularly clear in a detailed map of their colonies (see, for instance, map 3, in Butler, 1883,). These colonies formed a complex web stretching literally from one end of the Mediterranean to the other.

The work of Brown (1995) has provided fresh multifaceted evidence of Greek-Israelite connections. One facet involves texts:

> The unique excellences of Hebrew and Greek literature are most akin to novelties in biological evolution. . . . Israel and Hellas represent two poles of an unrepeatable emergence. . . . The doctrines of divine revelation and classical form express that special character for the two societies respectively. My novelty here consists in laying out the hidden connections between the twin centers of the new development. The argument of this book . . . should enlarge our notions of both theism and humanism; it should also bring us to see revelation and classicism as the two forms of a broader notion. (1995, 14)

Connections, therefore, exist. But perhaps they are accidental. Again Brown:

> Are the parallel features of the texts accidents, or the result of historical connections? Here I list what I regard as unmistakable indications (for those who have ears to hear) drawn from the texts that the two societies were in touch at one or more removes. . . . A few texts . . . are in effect *translations* of each other. . . . Others show abundantly that Israel and Hellas lived in *the same geopolitical world* of states and rulers, with the shared vocabulary of their *proper names*. Above all . . . the texts witness that the two societies were engaged in *parallel enterprises* with a *shared vocabulary of common nouns* (and a few verbs too). (1995, 14)

Brown (1995, 15) does not believe that he himself should undertake the comparing of epic narratives—Greek and Near Eastern (cuneiform)—but in effect his work helps to set the scene for such comparison, including the comparison of Greek epic with Hebrew narrative.

Conclusion

Politically, the Persian empire and the Greeks were distinct. But economically and culturally they were massively interwoven—particularly through the Ionian cities and through the interlocking of Persian roads and Greek ships. Together they effectively controlled much of the known world, lending it a certain unity. The Persians not only fought with the Greeks. They also made peace with them, traded with them, aided them, and welcomed them.

7   Greco-Persian Features

Theological Inquiry, Codification, and Historiography

Looking more closely at the Greco-Persian world, it is useful, when investigating the Primary History, to take account of some key features. These features include the spirit of theological inquiry, the codification of law, and the transition from epic to historiography. Among these features one in particular is reflected in the Primary History—Greek-style historiography.

Theological Inquiry

The spirit of theological inquiry is not unique to the Greco-Persian era, nor is it a feature that is easily documented, but it is appropriate to indicate its presence. Part of the story goes back to the initial Persian conquest:

> In 546 the Persians subjugated the Greek cities along the west coast of Asia Minor. Intellectually this had been the foremost area of the Greek world. Here the Homeric poems had taken shape; here the lyric poets had sung. Here too philosophy had begun about 585, with the speculations of Thales as to the possible origin of all things from some single element. . . . The important thing was his attempt to conceive nature as an intelligible order, a "cosmos." This intellectual daring was, in Ionia, fused with the new idea of individualism. . . . From Ionia the spirit of inquiry spread abroad when the Persian conquest produced a wave of emigrants. South Italy and Sicily became briefly the centers of philosophic thought. Xenophanes, who emigrated about 545, argued that the primary substance must be single, eternal, unchanging, conscious, controlling all things—in a word, God. Thus physics led to metaphysics and theology. The contrast is striking between this [physics-based]

monotheism and [the history-based monotheism of] Second Isaiah, roughly contemporary. . . . Both lines of thought led to attacks on idolatry and on popular notions of the gods. (Garraty and Gay, 1972, 168–169)

This background seems particularly helpful in discussing Genesis 1, a text that contains significant philosophical content (Samuelson, 1992).

Apart from theological inquiry—further aspects of Greco-Persian background could be usefully explored. One such feature is the social setting. It has been suggested, for instance, that one aspect of Genesis 1, its portrayal of order, may have been influenced by the social order of the Persian empire (Berquist, 1995, 139, 143).

However, two features are particularly significant: the codification of law; and the move away from epic poetry to a new form of prose.

The Codification of Law

There has always been uncertainty as to when and why Israel or Judea codified their law. At one level of course the Bible provides a clear answer: the Law was communicated to Moses on a mountaintop. But this is a simplification. Apart from customs, the origin of which is often forgotten, laws frequently originate from state authorities, and it is not clear how Sinai came to be regarded as the origin of biblical law (for discussion, see Crüsemann, 1996, 27–57).

The idea of a mountaintop commissioning is not unique. Hesiod received his call from the Muses while shepherding at a holy mountain (*Theogony*, 23–35). And "King Minos [of Crete] received the Law from Zeus on a sacred mountain, even as Moses did from God. Moreover, Minos is seconded by his master craftsman Daedalus, even as Moses is by Bezalel (Exod. 31:1)" (Gordon, 1963, 281).

The idea of a Mosaic origin is maintained by later books. It is recorded that after the exile, following King Artaxerxes' authorizing of Nehemiah to return to Judea, Ezra "the priest . . . the scribe" brought the Law to the people in Jerusalem and read it to them as if it were from Moses (Neh. 2:1–8; 8:1–3).

Given the idea of the mountaintop commissioning, it is understandable that the Bible gives no further account of the Law's origin. Instead it simply tells how the Law was communicated under the Persians. The origin therefore is shrouded in obscurity. Even the later communication is obscure: it is not clear what exactly happened when Ezra brought the Law to the people or at what date he did so (both the date and historical character of the book of Nehemiah are debated; see, for instance, Crüsemann, 1996, 334–339). What appears significant is that, while guarding the principle of divine origin, the bringing of the Law to the people is set broadly in the context of a Persian authorization.

Blenkinsopp (1992, 239–240), in discussing the origin of the Pentateuch, mentions an important factor: the Persian presence tended to encourage processes that gave self-definition to local peoples:

> During these two centuries . . . one aspect of . . . imperial policy was the insistence on local self-definition inscribed primarily in a codified and standardized corpus of traditional law backed by the central government and its regional representatives. . . . In Babylon, therefore, the New-Babylonian laws would have remained in force, and continued interest in the Code of Hammurabi may be deduced from copies made in the sixth and fifth centuries. As for Egypt . . . Darius I set up a commission of warriors, priests and scribes to codify the traditional Egyptian laws, the final draft of which was written up in Aramaic and demotic Egyptian. The composition of the commission charged with this task suggests an insistence on a legal system based on consensus. . . . Internal harmony was essential for the preservation of the *pax Persica* in the many and diverse ethnic groups in the empire.

This Egyptian codification strengthens the idea that, directly or indirectly, part of the impetus for composing the Law came from the circumstances of Persian rule, especially from Darius (Olmstead, 1948, 119–134; cf. Berquist, 1995, 138, 235; Crüsemann, 1996, 350–352, 356–358).

Persian law was twofold:

> There was a dual system of laws in the empire, the "king's law," applicable everywhere, and local laws which were codified by order of the king. . . . The concept of a universal "king's law" over the local "laws" of subject peoples was a legacy which the Romans followed and which, as far as we know, was an innovative feature of [Persian] rule. (Frye, 1984, 119, 135)

The "king's law" also involved codification—a process inspired significantly by the Hammurabi-based Mesopotamian code (Irving, 1979, 42). The idea of a long-term influence on Rome is not far-fetched. There was regular travel between the empire's Aegean coast and Italy; and Darius, early in his reign (522–486 BCE), "sent a sea-borne spying mission to southern Italy" (Irving, 1979, 39).

The connection between Persian law and Roman law does not impinge directly on the discussion of the origin of the Judeans' Law but it provides a broad context, a sense of the foundational role of Persia. Within this context Frye envisages the emergence of the Torah: "Darius's codification of the laws . . . is probably the beginning, for example, of the Jewish Torah as the law of the Jewish people. The king wanted a system of international law, which was the king's laws above the local laws, but he also wanted the local laws to be in good order" (quoted in Irving, 1979, 42). Consequently, in the search for the circumstances leading to the codification of the Pentateuch and the broader formation of the Primary History, Darius's emphasis on codification is significant. It provides a context of codification that is independently verifiable.

However, a further Persian-era factor is even more pertinent and verifiable.

The Transition from Epic Poetry to Historiography

When writing was first invented (in Mesopotamian Sumer, ca. 3000 BCE) its forms or genres were quite limited. It proved useful, for instance, for trade and administration, and for lists, inscriptions, and brief annual chronicles (the lists and inscriptions generally dealt with kings). But there were no Shakespeare-like dramas or Tolstoy-like novels, no detailed biographies such as Boswell's life of Johnson. Nor was there any complex historiography. Only slowly did the various literary genres develop.

Mesopotamia's primary literary genre was epic poetry—poetry that told of the exploits or travels of heroic figures, whether mythical or historical (Gilga-mesh, Atrahasis, Marduk, Sargon, Tukulti-Nitura) (van Seters, 1983, 92–96). Other important genres included written legislation (especially the code of Hammurabi) and written prose prophecy (van Seters, 1983, 96–99).

In Egypt, as in Mesopotamia, the development of literature eventually led to the description of people's exploits and travels. The genre used, however, was not heroic epic poetry but something close to a form of historical novel (van Seters, 1983, 160–172). The classic *Story of Sinuhe*, composed soon after 2,000 BCE, tells of an Egyptian courtier who went into exile in Asia, and, after many years, eventually returned. The account reflects historical conditions, and blends elements of biography and the novel.

The literatures toward the west—near the Phoenician coast and in Asia Minor (Ugarit, the Hittites, and the Ionians)—show varying degrees of affinity with Mesopotamia. The writings of ancient Ugarit consist largely of epic poetry, but are heavily mythological and have little relation to history. The Hittites, on the other hand, have annals or chronicles—some written in both Hittite and Akkadian—that are akin to the chronicles of Mesopotamia, and that, while stereotyped, do give a sense of the passage of history.

Among the Greek-language Ionians, what emerged was a mixture of epic poetry and history: the Homeric poems (the *Iliad* and the *Odyssey*, written perhaps around 700 BCE), while consisting of epic poetry and containing some mythology, reflected a significant sense of history (the Trojan war) and biog-raphy (the wanderings of Odysseus). About the same time, further west, in Greece proper, Hesiod wrote two more epic poems, and while one, *Theogony*, was largely mythological—it dealt especially with the origin of the gods, the world, and women—the other, *Works and Days*, was much closer to ordinary life. Attached to *Theogony* was *The Catalogue of Women*—a mixture of geneal-ogies and episodes (written apparently around 550 BCE, now lost, except for fragments). There is strong evidence that both Homer and Hesiod were in-debted to their eastern neighbors, especially to Mesopotamia (Feldman, 1996, 13–21; Burkert, 1992, 88–127). The wanderings of Odysseus, for instance, re-flect those of Gilgamesh (Feldman, 1996, 16–17).

In the sixth and fifth centuries BCE, some time after the epic poetry of Homer and Hesiod, literature underwent another development: as never before, poetry gave way to prose. In literary history, prose of its nature follows poetry (Frye, 1981, 8; cf. Lesky, 1966, 221).

In practice the development of prose meant that in various ways Homeric epic was turned into prose history. This transition—from Homer to history—was not arbitrary. As already mentioned, Homer's own work had already contained a historical dimension. In particular, it had begun to take a wide view of events and causes and to move beyond mythology:

> Historiography . . . arose among the Greeks . . . and from very diverse beginnings. For a long time their mythology served the Greeks for history, and [the development of historiography] took a long hard struggle. . . . It is quite conceivable that the Greek epics contained a good deal of historical material. . . . [In epic poetry] a start had been made . . . to tie the events and personalities together into a temporal sequence by means of genealogical cross-links. . . . But more important than all else, epic poetry was already looking beyond the unique and individual happening and asking what relevance it had to the world as a whole, asking also after the causes and connections of things, and looking for some ultimate meaning in the course of events. Homer is in this sense the "father of history." (Lesky, 1966, 218)

The social context of this change from heroic poetry to prose has been described by Plutarch (*Moralia: De Pythiae Orac.* 406B–E, esp. 406E). He tells how there was an overall movement from luxury to simplicity—away, for instance, from elaborate hairstyles and elaborate clothing; and furthermore, "language underwent the same transformation, the same stripping down: history abandoned the chariot of poetry, and by learning to walk on foot in prose succeeded in distinguishing truth from legend" (Flacelière's translation, 112).

Like Homeric epic, the new history-oriented movement came from western Asia—from the Greek-speakers of Ionia (Pearson, 1939; van Seters, 1983, 8–54). "Just as with poetry, philosophy and medicine, so with the writing of history the decisive impulse came to western Hellas from the Ionian coast" (Lesky, 1966, 332). Accordingly, when the Athenians needed a history, the person who supplied it, Hellanicus, was not an Athenian but a writer from the Ionian coast (from Lesbos, ca. 430). It was the area around Ionia, in fact, within the Persian empire, that gave birth to the three writers who in many ways pioneered the writing of historiography: Hecataeus, Hellanicus, and Herodotus.

Charting the World, Geographically and Genealogically: Hecataeus (ca. 565–490)

Born in Miletus, one of the intellectual powerhouses of Ionia, Hecataeus has been called "the first prose writer, or *logographos* . . . the man who foreshadows Herodotus" (Flacelière, 1964, 126). He composed histories that were heavily mythical and genealogical, but he is particularly distinguished for his role in trying to map the world. For these purposes he traveled widely. At times the travels were startling. He had been proud that he could trace his own lineage for sixteen generations, going back to a god, but in Egypt he met a priest who claimed to trace 345 generations (Lesky, 1966, 221). While his works have largely perished, the history (*Genealogies*, mythical-legendary) and especially the *Description of the World* (including travels, tales, and a map) still survive in hundreds of fragments and quotes (Pearson, 1939, 96). It is he apparently who started the tradition of beginning a history with his own name ("Hecataeus of Miletus . . .")—a tradition followed by Herodotus and Thucydides (Pearson, 1939, 97). And it is he who first refers to Egypt as "a gift of the Nile" (Flacelière, 1964, 126).

Charting the Nation's Role in the World: Herodotus (ca. 500–425, from Halicarnassus)

Like Hecataeus, Herodotus, too, was a traveler; he moved easily through the Persian empire and indeed through the known world:

> Peace reigned in the . . . empire in the mid fifth century. Conditions for travel were at their best; and it was possible for a gentleman of Halicarnassus to move freely about Egypt, Babylonia and the Levant, as well as to visit the Scythians, lecture in Athens and Olympia, and participate in the foundation of a new colony in Italy. . . . His travels were part of a grand programme of research. (Cook, 1963, 128)

To make matters yet easier, "everywhere he went he found Greeks or people who could speak Greek" (Flacelière, 1964, 167). His multifaceted *Histories* had a universal scope—it was virtually encyclopedic—but Herodotus emphasized the role of Greeks, thus giving the Greeks both an awareness of the world and a national pride (de Romilly, 1985, 63). He begins with two abductions—of a Greek princess to Egypt in pre-Homeric times, and of Helen to Troy—and then continues through the centuries into the time of the Persians. His interests were many, including natural history, cosmography, and geography, but his primary focus was on humanity as a whole (Flacelière,1964, 171).

Charting a City's Millennium: Hellanicus (ca. 480–400, from Mytilene in Lesbos)

Unlike the much-traveled Hecataeus and Herodotus, Hellanicus generally remained near his base. There he collected the writings of others, and produced prolifically—twenty-three large works. His own writings therefore, which survive only in fragments, constitute "literature which is wholly based on *litterae*" (Lesky, 1966, 330). His biggest challenge came when the Athenians, who knew relatively little of their own background, experienced a form of crisis:

As Athenian historical interest quickened, intelligent Athenians became aware how little knowledge they could muster of their own city's past. . . . In contrast with the Ionian cities, many of whom could boast of rich and eventful histories, Athens must have felt humiliated. A golden opportunity therefore presented itself to the courageous writer who could reconstruct the Athenian past, bring its legends into relation with reality, and prove to the world that there was such a thing as Attic history. It was a difficult task, needing the experience of a man well versed both in legendary and in historical lore. The ideal person would be a man who had done some work in elucidating the early history of other states and who had studied mythology from a rationalistic point of view. Such a man was Hellanicus, a writer with an established reputation. (Pearson, 1942, 7)

From quite limited materials Hellanicus produced a history that went back a thousand years. The surviving fragments of this work indicate some of its main aspects, including its basic organization (Pearson, 1942, 15). It had three parts, each treated differently:

1. The prehistoric/mythical period of the kings (before the Trojan war).
2. The intermediate period (to the middle of the fifth century).
3. The great civil war ("Peloponnesian," end of the fifth century).

The process of writing involved a striking degree of freedom. The construction of the prehistoric period, for example, was ingenious. Using diverse sources—among them the Hesiod-related *Catalogue of Women* with its mixture of genealogies and episodes—Hellanicus juggled and adapted his materials until he produced a schema that was complete (van Seters, 1992, 93–95). The resulting list of kings covered a period of about four centuries (ca. 1600–1200 BCE; Pearson, 1942, 17). The highpoint among these prehistoric kings was number ten—Theseus, circa 1300 BCE:

> The fragments reveal that Hellanicus was instrumental in establishing a tradition about Theseus, and especially in attributing to him certain characteristics which made him into something of an Athenian Heracles. [Hellanicus's] work of *Ktiseis* or *Foundings of Cities* had doubtless taught him something about the popular attitude towards national heroes. . . . Theseus was in a sense the founder of Athens. (Pearson, 1942, 18)

In developing the figure of Theseus, and in modeling him partly on the greatest of Greek heroes, the man-god Heracles, Hellanicus was not alone. But Hellanicus's role was important. (On "the invention of Theseus," see Morris, 1992, 336–361; cf. Arafat, 1996; Calame, 1990, 415–421; Garland, 1992, 82–98; Tyrrell and Brown, 1991, 161–170; and especially, Walker, 1995, 3–33).

Hellanicus, therefore, wrote with freedom, but apparently he was also attentive to the popular attitude. There is no representative commission, as in the process of Egyptian codification, but there is a form of listening.

The Convergence of the Primary History with
Greco-Persian Historiography

In the whole range of ancient literature (3000–400 BCE), the Genesis-Kings history finds its nearest analogue in the historiographical writing of the sixth and fifth centuries, especially in the works of Hellanicus and Herodotus. This does not mean that only Hellanicus, Herodotus, and Genesis-Kings fit a specific definition of history (the definition of history is controverted; see Younger, 1990, 25–46). Nor does it mean that Hellanicus, Herodotus, and Genesis-Kings are exactly the same kind of writing; in some ways they are hugely different. Nor does it exclude major affinities with other, older, literatures (Genesis-Kings, while its main literary genre is historiography, contains a synthesis of several genres).

But the historical literatures of the Near East do not match Genesis-Kings; they have neither its style nor scope. Grayson (1975, 1) highlights the difference of style: "The clarity and beauty of style found in the ancient Hebrew narratives is unique among historical documents from the ancient Near East." And in scope, too, the difference is great; Near Eastern historians never match the sweep and diversity of the Primary History. Thus, an analogue for the style and scope of the Primary History does not exist in the Near East.

But it does among the Greeks. The Persian-period Greek-language writers, including Greek historiographers, offer unique examples of style and scope. Hecataeus's mapping is a partial analogue for Genesis 10. In particular, the histories of Hellanicus and Herodotus share something fundamental with Genesis-Kings: an almost encyclopedic combination of length and breadth. They include not only whole centuries but in a sense the whole of life. Herodotus

> sketched the history of various peoples. . . . He did not confine himself to the simple narrative of events. To him "History" whose original meaning was simply "enquiry" or "research," included the geography of the known world, together with the natural history, and the social organization, customs and religious practices of the different races. . . . [He] . . . blended . . . breath of understanding, curiosity, scepticism and tolerance. (Cook, 1983, 128)

Such comprehensiveness is different from earlier forms of history, different, for instance, from the repetitive narrowness of the Mesopotamian chronicles (see Appendix 5). But in the Primary History, including Genesis, this comprehensiveness is matched, even surpassed.

Within this broad affinity, the literary genre of Genesis includes historiography, a form of history that contains diverse elements, including story, and also including myth in its most positive sense. (The word "saga" is less appropriate; it tends to be associated with recent kinds of oral culture, rather than with ancient literary forms, such as historiography.) The authors of the biblical history need not necessarily have known the work of Hellanicus and Herodotus—judgment on that issue awaits further research—but the work of these two fifth-century writers provides at least a broad context for understanding the emergence of Genesis-Kings.

The connection of Genesis with the writing of history had already been indicated by Wellhausen (1883). But Gunkel (1910, 1; cf. trans. 1994, 1), partly because his idea of history was narrow—unduly modern—and partly because he was so aware of other aspects of Genesis, opposed the idea that Genesis was any form of history; and it was not until the work of van Seters (1983, 1992) that the basic affinity with developed historiography was clearly recognized.

Yet a certain continuity between Greek historiography and biblical writing has long been recognized in principle—at least by Toynbee: "Ancient Greek or Hellenic historical thought began at the moment when the first rudiments of the poetry of Homer shaped themselves in Greek minds. It came to an end when Homer yielded precedence to the Bible as the sacred book of a Greek-speaking and Greek-writing *inteligentzia*" (1950, v).

What is essential is that Greek historiography makes the origin of the Primary History become less puzzling. The link is not primarily in some small example or detail, though, given work such as that of Brown (1996), the possible emergence of detailed examples is not to be excluded. What counts primarily is the Hebrew history *as a whole*: the entire Primary History fits well into the context of Persian-era Greek historiography.

8   Verifiable Sources

Historiography, Epic, Prophecy, Law, and Other

Initially, in modern research, it was presumed that all of Genesis's sources had been lost. Whether one believed the whole book was written by Moses or that it was a mixture of four hypothetical documents (those designated J, E, D, and P) there seemed to be no hope of laying one's hands on any of the underlying documents.

That situation began to change on December 3, 1872. Speaking in London, George Smith publicized some Assyrian accounts of the flood story (*ANET* xiii; Hess and Tsumura, 1994, 4–5). For the first time there was the prospect of reading and checking independent texts that could have been used in composing Genesis. Perhaps the biblical flood story depended on the Assyrian account.

As years passed it became clear that not only the flood story but much of Genesis 1–11 depended in some way on ancient texts that still survive, especially on epic poetry. Genesis 1–11 has absorbed, transformed, and synthesized various aspects of the *Epic of Gilgamesh,* the *Atrahasis Epic,* and the *Enuma Elish.* In Clifford's words, "Mesopotamian culture [was] evidently the model for most of the stories in Gen 1–11. . . . The similarity of the Atrahasis plot to Gen 2–9 is clear. . . . The biblical writers have produced a version of a common Mesopotamian story of the origins of the populated world" (1990, 2:2).

Nor were Mesopotamian cultural links limited to Genesis 1–11. The Covenant Code (Exod. 20:22–chap. 23), for instance, was found to be colored by a well-established tradition of law and codification which, in the code of Hammurabi, went back to eighteenth-century Babylon.

More recently a further world of influence has begun to emerge—that of Greek historiography (see preceding chapter).

At the same time, yet another source of inspiration has begun to be revealed—Israel's own prophets. The lives and visions of the prophets have provided material for Israel's early history, at least in the Pentateuch, including Genesis (see esp. Schmid, 1976; Brodie, 1981; van Seters, 1992, 1994, 1994a).

Bearing these things in mind, and having done further work, it seems reasonable to propose the following: Genesis used four main kinds of sources—historiography, epic poetry, prophecy, and law. These four, of course, do not exclude the use of many other sources.

Historiography

The primary dependence is not of content but of genre (form/type of writing). In other words, Greek historiography provided at least the broad literary context for the genre of Genesis. It does not yet seem possible to say that Genesis made direct use of a specific Greek historiographer, yet the possibility is worth investigating. It is normal for writers to secure copies of other works in their own genres.

Epic

The use of epic poetry was almost inevitable—both because it was probably the most famous literature in the world, and because historiography was descended from it (Lesky, 1966, 218). Examples of epic poetry from pre-550 BCE include not only the *Epic of Gilgamesh,* the *Atrahasis Epic,* and the *Enuma Elish,* but also, from around 700 BCE, the works of the two great Greek writers, Homer (the *Iliad,* the *Odyssey*), and Hesiod (*Theogony,* including the later *Catalogue of Women;* and *Works and Days*). None of these works—Mesopotamian or Greek—was written in Hebrew.

Since the dependence of much of Genesis 1–11 on epic poetry has already been established the primary problem concerns Genesis 12–50.

The claim to a specifically Jewish epic, perhaps oral in origin, cannot be excluded in principle (on the epic theories of Albright and Cassuto, see van Seters, 1983, 225–227), but—unlike the *Epic of Gilgamesh*, the *Atrahasis Epic*, and the *Enuma Elish*—there is no surviving literary evidence for such an epic.

Homer may seem alien to the Bible—a western intrusion into the Near Eastern world. But the division into west and east is a later construct, as is the very phrase "Near East." This east/west division does not correspond to the historical and sociological reality of the ancient world. As already seen (Chapter 6), the Homeric homeland was within the Persian network (note Brown, 1995). In today's perception the *Odyssey* may seem alien to biblical studies, but it is no more alien than Gilgamesh seemed to most biblical scholars of the nineteenth century. In fact, there is significant evidence that Genesis 11–50 made systematic use of the *Odyssey* (see Appendix 3).

Prophecy

The use of written prophecy was also virtually inevitable, for two reasons. First, these writings were available. It is very difficult to reconstruct a scenario, whether in Jerusalem or Babylon, in which a serious author would not have access to Israel's own prophetic writings—to the writings of those prophets who preceded and dominated the exile. Second, the prophets were central to Judaism; they were like its lungs; they—and their writings—kept it alive. An author who made methodical use of historiography and epic poetry is likely to have been equally methodical in using the prophetic writings.

Such in fact is the case. A close comparison of Genesis with the prophets indicates heavy indebtedness to written prophecy (see Appendix 2). In the final analysis, the heartbeat of Genesis is neither historiography nor epic poetry; it is prophecy. The genre of Genesis includes historiography, but it is not limited to it.

Both epic and prophecy consist largely of ancient poetry, and as such they are resonant with the rhythms of oral transmission. Genesis, however, while poetic and full of oral rhythms, is prose. It has taken high-flowing poetry and brought it down to the prosaic rhythms of daily life.

Law

Every society has laws or customs, and in ancient times some law codes were particularly famous—especially that of Hammurabi (ca. 1700 BCE). This general feature of human society was renewed by the Persians, especially by the long-reigning Darius (522–486; see Chapter 7). Whatever the complexity of Pentateuchal law (see Crüsemann, 1996; Levinson, 1997), it is probable that all these contexts—the general presence of laws, the existence of prestigious codes, and the empire's emphasis on law—contributed to the special place of law in the Primary History. However, as mentioned earlier (Chapter 5), there is also significant evidence that the Primary History itself—the larger narrative—is reflected in the various laws (Carmichael, 1974, 1979, 1985, 1996).

Other

Apart from historiography, epic, prophecy, and law, Genesis used other sources—among them some novellas or novel-like stories. This is particularly true of the Joseph story (see esp. Humphreys, 1988). In Irvin's words:

> . . . Literature of the ancient Near East . . . written earlier than the Old Testament can be used to gain information about the world of ideas [especially plot-motifs and traditional episodes] in which the Old Testament took shape . . . [episodes such as] the spurned seductress, . . . the interpreter of dreams, . . . the success of the unpromising, . . . [and] the treasure in the sack. (1977, 184–191, esp. 184)

Irvin is speaking not so much of the direct use of sources as of drawing on a general store of plot-motifs and episodes. The context, however, is that of literature, and so, for those who wanted them, these materials would have been available in a form that was written.

There is evidence, too, that Genesis used Ugarit materials. In the case, for instance, of the divine visit to Abraham (18:1–15) "the whole scene seems to be a monotheistic adaptation to the semi-nomadic early Hebrew setting of an episode from the Ugarit *Tale of Aqhat* (V:6–7)" (Alter, 77, citing Moshe Weinfeld). This overstates the case—the Ugarit text provides only one component—but the essence of the observation is true: Genesis 18 draws on the Ugarit account, or at least on materials shared by the Ugaritic account. The overall contribution of Ugaritic is considerable; it "represents better than any other second millenium language or literature the antecedents of the language and literature of ancient Israel" (Parker, 1989, 225).

Somewhat similarly is the case of Enoch: there are several links between the description of Enoch, the seventh figure in the antediluvian genealogy of Genesis 5 (Gen. 5:24), and the description, found in the Babylonian King List, of Enmeduranki, seventh of the ten long-lived antediluvian kings. Hence, "it is now clear that the figure of Enoch derives from Enmeduranki" (Day, 1996, 237).

Conclusion

Whatever the details of Genesis's sources, the overall impression is of a writer who, while adapting one central literary form—that of historiography—then drew on multiple sources to enrich the content. Yet the multiplicity of sources was not allowed to dominate. As Kselman says about the dependence of the flood story on ancient epics: "The ancient . . . material was consciously reshaped and altered in accordance with Israelite theological perspectives" (91). Foreign cultures, however prestigious, were not swallowed unthinkingly. They were consciously altered. The Greeks may have seemed dazzling, but the author of Genesis was not intimidated. Something further was still possible.

9   Toward Detecting the Process of Composition

To think that the Hebrews were simple people who, under their tents, recounted stories which were later put in writing or [to think] that the biblical books are the echo of purely oral traditions is to view the Bible in a way that is an aberration. A text like Genesis is magnificently crafted ("*magnifiquement surélaboré*"). It is not only written, it is written as no one ever wrote. I do not know, in all the world's literature, a text which makes use of such word technique, of such science of expression, of so much art.

André Chouraqui (1975, 455)

The question of Genesis's composition is inseparable from the larger question of how the Primary History as a whole was composed. And as the literary unity of the Primary History becomes clearer, so the picture of its composition begins to change. For instance, the account of finding the Law in the temple (2 Kings 22–23) seemed for many years to provide an anchor for discussing the history of composition. But, if the Primary History is a literary unity then the account of finding the Law in the Mount Zion temple (2 Kings 22–23) is probably no more historical than the account of giving the Law on Mount Sinai, and probably no more historical than the account of finding the apparently lost king in the temple (2 Kings 11). The two temple texts (2 Kings 11 and 22–23) are inherently connected; one is a reworking of the other (*Crucial Bridge*, 2000, 63–66). One cannot afford then to rely on a theory centered around the hypothesis of the finding of a certain part of the Law in the Temple. It is necessary to stand back and reassess the process of composition.

The problem may be divided under several headings: first, the general process; second, the general nature of the sources (oral or written?); third, the number of people involved in writing; and fourth, some specific procedures concerning form and depth.

The General Process

The Composition of the Primary History

There are four main theories on the origin of Genesis-Kings:

1. A form of Genesis-Joshua was first, and was expanded by deuteronomists.
2. Two independent works (Gen.-Josh.; the deuteronomic history) were combined and edited.
3. Deuteronomic history was first, and was later extended back to the beginning.
4. Several independent blocks were combined and edited.

Forms of these theories have been proposed by several scholars (see Boorer, 1989, 197–201; 1992, 7–34):

1. Wellhausen, Driver, Eissfeldt, Hölscher, Tengström, Schulte
2. Noth, Mowinckel, Cross, Weimar, Peckham, Schmid
3. Van Seters, Rose
4. Rendtorff (cf. Blum, 1984, 1990)

Boorer's analysis indicates that pivotal land-related texts in Deuteronomy were written after those in Exodus and Numbers (1992, 428–430). Her conclusions, which, in her own words, "directly contradict the position of Van Seters" (1992, 434), tend toward paradigm 1: a form of Genesis-Joshua was first, and was expanded by deuteronomists (1992, 440).

Even in the few years since some of these theories were proposed the state of research has changed significantly. The main development has been the accumulation of evidence that the Primary History is a literary unity and that that unity is pervasive (see Chapter 5). It is becoming more difficult, for instance, to speak of works or blocks which were independent. Texts which at first appear independent emerge as intricately interwoven with other texts. Furthermore, as already seen (Chapter 1), even where variations exist, it is also becoming more difficult, when discussing a single text, to speak credibly about distinct editors or authors.

Accordingly, without endorsing all of Boorer's conclusions, the present chapter tends as she does toward paradigm 1, but with important modifications. The proposal here is that, *apart from initial drafting and final editing*, there were three central steps:

INITIAL DRAFTING

The essential narrative (Genesis-Kings) was outlined—from creation to exile. The long history was set to run from the most ancient of Mesopotamian beginnings, namely creation, to a variation on the most prestigious of Greek endings, namely the fall of the city (cf. the fall of Troy, in the *Iliad*) (see Chapter 5; Speiser, lvii; Freedman, 1991, 9–10). To bridge this distance—more than three thousand years—the outline relied significantly on a tentative underlying chain of genealogies (Genesis), journeys (Exodus-Joshua), and reigns (Judges-Kings) ("reigns" of judges, and of kings). The period—creation to exile—may seem a long time to span, but in a world where Hecataeus recounted meeting an Egyptian who claimed to trace 345 generations it was not extravagant. The outline would have indicated events, basic themes, motifs, events, and characters.

STAGE 1

The outline was developed into a near-complete narrative: Genesis; much of the life of Moses (probably the book of Exodus); Joshua; Judges; Samuel; and much of Kings. The text built not only on the underlying chain, but also on itself. Each part generally developed or critiqued what preceded, especially what preceded immediately (see Chapter 5).

STAGE 2

The near-complete narrative was synthesized into a prophetic form—the Elijah-Elisha narrative. When the basic story line was essentially complete, from creation to the fall of the city, the process of building on preceding narrative took a new form. The entire narrative was synthesized into a new prophecy-centered form—into the Elijah-Elisha narrative. The text (1 Kings 16:29–2 Kings 13)—a distinct unit of virtually twenty chapters—builds systematically on virtually the whole Primary History, including the fall of both Samaria and Jerusalem; and it serves as an interpretive interlude for that history (*Crucial Bridge*, 2000, 29–78).

However, there is an exception. While the Elijah-Elisha narrative reflects Exodus, there is no clear indication that it reflects Leviticus, Numbers, and Deuteronomy.

The links between the Elijah-Elisha narrative and Exodus deserve a special study. Some are clear, others tenuous—see, for instance, shared references to Horeb (Exodus 3–4, 18–19; 1 Kings 19:8), meeting God (Exodus 33: 18–23;

1 Kings 19:11–13), anointing (Exodus 29:7; 30:26; 40:9–15; 1 Kings 19:15–16), building an altar (Exodus 24:4; 1 Kings 18:31), and a larger process of collecting and building (Exodus 25–31, 35–40; 2 Kings 12:1–17)—but while granting that some links need clarification and verification, the general principle of reliance on Exodus is solid. Not so, however, Leviticus, Numbers, and Deuteronomy.

STAGE 3

The whole narrative was capped by Mosaic law, including law that distilled the narrative itself. There is evidence that Pentateuchal law—apart from its possible links with specific social situations and various extrabiblical processes of codification, whether Babylonian, Persian, or other—reflects the larger biblical narrative; it mirrors much of the story of Genesis-Kings, including the Elijah-Elisha narrative (Carmichael, 1974, 1979, 1985, 1996). This implies that when the Primary History was essentially complete, the writer(s) went over it reflectively and composed law accordingly. The Mosaic law therefore is like a meditative distillation of the Primary History. Carmichael's proposal needs further scrutiny, but apart from the specific evidence produced by Carmichael himself, his thesis accords broadly with a traditional scholarly sense that some of the legal material, particularly in the present books of Leviticus, Numbers, and Deuteronomy is quite late. It also resonates with the overall dynamic involved in composing the rest of the Primary History, namely that of reflecting existing narrative. Leviticus, Numbers, and Deuteronomy are not alien to the Primary History. Though apparently written last, they were at the very center of the original draft.

The first parts of this center to be added were Numbers and Deuteronomy. These two books taken together have multiple echoes of the general unity formed by Genesis and Exodus. They interact with Genesis and Exodus, but in another language and with new material, including Joshua-Kings. It is as though, in the final stages of composing the Primary History, these two books reestablish the nation and rewrite the laws. Numbers reestablishes the nation that began to emerge in Genesis; and Deuteronomy rewrites laws in view of the whole history, especially Exodus. Numbers gives the people added quantity and cohesion. Deuteronomy gives added quality, a greater depth of mind, memory, and soul.

Leviticus appears to supplement Deuteronomy (see Crüsemann, 1996, 277–279). Thus it seems probable that Leviticus, with its climactic emphasis on worship and holiness, was the last piece to be set in place. While Deuteronomy went deep, Leviticus in a sense sought to go deeper. If Deuteronomy is the centerpiece of the Primary History as a whole, Leviticus is the centerpiece of the Torah.

To a significant degree this proposal builds on the JEDP theory. In simplified form, the JEDP theory often proposes two great stages (spread over centuries):

The combining of the basic story (JE, from creation to [near] the conquest)

The addition of D, and then of P

This proposal implies three stages (spread over years, but planned as a unity):

The composing of the basic story (from creation to exile)

The addition of prophetic reflection (Elijah-Elisha)

The addition of Numbers-Deuteronomy, and then of (priestly) Leviticus

FINAL EDITING

It seems best, as in most writings, to allow for a finalizing stage, which may have involved small adaptations.

The Place of Genesis within the Order of Composition

Van Seters (1992, xi) maintains that Genesis—a "Prologue to History"—was written after the main history was already complete: "[I]t was produced at a time close to, but also later than, that of the national history." This is possible in theory, but in practice the stronger evidence indicates otherwise. Deuteronomy, for instance, presupposes Genesis: the Deuteronomic laws concerning women are like a response to the women-related stories of Genesis (Carmichael, 1979) (Van Seters, 1999, even when discussing biblical law, writes as though Carmichael's many works on law do not exist). The Elijah-Elisha narrative clearly presupposes Genesis (*Crucial Bridge*, 2000, 42–46). So to some degree does the Torah as a whole: "The rest of the Torah would not be intelligible without the background provided in the Book of Genesis" (Sarna, xv). The conclusion is simple and adequate: Genesis was written with a view to the composition of the rest of the Primary History. And the rest of the Primary History provides clues to the meaning of Genesis.

The General Nature of the Sources: Oral or Written?

Genesis was based, above all else, on other writings—*great* writings. The basic model of production—writings based largely on other writings—is essentially the same as would be used later in Israel's other history, that of the Chronicler.

Niditch (1996, 128–129) distinguishes the processes used in the two histories, and in a sense she is right: the Chronicler's history has "an exact sharing of language" with its sources (1996, 129), something not found in the Primary History. But while the precise method of using sources may be different, the basic model is essentially the same: writings based directly on other writings. There is no need to invoke several processes. The Primary History drew on old poetry just as directly as the Chronicler drew on parts of the Primary History. The Chronicler, seeing much of the Primary History already written, could afford to follow closely, even to use the same language. The writer(s) of the Primary History, however, had to hammer out the history as no one had ever done it before, and so the materials had to be reworked much more thoroughly.

The sources of Genesis (summarized above in Chapter 8) are so diverse in genre and origin that the basic approach of the Primary History seems to have been encyclopedic. It vacuumed the world's literature, gleaning all that was well written and reshaping it in light of the great vision of the prophets (see Chapter 8; and Appendices 2 and 3). The precise way in which sources were used appears to have been quite orderly, but with allowance for radical adaptation, even for reversal.

The process of composition therefore was written—not just oral. It did indeed have an oral dimension. Like all ancient compositions (until the eighteenth century CE) it reflected the rhythms of oral speech and was written for the ear: it was aural, written for reading with the lips—rather than merely for the eye, as in much modern writing (Ong, 1971, 1–22, 255–261, esp. 1–4; cf. Ong, 1977, 214–216). But this oral dimension, this attentiveness to the ear, does not mean that it was primarily dependent on oral tradition. On the contrary it was as much a written composition as Shakespeare's plays. Shakespeare's work had a powerful oral/aural dimension but—regardless of the nature of his sources— every word was shaped by Shakespeare's pen.

The Number of People Involved in Writing

Theoretically at least it is possible that one person wrote the whole history. The quantity of text (about six hundred average pages, less in some translations) is roughly the same as for the histories of Herodotus and Thucydides. Indeed, many other historiographers produced far more.

Whybray (1987, 225–230) proposes one author for the Pentateuch. He summarizes the history of the scholarly breakthrough that saw the similarity with Greek historiography, and then (232–233) he moves toward his own conclusion, namely that a single postexilic author wrote the entire Pentateuch as a national history:

> Van Seters and Rendtorff and others . . . have failed to carry their views to their logical conclusion. There appears to be no reason why (allowing for the possibility of a few additions) the *first* edition of the Pentateuch as a comprehensive work should not also have been the final *edition*, a work composed by a single historian. In all Pentateuchal study up to the present it has been assumed that it is possible to detect the activity of successive authors or editors. Yet the variety of conclusions which have been reached by scholars from the time of Wellhausen onwards, of which the results achieved by such scholars as Van Seters are but the latest examples, arouses the suspicion that the methods employed are extremely subjective. The analogy with Herodotus

suggests that insufficient allowance has been made for deliberate variations of style and compositional method on the part of a single author.

The essence of Whybray's analysis is that variations in the text do not warrant the invoking of distinct authors; variations can be part of authorship. The example of prolific Hellanicus and his millenium-long history of Athens suggests that, in principle, one person could have undertaken the writing of the entire history of Judea, beginning with the prehistoric period.

The problem about attributing the entire History to one author is not quantity but quality. Much of the text—and Genesis is a prime example—is so dense and precise in its artistry that, like an illuminated manuscript, it must have been composed very slowly. Hellanicus, for instance, has been called a scribbler (Lesky, 1966, 330), a designation which is probably unfair to Hellanicus and is certainly inapplicable to the author of Genesis. The author of Genesis was not a scribbler. The writing of this one book must have taken years, and on its own it is an immense achievement.

Study of the composition of the Primary History could benefit from examining the procedures of known authors. Novelist Anthony Trollope could compose at the rate of 250 words in fifteen minutes; but for others a day's work might achieve three sentences—the case of James Joyce—or, for some authors, just one line (D. J. Taylor, 1999, 5).

The two most plausible scenarios in the case of the Primary History are of one gifted long-lived writer with a strong support team, or—as in the case of the Egyptian codification commission (warriors, priests, and scribes; Blenkinsopp, 1992, 239–240)—a team of writers working in close coordination on a single planned project. Aquinas, for instance, in composing his *Summa*, was a lone author, but with strong support, including several secretaries. The *Salmanticenses*, on the other hand—the Salamanca authors of a multivolume theology—worked as a team, in sequence, over eighty years (1631–1712), all following an initial outline (Couture, 1967).

Some Specific Procedures Concerning Form and Depth

To enter more closely into some of the dynamics of composition it is useful to focus on two of the text's features. These are, first, the choosing of an appropriate form; and second, the effort to give the text depth—to make it evocative and numinous.

The Problem of Choosing the Appropriate Form

It is a useful exercise to try to imagine the author(s) of Genesis-Kings in the process of deciding what form to use. Imagining what was not done helps to clarify what was done.

The author(s) had roots. There was no question of the modern phenomenon, developed especially by nineteenth-century romanticism, of "doing one's own thing," of trying to write almost purely from within. Freedom meant not imposing oneself on the world but absorbing the world; literature was an imitation (or mimesis) of reality—"a mirror of a world external to itself" (Trible, 1994, 10). The mirroring of the world meant also a mirroring of its great traditions, a rendering of sources into new form.

In pure theory the author could have chosen any of several forms—prophecy, epic poetry, factual history, a novel. Prophetic writing, such as that which came from Jeremiah and Ezekiel, was basic to Israel, and, as the second-century book of Daniel would show, prophecy was open to adaptation. So was epic. Epic poems—especially *Gilgamesh, Atrahasis*, the *Iliad*, and the *Odyssey*—were probably the world's most famous compositions concerning earlier times and people. In later centuries, the classic account of the origins of the Roman empire would also be written in the form of an epic poem—Virgil's *Aeneid*. The best-known account of that empire's fall, however, was written as if it were factual history (Gibbon's *The Decline and Fall of the Roman Empire*). And the most well-known account of Russia's titanic clash with Napoleon was written as a novel (Tolstoy's *War and Peace*).

In practice, however, these options were either unavailable or unrealistic. The genres of the novel and of factual history were not yet sufficiently developed to write a Jerusalem-oriented history (they would not be attempted until the nineteenth and twentieth centuries—in novels such as James Michener's *The Source*, and in the controverted scholarly effort to write the factual history of Israel).

Written prophecy, despite its prestige and adaptability, would probably have been strained unduly by a project that included the origins of humanity. And epic poetry, despite both its extraordinary power to evoke ancient times and its later revival by Virgil, was on the wane. By the sixth century many Greek writers regarded such poetry as unrealistic—too focused on external heroics and not sufficiently attentive to daily life and the self (Bowra, 1966, 56–79). Furthermore, much of what had once been expressed in epic poetry was now being rendered into prose (Lesky, 1966, 106, 218–21), and thus into the new form—historiography.

It was this form, descended from epic, which proved to be the most attractive to the writer(s) of the Primary History. As epic had already begun to look beyond the unique and individual happening to the world as a whole (Lesky, 1966, 218), so the author(s) of the Primary History would describe Jacob's life in such a way that he would be a symbol for all of humanity.

Yet the biblical use of the historiographic genre is not simple. The Primary History is so original and dense that, rather than speak exclusively of one genre it is better to speak of the transformation and cross-fertilization of genres (Damrosch, 1987, 41–47). Historiography is simply the overall covering that binds all the other genres together.

Depth: Making the Text Evocative and Numinous

THE TEXT AS EVOCATIVE

In discussing composition it is necessary to underline the subtle nature of the

text. In daily life communication often occurs *between* words—in the silences (Illich, 1973, 39–46, esp. 41)—and, unlike modern history, the frequent focus of Genesis is not on what it explicitly describes but on what it evokes. The same is true in much Old Testament writing (Clines, 1980, esp. 126) and also, for instance, in the Gospel of John (Brodie, 1993, 13). In art generally "the suggestion of a thing may be more convincing than a detailed portrayal of it. . . . We fill in a partially drawn figure. . . . If the context demands it, a face may seem to be peering intently even though it has no eyes" (Berlin, 1983, 136). In a photo, a face without eyes generally means that the photo has been interfered with; but not in art. A similar distinction applies between history and literary art. In history, gaps and contradictions generally mean that the writing is defective or confused; but not in literary art. In the words of Sternberg, "the literary work consists of bits and fragments to be linked and pieced together in the process of reading: it establishes a system of gaps that must be filled in" (1985, 186).

THE TEXT AS NUMINOUS AND CRYPTIC

The subtlety of the text extended beyond being evocative to being in some way numinous. At first it may not seem so. One of the temptations in trying to discern the process of composition is to imagine the author or text as in some way primitive. To some degree the text does in fact reflect a simpler way of thinking, or at least a way that regarded writing with a certain awe—as if it were numinous, or an icon (Niditch, 1996, 78–88).

But this reverence for writing sometimes led to results that were extremely sophisticated: it meant that, somewhat like the writers who invested great energy and artistic talent in developing illuminated manuscripts, ancient authors sometimes went to great lengths to invest their text with depth and meaning. Chouraqui expresses something of this phenomenon. While referring to technique, expression, and art, Chouraqui realizes that his awareness of these matters is general, that the crucial details remain elusive.

> What were the techniques of writing? . . . I believe we are scarcely beginning to discern them. This art corresponded to a science—very rigorous, traditional—which, apart from standard conventions, contained an inimitable science of relation, a perfect mastery of basic narrative, an art of symphonic composition where each word, each letter has correspondences which follow one another through the whole course of the text, and even a kind of arithmetic of words. We know that in neighbouring civilizations, among the Babylonians, even among the Sumerians and the Greeks, writing sometimes con-

stituted a veritable cryptogram. . . . As for the Hebrews, [their] techniques were much more refined than . . . simple parallelism. . . . They had an art of writing to which we do not have the keys. (1975, 455)

Chouraqui's words do not unravel the problem, but they are an indication of the kind of care and attention that may have gone into the process of composition.

Conclusion

The Primary History is like a pyramid. Both the book and the pyramid belong to a former world, to a way of building that now appears strange. The pyramid may seem at first like an extravagant monument—little more then a great mound of old stone. But when examined closely it shows unity, startling precision, inner space, and a sense of mystery.

The Primary History then is not some kind of parochial saga, nor some collection of campfire tales. Rather, it is like a distillation of human experience, with a wide-ranging synthesis of world literature and Israelite prophecy. Though composed during the years of the Persian empire, it placed its story in an ancient setting; and this setting, instead of diminishing the story, gave it a universal horizon.

10   Date, Place, and People: A Summary of Key Arguments

For the sake of clarity it is useful now to summarize the main arguments concerning the date, place, and people involved in the composition of Genesis.

The Date

As the claim to Moses' authorship faded, the estimated date for the writing of Genesis began to move. A partial analogue for such redating occurs in the case of the book of Daniel: though set in the sixth century BCE, research is essentially agreed that Daniel was written much later—in the second century BCE. Concerning Genesis, agreement comes more slowly.

Scholarship has already moved the date for the origin of Genesis by several centuries—from Moses to the exile or later—and so one century more or less may not seem to matter very much. But if Genesis-Kings is connected with Greek literature, a literature that was expanding rapidly, each century becomes important.

Two reasons seem particularly important in assigning Genesis primarily to a pre-exilic date:

First, the language of Genesis is distinct from postexilic language of the kind used, for instance, in Chronicles (cf. Hurvitz, 1988, 1995, 1997). In other words the language of Genesis seems distinctly old.

Second, the content also often seems old. Sarna (xv–xvii), for instance, speaks of "the singularity and antiquity of [Genesis's] traditions."

Yet there are good reasons for a Persian-period date, including the following:

1. *The Primary History as a whole, including Genesis, is of such a nature that it belongs with the broad genre of Greek historiography—a product of the Persian period.* Just as waltzes, for instance, do not belong to the middle ages—they can be traced to a specific cultural background (German-speaking central Europe, eighteenth–nineteenth centuries)—neither do extended quality historiographies belong to pre-exilic times. Even in size the Primary History matches the oldest extant Greek histories—those of Herodotus and Thucydides.

2. *The Primary History, with Genesis as an integral part, recounts fall-related events (Jerusalem's fall; exile; intimation of recovery).* The earliest possible date for such a composition is near or after the actual recovery, in other words, soon after the exile. However, the date may in fact have been later; there may have been a time-lag between the fall-related events and the time of composition. Such was the case in Berossos's history of Babylon: the history finished with the city's fall to Alexander (331 BCE), but the account was not written for about another seventy years (ca. 260 BCE). There is a good reason for ending with dramatic fall-related events rather than with subsequent news: it makes for a classic narrative. It is good drama in itself, and it sets the whole narrative on a plane with the *Iliad*'s account of the fall of Troy. In other words, a good writer knows where to conclude, and in fact the present arrangement makes an appropriate ending (Ben Zvi, 1998, 28–35). The Acts of the Apostles ends with Paul's dignified imprisonment, but that does not mean that Acts was written immediately during or after that imprisonment (Harrington, 1965, 172). It simply indicates that such endings make fundamental literary sense.

3. *Genesis depends on prophets, including exilic prophets.* An increasing number of scholars are showing that Genesis is dependent on some form of the exilic prophets. Von Rad (1962, I, 146), for instance, maintained

that the Genesis idea of the likeness of God (Gen. 1:26) was somehow dependent on Ezekiel 1 ("Ezek. 1:26 is the theological prelude . . . to Gen. 1:26"). Likewise, but more extensively, Genesis 2–3 apparently depends on Ezekiel 28: "Ezekiel's own invention has been taken over by . . . Genesis. . . . It is a mistake to try to derive both accounts from a common original" (van Seters, 1992, 119–134, esp. 121; cf. Fretheim, 359: "Some version of Ezekiel 28 was probably a source for the writer of Genesis 3"). And further signs of dependence on the prophets are emerging (see Appendix 2). Such dependence means that Genesis is later than the exilic prophets, including Second Isaiah.

These reasons converge in an unavoidable conclusion: the Primary History, including Genesis, was written after the exile.

Concerning the objections to a postexilic date—Genesis's language and antique traditions—these may be explained in another way.

First (Hurvitz): the absence in Genesis of distinctly postexilic language.

What Hurvitz proves is that there is a difference between the Hebrew used to describe the pre-exilic period (the Hebrew of Genesis-Kings) and that which describes the postexilic time (the Hebrew of Chronicles-Ezra-Nehemiah); Genesis—along with the rest of the Primary History—does not have any of the distinguishing features of the second body of prose.

But this literary distinction does not prove that Genesis is pre-exilic in date. What it indicates is that Genesis is part of a distinct literary project—one that recounted the time before the exile. With reasonable care, for instance, a twenty-first century author can compose a diary of a sixteen-century fugitive. The absence of modern vocabulary does not prove that a diary is old, merely that it was composed to evoke the ethos of another time. Likewise with Genesis: the absence of later words (or at least of specific words) does not prove that the text is old, merely that it was composed to suit and evoke a particular time. As already indicated (at the end of the preceding chapter) the text was composed so as to be evocative.

Second (Sarna): the presence in Genesis of ancient traditions.

Antiquity of a tradition does not mean that the book that records it is old. A new book can adapt an old document; the tradition from the document is old, but not the book. Many of the traditions and documents concerning Julius Caesar were very old and well known, but virtually every word of Shakespeare's *Julius Caesar* comes from Shakespeare himself. Furthermore, Genesis, even when using accounts of the past, seems more interested in addressing the present, so much so that the book is primarily a guide to the writer's own time rather than to the time described (de Hoop, 2001). Nor does a tradition's singularity necessarily indicate age; effective writing uses distinctive styles and elements for distinctive parts or periods. Thus within Genesis itself, for instance, the style and elements of chapters 1–11 are mythical or semi-mythical in a way that the rest of the book is not. A sense of something ancient or different occurs also at the beginning of Livy's history of Rome and in the opening chapters of the Gospel of Luke (see Chapter 1 on variation in style and language). This ancient tone does not prove that the beginning of a book is older than the rest of it; it simply means that the beginning has been written in a way that is appropriate to its subject and function.

The objections of Hurvitz and Sarna underestimate the author(s) of the Primary History. They do not allow for the kind of careful artistry that is readily accepted in many other writers.

Overall then, it is reasonable, given the three arguments listed above—and given that the Primary History predates Chronicles, written apparently ca. 350 BCE (Kleinig, 1994, 46)—to conclude that the time of composition was in or near the fifth century. The date that most easily accounts for the data is about 400—after Second Isaiah and Hellanicus, yet before Chronicles. But a somewhat earlier date is not to be excluded.

The Place and the People

The identity of the author(s) remains elusive. What seems reasonably certain is that the writing was not carried out in isolation. In the course of history, writers have often been linked to institutions—political, religious, educational, academic, media—and the same was probably true of the author(s) of Genesis-Kings.

The most likely link is with the Jerusalem temple and the Levitical priests who worked there. The temple, rebuilt around 520, may not have been as splendid as the pre-exilic temple, but, given the absence of the monarchy, its role was more important than ever. It was a focal point for all Judeans, and—crucially—the priesthood was linked with writing.

There are several indications of this priesthood-writing link and of a focus on the temple. At the center of the Primary History, as Moses' work comes to a close, his written words are entrusted first of all to "the priests, the sons of Levi" (Deut. 31:9). Likewise, the final focus of the Elijah-Elisha narrative falls significantly on the temple, especially on the pivotal role of the priest, who in diverse ways instructs both the soldiers and the king (2 Kings 11–12, esp. 11:9; 12:2–3). Ezra is introduced several times as equally scribe and priest (Ezra 7:1–6, 12; Neh. 8:1–2, 9). Furthermore, he is to appoint other scribes (Ezra 7:25) and he is associated with the Levites (Neh. 8:9, 13). The prominence of Berossos, Manetho, and Josephus—all priest historians—confirms writing's connection with the larger world of worship.

However, the role of the temple priests does not exclude other people and places. Some scholars have suggested that in the pre-exilic situation there was some form of coalition of priests, prophets, and others, including officials (Römer and de Pury, 1996, 87), and the same may have been true after the exile. Certainly the prophetic writings had a central role in the composition of the Primary History, and, in some basic way, the writers were imbued with prophecy.

Those responsible for the Primary History had access both to Israel's own writings and to a considerable range of international literature. This meant some form of library. Ancient libraries have been discovered or verified in diverse places. The Alexandria library, for instance, was richly endowed. The later Qumran community, despite its isolation, was apparently equipped for writing. So were the schools in ancient Athens (Culpepper, 1975). There were libraries also, for instance, in Mesopotamia (at Nineveh), Asia Minor (at Hattushah/ Boghazköy, the Hittite capital), and in Phoenicia (at Ugarit and Byblos) (Black and Tait, 1995, 2197–2209; Niditch, 1996, 60–69).

The temple, too, possessed scrolls and so must have had some form of library. Yet it is not at all clear that that library was a major institution (Lemaire, 1992, 1004–1005; Niditch, 1996, 53). From that point of view it is easier to imagine the place of composition as a great center such as Babylon. Furthermore, this Babylonian image corresponds in part to the picture of Ezra as bringing the Law back from Babylon (Ezra 7–8) and reading it to the people (Neh. 8). In fact, even if the primary place of composition was Jerusalem, Babylon probably contributed in some way (cf. Römer and de Pury, 1996, 88), and so did the whole social setting of the Persian empire. The writing of books, ancient and modern, often involves travel, at least to consult authorities and libraries. As already seen (Chapter 7), while Hellanicus worked from books, Hecataeus and Herodotus traveled. There is no reason why travel would not have been equally easy for Judeans. In conjunction with Babylon, Jerusalem had the necessary people—administrators, priests, sages, writers—and could summon the resources. Judean people had their own network, and, despite local difficulties, they were at ease in the larger network of the empire, at ease in the world. The terror of Assyria and Babylon was gone, and Greece's flowering culture was not yet seen as a threat. The focus of the writings is on Jerusalem, and Jerusalem became the main center for the larger tradition. Overall, it seems best to allow a role to both Jerusalem and Babylon.

The writers' technology and technique need further examination. Writing was probably humanity's most decisive invention, and the Jewish people would become known as the People of the Book, yet the study of Israel's history and sociology has generally not done justice to writing. De Vaux's masterful *Ancient Israel* (1961) for instance, scarcely mentions it. However, insofar as historians can come to saying what was technically possible and likely at the time of the writing of Genesis-Kings, there is a better possibility of getting a clear idea of how the writers worked. (On the role of writing, including schools and libraries, see Gelb, 1963; Negenman, 1969, 21–36; Lemaire, 1981, 1992; Ong, 1982; Gabel et al., 1996, 315–323; van Seters, 1992, 34–42; Millard, 1995; Crenshaw, 1998, 85–99.)

The character of the writers is elusive. Writers were a small minority, yet, few though they were, it was they apparently who shaped the tradition: "[T]he sociological study of tradition has argued . . . that the formation of traditions is the activity of an intellectual elite" (van Seters, 1992, 34). As a sociological term, "intellectual elite" is accurate, but as plain English it is probably misleading; it suggests snobbery. Most really great writers are not snobs; they consider themselves neither "intellectual" not "elite." They are intelligent humans who, the better they are as writers, the more they usually tend toward quiet dignity and toward solidarity with ordinary people.

Rulers of institutions are generally very conscious of writers, and sometimes try to pressure them or buy them off. Writers, however, are notorious, especially when they are really good, for maintaining artistic integrity.

GENESIS'S CONTENT AND MEANING

Human Existence and Its Many Aspects

The third part of the introduction has a key focus: What is Genesis about? What is its content?

The answer is not something specialized or remote. Genesis is concerned with human existence—in all its complexity. The first half of the book (1:1–25:18) sets the stage: at a certain level it describes the complex world or environment in which the drama of human life is played out. The second half (25:19–chap. 50) tells of the unfolding of that drama by recounting the life of Jacob, womb to tomb. Genesis also evokes some of the most basic elements of human life—especially time, space, and stages of age and perception.

Part III deals first with Genesis's emphasis on human life in general (Chapter 11). Then follows an examination of how Genesis deals with specific features—including history (Chapter 12), psychology (Chapter 13), spirituality (Chapter 14), and life's general complexity (including blessing, marriage, cities, and a sense of journeying) (Chapter 15).

Genesis's Central Concern

Human Existence under God

This chapter indicates that Genesis is primarily about human existence; such is its unifying focus. Genesis also depicts the flow of history—including origins, and the origins of a specific people—but it describes history in a way that is constantly adapted to the portrayal and evocation of the more permanent realities of human life.

The Two Threads—History and Humanity

Among the threads holding Genesis together two are fundamental—the thread of specific history, and the more general pattern of human life, human existence.

Specific history means the flow of events. It is the subject that school students sometimes dislike, and in Toynbee's oft-cited definition, history is "one damn thing after another." *Insofar as Genesis is a portrayal of specific history*, it is best divided into dealing with all nations (chaps. 1–11) and dealing with the ancestors of Israel (chaps. 12–50; Genesis does not use the terms "primeval" and "patriarchal").

But Genesis has another concern—a didactic purpose—namely the more general portrayal of human life or human existence, a subject one learns about long before school—in fact from birth—and about which one continues to learn till death. *Insofar as Genesis is concerned with this larger topic of life in general* it has a further structure—two halves (Genesis 1–25, and 25–50). As seen earlier (Chapter 2) each half contains a double drama. At this more general level, portraying life, each double drama has a separate function. The first sets the stage (it evokes humans' environment); the second describes the action, from birth to death.

Each half has its own unity.

The unity of the second half (25:19–chap. 50) is easy to see (this was already partly indicated in Chapter 2). The stories of Jacob and Joseph are in fact one story, centered largely on one person, Jacob (see esp. Coats, 1983, 259–61; 1976, 15–21). Within this double drama (Jacob/Joseph) the two dramas correspond to the two basic times of Jacob's life—youth and old age. Jacob's youth—taking "youth" broadly to include what today is called middle age—extends to both the birth of his last child, Benjamin, and the death of his father (25:19–chap. 36). His old age, dominated by the Joseph story, extends from the first explicit scene of old age (chap. 37) until his death and burial (chaps. 49–50).

At two points in the long biography, Jacob is in the background: first when he is very young (chap. 26); and again when he is old (chaps. 37–50, when center stage goes to the sons—to Judah, and especially to Joseph). Jacob's relegation to the background at these points (chaps. 26, and 37–50) may seem to indicate that the narrative is no longer presenting his biography. But the narrative is being true to life: at diverse stages of life people generally fade into the background—in early youth and in old age. The dominance of the figure of Joseph has the effect not of excluding Jacob but of covering his old age with the mantle of providence.

The Abraham story, however, is not a biography. Unlike the Jacob account—a narrative that spans all the basic phases of life and that tells clearly of parents and grandparents, of children and grandchildren—the Abraham story begins at age seventy-five and ends abruptly. It does not have life's full rhythm. The Jacob story therefore is the Bible's first biography (the story of Jeremiah may be older, but the Bible does not place it first).

Gammie summarizes Genesis 25–36 as "a relevant and still timely blueprint for the resolution of the ubiquitous problem of human strife" (1979, 132). Gammie's view is essentially right yet it is just a part of a larger truth: as the Bible's first biography, the Jacob story (Gen. 25–50) is a form of model not only for human strife but for all of human life.

The unity of the first half (1:1–25:18) is not as obvious. In the first half, for instance, there is no one figure, such as Jacob, to hold it all together. Instead there are the two foundational figures, Adam and Abram. This lack of obvious unity, however, is part of a larger coherent pattern—Genesis's overall spiraling movement from episodes to continuous narrative (Chapter 2).

Adam and Abram are not as far apart as may at first appear. The story of Adam flows, precisely, into that of Noah (the figures in Gen. 5 imply that the first person born after the death of Adam was Noah). And the line of Noah's sons overlaps, conspicuously, with the line that generated Abram (cf. 10:22–25; 11:10–18: Shem, Arpachshad, Shelah, Eber, Peleg). Through Noah, then—not to mention other factors—the Adam-Abram continuity is clear.

The Meaning of the Land/Earth (within 1:1–25:18)

One of the key factors holding Gen. 1:1–25:18 together is the emphasis on the ʿereṣ ("earth/land"). This is fairly obvious in the Adam/Noah story (chaps. 1–11): the stories flowing from creation and the flood are almost inevitably concerned with the ʿereṣ. But even in the Abram/Abraham story (12:1–25:18), the ʿereṣ is central. As Genesis 1 began with a double reference to the ʿereṣ (1:1–2), so also does the Abram story (12:1). The two panels of creation use ʿereṣ twenty-one times and seven times respectively. Each panel of Genesis 12–13 uses it nine times.

But, crucially, in the Abram story the meaning of ʿereṣ shifts. No longer does it always refer simply to physical land; Abraham is to leave the physical land '*ereṣ* he previously occupied (12:1a), and is to go instead to the '*ereṣ* "that I [God] will make you see." Seeing, then, is linked with the '*ereṣ*; not ordinary seeing, but seeing that is God-given, linked to Abraham's faith. Land is no longer simply a material object; it has another meaning, referring to a dimension or land accessible to a special form of seeing.

The idea of the ambiguity of land is not new. Brueggemann (1977, 2) distinguishes between land as actual earthly turf and land as symbolic ("a whole symbolic sense . . . to express the wholeness of joy and well-being characterized by social coherence and personal ease in prosperity, security and freedom"). Berquist suggests that "postexilic religion distanced itself from its natural roots in the land. . . . People wanted to be different from the old ways that had led to the destruction and to allow themselves to survive other potential disasters by making the religion abstract and institutionalized" (1995, 5, discussing Wellhausen). There may be some truth in this, yet while the connotations of the word "land" may have changed with the exile, the underlying idea, namely that reality has a dimension other than the visible, is hardly accounted for by the exilic disruption. That basic idea occurs already in the prophets, even in their various calls.

Habel (1995) speaks of six ideologies of land and he identifies each ideology with a diverse social group (the monarchy, Levites, ancestral households, prophets, tenant farmers, and immigrants). For Habel, the Abraham narrative is claimed by all six ideologies, but the claim of one group, the immigrants, is special and distinctive: "It is my contention that the Abraham narratives reflect a distinctive immigrant ideology that views the land as a host country and its inhabitants as potentially friendly peoples. The vision of the ideology in these charter narratives . . . is in conflict with most of the [other] ideologies" (1995, 115).

Without attempting to pass judgment on the sociological question—on the existence and circumstances of a specific immigrant group—it is clear that for Habel the Abraham narrative has a distinct vision of the land, a vision that is welcoming and friendly.

The Land/Earth: A Proposal

The proposal here is that the welcoming vision just mentioned—whatever its original sociological roots—has now become part of a further ideology, a theology which, in speaking of land, often evokes another dimension of reality, ultimately a dimension or land accessible only to faith.

One of the most striking indications that '*ereṣ* has another meaning occurs in the work of Boorer. At the end of her long technical study of the oath (concerning the promise of the land as oath), she comes to a basic underlying question—the meaning of land (1992, 449–450, emphasis added):

> The constant . . . reflection on the issue of Yahweh's oath of the land . . . has
> significant implications for . . . what is actually being conceptualized by the

word "land." The Mosaic generation was . . . portrayed as moving towards the land, arriving at its edge, but never actually entering the land. . . . Those composing these texts are writing always as if the oath of the land has not been fulfilled for them. But presumably at the time of the emergence of these reflections, those responsible for their composition were actually living in the land. This means that the reality of their life in the land is not commensurate with what is conceived as the fulfillment of the oath of the land, and *the "land" itself must be symbolic of something more than simply a piece of territory* or a geographical location.

But what is the wider reality symbolized by the "land"? And what does Yahweh's oath and its fulfillment actually mean? Perhaps the experience of life with which these texts constantly struggle is akin to that which is captured in the words of T. S. Eliot ["Four Quartets (East Coker)"] so many centuries later:

> In order to possess what you do not possess
>   You must go by the way of dispossession,
> In order to arrive at what you are not
>   You must go by the way in which you are not.
> And what you do not know is the only thing you know
>   And what you own is what you do not own
>   And where you are is where you are not.

Boorer's conclusion is an indication of the nature of the biblical text. Genesis is about history, but it is also about something far more elusive that history, far deeper. The story of Abraham represents "a breakthrough in the pneumatic mode" (Webb, 1981, 166).

Clarifying the Division between Genesis 1–25 and 25–50

The emphasis on land helps to clarify the nature of the distinction between Genesis's two halves. The first half (1:1–25:18) portrays the diverse levels of the 'eres, the two levels that together constitute humans' environment. It sets the stage for human existence. The second half (25:19–chap. 50) plays out the drama of life, from birth to death.

Within the first half, therefore—the opening double drama (1:1–25:18)—the Adam/Noah drama (chaps. 1–11) deals largely with a world that is very visible, a world which, despite goodness and grace, often seems dominated by sin and death. The Abram/Abraham drama (12:1–25:18), in contrast, shows that the human world has another aspect. Abraham, man of faith, has a deeper level of perception. He is aware of a dimension that is largely invisible, and he follows it even in the face of death.

In this way of dividing Genesis, Abraham belongs more with the Adam/ Noah story than with the long story of Jacob. Obviously, at one level, Abraham also belongs with Jacob. Abraham is an inextricable ancestor of Israel, he is the father in faith; but, at another level, he belongs with the larger human world. Likewise Jacob himself. At one level, the description of him is a biography; at another, it is a capsule of elements of Israel's specific history. The two portrayals—Israel's specific history, and human life in general (biography)—are interwoven in a delicate balance.

Relationship between the Two Levels

Of the two portrayals—patriarchal Israel, and human life—the second is more decisive: Genesis is governed primarily not by the flow of specific events but by the depiction of human existence. The portrayal of life commands the division of the book into two halves; and—more importantly—it commands the distribution of the patriarchs. There are three patriarchs—Abraham, Isaac, and Jacob—but as such, as three specific, distinct, figures, they do not decide the arrangement of the book; they do not receive a major division each. Instead, Isaac's story is brief and is divided between the stories of Abraham and Jacob, divided in fact between the two halves of the book. Within the first half he has one role (the miraculous son who crowns the faith-filled life of Abraham); within the second, he has another (the down-to-earth struggling father of Jacob). Thus, the description of the patriarchs, however important they may be, is so organized that it serves a larger purpose—the portrayal of human existence.

History—"the facts"—is something simple (Toynbee's "one damn thing after another"). As such history tends to narrate things in a way that is straight or flat. History, as such, would tend to give equal time to Abraham, Isaac, and Jacob. Initially, Genesis may seem to be written at that history-centered level. It uses the literary genre of historiography, and its initial episodic nature may give the impression of just one thing after another. But it moves beyond that level.

This relationship between these two intertwined portrayals is a further reason (in addition to what was said in Chapter 2) why Genesis 1–11 should not be referred to as "the primeval history." Such a designation privileges one level or portrayal—that of specific history—the level that Genesis itself puts in second place. The term "Adam/Noah story," though also a simplification, is more open to the ambiguity of the text.

Yet history, even in second place, is not something peripheral in Genesis. It is not a mere vehicle for a theological reflection on life. The history in Genesis is largely a history of origins, and origins were regarded as a window on the present, on what is timeless. "The time of the origin of a reality is a privileged moment in the ancient Near East; the original intention of Fate and the god is clearer then than at other times" (Clifford, 1990, 2:2). The best way therefore to give a clear view of something is to portray its origin.

History furthermore is an inextricable part of human life—so much so that at times the unpredictable forces of history tend to completely dominate life.

Genesis therefore, in portraying human existence, includes a sense of history. Genesis 1–11, for instance, "constantly reminds the reader of the historicality of things" (Combs and Post, 1987, 9). Yet the forces of history never dominate—neither in life nor in the shaping of the text. Joseph is the other side of the Isaac coin: the Isaac story fades, but the Joseph story flourishes. It is no accident that Jacob's old age is dominated not by some history-making pharaoh but by the providence that is embodied in Joseph. History is powerful, but it is not ultimate.

The Shaping of Genesis through Basic Life-Related Features

Given Genesis's focus on human life, it is not surprising that some of the basics in Genesis's structure are also some of the basics in the structure of life—time, space, and a sense of advancing stages (stages of perception or age). Time and space are foundational elements of human life. Life is composed of time—days, years, generations—and it is lived in space, in specific places. Life can be described as a journey. People are often defined initially through time and space ("an old man from Seoul;" "a young woman from Haifa"). To some degree these features overlap with the structure of history.

Space: Geographic Movement (from East to Egypt) and Its Ambiguity

The structure based on space involves movement from one place to another. The most obvious aspect of this movement is Genesis's spiraling progression from east to west, toward Egypt—toward "a coffin/sarcophagus in Egypt" (50:26). Yet there is an ambiguity: as well as a movement toward Egypt there is a powerful undercurrent of movement toward the cave of Machpelah (opposite Mamre, at Hebron).

Let us first consider Egypt. At one level, the whole narrative moves slowly westward toward Egypt. This movement toward Egypt is twofold, like two successive waves, where the second follows much of the path of the first but goes farther.

The initial wave is in the book's first half (1:1–25:18). Genesis 1–11 suggests a movement from the east, which passes through Mesopotamia but never gets far beyond it. The Abraham story goes farther and in various ways comes closer to Egypt.

In the second half of Genesis (25:19–chap. 50) the process seems to start over. Jacob, having gone to Laban, starts moving homeward—effectively in the general direction of Egypt (25:19–37:1). And in the later part of his life, in the Joseph story, the action moves, as never before, right into Egypt.

The presence of these two waves, these overlapping movements toward Egypt, is confirmed by crucial details, namely by the geographical indications that frame the four major dramas (Adam/Noah, Abraham, Jacob, Joseph). In other words, within each drama, these are the geographical locations that occur first and last (the references: 2:10; 11:31–32: 12:5–6; 25:17–18; 25:20; 37:1; 37: 12; 50:26).

From the East toward Egypt: The First Movement (2:10; 11:31–32; 12:5–6; 25:17–18)

2:10: "Yhwh God planted a garden in Eden, *in the east*."

11:31: "Terah [set out] to go *to Canaan*. But . . . Terah died in Haran."

12:5: "Abram . . . in Haran . . . came *to Canaan . . . at Shechem*."

25:17: "Ishmael [died] . . . Havilah to Shur . . . *Egypt* . . . to Assyria."

From the East toward Egypt: The Second Movement (25:20; 37:1; 37:12; 50:26)

25:20: "Isaac was forty when he took Rebekah . . . *of/from Paddan-aram*."

37:1: "Jacob settled . . . *in the land of Canaan*."

37:12: "His brothers went to shepherd their father's flock *at Shechem*."

50:26: "Joseph died . . . and was set in a coffin *in Egypt*."

The main point here is the overall movement from the east toward Egypt. In the whole first half of Genesis the geographical indications begin with "the east," and end *virtually* with Egypt ("Egypt . . . to Assyria," 25:18). In the second half, the indications begin virtually with the east ("Paddan-aram," 25:20), and end with Egypt itself. The focus therefore is Egypt. (The "coffin/sarcophagus in Egypt" is like a symbol of death—death from a worldly point of view.)

At another level, however, the focus of the story is not Egypt at all, but Mamre, at Hebron, the place which is associated with God's presence (13:18; 18:1) and which became the burial place (13:18; 18:1; 23:17–20; 25:9–10; 35: 27–29; 49:29–32; 50:13). The elaborate repetition of the name runs through Genesis like a haunting beauty—a magnet which in the end is more powerful than the richest land in wealthy Egypt. Somewhat like the transcendent-versus-earthly tension in the two creation texts (Gen. 1–2), the two burials in Genesis 50 provide two views of death: Jacob, leaving Egyptian rituals behind and defying normal geographic patterns, crosses the Jordan to God-related Mamre (50:1–12); but Joseph is just laid in "a coffin in Egypt" (50:26). This is an intimation of a contrast that will be much clearer in the transcendent Elijah and the more earthly Elisha (2 Kings 2 and 2 Kings 13:14–20).

The overall tension—toward Egypt, yet away from it toward Hebron—is captured, in distilled form, in Genesis 12–13: Abram goes to the attractive land of Egypt but he has to leave it, and he settles instead in Hebron. Genesis 12–13, therefore—the diptych that lies at the heart of 1:1–25:18—serves in part as a distillation or interpretation of the larger text.

The double focus—a movement toward Egypt, and a contrary subverting movement toward Mamre, at Hebron—is best seen in the context of the ambiguity of the broader concept of "land." At times "land" is visible, *obviously attractive*—like Egypt (13:10). But at other times, it suggests a realm *seen only through God*—as at Mamre (13:14–18).

What is important is the basic principle: in the structure of Genesis, space is important. The references to geography, including Egypt, may look haphazard, but they help to shape the narrative. In two great movements, one in each half of the book, there is an overall tendency toward Egypt. That movement, even if subverted at another level, contributes to giving the book its structure.

Time: The Flow of the Generations (tôlĕdôt)

The structure based on space is complemented by a structure based on time, especially on the listing of generations. It is a commonplace of Genesis studies that the book is held together by the periodic listing of generations (*tôlĕdôt*, Gen. 2:4; 5:1; 6:9; 10:1; 11:10, 27; 25:12, 19; 36:1, 11; 37:2). These generations reflect genealogy-based historiography, and they also involve time in a way that is eminently related to human life.

Something of the sophistication of these genealogies emerges in a single detail: when the figures in chapter 5 are calculated, it is found that, after the death of Adam (at age 930), the first birth is that of Noah. Many others apparently were born during Adam's long lifetime, but amid all the complexity there is a basic continuity: Adam gives way to Noah. The generations are the epitome of order and calculation.

Yet just as the space-related movement toward Egypt is undermined by a contrary movement toward Mamre, so, in a perplexing way, the orderly listing of genealogies is undermined by contrary indications. The undermining is clearest in the case of Isaac. The initial phrase, "These are the generations of Isaac" (25:19), instead of introducing Isaac, leads primarily to Jacob ("the . . . history . . . is rather the history of Jacob than of Isaac," Vawter, 286). The further major heading, highlighting Jacob ("These are the generations of Jacob," 37:2), is often concerned apparently not with Jacob but with Joseph. The apparent implication: however much history and life are governed by the flow of generations ("sunrise . . . sunset") there is a whole other dynamic at work.

To some degree this implication, this tension, is present at the beginning of Genesis: "These are the *generations* of the heavens and the earth—at their being *created*" (2:4a). Generating is a very earthy process, involving sexual activity. Creating, however, is reserved to God and is accomplished in Genesis 1 by a transcendent word. Amid the implacable advance of generations something transcendent is present. Time flows on but there is something greater than time. Or again, history is powerful, but it is not ultimate.

Stages of Age and Perception

The process of moving through time and space (through generations and places) provides a framework for other forms of movement—for advancing stages of age and perception. In other words, as one moves through years and places, one becomes older, and maybe wiser (more perceptive).

As already suggested, these basic human processes—of advancing in age and perception—help to structure Genesis. The division between the Adam-Noah story and the Abraham story corresponds largely to an advance in stages of perception: Abraham, man of faith, brings a new level of perception. And the fundamental division of the Jacob story (25:19–37:1; and 37:2–chap. 50) corresponds significantly to the fundamental human difference between being young and being old.

Overall, therefore, basic factors that give structure to human life give structure also to the book of Genesis.

General Conclusion

Genesis uses history and gives a sense of history, including a sense of origins, but, important as these aspects are in themselves, they also serve, within Genesis, to accomplish something more central, namely, the portrayal, almost timeless, of human existence—first, the portrayal of the human environment (the world, with its deep ambiguity, 1:1–25:18), then the portrayal of the full course of life, womb to tomb (25:19–chap. 50).

Genesis is united and structured not only by the broad context of life (its environment and life's full duration) but also by the fundamental elements that give shape to life—time (generations), space, and advancing stages of age and perception.

History, with all its vicissitudes, surrounds this portrayal of life, and at one level seems to swamp it. Yet it is not history that governs the structure of the book. And, in the final analysis—so Genesis implies—it is not the vicissitudes of history that govern human life.

Yet it is necessary now to look more closely at history.

12   Genesis and History

As just indicated (Chapter 11) Genesis's history-like thread is secondary to its portrayal of human life. History, while important, is not ultimate. What then is the relationship of Genesis to history?

Frye's answer is noteworthy: "If anything historically true is in the Bible, it is there not because it is historically true but for different reasons" (1981, 40). There is much truth in this. In dealing with the past, the Bible often shows radical freedom. It depicts the past, but its interest lies elsewhere, generally in something more permanent, something about the present. This principle may be illustrated in two ways, concerning the origin of humankind, and concerning the origin of Israel. According to the Bible, the earth and humanity were created about 4000 BCE, and Abraham entered Canaan about 2000 BCE. Modern research, however, has a more complex view.

The Origin of Humankind

From sources other than the Bible it is known that the universe is billions of years old: the universe itself, perhaps fifteen billion (or somewhat less); the immediate galaxy about ten billion; and the solar system, including the earth, about four billion (Sagan, 1977, 13; Corey Powell, 1992; Bolte and Hogan, 1995).

Humanity arrived late, not billions of years ago, but, in primitive form (hominids), about two million years ago, beginning apparently in Africa (Wilford, 1996, 1). The age of human beings proper, *homo sapiens*, is less than a hundred millennia. During that hundred millennia, it was only in the last ten, especially the last five, that agriculture and cities began to develop (Cheilik, 1991, 11).

If the age of the universe is compared to one year, then the solar system and incipient earth life were formed in September. Hominids appeared on December 30, and full-fledged humans, *homo sapiens*, late on the last day, December 31, around 10:30 P.M. The dinosaurs (lasting 140 million years) had come and gone the previous weekend. Agriculture and cities came later still, shortly after 11:59 P.M. The whole of history, from the invention of writing to the second millennium CE, has taken place in the final ten seconds of the universe's year (Sagan, 1977, 13–17).

The reason for going through all these details is to underline the chasm between actual history or prehistory and the biblical narrative. The splendid Genesis account (chaps. 1–11) not only does not know about the billions of years; it never tells the reader that its own account is not factual. The silence is not due to dishonesty, but because its interest lies elsewhere—in a portrayal that speaks to the present.

The Origin of Israel

From a strictly historical point of view it is not known when a grouping of human beings first formed the society that became the people of Israel. There are serious problems not only about the patriarchs but also about much of the period before the monarchy (on diverse approaches see, for instance, Hayes and Miller, 1977, 64–69; Whybray, 1996). And the questions continue to deepen. The title of a recent review of research reflects the elusiveness of Israel's history: "The Vanishing Solomon: The Disappearance of the United Monarchy from Recent Histories of Ancient Israel" (Knoppers, 1997).

Be that as it may—leaving aside distant origins (from Abraham to Solomon)—there is at least reasonable certainty that in the eighth century there were two well-established kingdoms, Israel and Judah. Later, when defeated Israel was partly settled by foreigners (Samaritans), Judah took over part of the identity of Israel. The biblical picture of Israel therefore is a Judean picture, filtered through Judean experience, and serving to build up the history of Judea and Jerusalem. The original history of Israel is largely hidden behind that filter.

This broad context—the filtering of Israel's heritage through the eyes of later Judea—clarifies Genesis's approach to history. It is no accident that, even in Genesis, a special role, including the climactic speech, goes to Judea's ancestor, repentant Judah (37:26–27; chap. 38; 43:1–10; 44:18–34; 49:22–26).

How much history therefore is there in Genesis? Its artistic nature and structure are styled. Stylization of course "does not, as one may think, imply concoction" (Halpern, 1988, 219).

The problem, however, is not only style; it is substance. For example: the betrothal of Rebekah (Gen. 24)—the most elaborate episode in Genesis, set at the center of the book—gives a substantive role to camels, especially to the extraordinary way Rebekah waters ten of them. But diverse evidence indicates that camels were not introduced into Canaan until a later time. It is not reasonable then to claim that the account of Rebekah's betrothal, however wonderful, is historical. Likewise the various episodes in which Abraham and Isaac are said to be involved with Philistines (21:34; 26:1,14–15). From all that is otherwise known there were no Philistines in Canaan until much later.

Again Genesis not only does not give the facts. It does not tell the reader that its portrayal is not factual. It is an artistic work, and even when it uses elements of the past it does so to portray something more permanent and more present.

There is a paradox about Genesis. It sounds like history, but is not. It gives the impression of a series of events, sometimes with many details, yet in the entire book of Genesis there is not one specific event that can be verified by history. There are, indeed, many long-term realities—from the cosmos to specific customs—but there is no individual happening, nor any individual person, who is otherwise known. Historically, the human race began not in the East but apparently in Africa. There is no independent collaboration for Abraham, Isaac, and Jacob. Even Joseph—the person who, according to Genesis, administered the Egyptian superpower and thus saved the world from famine—is unrecorded in all other chronicles and inscriptions; he is not even mentioned. In a sense, therefore, Genesis is unrelated to known history. One cannot use it reliably as a basis for Israel's beginnings.

Genesis and Historical Existence

Yet, in another way, Genesis is profoundly historical. It is like an artistic synthesis of history—complete with flood, famine, migration, war, and consuming fire. Unlike Greek mythology, which tends to take place in the skies of Mount Olympus or at the bottom of the sea, Genesis, by and large, is on the ground, at the human level. The people generally are ordinary people; their conditions and customs correspond broadly with the conditions and customs of real life. Historical investigation (including archaeology) sometimes contradicts the details of Genesis—for instance, concerning the camels and Philistines—but at other times it uncovers something that corresponds with practical aspects of the story. So the Genesis story gives a powerful sense of human existence, of its rootedness in historicality—in the unpredictable ebb and flow of daily life amid a troubled world. Historicality is not something accidental to human existence, it is of its essence. Genesis captures that essence.

Genesis, however, is more than history. While capturing the essence of historical existence, it also captures other aspects of human life, aspects that generally fall outside the analysis of historical investigation. Stated otherwise, Genesis deals with history not in a superficial way but in all its depth.

Genesis, for instance, in describing the call of Abraham, may not perhaps be recording the experience of a specific person called Abraham early in the second millennium, but "those who wrote the story had themselves had the experience it describes, 'for nobody can describe an experience unless he has had it, either originally or through imaginative re-enactment' " (Eric Voegelin, quoted in Webb, 1981, 167).

Furthermore, the idea of an original fall may not correspond to a specific event in history; and some of the apparent literary background (Ezekiel, 28; cf. Isaiah. 14? Hesiod's *Theogony*?) to the biblical picture of a fall may seem far away from history in both content and tone. But history, when looked at closely, is pervaded by various experiences of fallenness. In Hegel's analysis of human thought (*Logic,* 52–57, esp. 54, emphasis added), for instance, the quest for truth involves a move from innocence to loss of innocence, to a sundering:

> Upon a closer inspection of the story of the Fall we find . . . that it exemplifies the universal bearings of knowledge upon the spiritual life. In its instinctive and natural stage, spiritual life wears the garb of innocence and confiding simplicity. But the very essence of spirit implies the absorption of this immediate condition into something higher. *The spiritual* is distinguished from the natural, and more especially from the animal, life, in the circumstance that it does not continue a mere stream of tendency, but *sunders itself to self-realization.* But this position of severed life has in its turn to be suppressed, and the spirit has by its own act to win its way to concord again.

The important point for the moment is not the detail of Hegel's analysis but its general implication: the story of the Fall is not primarily about a distant historical event but about an inner process, which is generally not dealt with in historical writing. It is deeper than history, beyond normal historical criticism.

A variation on Hegel's approach occurs in the writings of another philosopher, Paul Ricoeur. Again, the tone is essentially positive:

> Every effort to save the letter of the [Adam] story as a true history is vain and hopeless. What we know . . . [from] science, about the beginning of humankind, leaves no place for such a primordial event. I am convinced that the full acceptance of the non-historical character of the [Adamic] myth—non-historical if we take history in the sense that it has for the critical method—is the other side of a great discovery: the discovery of the symbolic function of the myth. But then we should not say, "The story of the 'fall' is only a myth"—that is to say, something less than history—but "The story of the fall has the greatness of myth"—that is to say, has more meaning than a true history. (1967, 235–236)

At its beginning, therefore, Genesis emerges from something deeper than history. As the book goes on, the narrative becomes increasingly history-like (see Chapter 2 on spiraling structures). Yet that history is overtaken by another dimension—the relation of human existence to the larger providence of God; and so (as seen in the preceding chapter) the history-like structure of the three patriarchs yields to the providence-related story of Joseph.

Genesis, therefore, while adopting some of the features of one genre—historiography—does not limit itself to a narrow definition of history. Somewhat like Herodotus, but more so, Genesis blends diverse elements. Those who wrote the Primary History (Genesis-Kings, especially Genesis) relied partly on imperfect versions of physics and history. To that extent, Genesis's vision is imperfect; it needs improvement; it needs to be complemented by modern knowledge of physics, history, and other disciplines. Yet Genesis provides a paradigm for the effort to integrate science and theology (Fretheim, 338). Besides, Genesis did not pretend to be perfect; as a prologue to a long history its view would be modified by subsequent books. Nor has any later vision been perfect—not that of any evangelist (hence the need for four), nor of any medieval systematician, nor of any reformer, nor of any philosopher, theologian, religious leader, or litterateur.

One may complain that Genesis did not get everything right, or one may try to prove that Genesis was in fact always right. But such debates tend to miss the central reality: amid all the imperfect visions, that of Genesis is one of the greatest. Its strength is not in the areas of physics and scientific history, but—partly because of its attentiveness to some of the world's great traditions— it has an extraordinary awareness of what it is to be a human being, to be immersed in a world of history and spirit.

Overall there is loss and gain. On the one hand, Genesis is not history. On the other hand, it is history plus. It captures the essence of historical existence, and furthermore, it goes into depths that historical studies usually do not reach.

In the first place it goes into psychology.

13   Genesis and Psychology

> A reading of Genesis suggests how it was that psychoanalysis began as a predominantly Jewish discipline. Long before Freud, the authors of ancient Israel had already begun to explore the uncharted realm of the human mind and heart. They saw this struggle with the emotions and with the past as the theater of the religious quest.
>
> Karen Armstrong (1996, 8)

During the 1980s, when center stage in biblical research was often occupied by the contending claims of literature and history (including social science), a further voice was emerging from the background—psychology. This further voice was not something minor. Psychology is the aspect of Genesis which, more than any other factor, led to an explosion of interest in the book in the 1980s and 1990s.

Initially, the most striking developments were in Europe. In 1980, for instance, Maria Kassel of Münster published her study on biblical archetypes, an exposition which was based on Jung and which took most of its examples from Genesis (see Kassel, 1980). About the same time Eugen Drewermann of Paderborn began releasing a prodigious stream of writings on depth psychology, and many of these writings used Scripture, especially Genesis. In the three-volume study of the structures of evil (*Strukturen des Bösen*, 1977/1, 1977/2, 1978/3) the second volume subjected Genesis 2–11 to psychological analysis (for a long review of vol. 1, see Ruppert, 1979). Drewermann then undertook a massive two-volume study of the relationship between depth psychology and exegesis (*Tiefenpsychologie und Exegese*, 1984, 1985).

More so than Kassel, Drewermann was negative about the Bible's historical dimension, and, partly for this reason, his work drew a sharp response from the combined authorship of Lohfink and Pesch (1987). Drewermann responded by invoking the gospel: "By their fruits you shall know them" (1988). Though very popular in mainland Europe, the value of Drewermann's approach is still deeply disputed (see, for instance, the Gassmann and Lange booklet, *Was nun, Herr Drewermann?* 1993). The widening controversy, which eventually involved a sharp psychology-based critique of church doctrines and structures, has become "a case" (see Laurent, ed., *Le cas Drewermann. Les Documents*, 1993).

Before 1990, Drewermann's work scarcely crossed the Atlantic; there were virtually no English-language translations or reviews (for a rare review in English of *Strukturen des Bösen*, vol. 3, see Kimbrough, 1982). In 1991, however, Orbis Books, Maryknoll, published a short work—a collection of meditations—and in 1994 Crossroad, New York, followed suit (see Drewermann, 1991, and 1994).

The United States, however, had its own psychology-oriented movement. Largely independently, a group of scholars were discovering, with a fresh clarity, the psychological aspect of the Scriptures. Accordingly, in 1991 the Society of Biblical Literature set up its first psychology-based research unit: "Psychology and Biblical Studies." The development of this emphasis on psychology, both in the United States and elsewhere, has been summarized by Rollins (1995).

In 1993, the Pontifical Biblical Commission lent further support to the link between Scripture and psychology. In its review of interpretive methods, this international commission indicated at some length the need to engage psychology and psychoanalysis (Pontifical Biblical Commission, 1993, I, D, 3)—all part of a "methodological spectrum of exegetical work . . . which could not have been envisioned thirty years ago" (see Rollins, 1995, 12).

Recent Genesis studies that are psychological or psychology-related give the impression of a discipline beginning to blossom. The work of Zornberg (1995), which approaches Genesis through rabbinic tradition, is sometimes circuitous and wearying but ultimately enriching. The TV conversation conducted by Bill

Moyers (1996) was understandably uneven yet full of insights. Insightful, too, psychologically speaking, is the work of Armstrong (1996) and Visotzky (1996). Visotsky's description of Genesis as "an ugly little soap opera about a dysfunctional family" (p. 9) is grossly reductionist, yet his central thesis is noteworthy: the gap or dissonance between the roughness of the story and its reception or interpretation as something "nice" makes the book attractive (p. 10). The dissonance gives a form of depth, an extra dimension, which allows the "nice" person, while remaining nice, to feel that there is room also, somewhere, for what is not nice. And the co-authored study by Dreifuss and Riemer (1995) on the Abraham story offers a Jungian interpretation which, as well as respecting the biblical narrative, is brief and clear. Norman J. Cohen (1995, 14) is particularly focused on practical living: "Modern psychology has taught us that each human being has a complex personality made up of a variety of positive and negative traits. . . . The Genesis narratives . . . can serve as vehicles of insight into our own personalities as well as the dynamic tensions within our own families." Cohen then goes on to indicate, vividly, how Genesis can be healing.

An Example

In the psychological analysis of Genesis one of the areas that has been studied with greatest clarity is the first part of the Jacob story (25:19–37:1). This text has been interpreted in light of Jung, but the interpretation contains both occasional references to Freud and also an awareness of the old adage, "Know thyself," an adage that is Buddhist, Greek, and Christian.

The essence of this Jungian-related interpretation is as follows.

When a woman is born—the case applies equally to a man—she carries in her psyche a division; the space in which she lives consciously is small, but near her there is a curtain, thick yet permeable (composed of myriad strips) and beyond it, unconscious, lies a whole other space, a land of shadow. As she develops as an independent person, she desires more space, more deliberate union and integration. She wants to go beyond the curtain of present consciousness and live in her whole self—the wider land beyond the curtain, the land of shadow. But some first impressions of the unconscious shadow may be disturbing (Freud especially showed their negative aspect; the desire for union with one person may lead to wanting to eliminate someone else), so disturbing that she may turn back and spend the rest of her life living nervously inside the permeable curtain. The challenge is to go through and accept the whole world of the shadow—to enter it, wrestle with it, get to know and accept it. The shadow in fact is like a thick cloud—dark and overbearing on one side, but, on the other, full of light and opening out to the heavens, to an area far beyond the original cramped space. The full engaging of the shadow—the journey to awareness, to self-knowledge and self-acceptance, including death— brings a new, integrated, sense of one's own self.

In Jungian terminology this earnest wrestling with the shadow, this journey to calm self-awareness, is called individuation. Underlying the process of individuation is an emerging reality, personal and integral, the full person—in Jung's terms, the Self.

It is the thesis of some Jungian scholars (especially Kassel, 1980, 258–279; Kille, 1995) that one aspect of Jacob's story, especially his struggles with his twin Esau, involves a portrayal of the process of individuation. Esau is like Jacob's shadow, like the other part of himself. In dealing with Esau he wrestles and journeys, and finally, after many years and struggles, reaches reconciliation (chap. 33). The mysterious struggle at Peniel, on the night before reconciliation (32:23–32), is a climactic step in the process of individuation.

Toward Greater Clarity and Development

The emphasis on psychology is not only welcome; it is necessary. Much remains to be clarified, however, and to be developed. As examples of areas that need more attention one may mention the following.

1. *Building two stories.* Psychological analysis of Scripture sometimes bases itself partly on a literary reading of the text and partly on historical reconstruction—thus mixing methodologies. The result is that two stories become confused—rather like a psychotherapist who confuses the records of two clients.

Similar confusion may arise when, invoking midrashic tradition, the interpreter adds details that are not in the text. This, for instance, is the practice of psychotherapist Naomi Rosenblatt (1996). The added details may form a very interesting case, but it is no longer the case presented by Genesis.

2. *Imposing alien ideas.* Kassel has maintained that Abraham's near-sacrifice of Isaac was an expression of a struggle between generations, of a deep desire of a father to kill his son—the reverse side of the Oedipus Complex; "the father sees the son as a rival" (1980, 247).

Without doubt young people are sometimes capable of driving their elders to distraction and even to thoughts of murder. And perhaps, in analyzing parent-child relationships, depth psychology has uncovered a special murderous streak. Furthermore, humans do indeed occasionally tend to eliminate rivals.

But Genesis 22 has no glimmer of rivalry. The problem in Abraham's case is not that he may want to eliminate Isaac but to cling to him; the story emphasizes that he loves Isaac. When rivalry was present it was clear: Sarah, seeing Ishmael playing with Isaac, ordered that Ishmael and his mother be banished; and so they were. Abraham was initially distressed by this rivalry and the banishment order, but he implemented it after God assured him about Ishmael's future (Gen. 21:8–14).

If in chapter 21 the portrayal of rivalry is so clear then why in chapter 22 is there no hint of such rivalry? Chapter 22 points not to the presence of rivalry but to its absence. In this instance psychological analysis has taken an idea and imposed it on a text where it does not belong. The psychological analysis of the Abraham story by Dreifuss and Riemer (1995) is far more promising, far closer to the actual case presented by the text.

3. *The need for a broader horizon.* In the example given above, concerning Jacob and the process of individuation, one feature is striking: it does not include the second part of the Jacob story—concerning Joseph (chaps. 37–50). This suggests that the methodology being used needs clarification. The first question of the psychologist—as of the theologian, historian, or social scientist—is literary: What is the text to be interpreted? What is its extent, nature, and structure? From a literary point of view the Jacob story is inextricably interwoven with that of Joseph, and so a psychological analysis, to be credible in the long term, must follow the Jacob story beyond the reconciliation with Esau.

A similar question arises in the examining of Genesis 1–11. As Drewermann indicates (1977/2, 617), these early chapters involve a portrayal of human deficiency and failure. Psychological analysis, insofar as it was developed precisely for dealing with much of the sick side of life (neuroses) is attuned to understanding many of the ideas in these chapters. Drewermann's own extensive commentary on Genesis 2–11 (1977–1978) is a significant contribution toward such understanding.

But Drewermann omits Genesis 1. He does so no doubt in compliance with the historical critical method of dissecting the text, of assigning Genesis 1 to another author. The effect, however, is that he deprives Genesis 1–11 of its most positive chapter, its basic starting point—rather as the analysis of Jacob omits the Joseph story. The result is that psychological analysis, instead of learning from a literature that is wider than its own preoccupation with neuroses, tends to stay within its own relatively narrow frame of reference.

Genesis's point of departure—in Genesis 1—is not the sick side of life, but a calm symphony of goodness, dignity, and peace. Until psychological analysis is more open to the full dimensions of all that is positive in human existence it will not be able to deal adequately with Genesis. More specifically, until it incorporates the beauty of the Joseph story into Jacob's life it will not have done justice to Jacob—to his primordial biography.

An indication of the limitations of psychology in understanding literature is already provided by Welleck and Warren:

> Much great art continuously violates standards of psychology. . . . It works with improbable situations, with fantastic motifs. Like the demand for social realism, psychological truth is a naturalistic standard without universal validity. In some cases, to be sure, psychological insight seems to enhance artistic value. . . . But such insight can be reached by other means than a theoretical knowledge of psychology. In the sense of a conscious and systematic theory of the mind and its workings, psychology is unnecessary to art and not in itself of artistic value. . . . In itself, psychology is only preparatory to the act

of creation; and in the work itself, psychological truth is an artistic value only if it enhances coherence and complexity—if, in short, it is art. (1962, 92–93)

The general conclusion therefore is that psychology is one of Genesis's crucial components and that modern psychological analysis can do much in uncovering that factor. The psychological approach represents a major step forward. At the same time, there seems to be more in Genesis than much modern psychology can absorb or detect.

The more involves spirituality.

14   Genesis and Spirituality

In 1994, when the American Psychiatric Association published the fourth edition of the *Diagnostic and Statistical Manual for Mental Disorders*, the manual included, for the first time, an implicit acceptance of the importance of spirituality: there was mention of disorders based on religious and spiritual problems (p. 685).

This change is the tip of an iceberg. Freud, the founder of modern psychology, reduced God and religion to a psychological phenomenon. Since then, the same simplistic logic—reductionism—has tended to govern psychology. The resistance to spirituality was powerful, like a taboo:

> For most therapists it is far easier to discuss . . . sexual life . . . money . . . intimate love than it is to explore . . . prayer, meditation, and the discovery of meaning in the face of mortality. This difficulty in most clinical encounters can without exaggeration be called a taboo, first introduced during the training of the therapist and then transmitted in the clinical encounter with the patient.
>
> This taboo cannot be solely attributed to Freud's basic stance towards religion. It is similarly enforced in other psychotherapies, including those that advance the traditions of "value-free" positivist psychology and share little with psychoanalysis. Trainees, like patients, take subtle and not so subtle cues about what is proper or improper to address in therapy. No one ever told us not to pursue spiritual issues, but not one of our many gifted teachers ever suggested we do so. Does any typical psychiatric and psychoanalytical anamnestic interview ever include the exploration of the transforming images of God or the content and meaning of prayers across the lifespan? (Naom and Wolf, 1993, 197–198)

Now however, psychology and psychological analysis have begun to be some-what more open toward the spiritual level. This is particularly true at the level of counseling (Burke and Miranti, 1995). Furthermore, some authors, while dealing with the psychological dimension of Genesis, have laid the emphasis on spirituality (see, for instance, Ochs, 1994, 5–19). There is a move on to go beyond specialist dogmas:

> Today we are more likely to explore new "foreign territories of the mind" and to trust less in specialized truths handed down within any clinical sub-specialty. The field of psychotherapy has entered a post-dogma period that is more sensitive to the developmental needs of the patients and *their* (in contrast to the theorists' and therapists') reality. For example, the feminist critique of male biases in developmental and clinical theory exposed a uni-dimensionality in perspectives that ultimately concerned not only male/female issues but also such issues as ethnicity, class, and religion. (Naom and Wolf, 1993, 198)

It is not necessary here to analyze the changing relationship of religion to psychology/psychoanalysis (for this see Meissner, 1984, 1987; McDargh, 1993; and Jones, 1996, especially Jones's critique of reductionism, pp. 114–150). What is important is that Genesis, now discovered by psychologists, not be reduced to a narrow dimension that effectively excludes spirituality. Abraham at his best may become a symbol of sweet reason, an example of someone who is psycho-logically adjusted. Freud's analysis is often not far from modern psychology, and that analysis is not only reductionist; "it also implies there is some element of sham or pretense in our greatly valued higher activities" (Loewald, 1978, 75).

Accordingly, the purpose of this brief chapter is not to chart in any detail Genesis's world of spirituality, nor to clarify the age-long uncertainty about the meaning of the very word "spiritual" (see Smith, 1988, 9–48), but primarily to indicate that such a world exists and that Genesis engages it profoundly.

This is not to deny Genesis's limitations. It stumbles, as many artists and thinkers do, on the problem of evil. Part of its understanding of evil seems simplistic: there is an impression, especially in the account of the destruction of Sodom, that only evil people are punished by natural catastrophe. All the innocent are saved.

Yet this is not Genesis's full account of evil. The shadows begin in God's own creation, including the snake that God made; and Genesis generally sets evil in the context of a greater reality of goodness, even of awe, a reality which breaks the barriers of all simplistic thinking. It is no accident that the Sodom account (18:1–19:29) begins with the picture of Abraham's extraordinary gen-erosity to his unknown guests and that the whole account is colored by almost contradictory references to the mode of God's presence (three/two/one; God/angels/men). Genesis knows that the full answer to evil is not simple.

Be that as it may—for in the end it is always necessary, at some level, to let go of the problem of evil—it is still true that Genesis engages the deeper dimension of life, especially spirituality. To illustrate this further reality, it is appropriate to mention some of its features or aspects.

Aspects of Spirituality

The Story of God and God's Spirit

Apart from the delicate balance between the portrayal of specific history and the general portrayal of human life, Genesis contains a whole other dimension—the portrayal of the story of God.

The picture of God, however, is not simple. At first God appears utterly omnipotent, but, as the early chapters go by, God becomes more involved with humans: God walks; and eventually God begins to seem more limited. Before the flood, for instance, God grieves; and before the destruction of Sodom, God comes down to see what is happening.

The result is a picture of a God who, despite limitations at one level, is capable of giving a person a new strength or purpose. Cain, at his lowest, receives from God a protective sign, which enables him to survive. Abraham, amid a discouraging situation, receives a call which sets him on a new journey. The implication is of a higher presence, which in varying ways can lift someone.

As the narrative advances God's presence seems to fade (see Chapter 2, on spiraling structures), but in other ways God's presence comes to life, and it does so in very human ways—especially through the figures of Rebekah and Joseph.

Grace

When the world seems rotten and doomed, when the whole process of creation seems to have been a sad mistake, suddenly there is grace: "But Noah found grace in the eyes of Yhwh" (6:8). It is as though there is some radically positive reality which, in some aspects, is incalculable. Psychology can examine grace insofar as it has a psychological impact (Meissner, 1987, 3–60), but grace is more than its psychological impact. The effect of this grace, when combined with Noah's attentiveness, is that, amid the huge loss brought on by the flood, Noah manages to make a new beginning.

David Clines (1976a) offers two alternative readings of Genesis 1–11: (a) Humans tend to destroy what God has made good; or (b) No matter how much humans sin, God's grace offers a fresh start. Rather then see these two readings as mutually exclusive it is better to regard them as two aspects of a complex unity: humans destroy goodness, but God's grace gives a fresh opportunity.

Seeing as God Makes One See

One of the recurrent motifs of Genesis is that of seeing. There are diverse ways of seeing: Lot sees in one way, calculating the obvious richness of the land; but Abraham sees in another way—as God enables him to see (13:10–17). This accords with the original promise: God did not name a specific land; God promised the land "that I will make you see" (12:1). Here and elsewhere there is sufficient ambiguity to indicate that God is inviting Abraham to see reality in another way. Genesis never uses the word "enlightenment," but at times it is not far from that concept.

Second Birth

The birth of Isaac gives Abraham and Sarah a form of new life. Old Sarah—who for long seemed given to silence or, later, bitterness—laughs, breaks into poetry, and speaks directly (21:1–12). It is a story that crosses the boundaries both of history and psychology and that is understood most easily in the realm of the spirit. The new life that emerges from the old bodies of Abraham and Sarah is like a variation on the idea of how the spirit of Yhwh gave new life to the dry bones (Ezekiel 37).

The Question of Immortality

James Barr (1992) has made a strong case for the presence in Genesis of a promise of immortality. His thesis gets support not only from the enigmatic story of Enoch, who was taken by God (5:24), but also from the continuity between Enoch and Elijah (also taken by God, 2 Kings 2:1) and more generally by the broad literary continuity between Genesis and the Elijah-Elisha narrative (*Crucial Bridge*, 2000, 71–73). While Elijah himself was taken, Enoch-like, to heaven, the larger Elijah-Elisha narrative tells of raising others: first, the boy who appeared to be dead (1 Kings 17:17–24); then the boy who was definitely dead (2 Kings 4:18–37); and finally, climactically, the man who was on the way to burial (2 Kings 13:20–21). Both Genesis and the Elijah-Elisha narrative have indications of the soul as something distinct (Barr, 1992, 43; Overholt, 1996, 33).

John Day (1996) maintains that a gloomy idea of Sheol pervaded Hebrew thought till a fairly late stage. Yet, given the image of the tree of life (Gen. 2–3), he concludes that the picture is not so simple: "There can be no doubt that the early Israelites were familiar with the idea of immortality. . . . In my view, rather than saying the first humans are either mortal or immortal in the Garden, it is better to say they are potentially immortal" (1996, 236–237). From the beginning, therefore, the question of immortality is on the agenda.

As a tentative basis for further research it is useful to list some of the texts that suggest or evoke some idea of life as immortal or as surpassing predictable development:

The ambiguity of the concept of land (see Chapter 11).

The tree of life (2:9; 3:22).

God's taking of Enoch (5:24, intimating Elijah in the chariot, 2 Kings 2).

The fire amid the death-related darkness (15:17).

The role of (Sarah's) death in gaining the promised land (chap. 23).

The "still alive" motif (43:7, 28–29; 45:3, 26, 28; 46:30).

Jacob's journey, in a wagon met by a chariot (45:27; 46:5, 29), from a form of death (45:26) to meetings that are related to death (46:30) and judgment (47:7–10) and that lead to the good land (47:11).

The undermining of the dynamics of space and time (see Chapter 11) so that while at one level the story leads to death (literally to "a coffin in Egypt," 50:26), at another it is focused on Mamre—the place of God's apparition and of Sarah's field (18:1; 23:19).

Linked to immortality are other issues—especially transcendence.

Transcendence

Genesis deals with a dimension beyond history, with what Voegelin calls the pneumatic or spiritual experience of the divine calling and the manifestation of the One God as the source of order:

> [The call of Abraham] is an order that originates in a man through the inrush of divine reality into his soul and from this point of origin expands into a social body in history. At the time of its inception it is no more than the life of a man who trusts in God; but this new existence, founded on the leap in being, is pregnant with future. (Voegelin, 1956, 194; cf. Webb, 1981, 166)

Transcendence is the ultimate issue in Genesis. It is with a trumpet blast of transcendence that the book begins (1:1–2:4a), and, amid all the fears and follies of the characters' lives, the issue of transcendence runs through the text like a powerful river, often underground, often too deep to affect the surface, yet ultimately turning the wasteland of history into a place of hope.

Paradoxically, death can have the effect not of mocking transcendence but of revealing it, of bringing God closer. It is Adam and Eve's arousing of the shadow of death that introduces the picture of God as walking close to them in the Garden. It is Cain's incurring of the proximate threat of death that causes God to come closer still, touching him protectively. It is a family of premature death and barrenness (11:27–32) that provides the background for Abraham's journey into another kind of God-given land; and, after a life involving both courage and cowardice, it is a terrible onslaught of death, threatening Isaac and engulfing Sarah (chaps. 22–23), that finally brings Abraham to a unique level of serenity and graciousness: "God will provide."

The issue, of course, goes far beyond Genesis. It is transcendence and death which, in the final analysis, give hope—even to a modern activist. Václav Havel, in the course of analyzing hope, is led to the reality of transcendence:

> With a little exaggeration we may say that death, or the awareness of death—this most extraordinary dimension of man's stay on earth, inspiring dread, fear, and awe—is at the same time a key to the fulfillment of human life in the best sense of the word. It is an obstacle put in the way of human life in the best sense of the word. It is an obstacle in the way of the human mind to test it, to challenge it to be truly the miracle of creation it considers itself to be. Death gives us a chance to overcome it—not by refusing to recognize its existence, but through our ability to look beyond it, or to defy it by purposeful action.
>
> Without the experience of the transcendental, neither hope not human responsibility has any meaning.
>
> ... True goodness, true responsibility, true justice, a true sense of things—all these grow from roots that go much deeper than the world of our transitory earthly schemes. (1997, 2–3)

Havel adds that this message "speaks to us from the very heart of human religiosity" (1997, 3). One of the great expressions of that very heart is the book of Genesis.

15   Genesis as a Reflection of the Complexity of Life

Further Aspects of Content

Genesis is like an encyclopedia of life; it reflects all of human existence. As life is a many-splendored thing, so too is Genesis; it radiates in many directions. The aspects reviewed in the preceding chapters—history, psychology, spirituality—are but part of that larger reality. Such variety of interest is not unique. Homer, too, was encyclopedic (Havelock, 1963, 61–86).

This final introductory chapter indicates some of the further ways in which Genesis reflects the diversity of life. The emphasis is on *some*. Others could be examined, including, for instance, the role of work, prayer, kindness, love, death. Fretheim (329–330) summarizes certain basic themes. Sternberg (1985, 349) discusses old age. One could ask, for example, why, especially in comparison to Homer, Genesis has so few tears?

At key points, especially at the center and end (24:1–25:18, and chaps. 49–50, esp. 50) Genesis gives, as it were, a special flourish. There is increased emphasis not only on blessing, but on other features: an increase in the use of the particle of entreaty (*nā'*, "please/pray": six times in chap. 24, five in chap. 50); and, more strikingly, a change in the mode of transport: there is the great show of camels in chapter 24; and, in chapters 45–50, esp. 50, there are pictures, as never before of wagons, horses, and chariots.

Amid so much riches, a few aspects may be highlighted.

Genesis as Foundational

Genesis is a prologue not just to a work of history (Exodus-Kings) but in some sense to much of civilization. One of its recurrent emphases and story forms is that of human achievement (Westermann, I, 56–63). The book functions as an introduction to the whole biblical world (Adar, 1990). It helps to lay political foundations (Combs and Post, 1987). And, as is shown especially by Drewermann's monumental analysis of Genesis 1–11, it also helps to clarify human foundations—some of the basic features and dynamics of human life. So when Jung states that "our psychology, whole lives, our language and imagery are built upon the Bible" (cited in Rollins, 1995, 9), his words apply particularly to Genesis.

Harmony and Disharmony

The first reality for Genesis is harmony under God. Harmony appears at diverse times but particularly so at the book's beginning, middle, and end (creation; Rebekah; and Jacob's blessing-filled death). Harmony frames the book, surrounding even its most terrible episodes. Therefore, no matter what the circumstances, at a certain level evil does not dominate. Even when Abraham is being tested, his journey with Isaac has a striking sense of harmony, a form of serenity.

Much of Genesis, however, is not about harmony but about the disruption of harmony—about sin and its consequences, about crime and punishment. For Genesis, the appropriate response to sin is neither cover-up nor vindictive punishment. Rather, sin is to be exposed, addressed, and, if possible, healed. In the final analysis, Genesis's portrayal of sin and punishment is largely the same as that of Deuteronomy.

At one level, sin brings separation from God, yet sin causes God to become more involved. This happens, for instance, with Adam and Eve, with Cain, and also with sinful humanity, over whom God grieves (6:1–8). Thus, on every occasion there is an involvement of the divine. Toward the end of Genesis this involvement is less obvious, but it is no less central: God's presence is in Joseph, the one who, within Genesis, weeps most.

Blessing

Flowing out from God, from God's creation and providence, is the central reality of blessing. Blessing encompasses the book, especially the beginning, middle, and end (chaps. 1, 24, 49), and it is like a stream of divine energy and life. It is bestowed first on the fishes and birds—day 5—and afterward flows to and through creation and people. It surrounds not only a splendid story of betrothal, concerning Rebekah, but also Genesis's most detailed account of a death, that of Jacob. It is as though Genesis, having begun by showing the blessedness of creation, wants to emphasize that that blessedness does not fade.

Yet blessedness is not to be taken for granted. Sin brings a curse; Abraham goes through trials; and Jacob, to achieve blessing, has to participate in the effort to gain it. In God's process of blessing, the human factor is necessary.

Near the end, when Jacob summarizes his life for Pharaoh, he speaks of a blend of evil and blessing (47:7–10). He does not underestimate the evil, yet the emphasis falls, first and last, on blessing.

Marriage and Family

Much of Genesis's history is a form of family history, and there is a "pervasive concern for kinship and family, an order of creation" (Fretheim, 329). This concern provides the context for a more specific concern—marriage.

The Genesis portrayal of marriage begins in chapter 1 and is woven through much of the subsequent text, including the genealogies. This portrayal involves two basic aspects, sociological and theological.

Sociological. As with any text, Genesis reflects aspects of the sociological situation in which it was written, including aspects of the marriage situation. It seems likely, for instance, as indicated by Steinberg (1993), that Genesis's occasional approval of marrying within one's people reflects something of the postexilic situation when marriage to foreigners was contested.

Theological. Despite being colored by a specific situation, Genesis proposes implicitly a larger concept of marriage—a form of ideal that is based primarily not on local conditions but on a larger, theological, vision. In the primordial image of marriage (Gen. 2) the partners are simply man and woman; they are not members of a specific ethnic group. The primary background to Genesis 2 is not a particular sociological situation but Genesis 1—the two chapters form a literary unity—and in Genesis 1 the key pertinent factor is theological: there is continuity between the harmony of the couple, at the end of the second creation text, and the harmony of God, at the end of the first. In other words, marriage ultimately is founded not on sociological conditions but on a quality in God.

Despite its role as foundational Genesis seems flexible. Its ideal of marriage is monogamy (see, for instance, Gen. 2, and the marriages of Noah, Isaac, and

Joseph [7:7; 24:67; 41:45]). But at times this ideal does not work out. Jacob was intent on marrying only one woman, Rachel, but through force of circumstances he married two and had children by two more. Abraham also was essentially married to just one woman, but again, because of the circumstances, he had a child by Hagar. The impression is of a book that sees a clear ideal but makes allowance for circumstances.

In choosing a marriage partner there is again some flexibility. There are indications—in the cases of Isaac, Esau, and Jacob—that it is better to choose someone from among one's own people (24:4; 26:34–35; 27:46–28:2). Yet the peopling of the earth involved diverse intermarrying; Abraham's extra partner Hagar was an Egyptian (16:1–2); and Joseph's wife, the mother of Ephraim and Manasseh, was also Egyptian (41:45).

There is even greater flexibility in relation to eating meat. At first, Genesis suggests that vegetarianism is the ideal (1:29). But after the deluge it grants freedom to eat meat and fish (9:2–3).

Women and Men

The portrayal of human beings, women and men, is essentially positive. At the beginning they are created simultaneously and both are equally in the image of God (1:26–27). One of the unfortunate effects of the Documentary Theory was to give priority to a so-called Yahwistic document, which was said to begin with Genesis 2. Thus, in practice, Genesis was decapitated: the complex man-woman scene in Genesis 2 was removed from the clear positive context of chapter 1. The initial statement of equality in chapter 1 does not prevent Genesis from portraying patriarchy and sin-based domination by men—but it places a question mark before any form of inequality. Furthermore, in comparison with Hesiod (*Works and Days*, 47–105; *Theogony*, 570–620), Genesis is like a charter on the dignity of woman. Among the world's diverse scriptures there is none that places so clear a statement about the dignity and equality of the sexes on its first page. Genesis, therefore, despite its limitations, is one of the great portrayals of what it means to be a human being.

Women are less present in Genesis than in Homer. Their role—whether good or ill—is greatly reduced. The reasons for this reduced role are not clear. The roles of women in antiquity shifted considerably (Brown, 1995, 222–252).

Genesis shows the woman as taking the initiative in misleading the man (chap. 3), but it later shows the man, Abraham, as effectively taking the initiative in handing the woman over to Pharaoh (chap. 12). Genesis also shows Potiphar's wife as a seductress (chap. 39), but only after showing Judah, the eventual leader of Jacob's sons, as irresponsible and whoring (chap. 38).

One of the key figures in Genesis is a woman, Rebekah. She is not on the same level as the patriarchs; she is above it. Her role is set at the very center of the book—a key position in ancient book-writing—and the volume of text devoted to her entrance into the narrative is greater than for any other episode in Genesis. She appears and acts as if she were a physical manifestation of God's blessings.

The Larger Community (the Ethnic Group/ the World)

In principle, Genesis seeks to be inclusive—to include those who feel estranged. It moves from a sense of exile to a sense of belonging, under God. And it moves also from sibling murder to forgiveness and reconciliation. Thus, at various levels—while describing the complexity and pain of life—it gathers humanity toward meaning and peace.

Genesis's concern is not limited to the family. It seeks also the welfare of larger groups, including that of the world as a whole. By and large, foreign nations are regarded positively. They are not dismissed, as often happens in human life, through derogatory terms, nicknames, and negative projections. The Philistines, for Abraham, are essentially a peaceful presence. So are the Egyptians—whether as seen in Hagar or in Joseph's Pharaoh. God's care for all of humanity, begun in creation, extends, through the practical stewardship of Joseph, to all the hungry of later generations. "God's purpose in redemption does not, finally, center on Israel. . . . God's redemptive activity [is] . . . universal" (Fretheim, 355).

The universalism of Joseph's action is seen in the way his actions balance the initial fall. For instance, a woman once misled a man (Gen. 3), but Joseph countered that force (Gen. 39). A brother killed a brother (Gen. 4:1–16), but Joseph, though virtually killed by his brothers, led them to reconciliation (Gen. 42–45) and forgiveness (50:15–21). The man's sin earned him soil that was cursed, unresponsive (3:17–19), but, in face of world famine, Joseph's wisdom supplied food and saved people's lives (41:53–57; 47:25). Thus the Joseph story may be seen as a model of redemption (Steindl, 1989, 66–132).

Ambivalence toward Cities

Stories of building cities were an important part of ancient literature, and Genesis in turn tells of cities and city-building. But it seems ambiguous toward cities. City-building is associated with Cain (4:17), with Nimrod and Ashur (10:12), and with the over-ambitious builders of Babel (11:4). The story of Sodom (chap. 19) reinforces this negative impression of cities (see Kselman, 93). Curiously, this apparent antipathy toward cities complements Hesiod's emphasis on rural life (*Works and Days*, esp. lines 430–683).

The Centrality of Journeying

Genesis emphasizes journeying. In contrast, say, to some of Samuel Beckett's dramas, where characters tend to stand still, the book of Genesis is largely about people who move, who walk, who make long journeys.

This picture of walking can be associated with three diverse backgrounds. First, there is a well-known historical/sociological process: almost all through history, up to the present day, a certain percentage of people are involved in migration or in nomadism. In the twentieth century, for example, all five continents saw major migrations. Second, there is a literary background, in the journeys of epic heroes such as Gilgamesh and especially Odysseus. Third, there is a process of journeying or walking that is primarily a response to God. Even if one scarcely leaves one's native village, life may be described as a journey. Each pilgrim, however stable, has a private version of "Lead, kindly light . . . lead thou me on . . . down the arches of the years . . . down the labyrinthine ways of my own mind." (cf. John Henry Newman and Francis Thompson). The journey reflects something of God.

All of these factors—migration, the epic tradition, and response to God—are at work in Genesis; in diverse ways they impinge on the image of journeying or walking. The image of migration is particularly strong in Genesis 11: the opening picture is of people moving to the East (11:2), and the closing picture is of Terah's family moving toward Canaan (11:31). Such an emphasis, such a framing of chapter 11, forms the background to the journey of Abraham (12:1–4).

But this background of migration serves primarily to build a contrast; migration does not dictate Abraham's progress. When Abraham does follow such forces—by going to Egypt—the result is shameful. The migrations of Genesis 11 end in sin (Babel, 11:1–6) and death (Haran, 11:31–32). The journey of Abraham, in contrast, is inspired by God and directed toward blessing (12:1–4). In direct contrast with Babel, where people want to make their own name (11:4), Abraham's name comes from God (12:2). The journeys of Abraham, therefore, are not to be understood primarily within the context of natural forces such as migrations. Abraham is not primarily a migrant.

Nor again is Abraham primarily a wanderer. Wandering is ascribed to Cain, and it has more to do with guilt than with physical movement: "He settled in the land of Wandering (Nod)" (4:14–16).

Nor is Abraham simply another Gilgamesh. Wanderings such as those of Gilgamesh, while important, are not defining; they do not govern the text. Genesis sets its compass by another star, by another model of walking.

In Genesis the first person to walk is God: "They heard the voice of Yhwh God, walking . . ." (3:8). The movements that follow—by the snake and the couple—are ordered by God (3:14, 22–23). The next clear references to walking involves Enoch, who "walked with God" (until God took him, 5:22–24), and

Noah, the just and blameless man, who also "walked with God" (6:9). Somewhat similarly, Shem and Japheth walked backward—led not by their eyes but by respect (and so they are blessed, 9:23–26).

Within Genesis 1–11 therefore the emphasis, in the references to walking, is on a process which, in diverse ways, originates in God and is associated with God.

The evidence converges. Abraham's journey, his walking, is in contrast with ordinary human migrations, but is in continuity with God—with a way of walking which involves God, and with a call which comes from God.

The journeying Abraham therefore is primarily a reflection not of ancient migratory patterns but of the human journey, under God. And the journeys of Isaac and Jacob, which are in continuity with those of Abraham, are essentially of the same kind.

The Journey's Context: Between Creation and Providence

All this journeying (of Abraham, Isaac, and Jacob) does not occur in a vacuum. The surrounding dramas (those of Adam/Noah and Joseph) provide a larger context, one in which God provides the impetus not only for journeying but for all human involvement with creation.

In Genesis 1–11, humanity is first commissioned both to govern and to serve what God has created (1:28; 2:15), and the couple is then sent forth to serve the ground (3:23). After the flood, this mandate is essentially renewed (9:1–3). Thus, before Abraham's journey begins, there is already a sense of mission toward God's creation. The primary mission is to life at large.

In the Joseph account there is a further sense of mission. In various ways Joseph is sent (37:13–14); and he himself emphasizes, "God sent me before you. . . . God sent me before you. . . . It was not you who sent me here but God" (45:5–8). The purpose now is not so much creation as preservation ("to preserve life . . . to keep alive," 45:5–7). Thus the Joseph account, apart from being a unique story and placing a framework of providence around Jacob's old age, tells also of a larger gracious providence, which encompasses the whole world and which in a sense completes the work of creation.

The journeying therefore—in the dramas of Abraham, Isaac, and Jacob—is literally interwoven with a larger surrounding picture of creation and providence. Ultimately, Abraham-like journeying, however vulnerable it may seem, takes place in the context of a greater presence.

COMMENTARY

PART FOUR

BEGINNINGS

Genesis 1–11

The opening of Genesis is like an x-ray of the human world. Instead of concentrating on the surface of things—the wealth, the cleverness, the looks—it focuses primarily on what is underneath, on the deepest heart and on the way things relate. It also manages to give impressions of the surface—its stories are like an encyclopedia of available knowledge—but the primary emphasis is on the deeper dimension.

Its portrayal of this deeper dimension is imperfect. The picture of the woman, for instance, at best is open to misuse. Yet in its day this very picture contained a major advance—a vigorous protest against the kind of misogyny found in Hesiod. And while Genesis 1–11 did not have the detailed knowledge of subsequent centuries, yet amid the fluctuating oceans of modern information, its central insights still provide an important anchor.

The commentary on Genesis 1–5 beings with the two perspectives on creation (1:1–2:24). The panorama is vast and slightly shadowed, but it is harmonious. Then the harmony is shattered, culminating in murder (2:25–4:16). Eventually a form of harmony returns, not primarily through technology and music, but through a basic relationship to the God of creation (4:17–chap. 5).

Genesis 6–11 takes a hard look at creation. The flood story (6:1–9:17) indicates that people are rotten ("corrupted"), yet it ends not in bitterness but in compassion. Later, Noah's sons radiate exuberance, peopling the earth (9:18–chap. 10). But from Babel onward the exuberance beings to fade, both in city and family. Life crumbles (chap. 11).

Creation and Its Harmony (1:1–2:24)

Creation from God: The Grandeur (the Universe, 1:1–2:4a)
Creation for Humankind: The Groundedness (the Garden, 2:4b–24)

Introductory Aspects

The Basic Story Line (from Creation to Cain)

The initial chapters (1:1–4:16) consist at one level of three basic scenes: seven-day creation; the Garden of Eden; and Cain's killing of Abel.

The beginning is like an awesome trumpet blast: "God created the heavens and the earth" (1:1); and having given that resounding call, the opening account proceeds as it were to unfold it, to spell out how, for six days, God created (1:1–2:4a). Days 1–3 lead up climactically to the making of dry land and vegetation; and days 4–6, while echoing days 1–3, lead up, even more climactically, to the making of the animals and humankind. The high points, therefore, are land (day 3) and land animals, especially humans (day 6). Then, on the seventh/Sabbath day, God rests—a picture of harmony, divine harmony. The awesome trumpet blast reaches a certain calm.

The second scene, the Garden of Eden, builds on the first, and begins in turn to unfold it further. But the second is no trumpet. Instead, while the trumpet in the distance still echoes, the second scene comes in like a violin, closer to the human voice; and the two together blend, one responding to the other—a haunting concerto of trumpet and violin, touching some of the deepest chords of the human spirit. The second scene, while different in sources, style, and viewpoint, develops and unpacks the twin peaks of the first—days 3 and 6, with their dense pictures of land and animals (including humans). Furthermore, specific aspects in chapter 2 respond to aspects and details of chapter 1. For instance, where scene one had said "heavens and earth" (1:1), scene two responds with "earth and heavens" (2:4b), shifting the emphasis toward the earth. Where scene one had spoken of God's spirit hovering (1:2), scene two responds with God actually breathing life into a person (2:7)—again shifting the emphasis toward a more down-to-earth scene. And while scene one finished with a sense of harmony that is divine, God resting, scene two develops a picture of harmony that is human—the man with the woman. Linked to these climactic pictures of harmony are two central institutions: scene one provides the basis for the institution of the Sabbath, and scene two the basis for the more human-oriented institution of marriage.

The story goes on (2:25–chap. 3) to tell how much of the harmony was undone: the couple failed to hear what God had said and so they provoked tension concerning God, the ground, and one another. And they were expelled.

Subsequently, harmony suffered the ultimate breakdown: when they had two children, one killed the other (4:1–16).

The story is not a smooth straight line; it is not linear. There are inconsistencies or contradictions, and not only between scenes but even within them. Most strikingly, between scenes one and two there is apparent contradiction about temporal order: in chapter 1, priority of time goes to animals, but in chapter 2 to a human. And within the Eden scene there is some tension about spatial order: in chapter 2, priority of space goes to the tree of life—it is in the middle (2:9), but in chapter 3 the middle position is ascribed rather to the tree of knowledge (3:3). These central contradictions or tensions—about temporal priority and spatial priority—are a clue about the nature of the story: it is set in time and space, and as such it is an ordinary story. Yet, by immediately contradicting the elementary principles of time and space, it signals that time and space are not its ultimate framework. It is a time-and-space story, but with another dimension.

These contradictions have a particular effect: they alert the reader that at some level this history goes beyond the surface of events. A contradiction that seems particularly deliberate occurs at the beginning of the Joseph story, concerning the Ishmaelites and Midianites (37:25–36)—again a signal that something else is going on, that God is involved (45:5; see Introduction, Chapter 1, "Internal Contradictions," and comment on 37:23–30). The two sets of contradictions balance and complement one another—one at the beginning of Genesis 1–11, the other at the beginning of the Joseph story. The contradiction in the Joseph story is clearer—in accordance with the Joseph story's overall clarity. The time-and-space contradiction in Genesis 1–3 is less clear—in accordance with the relative obscurity of Genesis 1–11.

The implication of something beyond the measurableness of time and space is given at the very beginning—in the reference to spirit (*ruah*, spirit/wind). Like the wind, the spirit suggests a force—in this case a divine force—that is beyond calculation.

Apart from implying another dimension, the contradiction of time and space achieves something further. It establishes, from the beginning, a general principle for interpreting Genesis: even contradictions can have a purpose.

Literary Form

The above story, apart from having the structure of three scenes (seven-day creation, Eden, and Cain), has a further, overlapping, structure. The Eden scene falls easily into two parts, one matching creation, the other matching Cain-and-Abel, thus bringing the number of parts to four. These four parts constitute two diptychs—one of creation (1:1–2:24), the other of disharmony (2:25–4:16). This overlapping of structures requires clarification of the literary forms or types.

In the creation diptych (1:1–2:24) the two panels (1:1–2:4a; and 2:4b–24) are quite dissimilar, yet they are variations on a single literary form. In ancient literature, creation stories consisted of "two basic types" (Westermann, I, 22): stories about creation as a whole; and stories about the creation of something specific, especially about humankind. These are precisely the two types found in Genesis 1–2. First there is an account of creation as a whole, the process which takes seven days (1:1–2:4a). Then there is an account of the creation of humankind (2:4b–24). Genesis has combined the two basic types and adapted them to its own purposes. In particular, it has adapted the second so that it complements the first. Some features of this complementarity were seen already—the shift, for instance, from heaven to earth, and from Sabbath to marriage. Other features will be seen later. What is important is that, despite their serious differences, the two accounts follow the two basic versions of a single literary type. As such they are well placed to form a unity—a concerto.

The easiest explanation for the origin of this concerto is not that an editor found two musical scores—one for trumpet, one for violin—and combined them, but that, as is usual with concertos, it was written by a single composer.

There then follows another concerto, another diptych, but with a different literary type. Second only to creation narratives are the "narratives of crime and punishment" Westermann (I, 47–55). The terminology—"crime and punishment"—may seem unduly modern, but the idea is ancient, and the terminology is useful. Westermann (I, 48), in his first examples of this literary type, lists the two initial accounts of disharmony (in the Garden, and in the field [the murder]). Apart from sharing a literary form, the two pictures of disharmony have several other links (as will be seen later).

What emerges then in Genesis 1:1–4:16 is not only a sequence of three scenes but also—at another level—two diptychs, one of creation narratives, the other of narratives of crime and punishment.

Complementarity of the Two Panels

As already partly indicated, the two creation panels have a fundamental complementarity of viewpoints—one is primarily divine; the other, primarily human. Genesis has used the built-in differences between the two basic types of creation story as a vehicle for giving two approaches. The first shows creation as flowing out from God: "God created . . . God said . . . God rested." The second shows creation as more focused toward humankind: "As yet there was no man. . . . And Yhwh God fashioned the man . . . took the man . . . said 'It is not good for the man to be alone'. . . . fashioned the woman."

These two viewpoints are not arbitrary, not random choices from a wide range of possibilities. Rather, they are the two most fundamental viewpoints possible. One emphasizes the vertical dimension of creation, the other the horizontal. Either on its own would be one-dimensional. Together they form a radical completeness, and thus a radical unity. This principle of complementarity—the balance between the transcendent and the horizontal—is illustrated at length at a later stage of the Primary History, in the two figures of Elijah and Elisha. The portrayal of Elijah emphasizes transcendence; and Elisha emphasizes earthliness or humanity (*Crucial Bridge*, 2000, 6–7).

The unity of the two creation panels is primarily artistic and theological—not historical. As linear history, the accounts overlap and contradict. The theological unity hinges around the interwovenness of two fundamental realities—God the creator, in all of God's uniqueness; and God as involved with humankind. In the first panel, God's "making" is framed by God's "creating" (*bārā*), a verb reserved for God; in the second God simply makes "makes" or "fashions."

The opening lines (1:1; 2:4b) epitomize the relationship:

"In the beginning   God   created   the heavens and the earth."
"On the day   Yhwh God   made   earth and heavens."

Each word or phrase of the second line involves a precise complementarity with the first. Like "in the beginning," "on the day" is an initial designation of time, but it is more down to earth. One understands a day, but the notion of the beginning is elusive, almost beyond understanding. "Made" is a variation of "created," but again more down to earth, closer to human processes. "Earth and heavens" is a variation on "the heavens and the earth," but priority has shifted to the earth; it is mentioned first. And within this context of moving downward from the transcendent it is altogether appropriate that the divinity also be designated in a slightly different way: not the bare "God" but God with a further name, a name later connected clearly with involvement in the depth of human need (Exod. 2:23–25; 3:13–16).

Thus, the larger distinction between God the transcendent creator, and God as involved with humankind provides part of the explanation for the controverted divergence in divine names. "God" tends to reflect the divine in itself, as transcendent; "Yhwh" reflects the divine as engaged with humankind. As God's involvement with humankind, especially with humankind as troubled, becomes greater—in Genesis 3 and 4—so will the use of "Yhwh" become more dominant.

A further complementarity is that of time and space. Time and space may not be the ultimate realities for Genesis, but they are important; they provide an initial framework, and so they need to be established. The first panel—with its repetitive sequence of days, and its reference to seasons (fixed times), years, and days—emphasizes time. It builds up, first to day 3, then to day 6, and finally adds the Sabbath (Vogels, 1997). The second panel, with its sense of place—a garden, a middle/center, and four rivers (evoking the four corners of the universe, and the center of the universe)—emphasizes space (Soggin, 1997). The complementarity between time and space is second only to that between the divine and the human. (On other aspects of time and space, see Fields, 1997, 86–115.)

There is complementarity also concerning the nature of humankind and the relationship of man to woman. At first, humankind is seen as coming from God ("image," but with a sexual aspect), then as coming from the soil (but with God's breath). The two views—divine image, and earthy—complement and complete one another. And in the relationship between the man and woman, the first account emphasizes procreation ("increase and multiply"), the second companionship ("it is not good . . . to be alone").

Concerning the animals, what is ordered in panel one, namely that humankind should master the animals (1:26, 28), is implemented in panel two, when the human gives names to the animals—thus exercising mastery (panel two, 2: 20) (Wénin, 2001).

There is also a complementarity or connection concerning worship. While panel one, with its seven-day creation leading to (the) Sabbath, is generally regarded as connected to worship, the Eden scene also has various phrases that are reminiscent of the sanctuary. Like the sanctuary in the middle of people (Numbers 2), the tree in the middle is a source of life (for details, see Wenham, 1994).

Some aspects of the basic complementarity and balance between the two panels remain debatable. Some translators, for instance, see both accounts as beginning with a "When . . . then" clause (Clifford, 2:4–5; Speiser, 19); this translation problem is difficult and "cannot be resolved solely on the basis of grammar" (Childs, 1992, 111; cf. Scullion, 22). Some also see both accounts as having a climactic burst of poetry—one celebrating the closeness of humankind and God ("God created humankind in his image . . ." 1:27), the other celebrating the closeness of man and woman ("This one, this time—bone of my bones . . ." 2:23).

Apart from content, there is also a complementarity in style. The first has a clear repetitiveness which, when well read, is poetic and serene. The second consists of a more earthy prose. This diversity of style suits the diversity of content: poetic and serene for the panel that emphasizes God, and earthy prose for the panel that places greater emphasis on humankind.

Even the earth-waters relationship, which at one level is very diverse in Genesis 1 and 2, contains not only differences but also significant similarities— so much so that in the final analysis there is no sharp contrast between the cosmologies of the two accounts (Tsumura, 1989, 167–68; on the philosophy and science of Genesis 1, see Samuelson, 1992).

Differences notwithstanding, therefore, the two panels have a deep continuity. The second builds on the first, but in its own way. For Childs, the second panel "functions, not as a duplicate creation account, but as a description of the unfolding of the history of mankind. . . . The [second panel] functions on the level of *figurative language.* . . . [There was] little difficulty in reading the

[two] chapters as a unity until the Enlightenment" (1992, 113, emphasis added). Now, however, especially since the 1970s, there is a fresh sense of figurative language, and it is possible once again, at another level, to read the two chapters as a unity. Like woman and man, the two accounts are sometimes diverse, but there is only one human race.

Leading Elements

Genesis is instructive not only as a story but even more so in its artistry and symbolism. The full meaning of Genesis, of course, cannot be articulated; its full impact cannot be measured. But it is possible to mention some ideas, which in varying ways are indicated or evoked by the text, in this case by the creation diptych.

AN IDEAL OF HARMONIOUS UNION

Unlike much of modern existence, which is often alienated—alienated from God, earth, and people—Genesis begins with a sense of deep harmony. Both panels of the diptych share a governing vision of harmonious union—a harmony which begins in God, and which then flows into human life.

This harmony is first seen in the initial account (1:1–2:4a)—in the way God's word unfailingly brings forth creation (1:1–31), and especially in the way in which, on the seventh day, God rests (*šābat*, 2:1–4a). The heart of this rest, this calm, is a profound sense of the harmony between God and creation.

The second account shows God as extending that harmony to humans. To some degree, of course, man and woman in chapter 1 already enjoy harmony, at least insofar as they belong within the larger harmony of Genesis 1 ("The blessing [in 1:28] consists of the establishment and sanction of matrimony," Jacob, 11). But Genesis 2 spells out that harmony.

Amid language that is often mythical and patriarchal, the essence of Genesis 2 is simple: a man is given union with the earth and with a woman. Both earth and woman are close to the bone; modern people still argue about which is the more basic, relationship to the earth or to a companion. In Genesis 2, the man is bound up with both—even etymologically. He is *ʾādām*, not only echoing the generic *ʾādām*, humankind, of 1:26, but also *ʾădāmâ*, the ground. And he is *ʾîš*, a man, from whom is made the woman, *ʾiššâ* The two verbal links (*ʾādām*, *ʾădāmâ; ʾîš, ʾiššâ*) reflect deep affinities. Genesis 2 gives a certain priority to the affinity with the ground—it places it first—but the link with the woman, coming last, has a place of special prominence.

Initially, the man's relationship to the earth and the woman is one of harmony. The ultimate task may be to till the ground—literally to serve it (*ʿābad*, 2:5)—but the man's first experience, under God, is to rest in it: "Yhwh God took the man and caused him to rest (*nûaḥ* causative form) in the Garden of Eden to serve it and keep it" (2:15). And the first relationship with the woman is one of joy and union (2:22–24). The two types of harmony—with the earth and the woman—are part of a single drama, and together they complement and complete the original harmony in God.

WONDER

In contrast to nihilistic philosophies, nationalistic narrowness, and tabloid negativity, Genesis 1–2 is open and positive—a serene vision of the human race as one people under God, created for peace.

The beginning, the allusion to God's creation of heaven and earth (1:1), has a once-upon-a-time quality. As if to heighten attention, there is a moment of hesitation, a faint ambiguity as the reader absorbs the haunting image of the earth's shapeless emptiness, the darkness over the deep, the powerful yet uncertain presence over the waters—*rûaḥ ʾelōhîm* (mighty wind, or spirit of God).

Then, without the conflict that occurs in some other ancient creation accounts, the words flow forth—sure and clear: " 'Let there be light.' And there was light."

As the days roll on, the sense of wonder varies, ebbing and flowing with the oncoming tide of creation, reaching a new level on the sixth day with the solemn creation of humankind, and finally settling into a calm high point—the Sabbath rest.

In the second account (2:4–25) the wonder takes another form, closer to earth. The Garden haunts the mind, and the four rivers, particularly the first mysterious river in the land of gold and gems, evoke a sense, not of "Once upon a time . . . ," but of ". . . in a land far, far away." The subsequent story—being alone, the quest for a companion, the man's poetic exclamation at the sight of the woman—evokes the endless down-to-earth wonder of human love.

THE SOVEREIGNTY OF GOD

Associated with wonder, especially in the seven-day account, is the sense of the sovereignty of God. The word sovereignty is not used, but it is implied at every stage—in *bārāʾ*, "created," in the absence of conflict, and in the awesome procession of commands (their clarity, simplicity, and power). Even small aspects of nature—a flower, a bird—can draw people out of themselves toward an increased sensitivity with regard to a greater power, but the content of Genesis 1 is not just a small aspect; it is the fullness of nature in all its splendor—the ultimate parade.

The idea of God's sovereignty may seem so basic as not to merit attention. Yet in the maze of life, including the clutter of religious language and practice, it is often lost. Even in New Testament theology the idea was neglected (Dahl, 1975). But it is an idea that is foundational and powerful—as seen by its pivotal role in the emergence of Islam and Protestantism. It is pivotal also in the shaping of Genesis. Genesis is not just talking about distant origins; it is constructing a theological vision. Within that vision, sovereignty provides a solid foundation.

THE INTERWEAVING OF THE HUMAN AND THE NONHUMAN

Genesis 1–2 is attentive to nature; it provides "considerable evidence of what we today would call scientific reflection on the natural world" (Fretheim, 341). Human beings are so described that they are interwoven with the larger cosmos, especially with the plants and the animals. The first blessing goes not to humans but to the fishes and the birds (1:21–23). The sixth day, instead of being reserved exclusively for the making of humankind, is shared with the animals (1:24–31); and the blessing on humankind echoes the blessing already bestowed on the fishes and birds. Insofar as the first creation account is a genealogy (cf. 2:4a), the human race, with all its subsequent genealogies, shares a genealogy with the cosmos. Humans sometimes seem diverse, yet ultimately all humans share in one genealogy.

HUMAN DIGNITY

In a world where humans are variously abused and held in contempt, sometimes by democratically elected governments, the Genesis picture of humankind stands as a basic guide to human dignity. Not that Genesis is perfect; it is tinged with a men-first attitude ("male and female he created them," 1:27; in chap. 2, the man is made first). Yet the fundamental attitude to all humans— women and men—is one of the deepest respect. No other ancient religion or law code—from Hammurabi and Buddhism to Christianity and the Magna Carta—ever depicted so clearly on page one of its texts the basic principle of equality of the sexes and of all people. Even the American constitution, which was an important advance in the cause of respect for human beings, was not as universal: "all men are created equal" referred to white male landowners.

The foundational statement about humankind is that it is made in God's image (1:26–27)—a statement which, in its context, has echoes not only of divinity but also of royalty (see comment on 1:14–31). These echoes do not depend on gender or nationality or any other differentiation. The second foundational statement about humankind—lest people be carried away by a sense of their grandeur—is that humans are made of clay, clay with God-given breath (2:7). The resulting creature, however admirable and engaging, is fragile.

Associated with the picture of human dignity is an indication of human limits. Eating from the tree of the knowledge of good and evil is a symbol of trying to *experience everything* (literally trying to *know* everything). The effect of such eating, of such unlimited desire for experience, is not fulfillment but alienation, a kind of inner death (see comment on 2:10–17).

THE PRESENT REALITY OF THE PRIMEVAL HARMONY

The harmony evoked in Genesis 1–2 is not lost irretrievably; it is a permanent (or eschatological) ideal. Genesis does not speak explicitly of "a fall," and its image of expulsion (chap. 3) refers largely to an ongoing reality—to the way in which people, even when they are given a situation of harmony, spoil it, and so experience loss and alienation.

But the sense of loss is not final. The basic reality of God's creation is still present, still waiting to be rediscovered.

The rediscovery is sometimes slow, requiring deep freedom. A dramatic example occurs in the case of Gerard Manley Hopkins (1844–1889). He needed first to break through prevailing perceptions; "he sweeps the whole cultivated world of beauty of the Victorian age into the dustbin" (von Balthasar, 1986, 362). What he sees therefore

> is no cultural landscape, not at all a romantic or mythological landscape, but, as it were, a primeval landscape . . . a tense, utterly objective contemplation of the primal power of nature . . . a complete attentiveness that has nothing to do with romantic outpourings of the feelings but rather reminds one of the attentive eye of Goethe; with a desire for total objectivity that lays claim to the whole [person] through and through. A companion, with whom one must converse, is a hindrance to such total concentration. (ibid., 359–361)

The example of Hopkins may seem to say that one needs to be a gifted poet to attain radical attentiveness to God's creation, but the first couple, despite their uniqueness, are symbols of ordinary people. This rest is offered to all.

Structure (Table 2.3)

As already indicated in Table 2.3 (Introduction, Chapter 2) each panel consists of two or three main parts. The week of creation has just two such parts—but each part is divided into three (days 1–3, and 4–6; Sarna, 4). The picture of the Garden of Eden has three main parts—each divided into two.

THE FIRST PANEL (1:1–2:4A)

The balance between the two main parts (days 1–3 and days 4–6) is precise: light-lights; waters-fish; land-animals. Days 3 and 6 are two-part, an arrangement that gives a certain climactic effect. On day 6 this climactic dimension is developed: the creation of humankind is solemn and prolonged.

As the pattern develops, God's word literally expands: God says more, and the text increases in quantity. On the sixth day, for the creation of humankind, God reaches a high point in communication.

The conclusion (2:1–4a) is a careful tapestry of four sentences. The first and fourth sentences (2:1, 4a) are brief, and together they form a *frame:* they focus on creation itself (not on God), on how creation was completed (2:1) and generated (2:4a, "These are the generations . . ."). Despite the earthy connotations of "generations/breedings," the general tone of this brief framework is transcendent. The cryptic mention of "all their host" (2:1) reinforces this tone.

The conclusion's *center* (2:2–3) focuses on God, and here there is a delicate balance: while one sentence (2:2) shows God in a way which evokes human life (resting from work, from making things), the other (2:3) shows God in a way which emphasizes the transcendent or holy (blessing; making holy; resting not only from making but from creating).

The conclusion's delicate structure—of framework (2:1, 4a) and center (2:2–3)—helps to clarify the controverted role of "These are the generations . . ." (2:4a); this latter phrase is best seen as a conclusion, not as the beginning of panel two.

THE SECOND PANEL (2:4B–24)

The picture in the second panel is not quite so sovereign. The word "create" is no longer used (the last occurrence is in 2:4a). Things seem to happen independently of God (the flow, and the river, 2:6, 10); God's commands are open to being contravened (something that did not seem possible in the first panel); and, in making an appropriate counterpart for the man, God uses a process of trial and error.

A crucial clue to structure is repetition. In this text (2:4b–24) an element of repetition occurs, for instance, concerning the flow and the river: the picture of the river (2:10) seems to be a form of variation on the picture of the flow (2:6)—and, in accord with the less than transcendently sovereign picture of Yhwh God, both the flow and the river play their roles without waiting for Yhwh God to direct them.

Comment

Panel One (1:1–2:4a)

[1:1–2] **Introduction. The beginning—water and spirit.** The opening phrase (". . . God created . . .") may be read either as independent or as subordinate; in other words, either "In the beginning *God created* . . . ," or "In the beginning, *when God created* . . . , the earth was. . . ." The earliest translators saw it as independent ("In the beginning God created . . ."), and this seems best. As such it summarizes the chapter, balances 2:4a, and is comparable to the opening summary in 5:1 (Fretheim, 342; cf. Wenham, 11–13).

These opening words are resoundingly positive: God created everything—literally, "the heavens and the earth" (*ʾereṣ*, "earth/land"). At one level "heavens and earth" may be taken together, as a merism (the use of two opposite poles to express totality—everything; Sarna, 19), but at another level each word also has its own distinct significance; "the *sky* [or heavens] and the *earth* does not present itself with quite the same unity expressed by the word *kosmos*" (Sacks, 4). To create (*bārāʾ*) is exclusive to God, and so the implication is strong: whatever the hint of division (heavens/earth), ultimately everything is from God.

Genesis apparently is not describing *creatio ex nihilo*, creation from nothing (Sacks, 4; Scullion, 16; however, Jacob, 1, does hold for creation from nothing; and Wenham, 14, is circumspect: "The phraseology leaves the author's precise meaning uncertain").

The primary transition is not from nothingness to being but from chaos to order. The creation process begins with something like a formless waste: *tōhû . . . bōhû*. The first word, *tōhû*, suggests something shapeless, formless, uninhabitable; and it may also be related etymologically to *tĕhôm*, "the deep" (Clifford, 2:4). *Bōhû*, in rhyming with *tōhû*—forming an assonant hendiadys—simply reinforces its effect. The text may also be read as referring primarily to emptiness: the earth is "an empty place . . . unproductive . . . uninhabited" (Tsumura, 1994a, 328).

Incidentally, the opening words, "In the beginning . . . *tōhû . . . bōhû*," are somewhat akin to the opening of Hesiod's account of the origin of the gods (*Theogony*, 114–117): "Tell me, Muses . . . from the beginning (*ex archēs*). . . . At the very first was chaos (*chaos*), but then the earth (*Gaia*). . . ."

The initial picture in Genesis has three elements: "The earth was a formless waste, // darkness *on the face of the deep*; // and God's spirit hovered *on the face of the waters*." This picture is primarily art, not science. As art, the picture has a quiet tension, particularly in its balance between "darkness on . . . the deep" and "God's spirit on . . . the waters." The "dark . . . deep" tends to evoke a world of shadows, even of evil. In Near Eastern thought the sea's dark vastness sometimes made it a symbol of chaos or evil; and in the new Jerusalem, where evil is vanquished, there is no sea (Rev. 21:1). But such suggestions of evil are immediately countered: "spirit of God . . . on the waters" evokes much that is positive (the spirit [breath/wind/*rûaḥ*] is a great source of life—reviving even dry bones, Ezek. 37:1–14).

This striking picture—God's spirit amid the darkness—is like an intimation, a nucleus, of the vast drama that is about to unfold.

Of the three main elements in the introduction—the formless earth, the darkness, and the spirit—the first two are taken up in chapter 1. The final image, that of the spirit, finds a down-to-earth counterpart in chapter 2—in God's breathing of life into humankind.

[1:3–13] Days 1–3: Light, division, and land. The action begins with powerful simplicity—with the word and light, and without conflict. The impression (" 'Let there be light,' and there was light") is one of total sovereignty, of transcendence. The Hebrew for 'Let there be' is the same as for 'there was'—thus giving a perfect balance between God's commanding word and the subsequent reality.

The emphasis on light is not primarily scientific—even if, as some scientists have said, the world began with a Big Bang, which issued *light*. Rather it is a reflection of the primordial role of light in human existence. Hindus, for instance, have a feast of light (Divali), and Buddhists speak of the centrality of enlightenment. Given the role which light and darkness play in human life—from the child's fear of darkness to the long quest for enlightenment—Genesis touches the roots both of the physical world and of the human spirit.

God "sees" that the light is "good"—a positive picture which is akin to ancient Greek poetry (to Pindar; see Müller, 1997), but very different from the negativity of later Gnostics.

Not only is the light good; even the darkness loses its fearsomeness. God names the darkness, thus demystifying it (though the precise implication of naming is uncertain), and—insofar as sounds can suggest meaning—the Hebrew sound of the name, *lāylă* ("night"), seems particularly unthreatening. God's emerging world is making it essentially friendly.

Then, with artistry and simplicity, the narrator sums up the story so far: "And it was evening and it was morning; day one." In accordance with the Jewish custom for feasts, the day is regarded as beginning in the evening. (Normally the day was regarded as beginning with morning light.)

The second day looks totally positive: God inserts a great concave as it were into the waters, a dome, thus separating the waters above from the waters below and forming the basis for a vast living space. "The Hebrew word [for dome] is 'something hammered out flat,' e.g. gold leaf . . ." (Clifford, 2:4). "Homer refers to the heavens as *chalkeos* or *sideros,* bronze or iron made" (Scullion, 26). The sky is a gleaming dome—a concept shared by Israel and Greece (Brown, 1995, 106–113).

Yet unlike all the other days, this day is not described as good. The omission is small but significant, a faint glitch which suggests that there is something in this arrangement, something in the repeated idea of division between heaven and earth, which is troublesome.

The third day, however, is doubly good—first the dry land, and then vegetation, with special emphasis on fruit and fruit trees, and on seeds' power of propagation. There is a suggestion of procreation, and the scene is set to flourish.

[1:14–31] Days 4–6: Lights, animals, and the image of God. The relationship between days 1–3 and days 4–6 intimates something about Genesis as a whole: there is continuity but there is also progression. The "lights" (or lamps, *mĕ'ōrōt*) of day 4, for instance, echo the "light" (*'ôr*) of day 1, but they also go beyond it.

The purpose of the "lights" (1:14–19)—the sun and moon—is not only to divide day from night, but also to act as signs (*'ôt*) "for fixed times, and for days and years." Unlike "days and years," the fixed times (*môʿădîm*) suggest variety—times that are set or appointed, including festivals. The detail at the end—"and the stars"—adds a further variation. The sense of wonder, which was first evoked by the making of the light, is now renewed in another form.

The designation of the sun and moon as lights or lamps involves a process of demythologization: they are no longer gods or demi-gods; they are lamps for humans, especially for marking special days. The stars also are downgraded; they are not discussed further—a silence that "constitutes a tacit repudiation of astrology" (Sarna, 10).

The fifth day (1:20–23) adds further wonder—things that are alive ("living creatures"), namely fishes and birds. But the contrast—between the fishes below and the birds above—echoes the separation of day 2 (the waters below and the dome/firmament above); and, as day 2 had had a faint shadow—the absence of God seeing that "it was good"—so here, too, a faint shadow is noticeable: unlike the other days, the description of day 5 does not follow the pattern of increasing quantity. The account (1:20–23) is shorter than that of the preceding day (1:14–19). Thus, on two occasions (days 2 and 5) the creation account misses a beat.

Furthermore, the initial picture of perfect correspondence between God's word and reality ('Let there be light,' and there was light) is not repeated. As the days pass there are faint suggestions that some aspects of creation are slightly out of line: they either deviate ever so slightly from God's command or they take effect on their own. God recognizes that

> the world is incapable of the original type of unity which was demanded in the beginning. . . . Sufferings are [partly] due to [human] guilt . . . but these early verses [as far as 1:25] indicate that the most fundamental difficulties lie not in the [human] heart but in the heart of being. According to the simple meaning of the text the world was created perfect . . . [but] lying not too deep under the surface is another story. (Sacks, 14)

Yet the primary impression from day 5 is not of diminishment but of vitality. As well as swarming with life, it tells of something else that is new—God's blessing: "God blessed (*bārak*) them. . . . 'Be fruitful and multiply and fill. . . .' " It is a blessing which, in the account, is not only more striking than the diminished quantity, but which prepares the way for a blessing that is yet greater—that of day 6.

The making of humankind (1:24–31) occurs on the same day as the making of the land animals—thus implying a basic solidarity with the animals. And in the blessing there is further solidarity with the animal world: the blessing of humankind (1:28) echoes the blessing of the fish and birds (1:22).

Yet, at another level, the making and blessing of humankind stand apart; the making is more solemn, and the blessing more elaborate. The earth has a role in the making of the animals ("Let the earth swarm with . . . living creatures . . . ;" cf. 1:11, "Let the earth grow grass . . ."), but in this first chapter the earth has no role in making humankind. Humankind is made in God's image (1:26–27). The plural in God's decision ("Let us make humankind . . .") is probably best seen not so much as evoking a divine assembly but simply as a rhetorical feature—a plural of deliberation (Scullion, 28). In the ancient Near East the phrase "image of God" was often used of kings (Clifford, 4:5). In Mesopotamian creation stories, humans were usually depicted as slaves, but here the humans have echoes of both divinity and royalty. Given the context— God's creating—"image" also suggests that humans should reflect something of God's creative activity. Normally Israel forbade images of God, but Genesis 1 indicates an exception: "the only acceptable image of God is the human being" (Kselman, 85).

In dealing with humans there is no such phrase as "according to their kind"; there is essentially only one kind. "The Bible teaches unambiguously that only one human couple was formed in the beginning and that all [humans] are descended from it. This is the opposite of racism and emphasizes the unity of mankind" (Jacob, 10).

Yet among humans there is diversity. Unlike the account of the creating of the animals it is said that humans are created in two varieties, male and female, with no suggestion of a variation in rank or worth. "This humankind in its complementarity is a reflection of the deity. For feminist readers of the Scriptures, no more interesting and telegraphic comment exists on the nature of being human and on the nature of God. . . . The genders were meant to be equal at the beginning" (Niditch, 12–13).

The contrast between humans and other animals—the recording of sexual differentiation for humans but not for animals—indicates that "human sexuality is of a wholly different order from that of the beast. The [immediate blessing, 1:28] shows [human sexuality] to be a blessed gift of God woven into the fabric of life. As such it cannot be other than wholesome. By the same token, its abuse is treated in the Bible with particular severity" (Sarna, 13).

The blessing, while repeating what was said to the fishes and birds ("Be fruitful, and multiply and fill . . ."), goes on to speak of subduing the earth and having dominion over the animals. " 'Subduing' involves development . . . [and to] have dominion (rādâ) [implies] care-giving, even nurturing, not exploitation" (Fretheim, 346). But rādâ can also be read as indicating the rule, sometimes harsh, of a master over subordinates (Rüterswörden, 1993, 83–124). Being in God's image, humans are to relate to the earth as God does. "The text says something, at least implicitly, about the modern problem of ecology. The human race, collectively and individually, has a responsibility for the environment. The scientist, the technologist, and the industrialist cannot prescind from the consequences of their work" (Scullion, 21). The sense of respect for the environment is implicit in the relationship to the animals: humans are to govern them but, at this stage, no mention is made of killing them; food is vegetarian (1:29). Only after the flood—in the context of God accepting the deep-seated evil in the human heart—are humans told that animals, as well as plants, will be their food (8:21–9:3). Thus, meat-eating will eventually emerge as a form of healthy compromise.

Responsibility for the environment means work, and so work is something positive—a consequence not of sin but of being in God's image and of being blessed. "It belongs to human nature to work" (Scullion, 21). Unemployment therefore strikes at something basic in people.

[2:1–4a] Conclusion. The seventh-day climax of creation—rest. The conclusion balances four sentences (see discussion of structure), and within that balance the emphasis falls on God's rest (2:2–3). Thus creation reaches its highest level not in fireworks—in some impressive-looking action—but in rest.

This concluding picture of rest is partly etiological: it uses an event from the past to explain or suggest the beginning or cause (Gk. *aitia*) of a later phenomenon, in this case Israel's Sabbath rest. As such it sets a pattern for other Genesis conclusions that are likewise etiological.

But the deeper truth—behind both the creation account and the Sabbath ritual—is that rest, far from being some kind of lazy emptiness, is central both to God and to those who are in God's image. Rest—the deep quiet joy of simply being—is the highest point of God's creation.

Panel Two (2:4b–24)

[2:4b–5] Introduction. The growthless earth—without rain or human-kind. Whatever the complexity of the sources underlying Genesis 2:4b–24, the present text is "a new independent story," a story which has its own unity (Westermann, I, 186–190). There is indeed a form of independence. But independence does not exclude dependence. Independence from parents, for instance, does not negate their permanent effect on one's make-up.

Likewise here. The second panel (2:4b–24) is built on the first. While contradicting aspects of the sequence of panel one, it develops its essence. As already partly seen, the second account opens with echoes of the first:

"In (*bĕ*) the beginning God created the heavens and the earth. The earth was. . . ."

"On (*bĕ*) the day Yhwh God made earth and heavens . . . there was . . . on the earth. . . ."

Instead of a formless waste, the second panel tells of growthless land ("no shrub . . . no plant"). As the formless waste had once awaited the spirit and word of God, so the growthless land/earth awaits Yhwh God's rain and humans' service. The dark earth received light, and the growthless earth is about to receive water and tilling.

The essential relationship between the two creation panels is relatively simple. The second panel, while different in sources, style, and viewpoint, develops and unpacks the twin peaks of the first—days 3 and 6, with their dense pictures of a thriving earth, complete with animals and humankind. The second panel, telling of God's breathing life, also picks up, in variant form, the earlier image of God's spirit—an image which, within the elements of the introductory scene (1:2), is placed third, like days 3 and 6. The way in which the second panel develops the first is by writing a further picture, one which is modeled on ancient literature's second basic type of creation story.

In comparison with Genesis 1, the picture in Genesis 2 has its own distinct drama. It tells of someone who is brought into union with the most human-related elements of God's creation—soil and spouse. Genesis does not take an either/or approach to the soil and spouse. Through the Garden, it first secures the relationship to the soil/earth, and then goes on to establish the relationship to a spouse. The development of the two relationships forms a single story.

The language used in this account is partly mythical and patriarchal. Aspects of the Garden story are mythical. And the centering of the story on a man— "there was no man [*'ādām*] to serve/till the soil" (2:5)—may be seen as patriarchal.

Within Genesis 1–5 *'ādām* has diverse meanings: humankind (e.g., 1:26); a man (e.g., 3:8, 12); and a proper name, Adam (4:25; 5:5). When the word occurs at the beginning of the second creation panel its meaning is correspondingly ambiguous ("there was no human," or "there was no man"). Such is the text. To resolve this ambiguity it is necessary to examine the context.

The context supplies three indications that in this case *'ādām* refers to a man. First, the basic male/female distinction has already been clearly established in Genesis 1 (1:27–28). Thus the way has already been prepared for the presence of someone who is sexually differentiated. Second, in the closing part of the Eden story (Gen. 2–3) the tilling of the soil by an *'ādām* refers clearly to a man (3:17); therefore, given the close coherence of the story, the likelihood is that the same is true of the opening reference to the tilling of the soil by an *'ādām* (2:5). Third, in terms of basic story telling, the text makes better narrative sense if, from the beginning, the man is a distinct figure. In other words, "man" is not required by the isolated word *'ādām*, but it is more appropriate to the context, to the flow of the larger story.

It has been said that apart from having nostrils—and so, perhaps, a sense of smell—the human creature (*'ādām*) at the center of the drama in the Garden is undeveloped and without sexuality (Trible, 1978, 80). But the command about eating (2:16–17) presupposes someone who is developed fully—someone with hearing, sight, touch, and taste, as well as intellect and will. Such full development implies sexuality also; and so it is better to translate *hā 'ādām* not as "the (sexless) earthling/groundling" but as "the man," and to regard chapter 2, like much of Genesis, as colored by patriarchalism. Such limitations do not destroy the value of Genesis, especially since Genesis itself contains the seeds of revolt against human structures.

[2:6–9] Water and humankind, and then growth; a garden with trees. Here, as in Genesis 1, God's action is a precise response to the preceding lack:

in place of darkness there was light (1:2–3), and in place of no rain or human-kind there is water and a human being (2:5–7).

Creation here is not as smooth and sovereign as in Genesis 1. The course of events is more jagged, the characters more down-to-earth. The introduction (2:5) said the rain would come from Yhwh God, and service of the soil from humankind. And so one could expect something like: "Yhwh God caused it to rain, and humankind planted a garden." But instead the rain/water seems to start on its own ("A flow . . . watered," with no reference to God), and it is not a human being but Yhwh God who does the planting. Thus, even within this chapter, God's role is slipping from that of a God who orders the elements toward that of a God who does human work.

This proximity of God to human life is also suggested by the name Yhwh, a name associated with God's closeness to life (Exod. 2:23–4:17), and by the way Yhwh God makes a human being—with clay, like a potter (2:7).

Humankind in turn is more down-to-earth—less elevated than in Genesis 1 ("the image of God"). There is closeness to God—to God's handiwork and breath—but the emphasis is on closeness to the soil; humankind is made of earth to serve the earth.

The earth itself becomes more tangible. Eden (ʿēden), despite its broad mean-ing—"delight" (Westermann, I, 210) or "luxuriance" (Fretheim, 350)—gives an initial sense of a specific place. And there is also an initial sense of orien-tation: the Garden is "in the east;" and the tree of life is "in the middle." The earth is beginning to take shape.

The two special trees are like symbols of two vast dimensions of God's creation. If they had been the trees of, say, prestige and possessions, they would have been easier to understand. But they are greater than that.

The initial temptation concerns the tree of the *knowledge of good and evil*. "Knowledge" means experiential knowledge; "good and evil" (like "heavens and earth," a merism, all-inclusive) effectively means everything; the knowledge of good and evil suggests experience without limits. This limitlessness affects both mind and behavior. In mind there is a form of hubris, and in behavior there is a tendency toward limitlessness in the desire for experience—whether concern-ing power or possessions or relationships.

The tree of *life* is more basic. It is in the middle of the Garden with its four rivers; and this central position—somewhat like the central position of the later tabernacle amid the four directions (Numbers 2)—makes it an avenue of God's own life. The image of the tree of life was well known in the ancient Near East; "the sacred tree represented fertility or ongoing life" (Meyers, 1985, 1094). In Revelation (2:7; 22:2, 14, 19) it is a symbol of immortality, of life with God. By eating from the tree of life one would live forever (Gen. 3:22).

Initially, the trees present no problem. They are part of what appears to be a wonderful garden. Yet the mention of evil (or harm, rāʿ) is striking—the first such negative word in Genesis. Even if "good and evil" is merely a way of saying "everything," "evil" has a negative dimension; and, within this section (2:6–9) it is the last word.

[2:10–17] **The earth takes further shape, and so does life in the Garden.** As the account now stands, this second part—concerning the shape of the earth and of human life (four rivers, and the human role of serving the Garden, 2:10–17)—is in delicate continuity with the first part (2:6–9, the initial picture of the flow of water, and of placing humankind in the Garden).

The river becomes fourfold—"four world rivers" (Childs, 1992, 112)—thus evoking universalism (the four corners or quarters of the earth, 2:10–14; Clifford, 2:5). This river builds on the flow which waters "the whole face of the ground" (2:6). Like the flow, the account of the fourfold river makes no reference to God.

But immediately—after the accounts of both the flow and the fourfold river respectively—Yhwh God acts decisively. Having first intervened to fashion the man and place him in the Garden (2:7), Yhwh God now intervenes to engage the human and the trees more specifically. No longer are they just located in the Garden. The human has a specific role—to be at rest in the Garden, and to serve it (2:15). And the trees are for eating—except the tree of the knowledge of good and evil. This tree, it now emerges, will cause whoever eats from it to die.

The story has a suggestion of a sting in the tail. The concluding use of "die" (2:17) dovetails with the concluding use of "evil" ("good and evil," in 2:9). To try to experience everything will bring not greater life but death. "To die" here refers not to dying physically—something that, in this account, is natural to humankind—but to being cut off from union with God (Clifford, 2:5; Ezek. 18). In other words, the attempt to have everything, instead of producing a sense of union and vitality, generates alienation. The endless quest for more often involves absence from what one already has. One is so focused on non-reality that, as concerns reality (including God), one is dead.

Genesis never says that the couple in the Garden are immortal (despite Wis. 2:23 and Rom. 5:12). On the contrary, they would live forever only if they ate from the tree of life—something prevented by God (3:22). "In the ancient Near East not to die would mean that one would have to become a god since only the gods were immortal" (Clifford, 2:5). Physical death therefore is something inherent in life, something natural. In fact, one of the features of Genesis as a whole is a sense of the naturalness of death. Yet in accepting death as natural, Genesis also often sees death as in some way mysterious, as having a dimension beyond ordinary perception. The concept of immortality, while not explicit, was not far away (Barr, 1992, 43).

Despite the warning about trying to experience everything and about being cut off—"dying"—the overall tenor of the account is positive. Eden remains an attractive place. There is a great sense of ease and plenty.

[2:18–23] **The final stage in the shaping of life: the man and the woman.** As often happens in Genesis when there are three parts, this third part breaks away somewhat from the pattern of parts one and two.

Human aloneness leads God to say—for the first time—that something "is not good." Given the steady "it was good" in Genesis 1, this comment is all the more striking.

The subsequent creativity is impressive: God fashions the animals, and the man names them—thus recalling God's naming of the aspects of creation in Genesis 1 and a further indication of the gap between humans and animals (cf. Gen. 1:28). But, however impressive, this does not complete the man's existence.

The making of the woman shows her not only as the equal of the man (she is from man and corresponds to him); she is also the high point of creation. "The creation of woman from man does not imply subordination, any more than the creation of the man from the earth implies subordination" (Kselman, 1988, 88). Inequality will come only with sin. The man's naming of the woman does not necessarily indicate authority over her; Hagar names God (16:13).

The background to the biblical account of the creation of woman has often seemed elusive. "Curiously, the extant literature of the ancient Near East has preserved no other account of the creation of primordial woman" (Sarna, 21). To find a possible background text one has to look at the highly negative Greek account of Hesiod, ca. 700 BCE. In fact Genesis is like a rebuttal of the Greek account. For Hesiod (*Theogony*, 588–607 [cf. *Works and Days*, 52–114]) women are not only evil but lazy, not supportive in poverty (593, *ou symphoroi;* Loeb translation, "no helpmeets"); they do nothing while the man works (599, 603). For Genesis, however, women are not evil and lazy; they are appropriate co-workers: together men and women had been commissioned (1:28), together they work (2:20). While Hesiod describes woman as a beautiful evil to balance man's good (585), God describes both man and woman as very good (1:31), and Yhwh God says that it is not good for man to be alone (2:18). Hesiod then goes on to speak of marriage—mostly negatively (602–610)—but Genesis goes on to evoke marriage in a way that is essentially positive and joyful (2:23–24). If the author of Genesis knew of the negative ideas about women found in Hesiod then he has radically reversed them. It is right to decry Genesis-related sexism (Davies, 1998, 7–8), but it is also appropriate to acknowledge Genesis's contribution toward countering a sexism that was grosser.

[2:24] Conclusion. Leaving parents and becoming one with a wife. This picture—a man goes from parents to a wife—is a conclusion not only to chapter 2 (Westermann, I, 234) but to the entire diptych of creation. The man-woman harmony dovetails with two other culminating pictures of harmony—of the man with the Garden/ground (2:6–17), and, especially, of God with creation, at rest (2:1–4a). The position of the man-woman harmony—the third of three harmonies—highlights the role of the man-woman relationship within creation, and also gives a sense of an ending.

The sense of an ending is further emphasized by the way in which the man-woman picture leaves the distant past and moves into the present ("And so a man leaves . . ."). Like the phrase "lived happily ever after," which involves a shift in the sense of time (from one form of the past to another), the shift from past to present brings the twofold creation account down to earth—to its conclusion.

While the conclusion to the first creation account had an etiological aspect—it implicitly explained the institution of Sabbath rest—so this conclusion also is partly etiological; it explains, more clearly, the institution of marriage. Thus creation is so described that it flows into life's basic institutions.

---

17   Sin and Its Disharmony: Crime and Punishment (2:25–4:16)

Disharmony with God (2:25–Chap. 3)
Disharmony with One's Brother (4:1–16)

Introductory Aspects

The Basic Story Line

The story is one of the most famous in the world. While the naked couple were enjoying blissful innocence, a serpent cajoled the woman into ignoring God's word and into seeking a higher godlike status. Lured by this talk and by appearances—the attractiveness of the tree of knowledge—the woman ate, as did her husband, but the consequent opening of their eyes, instead of leading to higher status, led to shame, to covering themselves with fig leaves.

When God came around, he found them hiding and denying responsibility—shifting the blame. The result was a stinging recall to reality—to their actual status and to the results of their own actions. Their lives from now on will involve pain, especially in relationships and work. Yet they are not left hopeless. The serpent, who first misled them, does not master them. They may be stung—bruised at the heel—but the serpent is bruised in its head. And God, far from abandoning them, surrounds them, literally, with care—with good-quality coats.

Then, in a twist that is particularly puzzling, there is a reminder that, during all this drama, the couple—ordinary mortals—had been living in the presence of the tree of life—a tree that would have enabled them to live forever. Unlike the tree of knowledge, the tree of life had not been forbidden. But now, because they have eaten from the tree of knowledge, they are banished from the tree of life—banished from Eden.

When they have children, the children do as their parents had done, but in another form, and more intensely: Cain, dissatisfied with his status, kills his brother, and when confronted by God, evades responsibility. But for Cain, too, God cares. Then Cain moves—east of Eden.

Literary Form

As already indicated, both episodes may be classed as "narratives of crime and punishment" (Westermann, I, 47–55). Rather as the creation diptych (Gen. 1: 1– 2:24) was representative of the two basic types of creation narratives, so the crime-and-punishment diptych also is broadly representative. The first crime is primarily vertical, against God; the second is more horizontal, against another human being. Furthermore, these two crimes involve two of the most basic pairings in life: man-woman; and brother-brother. By portraying two basic couples and two basic kinds of crime or sin, the diptych as a whole is typical or representative.

The change in genre or type—from creation narratives to narratives of crime and punishment—brings a major shift in Genesis. The diptych of harmony now gives way to a diptych of disharmony. The word "sin" (*ḥaṭāʾt*) does not occur until 4:7 ("sin is crouching . . ."), but disharmony is already present in chapter 3. While the two creation panels showed humankind as increasingly involved with the congenial ground, the two crime-and-punishment panels show humans as increasingly alienated from the ground (3:17–19; 4:11–12). And relationships between the humans, instead of moving toward joyful union (2: 21–24), move from intimacy toward alienation (Gen. 2–3; Hauser, 1982), even toward domination and murder (3:16; 4:8).

Complementarity of the Two Panels

Two elements of complementarity have already been mentioned—concerning the focus of their crimes (respectively, vertical and horizontal); and concerning the people involved (two basic couples [man-woman, and brother-brother]). (A parent-child scene occurs after the flood, 9:18–29.)

Further aspects of complementarity are as follows:

One crime builds on the other. The alienation between humans, begun in the Garden (covering up, undue desire, and domination), becomes total in the murder. The relationship with the ground, already difficult in the initial punishment (3:17–19), becomes more so for Cain (4:10–12). The departure from Eden, begun in the Garden, goes further after the murder—in Cain's departure to a place east of Eden.

Here, too, there is diversity in the divine names. While the creation accounts varied between "God" and "Yhwh God," this diptych varies between "Yhwh God" and "Yhwh." Thus the move from "God" to "Yhwh," already begun in the first diptych, now reaches completion.

The essential clue to this move from "God" to "Yhwh" seems again to be the link between "Yhwh" and involvement with humankind, especially with human distress (cf. Exod. 2:23–3:15). The sovereign creator, whose word is supreme, is "God" (1:1–2:4a). But the more God is focused on humankind, and the more humankind is distressed, the more God becomes known as "Yhwh." In the story of Cain, when there is both distress and terrible alienation, the divine name is simply "Yhwh."

The affinity between the two panels (2:25–chap. 3; and 4:1–16) is detailed. For Westermann (I, 285) "the parallels . . . are . . . striking and thorough." At times these parallels involve a process of intensification. In the Cain story, for instance, "the sundering of the familial bond . . . is . . . paralleled and intensified" (Kselman, 1988, 89). (For more details, see Rudman, 2001.) Some of these parallels may be outlined, in varying degrees of clarity (see Table 17.1).

These detailed parallels (between 2:25–chap. 3 and 4:1–16) are important. It is often said that chapters 2 and 3 form a unity, and this is partly true, especially as regards the story line. Yet within chapters 1–4, the more radical continuity—in literary type and essential content—is first between chapters 1 and 2, and then between chapters 3 and 4.

Table 17.1. Primordial Sin. Complementarities

The setting

They . . . the man and his wife . . .	The man knew . . . his wife.
The serpent . . . of the field . . .	Sin crouching . . . into the field.
Fruit forbidden by God.	Fruit not regarded by God.
Problem: relation to God.	Problem: relation, through God, to Abel.
The drama on the face:	The drama on the face:
the eyes' delight, desire.	distress, face fallen.

Crime and punishment

After eating: they knew . . .	After killing: Where is Abel . . . ?
They heard the voice . . .	I do not know.
Where are you?	The voice . . . is crying to me.
I hid.	I must hide/be concealed.
Avoiding responsibility:	Avoiding responsibility:
It was the woman . . . the serpent.	Am I my brother's keeper?
Because you have done this,	What have you done?
cursed are you . . . cursed is the	Now you are cursed from the ground.
ground because of you.	

The aftermath

God's protective action:	God's protective action:
Clothes them.	Puts a sign on Cain.
God cast them out of Eden.	Cain went out from God.
Cherubim placed east of . . . Eden.	Cain dwelt east of Eden.

Leading Elements

These two stories (Eden, Cain) are among the most haunting in history. They touch basic threads of the human tradition and spirit, and they have inspired countless paintings. It seems strange then that later biblical narratives say almost nothing about them, not explicitly. They speak of Abraham, Isaac, and Jacob but not of Adam and Eve.

However, near the turn of the era, explicit reflection on Adam did develop. There were important references to the Eden story in the Septuagintal Book of Wisdom (of Hellenistic origin, perhaps 50 BCE), in 4 Ezra (late first century CE) and in St. Paul (see Barr, 1992, 16–20). The Book of Wisdom interpreted Adam and Eve as having been destined for immortality; death, therefore, was not something natural or from God; it came from the devil (Wisdom 2:3). Adam was described as having sinned, thus introducing a fall, a fall for everybody (4 Ezra 3:21). Paul confirmed the idea that death was alien, the result of sin; and, in explaining the role of Christ, Paul also centralized responsibility for sin and death on one man: "Sin came into the world through one man, and through sin death. . . . Adam prefigured [Christ]" (Rom. 5:12, 15). St. Augustine went further: in the course of doctrinal battles with Pelagians he developed the idea of "original sin"—understood as one specific historical sin, which was then transmitted at birth to all people. Others followed Augustine. The result was that "all too often readers come to Genesis weighed down by Augustine's or Milton's interpretation of the story" (Niditch, 14).

Furthermore, beginning perhaps around 100 or 200 CE, post-biblical writing began developing a whole literature about Adam and Eve (Stone, 1992, 58). In later Judaism the relationship to the idea of original sin is ambiguous: "[T]he main Jewish tradition, as we know it since the Middle Ages, has refused to accept any sort of doctrine of original sin. . . . [But,] interpretations that look quite like an idea of universal original sin did arise and can be found in Jewish traditions from between the Old and the New Testament periods" (Barr, 1992, 8).

However, all these interpretations, whether Christian or Jewish, are relatively late; "it is . . . possible to read the canonical Old Testament, taken in itself, in a way that sees nothing like original sin as an important element" (Barr, ibid.). In other words, the idea of original sin may reflect a significant insight, but that insight does not come directly from Genesis.

While later Jews and Christians used various traditions and doctrines to deal with Eden—including St Paul's portrayal of Christ as a second Adam—the question remains as to how the Primary History dealt with Eden. In particular, how did Genesis deal with it?

Genesis does not refer explicitly to Eden and Cain, yet neither does it ignore them. On the contrary, it resonates with them, but implicitly. In fact, these early scenes, before they haunt humankind, first haunt Genesis. They are like ghosts that need to be put to rest. The beguiling attractiveness that first misled the woman, for instance, later misleads the sons of God when they see the attractiveness of women (6:1–2), and with terrible results. The relationship between the couple, where one leads the other into disaster, is replayed in Egypt, concerning Sarai's attractiveness, but with roles reversed: it is the man who leads the woman into deviation (12:10–13:1). In other scenes, the Eden motif is partly or largely reversed (cf. Noah's nakedness, Hagar, Tamar, Potiphar's wife). The Cain motif also is replayed and reversed, especially in the relationships between Abraham and Lot, between Jacob and murderous Esau, and especially between Joseph and his murderous brothers.

Some other books of the Primary History continue engaging the motifs of Genesis 3–4 (see esp. Brueggemann, 1968; 1973, 54–63), but again they do not refer to them explicitly.

What is important is that, long before later Jews and Christians wrote about Eden, long before St. Paul's second Adam, Genesis itself was intent on redressing the evil portrayed in Eden and Cain. Centuries before all things were restored in Christ (cf. Eph. 1), they were, in a sense, already restored in Joseph (cf. Steindl, 1989, 66–132).

Unlike later tradition, which tended to focus largely on the first part of the diptych—on eating the fruit rather than murdering a brother—Genesis seems to lay slightly greater emphasis on murderousness and on the need to work toward reconciliation.

The struggle with the Eden-Cain syndrome emerges in Genesis as part of human life. Ordinary people work under its shadow and seek to overcome it. In one sense they are quite alone in this struggle; there is no guiding savior. Yet Genesis does have figures who break the mould of ordinary life—particularly Rebekah and Joseph. In diverse ways they are almost like incarnations of God's presence, guides through the struggles and famines of life.

What are these struggles and famines? What is the essence of the drama which, having begun in Eden, is often replayed, often redressed?

Eden was not another planet, not some form of superhuman existence. Descriptions of the Garden have often been "overly romantic" (Fretheim, 366). There is no reference to a fall—though the idea of a fall does occur "in Plato, in gnosis, in Plotinus. . . . The Adamic myth is a myth of 'deviation,' or 'going astray,' rather than a myth of the 'fall' " (Ricoeur, 1967, 233). As noted in the Introduction (Chapter 13), when Hegel (*Logic,* 54) speaks of a fall, he does so in the context of life: "Life . . . sunders itself to self-realization." The story about the origin of evil is essentially a story about ordinary people—people who are mortal.

As said above, concerning the allusion to Sabbath and marriage (2:2, 24), one of the ways of portraying present reality is through etiologies or stories about "firsts"—narratives that portray the origin or cause of something (Gk. *aitia* = cause). There are stories, for instance, about the origin of the world, about the first use of the lyre and flute (4:21), the first metalworkers (4:22), and the first vinegrowing (by Noah, 9:20). The story of Noah growing the vine tells something about the nature of vines—how wine can intoxicate—but it tells nothing about the complex history of wine-making. And the story of the first sins, likewise, tells something about the nature of sin—but nothing about the complex history of human wrong-doing.

Among ordinary people the ways of going wrong vary from person to person. Genesis accordingly does not pin the origin of evil on one person or thing. Apart from the man, there is the woman and the serpent. The phenomenon of deviation, which first emerges clearly in the Garden, reaches fresh intensity in the murder. The origin of evil has been "decentralized" (Ricoeur, 1967, 234).

Part of the evil has to do with insecurity about one's place. In a world that says you can have it all, Genesis 3–4 says otherwise: if you try to have it all you lose even what you have. The couple in the Garden tried to have it all, and lost. Cain wanted more than he had, and he lost further. The two crimes are connected: "[I]n arrogating to himself the divine sovereignty over life . . . Cain has repeated the sin of his parents by making himself 'like God' " (Kselman, 89).

The primary question here is not money or sex. The couple seem to have had a world of wealth and sensuousness. The implication at the end of chapter 2 ("they become one flesh") is of sexual union, natural and easy. The issue then is something more subtle or cerebral—the fundamental sense of one's place in the world, of one's relationship to others. The couple reject their given relationship to God. Cain rejects the given relationship to Abel. The result—the primary impression in the whole two-panel scene—is a descent from harmony to exile. At the end Cain is a hunted murderer, wandering and restless. Only God's intervention saves him.

At one level, of course, in seeking to have it all, one may manage to grasp everything that privilege can buy. It is possible to amass powerful wealth and to retain it for a long time. But already, long before such grasped wealth collapses or is taken, there is a more subtle form of exile: fear, desire, and guilt build a sense of alienation.

Whatever the details, one of the features of Gen. 2:25–4:16 is to dramatize a basic aspect of experience: life often brings a sense of exile, of not belonging, of being lost.

Structure (Table 17.2)

The first panel (2:25–chap. 3) consists of three main parts, and the second (4:1–16) of two. The Cain and Abel text is relatively brief—perhaps because the actors' status is shrinking, especially that of Cain.

PANEL ONE (2:25–CHAP. 3)

In the history of interpretation the picture of nakedness (2:25) has sometimes been treated as a conclusion to chapter 2, and, more recently, as a bridge be-

Table 17.2. Primordial Sin (2:25–3:24 // 4:1–16)

The break with God

Introduction: The two unaware (2:25)
The crime: the eyes' false regard: no limits concerning God (3:1–7)
   The serpent beguiles the woman (3:1–5)
   The eating, the opening of the eyes, and a form of shame (3:6–7)
The crime revealed (3:8–13)
   Yhwh God calls (3:8–10)
   Avoiding responsibility (3:11–13)
The punishment: enmity; the heel, the pain, the cursed ground (3:14–21)
   The serpent: because you have done . . . ; the woman (3:14–16)
   The man: because you have heard . . . (3:17–21)
Conclusion: out of Eden (3:22–24)

The break with one another

Introduction: The two brothers, diverging (4:1–2)
The crime: the lack of regard; no limits concerning a brother (4:3–8)
   God regards Abel's offering, not Cain's (4:3–5a)
   Cain's distress and the crouching sin (4:5b–8)
The punishment revealed and punished: cursed from the ground (4:9–15)
   The punishment stated (4:9–12)
   The punishment modified; the sign (4:13–15)
Conclusion: East of Eden (4:16)

---

tween chapters 2 and 3 (Westermann, I, 234, and others). But the role as bridge, such as it is, is secondary to the more basic function—that of introducing a whole new scene. Correspondingly, the preceding picture (the man going to his wife, 2:24) is a distinctive conclusion (see comment on 2:24). The word "naked" (*ʿārûm*) prepares especially for the cunning (*ʿārûm*) serpent, and "not ashamed" prepares for the opening of the eyes (3:7). The image of nakedness, therefore, belongs with chapter 3.

In the structure of 2:25–chapter 3, two details are difficult—how to divide the punishment (3:14–21), and whether to divide the conclusion (3:22–24). At one level the punishment is threefold (serpent, woman, and man), but at another it is just twofold—as indicated both by the twofold repetition of "Because you have done/heard . . . cursed . . ." (3:14, 17), and by the balance of quantity between the two parts (between 3:14–16 and 3:17–19).

The conclusion (3:22–24) balances two complementary actions—a *sending forth*, which seems congenial, almost human (it even echoes the human sending forth of the hand); and a *casting out*, which suggests severe separation, as if from something radically other or holy (cherubim with a flaming sword turning every way). In an earlier conclusion (2:1–4a) there was a somewhat similar variation. In that case the text consisted, apart from its framework (2:1 and 4a), of two central balancing verses—one which has human overtones (2:2: *rested from making*), the other which has a greater resonance of the transcendent (2: 3: *blessed . . . made holy . . . created*).

PANEL TWO (4:1–16)

In the Cain and Abel story, the introduction is considerably longer than the conclusion—a reversal of the situation in the preceding panel (cf. 2:25; 3:22–24). This reversal is part of a larger pattern: all the introductions and conclusions in 1:1–4:16 form a delicate interweaving of quantity and content. In various ways they complete and complement one another, sometimes contrasting sharply. As seen above, for instance, the third conclusion (3:22–24) has aspects of the first (2:1–4a). As for the fourth conclusion (Cain's going out . . . to dwell in Wandering, 4:16) and the second (a man's leaving of his parents . . . to cleave to a wife, 2:24), there is at least a balance in quantity, and also a contrast in content (togetherness/stability versus alienation/wandering).

Comment

Panel One (2:25–Chap. 3)

[2:25] **Introduction. Naked and not ashamed.** The introductory picture—naked and not ashamed—sets up a tension, an awareness that, even though shame has not yet come, it seems to be imminent. A somewhat similar tension occurs in the introductions to the creation stories (in 1:2 and 2:4b–5). As Westermann notes (I, 234–235), all three texts (1:2; 2:4b–5; 2:25) are like variations on "when there was not yet"—a literary pattern that was well established in Egypt.

An absence of shame is not necessarily a good thing; it can mean that a person lacks awareness—a meaning which accords with Betchel's view (1995) that Gen. 2:4b–3:24 is a myth of maturation. In making the decision about eating the fruit "the man . . . is utterly passive. The woman gives him the fruit and he eats it as if he were a baby" (Niditch, 14). The nakedness seems to have two levels: that of innocent newly "made" babies; and that of a blissful newly-married couple (2:24). Psychologically, these two forms of innocence/bliss are related (Peck, 1978, 85).

But, at another level, nakedness can also mean that there is no need for shame, that a person is genuinely at peace. Such seems to be the case here. The couple are in harmony with each other, with the Garden/ground, and with their maker.

[3:1–7] **The crime: the clever serpent and the removal of limits.** The couple's harmony lasts until, in their well-being, they begin to move away from their healthy limitedness and to confuse themselves with gods.

The serpent is clever, and cleverness is good, part of the general goodness of creation (Gen. 1). But the serpent is not in the image of God; it is not cleverness that makes one like God. In fact, the cleverness, though good in itself—made by God—helps to instigate evil. Thus the origin of evil—the greatest of puzzles—fades into the origin of good. Evil is not an independent force; it is part of a larger reality, which is essentially good.

The result of the cleverness is negative. Both the serpent and the woman misinterpret God's command. Amid the confusion the couple lose the sense of God's sovereignty and of a circumscribing framework. They try to reshape human existence; they seek to become something unreal—some form of god.

While the serpent represents a form of cleverness, the woman and Cain represent other human features. Cain apparently represents disordered aggression (including female aggression), and the woman disordered frailty (including male frailty). For Ricoeur: "The woman represents the point of least resistance of finite freedom to the appeal of *Pseudo*, of the evil infinite. Eve, then does not stand for woman in the sense of 'second sex.' Every woman and every man are Adam; every man and every woman are Eve; every woman sins 'in' Adam, every man is seduced 'in' Eve" (1967, 255).

What remains unclear is the root of the disorder. She wants to be like a god. But why? What is she seeking? Or seeking to avoid?

The deviation in the Garden is hardly sexual in the sense of referring to a sexual act between the man and the woman; the implication when they first met is that they enjoyed sexual freedom (2:22–24). Yet the deviation may have a sexual dimension; as a symbol the serpent had sexual connotations (Drewermann, 1977, 2: 69–124).

However, even if there is a sexual dimension, the essence of the problem appears to be a form of fear, or deep anxiety. Drewermann (ibid., 152–178) speaks of *Angst,* and Fretheim (360) of "anxiety about death. . . . The serpent responds (vv. 4–5) precisely at the point of exaggeration and vulnerability." Wenin (1998a, 16) likewise emphasizes fear: the man's first response to the woman, despite its enthusiasm, seems to contain fear: he reduces her to his own terms (2:23), as if unable to cope with her otherness, and with a lack within himself. This fear in face of lack provides the opening for the serpent to speak of a wider sense of lack (3:1–6; Wenin, ibid.). Thomas Merton, in an essay with a clanging title, "The Root of War Is Fear," touches the same problem : "At the root of all war is fear: not so much the fear men have of one another as the fear they have of *everything.* It is not merely that they do not trust one another; they do not even trust themselves" (1961, 112). One goes to war, or one moves imperceptibly into a low-key insatiable quest for security, always wanting more. The fear leads to mistrust, including a mistrust of God's word. Therefore the woman turns away from God's word. Built into this fear, this disordered quest for security, is an implicit violence—against whatever threatens security.

Among human needs and activities, eating is fundamental, thus making it a suitable representative for human conduct in general. If eating becomes unlimited, as it does in the Garden, then so in a sense does all conduct; and humans become the ultimate arbitrators of everything, of all good and evil. Humans may make their own world and their own rules—whether in a thousand-year reich or in private life.

The prospect looks inviting: "The woman saw that the tree was good for eating, and that it was an allurement to the eyes, and that the tree was desirable to make one wise." But this vision, though wonderful in theory, though echoing God's seeing of creation's goodness (1:4), misses something. By remaking the world according to one's clever calculations, one loses sight of a larger reality, a dimension that is beyond calculation. One loses a context which, while initially confining, is ultimately liberating.

When the couple eat without limit, no one condemns them immediately—neither God nor parent, state or church, friend or foe. But they know in themselves that something is wrong. In a sense, it is not God who expels them but they who expel God (Diana Culbertson, in conversation, Cleveland, May 22, 1997). They have damaged themselves, and their making of leafy loincloths seems to be an initial effort to protect themselves. At least this time their implied choice of tree is good; fig leaves are large.

[3:8–13] **The crime discovered: despite avoidance of responsibility, the need for the truth.** God's response to the crime involves a mixture of revealing and covering—like a nurse who wants both to see the full extent of a wound and also to treat it and bind it up. The first action, that of revealing, brings severe realism. The realism involves facing the problem—something that the couple does not want to do. In typical human fashion they shift the responsibility—the man to the woman, and the woman to the serpent. This flight from realism is compounded by irony: the man says he heard God's voice, but in biblical language "hearing God's voice" means obeying God—the opposite of what the man has done. However, God's search for the truth, unlike that of many human investigative agencies, is not conducted in a spirit of superiority or vindictiveness. On the contrary, when the couple are at their lowest, when in fear they seek the shelter of the trees, God also is seeking a form of shelter—by walking in the cool breeze of the day. In a real sense then, God speaks to them from where they are.

[3:14–21] **The crime punished—the permanent consequences.** Punishment takes two forms—permanent (or long-term, involving the permanent state of serpent, woman, and man, 3:14–21) and immediate (or short-term, expulsion from the Garden, 3:22–24).

The pronouncement of permanent punishment—a form of etiology—constitutes the third part or section of the larger narrative of chapter 3, and, as noted by some scholars (see Westermann, I, 257), the third section stands somewhat apart. (In Genesis as a whole, third parts generally stand apart.)

The permanent punishment is not light: a bruising battle with the snake; the woman's undue longing; men's domination of women; the painfulness of childbearing and of working the soil. As Trible notes (1978, 128), man's domination of woman comes not from creation but from sin.

All is not negative. In the struggle with the snake, humankind may indeed be bruised, yet, overall, it overcomes. The woman's new name, Eve, mother of the living, is resoundingly positive—quite unrelated to many of the negative depictions in later art and literature. And God is on humankind's side. God's actions—the revealing of sin and the covering of the couple with clothing—are positive. The revealing of the full dimensions of the sin is like giving a full diagnosis of an illness. And the covering is good in quality. This is no fig-leaf Band-Aid. This is genuine protection.

The texts lists several ills as consequences of sin—pain in childbirth, in relationships, in work. This may seem initially to clarify one of the greatest problems in life, that of suffering. Suffering comes as a result of sin. However, the problem is not so simple, and here Genesis displays one of its limitations. In this, it is close to Deuteronomy—another wonderful book, but, again, limited.

[3:22–24] **Conclusion. Expulsion from the Garden.** The concluding moment—when God sends the couple out of Eden (3:22–24)—has an element of severity, of casting out, but it is also a further act of protection, an act of solidarity. The danger is that having eaten from one tree they may make the situation worse by eating from the tree of life, thus seeking in another way to be gods. Such a step would further rupture the natural rhythm and healthy limits of human life.

Humankind is such that full control over life—over the tree of life—seems attractive, and not having access to it gives a sense of exile. But it is better to face the reality of human life than to spend one's life pining after an unreal dream.

The sense of God's solidarity with the couple is reflected in the double use of the verb "send forth" (3:22–23): lest the man "send forth" his hand to the tree, God "sends forth" the couple, out of the Garden. By acting in a way reminiscent of the man, God emerges not as an alien judge but as one who at some level is close to the two humans.

Panel Two (4:1–16)

[4:1–2] **Introduction. Cain and Abel—an implicit contrast.** Like the other introductions (1:1–2; 2:4b–5; 2:25), the beginning of the Cain-and-Abel story contains an element of tense expectation. The brothers form a contrast, and with that contrast there is a tension.

Cain is his mother's favorite. He is first-born, and despite the earlier warnings about childbearing (3:16), she seems to relish his birth. She speaks about him and the relationship of his birth to Yhwh in a way that she does not speak of Abel. Her producing of Cain, in conjunction with Yhwh, "suggests a creational theme" (Fretheim, 372). Abel, however, is like an afterthought, set by the wording of the text in the shadow of "his brother." His very name, *hebel*, suggests someone insignificant, even defective (Levin, 1991). Even when Abel does something new—he keeps flocks—attention immediately comes back to Cain, the tiller (literally, servant) of the soil. Thus in the introduction (4:1–2) it is Cain who is mentioned first and last.

Yet Cain's relationship to his mother is not healthy. She regards him as an object ("acquired")—a man to fill a lack—as she herself had first been treated by a man (2:23) (Wénin, 1999, 11). In such a situation, Abel is insignificant. Cain is mastered by his mother—a relationship intended for animals (1:28; 2:20)—and so he needs in turn to master the animal within himself; but he fails (4:7–8; Wénin, 1999, 14).

The contrast between the livelihoods—shepherd and farmer—echoes a specific historic tension, but that contrast also has a representative character. It evokes all those situations where diversity of occupation contributes to adversity. The primary tension, however, is not between people of diverse occupations; it is between siblings. The word "brother" is used seven times. This tension is something latent in every group of brothers or sisters, every community.

[4:3–8] The crime: from distress and fallen face to murder. When the brothers present their offerings, Cain is again first, and his gift is explicitly linked to Yhwh (4:3–4). But suddenly the order is reversed: "Yhwh had regard for Abel . . . but . . . not . . . for Cain."

In part, Yhwh's preference for Abel may be explained by the excellence of Abel's offering—the best ("fattest") firstlings of his flock—or by the curse attached to the ground (whence came Cain's offerings; Herion, 1995). But there is a further crucial factor: Yhwh's free choice—a choice that reverses the earlier favoritism accorded to Cain.

From the point of view of Cain and of many neutral observers, this is a disturbing development: God is unfair, and, more generally, life is unfair.

A more nuanced reading is that life's favors are unpredictable. Cain had once enjoyed the position of favorite, but when a pivotal preference goes against him, he rejects the situation: "Cain was very incensed, and his face fell."

Ironically, Cain then receives Yhwh's attention in a way that Abel never had (4:6–7): "Why are you incensed, and why has your face fallen?" It is in this episode, rather than in the Garden, that the word "fall" is used. The falling of Cain's face is a reflection of a deeper distress-filled fall within. Yet Yhwh is already at the scene—alerting, pleading, warning, encouraging: "Why. . . . If you do good, lift it up? And if you do not do good, sin is crouching. . . . You will rule it." Cain is down; and waiting for him, like a crouching animal, is "sin"—the first use of the word in Genesis. But he can be lifted up; he can

rule the crouching animal. Despite all that has happened in the previous episode—in the Garden—Cain seems to have as much choice in dealing with the
crouching animal as the couple had in dealing with the serpent.

The implication of something animal-like in both sins (the lying serpent; sin
as crouching—preparing to kill) touches a key factor in the human makeup,
what Hanaghan (1979) calls "the beast factor." Humans, despite their essential
goodness (Gen. 1), have a tendency to lie and to kill. Genesis does not hide
this fact. Rather it brings it into the open, spells out the murderous consequences of yielding to bestial fantasy, and then spends much of the rest of the
book (especially in the stories of Abraham, Jacob, and Joseph) showing the way
back from such deviation.

[4:9–15] **The punishment: Yhwh confronts and protects.** After the murder—rather as after the eating in the Garden—Yhwh's role is twofold. On the
one hand, again like a nurse or doctor attending a crying wound, Yhwh spells
out the full dimensions of the malady and its consequences (4:9–12). On the
other hand, in response to Cain's plea, Yhwh enables him to deal with the
terrible situation. Cain is doubly protected—by a threat of sevenfold vengeance,
and by a sign (4:13–15).

Within the context of the close-knit fabric of Genesis, the word "sign" picks
up one of the threads of creation—the lights in the heavens, which were "signs"
(1:14)—and "sign" links up also with the later sign in the heavens, the covenant
rainbow (9:13). As the sign of the rainbow moved beyond sin, indicating peace,
so, in some way, did the sign on Cain; it did not allow sin to be the final word.
Thus the creational theme, already noticed in Cain's birth, now continues. God
is giving Cain a further element of creation, some form of second birth.

In later centuries this positive sign was turned into something negative—
"the mark of Cain," a way of identifying an alleged criminal. But the original
idea was positive, and it contained an implicit protest against blood-feud—the
practice, found especially around the Mediterranean, of revenge through death,
thus provoking at times a cycle of avenging deaths.

The Cain-and-Abel story is scandalous to the extent that much of human
existence is scandalous. Life is unfair, and the innocent are slaughtered. Genesis
appears to have few illusions about solving the problem—either at the theoretical or practical level. But it does what a writer can do: it bears witness to
the reality—both to the drama that ignited the murder, and to the innocence
of Abel. Abel became the scapegoat—the target of Cain's disturbed emotions.
Also, as with the drama in the Garden, Genesis shows that the evil, instead of
being a completely independent force, is in some way related to God. God is
involved with Cain's birth and development, and God intervenes again with
Cain—to try to dissuade, to condemn, to protect. Surrounding the murder,
then, there is a real divine presence. This presence does not block human
freedom, but it shows that the murder has another dimension—that of a God
who pleads first for Abel, and then, in another way, for Cain. Murder is not

all, nor is despair. There is a form of dignity for both parties, and there is an effort to begin again.

[4:16] **Conclusion. The settled wanderer.** As a result of Yhwh's protection, Cain is able to do something he thought he could never do—settle down. As with the departure from Eden, there is an ambiguity in the final details: Cain "settled in the land of Wandering [= *nôd*]." He is indeed settled, but there is an evoking of homelessness, of exile, of division within. He has lost creation's sense of rest.

The Less-Than-Sovereign God: The Unity of 1:1–4:16

The two panels of disharmony (2:25–4:16), apart from forming a diptych of their own, are part also of a larger unity—from the first creation account to the departure of Cain (1:1–4:16). As already indicated, the variations in the divine name—the move from "God" to "Yhwh God" to "Yhwh"—suggest a pattern of increasing divine involvement in humankind and in human distress.

This change in the divine name—from "God" to "Yhwh"—is linked to a change in the divine word: like God's name, God's word comes more and more down to earth.

At first, the divine word is supreme, creating all things (1:1–2:4a). Then, in settling humankind in the Garden (2:4b–24), the divine command, while still respected, is open to being contravened, broken. Later, in the eating, it is indeed broken (3:1–7). Finally, Cain not only goes against it, but manages even to reverse it: his plea leads Yhwh to change the decree of punishment (4:6–8, 12–15). Thus there is a strong contrast between the transcendent freedom of the opening command, "Let there be light," and the pressurized closing command not to kill Cain; the God who once pronounced with total sovereignty becomes Yhwh who takes up the logic of a distressed murderer ("Therefore/Very well," 4:15). At the end, God's word is interwoven with the word of a banished wanderer.

Change is not limited to God's name and word; it occurs also in the portrayal of God's own self. As the story advances (in 1:1–4:16), as humans appear increasingly fragile and sinful, God appears increasingly close to human conditions. The first suggestions of closeness to humankind occur in creation's opening panel: humankind is in the image and likeness of God (1:26–27)—and so, implicitly, God is in some way like humankind; and God rests from work (2:2–3)—somewhat as humans do.

In creation's second panel, when humankind is more down-to-earth—made from the ground—God also is closer to the earth. The account begins (2:4b) with something of the framing phrases from the first account (1:1; 2:3–4a), but there is an important shift: the language of "creating" gives way to that of simply "making." This change, already begun after the creation of humankind (1:31–2:3), now reaches completion; and, as it does, priority of wording goes to "earth" rather than "heaven" (not God "created the heavens . . .", but Yhwh God "made the earth . . ."). Both God and humankind are connected with clay: in making humankind to work the soil, God also works in soil—fashioning humankind as would a potter.

In the third text (2:25–chap. 3), after eating the forbidden fruit, humankind is not only on the earth; it is in trouble—taking cover from fig–leaves and hiding in the middle of the trees (3:7–8). Yhwh God correspondingly walks in the breeze or cool of the day, away, so it is implied, from the noonday heat (3:8)—not only an anthropomorphism but a suggestion of vulnerability. Vulnerable humankind seeks one form of shelter, God another: they, behind leaves and trees of the Garden; Yhwh God, in the cool of the day in the Garden. Like them, God knows what it is to want shelter.

Finally, when Cain sinks even lower, God also reaches a lower state. Here, more than previously, Yhwh asks questions—something unthinkable in chapter 1 and unlikely in chapter 2. There had been a set of questions after the eating (3:9–13), but now there are two such sets (4:6–7, 9–10). In the first of these latter two sets, Yhwh finally seems even to plead ("If you do good, lift [your face/self] up?" 4:7). And after the second set, when Cain has been reduced to "wavering and wandering" (Fox, 1972, 18; Korsak, 1993, 14), Yhwh does something similar—wavers. It is at this moment, under pressure from Cain, that Yhwh has a change of mind. The change brings a threat of sevenfold vengeance—thus pulling Yhwh into the murky world of killing and retaliation. In a sense Yhwh has joined Cain. Yhwh is closest of all at the end: in putting the protective sign on Cain, there is an implication that Yhwh actually touches him.

The idea of the image of God now takes on a new dimension. Not only is humankind in the image of God, but in a sense, God takes on the image of humankind. When humankind is to till the soil, God also works with the soil. When humankind in its sinfulness needs shelter from leaves and trees, God walks in the cool Garden—in a form of shelter. And when the murderous Cain is condemned to wavering, God wavers in the condemnation and threatens vengeance to protect him. God is coming down to earth.

The overall unity of 1:1–4:16 is reflected in a detail that acts as a framework for the whole narrative. While the Creator's leading words concerned light, and lights as signs (1:3, 14—leading verses), Yhwh's last action is to put the sign on Cain (4:15). The first signs were in the highest heavens, the later one was on the lowest of humans, banished even from the ground.

18   Genealogies: From More Disharmony to Restoration (4:17–Chap. 5)

The Ten Generations of Cain and Adam (4:17–26)
The Ten-Generation Genealogy of Adam (Chap. 5)

Introductory Aspects

The Basic Story Line

Up to this point the story of humankind has been confined within just one small family. Suddenly, however, the horizon expands greatly across space and time—a picture of the development of civilization. Beginning with Cain, the succession of developments is dense and rapid: city-building, tent-dwelling, music, technology, and an intensifying spiral of violence and vengeance, even seventy-sevenfold (4:17–24).

Then the story takes a surprising turn. Just when the heritage of violent Cain seemed to be taking over the world, the narrative goes back to Adam and his wife, telling how, despite Cain's murder of Abel, Adam and his wife went ahead and had another son, Seth. And he in turn had a further son, Enosh. Enosh apparently was a good man. It was in his time that people began to call on Yhwh (4:25–26).

Then the story goes back yet again, even further, and in writing! Beginning "on the day God created humankind," it gives a written record (literally, a "scroll/book") of the generations of Adam (chap. 5). It not only reaffirms the birth of Seth and Enosh; it sets all three—Adam, Seth, and Enosh—in the context of blessing and of a great rolling genealogy of descendants, long-lived and illustrious, as far as Noah and his sons.

It is as though, just when the story of humankind seemed to have descended into a downward spiral of vengeance, someone recalled that Adam and his wife had made a fresh beginning. And then, building on that, someone else stood up and said, Yes, and here it is in writing, and in full!

The story contains contradiction: as will be seen, its lists of names (4:17–26, and chap. 5) simultaneously overlap and contradict. Such contradiction is ultimately of a piece with the contradictions in earlier episodes: it is a signal that the narrative is not just linear history. It has a transcendental aspect.

Literary Form (Mixed)

The story is told through the form of genealogies—first of Cain (seven generations, 4:17–24), then, briefly, of Adam-Seth-Enosh (three generations, 4:25–

26), and finally the full genealogy from Adam to Noah (ten generations, chap. 5). Genealogies, therefore, are the third major literary type in Genesis—after creation narratives, and narratives of crime and punishment.

In themselves genealogies may seem boring, but their function in society is often pivotal—the foundation, for instance, of identity ("roots"), fame, fortune (inheritance), relationship, positions of power, or lines of succession. A family tree, especially if annotated, can be like the barometer of a society's climate, a reflection of prevailing forces.

Genealogies were already established as a genre in the third millennium (for instance, among the Babylonians and Assyrians [(West, 1985, 12–13]), and, to a limited degree, features of Near Eastern genealogies occur in Genesis, such features as the occasional listing of seven generations, the standardizing of lists at ten, and the long life spans (Clifford, 2:7, 10). Even Genesis's first city, Irad (4:17), "corresponds to the Mesopotamian Eridu" (Clifford, 2:7). And the correlation between the seven generations of Cain and the ten generations of Adam may be an imitation of a further Mesopotamian feature—the correlating of lists of seven sages and ten kings, "even to the point of resemblance of names" (Clifford, 2:10; cf. Wilson, 1975; 1977, 148–166).

Some sense of the Near Eastern genealogies may be had from the Sumerian King List. It begins: "When kingship was lowered from heaven, kingship was first in Eridu. In Eridu, Alumim became king and ruled 28,800 years" (*ANET* 265; cf. Malamat, 1968). Having listed further cities and kings, the List continues: "These are five cities, eight kings ruled over them for 241,000 years. Then the Flood swept over the earth. After the Flood . . . Ga[]ur became king and ruled 1,200 years." Overall, the average reign drops from about 30,000 years before the flood to just over 1,000 after it.

However, apart from Sumer, Babylonia, and Assyria, genealogies were also a key feature of Greek historiography; they were a way of tying the story together (van Seters, 1992, 90–96), and Genesis's primary affinity is with Greek examples rather than with those of the Near East. The genealogies of Genesis "are much more closely comparable to the Hesiodic ones, both in their multilinearity and in their national and international scope" (West, 1985, 13). The affinity with ancient Near Eastern examples is relatively minor (Hess, 1994b).

In using genealogies, the text mixes them at one point with another form. The genealogy of Cain (4:17–24) is mixed or combined with an account of city-building, tent-dwelling, and technology development (4:17–26)—an account that at one level may be classified as an achievement story (Westermann, I, 56–62). In effect, the first genealogy is mixed with the account of the world's first economic and cultural boom.

The introduction of mixing—this mixing of genealogy and achievement story—is not an isolated phenomenon. It is part of something larger in art. As an artistic work progresses, it often begins to repeat and mix; while repeating, it becomes more complex. This may be seen especially in music, traditional dancing, poetry, song, and fireworks. Even within small units, Hebrew poetry tends toward repetition and intensification; and the prophetic books use a "strategy of complication" (Alter, 1985, 62–84, esp. 73). The Gospel of John, especially chapter 21, illustrates how prose can combine repetition with mixing and interweaving (Brodie, 1993, 184–187, 574–575, 577).

Within this framework of mixing literary types there now begins the mixing of divine names. Where previously there was a steady pattern (God, Yhwh God, or Yhwh), this diptych begins to mix the names: first "God," then "Yhwh (4:25–26; 5:1, 23–24, 29).

Complementarity of the Two Panels

The text is not simply a succession of three genealogies, all equally independent. At a certain level, the first two are bound together: the opening genealogy, based on Cain (4:17–26), forms a special unit with the subsequent little genealogy, which tells how Cain's victim, Abel, was replaced by Seth and Enosh (4:25–26). In particular, the name of Cain (4:17, 25) helps to bind these first two genealogies into a unity. Other details confirm that unity: taken together these two opening genealogies form ten generations (the requisite number for a full genealogy); and the wording of the statement by Adam's wife (4:25) echoes the wording of Lamech's speech to his wives (4:23–25).

The division, then, at another level, is not threefold, but twofold—two panels: first, the ten generations that are Cain-related (seven and three); then, the ten generations that begin on the day God created humankind. Again, therefore, what emerges is a unity that constitutes a diptych.

The first indication of this balance, this diptych arrangement, is the correspondence between the two sets of names (in 4:17–26 and chap. 5); they show pervasive overlaps and affinities (see Table 18.1).

Table 18.1. Genealogies: Characters, in Order of Appearance

Cain	Adam; God (twice)
Enoch	Seth
Irad	Enosh
Mehujael	Kenan
Methushael	Mahalel
Lamech (vengeance: 7 and 77)	Jared
Adah, Zillah	Enoch; God (three times)
Jabal, Jubal, and Tubal-Cain	Methuselah
Tubal-Cain's sister (i.e., Lamech's	Lamech (dies at 777)
daughter), Naamah	Lamech's son, Noah (brings comfort,
Adam	*nāḥam*, 5:29); Yhwh Shem, Ham, and
Seth; God	Japheth
Enosh; Yhwh	

The figure of Naamah ("pleasant/beautiful") is central and enigmatic. Apart from Eve, Adah, and Zillah, she is the Bible's first named woman.

As well as a balance between individual names there is also a balance between the genealogies' structures. The two basic genealogies (4:17–24; and chap. 5) both begin as linear—they trace a narrow perpendicular line from father to eldest son. But at the end they open out to become horizontal ("segmented"): each tells of three brothers (first, Jabal, Jubal, and Tubal-Cain; later, Shem, Ham, and Japheth).

The balance or complementarity includes other features:

Space and time. As in the creation accounts, there is complementarity between space and time—but in reverse order. The second panel (chap. 5), with its repeated references to days and years, is pervaded by a sense of passing time, a sense of life's quantity. In the first panel (4:17–26), however, no measure of time is ever mentioned, and the picture of technology—city, tents, music, metal—involves an emphasis on aspects of space, especially living space, and on life's quality. Taken together the two texts begin to fill out the world and its flow of time.

Divine-human complementarity. As in earlier diptychs, there is divine-human complementarity but—as with time and space—in reverse order. The first panel, which does not mention God until the end (4:25–26: "God . . . Yhwh"), is largely concerned with human affairs—the dwelling places and technology. The second text (chap. 5), however, mentions God six times (five times "God," and once "Yhwh").

The role of women. As a question for research, it may be worth asking whether there is a complementarity concerning the role of women. While women are important in the first panel, especially at the end (4:25–26), they have virtually no role in the second panel (chap. 5). This variation—between the presence and absence of women—follows the general pattern of the preceding diptych (2:25–4:16); the woman was important in chapter 3, less so in 4:1–16.

Whatever the details, the general conclusion is that while the basic story line proceeds in three steps (Cain, Cain's replacement, and Adam), the text has another level, which is twofold—diptych.

Leading Elements

FROM GENEALOGIES TO RESTORING HARMONY

On one level the genealogies tell a fascinating story of human origins and achievements—the emergence of town and tent and art, and the flow of the years and generations. Yet human achievement is not the primary focus. The genealogies tell of God's work; they are "the continuation of God's initial act of creation" (Kselman, 87), and, within both genealogies, the governing interest is on restoring harmony, rest.

In the first genealogy (4:17–26, taking all the Cain-related material as a unit), the reference to restoration is late and compact—in the closing figures of Seth (the God-given replacement of Abel) and Enosh (who first calls on Yhwh). Together these two figures, Seth and Enosh, restore both the horizontal dimension (replacing Abel) and the vertical (calling on Yhwh).

However, in the second genealogy the process of restoration is developed. This text (chap. 5) presupposes that the basics of restoration, of harmony, are already in place. It starts with the original vertical link (God's likeness in humankind), and, having implied that that original likeness continues in subsequent generations (Adam's likeness is found in his son Seth, 5:3), later goes on to tell of the deepening of that harmony. In the figure of Enoch it shows someone whose communication with God is extraordinary: "Enoch walked with God. . . . Enoch walked with God; and he was no more, for God took him."

In Enoch's grandson, Rest (*nōaḥ*, Noah [but see Westermann, I, 360]), the sense of harmony flows over into a deepening of the horizontal dimension— the down-to-earth sense of comfort or consolation, a consolation that comes "from the ground which Yhwh cursed." The sin-related cursing is recalled; at one level the sins are atoned for.

The sense of restoration, of rest, is increased by the way chapter 5 echoes something of the original account of harmonious creation—including the way the 777 years of Noah's father, Lamech, echoes the triple "seventh" at the end of creation (2:2–3).

HARMONY IS FROM GOD, NOT FROM MUSIC AND METAL

The brief account of the development of culture, especially of music and metalwork, is interesting. But it is followed by a picture of spreading violence (Lamech's vengeance). In the absence of God—Cain had left God's presence and Cain's genealogy does not mention God—music and technology are not enough to build genuine harmony. Only when God contributes and when Yhwh is called upon does restoration begin (4:25–26)—thus setting the scene for the deeper restoration implied in Genesis 5.

Structure (Table 18.2)

THE GENEALOGIES OF CAIN AND ADAM (4:17–26)

While the story of Cain was brief, his genealogy (4:17–26) is even more so, and so the structure is correspondingly simple, hardly demanding subdivisions. Yet it has a form of completeness—both in the number of generations (seven), and in the enveloping use of the name "Cain": "Cain . . . Tubal-Cain." The repetition of the word "wives" (4:19, 23) helps to clarify the division.

The conclusion (4:25–26) is both a partial repetition and a subversion of the introduction (4:17–18). The conclusion's length is considerable—given some

Table 18.2. Genealogies (4:17–26 // chap. 5)

Building and genealogies

Introduction: Cain's genealogy; the (godless) city (4:17–18)
  The godless civilization (4:19–22)
  The descent into violence (4:23–24)
Conclusion: Adam's genealogy; back to God/Yhwh (4:25–26)

Genealogy from Adam to Noah

Introduction: Adam's genealogy, in God's likeness (5:1–2)
  Five like generations (5:3–17)
  Enoch, walking with God, taken by God (5:18–24)
  Noah (Rest): after pain and curse, the bringing of relief (25–31)
Conclusion: Noah (Rest) and his sons (tenth generation, 5:32)

---

very short introductions and conclusions in 1:1–4:16—but that length seems to be connected to its role as a turning point, as something which, in diverse ways, surprises.

The overall unity of the Cain text (4:17–26) is like that of a downward spiral that turns at the end. The seven generations of Cain, godless and violent, give way to three generations that replace Cain's victim and which call on Yhwh.

THE GENEALOGY OF ADAM (CHAP. 5)

Discerning a structure is difficult here. Each generation gives three numbers (the year of begetting a son; the number of subsequent years; and the total). See Table 18.3.

The divisions in the table—before Jared, Methuselah, and Noah—reflect apparent divisions in the text. Number six, Jared, breaks the pattern: the 162 makes a radical break with the decreasing pattern of the first column; the 800 repeats the 800 of Adam (the genealogy's first repetition); and the 962 is a new high. So, if the generations are to be divided, it seems best to see Jared as beginning a second part.

Number eight, Methuselah, marks a further new high—969—thus suggesting the beginning of a third part. Furthermore, Methulesah comes after a certain culmination—the seventh generation, that of Enoch in all his uniqueness (in the genealogy of Cain the seventh generation had marked a culmination, 4:17–24). The second part therefore consists of just Jared and Enoch.

The third part consists essentially of Methuselah and Lamech (5:25–31). Like Enoch, Lamech stands out and has something of the effect of a culmination. As Enoch's total (365) was unique, so is Lamech's—777. Lamech's statement about his son Noah is a form of climactic pronouncement. And the message in that pronouncement is about coming close to God/Yhwh, over-

Table 18.3. The Years from Adam to Noah

	Years before begetting	Further years	Total
Adam	130	800	930
Seth	105	807	912
Enosh	90	815	905
Kenen	70	840	910
Mahalalel	65	830	895
Jared	162	800	962
Enoch	65	300	365
Mehuselah	187	782	969
Lamech	182	595	777
Noah	500		

coming the alienating curse, something which again echoes Enoch, but in a way which is much more down to earth.

The separateness of part three (Methuselah and Lamech) is clearer than the separateness of part two (Jared and Enoch). This accords with a larger phenomenon: when a Genesis text has three parts, whether within a single passage or within a whole dramatic act (such as Genesis 1–5), the third part is usually more separate.

The final verse—when Noah was 500 he begot Shem, Ham, and Japheth (5:32)—departs almost completely from the general pattern, and so would seem to be a formal conclusion. Like the introduction (1:1–2), it stands apart from the central body of the genealogy.

Comment

Panel One (4:17–26)

[4:17–24] **The seven generations of Cain: civilization's descent into endless vengeance.** The initial genealogy has its form mixed with that of an achievement story and so it wraps its seven generations around the story of the emergence of human technology—city building, tents, music, metal (4:4:17–22). Blended with the story of advancing technology is the story of Lamech's advancing violence (4:23–24). In fact the seven generations are framed by two murderers—Cain and Lamech—the second worse than the first. This Cain genealogy makes no mention of God—the first such extended omission in Genesis.

The main body of the text, centered on Lamech and his family (4:19–24), falls easily into two parts—one about the role of the three sons (Jabal, Jubal, and Tubal-Cain), the other about Lamech's intensifying vengeance (Alter, 1985, 5, 18).

In the role of the sons also there is an intensification:

Jabal . . . was the *father of* those who . . .

Jubal . . . was the *father of all* those who . . .

Tubal-Cain—*[himself the] forger of all.* . . .

The importance of Jabal and Jubal was indirect—in their descendants—but Tubal-Cain's far-reaching importance was immediate: he himself was the forger of all instruments of bronze and iron! So much metal provides an ironic background for Lamech's violent song.

[4:25–26] The three generations of Adam: arresting the descent and getting back to God. At the end of the Cain panel there is a turnaround: the brief Adam genealogy (Adam-Seth-Enosh, 4:25–26) begins to redress Cain's crime. "God," who had been absent from Cain's generations, is now mentioned. Finally, contact with "Yhwh" is reestablished: "they began to call on the name of Yhwh."

The continuity between the two genealogies (Cain's and Adam's, 4:17–24 and 4:25–26) is precise. Adam's wife not only refers back explicitly to Cain. She also articulates the idea of replacement (Seth replaces Abel). And in her statement—"For God has set . . . For Cain slew . . ."—the repetition of "For" (*kî . . . kî*) echoes exactly the repeated "For" (*kî . . . kî*) of Lamech (4:23–24).

The woman's role here is important. Eve is "a woman much maligned" (Dennis, 1994, 8–33), but her attitude at this moment is striking. Nothing had been said about her response to the murder in her family, but now, at last, she refers to Abel's death. This death could have led her to despair. Yet, she obviously went on with life, and when Seth is born she emerges as a woman who has moved "from tribulation to joy" (Deen, 1978, 2). Thus, in capsule form, she is a model for all the Bible's strong women, and for all people who rise above despair.

Panel Two (Chap. 5)

[Chap. 5] The ten generations of Adam: living in the likeness of God. The second table, the full-scale ten-generation genealogy of Adam (chap. 5), is a repetitive flow of names—people who generally live for close to a thousand years. In contrast to the Cain genealogy, where the only energy seems to be human (God is unmentioned, and the generations revolve around murder and technology), the Adam genealogy (chap. 5) is like an expression of God's command, given at creation (1:26–28), to increase and multiply. Unlike

Genesis 1, however, where ʿādām is a generic noun ("humankind"), ʿādām is now a proper name ("Adam"). This shift in meaning presupposes the drama of chapters 2–3.

Other ancient lists spoke of people who lived tens of thousands of years (Clifford, 2:10). In Genesis 5 the long life spans seem designed partly to evoke a sense both of indefinite time and of bygone giants (cf. 6:1–4); they also evoke a mythical past, which at some level suggests a closeness to divine origins.

But the mood here is not tied to a mythical past. There is a sense of coming to terms with the past's limitations and of moving forward. The second panel (chap. 5) unpacks the Adam-based turnaround and its references to God and Yhwh (4:25–26). Beginning with the three names at the end of chapter 4 (Adam, Seth, Enosh), chapter 5 implicitly spreads the role of God and Yhwh right across the generations.

First it reaffirms God's original likeness and blessing in humankind (5:1–2), implying that the likeness is transmitted through Adam and the like generations (5:3, and 5:4–31, esp. 5:4:20). The text is steady; there are no erratic changes, as in the Cain genealogy, to disrupt the continuity.

Then, when a change does occur, in the case of Enoch, its effect is not to negate that continuity with God but to strengthen it: God is present not only in distant origin and likeness, but in life's duration and at its end: "Enoch walked with God. . . . Enoch walked with God; and he was no more, for God took him" (5:21–24). God's taking of Enoch forms a pattern with the taking up of Elijah (2 Kings 2:9–10).

Finally, when attention turns to pain and curse, the end of chapter 5 comes back, as did the end of chapter 4, to the role of Yhwh (5:29; cf. 4:26). It also speaks of good conduct, namely giving comfort or relief (5:28)—the antithesis of the conduct of the vengeful Lamech.

As well as thus unpacking the Adam-based turnaround (4:25–26), the second panel also manages to go back to the Cain-based genealogy and redeem it, as it were: as the comparative list of names shows, most of the people in Cain's genealogy—practically all except Adah and Zillah (because the wives are not descendants?)—are echoed somehow in the new genealogy of Adam. "The two genealogies, juxtaposed, illustrate both the spreading effect of human sin and God's undiminished commitment to the blessing" (Clifford, 2:10).

Whatever the details (especially concerning Adah and Zillah), the overall pattern is clear: while the process of human degeneration, begun in the Garden and in Cain, continues in Cain's descendants as far as the bigamy and violence of Lamech, the reentry of Adam and his wife (4:25–26) marks a new beginning, a certain return to harmony; and chapter 5 elaborates that return. Chapter 4 ends with the picture of a newly-found call to Yhwh, and chapter 5 with Yhwh-related evocations of rest (nōaḥ, Noah) and comfort (nāḥam). Within the larger drama (chaps. 1–5), the final panel recaptures some of creation's sense of harmony and rest.

In chapter 5, the numbers for the years are such that the first person to be born after the death of Adam is Noah. The two form a continuity. Paradise has proved fragile, but it is not irredeemably lost.

Chapter 5 as a Conclusion to All of Genesis 1–5

Genesis 5 synthesizes aspects of the preceding chapters. Its initial sequence (Adam, Seth, Enosh) builds on the positive turnaround that follows the genealogy of Cain (4:25–26). Its later generations incorporate and reshape most of the people in Cain's list, redeeming them as it were, especially Lamech (4:17–24). Its climactic pronouncement about Noah indicates the coming, if not of redemption, then at least of rest and comfort—comfort from all the drama of the Garden and Cain, from all the pain and the curse (5:29; cf. 3:14–19; 4:9–15). Genesis 5 also has an echo of the second panel of the creation story ("On the day God . . . ," 2:4b; 5:1; note "This one . . . ," 2:23; 5:29). In addition, as if forming a framework or balance (an *inclusio*), chapter 5 has a special affinity with the first panel (1:1–2:4a)—particularly with its stately repetitive rhythm, with its idea of the likeness of God in humankind (1:26–28), and, in some complex way, with its ending:

God completed on the seventh day his work	Lamech called his name Rest/(Noah),
And he rested (*šābat*) on the seventh day	saying, "This one shall comfort us
from all his work which he had done/made.	from our doing/making
And God blessed the seventh day and made it holy because on it God rested from all his work . . .	and from the pangs of our hands
	from the ground which Yhwh has cursed."
	Lamech [lived] . . . 777 years.

Whatever the details, a key idea is clear: God's original rest brings blessing, and the child called Rest (Noah) brings comfort from the curse. The curse (3:17; 4:11) may have seemed to undo the original blessing (1:28; 2:3), but chapter 5 restores that blessing. The chapter had already restated the blessing positively (5:2). Now at the end, with Rest/Noah, it lifts the weight of the curse (5:29).

The overall pattern of Genesis 1–5 is one of a descent which, after creation's initial harmony (seventh, seventh, seventh—rest), spirals downward to the vengeance of Lamech (7, 77). But then, beginning with the first brief Adamite genealogy (Adam, Seth, Enosh), the descent is stopped, and there is a new equilibrium: a blessed Adam, an Enoch with God, and a Lamech who has both Rest/Noah and a life of 777 years.

Creation at the end is not without blemish. It carries within it the wounds of alienation and death—the scars and curses of Adam, Eve, Cain, and Lamech. The repetitive "he died" (5:8–31) can seem like a deathly tolling. Yet all this negative drama has been encompassed in a greater reality of blessing, rest, and relief.

The most plausible explanation for the composition of Genesis 1–5 is that—as with normal coherent literature—each passage builds on what precedes. In particular, chapter 2 builds on chapter 1 (it develops its high points and brings them down to earth); and chapter 5 builds on all of chapters 1–4. This explanation implies that the text is not linear; it contains depth and symbolism. It is art—coherent literature. Not just history, it deals also with the transcendent.

19 The Flood's Creation: More Sinful, More Compassionate (6:1–9:17)

Creation Undone (Chaps. 6–7)
Creation Remade (8:1–9:17)

Introductory Aspects

The Basic Story Line

Cosmic chaos, especially in marriage, is how the story begins. Some form of superhumans ("sons of God") indulge in a limitless number of bizarre marriages with human women. As a result God sets a limit to the extent of human life (120 years).

Then the story switches from marriage to the heart. The scene changes, as it were, from external chaos to its inner root. The heart in question, deeply evil, is human, but it also leads, for the first time, to the heart of God: God, pained at heart, regrets creation and decides to destroy it. The implication is that human life deserves not only to be limited but even to be wiped out. Creation is over.

Yet—surprise—the story introduces a figure of God-given grace: Noah.

When God tells Noah to build an ark, the process not only echoes the original creation; it also has its own harmony, with a covenant and couples: God promises to establish a covenant with Noah, and, within the context of that promised covenant, all the living creatures of the earth enter the ark, couple by couple. The story is careful to say, indirectly, that Noah and his sons had just one wife each (7:13), so the humans also were in couples. All these couples, walking in harmony into the ark, form a powerful contrast to the initial picture of marriage chaos.

But along with harmony there is doom—the apparently relentless flood. It begins in the year 600 (on the seventeenth of the second month). Having closed the ark, God goes away as it were—leaves the story—and the flood descends. In a slow repetitive scene—like the account of a nuclear cloud settling over the earth, settling, settling—the waters rise and rise. Eventually the waters cover the mountains by fifteen cubits (seven and a half yards)—enough to make sure no one survives. Not even giants (note the Nephilim, 6:4) could withstand fifteen cubits. Goliath was just over six cubits (1 Sam. 17:4), and Og, king of Bashan, the last of the Rephaim, was about nine (Deut. 3:11). Fifteen was too much.

But God remembered Noah. A wind caused the waters to recede, and gradually, beginning on the first day of a new century (the first of the first, 601), the earth dried. Just over a year after the rain began, the drying of the earth was complete.

When Noah went out and offered some animals in sacrifice, God was so pleased with the fragrance that he promised never again to punish people so badly. God's reason: because the evil in the human heart is so deep-seated. The same evil that originally led God to punish now leads God to compassion and fidelity.

Then, with a new command to increase and multiply, creation is reestablished, and with the new creation, reinforcing it, there is a covenant. God makes a promise of fidelity, and as a sign of the covenant he gives the rainbow—a colorful bridge that restores an appropriate link between heaven and earth. The story had begun with a heaven-earth relationship that was chaotic—the bizarre marriages—but now the heaven-earth relationship becomes one of covenant harmony.

The story has an extraordinary range—from the heights of the cosmos to the depths of the heart. It echoes ancient flood stories and so makes a great appeal to the imagination, but it also probes an inner world.

Given the enormity of the happening, it is not surprising that the account unfolds gradually. The text is dense and repetitive, building slowly through its various episodes. The terrible picture of the rising of the water, for instance, from the moment the water first lifts the ark until it finally tops the mountains by fifteen cubits, is described in four tense advancing stages (7:17–20).

As well as being densely repetitive, the account gives numbers in a way that seems inconsistent, even contradictory. In particular, the number of each species of animal entering the ark varies briefly but glaringly from two to seven twos (6:20; 7:2, 9). And the duration of the flood also seems to vary from 40 days to 150 days (7:17, 24; 8:3, 6). To some degree the discrepancy between 40 and 150 can be explained as referring respectively to the time of actual rain and the time of the subsequent cresting of the water. But the figures are so arranged in relation to one another (in 7:17, 24; and again in 8:3, 6) that initially at least they are jarring. At best the text is perplexing.

But the contradictions concerning numbers have a purpose. It is the contradictory number seven—seven pairs of clean animals—that makes possible the appeasing sacrifice. Had Noah stayed with just one pair of each kind of animal, he could not have offered the sacrifice that led God to move toward regarding the evil heart in another, compassionate, way. And if the number of days stayed at just 40, it probably would not have been possible for the new earth to emerge on the first day of a new century. It is the extra number of 150 that helps to fill out a year and bridge the gap between the start of the rain and the start of a new century—a new era. Thus it is the contradiction in the numbers that brings about the reconciliation and the suggestion of a whole new beginning.

A central idea emerges: forgiveness, the process of dealing with sin, requires rising above normal patterns of calculation. Normal calculating—counting in a superficial way, particularly counting injuries—leads to a dead end. Forgiveness moves beyond counting to another level of reality.

The contradictions in the numbers are not an isolated quirk. They occur within the context of a contradiction that is more basic and that frames the story: the reason that first leads God to punishment later leads God to a promise of compassion and fidelity. Initially, when God saw the waywardness of the human heart, God decided to destroy people (6:5–7). But later when, having smelled the fragrance of the clean animals, God again recalled human waywardness, God's decision was one of compassion and fidelity (8:21). Within God, compassion requires contradiction. Likewise in humans: compassion and forgiveness require the contradiction of normal calculations. A person has to stop counting and rise to another level of relating.

Literary Form (Mixed; Repeating)

Flood stories constituted a specific literary type—distinct from the three predominant literary types already seen in Genesis 1–5 (creation narratives, narratives of crime and punishment, and genealogies). In fact, flood stories abounded in ancient literature; there were hundreds of them (Westermann, I, 402).

Gen. 6:1–9:17 is a flood story of a particular kind: double, theological, and creation-related.

First, let us consider the idea of being double and theological. Some flood stories, especially those of Mesopotamia, are distinctive. They recount not only a flood but also a specific double involvement of the deity: they "begin . . . with the decision of the god or gods to destroy humankind by a flood and they end . . . with a modification of that decision" (Westermann, I, 402). The portrayal of the deity shows reflection; "the emphasis has shifted from the stark event of the flood to its theological significance" (ibid.).

It is this model—double and theological—that underlies the Genesis account. But Genesis goes further. What is double in Genesis is not only the kernel decision, but the overall structure. There are two major sections: a return to a form of watery chaos (chaps. 6–7) and the reemergence of creation (8:1–9:17). This progression—into water and out of it—causes a certain chiastic structure, centered on the phrase, "But God remembered Noah" (8:1). There is a crescendo and decrescendo (Westermann, I, 440). Details of this structure are debatable (compare Anderson, 1978, 23–29, and Clifford, 1990, 2:12), but the chiastic effect as a whole is clear and it helps to pull the entire text into a unity. Apart from being chiastic the deluge story is also a diptych, as will be seen. Thus the account is thoroughly double.

Second, the story is creation-related. In some Mesopotamian texts the story of a flood is linked to creation. In fact, "in a number of cases the flood narrative is identical with the creation narrative" (Westermann, I, 402; see Tsumura, 1994). This touches one of the key features of the Genesis flood: the entire account (6:1–9:17) echoes the preceding chapters, especially Genesis 1–3, and particularly Genesis 1. Panel one (chaps. 6–7) undoes creation; and panel two (8:1–9:17) remakes it. "The story of Noah and the Flood functions as a sort of second creation" (Barr, 1992, 77). This link to creation is examined below.

Furthermore—apart from being double, theological, and creation-related—this literary type is mixed with aspects of other literary types, including types already used. In particular, it repeats aspects of the creation narratives, and also has aspects of a story of crime and punishment (Westermann, I, 48).

This repeating and mixing at a basic level—the level of literary type—sets the scene for other forms of complexity, particularly the complexity and repetitiveness of the story line.

Complementarity of the Two Panels

The basic continuity between the two panels is clear, scarcely needing elaboration. The first panel tells of the flood's rising, the second of its abating. Together they form a kind of antithetic parallelism. It is precisely because of the many correspondences between the two parts that some authors see the whole as a chiasm (Anderson, 1978, 23–29, and Clifford, 1990, 2:12).

Other aspects of balance emerge by looking at other dimensions of the story, particularly its relationship to Genesis 1–5, and especially its relationship to creation.

Relationship to Preceding Chapters

The closeness of the flood story to the creation texts and to all of Genesis 1–5 involves three basic features—structure, contradictions, and content.

Despite greater volume and complexity, the structure of the flood story (see below) corresponds overall to preceding structures. While the panels of Genesis 1–2 contain, respectively, two main parts (in 1:1–2:4a) and three (in 2:4b–24), those of the deluge story are complementary: three main parts (in chaps. 6–7) and two (in 8:1–9:17).

The contradictions in the flood story have some affinity with those in creation. In creation the two basic contradictions concerned time and space—the normal framework for human calculations. In the flood the contradictions concern numbers. There is some inherent connection: time and space are often measured in numbers. One of the contradictions in the flood story—concerning the number of days—is clearly linked to the issue of time. (On details of the chronology of the flood, see Sarna, 376.) It is not clear whether the other, concerning the number of animals, is linked to space. (One of the most effective objections ever made against the historical truth of the flood story was based on space. In the 1860s a Zulu chief persuaded the local Anglican bishop, John Colenso, that so many animals could not fit in the ark, thus igniting a controversy that split the Anglican church in Natal.)

Incidentally, the repeated use of seven ("seven and seven . . . seven and seven . . . For in seven days") is in continuity with the triple use of seven in previous texts (2:2–3; 4:24; 5:31). The triple seven seems linked to rest—or its direct contradiction, vengefulness (contrast 4:24 and 5:28–31). The sacrifice, too, ends in a variation on the idea of rest: "As long as all the days of the earth, seedtime and harvest . . . day and night, shall not cease/rest" (šābat, 8:22). The sevens, therefore, are not something secondary; they are integral to the text, but they are artistic, surprising.

Thus there is a broad continuity between the creation-related puzzling references to time and space (Gen. 1–2) and the flood-related puzzling references to numbers (Gen. 6–9). In creation, God emerges as greater than space and time; in the flood story, this transcendence works for down-to-earth reconciliation: God eventually emerges as compassionate beyond the human way of calculating and counting.

The deluge story has several aspects of continuity with Genesis 1–3, among them the following:

The making of the ark (6:13–22) echoes the making of the earth. The building of the ark is a massive project, longer than a football field (300 cubits = 150 yards; a cubit, from elbow to finger tips, was approximately half a yard). But as well as being massive, the ark is like a fresh creation. As in Genesis 1, it follows, exactly, God's commanding word. Its three levels echo creation's implied three levels (sky, land, and water). Its covering echoes the firmament. Its contents are all creatures.

The increasing presence of the word is reversed (chaps. 6–7). One of the basic features of Genesis 1—the increasing role of God's word, increasing even in quantity—is reversed in the deluge story. God's word does have a role initially, in telling Noah to make the ark and to enter it, but, as the deluge comes closer (esp. in chap. 7), God's presence and word gradually fade away.

In chapters 6–7 there are several other lesser reversals or variations:

> The opening picture of sexual attraction—the sons of God seeing the daughters (6:1)—takes up where the story of creation concluded (the man's attraction to the woman, 2:23–24), but with a radical variation: the attraction, instead of leading to one marriage (2:24), leads to multiple whimsical marriages, deeply disordered.

> The disorder—humans are marrying "the sons of God"—echoes the disorder in the Garden, when the couple ate from the tree so as to be "like gods" (2:17; 3:5). Obviously the scene of bizarre marriages and giants also reflects other sources and strands (cf. Num. 13:33; Deut. 2:10–11, 20–21), including a possible mythological background, but its primary reference is its own context—the preceding chapters, especially the desire to be like gods.

> Yhwh's response to the disorder further echoes the second panel of creation. Originally Yhwh had blown the breath of life into the human being (2:7), but now Yhwh says, "My spirit shall not abide in humans for ever" (6:3). The original giving of the divine spirit is to be curtailed.

Thus while the opening picture of disorder (6:1–4) is new in Genesis, and probably has resonances of multiple sources, as it now stands it is so placed and formulated that it also resonates the Garden of Eden, or at least Eden's ruination. "At the beginning . . . humans strove to the level of divine beings, and God intervened. Humankind cannot be immortal. Here divine beings lower themselves to the level of humans, and God intervenes. A severe limitation on human longevity exists" (Sarna, 45).

The first two divine actions in Genesis 6—"Yhwh said . . . Yhwh saw . . ." (6:3, 5) echo the divine actions of the first day: "God said . . . God saw . . ." (1:3–4). But again there is a radical variation: what looks good now is not the light ("God saw that it was good") but the women ("The sons of God saw . . . that they looked good"). And what Yhwh saw was not good but evil: "Yhwh saw that the evil of humans multiplied" (6:6). The contrast continues:

1:31: "God saw all that he had made, and behold, it was very good."

6:12: "God saw the earth, and behold, it was corrupt."

At one point the deluge account refers explicity to creation but does so only to stand the idea on its head: "I will wipe out humankind whom I have created . . ." (6:7).

Table 19.1. Creation and the Flood

Genesis 1	Gen 8:1–9:17
God's *rûaḥ* on the waters	God sends a *rûaḥ*, so waters subside
Days 1–3	Part one (8:6–14)
Let there be light	Opening the window
The firmament	Releasing the birds
Dry land, plants	Olive branch; the land dries
Days 4–6	Part two (8:15–9:7)
	God: Come out . . . animals, birds
Lights to divide day, night;	Yhwh: All the days of the earth:
for seasons, days, years—	seedtime, harvest; summer, winter;
to shine on the earth	day and night shall not cease
Fishes and birds	
Animals, humans, blessing:	God blesses Noah:
Be fruitful, multiply . . .	Be fruitful, multiply . . .

Overall, then, the relation of the first half of the deluge story to creation is negative. Though the making of the ark itself is positive, echoing the making of the earth, much of the rest of chapters 6–7 involves reversals.

In the second panel (8:1–9:17), however, when the world emerges once more out of water, the echoing of the original creation is much clearer and more positive. As Genesis 1 began with water and led to two focal points—dry land and humankind (days 3 and 6), so does the emergence from the flood (8:1–9: 17). See Table 19.1.

As in Genesis 1, the text of the later creation (8:1–9:17, esp. 8:6–9:7) has two main parts, each with three sub-parts, and, as a whole, tends to increase in quantity. In particular, there is an increasing quantity of God's speech or word. (For further comparison of Gen. 8, 1–9, 29 with Gen. 1–2, see Kruger, 2001.)

Basic differences remain. In particular, the later creation does not have the serene rhythm of the original. But the flood's overall continuity with creation is central.

Leading Elements

PRIMEVAL RATHER THAN HISTORICAL

The link with creation helps to indicate that the flood account has a wide-ranging interest. Despite much discussion of its historicity, it is not possible to link it to a particular flood; "the flood narrative . . . is describing a primeval happening, not a historical event" (Westermann, I, 402). Even the geography is uncertain. The only place mentioned—the mountains of Ararat (8:4; not "Mount Ararat")—refers to the vast mountain territory of Urartu, north of Mesopotamia. The link with Mesopotamia is not central to the story. The Urartu mountains were once regarded as "the highest part of the world" (Clifford, 2:12); they reach 17,000 feet (Hamilton, I, 301). Apparently, the main idea for the biblical writer was that the ark came to rest on the world's highest mountains. Still, the mention of these mountains, however vague and symbolic, does begin to link the story of Genesis with the known world. The same was true of the rivers in the Garden of Eden; after some initial vagueness, they alluded to Mesopotamia (2:10–14). The geographical information, therefore, such as it is, has an affinity with Mesopotamia.

EVIL, GRACE, AND COMPASSION

The flood story is not only double and related to creation; it is also theological. Here especially Brueggemann's words apply: "the book of Genesis . . . is finally a theological statement. . . . Every scientific, historical, or literary analysis that misses this claim misunderstands the text" (1985, 338). The essence of the story, then, is not about a flood but about a theological reality.

The basic theological reality in question is grace. Grace does not come in some glib situation. It is when all is lost, when humankind is doomed, that the word "grace" (*ḥēn*) first appears in Genesis: "evil . . . evil . . . regret . . . pain . . . wipe out . . . regret—grace!" (6:5–8); "Noah found grace (*ḥēn*) in the eyes of Yhwh. These are the generations of Noah" (6:8–9). The initial pictures—of strange marriages and the evil heart (6:1–8)—are but a foil for the grace given to Noah. And with grace comes another new idea—integrity (justice/justness); "Noah found grace" is quickly followed by "Noah was a just man" (*ṣaddîq*, 6:8–9). The sequence—grace-just—is not an accident.

The root of the whole drama is the heart. The picture of the marriages implies that something is seriously wrong. At first, Yhwh simply limits the damage—reducing life's years (6:3), but then it becomes necessary to face the problem more fully: "Yhwh saw that the evil of humans multiplied upon the earth; and that everything fashioned in the thoughts of the heart was only evil all the day long" (6:5). This could be a formula for cynicism and atheism. But in Genesis the introduction of the full weight of evil leads not only to grace but to a new sense of God.

Obviously God has been present from the beginning, yet that presence often seemed distant. As the story progresses, however, the sense of God gradually changes. Already, in Genesis 2, the more earthy view of creation, the idea of God is more personal than in Genesis 1. In Genesis 3 and 4, as disharmony intrudes, the personal element goes further—God is seen walking, then putting clothes on the couple, and finally, in a gesture that comes closer still, putting a sign on Cain, thereby implicitly touching him.

But in Genesis 6, when awareness of evil intensifies dramatically, the personal aspect reaches a whole new level. God is upset, full of regret, with a heart in mourning: "And God was pained [or mourned] in his heart" (Gen. 6:6). The hearts are far apart—human and divine—yet one affects the other. "What we find here is not an angry tyrant, but a troubled parent. . . . Israel's God is fully a person" (Brueggemann, 77–78). "Fully a person" will later be expressed in Jesus, but, long before the Gospels tell of Jesus weeping over Jerusalem, Genesis tells of God mourning over the world. What is essential is that the awareness of evil leads to the conclusion not that God is absent but that God is more involved than was thought—involved with the heart and the grief.

God's involvement may be seen in one central detail. The evil "fashioning" (Hebrew, *yāṣar*) that goes on in the human heart, in the inner workshop, close to the smithy of the soul (6:5), contains a precise verbal variation of God's original fashioning of humankind (Gen. 2:8, *yāṣar*). Even the worst human fashioning—including human action—is somehow a distant or distorted echo of the original fashioning by God. There is no way therefore that God is a stranger to what is worst within the heart.

God's response is twofold—radical condemnation (the flood), and saving grace. Previous offences had brought curses (3:14,17; 4:11), but the full realization of all the evil in the human heart brings a new low. The flood is like the gathering of all the curses and condemnations that have ever been heaped on the damned world. God's "destroying" of the earth is essentially the completion of the "destroying" already wrought by humans (6:11–13). And as the flood gathers, God fades: within the text, God's word gradually diminishes (6:9–7:16). By the end of the first panel, when the flood is all-conquering (7:17–24), God is not even mentioned.

God's second response, after condemnation, is saving grace. God remembers Noah, and the final outcome is not condemnation but a deeper form of acceptance. There are affinities with psychotherapy, but with grace. Psychotherapy helps people to enter their own darkness. The deluge story, as well as entering into the darkness, also indicates a way out, through grace. The world, especially Noah, is led to face the abyss of evil; but instead of floundering indefinitely in the morass, God remembers, takes a new view, and starts again. The result is a new stability.

COVENANT AND MARRIAGE: BIZARRE MARRIAGES AND
ORDERLY COUPLES

Within the context of rebuilding stability, the flood story gives special attention to an implicit message about marriage and covenant—covenant being generally understood as an agreement sworn before the gods, so that the gods would guard it.

The chaotic picture of marriage at the beginning of the flood account (6:1–4) is not something completely new in Genesis. The Lamech story tells of bigamy (4:23), a situation which, while accepted in some societies, does not seem to accord with the general biblical ideal. In contrast to monogamous marriage, introduced in a context of harmony (2:18–24), bigamy is introduced in a context of extreme violence (4:23–24), a situation that does not recommend such a marriage arrangement.

Later (Gen. 12–50) the patriarchs are either monogamous (Isaac, 24:67; Joseph, 41:50), or take extra wives/women only under some form of pressure: Abraham from Sarai (16:1–2); Jacob from Laban (29:20–30). (The concluding picture of Abraham's extra wife, women, and many children, 25:1–6, is so placed—between his son's marriage and his own death—that, rather than being a portrayal of normal life, it seems like a riddle, perhaps a way of evoking some extraordinary fertility.)

In any case, the violence-related Lamech story had contained the first mention of bigamy. But the pre-flood situation has become much worse. There is no sense whatever of limits and so marriage is a matter of whim.

Like so much else in the flood story, the emphasis on marriage involves a variation on the original creation. The creation scene had concluded with a harmonious story of sexual attraction (2:18–23) and with a culminating snapshot of marriage (2:24). The flood story implicitly restores some of the sense of monogamy and harmony. The first mention of Noah's wife and the wives of his sons is framed by the first references to the covenant and the animals: "I will set up my *covenant* with you, and you shall come into the ark—*you, your sons, your wife, and your sons' wives* with you. And from all that lives, from all flesh, you shall bring *two of each* into the ark, to keep them alive with you; *male and female* they shall be" (6:18–19). Here, as at the end (9:9), the covenant in some way includes all living creatures.

The link between marriage and the covenant is confirmed by the flood story's structure: in the balance between the beginning and end (between 6:1–8 and 9:8–17) the key ideas are, respectively, marriage and covenant. The marriages at the beginning are a completely disordered form of the union between heaven and earth (6:1–4), but the covenant at the end brings that heaven-and-earth relationship to a form that is truly harmonious (9:8–11).

The closing covenant, while contrasted with the disordered marriages (6:1–4), echoes the first marriage (2:24): like the first marriage it is presented with a culminating "This . . . This . . ." (*zō't . . . zō't*, 2:23; 9:12,17). Marriage, therefore, is interwoven in various ways with both creation and the covenant. As Niditch (13) comments on the first couple in Genesis 2: "The conjugal couple is the foundation of social and cultural relationships for the writers of Genesis. Even [in] . . . the renewed chaos of the flood . . . (Genesis 6–9), social order remains afloat on the ark in the form of Noah and his wife, his sons and their wives (6:18)."

Future patriarchs and leaders will sometimes have more than one wife, but the implication both at creation (1:1–2:24) and in the remaking of creation (6: 1–9:17) is that stable monogamy remains the ideal. Genesis retains that ideal but is realistic enough to live with compromises.

An apparent ideal of a different kind—vegetarianism (1:29)—is no longer upheld (9:2–3). Yet the abandonment of vegetarianism, far from indicating a careless attitude to life, is used as a starting point for imparting an increased awareness concerning lifeblood, and especially concerning the value of human life, the life of one's brother (9:4–5). The ghosts of Cain and Lamech, in all their aspects, are not to be tolerated.

Structure (Table 19.2)

The first panel (chaps. 6–7). Apart from the introduction and conclusion, this panel has three main parts—two focused largely on the ark (6:9–22; 7:1–9), and the third on the actual flood (7:10–16). The divisions are confirmed by elements of repetition—for instance, Noah's obedience to *God* (6:22; 7:9, 16). Obedience to *Yhwh* (7:5), however, concludes not a main division but a subdivision.

The second panel (8:1–9:17). Here, as in the first panel of creation (Gen. 1:1–2:4a), there are just two main parts. The first leads up to the reemergence of the dry land, the second to the reemergence of humankind.

Comment

Panel One (Chaps. 6–7)

[6:1–8] Introduction. Amid moral chaos (bizarre heaven-earth marriages), surprising grace. The opening of Genesis 6—the sons of God took many women, and God regretted creation (6:1–8)—has continuities with the preceding text, but it also marks a sharp break. It is new in content and tone, and it opens a whole new horizon.

The ultimate literary and mythological background to this text seems dense and elusive. It may include overtones of ancient mythical motifs. Hesiod, for instance, tells how goddesses united with mortal heroes and bore children by them (*Theogony*, 963–1022, esp. 967–968, 1019–1020). And *The Catalogue of Women*—attributed to Hesiod and attached to *Theogony* (West, 1985, 136)—speaks of "the women . . . who were the finest in those times . . . and unfastened their waistbands . . . in union with gods" (West, 1985, 2). But the background, whatever it may have been, has been sifted and remolded into something new. As it now stands, the story fits well into its context and is reasonably clear.

The story begins with chaos, not the watery chaos of Genesis 1 (1:1–2), but moral chaos—the union of the sons of God with as many "good" women as they liked, mighty men multiplying ("giants . . . mighty," 6:1–4).

Table 19.2. The Flood (chaps. 6–7 // 8:1–9:17)

The flood rises: creation undone (chaps. 6–7)

Introduction: The mighty men. Bizarre heaven-earth marriages (6:1–8)
    Multiplication: mighty men, endless "good" wives (6:1–4)
    The heart (human/divine); wipe out all. But Noah . . . (6:5–8)
Make the ark: God speaks much: the ark and the covenant (6:9–22)
    Noah as just. Make an ark, evoking earth (6:9–16)
    A flood. Covenant promised: all in ark, in twos (6:17–22)
Enter the ark: Yhwh speaks a little (7:1–9)
    Aboard, just Noah! 7 pairs of clean . . . for in 7 days (7:1–5)
    Boarding. One pair of all (7:6–9)
Floodgates open (year 600). No speaking (7:10–16)
    Floodgates, fountains and rain—for 40 days (7:10–12)
    Into the ark: man and wife. One pair of all (7:13–16)
Conclusion: The mightier flood. No God mentioned (7:17–24)
    Multiplication of mighty waters, above mountains (7:17–20)
    All on earth die—except Noah (7:21–24)

The flood abates: creation remade (8:1–9:17)

Introduction: God remembers (8:1–5)
    God remembers Noah, so waters start abating (8:1–3a)
    After 150 days: the mountain tops are seen (8:3b–5)
Creation remade: the earth/land (8:6–14)
    After 40 days: sending the raven, and dove (8:6–9)
    After 7 days and 7 more: sending the dove (8:10–12)
    Year 601 (on 1/1 and 2/27): earth drying, dry (8:13–14)
Creation remade, especially humankind (8:15–9:7)
    God says, "Go out . . . all." So all went out (8:15–19)
    Clean offering. Yhwh smells, says "Never again" (8:20–22)
    God blesses Noah at length (9:1–7)
Conclusion: The heaven-earth covenant: God will remember (9:9–17)
    The covenant (9:8–11)
    The sign: God will see the clouds and remember (9:12–17)

The brief picture (6:1–4) has two steps, two stages of intensifying chaos: first, the sons of God marry women (6:1–2); then, the Nephilim, literally "the fallen ones," not only marry but have children (6:4). "Sons of God" and "Nephilim" are related terms. Elsewhere the Nephilim are described as giants (Num. 13:33). In God's response, too, there is intensification. First, life is to be curtailed (8:3). Then, as the situation worsens, life is to be abolished (8:6–7).

But just as the initial chaos of Genesis 1 was met by God's creative action, the moral chaos is met by grace (6:8).

[6:9–7:16] **The ebbing of creation and of God's word.** In the main body of panel one (6:9–7:16) the three parts—the making of the ark, the entering, and the flooding (6:9–22; 7:1–9; and 7:10–16)—are distinguished from one another by elements of repetition (e.g., 6:9 and 7:1) and by their diminishing quantity, a symptom of the ebbing of creation. As already noted (in comparing the flood and creation), central to the diminution in chapter 6 is the diminution in God's word: at first (during the making of the ark, 6:9–22) God speaks most of the time; then (7:1–9) about half the time (i.e., half the text); and when the flood comes (7:10–16), not at all. In the end, when all is submerged (7:17–27), God is not even mentioned.

There is also a diminution—miniscule but precise—in the various concluding statements about Noah's response to God's word (6:22; 7:4, 10, 16):

"Noah did this; according to all that God commanded him, so he did."

"Noah did according to all that Yhwh commanded him."

". . . as God had commanded Noah."

". . . as God had commanded him."

Both divine names—God and Yhwh—are integral to this single delicate pattern of diminution. The names have been combined. Such combining of names had begun in chapters 4 and 5 (4:25–26; 5:2, 22–24, 29). There is further combining (7:11–12) concerning the sources of water—not only springs and sluices (cf. Gen. 1:6) but also rain (as in Gen. 2:5).

Noah never speaks in the flood story. In making the ark and in coming out of it, he simply obeys God's word—as creation once obeyed (Gen. 1).

[7:17–24] **The waters—multiplied mightily.** At the end of the first panel (7:17–24) the picture is not of mighty men multiplying (as in 6:1–4) but of mighty waters multiplying, even over the mountains (7:17–20); and all creatures—human and animal—are wiped out (7:21–24). Thus the mightiness that seemed so impressive at the beginning is overcome at the end by a mightiness that is greater.

Within this balance of introduction (6:1–8) and conclusion (7:17–24), the one exception is Noah. At the end of their pictures of doom these two texts add, respectively, "But Noah found grace in the eyes of Yhwh" (6:8), and "There remained only Noah and those with him in the ark" (7:23).

Panel Two (8:1–9:17)

[8:1–5] **Introduction. Spirit over the earth: God's remembering spans the dividing abyss.** When God remembers Noah and the ark, and sends a spirit (*rûaḥ*) over the earth, the picture is like creation—like the spirit that hovered over the waters (1:2). The process of remembering, therefore, is hopeful, full of creative energy. In a slow repetitive spiral, the waters recede until finally the heads of the mountains are seen. The slowness of the process emphasizes the extent of the abyss.

The ark comes to rest (*nûaḥ*, a play on Noah) on the Ararat/Urartu mountains, once regarded as the world's highest (Clifford, 2:12). This image, coming to the highest mountains, and resting on them, is like a first tangible step in reaching down and establishing peaceful contact with the earth. And it is after this that the contact takes another dimension: the mountaintops are not just touched; they are seen.

[8:6–9:7] **Remaking the earth—and incorporating the evil heart.** The emergence from the ark has two basic parts: ensuring that the earth is dry (8:6–14); and God's re-establishment of the animals and humans (8:15–9:7). These two parts correspond significantly to the two basic parts of creation in Genesis 1 (days 1–3, and 4–6), especially to the focal days (day 3, the dry land; and day 6, the animals and humankind).

Probably the most significant difference between the making and remaking of the earth—between Genesis 1 and 8:6–9:7—is that the remaking delves deeper, particularly into the relationship between good and evil.

During the original creation (Genesis 1) the emphasis was on goodness. Only on two days—days 2 and 5—was there a suggestion that perhaps something was less than good (day 2 omitted the usual "it was good," and day 5 did not maintain the usual increase in narrative quantity). During the remaking (8:6–9:7), however, there is a greater awareness of evil. In the first part (8:6–14), for instance, when Noah, seeking the dry land, sends out birds, the first bird out is the raven (8:7)—an ominous creature. And in the second part (8:15–9:7), when all emerge from the ark, and the order is given again to be fruitful and multiply (8:17; 9:1, 7), there is an explicit awareness of human evil (8:21, "what is fashioned in a human's heart is evil from youth").

Yet the remaking account does not lack hope and goodness. On the contrary, the sense of goodness, if anything, is greater. The raven comes from within the ark—as though evil, somehow, is encompassed in God's providence. And the image of the raven is more than balanced by the drama, gentle and extensive, surrounding the dove (8:8–12).

In the second part (8:15–9:7), when human evil is so explicit, the greater emphasis is not on evil but on reconciliation and compassion. Human frailty arouses God's fidelity (8:20–22). Central to this new situation is the sacrifice: "Yhwh smelled the pleasing smell, and Yhwh said in his heart, 'Never again will I curse the ground because of humankind . . . '" (8:21). The reign of the curse has ended (Fretheim, 393). And the evil in the human heart—originally the reason for the global condemnation—becomes a reason for compassion.

This new reality, this world of compassion, comes from Yhwh's heart. Earlier, when the human heart was first mentioned (6:5), it engaged Yhwh's heart also—causing pain (6:6). Now, when the focus returns to the human heart, the engagement of the divine heart is all-encompassing: the evil is incorporated as it were. The evil is not denied or condoned, but there is a greater reality—a greater heart, which provides a new context for dealing with people. Never again will God walk out on humans.

The new blessing and recommissioning (9:1–7) echoes the original creation (1:20–31, esp. 1:26–30), but with changes. Unlike the earlier vegetarianism, it is now permitted to eat animals. There is a restriction, however, on blood; and there is a solemn triple admonition against shedding the blood of humans: "I will seek an accounting. . . . I will seek . . . I will seek. . . ." The subsequent warning ("Whoever sheds human blood, by humans shall his blood be shed," 9:6) refers to capital punishment. This recognizes the reality of such punishment; yet the idea of killing the murderer is tempered by God's earlier protection of Cain through a sign ('ōt; 4:15).

[9:8–17] **Conclusion. Rainbow over the earth: God will remember the covenant with humankind**. To emphasize fidelity, God makes a covenant with humankind.

The sign ('ōt) of the covenant is the rainbow. In one sense the rainbow is a disturbing sign, radically honest: its association with rain means that it recalls the flood—including evil and condemnation; it recalls humans' problem. But the rain-related aspect, instead of being isolated as though there were nothing else in life, is encompassed in the rainbow's greater reality—a wondrous vision of calm, color, and promise. Evil is surrounded by a larger world of grace.

The covenant encompasses all humankind and all creatures. It provides the context for the later covenants with Abraham and with Israel. Though animals may be used for food, the covenant gives them an important place.

As in panel one (chaps. 6–7), there is a balance between introduction and conclusion—between God's remembrance of Noah (8:1–5, esp. 8:1) and God's promise to remember the covenant (9:8–17, esp. 9:15–16).

Both remembrances are involved with seeing. The introduction leads to the seeing of the mountain heads; the conclusion, to the seeing of the bow in the clouds. The perspectives are diverse, intricately so. Among other things, one suggests looking down at the mountaintops; the other, looking up at the clouds. Yet the basic message is clear: the gap between heaven and earth, the gap which from the beginning did not seem good (1:6–8), is being bridged. The distance may seem great, but God remembers.

Excursus: The Deluge and the Theory of Two Sources

The deluge account contains much repetition and variation, and so some researchers have suggested that it is composed from two sources—J and P (for discussion, see Campbell and O'Brien, 1993, 213–223; note Halpern, 1995, 16–34). To obtain a sense of this explanation it is appropriate to quote at length from Kselman's summary of it (91, emphasis added):

The Flood story has traditionally been a parade example of the Documentary Hypothesis, by which the J and P versions of the Flood story can be identified and separated. The presence of more that one source can be seen in the doublets and in the irregularities and inconsistencies in the narrative. Such *inconsistencies* include, for instance, the distinction of the divine names

"Yhwh" in J and "Elohim" in P; . . . the pair of each species brought into the ark in P (6:19–20) against the seven pairs of clean and the single pair of unclean creatures in J (7:2–3); and the forty days and nights of rainfall in J (7:4, 12) over against the flood's cresting after 150 days in P (7:24).

Further, there are *duplicate accounts* of the divine command to Noah to enter the ark in 6:18–20 (P) and 7:1–3 (J), of the entrance into the ark by Noah and his family in 7:7 (J) and 7:13 (P), and the promise never again to destroy the earth in 8:21 (J) and 9:11 (P). More examples can be found in any standard commentary. . . .

The final product is not an unimaginative collection of material drawn from distinct sources, but *an artful unified composition* arranged chiastically around the central affirmation in 8:1 that "God remembered Noah."

This explanation, however, contains radical problems, problems that are both general and specific.

In general: the explanation is not coherent. It implies two opposite procedures—mechanical juxtapositioning (regardless of overlap or divergence) and artistic unifying. One procedure is slavish, the other imaginative. Behind these procedures are two opposite attitudes—scrupulosity and freedom. The contradiction in the explanation is far deeper than the contradictions in the text.

More specifically, the theory is not supported by the details. There are several problems (see esp. Ska, 1994; 1996, 259–260):

1. The purported J story is seriously incomplete. It contains no account of making the ark or leaving it. Such lack of completeness is not explained by a desire to avoid repetition. The author had no problem with repetition as such; some minor details occur twice.

2. The so-called "double" entry to the ark (7:7–9, 13–16) does not require two sources. The doubled text is part of a single coherent repetitive style—similar to the repetitiveness of Genesis 17 (17:23–27). Essentially the same is true of other so-called doublets: they are part of a coherent repetitive style. Repetition is a basic feature of narrative, especially of biblical narrative (Alter, 1981, 88–113). Repetition results from various techniques (Niccacci, 1994). The issue then is not whether there is repetition but whether it is possible to discern the repetition's variation or purpose. The two commands about entering the ark (6:18–20; 7:1–3), for instance, have several variations of context and content, but they are sufficiently similar to build something important: the sense—amid a collapsing world—of momentum and continuity. Nor do the two diverse types of bird (the raven and the dove, 8:6–12) mean two sources. In Tablet XI of the Epic of Gilgamesh, the Noah-like Utnapishtim sends out three diverse birds—a dove, a swallow, and a raven (Brichto, 1998, 114)—but that does not mean three sources.

3. The language of some purported J material, especially as regards order and sacrifice, would normally be reckoned as late or priestly.

For these and other reasons, scholars such as Blenkinsopp (1992, 77–78) and Ska (1996, 259) have moved to the idea of a single (priestly) account, which was later retouched. In other words, rather than dividing the text fairly evenly in two, they attribute most of it to a single author and reserve just a small percentage to an editor.

This is an important advance. A higher percentage of the jigsaw is fitting into place. As each piece fits there is increasing plausibility to the simple idea that the whole text is a unity. Such unity is indicated by further features:

1. *Chiasm.* Kselman speaks of the flood story as artful, and highlights one artistic feature—the chiastic arrangement (91).

2. *The inextricability of J and P.* There is significant continuity of the flood story with diverse aspects of Genesis 1–5, especially with Genesis 1 (see above, "Relationship to Preceding Chapters"), and this continuity strengthens the idea that J and P are inextricable. For instance, within 8:1–9:17 continuity with Genesis 1 (attributed to P) is not limited to so-called P material; it includes texts usually attributed to J—for instance, the opening of the window, the appearance of a fresh plant, the emergence of the dry ground, and especially the promise of the seasons (8:21–22, a variation on the arrangement of the seasons in 1:14–18). Thus, the alleged J material cannot be separated from dependence on P.

And alleged P material cannot be separated from dependence on J. For instance, the emphasis on violence and not shedding blood (6:13; 9:5–6, two P texts) fits best not with anything otherwise attributed to P but with material attributed to J—the violence of Cain and Lamech (chap. 4). This confirms other data of a similar kind: the alleged P material of chapter 5 builds on alleged J material in Genesis 2–4 (see Chapter 18, "Chapter 5 as a Conclusion to all of Genesis 1–5").

The effort to disentangle two hypothetical sources sometimes reaches incredible proportions. For instance, "in a pericope assigned mostly to P [7:8–9] but with inexplicable intrusions from J, we are asked to believe that an intrusion from P is present in the J intrusion" (Brichto, 1998, 134).

At times both divine names are so embedded in a single seam of narrative that they belong together. For instance, as the commentary on 6:9–7:16 indicated, the various concluding statements about Noah's response to God's word (6:22; 7:4, 10, 16) contain a precise diminution:

"Noah did this; according to all that *God* commanded him, so he did."

"Noah did according to all that *Yhwh* commanded him."

". . . as *God* had commanded Noah."

". . . as *God* had commanded him."

Within this carefully-wrought picture of diminution—itself part of a larger pattern depicting the fading of God's word—both divine names are integral.

3. *The increasing intelligibility of using two divine names.* As a general principle, the use of two names does not require two diverse sources. In the David

story, for instance, the variation of name—"David" and "King David" (e.g., 2 Sam. 7:17–18)—does not mean two sources.

Furthermore, some of the variations in the divine name are becoming understandable. In Gen. 1:1–4:16 the gradual change—God, Yhwh God, Yhwh—was seen to accord with an increasing involvement of God in human problems. The first mixing of divine names (4:25–26) occurred in the panel that first mixed literary forms (4:17–26). And in introducing the deity into the deluge story (6:5–8), the use of "Yhwh" rather then "God" makes sense: "Yhwh" helps to distance the deity from "the sons of God" in 6:1–4 (Brichto, 1998, 140).

It is possible that something similar applies in the repeated references to God's commands: God commanded, Yhwh commanded, God commanded, God commanded (6:22; 7:4, 9, 16). The variation between God and Yhwh may perhaps be linked partly to structure: obedience to the commanding role of *God* forms a conclusion to the three *main* sections of panel one (6:22; 7:9, 16). Obedience to the commanding role of *Yhwh*, however, concludes a *subdivision* (7:5).

4. *The coherence of repetition and variation.* The phenomenon of repetition and variation is understandable not only in light of later chapters (e.g., Genesis 17), but especially in light of the chapters that precede; the many repetitions and variations in the deluge story are a more complex form of the repetitions and variations that occur in Genesis 1–5.

Genesis 1 is laden with repetition and variation. The days follow one another with a smooth rhythm, yet there are variations: the omission of "it was good" on the second day; the fifth day's failure to increase in quantity; the subdivision of days 3 and 6 into two parts. The deluge story has more of the same, but without the serenity. Genesis 2–3 brings further and greater kinds of variation and repetition. The genealogies (Gen. 4:17–chap. 5), by mixing both literary forms and divine names, prepare the way for the more complex mixing that occurs in the deluge story.

5. *The purposefulness of the most perplexing variations, the contradictions.* As already indicated (in summarizing the story line), there are three virtual contradictions—concerning God's attitude to human evil, the number of animals (two, or two by seven), and the number of days (40, or 150)—but these apparent contradictions, far from breaking up the story, bring out its meaning: to make peace with this troubled world, to have the capacity for forgiveness and reconciliation, it is necessary for God, and implicitly for humans, to rise above superficial calculation, superficial counting.

In conclusion, the idea of the unity of the flood story is not new. Already in 1978 Wenham (347–348) was clear: "The syntax, literary structure, chronology and Mesopotamian parallels all point to the unity and coherence . . . of Genesis vi–ix." As time passes Wenham's essential thesis is increasingly justified.

The theory of two combined sources lacks internal coherence; it contains contradiction. Nor does the theory correspond to the external data. The story's structure is chiastic and unified. Despite the text's openness to repetition, the purported J source is seriously incomplete. The criteria for distinguishing the sources are inconsistent. Materials allegedly belonging to distinct sources are inextricably bound into a unity. The text's pattern of repetition and variation is part of a larger coherent phenomenon that is found elsewhere in other forms (for instance, in Gen. 1 and 17). The variation in divine names is becoming increasingly intelligible. And even the most puzzling features, the apparent contradictions, fit well with the basic story: forgiving humankind means letting go of some normal calculations.

The theory of artistic unity is initially difficult—it means entering into a world of art—but, piece by piece, it begins to make sense. The elaboration of the artistry is not complete, but with each added detail of understanding there is confirmation that this is the direction in which to search for the coherence and meaning of the text.

20 Noah's Sons: The World's Mixture of Curse and Blessing (9:18–Chap. 10)

Humankind in Embryo: Three Sons Contrasted (9:18–29)
Humankind at Large: Three Sons' Sons Contrasted (Chap. 10)

Introductory Aspects

The Basic Story Line (from Diverse Sons to Diverse Peoples)

The story is about the development of the human tree—first about its roots (Noah and his sons; 9:18–29), then about its branches (the sons' descendants—a whole table of nations; chap. 10). The "table of nations" shows humankind as greatly multiplied, and, since multiplication was first associated with blessing (Gen. 1:22, 28), this is like a story of great blessing.

The first panel (9:18–29) tells how, when Noah, having planted a vine, was surprised by wine and lay naked, his three sons showed radically diverse attitudes toward him. Ham, father of Canaan, was contemptuous, but Shem and Japheth showed respect by looking away and covering him. The result is a sharp contrast: Ham is cursed, but Shem is associated with blessing. The third brother, Japheth, is grouped with Shem ("in the tents of Shem"), and so the basic contrast is between cursed Ham/Canaan and blessing-related Shem.

The second panel (chap. 10), the table of nations, a form of genealogy, looks like a picture of the nations of the known world. These nations, a total of seventy—seventy for fullness (cf. the seventy in Jacob's family, 46:27)—are presented as divided between the descendants of Shem, Ham, and Japheth. In simplified terms, Japheth peopled the north and west (from the Caspian Sea to Asia Minor and Greece), Ham, the south and east (from north Africa, through Canaan, to the Persian Gulf), and Shem, father of Eber, the center. The table contains some unknown names but it reflects genuine elements of history and geography (for details, see Clifford, 2:14; Sarna, 70–80).

To some degree, the story is extraordinary. The table of nations "is unique and has no parallel either inside or outside the Old Testament" (Westermann, I, 501); it is a "serious attempt, unprecedented in the ancient Near East, to sketch a panorama of all known human cultures—from Greece and Crete . . . through Mesopotamia . . . to northwestern Africa" (Alter, 42). However, insofar as Genesis 10 combines elements of world review, myth, and genealogy it corresponds partly to much of the work of Hecataeus of Miletus (ca. 520).

The story is puzzling. First, there is apparent confusion about the relative age of Ham: he is introduced as if he were second among the three sons ("Shem, Ham, and Japheth," 9:18; cf. 5:32; 10:1), but then he is depicted as the youngest ("when Noah . . . knew what his youngest son had done to him," 9:24). There is also apparent confusion about the relative location of Ham's descendants. In any ordinary ethnic classification of nations, Shem (Israel) and Ham (Canaan) would belong together; both are semitic. But instead of placing them together, the text uses them as a basis for dividing much of the world. There is, then, an apparent contradiction: they belong together ethnically, yet they divide the world. As Speiser notes (1962, 235–236) it is not clear what is the basis of the table's division or classification.

The apparent contradictions concerning Ham's relative age and location make more sense when seen in the context of earlier puzzles, especially those concerning time and space (in Genesis 1–3). As God and God's creation contain a level that is beyond space and time, so also does curse/blessing and multiplication. The contradiction concerning Ham's age is a signal that the text has other dimensions.

However, to appreciate the unity of the text (9:18–29; chap. 10), it is necessary to look at it more closely, first at its literary types.

Literary Form (Mixed; Repeating)

It is necessary first to set the context. The initial four diptychs (1:1–9:17) relied largely on four diverse literary types—concerning creation, crime and punishment, genealogy, and a flood. Within each diptych there was essentially just one literary type, and, within Genesis, it was new.

Here (9:18–chap. 10) one might hope for the same—essentially one literary type, and new. But the situation is not so simple. As already mentioned, art often tends toward complexity. Already, even in the third diptych (the two genealogies, 4:17–chap. 5) there was some complexity, a mixing: the Cain genealogy was interwoven with a further literary type—an achievement story. (That initial phenomenon of mixing opened the way for other aspects of mixing, including mixing of the divine names.) And the flood account involved both mixing and repeating.

Now, in the final two diptychs of Genesis 1–11 (9:18–chap. 10; and chap. 11), the basic patterns involve further mixing. They also involve repetition: they use literary types that were used already in preceding chapters.

This fifth diptych, concerning the sons of Noah (9:18–chap. 10), illustrates the change. The text goes back to previously used literary types, and it mixes two of them in one diptych—first a narrative of crime and punishment (Ham's intrusion on his naked father, 9:18–29), and then a form of genealogy (the table of nations, chap. 10). In this case (9:18–chap. 10), the phenomenon of repeating and mixing breaks new ground; instead of being a secondary feature, this repeat-and-mix process becomes primary. The two panels are repetitions of earlier types; and they are different from one another: the first is primarily a narrative of crime and punishment (9:18–29); the second, is primarily a genealogy (chap. 10).

The diversity of types is not total. Aspects of sameness or oneness still remain. The beginning and end of the crime and punishment story (9:18–19, 28–29) are like parts of a genealogy. But these aspects have now become secondary. Essentially, the literary types of the two panels are diverse, mixed.

Diversity of literary form may seem to preclude unity, but if the diversity fits into a larger unified pattern of increasing complexity, as it does, then the diversity makes sense.

Complementarity of the Two Panels

The primary clue to the basis for dividing the table of nations (chap. 10) lies not in ethnographic research but in the immediate literary context—in the preceding account of the radical divide between Ham and Shem, between cursing and blessing (9:18–29). In other words, the table of nations—while giving at one level a valuable sense of the world's diversity, and while containing genuine elements of history—is primarily concerned with something else, with a deeper level of reality, namely with people's relationship to curse and blessing. This is a level, which, as with other basic aspects of Genesis, is beyond calculations of time and space.

The table of nations, of course, never refers to curse or blessing. Yet in varying ways it reflects the story of Ham's offense. Some of the links between the two panels are as follows:

1. *The primary contrast between Ham and Shem.* As already mentioned, the primary division in both panels is between Ham and Shem. Furthermore, in both panels, the nature of the Ham-Shem division has a sharp edge. In the

first, Ham is to become Shem's utter servant. In the second (chap. 10), Ham's descendants include most of Shem/Israel's greatest enemies—Egypt, Babylonia, Assyria, the Philistines, and Canaan.

The effect of this portrayal is to defang the enemies, to demystify them: if Ham/Canaan is to be reduced to utter servitude (panel 1), then Ham/Canaan's imposing descendants in chapter 10 need not be feared.

2. *The role of Japheth—secondary and Shem-related.* In the episode of Shem's offense, Japheth is in some way secondary to the other brothers; in fact, he is assigned to the tents of Shem (9:27). In chapter 10, there is a related phenomenon. The list for each of the three brothers has essentially three parts:

"The sons of X . . ." (10:2–4, 6–7, 21–23).

"X begot . . ." (10:8–19, 24–30).

"(From) these . . ." (10:5, 20, 31).

But not for Japheth; the large central section ("X begot . . ."), so striking in the cases of Ham and Shem, is missing in Japheth; his list seems defective, in some way secondary. But then, curiously, his name turns up in the list of Shem: "To Shem also children were born . . . he . . . the older brother of Japheth" (10: 21). The presence of Japheth's name in Shem's list is the literary equivalent of dwelling in the tents of Shem.

Thus the two primary relationships between the brothers—Shem's central contrast with Ham, and Shem's incorporation of Japheth (9:18–29)—help to account for the curious shaping of the table of nations.

3. *The dramatis personae.* These are the only two texts that are built around Noah's three sons. The link is all the greater because "Noah's sons may be understood in both individual and eponymous terms, thus preparing the way for the table of nations" (Fretheim, 403). The interchanging of Ham's name with Canaan—otherwise puzzling—confirms this link with the subsequent genealogy.

4. *The framework.* The framework of the second panel ("after the flood," 10: 1, 32) echoes the first ("from the ark," 9:18; "after the flood," 9:28; 10:1, 32). And the introduction to the first announces the second: it looks forward to the peopling of the earth (9:19), and specifically to Ham's fatherhood of Canaan (9: 18, 25–27; cf. 10:6, 15–19).

5. *The sexual or generational dependence.* The second panel depends completely on the first—not only on Noah and the three sons, but precisely on the role of sexuality; without sexuality, there is no genealogy. Obviously a genealogy need not refer explicitly to sexuality, but an emphasis on sexuality, when it happens, is appropriate. In Gen. 35:21–29, for instance, the truncated genealogy begins with a picture of warped sexuality—incest. This emphasis on sexuality is particularly appropriate before giving the table of nations. The two panels are like root and branch: chapter 10 is like a great family tree with branches

spreading out to the whole world; the naked Noah and his three sons are like that tree's roots.

6. *The sandwiched position of Ham/Canaan.* As will be seen in the later comment, the position of Ham/Canaan in the initial introduction (9:18–19) corresponds broadly to the central position of Ham/Canaan in the table of nations (10:6–20): it is sandwiched between characters who are associated with what is good—between repeated references to Noah, man of grace (9:18–19); and, in chapter 10, between Japheth and Shem, men of blessing (cf. 47:7–10).

Hence, the list of seventy nations—while it looks matter-of-fact and does give an idea of how the world was seen—is so arranged that it reflects a further reality, namely the dynamics between the three brothers, and especially the dynamics around curse and blessing.

Relationship to Preceding Chapters

The dramatis personae of the naked Noah story complements that of earlier crime-and-punishment stories. It completes a primordial triad of human pairings: first, man and woman (chap. 2–3); then, two siblings (chap. 4); and now, parent and children.

It also echoes these earlier stories. It provides a further instance not only of crime and punishment but also of subsequent curse. The tension between Cain and Abel echoes in the division between Canaan/Ham and Shem (including Japheth). In particular, there are multiple links with the scene in the Garden —between looking at the nakedness of Noah in the middle of his tent (9:22, "Ham saw . . ."), and the naked woman looking at the tree (2:24–3:21, "the woman saw . . ."), a tree that was in the middle of the Garden (2:9) (in Hebrew the words for naked are diverse). The fruit of an unusual tree undoes the couple, bringing shame to their nakedness; and another kind of unusual tree, the vine, undoes Noah, thus revealing his nakedness to a shameful gaze. After the nakedness come covering and cursing. The curse, however, is announced by Noah, not by God (as in 3:14, 17; 4:11)—an initial reflection of the gradual process by which, as Genesis develops, God's role moves into the background.

As well as cursing, both texts tell of radical tension and a positive message. In the Garden there is a primordial struggle between the cursed serpent and humankind (the woman's offspring); and at Noah's vine there is a radical contrast between the cursed Canaan and the blessed Shem. The final, positive, message is of gaining a form of power over the one who brought the curse: the woman's human offspring will crush the head of the serpent; and Shem will enslave Canaan/Ham.

The Ham-Shem tension, therefore, is not just personal or political—not just the contrast between two brothers, or two specific peoples (Canaan and Israel). It echoes the primordial tensions in humankind as a whole, those between Cain and Abel, and especially those between the serpent and the woman's offspring.

Within the second panel (the table of nations, chap. 10) the individual who receives the most attention is Nimrod (10:8–12). The brief portrait of him ("mighty . . . mighty . . . mighty"), while it draws on extrabiblical material, also incorporates an echo of the city-building of Cain's son, Enoch (4:17), and especially an echo of the mighty men who preceded the flood (6:4, "mighty;" cf. the related use of "grew mighty . . . mighty . . . mighty," 7:18–20).

The second panel's opening phrase, "These are the generations . . ." (10:1), was first used in the account of creation (2:4a).

Leading Elements

What begins to emerge is not only that the two panels are a literary unity, but that in varying ways they echo a primordial struggle. At one level the text may be concerned with humankind's rich diversity, with its many nations, but at another level, a level that is more decisive, its concern is with humankind as a whole. Thus, even in depicting the division between the world's nations, it undermines that division; it subjects it to a dramatic struggle that is more radical, something shared by all humans.

That primordial struggle is against the curse, something variously associated with the serpent, with Cain, and with Canaan/Ham. This curse does not triumph; Canaan is to be reduced to the service of Shem, and with Shem there is God and blessing. Shem is the father of Eber (Hebrew), ultimately of Abraham and Israel, and so the blessing of Shem points to the future blessing of Israel.

Canaan then is largely eponymous or representative (Fretheim, 403). The cursing of Canaan is not primarily the cursing of an individual—not an individual's condemnation to slavery—but is part of the larger struggle against what Canaan represents.

Shem is not alone. With him, in his tents, is Japheth. Even if this sharing of tents has a local overtone—an allusion to Israel sharing specific land with another nation—its primary reference is to the way in which other nations (the sons of Japheth) will share the blessing of Shem and of Israel. This theme—the nations' sharing in the blessings of God's chosen ones—is scattered through the whole book of Genesis.

Structure (Table 20.1)

THE FIRST PANEL (9:18–29)

The first panel, concerning Noah's drunkenness and nakedness, has two main parts. These deal respectively with the crime and its punishment. The introduction (9:18–19) and conclusion (9:28–29) both refer back to the ark or flood.

Table 20.1. Noah's Sons (9:18–29 // chap. 10)

Naked Noah: the three sons contrasted

Introduction: Noah's three sons, "from the ark" (9:18–19)
Noah's vine/tree: nakedness and unwarranted seeing (9:20–23)
Cursed Ham/Canaan and blessed Shem (including Japheth) (9:24–27)
Conclusion: Noah's life, death, "after the flood" (9:28–29)

The nations: Noah's sons' sons implicitly contrasted

Introduction: Noah's three sons "after the flood" (10:1)
Japheth: a defective list (10:2–5)
Formidable Ham/Canaan: (10:6–20)
Fateful Shem (including mention of Japheth) (10:21–31)
Conclusion: these are the nations "after the flood" (10:32)

THE SECOND PANEL (CHAP. 10)

The second panel has three parts, one for each of the brothers. Subdivisions of Ham/Canaan (10:6–20) are tentative.

Comment

Panel One (9:18–29)

[9:18–19] Introduction. Noah's three sons as the root of all humankind. In many ancient flood stories, "the whole of humankind derives from those saved from the flood" (Westermann, I, 482), and so it is with Noah's sons. The introduction tells that "from these [three] the whole earth spread out [or was peopled]." In a sense humankind is starting again. As the initial beginning (at creation) was followed by the episode of the tree and the nakedness, so this new beginning is followed by the episode of the vine and the nakedness.

As sometimes occurs in Genesis's introductions, there is a hint of tension. The listing of the three sons, "Shem, Ham and Japheth," is followed by the jolting detail that "Ham was the father of Canaan." In biblical tradition, "Canaan" often evoked an evil adversary. Yet evil is not supreme. The mention of Canaan is sandwiched between a reference to Noah's ark and a second apparently unnecessary reference to Noah. Noah was the man of grace and justice (6:8–9). The allusion to evil is surrounded by allusions to good. The details may look casual, even repetitious and awkward, but they have a purpose, and they are a first indication that the following incident has deep dimensions.

[9:20–23] Noah's nakedness: Ham/Canaan's offense and Shem's devotedness. The episode describing Noah's offense begins by referring to Noah as "a man of the ground" (*'îš hā-'ădāmâ*)—a detail which, at one level, recalls the origin of humankind (2:6). Noah's planting provides both an etiology of the vine and an echo of the earlier troublesome tree in the Garden. There is no moral condemnation of his drunkenness and nakedness—any more than of the couple's nakedness. The trouble starts therefore (both in Eden and here) not with the nakedness but with an intrusive visitor—the serpent (in chap. 3) and now Ham.

Ham's intrusion on his naked father may be related to distant accounts— perhaps to a Zeus-Chronos story in which the son interferes sexually with the father (Alter, 40), and certainly to the description of how Lot's daughters sleep with their father (19:30–38)—but any such literary relationships have been adapted to the requirements of the present context, especially the context of the earlier story of the naked couple and the serpent.

Then the intrusive visitors, the serpent and Ham, spoke to others, enticing them. But the reactions are diverse. While the tree's looks caused the couple to give way to the serpent, the two brothers, Shem and Japheth, resisted Ham/ Canaan and his invitation to look. Unlike the couple, the two brothers have a healthy sense of limits.

The limits in question vary, at least at first sight. In the Garden, the limits concern life in general; by seeking knowledge of good and evil, the couple want experience of everything. In Noah's tent, the limit broken by Ham/Canaan seems more specific; it is obviously related to sexuality. In discussing the nature of Ham/Canaan's sexual offense it is possible to imagine that he did something sexually violent to his father, but the biblical text, which is not shy about reporting violence and sex, says nothing about any such action. It is more plausible then to take the text first of all in its literal sense: the offense lay in a lack of appropriate control of the eyes; "it is entirely possible that the mere seeing of a father's nakedness was thought of as a terrible taboo" (Alter, 40).

However, the sexuality in question is so basic (that of one's father), and the context is so broad—the discovery of wine, evocative of the vibrancy of life (Kazantzakis calls wine a miracle)—that it seems better to regard the issue as having a further dimension, as extending beyond sexuality to include something about life in general. Life, including sexuality, and especially including one's parents, is not to be looked at only in the raw. The two brothers show a respect that at one level is ridiculous. They do the opposite of what is expected in normal life; they walk backward, and they do not see where they are going. But in this riddlesome approach to their father, ultimately to life, they have a better sense than the intrusive Canaan of what their father and life are about. Respect for the larger dimension of life brings Shem and Japheth into the realm of God's blessing.

[9:24–27] The cursing of Canaan and the blessing of Shem and Japheth. As in the Garden, so here the emphasis on nakedness is followed quickly by judgment. In the Garden God appears and searches for the couple. Here Noah wakes and he knows what has happened. Then comes the cursing (of the serpent and Canaan); next, the picture of overpowering or enslaving the tempter (serpent/Canaan); and finally the positive message—ultimate victory for humankind, and blessedness for Shem. In chapter 3 the picture of that victory is obscure (crushing the head), but here the sense of blessedness is clear.

Shem is ancestor of Abraham (11:10–26), so there is a promise of blessedness for Abraham and ultimately for Israel. And Japheth is to dwell in the tents of Shem.

The role of Japheth is elusive. His name "may be the same as . . . Japetus . . . [from] Greek mythology" (Sarna, 45). Some suggest that Japheth represents those who, apart from Canaan, were Israel's closest neighbors, namely the Philistines (Speiser, 63). Vawter (141) suggests the Hittites, because to pronounce such a blessing on the Philistines is impossible. Von Rad (138–139) holds for the Philistines, for the Philistines did in fact share the land with Israel, and this sharing was "a great riddle in God's guidance of history" (von Rad, 139).

The trouble with this debate—Philistines? Hittites?—is that it is based on a reconstruction of the history of Israel rather than on the first clue to meaning—the context. The primary context in Genesis 9 is not the history of just one country; it is the primordial history of humankind, and the way in which humankind at large deals with life, especially the way in which blessing outweighs curse, enslaves curse.

In the light of Genesis 3 and the recommencement of humankind after the flood, Ham/Canaan and Shem represent two opposites, two poles of humankind; they have a local dimension, but they also represent curse and blessing. Japheth, however, is indefinite, not one group, but someone whose name ("Japheth" = Expansion) refers to a whole mass of humankind, a humankind which shares in the tents and blessing of Shem, ultimately in the blessing of God.

What is happening obscurely in the story of Japheth is something that in varying ways occurs throughout Genesis. There is an implication that God's blessing, though focused on individuals such as Shem and Abraham, is ultimately for all of humankind.

[9:28–29] Conclusion. After the flood, Noah's life and death. The conclusion comes back to Noah, to the memory of the flood, and to a total of years (950 years, "and he died") reminiscent of the pre-flood genealogy and its emphasis on the primordial idea of the likeness of God (chap. 5; cf. 1:26). The effect of this primordial-style conclusion is to anchor the story of Ham's offense all the more firmly in the ancient context, a context with implications for all of humankind.

Panel Two (Chap. 10)

[10:1] Introduction. "These are the generations . . . after the flood." The introduction fits well with the diptych's larger framework (with the other introduction and the conclusions, 9:18–19, 28–29; 10:32), and it looks to the future—to the emerging generations. But again, like the preceding panel, it keeps an echo of the past—of the flood. Even the phrase "These are the generations" is not new; it occurred at the end of the first panel of creation (2: 4a)—just before the account of the making of humankind.

What is important is that the introduction, instead of saying something like "This a table of the world's nations," gives a heading that resonates more with humankind at large rather than with its individual nations. Thus while the text that follows does indeed contain an extensive list of nations, a three-part "table" that reflects aspects of history and geography, that table has been adapted to fit another purpose, to express a more basic truth about humankind as a whole.

[10:2–5] **Japheth: largely north, and west, toward Greece. A defective list.** The Japheth list reflects in part the nations to the north and west—especially those between the Caspian Sea and Greece.

The principle that governs the list is not only historical; it is also literary and theological. Japheth's line of descent corresponds significantly with the place of Japheth in the episode of Ham's offence. There he received less direct attention than Shem and Ham, and the same occurs in this text. Though mentioned first here, he again receives short shrift; the list (10:2–5) is defective; there is no central section as in Ham (10:8–19) and Shem (10:24–30). And later, Japheth's name is placed in Shem's list (10:21). Thus Japheth, from a literary point of view, is placed in the tents of Shem—in Shem's section.

[10:6–20] **Ham/Canaan: south and east—including great powers. An imposing list.** This list, the biggest of the three, covers a vast sweep—from north Africa to Mesopotamia—and includes many great powers.

Again the shaping of the historical and geographical data is influenced by literary and theological factors. The most obvious literary influence is from the preceding Ham episode (in chap. 9): Ham's centrality and his aggression in dealing with his father helps to explain the nature of this long imposing list. But there is influence also from earlier chapters, especially from the picture of the mighty men who preceded the flood (6:1–8). And the implied enmity between Ham/Canaan and Shem (9:25–26), itself an echo of a deeper enmity (3: 15), helps explain why the Ham/Canaan list contains many of Israel's most powerful traditional enemies—Egypt, Babylonia, Assyria, the Philistines, and Canaan.

Dominating that list is Nimrod—the earth's first mighty potentate and the founder of a kingdom that included Babylonia and Nineveh (10:8–12). Nimrod is introduced as like an archetype (Alter, 43). He should have been a terrifying figure—the personification or incarnation of overwhelming power. But the story demystifies him. In the figure of his ancestor Ham, the weakness of his foundations have already been seen; ultimately his fate is not mightiness but servitude. The description of him as "mighty . . . mighty . . . mighty" recalls the mighty men who were washed away by the mightier flood (6:4; 7:18–20). To emphasize God's presence, Nimrod's hunting is placed "before Yhwh," in other words, subject to Yhwh (10:9).

Hence, while the portrait of Nimrod may have drawn on multiple sources (the Mesopotamian cities named Nimrud; the epic figure of Gilgamesh; and various kings and kingdoms), the present biblical portrayal of him is distinct and is fully integrated into the larger biblical narrative. He is a synthesis of raw power, but his power loses its terror, and so correspondingly does the list of enemies and all other mighty rulers.

Both Ham and Nimrod (Ham's grandson) represent superficial views of the world—a world in which the wonder evoked by wine-related sexuality is set at naught, and in which intimidating power seems to be everything.

[10:21-31] Shem, father of Eber (= Hebrew). The contrast between Ham/Canaan and Shem—one cursed, the other associated with the God of blessing (9:25-27)—is reflected also in the list of Shem. While the line of Ham/Canaan/Nimrod degenerates into that of Sodom and Gomorrah (10:19), the line of Shem leads to Eber (Hebrew) and his eldest son Peleg (Divide), both of whom will reappear in the genealogy that leads toward Abram (11:14-19).

The curious allusion to Divide (Peleg)—"for in his days the earth was divided" (10:25)—refers at one level to the physical dividing or scattering of peoples, or perhaps to the dividing, literally "splitting," of the earth, for instance through a cataclysmic earthquake (Alter, 44).

Incidentally, as a speculative question it seems worth asking whether, at another level, Peleg intimates division of a more radical kind, namely between diverse attitudes—attitudes that eventually bring curse or blessing. Peleg represents a certain parting of the ways: his name is the last from the table of nations to enter the genealogy leading to Abram (10:25; cf. 11:18; his only brother's line ends in an eastern mountain, 10:26-30). Abram will bring a certain dividing of the earth—a division between blessing and cursing (12:3). It was a division that was already prepared in the contrast between Ham and Shem.

This division between curse and blessing does not imply some narrow dualism or exclusivism. The figure of Ham/Canaan, echoing the couple in the Garden (and echoing elements of Cain), represents an aspect of humankind at large. And Shem is accompanied by Japheth—a brother whose list is defective but whose name means Expansion. Together the lists of Japheth and Shem surround that of Ham. And Ham, with Nimrod and all the enemies, has already been demystified. Thus the initial sandwiching of Ham/Canaan between two references to Noah (9:18-19) is now repeated at a larger level—in sandwiching the whole Ham/Canaan line of descent between the lines of two people who have been blessed, namely Japheth and Shem.

As a result the world becomes a less threatening place. The sense of grace and of renewed blessing that marked the story of Noah continues in the story of the respectful attitude that led Shem and Japheth into the realm of blessing. The shadow of Ham/Canaan may loom large both near Noah's tent and among the nations, but in principle, Ham has already been contained, and Canaan ends near

Sodom and Gomorrah (10:19). Nimrods have their effect, perhaps their place, but they are not the measure of reality. God's overpowering of the mighty, first seen in the flood, continues in varied form both in Nimrod and in those who follow him in history. The complexity—which, like the complexity of the world, may seem intimidating—comes essentially to a total of seventy, a number that connotes something positive, something full and unified. It is possible then to read the list of nations, not as something turgid or intimidating, but as a map inviting people to accept the blessed command to fill the earth (9:1).

[10:32] **Conclusion. Clans, generations, nations.** The conclusion, while echoing the introduction, is more expansive: not just "generations" (10:1) but "clans, generations, nations . . . nations spread abroad on the earth." Such expansiveness is like a positive affirmation of the world.

21   Failed Tower and Fading Family: Life's Fragmentation (Chap. 11)

The Towering City Fails (11:1–9)
The Great Genealogy Fades (11:10–32)

Introductory Aspects

The Basic Story Line

The story tells of a journey that comes to a halt. The human race, speaking one language, stops and becomes engrossed in an ideal world: all the people, using the best of human resources—language and technology—join together to build the ultimate city, with a tower reaching to heaven, a city that will provide them with their destiny ("name"). Cities and impressive buildings—from Luxor to Paris, from ziggurats to skyscrapers—have often captivated human imaginations—and the Babel story tells of this captivation reaching its ultimate stage, where it becomes the be all and end all of human existence. Like the thought of the ultimate city, then, the story of Babel is fascinating.

What emerges as the story goes on is that the great project is narrow. It leaves no room for anything beyond what is humanly calculable. And so God comes down and scatters the people, sending them away into a world that is diverse and wide—beyond the power of their language and technology. The particular way in which God does this—by confusing their language—is used to account for the diversity of languages.

The people's failure was in a form of idolatry—turning a human project, however splendid, into their complete destiny. God's purpose was for something greater—something that involved filling the earth (1:28; 9:1). Even today when the world has been explored, the idea of filling the earth remains as a reminder of a purpose that surpasses narrow plans, breaking those plans in order to reach something further.

The failure of the city is followed by the threatened failure of the bloodline: the genealogy of Shem (11:10–32) not only shrinks to ordinary lifespans (11:10–26); it also comes face to face with premature death, barrenness, and a family journey that peters out (11:27–32). The bloodline is going nowhere. It comes to a halt in Haran—essentially the same name as that of the young brother who died prematurely. Haran is literally the last word.

Thus, city and genealogy both fade. "The glories of our blood and state are shadows. . . ."

Unlike previous diptychs, chapter 11 does not contain an internal contradiction, but the Babel story contradicts what precedes: the human race, instead of consisting of diverse peoples with diverse languages as was said clearly in chapter 10 (esp. 10:3, 20, 33), seems united—having one language (11:1). At some level, the relationship to the preceding chapter is dialectic (Alter, 45). It is as though life itself contains a contradiction. On the one hand, life is exuberant; it generates surprising vines and expanding nations (9:18–chap. 10). On the other hand, life crumbles (chap. 11).

Among the diptychs of Genesis 1–11 this is the shortest. Particularly short is the story of the tower—the tower that was supposed to reach the heavens. The genealogy (11:10–32), though longer, is even more bereft: it is the only panel in Genesis 1–11 where God is never mentioned; and no one ever speaks. The word has gone.

Literary Form (Mixed; Repeating)

Here, as in the preceding diptych, the literary form of the two panels is mixed: first, an episode of crime and punishment (the tower of Babel, 11:1–9; Westermann, I, 53, 535–536), and then a genealogy (11:10–32). The later part of the genealogy (11:27–32) is like the Babel narrative—a story-type narrative.

As well as being thus mixed, the diptych contains further complexity. The Babel story combines several motifs (language, technology, scattering), and the genealogy is double (first the generations of Shem, then the generations of Terah).

The overall complexity seems connected to the diptych's role as a conclusion—the closing of the initial history (Gen. 1–11). Conclusions generally try to draw things together, and so it is here.

Complementarity of the Two Panels

At first sight the two panels may appear unrelated—one a sharp drama, the other a colorless genealogy. Yet there are indications of unity.

1. *Kinship to unified texts*. Genesis 11 is akin to two unified texts, and this kinship helps to clarify its own unity. It is akin first of all to the diptych concerning Noah's sons (9:18–chap. 10). Here (9:18–chap. 10) the mixture of literary types—a crime-and-punishment story, and a form of genealogy—provides a precedent for the mixture of literary types in Genesis 11.

Chapter 11 is also akin to the genealogies of Cain and Adam (4:17–chap. 5). The Cain genealogy begins with city-building and technology (4:17–22); and the Adam genealogy (chap. 5) is linked to that of Shem. In outline:

4:17–chap. 5:   A city-building genealogy.   And a final genealogy (Adam–Shem).

Chap. 11:   Building a city tower.   And a final genealogy (Shem–Abram).

The kinship of Genesis 11 with 4:17–chap. 5 is confirmed by general position. Within Genesis 1–5, the Cain-Adam genealogies form a third, closing, diptych; and within Genesis 6–11, the diptych in chapter 11 is also third and closing. Both these third-placed diptychs are unusually distinct from what precedes them. They break away, as it were, one from the first couple and their sons, the other from Noah and his sons. Thus, the unity of 4:17–chap. 5 provides a strong precedent for the unity of chapter 11.

2. *Shared continuity with the table of nations (Gen. 10)*. Both panels develop elements from the preceding table of nations (chap. 10). The ambitious building of the city tower at Babel in the land of Shinar involves a variation on the mighty Nimrod. The beginning of Nimrod's kingdom was "Babel . . . in the land of Shinar . . . he built . . . Reheboth-Ir [= the wide-street city] . . . and Calah, that is the great city" (10:10–12). And the genealogy of Shem (11:10–17) distills the basic sequence of chapter 10: "Shem, Arpachshad, Shelah, Peleg" (10:21–25). Thus both panels of chapter 11 have roots in chapter 10.

3. *The shared location—Babylonia/Chaldea*. In all the preceding episodes (Genesis 1–10) the location of the action was either unmentioned, vague, or regional (Ararat and Nimrod are regional, but approaching specificity). In chapter 11 the specificity is greater: the panels are linked primarily not only to a particular area, but to the same area—Babylonia/Chaldea. Within the narratives of each panel there are two well-separated references:

11:2, "in the land of Shinar" [= Mesopotamia in 10:10].

11:9, "its name was called Babel."

11:28, "in Ur of the Chaldeans [Babylonians]."

11:31, "from Ur of the Chaldeans."

4. *The shared movement*. The shared location (Babel/Chaldea) is part of a larger affinity: both panels—not merely the first—contain a story line. The second story, concerning Terah and his family, occurs in the later part of the genealogy (11:27–32). Hence while the primary literary types are mixed, at a secondary level there is greater affinity.

More specifically, the references to Shinar/Babylon/Chaldea occur within a larger picture of movement—eastward to Babylonia (11:2), and from Babylonia to Canaan (11:31). To some degree, this larger picture simply reflects "the book's perspective that all the nations originated in the East (Gen. 3:24; 4:16)" (Clifford, 2:19). But the references within chapter 11 have a particular continuity:

11:2   "And . . . as they tented . . . eastward,
        they found a plain in . . . Shinar . . . and they settled there
        (wa-yēšĕ<u>š</u>bû šām)."

11:31   "And Terah brought them forth . . . from Ur of the Chaldeans but when
        they came to Haran, they settled there (wa-yēšĕ<u>š</u>bû šām)."

The repetition of "And they settled there" provides a precise framework for the whole diptych, sealing the unity of the two panels.

There is strong evidence then that the two panels form a unity.

Yet an impression of fragmentation remains. Many commentators not only split chapter 11 into two unrelated episodes; they also assign its conclusion (11:27–32) to the Abraham story.

However, the impression of literary fragmentation has a certain appropriateness. It coincides with the diptych's message: life is fragmented and frail, and it is ultimately overshadowed by death. Fragmentation and fading occur in the scene not only as ideas but as part of the scene's literary fabric, as part of the way it is composed. Thus, while, at one level, Genesis 11 is fragmented and defective, at another it is delicately unified. The brokenness of life, even the fading of God and of speech, is encompassed by a structure, a word, which at some level holds it together.

Relationship to Preceding Chapters

The discussion of the diptych's unity has already mentioned its main connections with preceding chapters: the same mix of literary types as in the diptych on Noah's sons (9:18–chap. 10); a variation on the building-genealogy sequence of 4:17–chap. 5; and use also of the building and genealogy elements from chapter 10 (see van Walde, 1994, 104–109).

There is a connection also with the creation story. The pretentious decision to build to the skies, "Let us bake bricks . . . Let us build ourselves . . . Let us make ourselves a name" (11:3–4) contains a distorted echo of God's original decision to make humankind ("Let us make humankind in our own image," 1:26).

The most radical continuity, however, is between the Babel story and Genesis 3 (Westermann, I, 554–555). The pretentiousness that once spoiled the dreamlike Garden of Eden now spoils the practical world of work and technology. The hubris of the first couple has become the hubris of all. Both texts begin with an idyllic situation (naked and unashamed; one in language), but then, through a discussion, there develops an ambition which in effect seeks to replace God (in the Garden, they wish to be like gods; at Babel, the city is to become a new self-made space, an alternative to God's space). The ultimate motivation in both cases appears to be fear: fear of death (in chap. 3); and fear of being separated or scattered (11:4).

Then God arrives, walking in the Garden, coming down to see the city, and what previously was idyllic—the nakedness, the language—is now confused. Instead of achieving their godlike ambition, those who are confused are banished from their unreal dream—out of the Garden, over the face of the earth.

Leading Aspects

At one level, as a museum piece, the Babel story connects with the past—with the building of towers (ziggurats) and with the ancient diversity of languages— but, at another level, as a meditation, its primary focus is toward what is true now: the shattering of groups and plans is not necessarily a bad thing; it may open the way to something broader, to a truer destiny. "Diversity inheres in God's intention for the world. . . . Unity will be forged most successfully in getting beyond one's own kind on behalf of the word in the world" (Fretheim, 414).

God's scattering of the people—the breaking of unity—has been used to justify racial apartheid. But the unity in question was idolatrous, a unity without God. The need to destroy idolatrous unity does not mean that unity as such is to be destroyed. In the words of Desmond Tutu, addressing an all-white government commission of inquiry in Pretoria, in 1981: "It is a perverse exegesis that would hold that the story of the Tower of Babel is a justification for racial separateness, a divine sanction for the diversity of nations. It is to declare that the divine punishment for sin had become the divine intention for mankind" (Sparks, 1990, 291). When the sin has been punished, when the false unity has been destroyed, the original ideal remains, namely the unity of all humankind, all races, under God. That unity was the implication of the creation account, and that also will be the implication of the call of Abraham (12:1–3); his blessing is shared by all.

Structure (Table 21.1)

Despite its brevity, the Babel story has a complete structure: introduction, conclusion, and three parts, the third of which is twofold—an abbreviated version of the structure found in the first creation story.

PANEL ONE (11:1–9)

The three-part structure of the Babel story is sequential: it sees the text as progressing, in sequence, from beginning to end. The Babel text may also be

Table 21.1. Failed Babel and Fading Family (11:1–9 // 11:10–32)

Building Babel: the city fails

Introduction: one language in the whole earth (11:1)
As a journey stops, an initial ambition: developing technology (11:2–3)
The next ambition: a city, with a tower to the sky; make a name (11:4)
Yhwh's response
   This ambition has no sense of limits (11:5–6)
   Scattering the people (11:7–8)
Conclusion: Language confused; scattered in the whole earth (11:9)

Shem's genealogy: the family fades

Shem's generations: defective (nine), diminishing (11:10–26)
The Terah family (11:27–32)
   The people: premature death (Haran), and barrenness (11:27–30)
   A journey that stops (ending in Haran, 11:31–32)

seen as chiastic, where the emphasis is not so much on the beginning and end but on the middle (Fokkelman, 1975, 22). As often in biblical texts, the two structures—sequential and chiastic—overlap and complement one another. The water on the shore, for instance, can have complementary patterns, one caused by a passing ship, the other by the wind (Giblin, 1985).

PANEL TWO (11:10–32)

The genealogy seems to be defective. It has nine generations (for Shem), not the standard ten; and apparently has no introduction or conclusion (unless perhaps 11:10a and 11:32).

Despite its limitations, the genealogy is double or twofold—first "the generations of Shem" (11:10–26), and then "the generations of Terah" (11:27–32). The Terah section in turn is twofold (first, the people; then the journey). As for the list of the nine generations of Shem (11:10–26), it is not clear, at least not to the present writer, whether or how it should be divided. Perhaps it falls into four generations and five (after the fourth generation there is a shift to Peleg and to much smaller totals).

The genealogy's two parts (11:10–26; and 11:27–32) have diverse styles— thus causing some commentators to separate them—but, on closer inspection, they form a unity. Each part begins with the distinctive "These are the generations of . . ." (11:10, 27), and each concludes with some form of the word "Haran" (11:26, 32). The repetition, within one panel, of "These are the generations . . ." occurs also in the complex genealogy of Esau (36:1, 9). The idea of a double genealogy (Shem-Terah)—two distinct genealogy-related texts within a single panel—finds a partial precedent in the Cain-Adam genealogy (4:17–26). The concluding part of the genealogy lists three sons (Abram, Nahor,

and Haran—three "executive" sons, 11:26), a feature found also in the genealogies of Cain (Jabal, Jubal, and Tubal-Cain, 4:20–22) and Adam (Shem, Ham,
and Japheth, 5:32).

For those who understand genealogies, the deficiency in the list of generations is so stark—nine generations instead of ten—that Genesis's first translator, the writer of the Greek Septuagint, inserted an extra generation. Yet the
deficiency probably has a purpose. It accords with the larger picture of the
Shem-Terah clan as fading—fading in life span, in fertility, and in ability to
reach a desired destination. Like the failure at Babel, but more so, this fading
process expresses the inadequacy of human energy, and so it evokes the consequent ebbing of life, and the shadow of death.

Again the text is not only a form of history; it is also artistic, poetic.

Comment

Panel One (11:1–9)

[11:1] **Introduction. One in language and words: a world that is idyllic
but unreal.** The brief introduction suggests an idyllic state—the whole world
had one language, literally, one tongue. In the Garden (2:24–25) there was a
different kind of idyllic picture, that of the couple who formed one body, and
who were naked but unashamed. This echo of creation suggests language's
extraordinary role, its place as a defining element of humankind at large.

[11:2–4] **Technology for a towering city, for redefining humankind.**
The action begins with a decision to settle down, as though all humankind,
speaking one language, decided to settle in one place. (For the moment the
complexity of chap. 10 is left aside.) This decision to settle seems innocuous,
yet it does not accord with the original plan of creation to "fill the earth" (1:
28). Instead of following the divine momentum, they stop and try as it were to
establish a private world.

The sense of a private world is reinforced by what follows. They become
absorbed first in the technology of brick-making, and then in city-building,
including a tower reaching to heaven. The image of the tower may have been
prompted in part by the temple towers of Mesopotamia, but the primary inspiration for the idea of the tower "was not monumental architecture but literary
tradition. . . . We need look no further than the account [in *Enuma Elish*, VI,
60–62] of the building of Babylon and its temple" (Speiser, 75) (on Babel and
Troy, see Appendix 3 comparing Genesis 11–13 and Od. 1).

More important, however, than the story's source—whether architectural or
literary—is the story's content, especially the attitude of the builders. On the
one hand, they are being very successful. Their language and technology are
flowing. The language contains wordplay, and the building technology sounds
impressive. The interweaving of the two—the wordplay and the technology—

suggests great energy and achievement. These humans, it may seem, are at their best.

It is no accident that subtlety of language, including wordplay, reaches a highpoint in Genesis 11. It is a way of exhibiting, through the narrative's quality, through its form, what the narrative is describing—a situation where people feel they have a complete command of language, and ultimately of reality.

On the other hand there is a shadow over their work. As already noted, their words ("Let us bake bricks . . . Let us build ourselves . . . Let us make ourselves a name") have echoes of God's making of humanity ("Let us make humankind . . ."). Such echoes can be a positive sign—a reinforcing of God's original decision for humans. But they can also suggest a replacing of God's original decision. That in fact is what is happening. There is an "arrogant abuse of technology" (Westermann, I, 53); and "the prose turns language into a game of mirrors" (Alter, 47). The builders' vision has become narrow—something seen in their decision to make their own "name" or destiny. It is God who makes a name great (12:2). They think they have the measure of the cosmos and that they can redefine humankind. There are shades not only of Genesis 3 but also of Communism, Nazism, and other human structures, including some religious structures.

[11:5–8] **The city flounders: scattering the builders to a wider world.** When Yhwh arrives on the scene there is an implication of both closeness and distance. On the one hand, Yhwh is close—close physically, having come down to see, and close in language. God's words, "Come, let us . . . ," imitate those of the people. On the other hand, there is a great distance. Even to see what the people are doing, Yhwh has to come down. And there is no direct communication.

God's coming down, just to be able to see the great tower, is humorous; but the mixture of closeness and distance has a poignancy, an evoking of breakdown in relationship.

The verses that follow compound that sense of breakdown. Not only does God decide to confuse (or babble) their language, but the very account of doing so seems confused, lacking in continuity (Westermann, I, 535). In particular, the decision to confuse (11:7) is followed not by an account of doing so but by an account of doing something else—scattering (11:8).

The result is that unlike the communicative purposeful flow which pervaded the initial part of the story (11:2–4), a flow which at one level was directed upward, this later section (11:5–8) begins with a going downward (by God) and then descends further into fragmentation—into confusion and scattering.

There is some sense of paradise lost. God's confusing and scattering "resembles the expulsion of the man and the woman from further contact with the tree of life, lest they eat of that tree too (3:22–23)" (Clifford, 2:15). But the paradisal city was ultimately unreal, and God's scattering of it, though at one level a punishment, at another is an act of release.

[11:9] Conclusion. The present situation: Babel, languages, and scattering. As sometimes happens in Genesis (cf. 2:24), the conclusion is etiological: it uses a past story to explain the present. Here it explains the name Babel (Babylon), the diversity of languages, and the scattering of people throughout the world. The explanation of these features is not strictly historical, but theologically it sets them in place: however complex their origin, however daunting they may appear, they are subject to God. As Nimrod and his great city were demystified (10:8–12), so Babylon, exotic languages, and far-flung nations are brought down to size. The wonder of such things will not cease, but at this point what needed emphasis was their limitation. They may be wonderful, but in the end, under God, they are fragile.

Panel Two (11:10–32)

[11:10–26] The generations of Shem: short and shrinking. At first sight the genealogy from Shem to Terah looks impressive. As well as building with precision on the Shem line in chapter 10 (10:21–25: Shem, Arpachshad, Shelah, Eber, Peleg), its leading character, Shem, appears to echo some of the energy of creation (11:10–11). He takes up where the God-related and primordial Adam-Noah-Shem genealogy leaves off (chap. 5). He is associated with the earth-shaking flood (10:10, "two years after the flood"); and his years (five hundred) recall the great Noah (5:32).

But the generations that follow Shem dwindle. There are essentially only nine (nine begettings), not the standard ten (as in chap. 5), and the numbers fall: 500, 403, 403, 430, 209 (Peleg), 207, 200, 119. In the Adam-Noah genealogy (chap. 5) there was no such steady decline. Methuselah, with 969 years, was near the end. The overall impression is of a generating process which, whatever its original energy, is now failing.

[11:27–32] The generations of Terah: failure in progeny and land. The account of "the generations of Terah" is largely concerned with two things that often give a sense of strength and stability, namely progeny and land. Terah's hopes of progeny revolve around his three sons, Abram, Nahor, and Haran (11:27–30); and his hopes of land depend on his attempt to journey from Ur of the Chaldeans (approximately seventy miles south of modern Baghdad) to "the land of Canaan" (11:31–32).

But these hopes are fragile. Of the three sons, the youngest, Haran (*hārān*), dies prematurely, and the shadow of that death—or at least of that name, "Haran"—seems to haunt the family. The wife of the middle brother is "Milcah, the daughter of Haran." The wife of the oldest brother, Abram, is Sarai: "Sarai was barren; she had no child." Sarai, being the last name in the paragraph, stands out. She receives no ancestry, and her barrenness is emphasized by "she had no child." The picture of her is stark: "Not only are her ancestors unknown, but the possibility of her having children is doubtful" (Jeansonne, 1990, 14).

As for the effort to reach the land of Canaan, the journey peters out inexplicably and ominously: "when they came to Haran (*hārān*) they settled there . . . And Terah died in Haran." There is a difference between the personal name Haran (*hārān*) and the place name Haran (*ḥārān*); the initial *h* reflects two different Hebrew letters (aspirated *heh* and fricative *ḥet*; Alter, 49). But, in a book that plays with words, such closeness between two names suggests continuity. The continuity is confirmed by their position: the two parts of the genealogy conclude respectively with Haran (*hārān*, 11:26) and Haran (*ḥārān*, 11:32). The two names dovetail.

The issue is not trivial. The personal name Haran evoked death; it belonged to someone who died prematurely. Hence, "died in Haran" is almost like "died in death." So ends the genealogy. This progeny lives in death's shadow.

Thus the genealogy and the plans of Terah, Abram's human father, end in a place of death. Abram, with his barren wife, is left in the shadow of the dead brother. At the end, human effort and life seem to be falling apart.

Such is Genesis 11: things fall apart. Babel is a powerful symbol because it is a substitute for God, more graspable than God's own self, and therefore, at first sight, more alluring. Here one can settle down, speak peacefully, enjoy civilization, and touch the sky. It is like a dream.

It is in fact an illusion—like a glamorized Arcadia or an unreal Atlantis. For humans there is no abiding city, however much, with dreams and technology, one may pine for one. Cities may be great, but they are no substitute for God. One may settle in them, but only to a limited extent; a city does not satisfy one's entire being. God is far greater, and reality much more complex. Family trees, too, may be impressive, but eventually in various ways they, too, fade.

PART FIVE

THE STORY OF ABRAHAM

Genesis 12:1–25:18

Abraham is central to Judaism, Christianity, and Islam. He encapsulates the way in which, by listening to the deepest level of reality, a person may arise from a landscape of death and journey to new life. The result is blessing—blessing for oneself and blessing for many others.

The narrative, almost fourteen chapters, falls fairly easily into seven units of about two chapters each, seven diptychs. The opening three units (chaps. 12-13; 14-15; and 16-17) recount the initial trials. Abraham struggles with changing fortunes, and Sarah hovers on the edge of bitterness.

The remaining four units bring powerful encounters with the forces of life and death. First there is a great catastrophe, the burning of a whole city—an event that causes much soul searching for Abraham (most of chaps. 18-19). Then, in contrast, there are a series of births, events which, at least in the case of Isaac, bring great joy (19:30-chap. 21). The result is that when Abraham is faced with the greatest challenges of all—the offering of his son and the death of his wife (chaps. 22-23)—he responds with a striking degree of serenity. At the end, through Rebekah and in his death, he is surrounded by blessing (24:1-25:18).

22 Abram Journeys and Sees the Land (Chaps. 12–13)

The Trial of Seeing beyond Beauty (12:1–13:1)
The Trial of Seeing beyond Wealth (13:2–10)

Introductory Aspects

The Basic Story Line

This account (Gen. 12–13) begins one of the great stories of human history. Despite a background of death, barrenness, and failed objectives (11:27–32), a man picks up his life and sets off into the unknown. Here is no facile undertaking. He is given no clear destination, and he lives out of a tent, moving frequently. Within his household, his closest companions are a wife who is barren and a nephew whose father died prematurely. The man is old. The place he goes is already occupied. And, out of the blue, there is a famine, bringing threats both of starvation and murder. His existence is fragile.

Yet he moves with purpose. He is sustained not by whim or empty wish but by attentiveness to the God who first made the earth and blessed it, and who now sends him forth so that he, amid his fragility, will be for all people a source of blessing.

His conduct is not perfect. When the famine causes a crisis, he succumbs to fear and in effect betrays his wife. Yet he rallies and resumes his hopeful journey. When there is a second crisis—a dispute over land—he does better, and at the end his sense of God's purpose is stronger than ever.

Literary Form

The literary form (of chaps. 12–13) is probably best described as a kind of travel narrative—a condensed variation on some of the travel narratives found in diverse forms of ancient writing, from epic and prophecy to the origins of Greek historiography (Lesky, 1966, 219).

Mixed with the travel narrative, however, is another form, that of the test or trial, one of the Bible's well-established conventional scenes. Such trials may be initiatory (like Jesus' temptations, for instance; cf. Alter, 1981, 51), but not necessarily so. Rabbinic tradition highlighted the idea of trial and spoke of Abram's trials as numbering ten (Cassuto, II, 294–295; Clifford, 2:18). The emphasis on ten says less about precise quantity than about quality: Abram was tested thoroughly. In particular, he was tested first and last—here and when asked to offer Isaac (chaps. 12–13; chap. 22).

During Abram's journey (chaps. 12–13) the primary trials concern beauty and wealth—Sarai's beauty and the wealth of the land.

209

Complementarity of the Two Panels

Abram's journey (chaps. 12–13) brings the Genesis story to a new setting—the land between Canaan and Egypt—and thereby introduces some of the excitement of a story of exploration. In the first panel (12:1–13:1) he goes to Shechem (to the Oak of Moreh), Bethel, the Negev, and Egypt (12:1–13:1); in the second, to the Negev, Bethel, and finally to Hebron (to the Oaks of Mamre; 13:2–18). The journey has a chiastic effect, which draws it into a unity:

Shechem, Oak of Moreh
    Bethel
        Negev
            "went down" to Egypt
            "came up" from Egypt
        Negev
    Bethel
Hebron, Oaks of Mamre.

The verb used for journeying (*nāśaʾ*) means, literally, to pull up tent pegs—a detail that captures the stage by stage nature of Abram's movement. There is frequent use, too, of the verb "to go/walk." This exploration, therefore, is not a superficial tour. Abram's journey is vivid and down to earth.

Relationship to Preceding Chapters

Abram's journeys provide a hint or foreshadowing of journeys to come—those of Isaac, Jacob, Israel (in Egypt), Joshua, and David (in Hebron); and his "visionary possession of the land foreshadows that of Moses" (Clifford, 2:20–22; Cassuto, II, 305–306).

However, as well as foreshadowing the future, these two chapters also echo the past. The account of Abram's journey (chaps. 12–13) is so formed that it distills and reshapes the essence of the Adam-Noah history (chaps. 1–11). Almost every phrase gathers up memories of the past and gives them a new orientation.

For instance, the introductory declaration—"God said . . . 'Go forth from your land . . . I will bless . . . bless . . . All . . . shall bless' "—distills aspects both of the original creation, especially its blessing (1:22, 28; 2:3), and also of Noah's role in remaking creation. As Noah implicitly left the old world, so also, but much more explicitly, does Abram.

The sense of complete accord with God's word, found both in creation (chap. 1) and in Noah (6:22; 7:5, 9,16) recurs in new form in Abram: "Yhwh said to Abram . . . And Abram went as Yhwh had spoken to him" (12:1, 4). Even the word's instantaneous fulfillment—for example, " 'Let there be light,' and there was light"—finds a curious echo in Abram's journey: "They went forth to go to the land of Canaan, and they came to the land of Canaan" (12:6).

The shift from God's commanding word (12:1–3) to a sense of place, including trees (esp. 12:6–9; 13:14–18, north, south, east, and west), corresponds to something of the transition from the first creation account to the second, with its trees and four rivers (2:4b–24, esp. 2:8–14).

The diptych on primordial sin (2:25–4:16) is particularly important in chapters 12–13. It provides a form of framework. The first panel (12:1–13:1), with its various motifs—seeing, the woman, attractiveness, death, deception—echoes the event in the Garden (chap. 3). In the Garden, the woman led the man; in Egypt, the man leads the woman. Even Pharaoh's angry reaction ("What have you done?," followed by expulsion) is modeled partly on Yhwh God's reaction in the Garden.

The second panel, in which there is "quarrelling between . . . brothers" (13:8), reworks aspects of the Cain and Abel story, but with a radical change: Abram ensures that the animosity leads not to murder but to generous separation.

Without attempting a detailed analysis (see Wénin, 1998, 438–450), the general picture emerges: while the two events in 2:25–4:16 show a degeneration—the murderous second panel is worse than the first—the two Abram episodes show a process of learning. In the first crisis, Abram fails—fails to trust Yhwh—and is duly expelled. But in the second, his generosity wins the day; and his eyes receive new sight. This is not the opening of the eyes that leads to shame (3:7), but the God-given lifting up of the eyes that brings a new vision (13:14–16). In the Garden, the opening of the eyes led to hiding among the trees, away from Yhwh God (3:8). But now Yhwh invites Abram to walk through the land (13:17).

The dense repetitious picture of Noah gathering the creatures of the world into the ark colors the slightly repetitious account of Abram bringing wife and possessions "and all the persons (*nepeš;* cf. 1:20–24; 2:7) they had made" to the new land (12:4–5).

There are echoes of earlier phrases. For example:

"The . . . giants were on the earth (ʿereṣ) in those days" (6:4).

"The Canaanites were then in the land" (ʿereṣ, 12:6);

The giants and the Canaanites belong to the same literary thread: giants, mighty men, Ham/Canaan, Nimrod, Canaanites (6:4; 9:18; 10:6–9, 15–19).

Furthermore, "I will make your name great" (12:2) is both an echo and a reversal of the disordered ambition at Babel to make one's own name, one's own identity and destiny (11:4).

The Abram, therefore, who sets forth contains not only an intimation of history to come. He also carries within him the blessings and primordial sins of the world. He may be the ancestor of a special people, but his roots extend to every corner of humankind, and his journey, whatever the stumblings caused by the weight of the world's sin, is a journey for everybody.

Leading Elements

THE ROLE OF PROMISE

Abram's larger role in Genesis has already been summarized briefly (Introduction, Chapter 11). He is the man who, against the background of many failures (Gen. 1–11), brings an awareness of another dimension, thus inspiring faith and a *joie de vivre*.

This other dimension is connected with a new emphasis on promise—the promise of God's word. God's word had already been active in Genesis 1–11, especially in bestowing creation and creation-based blessing. Those creation-based blessings continue in the Abram story, and there is some continuity between what was blessed and what is promised; blessings were directed toward creation and procreation; promises dealt with land and progeny (for details on the promises, see Fretheim, 418–419).

But blessing and promise are not exactly the same; promise adds something new. Blessings can be counted. Promises are less calculable; one must trust. "The story of the fathers is an education in patience" (Jacob, 84). The issue then is not simply what is promised, but the nature of promise: it draws a person beyond the calculable and into a realm that surpasses normal human perceptions. Fretheim (418) emphasizes "the way in which promise *functions as promise*," and he indicates (419) that promise moves a person from the realm of creation into that of redemption. In effect, whatever the circumstances, the promises bring hope.

This movement—beyond standard perception—requires faith. The word "believe" is not used initially, yet from the beginning some element of faith is implicit.

The nature of promise and faith, the way in which they leap beyond the calculable, explains the sharp beginning to the Abram narrative. Without introduction, God speaks, making a great promise (12:1–3). The divine word is disjunctive. God's word, this faith-evoking promise, does not destroy normal life and blessing, but it goes beyond it. The disjunction is positive.

SECOND LEVEL

The journey has a second level—a story about seeing, particularly the contrast between superficial seeing and the seeing that is given by God. It is especially within this second level that the trials arise concerning the seeing of beauty and wealth.

The first panel tells of seeing beauty. The Egyptians "see" Sarai. But the result of this form of seeing is a list of negatives: danger to Abram's life; Abram's lies (pretending to be Sarai's brother); cooperation in the lie by Sarai; Pharaoh's taking of Sarai as a wife; plagues on Pharaoh and his house; and Pharaoh's angry expulsion of Abram and his wife.

The second panel tells of seeing wealth: Lot "lifts his eyes" and "sees" a region that looks obviously watered and wealthy. But it evokes negative experiences—the Garden and Egypt—and it draws Lot into a place of great evil.

In contrast to the seeing of beauty and wealth, there is the seeing that God grants to Abram. "The land" to which Yhwh calls Abram is described first of all not as Canaan but as "the land that *I will make you see*" (the causative form of *rāʾâ*, "see"). Then, when Abram arrives in the land, Yhwh "*was seen*" (again "see," passive form). Finally, when Lot has gone, following his own eyes, God takes charge of Abram's process of seeing: "Lift up your eyes and see." It is then, with God guiding his vision, that Abram sees the land with fresh clarity—north, south, east, and west—and he does so in a way that goes beyond spatial calculations. Lot has taken the best, yet Abram is to receive all.

The placing of Sarai near the beginning of the Abram story (Gen. 12:10–20) is no accident. Each of Genesis's four major dramas (Genesis 1–11; Abraham; Jacob; Joseph) has an initial emphasis on women. And as a woman had a role, along with Adam, in the initial loss of blessing (Gen. 1:1–4:16), so a woman, Sarai, will have a role, along with Abram, in recovering the blessing (Wénin, 1998).

Structure (Table 22.1)

THE FIRST PANEL (CHAPS. 12–13:1)

The first panel comprises not only chapter 12, but also 13:1, Abram's return from Egypt (Clifford, 2:21). The panel begins and ends with commands to

Table 22.1. Abram's Journeys (12:1–13:1 // 13:2–18)

The promise: crisis over beauty
Introduction: Yhwh sends Abram; blessing (or curse) for all (12:1–3)
The promise. Journeying and seeing Yhwh (12:4–5)
Following Yhwh's command (12:4–5)
Seeing God, invoking God (12:6–9)
Egypt. Seeing beauty and its danger (12:10–17)
Look: seeing beauty leads to danger (12:10–13)
Seeing beauty leads to the taking away of Sarai (12:14–16)
Conclusion: Pharaoh expels Abram: "Look . . . Go!" (12:17–13:1)

Crisis over wealth: the promise intensified
Introduction: starting again (differently); an altar (13:2–4)
Lot: a wealth-based dispute (13:5–9)
Lot: a wealth-based seeing and choosing (13:10–13)
Abram: a God-given seeing. Promise intensified (13:14–17)
Conclusion: journeying to Hebroń, to an altar (13:18)

Abram to go from the country—the first command by Yhwh, the later command by Pharaoh (12:1, 20). What was promised in God's command—that Abram would affect people in all the earth, for better or worse—is already partly fulfilled in Pharaoh.

Details confirm the unity of this panel (12:1–13:1). The going up (13:1) balances and completes the going down (12:10). "Negev," as the final word (13:1), dovetails with the concluding use of "Negev" in 12:9. The phrase "his wife and all that he had" ties 13:1 to 12:20.

Within panel one, there is a sharp division between its two main parts—one is set in Canaan (12:4–9), the other in Egypt (12:10–16)—and so these two parts are sometimes seen as distinct episodes. This sharp division, this fragmentation, should probably be viewed in conjunction with the divisions within chapter 11. In that chapter, the narrative moves from a first panel, which is reasonably unified (Babel, 11:1–9), to a second panel, concerning Shem-Terah, which is sharply divided, fragmented (11:10–26; and 11:27–32). Now, in this diptych (chaps. 12–13), the narrative moves in the opposite direction—from a first panel, which is sharply divided (12:1–9; and 12:10–13:1), to a second panel, which is reasonably unified (13:2–18). At some level the process of fragmentation is being reversed. It is probably not an accident that when Abram is tested in these two panels (concerning Sarai, 12:10–13:1, and wealth, 13:5–15), he fails the first test, but meets the second. At some level he himself is moving away from fragmentation. He has started on his journey, following God's word, but as the incident in Egypt shows, he does not yet trust God fully.

THE SECOND PANEL (13:2–18)

With its three main parts, the second panel has a more obvious unity, and Abram's character likewise shows greater coherence.

THE PROBLEM OF THE DIPTYCH'S BEGINNING:
12:1 (NOT 11:27)

The beginning of the Abram story has two overlapping structures: one, based primarily on theology, begins at 12:1; the other, based primarily on historical sequence, begins with the place of Abram within Terah's family, in 11:27–32, and then tells more about Abram in chapter 12.

If Genesis is primarily history, then the story of Abram, being primarily a historical document, begins at 11:27. But if the story of Abram, while having a historical dimension, is primarily a story of faith, then the primary division is theological, in other words, the moment of God's call (12:1). Several factors corroborate beginning at 12:1:

1. In the reading and preaching of the old Jewish synagogue tradition, the division was made at the call of Abram, 12:1 (Mann, 1940, 96). The same occurred in the preaching-oriented medieval division into chapters.

2. Genesis as a whole is not a straight narrative sequence. While it uses a historical genre and has a historical dimension, history is not its primary interest. One of the theses of this work is that Genesis is theology-oriented literary art (see Introduction, Chapters 2 and 11).

3. The abruptness of the call (12:1–3), its disjunctive nature, is appropriate as a beginning to a disjunctive story, a story which tells of someone who lived essentially at the level of faith. Faith and grace do not break away completely from nature (including natural sequence); they build on it. Yet they do involve a distinctive change, an element of disjuncture.

4. Chapter 11 has its own unity; it forms a diptych (see discussion of Genesis 11, Introductory Aspects).

5. The repetition of "These are the generations" within the genealogy of Shem (11:10–32, in vv. 10, 27) does not mean that that genealogy is not a unity. A similar repetition occurs in the genealogy of Esau (36:1–37:1, vv. 1, 9), a text that is a basic literary unity.

Comment

Panel One (12:1–13:1)

[12:1–3] **A blessing for the whole earth.** Echoing the command that first made the earth (ʿereṣ), God commands Abram to leave the familiar ʿereṣ ("earth/land"), and to go elsewhere: "to the land (ʿereṣ) that I will make you see." In this new space there is promise of blessing not only for Abram, but through him for "all the clans of the ground" (ʾădāmâ).

In being asked to leave his father's house, Abram faces a challenge which, among other aspects, has a psychological dimension: "The 'father's house' symbolizes the collective masculine principle of security and honor, family continuity, and tradition passed on from father to son. . . . The personality that is driven toward change and development—toward individuation and psychic wholeness—must break free of this setting" (Dreifuss and Riemer, 1995, 9).

The horizon that beckons is not limited to a specific place or nation; there is no explicit reference to Canaan or Israel. Instead the vista opens out indefinitely. The land is simply "the land that I will make you see." And the "great nation" is linked—through Abram's "great name" and blessing—with "all the clans of the ground/earth." The sharpness of the beginning—no introduction, no divine self-identification—is a literary way of expressing the nature of the promise, the way it breaks normal expectations and patterns.

One of the patterns of creation was the giving of blessings, and it is conceivable that a new pattern, that of promise, would upset the pattern of blessings. The effect of the promise, however, instead of setting blessing aside, is to intensify it.

The curse ("him who damns you, I will curse") is not an expression of any malevolence, but primarily a warning of what is at stake, like saying that whoever does not accept food will starve. Whoever does not accept the blessing borne by Abram will be utterly deprived of blessing—cursed.

[12:4–5] **The journey begins—prompt but burdened.** The beginnings of journeys are often eager, and so it seems with Abram. There is no hint of questioning or hesitating; instead he "went as Yhwh had spoken (verb, *dābar*) to him." His guide is Yhwh's word, and so his departure evokes many generous beginnings.

But his journey will not be simple. The first faint note of complication comes immediately: "and Lot went with him." There is no indication that anything is wrong, but this was not expected. Lot's name is placed next to that of Abram (". . . Lot. And Abram . . ."). To some degree he seems to shadow Abram.

There is a further fact: "Abram was seventy-five years old. . . ." The problem is not only one of possible infirmity. Seventy-five is often associated not with the beginning of a life but with its end, with the time of death ("our life span is seventy years, or eighty for those who are strong," Ps. 90:10). The evoking of death is then compounded: ". . . when he went forth from Haran." Haran had negative connotations: it was the place where the failed journey to Canaan had stalled, the place of his father's death (11:32). And it was also, essentially, the name of his brother, Haran—prematurely dead (11:28).

"Abram took Sarai his wife . . ."—comforting perhaps, but that is not said. The only thing known about her is her barrenness: "Sarai was barren; she had no child" (11:30). If the connotation of "seventy-five" and "Haran" was unclear, left hanging in the balance, Sarai's barrenness tips the scales heavily toward negativity. The evoking of death is combined with someone known to be barren.

Abram also took "Lot his brother's son. . . ." Thus, the the story comes back to Lot, but with a new detail: "his brother's son"—the brother who died prematurely, Haran (11:27). The connotation of Lot's presence, so uncertain at the beginning, now begins to emerge: he carries something of his brother, something of premature death. The shadow is beginning to take on some shape. The details will emerge later.

And Abram took ". . . all their possessions . . . and the people that they had made in Haran." "People" refers to those who worked in the household as servants or slaves. Unlike later North American slaves, "subsequent stories in Genesis make clear . . . these slaves had certain limited rights, could be given great responsibility, and were not thought to lose their personhood" (Alter, 51). Such possessions and people are important assets; they seem to give security. But they have an association that is negative: they had been acquired "in Haran"—a place linked with death.

Overall, therefore, Abram's departure is ambiguous. He is following God's word, but the baggage he carries—his years and people and places and possessions—is not light. Whatever his eagerness, at some level he bears a heavy weight.

Yet just when it all may seem too much—the weight too heavy, the journey too long—the narrative lifts him: "They went out to go to the land of Canaan, and they came to the land of Canaan." All in one simple sentence. Whatever the weight, the word is stronger. As noted already, the immediacy of the effect ("They went out to go to . . . Canaan. And they came to . . . Canaan") is like an echo of the immediacy of creation ("Let there be light. And there was light").

[12:6–9] **Shechem and Bethel: journeying in a land that is accessible yet elusive.** Once arrived in Canaan, Abram's progress is steady. First, he passes to a central place—Shechem and the Oak of Moreh (12:6–7). Then, in a second stage, he pitches his tent on a mountain east of Bethel (12:8). And so on, stage by stage, to the south—the Negev (12:9).

At both of the stages that are highlighted—Shechem, and the mountain east of Bethel—Abram becomes actively engaged with God. First, "Yhwh was seen by Abram"; and later, as if returning the communication, Abram "called on the name of Yhwh." And on both occasions Abram builds an altar, first because of the divine initiative (*after* Yhwh was seen), and later on his own initiative (*before* calling on Yhwh). The pattern therefore has a certain clarity and completeness—divine initiative followed by human response. And on it goes, stage by stage, to the Negev. Faith is not mentioned explicitly, but at least there is external worship. This is a steady pilgrim.

Yet all is not well—at least at Shechem. Abram's arrival there, when one might have expected a sense of achievement and peace—at last the promised land!—is marked by a dissonant note: "The Canaanites were then in the land." Quite apart from echoes of earlier texts—echoes of "there were giants in the land in those days" (6:4) and of Ham/Canaan's descendants (10:6–19)—this sudden reference to the Canaanites is something of an unpleasant surprise. And then, when Yhwh speaks—"To your descendants I will give this land"—the message is ambiguous. If the accent is on "your," the promise is reassuring, but if on "descendants" then Abram's personal fate becomes uncertain. The Shechem event, therefore, sends a message: despite the promise, Abram's life is not facile; already he has to deal with unexpected people and with uncertainty. Still, he carries on to Bethel, and he recovers his rhythm, "journeying and tenting toward the Negev."

[12:10–13:1] **Famine, failure, and expulsion.** The next events seem to make a mockery both of the promise and of Abram's journeying. Without warning, the land becomes a place of famine. The land, at least the physical land, is not dependable. Then the journey takes an unforeseen route—Egypt. Next, Abram gives in to fear and lying. And finally, beautiful Sarai is taken into Pharaoh's palace, so that Pharaoh says later, "I took her as my wife" (12:18). (At this point the text says nothing about Sarai's age. To inject here a calculation of her age is to spoil a delicately-drawn impression of a beautiful woman.) The implication is that for a time Sarai became Pharaoh's wife. Commentator Benno Jacob (89) tries to soften the scene: "It must be understood that everything was done in a pleasing and courteous form as suitable to a royal court."

Sarai has still not spoken—somewhat like the man in the eating of the fruit. There is no indication of what it was like for someone who previously was known only as barren and childless to find herself being the toast of the most prestigious society in the world. And there is no indication of what it was like for her as Pharaoh's wife. Abram does well out of the situation: "he gets a huge bride price" (Dennis, 1994, 39).

Abram's deception, instead of bringing blessing to Egypt, brings plagues. He becomes rich, but the tale is one of moral disaster. Pharaoh seems more moral than Abram. The expulsion at the end (12:18–13:1) has overtones both of the original expulsion from the Garden of Eden (3:13–14, 23) and of Israel's later departure from Egypt.

From a literary point of view this scene of the endangered wife (12:10–13:1) is a type-scene: a fixed sequence of narrative motifs are modified according to the needs of the context (Alter, 52). Later episodes (chaps. 20 and 26) will show other modifications.

Panel Two (13:2–18)

[13:2–4] **Beginning again—but not at Shechem. A geographic puzzle.** After Egypt, there is a sense of a fresh beginning. Abram, it now emerges, has not only livestock, but also silver and gold. This could bode ill. It raises the specter that Abram is governed by the desire for riches, and that the moral confusion that surrounded Sarai's beauty is now about to be expressed in his attachment to wealth. But the story intimates that something is changing. In a perplexing introduction (12:3–4) it tells that Abram went back to where he had been "at the start . . . at first." But in fact he does not go back to the original place—to Shechem. Instead "he went . . . as far as Bethel . . . to the place where his tent had been at the start, between Bethel and Ai, to the place where he had made his altar at first." The implication is of beginning again, but in a way that is different—a way that departs from Shechem and also challenges normal perceptions of geography. This geographic puzzle—the challenge to ordinary perception—prepares for what follows.

[13:5–17] **Contrasts in vision: Lot and Abram see the land.** Having experienced the ambiguity of beauty—how it can bring danger, deception, dishonor, and plagues—Abram now has to face the ambiguity of wealth. Lot's abundance of livestock leads to a quarrel about land. The root problem, however, is not land but wealth; "they had become too rich" (Jacob, 91). And, adding salt to the wound, there is a reminder, not only of the Canaanites, but also of the Perizzites, previously unmentioned in Genesis. The shadow of the mighty giants and of Ham/Canaan/Nimrod grows ever longer.

In the quarrel with Lot, Abram could have invoked rank. Instead, in a spirit of brotherhood and with great freedom he allows Lot to choose. Lot lifts his eyes, and looking "till you come to Zoar," chooses carefully but superficially. Modern guides still show the superb observation point from which, according to tradition, Lot chose his land. The biblical description of his viewing contains elements that suggest something unreal or unresolved. The wording refers to Sodom (later destroyed), the Garden (lost), and Egypt (rich, but enslaving). "Lot does not perceive accurately the reality of things. . . . In view of Israel's wandering in the wilderness begging to return to Egyptian fleshpots, Egypt represents a desire for a preredemption state of affairs" (Fretheim, 434). Eventually Lot's actions follow his vision: he moves toward Sodom, near it.

Abram takes what is left. His eyes, lifted by the word of God, see as never before, in every direction. And the promise, instead of being diminished, is enhanced. For the first time the land is now promised "forever" (13:15). Abram's vision, while it includes legal procedures (especially walking the land; Alter, 57; Fretheim, 434), sees beyond human legality.

[13:18] Settled by the oaks—but in Hebron. At the end, Abram moves, but despite the earlier emphasis on going back to the initial place (13:3–4), he still does not return to Shechem and the Oak of Moreh. Instead he settles "by the Oaks of Mamre, which are in Hebron." In every sense he seems to have found a new place. At Mamre, in Hebron, the final word is "Yhwh" ("and he built there an altar to Yhwh"). Hebron will be central—the place of God's visitation (18:1), the place even of Sarah's burial, and a haunting focal point for the whole book, until at last it is the place to which all the chariots carry Jacob (50:4–13).

---

23   War—and Vision of a Covenant (Chaps. 14–15)

Amid an Enslaving War, a Blessing (Chap. 14)
Amid Uncertainty and Enslavement, a Covenant (Chap. 15)

Introductory Aspects

The Basic Story Line

In the words of a film title, Abram in this account is like "a lion in winter." The film told of a brave king in old age.

At first there is no mention of old age. Chapter 14 shows Abram simply as a lion—a surprising development considering how fearful he had been when he first approached Egypt (12:10–14). But now, when much of the world seems overpowered by indomitable war-makers, Abram puts himself and his household on the line and, overpowering the war-makers, restores peace.

This story of war and peace (chap. 14) contains great color and musicality. The initial list of names and campaigns has a once-upon-a-time quality, which when read aloud hovers between the frightening and the humorous (14:1–12)—a story that is truly fabulous. When all seems lost Abram daringly turns the tables on the invaders at night (14:13–16), and in the peaceful denouement, in dealing with the kings of Salem and Sodom, he shows himself strongly as a man of graciousness and principle (14:17–24).

But suddenly, in chapter 15, the lion seems frightened. He speaks about going away, a reference, many commentators believe, to going away in death. And the subsequent conversation refers explicitly to old age and death (15:15). The threat of death unnerves him in a way that powerful armies did not. And so there is, as it were, a second campaign, not against invading armies but against invading death.

While the first campaign (chap. 14) was far-reaching, even far-fetched, it had a basic clarity. But the later struggle (chap. 15) is obscure. It begins as a vision and is fought on a different kind of terrain, much more internal. The explicit issues are those of progeny and land. Abram wants a child of his own, and the child(ren) will inherit the land. But the child and the land are not just external issues—something to do with the future of other people. They are linked to Abram's own fate, to his struggle with impending old age and death. And so, while discussing progeny and land, he struggles toward a resolution of his own anxiety.

This internal-oriented struggle is almost as colorful as the campaign against the invading hosts. Having formerly engaged the enemy at night, Abram now cuts up several animals and becomes engaged by God in a profound night action, which bestows a covenant and, apparently, a particular form of peace. At the end, the litany of names is not of invading kings but of many peoples encompassed by God's covenant.

Literary Form

The two panels are vivid and diverse. The first (chap. 14) tells of the extraordinary campaign of four kings who, on their way to crushing five kings who had rebelled, sweep around to defeat several other peoples. But the last victory goes to Abram and his covenanted allies. In a night action they not only rescue Lot, along with his possessions and people, but also defeat the all-conquering kings, and even pursue them north of Damascus. The picture is like a panorama.

This narrative (chap. 14) cannot be linked reliably to any specific historical context. Furthermore, some of the names seem symbolic; "the names *Bera* and *Birsha*, kings of Sodom and Gomorrah, seem to be derived from the words for evil and wickedness in Hebrew" (Jacob, 94). But chapter 14, while not having a clear context in history, does have a tangible context in literature: it is modeled, partly, on reports of military campaigns; parallels exist (cf. Clifford, 2:23; Younger, 1990). Its basic literary type, therefore, emerges as that of a war report (a *Kriegsbericht*, Schatz, 1972, 275).

The campaign makes no mention of God, but on the way home, meeting the king of Sodom and Melchizedek, Abram is blessed in the name of El Elyon, the God of heaven and earth, and then, in an extraordinary show of integrity, he raises his hand in an oath and forswears ill-gotten gain. The chapter highlights "new facets of Abram's character. The one who displayed fear and evasiveness in Egypt now shows himself to be decisive and courageous" (Sarna, 103).

The second panel (chap. 15) is almost the very opposite—not a vast war in which God never speaks, but a private vision, where God, alone with Abram, speaks deeply. The basic literary type here is that of a call or vision ("the word . . . came to Abram in a vision," 15:1) (see Hagelia, 1994, 211). Fretheim (444) speaks of a theophany, and lists its formal features. The conventional scene of a vision contains six motifs: divine confrontation, introductory word, commission, objection, reassurance, and sign (Habel, 1975). In chapter 15, this convention has been adapted: the words of promise are twofold, and therefore to some degree the motifs are repeated—first, in the promise, complaint, and answer (15:1-6); then, in the promise, request for a sign, and answer (15:7-21). Unlike the prophets, whose visionary commission is usually specific, Abram's mission is more general.

In its own way, however, the vision also, like the war report, is a panorama. It reviews the two foundational promises—of progeny and land—and does so in a way that sweeps far and wide. The promise of progeny is linked to the far-flung uncountable stars (15:1-5). And the promise of the land is spread across a great expanse of time and space—across four hundred years, and from the Nile to the Euphrates (15:7-21).

Hence, while the two panels are diverse in nature or genre, they have a breadth which draws both of them to distant horizons. Ha (1989, 216) concludes that chapter 15 did not know chapter 14, but Hagelia (1994, 4) believes otherwise: "Chapter 15 links well to chapters 12-13 and 14." More specifically, "the kings' responses [in chap. 14] prepare us for the response of God in chap. 15" (Fretheim, 438).

Here, too, as in earlier chapters, the predominant literary types are not exclusive. Genesis 14-15, as well as telling of war and vision, also contain a trial story (cf. Cassuto, II, 295). The issue now is not wealth or beauty but security. In diverse ways Abram is challenged to place his life on the line, to let go—first in rescuing Lot, then in facing aspects of impending death.

The result of letting go is not emptiness but an experience first of blessing (returning from the war, 14:17-20) and then, having faced the vision involving his own death (15:18), of covenant.

Complementarity of the Two Panels

The two chapters balance one another. While chapter 14 lays the primary emphasis on the enslaving powers, it gives a secondary role to the protective God, the God Most High of skies and earth, in whose name Abram resists the rewards of the king of Sodom. Chapter 15 lays the primary emphasis on the protective God, Yhwh who shields and shows the skies, but it gives a secondary role to the nations that enslave or threaten.

The litany of places and peoples at the beginning of panel one (14:1–7) finds a counterpart at the end of panel two (15:18–21). The two litanies form a framework which holds the two chapters together.

The primary issue in the war (chap. 14) is enslavement or servitude. The rebellion of the five kings occurs after years of serving (ʿābad) Chedorlaomer. But Chedorlaomer and his allies seem able to enforce the servitude and conquer all before them, including Abram's nephew (14:4–5, 11–12). The subsequent chapter, the vision (chap. 15), gives a related picture, a daunting image of servitude: Abram's descendants have to serve (ʿābad) for four hundred years (15:13).

However, those who enforce servitude are finally beaten. In chapter 14 Abram defeats the conquerors (14:15). And in chapter 15 Yhwh says to Abram, "But on the nation which they serve (ʿābad), I will bring judgment" (15:14). The freedom Abram brings to the enslaved in chapter 14 is a harbinger of the freedom promised in chapter 15.

Abram brings back (šûb) Lot and his possessions (rĕkûš) and his people (14:16). Abram's descendants, with great possessions (rĕkûš), will be brought back (šûb) (15:14:1–15).

While chapter 14 tells of a military campaign, which threatens Abram's people, chapter 15 begins with a corresponding military metaphor—Yhwh is Abram's shield (15:1). Combat (chap. 14) tends to engender awareness of death (chap. 15).

In both panels the climactic action takes place at night—Abram's liberating attack (14:15), his vision of the stars (15:5), and the passing of the fire in making the covenant (15:17–18). Previously in Genesis, nothing had happened at night.

In both texts the night is associated with vivid actions, including diverse forms of bloody dividing. Abram's most vivid action in chapter 14 consists of marshalling his men—literally emptying them or unsheathing them, as one unsheathes a sword—and dividing his forces to catch the enemy in a pincer movement (14:14–15). Abram's most vivid action in chapter 15 consists of splitting various animals, and later, during the night, fire goes between the parts (15:9–11, 17). There is some form of complementarity between the night force, which pincers the enemy, and the night fire, which goes through the divided animals.

The picture of a covenant (bĕrît) oath, so strong in God's dealing with Abram (15:9–21), is prepared for in Abram's own conduct—in the covenant (bĕrît) with his allies (14:13, 24), and in his swearing (14:22–23, he raises his hand before God Most High not to accept Sodom's wealth). Abram, in effect, makes a covenant with Melchizedek (Elgavish, 2001). Apart from the story of Noah, no previous Genesis episode had mentioned a covenant; and there was no reference, anywhere, to an oath.

Abram's acceptance of El Elyon, God Most High, "owner of heavens (*šāmayîm*) and earth" (14:22) prepares for his acceptance of the God who tells him to look at the heavens (*šāmayîm*, 15:5). Thus while the title El Elyon may have been Canaanite in origin, it has been so integrated that it forms a background for Abram's act of faith in the God who shows him the heavens and the stars.

Melchizedek's name (*malkî-ṣedek* of *šālēm*) has affinities with chapter 15—with Abram's righteousness or rightness (*ṣĕdāḳâ*, 15:6), and with his going in peace (*šālôm*, 15:15). It is as though, when the struggles are over, especially the struggles against servitude, something peaceful comes to Abram—on the one hand the figure of Melchizedek, and, on the other, rightness and peace.

Relationship to Preceding Chapters

The distinctness of chapters 14–15 may be seen further by comparing and contrasting them with chapters 12–13. Egypt apart, the journey of chapters 12–13 seemed to set Abram on a confined stage. But now, suddenly, the stage opens up to include kings and peoples from far and near: the text (chaps. 14–15) begins and ends with litanies of kings, kingdoms, and peoples (14:1–4; 15:18–21). The incident in Egypt had been set at the center of chapters 12–13, but in chapters 14–15 the litanies of kingdoms form an encompassing framework. In the overall fabric of the text (chaps. 14–15) the name of Abram is literally surrounded by alien peoples.

A further contrast with chapters 12–13 is the emphasis on time. While Abram was moving from stage to stage there was a clear sense of space, but none of time (the only time reference—Abram's seventy-five years—is a conundrum). Chapters 14–15, however, speak considerably of time—the years of Chedorlaomer's servitude, the night of rescue, the future years of servitude, and the stages from sunset to darkness (13:4–5, 15; 15:12–17).

Abram's involvement with the nations (chaps. 14–15) builds on aspects of the story of Noah and his sons (chaps. 6–10), especially on the reference to the giants, who were on the earth in those days (6:4), and on the table of nations (chap. 10).

chap. 10	*chap. 14*
	[Abram . . . by the Oaks of Mamre, 13:18].
[There were giants . . . in those days, 6:4].	It was in the days of . . .
Nimrod . . . Babel . . . Shinar . . . went forth into . . . Nineveh . . .	Amraphel king of Shinar . . . They made war on . . .
	Sodom, Gomorrah, Admah, Zeboiim

Misraim begot the Ludim, the Anamim . . . [or Ludites, Anamites]	They struck . . . the Rephaim . . . Zuzim . . .
Canaan begot . . . Jebusites, Amorites, Girgashites . . . Canaanites	They struck . . . the Amalekites . . . the Amorites . . .
Sodom, Gomorrah, Admah, Zeboiim	Then . . . Sodom, Gomorrah, Admah, Zeboiim
Shem . . . father of . . . Eber	He told Abram the Hebrew . . . Mamre the Amorite . . .
	15:19–21: . . . the Kenites . . . Rephaim . . . Amorites . . . Canaanites . . . Girgashites . . . Jebusites.

This is not parallelism. The events of chapters 14–15 are very different from the content and genre of chapter 10, almost as different as leaves from their supporting branch. But one does grow out of the other. The references to mighty men, great powers, and many nations (6:1–4; chap. 10) provided one component for Abram's encounter with powers and nations.

Structure (Table 23.1)

Panel one (chap. 14) is marked by the presence of ten kings, especially by Chedorlaomer and the king of Sodom (14:1, 5, 17, 21). Their primary feature is that they enslave. Chedorlaomer's coalition enslaves in a way that is obvious, and the king of Sodom seeks to enslave in a way that is more insidious—he tries to enrich Abram. This continuity, concerning enslavement, helps in detecting the structure of chapter 14.

Table 23.1. War, and Intimation of Death (chap. 14 // chap. 15)

War against enslavement

Introduction: war; the kings and the revolt against servitude (14:1–4)
Kings attack, and take Abram's nephew, Lot (14:5–12)
Abram counterattacks, and brings back his people (14:13–16)
Blessing: Melchizedek blesses by God Most High (14:17–19)
Conclusion: Abram's moral revolt against the king of Sodom (14:21–24)

Facing death: covenant promise against enslavement

Introduction: A vision, promising many children. Abram's faith (15:1–6)
The death-related (covenant) ritual (15:7–11)
A promise about bringing Abram's people back from servitude (15:12–16)
Conclusion: the covenant, promising a land of many peoples (15:17–21)

The process of dividing is helped further by details—the time-related repetition of "in" ("in the days/fourteenth year"), and the repetition of "Sodom" (14:12, 17, 21).

Panel two (chap. 15) consists, at a certain level, of two distinct parts, and no more—the promise of progeny (15:1–6) and the promise of land (15:7–21). But the two parts form a unity—they are separated only by "And he said to him," so that one continues the other. Besides, they are divided by another criterion—that of time: just as the beginning of chapter 15 is marked by a reference to passing time ("After these things . . ."), so the going down of the sun acts as a divider (15:12, 17). Ha, having shown the complexity of chapter 15, concludes: "The compositional unity of Gen. 15—from the literary, structural and thematic perspectives—marks it as the work of one single author" (1989, 215).

Comment

Panel One (Chap. 14)

[14:1–4] **Kings—north and south.** The four great kings enter with a flourish. Their names are like an imposing procession, a drum roll. And their introduction, "And it happened in the days of Amraphel king of Shinar . . . ," has echoes of "The giants were on the earth in those days" (6:4).

Among their kingdoms, the two that can be identified—Shinar (Babylon) and Elam—are in southern Mesopotamia. But the only other identifiable element, Tidal king of the Goiim (apparently = Tudhaliya), is Hittite—far from southern Mesopotamia. Goiim simply means "nations." The four kings therefore suggest a far-flung coalition from the powerful north.

Insofar as these kings and the other names in chapter 14 constitute a list of peoples, they are in broad continuity with the table of nations (chap. 10). More specifically, the four kings come from the same general region as mighty Nimrod (10:8–12)—the region from which so many of Israel's enemies would come.

The five kings who are attacked belong to cities at the southern part of the Dead Sea. Four are listed together in the table of nations (10:19, Sodom, Gomorrah, Admah, and Zeboiim) and the fifth, Bela, "that is Zoar," was at the end of Lot's vision (13:10, "till you come to Zoar"). The first four will be destroyed (19:20–24), but Zoar has a history of its own, from the seeing of Lot to the seeing of Moses (Gen. 13:10; 14:2, 8; 19:22–23, 30; Deut. 34:3).

The issue in the war—rebellion against servitude—will be particularly important to Abram and to his descendants.

[14:5–12] **Kings at war: might, farce, and greed.** The drum beat intensifies. Diverse elements add to it. The succession of the years builds momentum: "Twelve . . . thirteen . . . In the fourteenth. . . ." The invasion is sweeping and triumphant. Instead of coming straight, the four kings make a great detour east and south of Transjordan, defeating several peoples before turning back to face the five rebellious kings. And when the kings line up for battle, the names are repeated—the names of the five briefly, but the names of the four in full—and so the drum roll intensifies yet more. Then there is a climactic summary: "Four kings against five." The effect is like a clashing of cymbals. It is time for military heroics.

What happens is farce. Von Rad (177–178) "doubts . . . that this was reported with humor." But the event is absurd. The five kings fall into holes and run over mountains.

Yet the farce has a grim aspect; it shows that the four great northern invaders are all-conquering. They are also rapacious: "They took all the possessions of Sodom and Gomorrah. . . . They also took Lot and his possessions. . . . He was in Sodom." The repetitive phrasing is such that Lot is locked into Sodom and its possessions. It is not only the four great kings who are rapacious.

[14:13–16] Abram and Mamre: covenant, courage, and ingenuity. When the focus returns to Abram he, too, echoes the table of nations. He is called Abram "the Hebrew," a term which, insofar as it reflects a "relation to members of other national groups" (Alter, 60), echoes the table of nations, especially Abram's descent from Shem's son Eber (10:21). With Abram is "Mamre the Amorite." Mamre was alluded to at the end of the previous episode (13:18), but the Amorites first appear among those descended from Canaan (10:15).

Abram's relationship to Mamre, and to Mamre's two brothers, is governed by a covenant, thus forming as it were a covenant of brotherhood, and when he hears of Lot, his own brother, the covenant works to Lot's benefit.

Abram risks everything in his house for his brother. Literally, "he emptied out" his trained men. He also shows ingenuity in the way he deploys his forces and attacks at night. And he presses his advantage, pursuing the enemy. The mighty enemies, now vanquished, are scarcely mentioned. Attention stays with Abram, with "Lot and his possessions," and—a new element—with "the women and the people."

[14:17–20] Melchizedek's blessing. The king of Sodom, "having recovered from his asphalt bath" (Jacob, 97), acts as leader of the Canaanite coalition, and comes to meet Abram. But Melchizedek, a king who apparently is higher among the Canaanites, intervenes. Melchizedek ("righteous king"), king of Salem, brings Abram a gracious meal—surely welcome after the dangerous foray. He was a priest—Genesis's first mention of a priest—and he blesses Abram in the name of the chief Canaanite god, El Elyon, "God Most High." Abram, responding, pays tithes to Melchizedek—the first foreigner to receive blessings through Abram. Commentator Benno Jacob (97) is humorously skeptical about Melchizedek—he sees him as opportunistic, receiving booty from Abram—but the text, context, and later tradition view the priest-king positively (Sarna, 380). At one level, the level at which Genesis reflects the later history of the priesthood, this episode shows Abram, like a later worshipper, as paying what is due. But more importantly, at the level of the basic narrative, set in distant history, the figure of the gracious Canaanite priest-king provides a testimony to goodness in the midst of war and foreigners. Thus Abram's links to Canaanites, already established through his covenant with Mamre and his brothers, are strengthened. "Whatever Melchizedek's theology, Abram elegantly coopts him for monotheism by using *El Elyon* in orthodox literal sense (verse 22) when he addresses the king of Sodom" (Alter, 61).

[14:21–24] **Abram withstands Sodom, but remembers Mamre.** By now, apparently, the king of Sodom has become nervous. He has seen Abram give away a tenth of the booty and, fearing that Abram will take everything—booty and people—makes an offer of seeming generosity: "Give me the people, and the possessions take for yourself." Thus, "the king tries to save at least the most valuable part for himself. . . . [His] brief and sullen speech, not sweetened by polite phrases, seems to say that these pious gestures [between Melchizedek and Abram] are mutual aid at his expense" (Jacob, 97). But Abram, despite his acceptance of Melchizedek's food and blessing, does not blindly accept all that is Canaanite. On the contrary: "For me, nothing." And he swears in the name of the Canaanite god, thus showing that he knows how to distinguish among things Canaanite. And, remembering his covenanted Canaanite allies, he asks that Mamre and his brothers get their share.

What is important here is not the motivation of either Melchizedek or the king of Sodom—both are elusive, probably deliberately so—but the integrity of Abram. The motivation of kings and high priests is ultimately their problem, and Abram cannot be responsible for it. What he can do, however, in dealing with them, is be true to his own calling and act honorably. The essence of Genesis 14 is to show that whatever the nature of the surrounding darkness— whether the maelstrom of war or the uncertain motivation of authorities— Abram keeps his course: "For me, nothing."

Panel Two (Chap. 15)

[15:1–6] **The promise of progeny: crisis and faith.** The episode is "a vision," and though the reference to the vision is brief, it is important; it sets the scene. It also places what follows within the general context of seeing—of God making Abram see (cf. 12:1, "The land that I will make you see").

Yhwh speaks as "your shield"—an image which echoes something of the military campaign of the preceding episode (chap. 14). In a war-like world, Yhwh protects. And Yhwh will give Abram a "very great . . . reward"—an obscure reference to some form of payment or hire for Abram. At the end of the preceding episode, Abram's allies had received a "share," but Abram had taken nothing.

Now comes the crisis: "My Lord Yhwh, what will you give me, for I go childless. . . ." "Go" in this context means die (as in Ps. 39:13; Clifford, 2:24).

Abram fears he will die childless. The crisis, however, is not just about a child; it is also about the word of Yhwh and about the threat of death itself. Abram may have been victorious and noble in the military campaign, but night battles tend to evoke the worst. Battle can bring a crisis concerning death (Sheehy, 1974, 2–10; cf. Isa. 37:36–18:1).

God's answer is indirect. Instead of remaining within Abram's knotted world, within his doubt and frame of reference, Yhwh "brought him outside," and he challenged him to look at the heavens and count the stars.

A similar drama occurs in Job, but at far greater length. The answer to Job's questioning—insofar as there is an answer—does not come within the framework of Job's thinking, but through the voice from the whirlwind, which effectively brings Job into another world (Job 38–42).

Abram "believed" in Yhwh. Intellectually the problem is not solved, but Abram knows now that there is something far greater than his intellect, something far beyond what he can count or calculate, and so, rather than limit his horizon to the short scope of his own intellect, he trusts in that other greater reality.

Such an act may appear as a throwing away of his own power of thinking; it may seem to be a form of self-betrayal or even an intellectual self-mutilation. But the very opposite is true. It is by making this leap into the reality of the greater world outside that Abram reaches his true self, that he comes to what is deeply right: Yhwh "reckoned it to him as rightness." Full rightness or integrity ("righteousness") is not something that a human can achieve completely alone. Such a step involves awareness of something greater than oneself, something in which one trusts. One relies ultimately not on one's own counting but on another's reckoning.

St. Paul will use this moment to explain Christian faith (Rom. 4; Gal. 3:6–9). It is appropriate, however, while being aware of its Christian relevance, to stay with Abram. The awareness of the stars, of the universe, is not something peripheral to faith. It was in such a moment that Abram, the father of faith, first explicitly believed. The God here is first of all the God of heaven and earth, the God by whom Abram had sworn in the previous episode (14:22), the God who now shows him the heavens. It is by rootedness in this God that faith can flourish.

[15:7–21] **The promise of land: covenant, death, and knowing.** While the preceding paragraph (15:1–6) had spoken of Abram's reward, the topic now is Abram's inheritance—the land. And as the discussion flows easily into this question of the land, Abram's focus moves from the great universe to the flow of history, including his own personal history. He also moves from believing to the issue of knowing: "How [or through what] am I to know . . . ?" (15:8). He already believes, yet he wants a sign.

What follows may at first seem macabre—a grim ritual of death. At Yhwh's instruction, Abram takes three mature animals—a heifer, she-goat, and ram—

halves them down the middle, and then he and God lay them out facing each other, leaving a lifeless passageway between the parts.

To some degree the explanation is simple. God is making a covenant or agreement, and one of the rituals for making a covenant was to cut animals in two and walk between them—thus invoking similar death on any of the parties should they violate the covenant (Jer. 34:18; Clifford, 2:24). The cutting seemingly contributed to the Hebrew idiom "to cut a covenant."

But in chapter 15, death is not only a ritual threat to ensure God's compliance. Animal sacrifice has a positive meaning; in Jungian terms it represents the sacrifice of the animal nature, of the instinctual libido (Dreifuss and Riemer, 1995, 31). And death itself is an important part of the scene. The scene-setting paragraph (15:1–6) introduced Abram as facing the ultimate prospect of death. The next paragraph (15:15) tells of his going to his fathers and being buried. The sleep that comes on him is not some easy rest or trance; it is "dread and great darkness" (15:12), to be followed, when the sun has gone, by "thick darkness" (15:17). The lifeless passage surrounded by thick darkness is the passage to death.

And the scene in fact is not macabre. The evoking of death is surrounded by elements, which, with varying degrees of clarity, suggest something positive.

First (15:7–11), the divided animals are accompanied by birds, which are *not* divided. And when carrion birds come down on the corpses—birds which would have reduced the corpses to carrion meat—Abram drives them away.

Next (15:12–16), the deep sleep, despite its dread and great darkness, "is a prelude to divine intervention" (Clifford, 2:24), like the deep sleep that brought forth the woman, the mother of the living (2:21–22; 3:20). The sleep therefore has a positive role. What emerges, however, from this sleep is not a woman, but a picture of the people going from long servitude to great possessions, and of Abram going to a peaceful death.

The servitude is to last four hundred years, reckoned here as four ages. This implies that an age is a hundred years, but a full explanation would probably need to unravel the intricate relationship between the fate of the people and that of Abram. Besides, the four hundred and the four need to be examined in the context of Genesis's other references to four hundred and four (e.g., the City of Four, 23:2; and the four hundred shekels/weights, 23:15). Four sometimes connotes universalism (the four corners of the earth).

Here, too, as with the carrion birds, there is a negative note—the iniquity of the Amorites (15:16). These two negative images—the carrion birds and the iniquity of the Amorites—are connected, in their respective contexts, with other, positive, elements. The carrion birds are like the shadow side of the undivided birds (15:10–11). And the iniquity of the Amorites, which is not "complete up to now" (šalēm . . . 'ad-hēnâh, 15:16), is like the shadow side of the preceding references to Abram going in "peace" (šalôm) and the people coming back "to here" (hēnâh, 15:15–16). It is as though the evil is in some way tied in with the positive. In the preceding chapter, Abram was in covenant with an Amorite (14:13). Part of the understanding here is that "iniquity . . . is conceived of quantitatively" (Clifford, 2:24), and for the moment the iniquity has not reached such a degree, such a quantity, that it is necessary for God to intervene.

Finally (15:17–21), when the sun has gone and it would seem that all that remains is the deathly passage now wrapped in thick darkness, fire emerges and passes through the dark passage of death. The fire reflects God, God who is not only making a covenant, but also giving life where there had been death, and promising an extraordinary land—stretching from one great river to another (the Nile and Euphrates, the two greatest known rivers), and tapering off into a vast horizon of ten peoples. (The scene—the smoke, fire, darkness—intimates the later covenant on Sinai, Exod. 19.)

Unlike the question of believing, where it is said directly that Abram believed (15:6), it is never said, as directly, that Abram knew. But he asked how he should know (15:8), and he was told with emphatic directness, "Know! Know that your descendants . . ." (15:13). To a significant degree the process of knowing seems to be one of experience. If Abram is to come to know, he will do so through all that the covenant ceremony evokes, including death, birds of prey, servitude, and the end of his day. In this covenant the only one who is bound is God; and Abram's knowing, such as it is, comes from God.

24   Personal Conflict, and Vision of a Deeper Covenant (Chaps. 16–17)

A Personal Conflict Excluding Foreign Slaves (Chap. 16)
A Vision Including Such Slaves (Chap. 17)

Introductory Aspects

The Basic Story Line

The story tells how a woman who was an apparent failure and who had never spoken finally took action. In accordance with a custom that was permissible but hazardous, Sarai opted for surrogate motherhood. Using the little power she had, she gave her foreign slave, Hagar, to Abram in the hope of having a child through her. The scheme succeeded, but it engulfed the house in bitterness and tension. Sarai and Abram both suffered, but so especially did the weakest one, the pregnant slave. Despite her terrible vulnerability, she ran away.

But just when all seemed lost, the story turned around. First, God's messenger spoke at some length to Hagar and, by giving her a new sense of herself, persuaded her to go back to Sarai and Abram, where she gave birth to her child. Then (chap. 17), when the child was on the verge of adulthood, God spoke again, to Abram, and gave a covenant, which effectively lifted the status of all the people in the household. Abram and Sarai received new names—signs of new fertility—and the covenant was such that it included slaves. At the end, the sign of the covenant, circumcision, was received simultaneously by Abram and the slave's son.

As a result of the story, Sarai leaves her silent isolation; and the sense of the covenant, already established through the cutting of animals (chap. 15), now reaches a new level of inclusion and of moral depth.

Literary Form

The literary forms of chapters 16–17 are diverse. Chapter 16, which at first may seem like a soap opera, is probably best regarded as a conflict narrative (Westermann, II, 235). Chapter 17, however, is a further form of vision ("... Yhwh was seen by Abram," 17:1). It is "a typical theophanic narrative" (Fretheim, 458).

Complementarity of the Two Panels

Given the diversity between the two chapters it is easy to invoke diverse sources. But Genesis 17 belongs to its present context (Ska, 1989, 114), and, besides, a literary artist may use diverse styles to describe diverse moments. In this case the petty conflict (chap. 16) and the noble covenant (chap. 17) are like two sides of the same coin, antithetic parallels. One side tells how, with Abram's consent, Sarai ill-treated her foreign slave and effectively expelled her. The other side tells how Abram, having embraced blamelessness, embraces also a covenant that includes foreigners and slaves. The two chapters present a sharp contrast in moral conduct—specifically with regard to foreigners and slaves. Contrasts are instructive, and, by forming a contrast that is so precise, the two parts belong together.

The contrast, however, must not be overdrawn. Both texts give surprising announcements—concerning the birth of Ishmael, son of the foreign slave (16: 7–13), and concerning the birth of Isaac (17:15–22). And both conclude with episodes involving Ishmael—his birth (16:15–16), and his circumcision (17:23–27).

Nor is the Hagar story all conflict. Its later part, when the messenger of Yhwh speaks to Hagar (16:7–14), is already a form of vision, effectively a preparation for Abram's divine encounter (chap. 17).

Taken together the *conflict* and the *vision* (chaps. 16–17) are a development of the *war* and the *vision* (chaps. 14–15). But while the war was hugely public, the conflict is intensely personal.

Relationship to Preceding Chapters

RELATIONSHIP TO ASPECTS OF GENESIS 1–14

Sarai's action—telling Abram to go to Hagar, and then giving her to him—may indeed have been sanctioned by custom (as reflected in fifteenth-century Nuzi texts; Clifford, 2:25; Speiser, 119–121), and it had a good result, namely Ishmael. Nonetheless, her action has negative overtones—an edge of bitterness and of lack of faith—and it has an echo of the debacle in Egypt. There Abram had effectively given her to Egypt's ruler; now she gives him to an Egyptian slave.

More fundamentally, her action also contains a variation on the scene in the Garden: the woman takes the initiative, seeks to be built up, and gives to the submissive man, who hears the voice of his wife. But, again, the resulting drama of the eyes ("her eyes . . . your eyes") is disillusioning, and leads to a form of expulsion—Hagar's flight.

The angel finds Hagar in the wilderness, and after questioning her, sends her back. Here, too, there are multiple resonances of the scene in the Garden, but with a difference: the Garden scene is reversed. The mission of the messenger/angel—unlike that of the cherubim guarding the tree of life—is not to ensure her expulsion. The angel's questions ("Where . . . ? And where . . . ?") may have echoes of Yhwh God's questions in the Garden ("Where . . . ? Who . . . ?") but their effect is not to drive her farther away. And when the angel then makes a triple pronouncement ("Go back. . . . I will greatly multiply. . . . Behold you have conceived. . . .") the form and words may indeed echo Yhwh God's triple pronouncement (to the serpent, the woman, and the man), but their message to the woman is the opposite. She is told not of a great multiplication of pains in conceiving and bringing forth children, but of a great multiplication of descendants and the conceiving of a child called Ishmael.

The result is not that the man names the woman but that the woman names God—El Roi, the God of Seeing. The negative dramas surrounding the process of seeing (the Garden; Egypt; Lot; Sarah) are now reversed in the unlikely figure of Hagar.

The description of Ishmael—his conception, his role as a response to affliction, his tension with his brothers ("wild ass" suggests someone difficult), his dwelling (16:11–12)—distills many of the aspects surrounding those born after the expulsion from the Garden (especially Cain, Seth, and Noah, 4:1–16, 25–26; 5:29). But again the negative drama of the past is now reversed: despite echoing Cain's tension with his brother, the picture of Ishmael is essentially positive.

This reversal is not completely new. Already within chapters 1–5 the downward slide, which culminated in Cain and Lamech (4:1–24), was turned around—first in the births of Seth and Enosh (4:25–26), and then in the genealogy from Adam to Noah (chap. 5). But now the reversal is accomplished though someone on the margin of the world—a woman, a foreigner, a slave.

The following episode (chap. 17)—the covenant that is blameless—reflects aspects of the story of Noah (6:1–9:17). Like Noah, Abram is to walk before God and be blameless (6:9; 17:2).

Rather as God's covenant to Noah was all-inclusive, involving the saving of all creatures (6:18–21), so now God's covenant to Abram is far-reaching. It includes a multitude of nations (hence Abram's new name) and also those within Abram's household who are foreigners and slaves (17:4–6, 12–13). Any soul who is not in the ark or not in the covenant will die or be cut off (7:21–23; 17: 14).

For both covenants there is a sign—the rainbow (9:12–17) and circumcision (9:10–11).

God's announcement that Sarah will give birth (17:15–22) has echoes of the rebirth of the world after the flood (8:15–9:11): many creatures/people come out (out of the ark; out of Sarah); there is blessing, fruitfulness, and multiplying (9:1, 7; 17:16, 20); and there is a suggestion of worship and of speaking in the heart (8:20–21; 17:17).

The Noah story itself is a story of reversal: the world, which had been condemned, is brought back; the heart, which seemed thoroughly evil, becomes a motive for forbearance (6:5; 8:20–21). In the Abraham story that reversal is brought further. The heart is not only mentioned, but is mentioned in relation to someone who, as well as apparently worshipping (Abraham falls on his face), is also laughing (17:17). In other words, the heart, once seen as so evil, moves not only to worship but toward laughter.

The conclusion, the circumcising (17:23–27), reflects an aspect of Noah's conduct—doing exactly as God commands (6:22; 7:5, 9; 17:23).

RELATIONSHIP TO THE COVENANT OF GENESIS 15

To some degree the second covenant (chap. 17) repeats the first (chap. 15). Yet it goes further, and it does so in several ways—concerning Abram, the promise, and God's own self.

Abram's role in the first covenant (chap. 15) was quite limited. The obligation fell primarily on Yhwh, and all that was required of Abram was faith. But even though in one way faith is enough—it makes a person right (15:6)— God now comes back and supplements it with a covenant that requires blameless conduct, and that conduct involves care to include foreigners and slaves. In chapter 17 the covenant comes closer as it were, even physically: "The contractual cutting up of animals in chapter 15 is now followed by a cutting of human flesh" (Alter, 73).

The promises take further shape. On the one hand they become more precise, with a clearer identification of the land with Canaan ("the land of your sojournings," 17:8), and a clearer reference to the birth of a son from Sarah (17:15–19). Such precision—this land, this person—tend to make the promise seem narrow.

But at another level, the promise becomes wider than ever. Abram's new name, Abraham, is associated with phrases that seem limitless—"a multitude of nations . . . a multitude of nations" (17:4, 6). And the promise regarding Ishmael ("I will bless him and make him fruitful and multiply him," 17:20) suggests some form of further creation (cf. 1:28; 9:1).

With regard to God, chapter 17 lays more emphasis on divine sovereignty, on the way in which God completely surpasses human calculation. The sovereignty is seen first in the style—solemn, repetitive, lofty. It is seen also in the content; in chapter 15 Abram was trying, as it were, to expand Yhwh to match his own human requirements, but in chapter 17 God is so far beyond Abraham's calculation that Abraham laughs and tells God not to go too far, that Ishmael will be enough.

With regard to the divine name, the use in chapter 17 of "God" rather than "Yhwh" fits with larger patterns—especially the general way in which chapter 17 seeks to deepen the covenant, and the way in which, after the negative beginning of the Hagar story, the scene as a whole (chaps. 16–17) moves toward a greater divine presence and a greater sense of divine sovereignty. As in Genesis 1, "God" tends to evoke God as sovereign.

Leading Elements

This is the third diptych in the Abraham story, and like other third diptychs (4:17–chap. 5; and chap. 11) it moves well beyond what precedes. It is ten years later (16:3), and Abram's age, not mentioned since the beginning (12:4), is now given twice—in successive verses, which link the chapters (16:16; 17:1). Sarai likewise, not seen since Egypt (12:14–20), now reappears in both chapters, and in a new light. Both Abram and Sarai receive new names.

This diptych brings a new awareness of inclusiveness. To some degree Abraham's original call (12:1–3) was inclusive of all people, but now the idea becomes clearer. The setting does not have the panoramic geography of chapters 14 and 15—at one level all the action is restricted to Abraham's household—yet it alludes more clearly to new horizons. It refers to a multitude of nations, to kings of peoples, to twelve princes (17:5, 16, 20). The covenant, given new depth and moral strength, now explicitly includes the weakest—the foreigners and slaves. Hagar at one stage is a foreign woman slave refugee.

During the two-panel scene, God's mode of presence changes. At first, when Sarai is in charge (16:1–6), God says nothing. Sarai speaks of Yhwh twice, first in a way that is very negative (as preventing her from having children, 16:2—

her first words in Genesis); then, in a way that has a mixture of bitterness and hope (God is the hoped-for judge of her suffering, 16:5).

Later, as the Hagar episode goes on, the messenger speaks in such a way that God's voice emerges increasingly, first in two short questions (16:8), and then in three utterances, which are increasingly long and positive (16:9–12).

When the angel has finished, the sense of God takes a further step forward: the one who had spoken to her is called not "the angel of Yhwh," but simply "Yhwh" (16:13).

The next reference to God—apart from the elusive terms "El Roi" and "El Shaddai"—is again to Yhwh: "Yhwh was seen by Abram" (17:1). Then, after Abram shows himself as disposed to being blameless, God is finally called Elohim, "God." And then "God" speaks at length—in three increasingly long sections (17: 4–8; 9–14; and 15–22).

The contrast between the two chapters, therefore, is not simple—as though one used "Yhwh" and the other "God." Rather there is first a steady increase in the presence and word of "Yhwh" and then an increase in speech from "God."

Structure (Table 24.1)

The Hagar text (chap. 16) has two main parts (Sarai, 16:3–6; and the messenger, 16:7–14); and the covenant text (chap. 17) has three.

PANEL ONE (CHAP. 16)

When a chapter has only two main parts (as in chap. 16), each of these parts generally falls into three subsections, but the part devoted to Sarai (16:3–6) seems to have only two such subdivisions. However, the part devoted to Hagar (16:7–14) does have three subdivisions—the third, as usual, being somewhat apart (16:13–14). The apparent deficiency in the structure of the Sarai text may be a reflection of the status of Sarai herself, of the way she feels small ("less"). In any case, even in the quantity of text, Sarai is less than Hagar.

PANEL TWO (CHAP. 17)

The three parts of chapter 17 are distinguished particularly by the changing emphasis on God (17:3b–8), Abraham (17:9–14), and Sarah (17:15–22). The diminishment of Sarai in chapter 16 is counterbalanced by the length of the third, Sarah-centered, part of chapter 17 (17:15–22). The two long texts in question (16:7–14; 17:15–22) deal not only with Hagar and Sarai respectively, but also with the annunciations of the births of Ishmael (16:9–14) and Isaac (17:17–22).

Table 24.1. Conflict Concerning Foreign Slaves (chap. 16 // chap. 17)

Conflict: expelling the foreign slave, Hagar

Introduction: Sarai proposes Hagar to Abram (16:1–2)
Sarai's suffering prayer and expulsion of the foreign slave (16:3–4)
   Sarai becomes less in Hagar's eyes (16:3–4)
   Sarai afflicts Hagar, who flees (16:5–6)
Hagar's suffering and encounter with God (16:7–14)
   An angel meets Hagar, fleeing (16:7–8)
   The angel's triple statement; annunciation of Ishmael's birth (16:7–12)
   Hagar acknowledges the seeing of God (7:13–14)
Conclusion: Hagar bears Ishmael to Abram (16:15–16)

Covenant: including foreign slaves

Introduction: Thirteen years later: a conduct-based covenant (17:1–3)
God: I—and my covenant (17:4–8)
   Abraham, a new name, including many nations (17:4–6)
   My covenant: I will be their God (17:7–8)
God: you (17:9–14)
   The covenant for you—circumcision (17:9–11)
   The covenant includes slaves and foreigners (17:12–14)
God: Sarai (17:15–22)
   Sarah, a new name (17:15–16)
   The announcement of the birth of Isaac (17:17–22)
Conclusion: Ishmael at thirteen; Abraham is circumcised (17:23–27)

Chapter 17 is framed by references to Abraham's age—ninety-nine (17:1, 24). Furthermore, the whole chapter tells of a single appearance of God to Abram.

The conclusion (17:23–27) has four finely balanced subsections (17:23, 24, 25, and 26–27)—somewhat like the conclusions of creation (2:1–4a) and the deluge (9:12–17).

Comment

Panel One (Chap. 16)

[16:1–2] **Sarai's lifeless God.** Thus far Sarai has not spoken. However, with minimal words, the narrative has drawn an enigmatic picture. There are two salient facts. From one point of view, that of a world where childbearing was central, she is radically inadequate. From another point of view, she had been the toast of the world's leading society—Egypt and its court. When the narrative now comes back to her, the opening verse echoes aspects of these two facts—she "had not borne . . . And she had an Egyptian slave-woman." Her Egyptian adventure may be over, but she has a reminder of it.

With regard to God, she is as empty as her womb. It is as though there is a correlation between the lifelessness in her body and the lifelessness in her soul. She does not deny God's existence—the existence of some deity was generally not an issue—but her sense of God is negative: "Behold, Yhwh has prevented me from bearing [children]. Go. . . ." Yhwh for her is subordinate, passed over in a virtually subordinate clause, and insofar as Yhwh is real, Yhwh is the source of lifelessness, and implicitly, of a form of cruelty.

She feels small. "Go to my maid," she says, "perhaps I shall be built [or built up] from her." The building refers first of all to something personal ("perhaps *I* shall be built . . .") but it may also refer to a corporate building up— the building up of a people; Sarah is watchful that, through her, a people be built up (Jeansonne, 1990, 19). Something similar will happen with Tamar; Tamar will show more determination and resourcefulness in building Judah's people than Judah himself (chap. 38).

Yet, ambitions of building can have an ambiguous character. The builders at Babel had sought a self-made identity, and Sarai, in her own way, apparently seeks to be built up in a way that bypasses her lifeless deity.

[16:3–6] **The mistress (gĕbîrâ) becomes less—and angry.** The idea of being built up turns out to be an illusion. In fact the opposite happens. Sarai is now described as Hagar's mistress, (gĕbîrâ) akin to gibôr, "mighty." This could be ominous. Thus far Genesis has overpowered or demystified the mighty (6:4; 7:18–20; 10:8–9). In the event, Sarai, instead of being built up, "became less" (16:4), less even in the eyes of a slave.

Her fall is now complete. She has gone from being admired by Egyptian high society to being looked down on by an Egyptian slave.

She feels misused, and she directs herself to Abram: "This outrage (ḥamas) against me is from you!" This word (ḥamas) suggests not only wrong, but even violence. It may appear that she is throwing a tantrum and taking it out on the nearest person. But there is profound suffering, and in the virtual absence of God, she has no sense of direction.

Then she looks at herself: "I, I gave my slave woman . . . ," and, having summarized (and apparently relived) what happened, she comes back again to the consequences: ". . . I became less in her eyes."

Next, she comes to the deity: "May Yhwh judge (šāpaṭ) between you and me." However deep the anger, confusion, and suffering, this desperate prayer is a significant step forward. It is as though the depth of her fall has woken something. There is a now a glimmer of hope that the deity might eventually do something for her, give her justice.

But she lets the moment pass. Her sight ("what is good in . . . [her] eyes") is perverted and she unleashes her frustration on the weakest, on the slave. The motives of both women are complex, and both suffer (Jeansonne, 1990, 20), but

Sarai is stronger. She "regards Hagar . . . as no more than a possession" (Darr, 1991, 133). While all three bear some blame in the domestic conflict (Sarai, Abram, and Hagar), "Sarah bears the greatest portion of guilt" (Darr, 1991, 148–156, esp. 152). Hagar is "in her hand" and she afflicts her so badly that the slave runs away.

[16:7–16] A spring in the wilderness: Hagar sees. As well as being woman, foreigner, and slave, Hagar also becomes a refugee. The road she is on, "the way to Shur," goes toward Egypt. The terrain is wilderness. The word šûr, "Shur," may also be read as a verb, "to see," a word that links with the rest of the Hagar story (Alter, 69).

Suddenly, immediately, someone intervenes: "The messenger of Yhwh found her . . ."—virtually Genesis's first angel (cf. 3:24; in the Old Testament the messenger or angel mediates the divine word, or constitutes God's own self in human form). There was never a suggestion that Sarai was visited by the messenger of Yhwh. Sarai had uttered a desperate prayer for Yhwh to judge, but ironically, Hagar, who was in her hand, needed judgment even more, and it is to Hagar that the angel goes.

With the messenger of Yhwh there is life, "a spring of water." Unlike Sarai, who associated Yhwh with lifelessness, Hagar's messenger is associated with something close to life, even in a desert.

But the messenger does not convey life in any simplistic way. The messenger implicitly reminds Hagar that she is Sarai's maid, and then poses two questions: "Where have you come from? And where are you going?" (16:8). At one level, these questions are prosaic, but at another they are probing, requiring a review of much of one's life. Hagar said, "From the face of Sarai. . . ."

The messenger's triple response sends her back to the affliction, to Sarai's face or presence. Hagar will learn to live with Sarah's antagonism. Her son, too, will live with antagonism. The angel announces that the son will have to deal with the face or presence of his brothers (16:12). The experiences of mother and son are related by verbal echoes:

"From the face of Sarai my mistress; I, I am fleeing."

"Toward the face of all his brothers he shall dwell."

Sarai may represent a form of affliction, but for Hagar there is a way of dealing with it, a way of facing Sarai that is life-giving. And something similar will be true for her son. Given the positive tenor of the angel's message, there is an implication that Ishmael's closeness to his brothers, however difficult, will itself be positive. "Ishmael" means "God hears/has heard."

At one level this closeness is physical; Ishmael will live beside the land promised to Abraham. "His hand against all" expresses some of his powerful raw energy. But the physical closeness seems to be the indicator of a further, moral, closeness; Ishmael will share something with his brothers. Later (17:18) Abraham asks that Ishmael live "before the face" of God—a further indication that "the face" is more than physical.

Hagar apparently hesitated when the messenger first told her to return to Sarai and affliction. But as the messenger continues, addressing her three times, Hagar comes to a fresh perception.

Hagar "called the name of Yhwh who spoke to her, 'You are the God of Seeing' (El Roi)," but the Hebrew wording of her explanation (16:13b) is corrupt or at least cryptic: "Have I not seen here also after [his] seeing me?" (cf. Clifford, 2:25: "Have I not from here seen after seeing me?" Alter, 71: "Did not I go on seeing here after He saw me?"). In much biblical tradition it was not possible to see God and live, but Hagar, despite her divine vision, still lives, and she is grateful.

The issue, however, is not only that she has seen God and lived, but—as indicated by the preceding phrase (16:13a, "God of Seeing") and by the earlier seeing motif (12:1, 7; 13:14–15; 15:1, 5; 16:4, 6)—that God is a God of seeing; and she now knows that God sees her and makes her see. The result is a new sense of reality and of herself.

For with seeing comes life; " 'see' has the sense of see and rescue" (Clifford, 2:25). The spring, now called a well, is named not just "the Well of the One Who Sees Me," but "the Well of the *Living* One Who Sees Me." The implication is of a life-giving down-to-earth presence.

Then, as if to concretize that down-to-earth presence, the text adds, "Behold, it is between Kadesh and Bered." Bered is otherwise unknown, but Kadesh, forty-five miles south of Beer-sheba, was very familiar.

The conclusion, when Hagar bears Ishmael, is brief (16:15–16), but it seems to bring Abram to life. He is eighty-six, but his name is mentioned four times (in two short verses), and he gets the name right: "God Hears" (Ishma-el). Hagar's name occurs three times. There is no reference to Sarai.

Panel Two (Chap. 17)

[17:1–3a] Abram at ninety-nine and the God of life. The introduction (17:1–3a) indicates something new. Abram is a startling ninety-nine, and God is not only seen but uses a new name (El Shaddai). Furthermore, there is a new challenge for Abram: to be like another Noah ("Walk before me and be blameless;" cf. Noah, 6:9). His response, falling on his face, indicates a readiness to accept the challenge.

Yet all is not new. The opening (17:1) reflects the end of chapter 16:
16:16: "Abram was eighty-six years old when Hagar bore Ishmael to Abram."
17:1: "Abram was ninety-nine years old and Yhwh was seen by Abram."

The similarity, within successive verses, is so close and obvious as to suggest a correlation between the two sentences, specifically between God and birth (the birth of Ishmael and seeing God). Chapter 16 had started with Sarai implying a correlation between God and nonbirth (16:2). The effect of both beginnings is to strengthen the idea that, in the Abraham narrative, birth is related to God and to the seeing of God.

There is further continuity between chapter 17 and the later part of chapter 16. Most of chapter 17 is cast in the form of an appearance of God, an account of God being seen. But the major breakthrough in seeing had occurred with Hagar (16:7–17).

The meaning of El Shaddai (17:1) is unclear, perhaps God of the Mountain (from Akkadian *šadû*; Speiser, 124), or God of Might. The name—also tentatively associated with fertility—was considered by the biblical writers as archaic (cf. Exod. 6:3; Alter, 72). When used elsewhere in Genesis (28:3; 35:11; 43:14; 48:3) it tends to be associated, as here, with good fortune, especially with abundant company and with some form of protected journey (it occurs also in Exod. 6:3; Ezek. 10:5). Its position here (17:1) seems to form a pattern with other references to God—as El Elyon (14:19, 22), as shield (15:1), and as El Roi (16: 13–14).

[17:3b–8] **The covenant of the sovereign God.** The covenant that God now offers does not negate the earlier one (chap. 15), but it deepens it. The divine name, "God," is more elevated, the style of address is more repetitively solemn, and Abram is required to be blameless. Furthermore he receives a new name—"Abraham." "Abram" and "Abraham" are variants of one name, but the longer variant, *'ab-rāhām*, has an assonance with *'ab hămôn*, "father of a multitude," and so in 17:5 it now receives that meaning.

The range of the covenant becomes even greater when God speaks of "a multitude of nations," of "kings," and of a covenant that is "everlasting." The use of "nations" and "kings" (a pairing found in Isa. 41:2; 45:1; 60:3; Jer. 25: 14) "suggest[s] perhaps that [the text] . . . is underscoring Abraham's role in world history" (Clifford, 2:26).

There is, in fact, a tension between the sense of the covenant as vast, everlasting, and the covenant as focused on something limited in time and space— "the land of your sojournings, all the land of Canaan" (17:8). The text seems to be operating on two levels. On the level of what is immediately tangible, the land is a place for now, a place to sojourn. On another level, the land is something far greater, for multitudes of nations forever.

[17:9–14] **The covenant of circumcision, foreigners and slaves.** The ambiguous range of the covenant now becomes clearer. As a sign of the covenant, God chooses circumcision, a ritual which, far from being exclusive, was common to many peoples (for details, see Sarna, 385–387; for a personal account of being circumcised, see Mandela, 1994, 24–29). Something similar had happened in the case of Noah: the sign of the covenant, the rainbow in the clouds, had been open to all people. In Noah's situation such openness was understandable; but even now, with Abraham, the sign, in fact, is not exclusive.

What follows underlines that the covenant is not limited to Abraham's physical descendants. God insists that the sign of the covenant be given to all those in Abraham's household—including those born in the household or bought from foreigners, in other words, including slaves whether domestic or foreign.

Women were included insofar as they were members of households where the males were circumcised. In this diptych, the roles of Sarah and Hagar give women a leading position.

Circumcision, therefore, as depicted here, is inclusive. Yet, insofar as circumcision goes against nature and nature's pleasure—it involves a painful bloodletting—it sets a person apart from nature:

> Circumcision originates in the need to segregate humanity, previously at one with nature, to set humans apart from the world and its natural laws. . . . The inevitable bloodletting that occurs in the Jewish rite symbolizes spiritual sacrifice. . . . By offering both facets of himself to the divinity, the circumcised man transcends the sphere of mere corporeal existence and enters that in which the psyche, too, fulfills itself. (Dreifuss and Riemer, 1995, 55)

It is no accident then that, when Abram agrees to circumcision, he and Sarai receive a name change. "Circumcision has become a metaphor denoting spiritual and ethical purification" (ibid., 56). Abram and Sarai are moving to a new level of spiritual development.

[17:15–22] **From incredulous laughter to the laughter of joy.** God extends Abraham's horizons yet further by renaming Sarai as Sarah (dialectical variants of one name, meaning "Princess"), and promising her blessing, which here means fertility—a son, and even "nations, kings of peoples."

It is at this stage that Abraham laughs and asks in his heart what God is doing, asks about bringing a child into the world at age one hundred and, in Sarah's case, at ninety.

His previous problem, in his crisis before the first covenant (15:1–6), was that God was not meeting his expectations, was not giving him what he wanted out of life. His sense of his life was failing; and he needed an act of faith to keep going. In a sense he had wanted too much.

The problem now is that he wants too little. After thirteen years of Ishmael, he thinks he knows what life and God have to offer, and the difficulty is to awaken into realizing there is more.

When he tells God he will settle for Ishmael and for seeing Ishmael do well ("Just let Ishmael live before your face"), God protests, "But [no]; Sarah your wife will bear you a son and you shall call his name *yiṣḥāq*, "laugh" (*or* "he laughs;" "literally, 'May God laugh in delight, smile upon!' "—Clifford 2:26). Abraham's laugh had been the laugh of disbelief, but God is promising laughter of another kind, something that, for Abraham, is difficult to accept. Subsequent chapters bring out diverse meanings of this laughter-related verb. These meanings include "joyous laughter, bitter laughter, mockery, and sexual dalliance" (Alter, 75).

Here, in speaking of progeny, there is an ambiguity. God promises the covenant to Isaac, but the promise to Ishmael, instead of being abandoned, is expanded, like a further creation ("bless . . . fruitful . . . multiply . . . He shall beget twelve princes," 17:20). Some of the same ambiguity was seen earlier (17:

8) about the land. God is building toward physical descent from Abraham and Sarah, and simultaneously encompassing a far wider world.

[17:23–27] **Circumcision—with Ishmael, and with foreign slaves.** The account of Abraham's circumcision is coupled, in matching phrases, with that of Ishmael (17:24–25). Furthermore, not only is Ishmael thirteen; there is a thirteen-year period in Abraham's life also; notices of his age occur at eighty-six and ninety-nine (16:16; 17:1). It is as though Abraham, at some level, is also thirteen—about the right age for circumcision. Circumcision was a rite initiatory to fertility (puberty or marriage), except that in Abraham's case fertility is also linked to seeing God.

The account of the circumcision of both Abraham and Ishmael is in turn framed by references to the broader process of circumcising, which encompasses *all* of Abraham's household, including the foreigners and slaves (17:23, 26–27). This framing format—the same as occurs at the end of creation (2:1–4a) and of creation's restoration (9:12–17)—confirms the sense of a covenant, which at some level is wide-ranging, even universal.

---

25   Sodom: Generosity-Based Justice (18:1–19:29)

Abraham's Generosity: A Basis for Justice (Chap. 18)
The Rescue of Lot: Justice as Generous (19:1–29)

Introductory Aspects

The Basic Story Line

This story goes from care to catastrophe. It begins with Abraham's extraordinary hospitality to strangers, his attentiveness even to their feet, and it ends with whole cities being consumed by fire.

The opening seems lethargic: a man sitting by a tent entrance, at the hottest part of the day—like a slumbering scene from a scorching desert. Already the story has a form of fire.

But the heat and its lethargy do not prevail. Seeing the strangers, Abraham comes to life and pours hospitality on them in a way that is admirable, breathless, and amusing.

His visitors, if he knew it, are divine—God in the form of three men. After the meal they quietly stage an annunciation: Sarah will have a son. And Sarah, against heavy odds—her own kind of lethargy, her bitterness—listens. And she begins to come to life.

The story thus far is one of great vitality. The divine visitors are an occasion of generosity and surprise. In different ways both Abraham and Sarah rise up from a kind of lifelessness, and they do so in a fashion that is eye-catching.

But then the story changes, switching suddenly to a picture of lifelessness that is utterly unresponsive—a city so corrupt that God is thinking of taking drastic action. Should God hide it from Abraham?

It now emerges (18:16–21) that God is somehow very close to Abraham. God has known him (18:19), and this knowing leads to a particular way of living—a way of deep justice. Implicitly, Abraham's wonderful generosity is now seen, not just as cultural or personal, but as the outflow of this knowing of God. In some way his generosity flows from God. Furthermore, as God knows Abraham, so, in some way, Abraham knows God. God's drastic plan is not hidden from Abraham.

And so, with great boldness, Abraham argues with God about the fate of the city—about the justice of killing innocent people. God listens. There is great irony here, since the generosity that drives Abraham to plead with God derives ultimately from God's own self.

But the people are not innocent. The whole city is corrupt, bent on homosexual gang rape. Abraham's few relatives, being less corrupt, are saved, and the city is consumed by fire from God.

At the end Abraham looks down on the terrible scene. He sees smoking devastation, but he is aware that the scene has another dimension. He had talked this through with a God more generous than himself, and the smoke has reminiscences of another smoking scene, when, in the face of growing awareness of his own ultimate death, God had made a covenant with him (15:17–18).

Literary Form

The two basic underlying literary types are those of a vision (chap. 18) and a crime-and-punishment story (19:1–29). In the down-to-earth, vision-like scene, when Yhwh appears to Abraham in the form of three visitors, the primary emphasis is on generosity. Abraham falls to the ground not so much in awe and worship as in hospitality. The energy that is normally turned toward God is now directed into practical expression, into down-to-earth generosity.

This generosity is not limited to Abraham. It is based on the surpassing generosity of God, as will emerge in the subsequent conversation (18:9–33). God's generosity is seen, for instance, in the blessings promised to the incredulous Sarah (18:9–15). At the end of the panel, when Abraham has finished questioning God (18:33), the phrasing is turned to show that the direction of the conversation was not from Abraham to God but from God to Abraham ("when Yhwh . . . had completed speaking to Abraham"). In a sense, it was God who had been pushing Abraham to ensure that justice would be generous. Thus while Abraham is generous and just, God is even more so.

Interwoven with the vision is a further type-scene, that of an annunciation of birth, but the usual features of an annunciation scene have been adapted to lay greater emphasis on the divine or miraculous (Alter, 78).

The crime-and-punishment story (19:1–29), concerning Lot and the destruction of Sodom, is an illustration of justice. Sodom is destroyed, but not callously. Justice is observed scrupulously, making sure no innocent person is punished. In fact, there is unmerited generosity. Lot's hospitality (19:1–3) is not as generous as Abraham's, but God treats even this relatively ungenerous person with great mercy and kindness.

Complementarity of the Two Panels

Letellier (1995, 39–42) summarizes aspects of continuity or complementarity between the two panels. His title captures one such aspect: *Day in Mamre, Night in Sodom*. There are several other continuities (Hamilton, II, 30).

Relationship to Preceding Chapters

The entire diptych (18:1–19:29) has numerous affinities with the flood story (6: 1–9:17). God's great punishment now, however, is not by flood but by fire. As the flood was a major turning point within Genesis 1–11, so is the destruction of Sodom within the Abraham story. There are numerous linking details (Alter, 88).

The previous episode (chap. 17) saw Abraham becoming like Noah—walking blamelessly before God (17:1). Now, Abraham's Noah-like quality is put to the test: he faces the destruction, not of the world, as Noah did, but of two cities; and not by water but by fire. The flood story, despite all its negativity, was primarily about compassionate grace, a precedent for this story's emphasis on generosity, on generous mercy.

The interwovenness of the Sodom episode with other biblical texts is best described by Alter (1986), who concludes: "the Sodom episode reaches back multifariously into the Abraham narrative, and further still to the Deluge and ultimately the creation story, and forward to the future history of Israel . . ." (1986, 38).

Leading Elements

The seriousness of the issues in this diptych has been highlighted by Letellier (1995, 248–254), who speaks of "the symbolic substratum" of the text, and by Fields (1997, 27–53), who highlights the attitude to strangers. The submotifs concern time and space, and the treatment of outsiders (Fields, 1997, 54–115).

Generosity and justice, the two elements highlighted here, belong together. Unlike the Greeks, who tended to visualize justice as an expression of precise measurement, symbolized by the weighing scales, Genesis shows justice as flowing from generosity. Hence, while the destruction of two cities raises questions about God's justice, the tone of the narrative is not apologetic. The purpose is not just to show that God's justice meets human standards, the standard of the precise weighing of guilt, but that God's justice is something greater and richer, something based not on the weighing scale but on an immeasurable generosity. The same crucial idea pervades the prophets: God's justice is founded not on begrudging measurement but on a mighty stream of mercy (Heschel, 1962, 212).

In this whole diptych God appears in diverse forms—as Yhwh, as three men, as Yhwh and two men or two angels, and as "God." One of the purposes of this interchanging is to show diverse aspects of God; "the fluidity of actors . . . is a narrative means of describing both the nearness and mysterious elusiveness of God" (Clifford, 2:28). A further purpose is to indicate, on the sensitive issue of justice, that God is not some distant despot, but is thoroughly intermingled with the reality of human life. This intermingling or interweaving reaches a further level at Sodom (chap. 19), when the term "men" is used of both the would-be rapists and of the divine messengers.

Structure (Table 25.1)

PANEL ONE (CHAP. 18)

The first panel narrates a single episode, a visit, framed by Yhwh's arrival and departure. Curiously, each of its three main parts seem to have three subdivi-

---

Table 25.1. The Story of Sodom (chap. 18 // 19:1–29)

Abraham's generosity: a basis for justice

Introduction: Yhwh appears; Abraham's generous meal (18:1–8)
The future of Sarah—a child (18:9–15)
The future of Abraham—teaching his children justice (18:16–21)
Abraham pleads for justice (18:22–32)
Conclusion: Yhwh goes away; Abraham goes home (18:33)

Rescuing Lot: justice as generous

Introduction: Lot's hospitality and meal (19:1–3)
Crime: The injustice of the whole city (19:4–14)
   Wickedness: Lot comes out at the entrance and shuts the door (19:4–6)
   Wickedness intensifies: blinded, not finding the entrance (19:7–11)
   Destruction announced. In their eyes, Lot is joking (19:12–14)
Punishment: Sodom's three-stage destruction (19:15–28)
   Dawn: Angels rescue Lot—with mercy and kindness (19:15–22)
   Sunrise: Yhwh destroys the city (19:23–26)
   Morning: Abraham goes to where he had stood (19:27–28)
Conclusion: God remembered Abraham, and rescued Lot (19:29)

---

sions, rather than just two (divisions occur after vv. 10, 12, 15, 18, 19, 21, 26, 30, 32).

PANEL TWO (19:1–29)

A single episode, the second panel describes the overthrow of Sodom. Its first main part (19:4–14), Sodom's crime, is divided by varying images of the people of Sodom being shut off from seeing and knowing. Lot shuts the door, which they want to enter (4:6); then they are blinded so that they cannot find the entrance (4:11); and the eyes of his sons-in-law are such that they do not grasp that he is offering them a way out.

The second part, Sodom's punishment (19:15–26), is divided by advancing time—dawn, sunrise, morning—but the first subdivision, emphasizing mercy and kindness (19:15–22), is disproportionately large and to some degree contains its own subdivisions.

Comment

Panel One (Chap. 18)

[18:1–8] Three guests in the heat of the day: the generosity of Abraham and Sarah. The scene begins at the place where Abraham had first settled— by the Oaks of Mamre (in Hebron, 13:18). The setting may seem lethargic; it is the hottest time of the day, and Abraham is not on his feet; he is just sitting at the entrance of his tent. No mention is made of his age (ninety-nine). Then a guest appears.

The guest is God in the form of three humans, and Abraham addresses them first as singular, then as plural. Throughout the whole diptych God's form changes—varying from one to three to two—intertwining in diverse ways with humans. This intertwining is particularly important when, as a catastrophe strikes, God may appear to be utterly absent.

The scene is one of the most significant and striking in the Bible. Abraham's response to the sudden appearance of the three men is admirable and amusing; his hospitality is "prodigious" (Gossai, 1995, 46). His response is also puzzling. How can someone so old have so much vitality? As one observer commented, "In this scene, Abraham is like a boy" (Nicholas King, in conversation, Pietermaritzburg, Natal, May 26, 1995). A clue to Abraham's vitality is in his position: "The tent door symbolizes Abraham's psychic receptiveness" (Dreifuss and Riemer, 1995, 57).

In fact the scene does contain a boy (boy/lad/young man, *na'ar*, 18:7), and the boy's activity—in preparing the calf—is so interwoven with that of Abraham that, at one level of reading, it appears that it was Abraham who did the work of the boy: "Abraham ran and he took a calf . . . and gave it to the lad and he hurried to make it ready. And he took curds and milk and the calf which he had made ready. . . ." Some translations inject "who" after "lad," thus removing some of the ambiguity, but the ambiguity is important; it is a way of saying that, in a sense, Abraham is indeed a young man. At the end of chapter 17 he had been circumcised in close association with the thirteen-year-old Ishmael (17:24–25). Now he shows the vigor of that age.

As well as vigor, there is graciousness, and there is attentiveness to detail—from the feet to the heart (18:4–5, "wash your feet . . . refresh your hearts"). In the introduction to the flood story, the heart seemed hopelessly corrupt (6: 5–6), but Abraham undertakes to refresh it. And he seems so attuned to his guests that they simply tell him to do as he says. There is a harmony between their quiet authoritative words and Abraham's words and actions.

Associated with this vigor and harmony is a seemingly insignificant detail—Abraham's access to the entrance of the tent. At one level Abraham's access to the tent is to be taken for granted. But in the second panel, access to an entrance becomes a central factor; it is what the men of Sodom do not achieve (19:6, 11). And the sons-in-law also are outside (19:14). The nature of this access will become clearer in the next episode—with Sarah.

[18:9–15] **Sarah at the entrance: hearing, laughing, and then fearing.** The first indication that these guests are extraordinary comes when, apparently without being told, they use Sarah's name: "Where is Sarah?" The question is commonplace, but it is also one of the basic questions of the larger narrative: after all her trials and bitterness, where indeed is Sarah? It is a variation on the divine messenger's questions to Hagar (16:8): Where are you coming from? And where are you going? In both cases the divine visitors (in chaps. 16 and 18) go on to announce the birth of a son.

At some level Sarah is close to Abraham. The evoking of a boy in Abraham is followed by the announcement of the birth of a son for Sarah, and she in turn asks in effect if she can have the experience, the pleasure, of a young woman ("After I am worn out, shall I have pleasure?"). In other words, she is not simply an old woman who is having a child; in some sense she is becoming young again.

Sarah was last seen emerging from silence in a knot of bitterness and anger, hounding away Hagar, calling for justice (16:1–6). She could have reverted to silence and bitterness. But Hagar had returned to her, God had given her a new name, and Abraham, when he needed fine fresh bread, hurried to the tent to ask Sarah to prepare it.

Yet in the preceding chapters Sarah has scarcely been seeing actually doing anything. The last active verb used of her involved Hagar: "Sarai . . . afflicted her. . . ." Now, tantalizingly, even though Abraham asks Sarah to prepare bread, nothing more is said about that bread—unlike the calf. The text does not say she did anything, nor is the bread mentioned in the final list of what is served. Her role is unclear. "Sarah, the woman of little faith, symbolizes doubt. . . . She stands for one who dwells in a particular setting and cannot dissociate from it . . ." (Dreifuss and Riemer, 1995, 59). The association of Sarah with doubt occurs also in ancient Jewish tradition: "The commentators are uneasy with her for her slower and perhaps doubting response to the message about Isaac" (Miller, 1984, 41).

And so the guests' question is like a crossroads: "Where is Sarah?" After that comes the promise of a son "as the year/time comes around." And then there is the crucial information: "Sarah heard (šāma') at the entrance of the tent." Hearing is the heart of the process of accepting God, as witnessed in the Shema ("Hear, O Israel . . . ," Deut. 6:4–6). This is the pivotal word in the whole portrayal of Sarah. The placing of this act at the entrance of the tent confirms the idea that the entrance is significant—evocative apparently of some form of opening or openness.

She laughs in incredulity—a variation on one of the features of a theophany.

As the guest keeps talking, however, there is further evidence of something unusual. The guest, clearly identified as Yhwh, again shows extraordinary knowledge—aware not just of Sarah's name but of her response and her laughter. Yet, the guest, in relaying Sarah's reaction to Abraham, edits it diplomatically, omitting anything that could discourage Abraham from begetting a child, particularly the references to tired bodies and old age (Alter, 79).

When the guest says "Is any word too difficult for Yhwh?" something further seems to shift within Sarah, and her laughter turns to fear, awesome fear. It is the first indication that the reality of God has come home to her. The imminent birth inside her is not just physical.

Later she denies laughing, "not because of her fear of punishment, but out of respect. It shows good breeding to feel shamed . . . and to say 'I did not do it.' It is actually not a concealment, but a confession that she had done wrong. She would have preferred not to have laughed" (Jacob, 118). The shame at having her laughter heard is like that of a young girl.

[18:16–21] Abraham accompanies the guests toward Sodom: Yhwh's soliloquy about knowing. Maintaining hospitality, Abraham accompanies his guests toward Sodom, and the emphasis shifts from hearing to knowing. At this stage, Abraham does not speak. Instead, there is a form of divine soliloquy.

As in the previous episode ("Where is Sarah?"), Yhwh begins with a question—"Shall I hide from Abraham what I am doing?"—and then repeats the substance of Abraham's initial call (12:2–3). Despite the repetitiveness, this question breaks new ground. It implies that Yhwh not only communicates but also hesitates about withholding, about not giving the whole truth. The implication of such sharing is that between God and Abraham there is a relationship of friendship: "In the ancient Near East, a servant of the god or king was also a friend, privy to his master's plans" (Clifford, 2:29). It also sets the scene for the later declaration (20:8) that Abraham is a prophet.

Then Yhwh speaks of knowing: "For I have known him . . ." (18:19). But the knowing is not abstract; it is about Abraham's role as commanding—of teaching authoritatively—the way of righteousness and justice (ṣĕdāqâ, mišpāṭ).

This emphasis on righteousness and justice reflects the covenant's requirement of moral obligation. This picture of knowing Abraham and of Abraham teaching his children contains an implication: there is harmony between Yhwh knowing Abraham and Abraham's subsequent conduct. God's knowing flows through Abraham.

And having thus exalted the knowing of Abraham, the narrative goes on to give the other side of the coin—Yhwh's need to know more, specifically to conduct a judicial inquiry about the cities (18:20–21). Thus the knowing of Abraham and Yhwh are interwoven.

[18:22–33] **Bargaining for justice: Yhwh speaks to Abraham.** The full extent of the interwovenness of Abraham and Yhwh emerges when Abraham first "stands" before Yhwh, then "draws near," and finally challenges God on the issue of justice. The discussion is precisely about justice, not about Sodom as a city. The scene has the drama of a courtroom when someone steps forward boldly to plead a case.

The bargaining, concerning the requisite number of just people to save the city, falls essentially into three parts, bringing the number first to fifty, then to thirty, and finally to ten. The language of *just* and *wicked/evil* is moral, but, in this legal debate, such language also has the legal meaning of *innocent* and *guilty*. The issue: Does God punish the innocent? Abraham is careful. In pleading the case he "deploys a whole panoply of the abundant rhetorical devices of ancient Hebrew for expressing self-abasement before a powerful figure" (Alter, 82).

It is Abraham who begins the discussion, and he twice emphasizes his own initiative ("Behold . . . I have taken it upon myself," 18:27, 31). Yet, at the end, the discussion is described not as Abraham's bargaining with Yhwh, but as Yhwh's speaking with Abraham: "Yhwh went away when he had completed speaking to Abraham" (18:33).

The implication is that God has not only let Abraham know what is going to happen—the question asked earlier ("Shall I hide from Abraham . . . ?" 18:17) —but also, as an expression of union with Abraham (of knowing him, 18:19), God has led Abraham into the thick of the discussion about justice. The purposefulness of God's procedure is emphasized by the word "completed" ("when he had completed speaking . . ."), the word used at the conclusion of harmonious creation (2:1). Abraham has been pushing to achieve justice, yet, as noted earlier, in a sense it is God who has been pushing within Abraham, pushing not so much to ensure justice, for God would do that in any case, but to bring Abraham, the future teacher of justice, to a knowledge of God's ways. The apparent bargaining is God's revelation to Abraham.

One of the puzzles in Abraham's bargaining is why he stops at ten. Do individuals not count? Why not challenge God about saving the city for the sake of one person? Individuals do count, as was seen in Abraham's earlier rescuing of Lot (chap. 14) and as will be seen again in the later rescuing of Lot and his family from Sodom (19:15). But a city, of its nature, means a community; it needs a quorum, or minimal critical mass (cf. Fretheim, 478; Sarna,

134). The minimum needed in later synagogues services, for instance, was ten. If there is not a minimum community, then the city is no longer truly a city, and so it is open to destruction. All that remains is to save those individuals who are capable of being saved.

Panel Two (19:1–29)

[19:1–3] **Two guests in the evening: the limited hospitality of Lot.** The action begins at the city gate, adjacent to the busy square that was the center of diverse occupations—commercial, legal, and social. At evening, however, the time of the messengers' arrival, as the unlighted square grew dark, the atmosphere in such a square could be unnerving.

The arrival of the two messengers at Sodom, where Lot was sitting in the gate, has obvious similarities with the arrival of the three men at Abraham's tent (18:1–8; for details, see Wenham, II, 43). But there are significant differences also. In particular, Lot does not run, there is no fine tender calf, and there is not the same sense of harmony (at first they say "No," so that he really has to press them to turn aside). The overall impression is that there is communication between Lot and the messengers, yet its quality is wanting.

[19:4–14] **The men outside the entrance: another kind of knowing.** Lot's limitedness in communicating prepares the way for those whose mode of communicating is of yet another kind, the men of Sodom who want sexual intercourse ("to know") with the two guests. Everyone in Sodom is present, leaving no chance of finding the ten necessary to save the city. When Lot goes out to them at the entrance and shuts the door behind him, the scene becomes one of people who, with minds set on a particular form of knowing, are blocked from the entrance (19:4–5).

There are two issues at Sodom—sexual conduct and hospitality. It is arguable that the homosexual issue is "minor" and has been "overworked" (Gossai, 1995, 75). For Lot, when he speaks to the men of Sodom (19:6–11), the primary issue is hospitality; he does not want his hospitality abused. And so, to protect his two guests, he offers his two daughters to the crowd.

Lot, however, is not an authority on hospitality, as was seen in his initial reception of the two guests. And so his actions, including his offering of his daughters, are suspect. The offering of the daughters therefore is not to be explained solely as an expression of hospitality. It springs also from Lot's character, including a narrowness of vision which emerged in his choice of land and in his initial move toward Sodom (13:10–13). There is uncertainty, too, about his accuracy and truthfulness. He addresses the men of Sodom as brothers, but they effectively reject such kinship (19:7, 9). And he refers to his daughters as virgins but, unless there are further unmentioned daughters (which seems unlikely), his daughters are already married or at least betrothed (19:14).

When he offers his daughters, the men of Sodom reject his reasoning completely and they "press him much"—an ironic echo of how he had pressed his guests—so that it is left to the guests to rescue Lot. Then the guests, far from bringing the two daughters out to appease the crowd, strike the men of Sodom with blindness, leaving them, again, outside, wearily seeking the entrance.

In a narrative that emphasizes seeing, blindness is particularly significant. In this case, it is associated with disordered sexual desire, as though such desire blocks seeing. Sexual obsession blurs one's vision of reality.

It is not clear whether the primary issue here is homosexuality or gang rape. It is arguable that the main motivation of the attackers was not lust but a larger sense of hostility. Had the motivation been lust, then, according to some premodern Jewish views, the attackers would have accepted the offer of the women (Gilders, 1997, 7). In contrast, if the primary motivation was lust of a particular kind, namely homosexual lust, then the rejection of the offer of the women is understandable. It is hard to escape the impression that the scene contains a negative feeling about homosexuality. Certainly, in contrast to the positive setting that was given to the origin of marriage (2:24), it is an unsavory situation in which to introduce the topic of homosexuality. Curiously, the first instance of bigamy is also set amid violence (4:23–24).

However, the specific form of homosexuality that is condemned here is violent. There is equal condemnation for violent heterosexuality: the two angels intervene soon after Lot offers his daughters to the crowd (19:7–11), and in Judges, when violent heterosexuality leads to a woman's death, those responsible are severely punished (Judg. 19–20). It is possible therefore for a commentator to conclude that Genesis 19 "does not talk about homosexual activity or orientation generally, or about nonviolent sexual behaviour" (Fretheim, 477).

Then the sons-in-law are questioned, those who "take his daughters" (19: 12–14). But they, too, are outside—Lot has to go out to them—and their sight also is not clear: Lot was "as one joking in their eyes." The word for joking is a variation on "laughing": Sarah laughed at the idea that God could be so positive; the sons-in-law see laughter in the idea that God might be so negative. The reason for their relative blindness is not clear—perhaps it has something to do with the relative crudeness of how they relate to the daughters (they "take" them)—but they are in essentially the same position as the men of Sodom: they are outside and somehow not seeing.

[19:15–28] The overthrow of the cities: haggling, looking back, and looking down. The next day brings the disaster—first the dawn, when the messengers evacuate Lot and his family; then, sunrise, when Yhwh sends brimstone and fire; and finally, morning, when Abraham goes to where he had stood before.

Lot's limited awareness becomes no clearer as the disaster nears (19:15–22). Not even the experience of the evening before—of being rescued from the mob—has taught him to trust the angels. They urge him to arise, take his family, and leave, but instead of listening to them, "he lingered." And so "in Yhwh's pity for him," they took him and his family by the hand, and brought them out.

Even now, he cannot cut cleanly. When they tell him to flee to the mountain, he haggles, knowing their kindness. Part of his problem is that "he does not want to leave the city for the country" (Clifford, 2:30); "accustomed to an urban setting, he is terrified at the idea of trying to survive in the forbidding landscape of cliffs and caves to the south and east of the Dead Sea" (Alter, 87). Lot's preference for the city is also like the obverse side of Genesis's tendency to prefer the countryside.

Finally, Lot extracts from them enough time to go to a town called Little (Zoar). In fact Zoar was at the limit of his original view of the land (". . . as far as Zoar," 13:10). Apparently his vision has never expanded.

The detail of the divine kindness is shown in waiting for the difficult Lot to reach Zoar, but once he arrives, the brimstone and fire come down. The description of the fall of the brimstone ("from the heavens") puts full responsibility on Yhwh and emphasizes the destructiveness (19:23–25).

Lot's limitedness, his closeness to Sodom, is highlighted in a final detail about the destruction: his wife looks back at the catastrophe, thus indicating "her desire to return to the city" (Jeansonne, 1990, 39), "her longing to go back to her old life" (Deen, 1978, 9), and she becomes a pillar of salt (19:26).

The pillar of salt has two explanations—geographical and psychological. Geographically speaking, the area contained various formations of salt, including, apparently, pillars that were somewhat akin to human shapes. The story of Lot's wife is like an account of their origin, an etiology.

Psychologically speaking, the pillar of salt is a pillar of death (in that area salt means death; the Salt Sea is the Dead Sea). By looking backward on what is destroyed, gone, dead, Lot's wife herself becomes dead. Her transformation is a further example of the importance in this narrative of seeing. She is like someone who, instead of looking forward, spends life pining about tragedy and about the past—about a former life or love or church ("When I . . ."; "When we . . ."). At some level such people are dead, dead pillars.

Her fate does not mean that death, destruction, and loss are to be obliterated from one's mind. The next episode shows that Abraham also looks at the scene of destruction (19:27–28). But his vantage point is different. Instead of looking back he looks down, and does so from the place, many miles from Sodom, where he had stood facing Yhwh, insisting on justice. The implication is that instead of seeing the overthrow of the cities as purely destructive, he has some sense of a larger context and of a larger justice. Besides, the smoke from the overthrow is somehow familiar: "and he saw, and behold, the smoke of the land went up like the smoke of a furnace"—effectively like the smoking oven, the smoke and fire which first made the covenant (15:17–18). This covenant was connected with the first rescue of Lot (14:13–16). Amid the fire and smoke, therefore, Abraham saw something more—a presence which in his own time of crisis had made him aware of another dimension.

The story of the flood ended with the rainbow, the water-related sign of the covenant. And this story of the fire ends with a smoking furnace, the fire-related reminder of another covenant (chap. 15). Thus the water and the fire, both potential sources of terror, have been turned around to become reminders of God's covenant, sources not of terror but of reassurance.

[19:29] God remembered Abraham. The four-part conclusion is chiastic, like some earlier conclusions (2:1–4a; 9:12–17; 17:23–27). The center of that chiasm has a certain simplicity:

> God remembered Abraham,
> and he sent forth Lot out of the midst of the overthrow.

This is a variation on God's remembrance of Noah (8:1), an assurance, whatever the complexity of the situation, of God's compassion and justice.

Aspects of that justice remain puzzling.

The most obvious disharmony (sin) of the men of Sodom is sexual obsession—an imbalance which prevents them from seeing clearly and which shuts them out from a larger world. To some degree, Lot shares their situation. From the beginning he used his eyes superficially (13:10–13), and the limitedness of his vision is manifested in his narrow hospitality (19:1–3), in his offering of his daughters (19:8), and in his petty haggling about where to go (19:15–22). There are vision problems, too, among his family—in his sons-in-law and wife (19: 14, 26). These latter are closer still to Sodom and so they share its fate.

What emerges is that while the most obvious disharmony is sexual, the figures of Lot and his wife suggest a wider context, a more radical form of distorted vision. When Lot first looked at the area, all he saw was what was obvious—the fertile land (13:10). And when his wife looked back, apparently all she saw was death (19:26). Thus, one saw life, and the other saw death, but both perceptions were superficial. And it is within the framework of that radical misconstrual of life and death that the blurred vision of sexuality occurs. In other words, superficiality concerning life and death provides the context for superficiality about sexuality.

Apart from the issue of sexuality, there is the larger question of the fate of the cities. The Noah story saw people being obliterated by water. In this account people are obliterated by fire. Even if one grants that all those who died were serious sinners, the punishment seems harsh. And in most comparable catastrophes, the presumption is that not all the people are serious sinners. The innocent also suffer.

To this question there is no answer, at least not on the level of easy perception. Much suffering seems to cry out not about God's presence but about God's absence. If the hard-bargaining Abraham says nothing, it is only because he has learned another way of seeing and has learned to trust.

26   **Abraham and Isaac among the Nations
        (19:30–Chap. 21)**

Lot's Foreign Children and Abraham the Foreigner (19:30–Chap. 20)
Abraham's Child and the Foreigners (Chap. 21)

Introductory Aspects

The Basic Story Line

The first picture is stark. It tells how the incest of Lot and his daughters gave rise to the Moabites and Ammonites.

But the next picture is very different: Abimelech and his people, down in Gerar, are like Abraham at his best, speaking to God and seeking justice. Here Sarah seems at first to be endangered, as she once had been in Egypt, but, through the combined work of God and Abimelech, Sarah comes out smelling like a rose.

Then, amid old age and laughter, Sarah gives birth to Isaac—thus raising the prospect of yet another people, the people of God's promise.

The birth of Isaac brings a curious twist. The story, instead of concentrating on this long-awaited child, switches back to incidents concerning other peoples. First, there is an incident with implications for Egypt: the expulsion of Hagar the Egyptian and the marriage of her son to a woman from Egypt. And then there is an incident involving Abimelech and the land of the Philistines.

Thus, the centerpiece of the story is the birth of the child of Abraham and Sarah, but this birth—however personal for his own family and nation—is not a narrow event. It is linked to surrounding nations. Even Sarah, in her joy, proclaims that her birth-giving is open to all (21:6): "Everyone who hears will laugh for me."

Literary Form and Complementarity

The panels of this diptych begin with contrasting images of children being born—the children of Lot (Moab and Ammon, 19:30–38), and the child of Abraham (Isaac, 21:1–7). The previous scene also (18:1–19:29) had been headed by an Abraham-Lot contrast (diverse pictures of hospitality, 18:1–8; 19:1–3), but here, in Lot's last appearance, the contrast reaches its high point and so is sharper. Lot's children come from incestuous coercion; Abraham's child comes in God's time, amid harmony and laughter. Lot, in a cave, with just two daughters, seems fearful and enclosed, knowing nothing. Abraham, however, appears unconfined and his wife Sarah calls out poetically—sings almost—for all to hear. One episode is of shame, the other of joy.

Given these balancing pictures of birth it seems best to consider both texts (19:30–38; 21:1–17) as birth stories. The first may indeed be defective ("not really a narrative," Westermann, II, 311), but the second is standard (ibid., 331).

Associated with both are aspects of a second literary type—the travel narrative. A variation on this travel type was already seen in chapters 12–13, and variations on elements of chapters 12–13 reappear here, especially the danger to Sarah (12:10–13:1) and the dispute (13:5–13). The Sarah episode is now rewritten (chap. 20), and (in chap. 21) the dispute takes two forms—sharp (between Sarah and Hagar), and more relaxed (between Abraham and Abimelech).

Despite their differences, both birth episodes share a relationship to other peoples. The children of Lot are the Moabites and Ammonites—foreign peoples. Abraham's child is called *yiṣḥāq*, Laugh, but the first child recorded as actually laughing is the son of a foreigner (Hagar, the Egyptian; 21:9). In some sense, the laughing Egyptian shares Isaac's name. And of course he also is the child of Abraham. Furthermore, Isaac's birth and weaning are the prelude for recounting the growth not of Isaac but of the Egyptian, a child who is also destined to become a great nation (21:20–21; he is never called Ishmael here). Hence, despite the expulsion of the Egyptian and her son, the fates of the two children are interwoven.

Apart from the foreign peoples who are related through the children, there is the eminent foreign personage who is related to Abraham and who to some extent dominates both panels—Abimelech (chap. 20; 21:22–34).

In the contrast between the two birth episodes, there is no doubt where Abimelech belongs. Though he first appears immediately after the Lot episode (chap. 20), he is far from its ethos. The Lot incident, centered on two successive days, is full of incestuous shame. Abimelech, though he sends for Sarah, reveals, over two successive days, that he is full of innocence; and Sarah emerges, as never before, not with shame, but vindicated and with honor.

Abimelech's place, therefore, is with all that Abraham and Sarah represent, and so, after the Isaac-Egyptian episodes, he reappears (21:32–34). Here he brings together elements of both panels—especially the innocence and kindness (*ḥesed*) of the first (cf. 20:4–5, 13), and the key role of the well in the second (cf. 21:19)—but, more than that, he moves the relationship with Abraham to a new level, to intensifying stages of covenant.

At the end (21:32–34) there is further surprise. He apparently is a Philistine, and when someone plants a tree and calls on the name of Yhwh, the text omits the subject of the verb (21:33) and so one scarcely knows who is praying—Abraham or the Philistine.

Relationship to Preceding Chapters

The basic sequence here—from natural disaster (fire, chap. 19) to incest (Lot and his daughters) to an emphasis on the nations—is akin to the sequence that followed the flood: Noah's nakedness and Ham; and the table of nations (9:18–chap. 10).

The scene of the endangered matriarch (chap. 20), one of three such type-scenes, has several continuities and contrasts with the other two instances (in 12:10–13:1; and 26:1–12; Alter, 52). Likewise, the scene of Hagar in the wilderness (21:8–21) is a development of the scene in which Hagar first ran away (chap. 16).

Leading Elements

ABRAHAM AND THE NATIONS

This two-panel scene (19:30–chap. 21) is not the first involving other nations. Most of Genesis 1–11, especially chapter 10, deals with the world at large. And in the first half of the Abraham story (chaps. 12–17), there is, at its center (chaps. 14–15), an account which includes Abraham's encounter with the nations, an encounter which, though largely adversarial, contains, especially in the final list of nations (15:18–21), an ambiguity with a more inclusive view.

Here the Lot episode is negative, but it acts as a foil for a positive presentation of two of Israel's greatest enemies—Egypt and the Philistines.

The birth of Isaac therefore, while it is foundational for Israel, is not for Israel alone. Isaac's birth and Sarah's joy are at the center of new life for Egypt and for the land of the Philistines. This broader dimension gives new meaning to the promise that Abraham will be the father of a multitude of nations.

SPOUSAL ḤESED AND PARENTAL TEARS

This diptych highlights aspects of personal relationships scarcely seen previously in Genesis: kindness *ḥesed* and tears—Sarah's *ḥesed* to Abraham (20:13), and Hagar's tears for her child (21:16). The idea of *ḥesed* reappears in chapter 21 (21:23). Thus the pictures of the Egyptian and Philistine evoke basic forms of love.

Structure (Table 26.1)

Despite the complexity of the text the structure of the finished text is reasonably straightforward.

Comment

Panel One (19:30–Chap. 20)

[19:30–38] Lot's children: Lot's unknowing and the forced birth of Moab and Ammon. In the end Lot's illusory vision collapses. The city of Zoar,

Table 26.1. The Birth of Isaac (19:30–20:18 // chap. 21)

Lot's children and the foreigners

Introduction: The shameful birth of Lot's children (19:30–38)
Abimelech and Sarah: Not shame but innocence (20:1–7)
Abimelech and Abraham: Innocence reaffirmed (20:8–13)
Conclusion: Sarah's honor opens the way to many births (20:14–18)

Abraham's child and the foreigners

Introduction: the birth of Abraham's child, Isaac (21:1–7)
The Egyptian and her son are to be cast out (21:9–13)
The Egyptian and her son in the wilderness; the son grows up (21:14–21)
The Philistine and his commander: in covenant with Abraham (21:22–31)
Conclusion: solidarity with the Philistine, Abimelech (21:32–34)

---

which he had seen so long ago (13:1), and to which he clung despite the angels' words (19:17–22), turned out to be a place in which he could not settle. So, not from obedience but from fear, he left Zoar and went to the mountain. The mountain, therefore, is not something he embraces but something to which he is compelled. There he lives, in a cave—apparently without a view of the land. And suddenly, he is described as old.

With him are his two daughters—the two whom he would have given to the mob (19:8). On successive nights, they make him drunk with wine and use him to become pregnant, thus giving birth to the peoples of Moab and Ammon. Their forceful procedure, in seeking progeny, contrasts with the essentially trusting attitude of Abraham.

This scene, coming after the destruction of Sodom and Gomorrah, has overtones of the scene that followed the flood, when Ham's seeing of the nakedness of his father, drunk with wine, prepares for the birth of various peoples (9:18–chap. 10).

Part of the effect of this incestuous scene is to ridicule the peoples of Moab and Ammon. However, from the Israelite point of view, the ridicule is something of a boomerang: Lot is not some distant figure; he is the nephew of Abraham, someone whom Abraham regarded as a brother.

In fact the focus of this episode is on Lot, and not because he does anything but because he does so little. Virtually the last things attributed to him are being afraid and being old. The drink and sex are passive, and he is heard from no more.

It is ironic that someone who had once lifted up his eyes and chosen the best-looking land so carefully should last be seen in a cave, at night, and unknowing. He is not only old; he seems dead before his time. The structure of the text—its description of the two daughters taking turns with Lot on successive nights—has a form of repetition that is lifeless. They sleep with him, but he does not know; he has sex without being aware of it. One could hardly find a more expressive symbol of unawareness, of life passing one by. He had been so intent on the surface of life that he had missed the deeper dimension. The contrast is acute between this drunken sex and the graceful alertness of Abraham.

[Chap. 20] **Abraham the sojourner/foreigner, and the foreign Abimelech's vindication of Sarah.** Like Lot, Abraham also moves "from" where he had been and "settles," but in contrast to his nephew—afraid, old, in a cave— Abraham now appears full of life and adventure. Instead of going into dark retreat with close relatives, he "tented onward from there to the land of the Negev, and settled between Kadesh and Shur." The Negev is wilderness, and the area from Kadesh (about forty miles south of Beer-sheba) to Shur (near Egypt) is extensive. The only clue as to his location in this vast wilderness is that "he sojourned (*gûr*; noun, *gēr*) in Gerar (*gĕrār*)." Though the table of nations (10:19) places Gerar near Gaza, it is geographically unknown. However, in a narrative that plays with words, it tends, whatever its historical status, to strengthen the idea of sojourning, of living like a foreigner in transit, with a healthy nonattachment to things. Lot, in contrast, had tried to cling to his world.

The Gerar incident—in which Abraham says Sarah is his sister, and the king sends for her—recalls Pharaoh's taking of Sarah (12:10–20), but, as frequently happens in the unfolding narrative of Genesis, this episode is a form of reversal. The king, warned in a dream (Genesis's first dream, granted to a foreigner), does not touch her, and the whole incident, instead of being a variation on Eden's sin and expulsion (as was the Egyptian experience), shows that the king is like Abraham at his best—blameless, and arguing with God about punishing the innocent ("the just," 20:4–5; cf. 17:1; 18:23). As with Abraham's arguing or bargaining, the king's blamelessness comes from God (20:6; cf. 18:17, 33). Abimelech's plea for a whole nation, rather than just for himself, seems strange at first but makes sense as a continuation of Abraham's plea for a whole city. "The apparent deformation of idiom has a sharp thematic point" (Alter, 93).

The royal servants all fear God, as does Abimelech their king; they are the antithesis of Sodom. When Abimelech speaks to Abraham, his indignation is reflected in his flow of words: "Abimelech said . . . And Abimelech said. . . ."

Abimelech is blameless but "in the ancient deed-perspective of the story, he is, however unwittingly, still under the death sentence for the act of abduction of a man's wife" (Clifford, 2:32). However, the sentence of death, instead of casting a pall over the situation, allows Abraham and Sarah to emerge in a new light.

In some respects, Abraham seems weak in dealing with Abimelech. He has made a huge blunder. He thought that Gerar was godless, an evil kingdom, perhaps like Sodom and now he struggles to undo the damage. In the king's words, he almost causes "a great sin," apparently meaning adultery (Clifford, 2:32). He is not as self-centered as in Egypt, where his explicit motivation was to save his life and do well (12:12–13), but he quibbles about Sarah's status—if not his sister, at least his half-sister—and he seems to have slipped back some-what since he interceded with God on behalf of threatened Sodom (18:16–33).

At the same time, once he is confronted by the king, some of the qualities seen near Sodom achieve greater clarity. His ability to sense what is coming is linked to prophecy; and his intercession is called prayer. As a prophet who prays—Genesis's only explicit reference to a prophet—he apparently wrestles as never before with the threat of death. Death had not turned away from Sodom, but now it is indeed turned away from Abimelech, and the barrenness is likewise turned away from Abimelech's household. (As a sanction for Sarah, all the wombs of the royal house had been closed, 20:7, 17–18.) In diverse ways, whether in prophecy, prayer, or conversation, Abraham has learned to speak more appropriately. His reference to "the gods" rather than "God" (20:13) is an apparent adaptation to the presumed religious beliefs of Abimelech. Far from being expelled, as happened in Egypt, Abraham is told that the land is before him: "settle wherever is good in your eyes."

Sarah now emerges with great honor (20:4, 14–18). She is untouched; she is vindicated in the eyes of all. The precise function of the king's thousand silver pieces is unclear: it is called "a covering of the eyes," possibly referring either to a covering of Sarah's eyes—a mask or eye-veil to protect her—or to a covering or blocking of the eyes of those who would condemn her for this incident. The noble king's generosity surrounds her as it were, and gives her protective prestige.

Furthermore, the safeguarding of her womb means the opening of the wombs of the whole royal house. Not only has she gone from being barren to being on the verge of childbirth. She has also become, in her own way, the foundation for the fertility of the whole royal house of a foreign nation.

Panel Two (Chap. 21)

[21:1–7] **Abraham's child. Harmony and laughter: the birth of Isaac.** Having told of Sarah's vindication and her role in the fertility of the royal house, the narrative goes on to tell of her giving birth to Isaac.

The first part of the account (21:1–5) emphasizes harmony. Everything happens as Yhwh had said, and at the right time: in the season Yhwh had said; on the eighth day as God had commanded; when Abraham was one hundred years old. The sense of harmony is heightened by a form of repetition that is almost poetic:

> Yhwh provided for Sarah as he had said,
> and Yhwh did to Sarah as he had spoken.
> And Sarah conceived and bore to Abraham a son in his old age,
> at the set time that God had spoken of to him.

The initial emphasis on Sarah, as seen in the preceding lines ("Sarah . . . Sarah . . . Sarah . . ."), is immediately balanced by a corresponding emphasis on

Abraham ("Abraham called . . . Abraham circumcised . . . Abraham was a hundred years . . . ," 21:3–5).

But in the second part (21:6–7) the emphasis comes back, climactically, to Sarah, and—long before Hannah (1 Sam. 2:1–10) and Mary (Luke 1:46–55)—she cries out with joy:

> God has made laughter for me;
> everyone who hears will laugh for me . . .

According to Jewish legend Isaac's birth brought joy to the world (Ginzberg, *Legends,* quoted in Darr, 1991, 106):

> The whole world rejoiced,
> for God remembered all barren women at the same time with Sarah.
> They all bore children.
> And the blind were made to see,
> all the lame were made whole,
> the dumb were made to speak,
> and the mad were restored to reason.

The episode as a whole is in multiple contrast to the birth episode in the opposite panel—the birth of the children of Lot, with its inert repetition, its fear, its radical disharmony. It is a symptom of the relationship between these two birth episodes that while the Lot account uses the word for birth (*yālad*) just twice—once for each child—the Abraham text, in its vitality, uses it five times.

Isaac's circumcision—the sign of the covenant—prepares the way for the making of the covenant with Abimelech (21:27, 32).

[21:8–21] **The Egyptian, too, is to become God's nation.** The birth of Isaac is followed by the account of a boy growing up, but ironically the boy is not Isaac but Ishmael, son of an Egyptian. And the subsequent action involves Abimelech, who now emerges as a Philistine.

The action begins at Isaac's weaning, probably about three years after his birth. At the festive meal to celebrate Isaac's emergence, Sarah saw that the son of "Hagar the Egyptian" was laughing/playing with her son—the same multifaceted verb first used when Abraham bowed down and laughed incredulously (17:17). The verb's playfulness can have a sexual connotation (cf. 26:8). Thus one may argue "in the light of . . . Genesis' . . . abhorrence of corrupt sexual behaviour [that] . . . Sarah saw Ishmael . . . performing sexual acts with Isaac . . . and so the legal link between Hagar and Abraham was brought to an end" (Fleishman, 1997–1998, 96, 100). But Alter (98) thinks a sexual connotation is unlikely, and certainly Ishmael, while expelled, still seems related in some important way to Abraham. Their genealogies—Abraham's and Ishmael's—form a literary unity (25:1–11).

The laughing of Ishmael may involve a disturbing mockery. Or more simply, given that laughter is at the center of Abraham's heritage, the sharing of laughter with the Egyptian's child is an indication of a sharing of heritage.

Sarah's insistence on sending away the slave-woman and her son may seem at first to spring, if not from bloodymindedness, then from neurotic insecurity. And her way of referring to Hagar and Ishmael—avoiding their names and referring to their slave status—is less than gracious. But at a certain level, Hagar's son is a threat to the inheritance, and Sarah is struggling for survival. "Her own future is tied up with her son's; she is fighting for her life" (Clifford, 2:33). And she is able, finally, to speak with a powerful clarity and assertiveness. She will no longer deal indirectly, as when she so mistreated Hagar that she ran away. Sarah knows what she wants; she also knows at some level what is right; and she says so in words that are strong and decisive.

Her struggle for survival may involve, at some level, a certain challenging of death. At her age, inheritance would seem to matter only for her son. If it matters for herself, then the inheriting will be close to her death.

It is not Sarah alone who has become more clear and assertive. Abraham also is no longer a pushover. His response to Sarah is not passive compliance as in the original mistreating of Hagar (16:2, 6) and as once happened in Eden (3:6). Instead, using his own eyes, he is deeply upset. But God tells him, "Hear her voice" (21:12)—again the opposite of the scene in Eden, where hearing the woman's voice led to condemnation (3:17). In fact, here God adopts some of the woman's own message. In this case, the woman's voice contains a basic truth: the distinctive development of the Egyptian and her son will be best achieved if they go away, if in effect they go free. God will set up the son of the slave-woman as a nation, as Abraham's descendant.

The expulsion of Hagar and her son into the wilderness (21:14–21) is modeled partly on her flight toward Shur (16:8–14), and, like that original flight, it also echoes aspects of the expulsion from the Garden (2:25–chap. 3).

Chronologically the boy should be about sixteen, but Hagar seems to handle him as if he were a small child. This may, perhaps, be a way of connoting his closeness to the little Isaac, something already suggested by his laughing or playing with Isaac (21:9).

Unlike the flight toward Shur, there is no immediate angelic drama, no immediate spring. Instead, Hagar is sorely reduced, without water, facing the boy's death, and crying (21:16–16).

It is the boy who saves the situation, at least insofar as it is his cry that God hears. Thus he fulfils his name—God hears, Ishma-el. And then, in capsule form (21:17–19) the angelic drama takes place once more; and again Hagar sees in a new way.

However, the shift of emphasis to the boy remains (21:20–21): "God was with the boy/lad. . . ." His settling in the wilderness may seem eccentric, but it reflects Abraham's earlier action of settling between Kadesh and Shur (20:1). In fact the wilderness in which he settles, Paran, touches or overlaps the area between Kadesh and Shur.

In Ishmael's initial isolation (cast out, *gāraš*, 21:10; and sent forth, *šalaḥ*, 21:14), a bowshot had once separated him from his distraught mother (21:16), but later he became a master at the bow (and thus at traversing the length of a bowshot, 21:20). The same two verbs (cast out, *gāraš;* sent forth, *šalaḥ*) had been used of the expulsion from Eden (3:23–24), but in that case the weapon—the sword—had reinforced the expulsion. Whatever the full connotations of Ishmael's expert bow, it seems essentially positive. Though he was in the wilderness, God was with him ("God was with the boy," 21:20)—almost exactly the phrase that Abimelech will soon use of Abraham ("God is with you in all that you do," 21:22). Despite the separation of Abraham and Ishmael, God is with both.

Hagar the refugee remains a haunting figure. "Did she find happiness one day, as the rabbis claimed?" (Darr, 1991, 156). It is not clear. Yet the final details are telling (21:21): "He [Ishmael] settled in the wilderness of Paran [eastern Sinai], and his mother took a wife for him from the land of Egypt." Her action is bold, "the only time a mother does this in the OT" (Fretheim, 489), the sort of thing otherwise done by men of standing—for example, by Abraham and his servant (chap. 24), or by Laban (chap. 29). In other ways, too, she is "a woman with an attitude," in the best sense (Rulon-Miller, 1998).

Her action, however, is not only one of boldness or power. It is also a return to her origins, to herself. Egypt was her home, and in another Egyptian woman—her chosen daughter-in-law—there is a world that is her world also, and a world that by her action she now embraces. But she had known a further world, where a woman had taken her and given her to a man. So now, when she in turn takes a woman and gives her to her son, she is in a sense going back to a place from which she once fled, and from which she had once been sent away. This time the divine voice does not send her back physically (as in 16:9–16); there is no return to being subject to Sarah. But the God who opened her eyes in the wilderness has enabled her so to see her fate that, from her new situation, she can act with independent boldness and embrace it.

[21:22–32a] Abimelech the Philistine: taking a well and making a covenant with Abraham. Abraham's closeness to someone Egyptian is followed by an account of his covenant-making with Abimelech. Previously (chap. 20) this closeness to Abimelech was not as clear. The king had indeed been good to Abraham, granting him the freedom of his land (20:15). But now Abraham has prospered so much that Abimelech wants to ensure that he will not exploit his prosperity at the expense of himself (Abimelech) and his family.

The covenant-making (21:22–32) occurs in three steps:

The oath: Abimelech asks Abraham to swear an oath of kindness (*ḥesed*, 21:22–24).

The covenant: Abraham's reproach about a well leads to Abimelech's statement of innocence and to a covenant (21:25–27).

The oath and covenant: Abimelech accepts seven ewe lambs so as to be a witness that Abraham had dug the well. Then, at Beer-sheba, they swore an oath and made a covenant (21:28–32).

The text is dense and overlapping, and some scholars have suggested that it conflates two accounts. However, much of the diversity comes from the context of the rest of the scene:

The initial emphasis on doing kindness (*ḥesed*, 21:22–24) echoes Abraham's earlier explanation to Abimelech—about asking Sarah to do kindness (20:13).

Abimelech's innocence about the taking of the well (21:25–27) echoes Abimelech's innocence about the taking of Sarah (20:2–8) and combines it with the well image from the preceding Hagar episode (21:19).

Abimelech's role as witness to the well (21:28–32) echoes his earlier role as vindicating Sarah (20:16).

Overall, therefore, the earlier drama surrounding Sarah (chap. 20) has been distilled and refocused around Abimelech. The refocusing has been achieved partly by integrating the pivotal image of the well from the Hagar episode, but especially by adding a new dimension, the covenant.

This combining of elements—of covenant theme with aspects of Sarah—is not strange. As wife to Abraham, Sarah was implicitly in a form of covenant with him. Now, in dealing with Abimelech (chap. 21), that implicit covenant aspect has been made explicit. It is not only Sarah, but Abimelech also who, in his own way, is in covenant with Abraham. Abraham's relationship to Sarah is echoed at some level in his relationship with Abimelech.

The three covenant-related references—the oath, the covenant, and then the combined oath and covenant—form a threefold intensifying pattern, which draws the whole text (21:22–32) into a unity.

The location, Beer-sheba, also draws the text into a unity; the name captures aspects of all three stages of making the covenant. "Beer" reflects the well (*bĕ'ēr*), and "sheba" reflects both the swearing (*šāba'*) and the seven (*šeba'*). Curiously, there is no reference to Gerar. Perhaps Gerar's possible connotation of someone foreign seemed inappropriate to the context of a covenant.

The episode's opening allusion to the time ("at that time . . . Abimelech," 21:22) ties in with the chapter's initial emphasis on God's harmonious time (at the birth of Isaac, 21:2–5). Abimelech is within that harmony.

With him is his army commander. Foreign armies can suggest terror, but not here; the covenant, founded first of all on kindness (*ḥesed*), on an oath not to deal falsely, will demystify the possible terror.

But the kindness is not soft-minded. Abraham's swearing of kindness is followed immediately by a reproach (concerning the taking of the well, 21:25). Apparently *ḥesed* is to be the basis not for covering things up but for frank discussion. As a result of this frankness the agreement is not abandoned but rather is strengthened: they make a more formal covenant.

However, even the formal covenant is not enough. There is a third stage when Abimelech accepts the seven ewe lambs and becomes a witness to Abraham (21:28–32). Thus Abimelech will not only be in covenant with Abraham but, by being a witness, will carry that agreement to others.

Who those others might be is not said—until one comes to the conclusion.

[21:32b–34] Conclusion: the name of Yhwh in the land of the Philistines. The conclusion brings a surprise: not only is Abimelech in solidarity with Abraham, but Abimelech apparently is a Philistine and he brings that solidarity to the land of the Philistines.

Like some other conclusions (2:1–4a; 9:12–17; 19:29), the structure is chiastic. There is a framework involving references to "the land of the Philistines" (21:32b, 34), and at the center an enigmatic account of planting a tamarisk tree, an evergreen, and calling on the name of Yhwh, the Everlasting God (El Olam, another ancient title applied to Yhwh, 21:33).

In a curious way Abimelech and Abraham separate and yet, at a certain level, stay together. Abimelech and his commander "go back (*šûb*)" to the land of the Philistines, apparently a form of returning home, as Hagar and her son had gone homeward. Abraham, though he stays where he is—he sojourns many days—is likewise in the land of the Philistines. And the activity in the center, about planting a tree and calling on the name of Yhwh (21:33), has no subject. The phrase "he planted" could refer either to Abimelech or Abraham. Some translations, anxious to clear up the ambiguity, inject "Abraham." But it seems better to leave the ambiguity, for it touches a basic idea: it is not only Abraham who plants evergreen trees and calls on Yhwh; Philistines, who have a solidarity with Abraham, do so too. This concluding reference to the land of the Philistines (21:34) dovetails with the concluding reference (in 21:21) to Egypt.

27   Facing Death (Chaps. 22–23)

The Offering of the Son (Chap. 22)
The Death of the Wife (Chap. 23)

Introductory Aspects

The Basic Story Line

The first episode is famous: as a test, God asks Abraham to sacrifice his son
Isaac, the child of promise; and after a wrenching account, an angel intervenes
at the last moment and renews the promise. The promise is further strengthened by a form of good omen, the news that his brother has had twelve sons.
Thus the episode goes from the impending death of an only child to a sense
of children abounding.

But while Abraham was spared his son, he was not spared his wife. In the
second episode Sarah dies and Abraham mourns. Yet here, too, there is a turnaround and again the shadow of death gives way to something positive, not to
children but to land. In seeking a burial place Abraham acquires a field of great
price, four hundred shekels. As the twelve children of the first episode intimated
the people to come (the twelve tribes), so the field of four hundred shekels
intimates the future possession of the land.

This double encounter with death means not that Abraham is impoverished
but that the promise of progeny and land is stronger than ever; stronger and
closer.

Literary Form

The predominant literary types are those of a trial (chap. 22) and a dialogue
contract (chap. 23; Westermann, II, 354, 371). The dialogue contract secures
Sarah's burial place—a field with a cave.

Complementarity of the Two Panels

TWO PENDULUM MOVEMENTS

The overcoming of death is reflected in a pendulum effect at the center of both
panels. In the Isaac episode this pendulum effect is a journey to the mountain
and back again. Abraham explicitly tells his two accompanying boys (young
men) that he and Isaac will go to the mountain to bow down (*šāḥāh*), implying
worship, and that they will then come back again; and so he does; "he came

back and they arose (*qûm*) . . ." (22:5, 19). Bound in with this coming back is Abraham's sense of assurance that Isaac will not be conquered by death: "we will bow down and we will come back. . . ."

In the Sarah episode the pendulum effect is vertical: not over and back but down and up, a form of descent and ascent. Abraham's buying of the burial property is achieved through a series of leading verbs (23:3, 7, 12, 16, 17, 20), which suggest descent and ascent:

Abraham arose (*qûm*) . . .

Abraham arose (*qûm*) and bowed down (*šāḥâh*) . . .

Abraham bowed down (*šāḥâh*) . . .

Abraham weighed (*šāqal*) . . . 400 weights (*šeqel*) . . . standard (weight)

And the field arose (*qûm*) . . . to Abraham [i.e., went over to him] . . .

And the field arose (*qûm*) . . . to Abraham . . .

The action of arising gradually gives way to bowing down; and then, after the weighing of a great weight, the narrative returns to the action of arising. The emphasis on weighing and weight seems to reinforce the sense of a downward movement.

The center of the pendulum movement in both episodes is the bowing down (*šāḥâh*). And in both cases the central drama takes place in three stages: there are three stages on the road to sacrifice (22:3–10); and three stages until Ephron agrees to sell the burial field (23:3–15).

ALONE, AND AT THE CENTER OF THE PEOPLE

The bowing down occurs in diametrically contrasting settings. When Abraham goes to bow down with Isaac, he goes to a place of the greatest solitude—an unknown land, an unnamed mountain, to face the death of his beloved. But when he goes to bow down after the death of Sarah, his progress is not into isolation but into intense involvement with the people:

And Abraham arose . . .
and spoke to the Hittites (v. 3),

Abraham arose and bowed down
to the people of the land, to the Hittites. . . .
And Ephron was sitting in the midst of the Hittites.
And Ephron the Hittite answered Abraham
in the hearing [literally, ears] of the Hittites,
of all who came in at the gate of his city (v. 7).

Abraham bowed down
before the people of the land.

And he spoke to Ephron
in the ears of the people of the land . . . (vv. 12–13).

"Hittites" had become a very broad term, sometimes used of the population as a whole (Clifford, 2:37). When Abraham bows down he effectively does so "in the midst" of the Hittites, before "all who came in at the gate." No place was more public. Socially, the gate was a kind of central plaza, so Abraham now bows down at the center of the people.

There are further balancing details. Chapter 22, for instance, emphasizes seeing (eyes), chapter 23, hearing (ears). Thus the contrast between the aloneness on the mountain and the social involvement at the city gate is part of a larger pattern of balance and complementarity.

Relationship to Preceding Chapters

Chapter 22, with its scene of rising early in the morning, echoes other early mornings—Sodom's destruction (19:27), and especially the dismissal of Hagar and Ishmael (21:27). The role of Abraham and the three boys (two servants and Isaac, 22:3) seems to echo Genesis 18–19 (God and the three men), especially since chapter 18 refers to a boy (18:7). The angel (22:11–19) continues the angel element of earlier episodes, especially those concerning Hagar (16:7–14; 21:14–20). Between the angel's saving of Ishmael in the desert (21:14–20) and the angel's saving of Isaac at Moriah (22:11–19) there is "a whole configuration of parallels" (Alter, 106).

However, the diptych as a whole (chaps. 22–23), the last in which God speaks to Abraham, has a special affinity with its opposite number, the diptych in which God first speaks to Abraham (chaps. 12–13). In simplified terms, the journey which involved the dishonoring of Sarah (chaps. 12–13) has been replaced by a journey of great integrity (to Moriah, chap. 22), and by a purchase of land which, after death, greatly honors Sarah (chap. 23). Sarna (150) spells out some of the details:

> Chaps. 12 and 22 share many connecting links. God's first call to Abraham is introduced by the declaration, "Go forth . . . to the land that I will show you;" and His last [call, in chap. 22] employs almost identical language, "Go forth . . . to the land of Moriah [Seeing]. . . ." The Hebrew phrase *lekh lekha*, "go forth," does not occur again in the Bible, a fact that underscores the deliberate and meaningful nature of its use in these two passages. In both instances the precise ultimate destination of the trek is withheld, and in both the tension of the drama is heightened by the cumulative effect of several Hebrew epithets, the last of which is the most potent: "your land, your homeland, your father's house;" "your son, your favored son, Isaac whom you love." Both episodes culminate in promises of glorious posterity, the second one [22:13, 17–19] containing striking verbal echoes of the first [12:3; cf. 13:

14–17]. One blessing was received at the terebinth of Moreh [12:6], the other at the similar sounding Moriah; and at both sites, it is stated Abraham "built an altar there [12:7,8; cf. 13:18; 22:9]."

Other elements may be mentioned, such as God's use of "please/pray" (13: 14; 22:2; otherwise used only three times in the Bible), and Abraham's lifting of his eyes (13:14; 22:13). The subsequent gracious buying of land to bury and honor Sarah (chap. 23) consists partly of a reversing of Abram's dishonorable conduct toward Sarah in Egypt (12:10–13:1).

Leading Elements

In comparison to all that precedes, this two-panel scene has a distinct and climactic intensity. At stake for Abraham is nothing less than the lives and deaths of the two people closest to him, his child (chap. 22) and his wife (chap. 23).

God's testing of Abraham has been the subject of much interpretation, most famously by Rembrandt, Kant, Kierkegaard, and Auerbach (on the history of interpretation, see Westermann, II, 353; on Rembrandt, see Fretheim, 499; on Kant, see Clifford, 2:35; on Kierkegaard, see Gellman, 1994; Dreifuss and Rie-mer, 1995, 135–138; Sacks, 163–164; on Auerbach, see Auerbach's *Mimesis* (1953), and Gros Louis's critique of Auerbach, 1982, 71–84). Apart from its use by famous names, the testing of Abraham has had a major role for later generations, especially in Jewish tradition (Sarna, 393–394).

Israelite law provided a certain context for the test. The idea of offering the first-born son to God was not strange. In principle it was well established (Exod. 22:29: "You will give me your first-born sons). But in practice people were not asked to do so; they had to sacrifice an animal instead (Exod. 34:40: "You will save/redeem [with an animal sacrifice] all your first-born sons"). These two laws balanced one another, serving both to establish the sovereignty of God and to safeguard human life. In Abraham's case it seemed as if he might actually sacrifice his son, but then, in accordance with usual practice, he offered a ram instead (22:13).

The prevention of the actual sacrifice of Isaac is sometimes seen as a statement against child-sacrifice—child-sacrifice existed in Canaan—but such an aspect is secondary at most. Brichto (1998, 293–287) contrasts Genesis 22 with Greek-drama scenes that involve god-related threats to sacrifice someone. In the Greek dramatic tradition certain forms of love often played havoc with lives. The effect of Brichto's contrast is to show both God and Abraham as calm. Yet, similarities with Greek scenes are significant (Brown, 1995, 216–218).

The assessment of Abraham's action by both Jewish and Christian tradition has been essentially positive, though with varying emphases. Christian tradition focuses on the interaction between God and Abraham, on the spiritual drama. Jewish tradition has placed greater emphasis on Isaac, sometimes referring to the whole episode as the Binding (Akeda) of Isaac (from ʿāqad, "to bind"), thus highlighting the emotional drama. Both emphases—spiritual and emotional—are important. If there were no emotional issue, there would have been less demand on the spirit.

Amid the complex discussion two issues are particularly crucial, one theological, the other psychological. The theological issue is not the relationship of moral law to divine law but whether any emotional tie, even parental, should come before God. More simply: does human love take priority over God? Trible (1996, 227) expresses the issue as one of idolatry:

> The text . . . tell[s] us he loves Isaac. . . . The story has to do with idolatry—the idolatry of the son. Once God had given the gift of Isaac to Abraham, does Abraham focus on Isaac and forget the Giver? The climactic line is "Now I know that you worship God," with the implied "and that you do not worship your son." If we borrow categories from Zen Buddhism, we can see how the story moves through three levels: attachment, detachment, and nonattachment. Abraham is so attached to this child that the issue of idolatry becomes acute for God. . . . It's a matter of the nature of faith.

The issue then is not the prevention of an immoral act—the killing of a child (this issue is important yet distinct)—but the letting go of control, even control over what God has promised. Abraham's test consists in "a willingness to surrender to God that which is most precious to him" (Moberly, 1992, 44).

The test has affinity with other biblical dramas; it "reminds us of the book of Job. It is the same problem; is there an unconditional devotion to God which could sacrifice everything and survive the hardest test?" (Jacob, 142). The New Testament (Matt. 10:37) turns the idea around, asking that one let go not of one's child but of one's parents: "Whoever loves (philō) father or mother more than me is not worthy of me." The Genesis story, however, with its wrenching emotional drama, conveys the radical spiritual challenge more effectively.

In psychological terms, the issue is one of the ego: "It is the ego of Abraham that has to be sacrificed on that mountain" (Cohen, 1996, 227). This sacrifice of the ego is part of the process of individuation (Dreifuss and Riemer, 1995, 103):

> One of the climaxes of the process of individuation . . . is the sacrifice of projections, the relinquishing of control over and expectations of another person, the ability to dissociate oneself from the object of one's projections. Abraham embarks on this terrible episode bearing the burden of Isaac's life (projection), and returns to the young men as one—different, whole and aware that he has parted with Isaac forever. Thus he returns alone.

Despite this aloneness, Abraham has not been impoverished. When God first asks him to take his son, God says please ("Take, pray [nā], your son . . . ," 15:2). In the other rare instances where God says please (13:14; 15:5; 31:12; cf. Exod. 11:2) the word is used "in the sense of inviting someone to accept a gift"

(Sacks, 164; Hamilton, 101). So when God asks Abraham to please take his son, Abraham does so calmly.

In the case of the threat to a city of sinful strangers, Abraham had argued with God at length (18:22–32). And in the case of parting with Ishmael, he had been upset, so that God needed to reassure him (21:11–13). Now, however, when there is a threat to the very life of the one he loves, he has seen enough not to be afraid.

The saving from death, so clear in the Isaac story, raises a question of whether the Sarah story also contains some form of overcoming death? And what, in such a context, is the meaning of the pattern of going down and arising?

Another issue is relationship to foreigners. The emphasis of the Sarah episode on the Hittites, right to the end (23:20), seems to be of a piece with earlier emphases on the Egyptians and Philistines (19:30–chap. 21, esp. 21:21, 34). Thus the Abraham story, as it moves toward its close, does not turn in on one group or nation. Rather it opens out to all kinds of foreigners.

A further issue is that of the relationship between love and death, two basic realities that seem interwoven in Genesis 20–23. Love here is of two kinds: parental (21:14–21; cf. chap. 22), and spousal (20:11–13; chap. 23). This love-death issue features not only in psychology (for instance in Rollo May's *Love and Will*, 1972, 99–121) but also in Scripture, most noticeably in the Song of Songs (Pope, 1977, 210–229).

At the core of both texts (chaps. 22 and 23) is an encounter with death. At some level, Abraham has to be ready to allow Isaac to die; he has to deal with potential death. And in the case of Sarah, he has to deal with actual death. Yet death does not dominate these episodes. Death can bring a sense of absurdity and confusion, even despair and bitterness (and so Auerbach, 1953, 10, imagines Abraham as bitter). But the reality of Genesis 22–23 is precisely the opposite: Abraham is serene (chap. 22) and gracious (chap. 23). The saving of Isaac is followed by the renewal of the promise of progeny (22:15–18), and the death of Sarah opens the way to finally entering into possession of at least some of the promised land (23:17–18). The prevailing mood throughout the whole diptych is one of harmony.

For one half verse (23:2b), immediately after Sarah dies (23:2a), Abraham mourns. He does so fully—wailing and weeping. But, unlike some Homeric scenes, he does not wallow in the sadness. Both death and mourning are recounted concisely (23:2). Then he picks himself up. The picture of the mourning—brief, full, and appropriate—has the effect not of disrupting the overall sense of harmony, but of confirming it, of integrating mourning with harmony. Such harmony in the face of death means that in some way death is overcome.

Structure (Table 27.1)

Chapter 22 is a tightly woven unit. At one level, the conclusion is ill-fitting: Abraham is told, after his test, that his only surviving brother has had twelve

Table 27.1. Facing Death (chap. 22 // chap. 23)

The offering of the son

Introduction: God—offer your child (22:1–2)
Trial: the three-stage journey to an unnamed mountain (22:3–10)
Trial: the angel—do not touch the boy (22:11–14)
Blessing: the angel—I will shower blessing (22:15–19)
Conclusion: blessed news; a brother's twelve children (22:20–24)

The death of the wife

Introduction: Sarah's death (23:1–2)
The three-stage quest for the field: bowing down (23:3–15)
Weighing, and the acquiring/rising of the field (23:16–18)
Conclusion: Sarah's burial (23:19–20)

children (22:20–24). But even in breaking the mould of the story, this has the effect of an appropriate surprise. It indicates that "Abraham's whole family is blessed" (Clifford, 2:36). Thus it partly fulfils what the angel promised: "I will bless you . . ." (22:17).

Comment

Panel One (Chap. 22)

[22:1–2] Abraham's trial: the offering of the beloved in the land of seeing. "After these things . . . God tested Abraham." In this story there is never a question of killing Isaac. "The reader shall know from the outset, what Abraham does not know: that the stupendous demand made of him shall be only a test" (Jacob, 142). The focus then is not on Isaac but on Abraham.

Yet God's command is open to misinterpretation, to imagining God as promoting killing rather than testing, and so it has led to great debates. But the essence of the test expresses a central human dilemma: does human love, even a unique love, come before God? Isaac is unique. Besides, Ishmael has gone, and at this stage Abraham has no other children.

This is Genesis's first use of the word "love" (*'āhab*). Previous episodes, especially the preceding scene, had broached the subject—in Sarah's kindness (*hesed*) to Abraham (20:13), and Hagar's weeping for her son (21:16). Now that the verb to love is explicitly used it is not taken lightly. In the person of Abraham, it is tested.

A related phenomenon occurs in the Bible's first references to women's beauty—in the implicit reference before the flood (6:2), and in the explicit reference in Egypt (12:10–20). Women's beauty is introduced as a possible cause of radical disorder and suffering.

Love might have done the same to Abraham. In the beauty-related episode in Egypt he had failed badly (chap. 12), but already in the dispute with Lot (chap. 13) he had reached another level of seeing, and the offering of Isaac is to take place in the land of Seeing (Moriah). Thus the offering up of the beloved, which within the limits of ordinary perception makes no sense, can be understood within the realm of a form of perception that goes further, the realm of God's seeing.

What he is being asked to do is to bring his love to another place. The place is not specified (see esp. Sarna, 391–392). Chronicles will identify Moriah with Jerusalem (2 Chron. 3:1), but such an identification belongs to the Jerusalem-related theology of Chronicles, not to Genesis. Yet it seems that just as the figure of Melchizedek, the gracious priest-king of Salem, contains an allusion to the Jerusalem priesthood, so the mountain, too, alludes to Jerusalem. Both mountains are related to an emphasis on seeing, to sacrifice, and to the name "the mountain of Yhwh" (Moberly, 1992, 47).

However, Genesis is careful not to mention Jerusalem; to do so would inject the clutter of a specific city into a scene which, at this moment, has another focus. Genesis has its own purpose, the evoking of a realm that is not geographically limited. The mountain, instead of being located, is indefinite; God will say where to go. Abraham is being asked to bring his love to a land of God's seeing and saying. His response, "Here I am" (22:1; cf. 22:7, 11) shows complete willingness (cf. Isa. 6:8, "Here I am. Send me").

The reticent evoking of Jerusalem has its purpose. It means that for those who live in or near Jerusalem, for those who turn toward it, it may indeed be a place with a city's usual limitations, but it was once a wondrous mountain, and at some level, it remains so.

[22:3–10] **The serene journey.** It is not only the reader, informed that this is a test, who has special knowledge about God's command. Abraham also has learned. When he rises early in the morning, it is not for the first time. Twice already he has arisen early following soul-searching encounters with God, first after the bargaining concerning the fate of the just at Sodom (19:27; cf. 18:22–32), and then after the distress concerning the sending away of Hagar and her child (21:14). Through those anguished struggles he has come to an awareness of God's word, God's ways.

The contrast with the sending away of Hagar and her son is particularly sharp. There is no indication here (chap. 22) of what was said plainly there, that sending away a son was bad in Abraham's eyes (21:11). If the sending away of Ishmael seemed bad to Abraham, the command to offer Isaac should have been doubly so. But of such a perception on Abraham's part, the text does not give a glimmer.

The chopping of the wood is unnerving, lest the same happen to Isaac. While Isaac carries the wood, Abraham himself, as if protecting Isaac, carries the two objects most likely to cause damage, namely the fire and the knife. Isaac, in inquiring about the lamb, refers to the wood and the fire, but omits any reference to the most frightening element, the knife.

It is easy to imagine Abraham as agonized or bitter. Such images express a general truth: death and loss tend to generate agony and bitterness; they hurt terribly; and aspects of that agony and hurt appear in Abraham's dealings with Sodom and Hagar.

But now Abraham has moved to a further stage. The picture here is of someone who, having come through questioning and disturbance, has moved to another level of awareness, another realm of seeing.

The biblical account of the journey, far from suggesting bitterness, is one of great calm. Abraham undertakes the journey methodically. He attends to the details—the donkey, the wood, the fire, and the knife. When he speaks, he does so with confidence and gentleness: "Let us worship/bow down and let us come back. . . . Here I am, my son. . . . God will see to the lamb. . . ." Even when the altar is built, he seems unruffled. He lays out the wood, not in distraught confusion, but "in order." And the remaining actions appear equally serene, even to the taking of the knife.

The sense of harmony is confirmed by the length of the journey. The journey is not a brief moment. The reference to "the third day" suggests something orderly and extended. Clifford (2:35) suggests that the reference to the third day "may be the halfway point of a seven-day journey ending in the arrival at the mountain." If so, then the serenity of Abraham is probably an echo of the harmony of creation.

The extent of Abraham's union with God emerges further in the identification of the mountain. God promises to tell Abraham which mountain, but God never needs to intervene. On the third day Abraham just lifts up his eyes and sees it (22:4). His seeing now reflects the seeing of God. In some way God is within him.

Isaac, too, is part of this union of spirit. He knows that superficially something is missing in the arrangements ("Where is the lamb . . . ?"), but he shows no hint of doubt about the rightness of what God and his father are doing. He is himself God's child; if his father walks with God to the mountain, so does he; he and his father walk "together" (22:6, 8). He does not drag his father away from God. On the contrary, he reinforces their union. Abraham's reply to Isaac, "Here I am," is the reply he, Abraham, had already given to God. Isaac's compliance with being bound indicates further confidence, indicates "his own willing submission to God's command revealed to his father" (Wenham, II, 115).

Abraham's sight is God's, and his child also is God's. At some level he knows God well enough to know God's child is secure.

[22:11–14] **The angel intervenes.** The angel who calls from the heavens declares what is at stake: the fear of God, reverential awe, comes before all else in life, even before a beloved. Abraham's positive fear of God, instead of being a killjoy, brings a further sense of life and its blessings. When he lifts up his eyes he sees a ram, thus supplying the needs of the sacrifice. Abraham had said God would "see" to the offering, and so he names the place "Yhwh Sees," meaning God both sees and provides (22:13–14). The resultant saying, "On the mountain of Yhwh there is seeing," is ambiguous: "It is not clear whether it is God or the person who comes to the Mount who sees/is seen" (Alter, 106), an obscurity akin to Hagar's saying about seeing (16:13). One implication is that even at the terrible mountain of loneliness and deathly loss, there is seeing and providing. In some sense, at death God provides.

The substitution of the ram accords with the above-mentioned Israelite practice of substituting an animal for the first-born (Exod. 22:29; 34:40).

[22:15–19] **The renewed promise of blessings.** The angel now solemnly renews the promise to Abraham, and does so in a form that is yet more abundant: "descendants like the stars . . . like the sand . . . ," including inheriting the gate of their enemies, and bringing blessing on "all the nations of the earth." This is the seventh and climactic statement of the great promises (cf. 12:2–3, 7; 13:14–17; chaps. 15, 17, 18).

Within the story of chapter 22, the role of the promise of blessings is similar to that of the blessing given by Melchizedek to Abraham as he returned from an earlier trial, the war (14:17–20). Neither blessing fits within the standard confines of the conventional trial scene. Rather they extend the convention of the trial, integrating it into a larger unity.

[22:20–24] **Conclusion. A brother's children, intimating Abraham's.** Finally, in the conclusion (22:20–24), the promise of many descendants comes a step closer: Abraham is told that Nahor, "his brother," has had twelve children—eight through Milcah, and four through his concubine. And, bringing the promise yet closer, the second part of the conclusion notes repetitively and elaborately that Nahor was "the brother of Abraham" (22:22b–24). The emphasis intimates what is to come for Abraham himself, and does so after an episode in which he was ready to let go of everything. He has gone from almost losing his only child, Isaac, to the sudden news of twelve extra children.

At the structural center of those twelve (between the eight and the four), there is an extra name—Rebekah—Isaac's future wife.

And in those twelve children—the eight and the four—there is already an outline of the twelve sons of Jacob, eight from his wives, and four from his concubines. From the virtual namelessness that governs its beginning, the chapter has swung around to becoming reassuringly specific. Not only has Isaac been spared; at some level, the children of Jacob are already on their way.

Panel Two (Chap. 23)

[23:1–2] **Sarah's death, evoking fullness of life. Abraham mourns.** The announcement of the time span of Sarah's life, 127 years, brings an evoking not of tragedy (Dennis, 1994, 61) but of overflowing fullness. As well as achieving the full span of 120 (as set by God, 6:3; and fulfilled in Moses, Deut. 34:4), she has an extra seven, itself a symbol of fullness. And the unnecessary-looking repetition of the reference to her years of life ("the years of the life of Sarah," 23:1b) heightens yet further the sense of a full life. The effect is all the greater because she once was described as barren.

Not only in time but also in space or geography there is a fullness about her death. Her place of death, Hebron, is preceded by a new designation, the City of the Four (Kiriath-arba), and followed by the unnecessary-looking information that Hebron was "in the land of Canaan." Just as seven has a general sense of fullness, so, when dealing with space, does four (four corners of the earth; four rivers in Eden, Genesis 2; four directions around the tabernacle, Num. 2:3, 10, 18, 25). And "the land of Canaan" is not just an address; it has been associated in various ways with God's great promise. Sarah therefore does not shrink away in a corner of nothingness. Her death, however quiet, has evocations of great life and of a broad land.

For Abraham the loss seems acute. He wails and weeps for her. This suggests that he followed ritual mourning customs of lamentation, but there is no suggestion that the mourning is unreal. It is real, but he does not prolong it unduly. The initial rising probably contrasts with the mourning; "he was prostrate beside his wife's body" (Clifford, 2:37).

[23:3–15] **Buying the burial property: Abraham's descent among the people.** There is nothing shabby about the procedure surrounding Sarah's burial. When Abraham buys burial land he does so with impeccable legality and with a certain elegance; the gathering at the gate is like a town council (see esp. Sarna, 156–157; Speiser, 172). The transaction is solemn, yet with a touch of humor (Darr, 1991, 111). The solemnity is increased by such touches as "Pray . . ." (23:6, 17; cf. Alter, 109). Initially all Abraham wanted was the cave. Ephron manages to include the field, and thus to make a huge sale. Eventually Ephron refers to the field as "land" (ʿereṣ, 23:15) thus ironically evoking God's promise. Ephron is "intimating, by way of a term that also means 'country,' that Abraham is free to imagine he is getting more than a field with a burial cave for his money. . . . Many interpreters view this whole episode as a final gesture of the aged Abraham toward laying future claim to possession of the land" (Alter, 111–112).

As a "stranger and sojourner" Abraham "needed the natives' permission to conduct business with the same right as the natives" (Clifford, 2:37). In fact they regard him as a prince/elect of God (23:6), unlike the way the men of Sodom regarded Lot (19:9).

But the elegance is not just a superficial ritual. As already indicated, the procedure involves both a pendulum effect of descent and ascent and an increasing involvement with the people.

[23:16–18] **Weighing the weights and acquiring the field in all its border.** Instead of saying simply that Abraham paid the required price, the account spells out the process. It recounts both Abraham's hearing of Ephron, and the actual paying. The paying has a resonance of weightiness: "he weighed out the silver . . . four hundred weights/shekels of silver, according to the standard (weight) of merchants." (The silver shekel varied from about eight grams to sixteen, around half an ounce). The repetition ("weigh . . . weight") is compounded by the number—four hundred, "probably . . . exorbitant" (Darr, 1991,112). In contrast, Jeremiah bought a field for only seventeen shekels (Jer. 32:7). Perhaps it is no accident that four has a connotation of universality. It is appropriate in any case that the promised land should have a suggestion of universality; it is for all peoples.

The picture of Abraham weighing out such a weight blends in with the preceding picture of Abraham's descent, his bowing down among the people (23:3–15). In some sense he is involved in a going down, a heaviness.

But then the account swings around: "And so was set up [literally, there arose, qûm] the field of Ephron. . . ." At one level, "arose" simply means that the field achieved a new status, that is was made over to Abraham. But the word has a further dimension. Genesis uses not only the same verb (qûm) as was used when Abraham first arose and began the process of descent (23:3, 7), but the same part of the verb (wayāqām, imperfect, Qal). Thus the element of arising, which, during the process of descent and weighing, had faded away, now returns: the field arose. The descent is reversed.

The sense of reversal is heightened by the subsequent description of the field, by the field's evocation of vitality and spaciousness (23:17–18). It is a field that faces Mamre, the place last mentioned in connection with Yhwh's appearance (18:1). And the field has trees, and, round about, has a border (gĕbûl), a word otherwise used of the limits of a country (10:19, "the border of the Canaanites"). Furthermore, this field is associated with many people: it was acquired "before the eyes of the Hittites, before all who came in at the gate of his city" (23:18). The final detail, "his city," as though the city was now Abraham's, corroborates the sense of reversal.

[23:19–20] Sarah's burial, again evoking life. Abraham buries Sarah in a "cave," a location which in itself suggests a place of darkness and confinement. But now, instead of being called "the cave of Machpelah," as when first mentioned (23:9), it is "the cave of the field of Machpelah," a factor that adds vitality and sets it more properly in the land. And the location of the field, as well as recalling Mamre, echoes the geographical overload of the introduction. Compare:

23:2: "the City of Four, that is Hebron, in the land of Canaan."
23:19: "facing Mamre, that is Hebron, in the land of Canaan."

The overloaded introduction had a purpose—to evoke a fullness of life; and now something of that fullness is attached to the field of burial.

Then the text concludes: "And the field arose (qûm) . . . to Abraham," again meaning the field was made over to him, but again with an overtone that helps to complete the reversal of Abraham's earlier descent. The result is that Sarah's death and burial, instead of being overwhelmed by mourning, is surrounded primarily by evocations of life (see "The Question of Immortality" in Chapter 14).

That life is not for herself and Abraham alone. As mentioned earlier, the last word is "Hittites" (23:20)—rather as "Egypt" and "the Philistines" were the last words in the episodes after Isaac's birth (21:21, 34). In some way many others are involved.

| 28 | Rebekah, Betrothal, and Genealogy (24:1–25:18) |

The Double Betrothal (Chap. 24)
The Double Genealogy (25:1–18)

Introductory Aspects

The Basic Story Line

The narrative recounts both betrothal and genealogy—the betrothal of Rebekah (chap. 24), and then the concluding genealogies of Abraham and Ishmael (25: 1–18). The Rebekah episode is the most elaborate in Genesis, and has a great sense of harmony.

The story begins when the old servant swears to old Abraham that he will seek a kindred wife for Isaac. Arriving at the well of Nahor at evening, the servant sets up a demanding test for discerning the wife, in some ways a test of God and of God's dealings with Abraham. No sooner said than done: Rebekah arrives and passes the test with flying colors, not to mention flying feet and strong arms. She is a "doer" (Teugels, 1996, 289–291).

Inside the house the mood threatens to be dominated by Rebekah's greedy-eyed brother, Laban. However, in a long speech, the longest in Genesis, the servant recalls a world of blessing, both the blessings showered on Abraham and the generosity shown at the well, and the night ends not with any greed but with elaborate sharing of gifts, food, and drink.

Next morning Laban is inclined to hold on longer to Rebekah, but she is as clear-eyed as ever and, amid portentous blessings, she mounts a camel, leaves her home, and follows the servant.

Later, in the context of a second well, to the south, the focus of the story shifts from Abraham to Isaac. Isaac sees the approach of the distant cavalcade, and Rebekah sees the distant Isaac. Then the two come together in a tent.

But Abraham is not forgotten. The second panel (25:1–18) comes back to him and to a surprising picture of vitality and of generating: he has a second wife, concubines, and several children—ancestors apparently of many peoples. Isaac is still special, but even at Abraham's death, Isaac is accompanied by Ishmael, and it is with an emphasis on Ishmael and his descendants that the Abraham story ends.

Thus at one level the center of the whole diptych is the search for a wife for Isaac, yet at another, the focus is not on Isaac but on Abraham and on Abraham's wider range of descendants.

Literary Form

The two final panels of the Abraham story follow two diverse literary conventions, those of a betrothal (chap. 24), and a genealogy (25:1–18).

Variations on the betrothal convention occur, for instance, in the stories of Jacob (Gen. 29:1–14) and Moses (Exod. 2:15–22) (Alter, 1981, 51–58). Combined with the betrothal scene are aspects of a commissioning: Abraham commissions the old servant (cf. Jer. 1; Exod. 2:23–4:17).

Variations on the genealogy occur in five other Genesis passages (4:17–26; chap. 5; 11:10–32; 35:21–29; and chap. 36). All five are conclusions or parts of conclusions: they occur respectively at the end of Genesis 1–5, the end of Genesis 6–11, and the end of the first half of the Jacob story (35:21–chap. 36). Moreover, all five are either double (two genealogies in one) or paired (paired with another genealogy). The Cain-Adam genealogy (4:17–26), for example, is double—first, the genealogy of Cain (4:17–24); and then the shorter genealogy of Adam (4:25–26). Likewise, the Shem-Terah genealogy (11:10–32), the passage that concludes Genesis 1–11.

Of these five other genealogies, three record death: chapter 5, with its repetitive "and he died;" Terah's genealogy (11:27–32); and 35:21–29, which recounts the death of Isaac. The Abraham-Ishmael genealogy likewise recounts death.

Overall, therefore—as concluding, as double, and as recounting death—the Abraham-Ishmael genealogy accords with the broader genealogical patterns of Genesis.

Complementarity of the Two Panels

The pairing of a long betrothal (sixty-seven verses) with a genealogy (eighteen verses) may seem surprising, particularly insofar as the two texts use diverse perspectives. The betrothal focuses on one event, in colorful detail, while the genealogy does the opposite; it sweeps quickly across whole generations.

Yet the pairing of conventions of uneven length is not unique. In the story of Moses, his brief betrothal (eight verses, Exod. 2:15–22) is paired with his extensive prophetic call (forty-two verses, Exod. 2:23–4:17). Besides, betrothal and genealogy are almost inherently connected, like getting married and generating children. When Rebekah is setting off to marry Isaac, her own people wish that she will become the source of whole multitudes (24:60). It is appropriate, then, that the next panel mentions many peoples and generations.

Relationship to Preceding Chapters, Especially Genesis 1–2

As well as echoing the beginning of the Abraham story (esp. 12:1–3), and linking with several aspects of Genesis 12–50 (Gillmayr-Bucher, 2001), this diptych of betrothal and genealogy also contains a broad echo of the whole creation scene.

First, there are some similarities that are very general. The overall sense of harmony that pervades chapter 24 is akin to that of the first creation panel (1:1–2:4a). Creation's sense of God, as being in supreme control of everything, finds an echo in God's guidance of the servant's mission. And the second creation panel (2:4b–24), with its emphasis on space and with its four rivers, may have contributed to aspects of the genealogy—its mention of diverse places and its unusual fourfold structure.

Second, there are a number of more detailed affinities:

The repeated cosmic invocation at the beginning ("Yhwh, the God of the heavens and the God of the earth," 24:3, 6).

The emphasis on blessing (and being blessed, 24:1, 27, 31, 34, 48, 60; 25:11).

The highlighting of the man-woman relationship.

The importance of finding the right companion/spouse for the man.

The leaving of home to be with one's spouse.

A sense of great numbers and variety (25:1–18).

The goodness of things: "every good thing" (24:10); "good old age" (25:8); Rebekah as "very good" (24:16).

The "completing" (*kālâh*) of the good work (by Rebekah, 24:19–22; cf. 2:1).

Leading Elements

TWO DIVERSE BETROTHALS

The key to the whole diptych lies not only in the literary conventions, in the broad patterns, but also in the way these conventions have been adapted. Adaptations to a convention generally reveal a specific purpose (Alter, 1981, 50, 62).

The betrothal scene speaks of two unions, not only that of Isaac and Rebecca, but also that of God and Abraham. It is this latter union—of God with Abraham—that receives priority. Only at the end (24:62–67), when Isaac enters the scene, and when a second well is mentioned (24:62), does the focus turn directly on Isaac and Rebekah.

During most of the betrothal scene (24:1–61), therefore, even at the first well, the primary relationship is that between Abraham and God. The opening verse (24:1), for instance, is not about Isaac and Rebekah, but about God's blessing of Abraham. The "thigh" (24:2, 9), a euphemism for the genitals, is not that of Isaac, but of Abraham. At the well, the love that is recognized (*ḥesed*, *'emet*, "kindness and faithfulness") is God's faithful love for Abraham (24:27). In the second recounting of the meeting at the well, during the servant's climactic speech (24:34–49), the primary emphasis is on that faithful love being returned. In this scene, therefore, the foundational love is that of God. The author has adapted the convention of the betrothal so that the primary reference is spiritual not physical. The Gospel of John does likewise: Jesus' meeting with the woman at the well involves spiritual betrothal (John 4:1–42).

The relationship between Abraham and Yhwh is not just a background theme. It is depicted obliquely but vividly in the meeting of the old servant and Rebekah, especially in their running (24:17, 20). The old servant represents Abraham. In successive verses both are introduced as "old" (24:1–2), and the servant has all of Abraham's responsibility and goods (24:2, 10). Rebekah, at a certain level, is like God; she is God's manifestation. Her identity and her qualities—grace and great generosity—are a revelation not only of herself but even more so of God, of Yhwh's love and guidance (24:26–27).

Apart from representing Yhwh, Rebekah of course is also a specific woman, vibrant and decisive, and the Yhwh-Abraham relationship opens the way to the marriage of Rebekah with Isaac. But the broader emphasis in chapter 24 is on God's dealing with Abraham. Chapter 24 is the summit of God's blessing of Abraham.

The other part of that summit is the genealogy (25:1–18). The genealogy, recounting many children and an ideal death, suggests immense blessing, thus complementing the betrothal and completing it. In essence, while chapter 24 tells of Abraham's betrothal, the genealogy tells of his children.

THE RESULT OF THE GREATER BETROTHAL: CHILDREN THROUGHOUT THE WORLD

Unlike the betrothal of Rebekah and Isaac, with its orientation toward a specific people, the betrothal and genealogy of Abraham opens the way to very diverse kinds of children, located almost everywhere.

The first part of the genealogy, Abraham's children by Keturah and by an unspecified number of concubines (25:1–6), suggests whole peoples, great variety, and wide expansion. And even the later part of the genealogy, concerning Ishmael and all his descendants, belongs ultimately to Abraham: Ishmael is introduced as "son of Abraham" (25:12).

At the end, the range of the Abraham story is universal. In its own way it encompasses both the world and death. Its encompassing of the world is evoked by the apparently endless variety of the children suggested in the final genealogy. Isaac remains central (25:5, 11), but the others are also important and far-flung.

Two details may be particularly linked to universality: the sending of the concubines' children far away to the east (25:6; in the perspective of Genesis, the east is the source of the human race); and the final tantalizing details about the location of the people of Ishmael (25:18a; the naming of the location uses not one name but four, names which individually are prestigious or widespread, and which when taken together, evoke something of the four rivers of the Garden of Eden and the four corners of the world; see later comment on 25: 17–18). Even the structure of the genealogy, at one level at least, is fourfold.

The encompassing of death is seen in the way Abraham's death is surrounded by a sense of goodness and fullness. And its aftermath, for Isaac, is not bitterness but blessing (25:11). Ishmael's death is not so obviously surrounded by goodness; in fact there is a clear contrast between his death and that of Abraham. Yet, in the final analysis, Ishmael's death, like Ishmael's children, is related to Abraham.

THE PLACE OF REBEKAH WITHIN GENESIS AS A WHOLE

The story of Rebekah (sixty-seven verses) stands out at the center of Genesis. The account forms a striking interpretive interlude, partly comparable in its literary function to the role of the transfiguration at the center of the Gospel of Mark.

On the one hand, the Rebekah story is thoroughly embedded in the larger text of Genesis, in the accounts of the patriarchs. The story evokes the God of creation ("Yhwh, God of the heavens and God of the earth," 24:3, 7), recalls the call of Abraham (24:7), and summarizes Abraham's blessings (24:1). It also anticipates aspects of later stories—the character of Laban (calculating, delaying, 24:30, 55), and the leisurely detailed style of some of the narratives of Jacob and Joseph.

On the other hand, the Rebekah story is unique. Most obviously, as a single episode, it is uniquely lengthy, well beyond anything else in Genesis. It follows Genesis, yet breaks the mould. It tells of Abraham, yet leaves him behind. He speaks for the last time in 24:8, an injunction not to go back to his original country. It is also uniquely woman-centered. Though most of the characters in the story are men, the figure of Rebekah stands at center stage, like a radiant personification of God's covenant love (*ḥesed*, "kindness / steadfast love / covenant love") (24:12, 14, 27; cf. 24:48, "kindness and truth"). She is an ideal woman (Gillmayr-Bucher, 1998), and she is the "divinely-sent helper. . . . The 'divine hand' is . . . in her life" (Teugels, 1996, 295).

Table 28.1. Rebekah, Betrothal, and Birth (chap. 24 // 25:1–18)

The double betrothal

Introduction: Abraham's thigh, and a wife for Isaac (24:1–9)
At the well: Rebekah's Kindness (24:10–27)
  Let kindness be the sign (24:10–14)
  Rebekah's kindness (24:15–21)
  The servant acknowledges God's kindness (24:22–27)
In the house: Laban (24:28–54)
  Laban's kindness, based on gold (24:28–32)
  Central speech: Recounting kindness, that kindness be returned (24:34–49)
  Response to the speech (24:50–54a)
Next morning: Rebekah's decision to depart (24:54b–61)
  Laban and mother tend to cling to Rebekah (24:54b–56)
  Rebekah's clear decision to go (24:57–59)
  Rebekah's blessed departure (24:60–61)
Conclusion: A second well and meeting—Isaac and Rebekah (54:62–67)

The double genealogy

Abraham's descendants (25:1–6)
Abraham's death (25:7–11)
Ishmael's descendants (Ishmael, son of Abraham, 25:12–16)
Ishmael's death (25:17–18)

The centrality of the idea of covenant love is corroborated by the fact that the story follows the literary convention of the betrothal scene, the most elaborate betrothal scene in the Bible. The story of Rebekah's betrothal, her covenanted love, interprets the larger story of the covenant love, which implicitly encompasses Genesis, encompasses even the Primary History (2 Kings 13:23).

Structure (Table 28.1)

PANEL ONE (CHAP. 24)

The clarity of the story makes for easy detection of the structure, as does the first creation story. (However, note Teugels's slightly different structure, 1996, 285). The introduction (sending the servant, 25:1–9) and conclusion (Isaac meets Rebekah, 24:62–67) stand apart, and the intervening journey falls into three distinct flowing episodes, each with three parts. The central piece, the climactic speech (24:34–49), itself contains three parts, the central one being the recounting of the sign—Rebekah's kindness (24:42–46).

PANEL TWO (25:1–18)

The genealogy does not seem to have a formal introduction or conclusion in panel two. Instead, the text appears, curiously, to fall into four parts, a structure that breaks the mould. Within these parts one may subdivide at verses 5 and 11. Other subdivisions seem less sure. At the end the text shrinks.

Comment

Panel One (Chap. 24)

[24:1–9] **The old servant, and the puzzle of the land of Abraham and his kindred.** At one level the introduction seems straightforward. The old Abraham sends the old servant, under oath, to find a wife for Isaac. The wife must come from his own land and kindred, not from the Canaanites or his land of origin.

Yet the episode is perplexing. First of all, in the mode of swearing the oath the servant places his hand under Abraham's thigh (the genitals), a rite that "may place the one who swears under the penalty of sterility if the task is not carried out" (Clifford, 2:38). But the servant is old ("the old [one] of his house"), so the threat of sterility seems virtually meaningless. Even if the sanction is not precisely the threat of sterility, there seems to be something incongruous about two old men engaged in a rite that is linked to fertility.

Besides, the old servant's destination is not clear:

ABRAHAM: "Go to my land and my birthplace. . . ."

SERVANT: "[If necessary], shall I [go] back to the land from which you came?"

ABRAHAM: "[No], Yhwh . . . took me from my father's house and from the land of my birthplace. . . ."

Thus, the servant must go to Abraham's land and birthplace but must not go back to his land and birthplace.

One may try to explain the problem by saying there were two ancestral homes in diverse geographical places. That idea is eminently plausible and clear, but it is not what Genesis says. At this stage, Genesis does not mention any geography or places. Instead it speaks of "land and birthplace" and then contradicts "land and birthplace."

A clue to the contradiction comes from the Genesis account itself, from Abraham's original journey (12:1–3). The two journeys (24:1–9; 12:1–3) open the first and last diptychs respectively of the Abraham story, and in some ways they are connected. They speak of Yhwh's blessing and of sending someone to another land.

But—and this is the crucial clue—the original land of destination is not named. Even though Canaan will be used as a place to live, the land is "the land that I will make you see (12:1);" and the focus in the whole opening diptych (chaps. 12–13) is not so much on Canaan as on another dimension of seeing, in other words, on another land.

In this closing scene also (24:1–25:18), "land" is being used in two senses: the physical meaning, Abraham's place of origin, to which the servant must not go; and a meaning that includes a further dimension, the land of seeing to which he now belongs. Thus, wherever Isaac's wife is to come from—and she must come from a specific geographic place—she must also inhabit this land of seeing, she must be aware of this further blessed reality.

This explains why Abraham, instead of giving geographical directions to the servant, says that Yhwh, who first guided him to the land of seeing, will now send his angel before him. The angel had also helped Hagar to see (at Beer-lahoi-roi, the Well of the Living One Who Sees Me, 16:7–14).

The presence of an extra dimension helps to explain the old man's fertility-related oath. Physically, an old man has virtually no fertility. But if there is another sense to land and kindred, something beyond the physical, then there is another form of life, and thus another form of fertility. One may be old, therefore, and still be fertile, still be involved in a form of betrothal.

[24:10–27] Rebekah. At the well, at evening: Rebekah's graciousness as a revelation of God. The servant's journey suggests overflowing providence. He has great riches (ten camels; ten connotes fullness); he has some of all of his lord's goods; and, as with Abraham's original journey to Canaan (12:5), his arrival at his destination, Aram-Naharaim (somewhere in central Mesopotamia), is recounted instantaneously (24:10).

At the well the servant goes through three stages of perception. First (24:11–14), he asks for a sign that, as an indication to him both of divine kindness (*ḥesed*) and of Isaac's future wife, a girl or young woman (*naʿărā*) will respond in a specific way. When asked for a drink, she will spontaneously offer to water the camels also. Then (24:15–21), when Rebekah fulfils the requirements of the sign, and does so with beauty and energy, the servant gazes silently, wondering. Finally (24:22–27), when Rebekah has watered the camels fully—no mean task—and disclosed her identity, thus confirming the sign, the servant bows down in acknowledgment of God's "kindness and truth" (*ḥesed, ʿemet*). Rebekah, therefore, discloses not only her own kindness and identity, but also the kindness of God.

[24:28–54a] Laban. In the house, with Laban: the revelation is contrasted and developed. The focus now moves significantly from Rebekah to Laban. Rebekah's deed at the well is recounted, but she is no longer leading the action. Laban, in contrast, is highlighted first and last (24:29, 50). Reference is also made to Rebekah's mother.

Laban acts as if his father were not there, so perhaps the brief reference to the father's presence (24:50) is a scribal gloss. It could also be that, while the father is still alive, the pushy Laban has taken over. It is not only Laban who will appear again in later events; so will the question of a father being pushed aside (namely, Jacob; cf. chap. 34). It is appropriate then that that motif be intimated now in the absence or pushing aside of Laban's father.

The servant, when brought into the house by Laban, recounts what has happened. His blessednesss-laden speech is the longest in Genesis (24:34–49). It tells of Abraham and the journey to Nahor, and is longer even than Judah's grief-laden speech to Joseph, telling of Jacob and the journey to Egypt (44:18–34).

This long speech (24:34–49) repeats much of what has already been recounted in chapter 24 and so it is highly repetitive. But there are changes in details (Alter, 113, 119, 120). The covenant language of Abraham's instructions to the servant (24:7) is discreetly left out. The order of two events—giving the ring and inquiring about family—is reversed (24:22–23; cf. 24:47), lest the giving of the ring before inquiring about family seem presumptuous. There is also a shift of ideas, namely from God's kindness to responding to that kindness. The emphasis on blessing forms a frame around the speech (24:35, 48). Years later, Jacob's brief reply to Pharaoh is also framed in blessing, though somewhat obscurely (47:7–11). It is this reply that gives central clarity.

The repetition itself seems to have a purpose. It shows correspondence—the literary correspondence between what is said and repeated—and this correspondence appears, in the context, to reflect one of the ideas in Genesis 24, namely that of harmony. There is some form of deep harmony between Abraham and God.

The presence of Laban develops the sense of the revelation. First, his level of seeing—his focus is on the gold (24:30)—forms a contrast with Rebekah's spontaneous generosity. Also, as Rebekah's brother, he is in a position to approve the marriage, and so, whatever his motives, he advances the providential journey of Rebekah to Isaac.

[24:54b–61] The morning: Rebekah again hastens the providential marriage. Rebekah again becomes the decisive figure. In the morning, when there is a difference of opinion about going back to Isaac—the servant wants to cooperate quickly with the providential mission, but Laban and his mother want to cling to Rebekah—Rebekah herself makes the decision: "I will go."

Her departure is like a triumphal procession, with overflowing blessings, with her nurse and her female companions, on the camels. As in other societies, retaining one's wet nurse was a sign of social status (Alter, 121).

[24:62–67] In the Negev [desert], at evening: the seeing, the veiling, and the loving. The picture of Isaac walking in the evening is full of ambiguity and hauntingly beautiful. Apart from the uncertainty about what he is doing—the Hebrew verb (*sûaḥ*) is unique and unclear—his situation can be read in diverse ways. On the one hand, he is in a desert area, the Negev, at evening time, a place and time that suggest emptiness, darkness. On the other hand, he is introduced as having been at the Well of the Living One Who Sees Me, and he is in a field—locations that are more indicative of life and growth.

It is while he is in the field that he lifts his eyes and sees camels. And Rebekah lifts her eyes and sees a man. The mutual seeing, though not fully clear (he sees camels; she sees a man), is a capsule form of the earlier revelatory meeting at the well, and a high point in the whole drama of seeing.

Rebekah's veil prevents immediate full seeing, but when Isaac takes her as wife and loves her, the implication is that the seeing is completed. Thus the seeing, in the final analysis, is not abstract or gnostic; it is love.

Panel Two (25:1–18)

[25:1–6] Blessedness during life: Abraham's descendants through Keturah and the concubines. After the long slow drama of the birth of Isaac, the account now tells surprisingly about a sudden flow of offspring from Abraham. Children are born first through his new wife Keturah, and then—something quite distinct—through his concubines. Some of the children's names are those of tribes or peoples (Clifford, 2:40). In the Keturah list "Abraham figures as the progenitor of the semi-nomadic peoples of the transJordan region and the Arabian Peninsula" (Alter, 124). (The Chronicler's identification of Keturah as a concubine [1 Chron. 1:32], like the Chronicler's identification of Moriah with Jerusalem [2 Chron. 3:1], represents the viewpoint of the Chronicler's theology, not necessarily the viewpoint of Genesis.)

This combination—wife/wives and concubine(s)—brings Abraham into the same pattern as his brother Nahor (22:20–24), and also prepares for Jacob (29:31–30:24).

The two sets of children—from the second wife and from the concubines—also indicate the spreading of Abraham's children through time and space. The children through Keturah are recounted to the fourth generation (25:2–3). And the children of the concubines are sent far to the east, the presumed place of origin of human beings (25:6).

The impression, in the shaping of the text, is that all these children were born during Abraham's lifetime—they are all listed before he dies—and the sending of the concubines' children to the east occurs, explicitly, "while he was still alive."

The overall effect is to suggest great blessing. The sense of blessing is heightened by the emphasis on gifts: while Abraham "gave" all he had to Isaac, he also "gave gifts" to the sons of the concubines (in Hebrew, as in English, "give" and "gift" are related). Thus the concubines' children have a share of the blessed gifts that go to Isaac.

[25:7–11] Blessing in death. Abraham dies and Isaac settles. The death of Abraham is recounted in a positive way, a fact heightened by comparison with the subsequent account of the death of Ishmael:

These are the days of the years	These are the years
of the life of Abraham which he lived	of the life of Ishmael
—175 years (v 7).	—137 years
Abraham expired and died	He expired and died,
in a good old age (*śêbâ ṭôbâ*),	

old and full,

and he was gathered to his people (v. 18).	and he was gathered to his people. (v. 17)

The material that is special to Abraham—including "the days of" and "which he lived"—has the effect of expanding the picture of Abraham's life, of simply emphasizing his days and his life. The idea that old age is good repeats what was said earlier when Abraham seemed afraid of the future (15:15).

"Gathered to his people" (25:8, 17; said also of Esau and Jacob, 35:29; 49: 33) is used in the Pentateuch only and "probably alludes to Sheol or some other form of afterlife" (Fretheim, 515).

Abraham's burial, with both Isaac and Ishmael present, is in the cave of Machpelah—with details to recall both the ceremonial buying from the Hittites, and the memory of Sarah (25:9–10).

Finally, Abraham's death does not leave Isaac forlorn. On the contrary, he is blessed ("God blessed Isaac"), and he settles at the Well of the Living One Who Sees Me (25:11).

Again, as in life, so in death; the overall impression is of blessing. In the reference to good old age this impression of blessing is implicit. And at the end, in the mention of the post-death blessing of Isaac, it is explicit.

[25:12–16] **The descendants of Ishmael.** As the descendants of Abraham were listed, so are those of Ishmael. Some of these children's names occur elsewhere as the names of tribes or places (Clifford, 2:42).

Even when attention switches to Ishmael, Abraham is not forgotten; there is a reminder that Ishmael is the "son of Abraham" (25:12). And the number of Ishmael's children, twelve, links him both with Abraham's brother, Nahor, who had twelve children (22:20–24), and with the later sons of Jacob. Thus however distant Ishmael may be, at some level he remains within the tradition of Abraham.

[25:17–18] **The death of Ishmael, and the puzzle of his location.** The final references to Ishmael's life and death, while briefer than the references concerning Abraham (see comment on 25:7–11), contain one very positive detail—living until 137. This is less than Abraham, but ten years more than Sarah in all her fullness of life (see comment on 23:1–2).

The moment after Ishmael's death presents a contrast with the death of Abraham:

Abraham	*Ishmael*
And he was gathered to his people.	And he was gathered to his people.
Isaac and Ishamel buried him in the	They dwelt from Havilah to Shur,
cave of Machpelah . . . and Sarah.	which faces Egypt till you come to Asshur.

Instead of linking "his people" with a specific burial place (the cave . . . and Sarah), the Ishamel account tells where the people dwelt, and does so in a way that is puzzling: "from Havilah to Shur, which faces Egypt till you come to Asshur." The designation seems overloaded. Even if one reduces Havilah and Shur to a single name, the text is still perplexing (see, for instance, the *NAB*, "from Havilah-by-Shur, which is on the border of Egypt, all the way to Asshur"). It seems better, then, since fusing of names does not clarify the text, to take the names as being four.

All four are weighty:

> However many Havilahs are known to geographers, the only previous Genesis reference to Havilah as a place-name is in the Garden of Eden, as the land of the first river—a land of gold and precious stones (2:11).

> Shur was associated with the angel's appearance to the Egyptian slave woman, at the Well of the Living One Who Sees Me (16:7, 14), the well where Isaac settled (25:11; cf. 24:62). It was later associated with Abraham in a context that emphasizes the connection of Abraham and Isaac with the nations, especially with Egypt and the Philistines, 19:30–chap. 21, esp. 20:1; 21:21, 34).

> Egypt, over the millennia, was the most prestigious country in the ancient world.

> Asshur (Assyria), apart from the table of nations (10:11, 22), has been mentioned only in the Garden of Eden, in association with the third river (2:14).

Whatever the final details of their significance, the effect of the four names is to provide a form of variation on the four rivers of Eden, and thus to evoke the whole world, the four corners of the earth. It is as though the original idea of four rivers or corners has been adapted to include aspects of developing history, especially as that history includes significant events near Shur and Egypt.

Ishmael's people, therefore, seem in a sense to dwell everywhere.

The final detail (25:18) is also puzzling: "Facing all his brothers, he [Ishmael] fell" (*nāpal*). "Fell" is sometimes translated less literally, for example, as "encamped" or "settled," yet the context is Ishmael's death, and "fell" corresponds partly to that context. ("Fell" is also used of Rebekah's descent from her camel, 24:64.)

"His brothers" apparently refers to his brothers through Abraham, in other words, Abraham's other children. Such is the implication of the context, of the whole Abraham-Ishmael balance of this section (25:1–18), and of the pairing of Isaac and Ishmael at Abraham's burial (25:9).

At one level, therefore, when compared with that of Abraham, the death of Ishmael seems wanting. Yet Ishmael's death, far from being isolated and meaningless, is closely bound with Abraham's and fills out the whole Abraham account. His people and fall—whatever "fall" connotes—seem to reach out to the whole world and to gather it in so that he is facing his brothers. Isaac is Abraham's special child, yet there are children of Abraham everywhere. In some enigmatic way this final diptych (24:1–25:18) has multiple resonances of the diptych of creation (1:1–2:24). Creation is reflected in the most down-to-earth realities.

PART SIX

THE STORY OF JACOB

Genesis 25:19–37:1

Jacob is like a foundation stone. The full account of his life—a striking double drama, set near the beginning of the Bible (Gen. 25:19-chap. 50)—is like an initial guide to the practicalities of human existence. This part of the commentary concentrates on the opening drama (25:19-37:1).

The drama consists of six two-part scenes or diptychs. First there is an account of diverse facets of the family and world into which Jacob is born (25:19-26:33). The next scene focuses more directly on Jacob himself—on wresting a blessing from his older brother and on journeying abroad to work and marry (26:34-27:45). Then, in a further development, there is a portrayal of Jacob as flourishing—in both children and flocks (25:31-chap. 30).

In the later scenes, however, the flourishing falters. Jacob's journey toward home is shadowed by increasing fear (chaps. 31-33). For a while he makes a remarkable recovery: though the rape of his only daughter leaves him powerless and virtually speechless, he responds to a divine call to move on (34:1-35:20). But then, following an episode of incest in the family, he seems to shrink, and the only one who flourishes is his older brother (35:21-37:1).

Isaac's Jacob-Oriented Journey (25:19–26:33)

The Family: Problems of Birth and Beauty (25:19–26:11)
The Outside World: Problems with Contending Philistines and
Wealth (26:12–33)

Introductory Aspects

The Larger Jacob Narrative

The biblical account of Jacob is a form of biography, womb to tomb, and as such it extends clearly as far as Genesis 50 (25:19–chap. 50). But it is not all clear and simple. The narrative is complex in its content and levels. Its content includes other important characters, especially Isaac, Joseph, and Judah. And it has several levels. As a biography it tells the story of just one person. As an account of someone who is corporate, it tells the story of a whole people (Jacob is Israel). And insofar as Jacob's biography is a paradigm of human existence, his story portrays human life as a whole.

While it is useful to discuss the background of the Jacob story, especially the relationship to Hosea 12 (de Pury, 2001; Wahl, 1997), such discussion needs to be set in the context of Jacob's place within Genesis (see Introduction, esp. Chapter 11), and in the context of the virtual impossibility of separating strata from within a finished text (see Appendix 1).

In the Jacob story the focus on life as a whole emerges from the beginning. The diptych account of the journeys of Isaac (25:19–26:33) is unusual: its ultimate function is not to describe Isaac but to set the scene for his son Jacob. Isaac does not receive the attention due to him historically as one of three founding fathers. Rather, in a move which subjects the interests of history to those of theology-oriented literary art, the portrayal of Isaac is subjected to the portrayal of Abraham and Jacob, and thus to the larger portrayal of human life. Hence, while the narrative begins with an Isaac-centered historiographical introduction ("These are the generations of Isaac . . . ," 25:19), it promptly switches to the birth of Jacob and to an implicit statement about the difficulties of human birth and existence. The children clash in the womb, and Rebekah's anguished question, "Why go on living?" (*or* "Why/who am I?" 19:22), is applicable to the larger question of human existence. Aspects of Jacob are like those of Oedipus (Nicol, 1996).

The Basic Story Line (25:19–26:33)

The story recounts the beginning of the life of Jacob. It is a troubled beginning, with barrenness, a difficult pregnancy, and contention between twins. Yet all is not negative. Rebekah may indeed seem barren, but Isaac prays to Yhwh and she conceives.

As the twins grow the contentiousness develops. Their ways of life are diverse: Esau is a hunter, "a man of the field"; Jacob is more settled in tents. Esau is loved by his father, and Jacob by his mother. And once, when Esau was exhausted and indifferent, Jacob made him forswear his birthright. Then there is further trouble—famine in the land, and danger to Isaac because of his wife, Rebekah. But here again the trouble is accompanied or preceded by an encouraging communication between Isaac and God. God instructs Isaac and promises land and progeny. As for the danger to Isaac and Rebekah, they are protected by a royal command from Abimelech, the Philistine king in Gerar. The result is that Jacob's family, despite its contention and trouble, is surrounded by forms of mercy.

Then, in panel two (26:12–33), the story leaves the confines of Jacob's family and opens out to a much wider picture of contention—a struggle between Isaac and the Philistines. The Philistines become envious of Isaac's riches, and having effectively cut him off from his father's wells, they send him away. Isaac, therefore departs into a kind of exile.

This exile, first in the wadi of Gerar, then in Beer-sheba, is difficult. Despite gaining access to water, the finding of wells is accompanied by quarrels and by names related to these quarrels, and it is only as time goes by, particularly with the move to Beer-sheba, that there is a renewed sense of God-given space and protection.

Then, at the end of the exile and the quarrels, there is a reconciliation. The Philistine leaders come to Isaac, acknowledge that God is with him, and having made a covenant, depart in peace.

The contention with the Philistines—blocking a father's heritage, exile, finding water, quarreling, moving, and reconciliation—is both an expansion of the contention already present in Jacob's family and an intimation of what is yet to come in Jacob's life.

Literary Form

The diptych involves a mixture or synthesis of at least two literary types: primarily the travel narrative or itinerary, and secondarily the birth story. The birth story, despite its smaller volume, dominates the opening, and to that extent, dominates the whole narrative. Furthermore, the birth story includes a variation of an annunciation type-scene: the annunciation is made after the pregnancy and is concerned not with the birth but with the future struggle between the twins (Alter, 126). The picture of twins is part of an ancient literary motif (Kuntzmann, 1983).

The emphasis on travel is clear in the sojourn among the Philistines (chap. 26; Westermann, II, 423), but even at the beginning, when Isaac is introduced with references to his wife's distant origin in Paddan-aram (25:20), and when the same wife goes to consult Yhwh (25:22), there are indications of travel.

Researchers now recognize that the account of danger to Rebekah (26:1–11) is "a literary imitation" of the accounts of danger to Sarah (12:10–13:1; chap. 20; Westermann, II, 424; cf. Murphy 2:45). This woman-centered imitation in turn is part of a larger continuity. The entire itinerary narrative, including its birth story (25:19–26:33), is an imitation of the two itineraries that frame most of the story of Abraham—the original journey, with its famine-related visit to Egypt (chaps. 12–13), and the later birth-related journey to Abimelech and the Philistines (19:30–chap. 21). The form and content of the earlier itineraries have been adapted to suit the absorption of new sources and the portrayal of a new picture.

The story of Isaac among the Philistines (esp. 26:12–33) provides "an interlude within the more comprehensive story" (Fretheim, 526). In other words, the account of Isaac among the Philistines functions somewhat as does the account of Judah among the Canaanites (chap. 38). It provides an early interlude to allow the story to develop. As the Judah story (chap. 38) intimates some of what follows, especially concerning Judah himself, so Isaac's clash with the Philistines—a clash involving property, envy, expulsion, and reconciliation—intimates much of what will happen between Jacob and Esau, namely the taking of the blessing, anger, expulsion, and eventual reconciliation (Alter, 131, 134, 135).

Complementarity of the Two Panels

The picture, in its two panels, sets the scene for the long story of Jacob. Panel one (25:19–26:11), concerning marriage, birth, children, and wife, is primarily family-oriented. Even when an outsider, Abimelech, intervenes, he does so largely from a distance, and the effect of his intervention is to safeguard the marriage. The whole panel is framed by repeated use of the word "wife" (25: 20–21; 26:7–11).

Panel two (26:12–33) is oriented not toward the family but toward a much more complex outside world, a world that involves a high level of contention; Isaac is in contention with the envious Philistines. Already in panel one some contention is present, in the struggle between the two boys, but in the second panel contention and conflict are central. As the marriage is safeguarded at the end of panel one, so, at the end of panel two, the conflict is resolved.

Relationship to Preceding Chapters

This diptych has strong echoes of what precedes. The barrenness of Rebekah, briefly told, distills part of the story of Sarah; and much of what is said of Isaac echoes Abraham: "All the actions [of Isaac] reported here . . . delineate him as a typological heir to Abraham. Like Abraham he goes through the sister-wife experience, is vouchsafed a covenant promise by God, prospers in flock and field, and is involved in a quarrel over wells" (Alter, 131).

The initial food-related encounter between Jacob and Esau, the food that cost Esau his birthright (25:27–34), has some echoes of the primordial loss (Genesis 3) and rivalry (Gen. 4:1–16).

Leading Elements

In this diptych, two of the most obvious sources of trouble are beauty and wealth. Rebekah's beauty threatens the welfare of the marriage, and Isaac's wealth incites the Philistines' envy and hostility. Thus the same two threats that hung over the beginning of the Abraham story are now set, through Isaac, at the beginning of the Jacob story.

Connected to these disruptive threats, underlying them, at least in the flow of the story, is the more radical and enigmatic struggle between the two children, Jacob and Esau. This struggle is not petty. Esau—apart from his roles as an individual and as a representative of a specific people (Edom)—contains aspects that evoke shades of the serpent (chap. 3): his cloak of hair (somewhat animal-like), his closeness to the field, his disastrous focus on food. Other elements of the birth confirm an echo of the Garden—the pains in childbearing, and a struggle involving the heel. The wrestling between Jacob and Esau, therefore, echoes not only a struggle between two specific peoples but the struggle of the whole human race.

In much of this Isaac-centered story two features are curious. On the one hand, Jacob is left in the background, and virtually nothing is said of the immediate father-son relationship (Isaac-Jacob). On the other hand, much is said or suggested about Isaac's own relationship with *his* father, Abraham, or at least of Isaac's relationship with his father's heritage, the wells Abraham had dug (26:15–25). Perhaps the two features are connected; Isaac's struggle with the heritage of his father may perhaps reflect or evoke a father-related struggle within Jacob. In any case, the young Jacob fades from the picture (as Joseph does in Gen. 38). Jacob's position in the background seems appropriate: as far as the public is concerned—and panel two is very public—children are generally in the background.

This diptych shows part of a larger phenomenon, namely that "the traditions of Genesis 25–36 reveal an astonishing degree of empathy with Israel's antagonists" (Gammie, 1979, 130). Such empathy is a feature of Genesis as a whole.

To some degree this diptych is programmatic for the whole of Jacob's biography, programmatic for human life. It is no accident that panel one begins with a double use of "generate" ("generation," "begot," 25:19) and ends with a double use of "die" ("dying he will die," 26:11). And while panel one thus encapsulates life (as Genesis 1 encapsulates creation), panel two unpacks some of life's leading aspects, especially the checkered process of relating to the larger world, including one's father's wells and God.

Structure (Table 29.1)

The most difficult step, structurewise, is finding the division between the two panels, especially deciding whether the account of Isaac becoming great (26:12–14) belongs with the first panel or the second.

The evidence indicates the second. Isaac's greatness provides the starting-point for the conflict with the Philistines, a conflict that frames the second panel.

The resulting division (25:19–26:11; and 26:12–33) is corroborated by details. Within the first panel, there is a framing balance between the many opening and closing references to Isaac and his "wife" (25:20–21; and 26:7–11). And in the second panel there is a framing balance between the opening and closing references to "finding" and "servants" (26:12–14; and 26:32). In the first panel, Isaac's world, despite his travels, is confined essentially to wife and children. But in the second, when he has servants, he appears to be in charge of a much larger household and to engage in much more complex relationships.

Ending the first panel at 26:11, a command about the man and his wife, finds some support in the first diptych concerning Abraham (chaps. 12–13). Abimelech's command about the man and his wife is comparable with Pharaoh's

---

Table 29.1. Isaac's Jacob-Oriented Journey (25:19–26:11 // 26:12–33)

Isaac and the family: beauty

Introduction: marriage, conception, pregnancy, birth (25:19–26)
The children grow up (25:27–34)
   Contrasts of character and love (25:27–28)
   Esau gives up his birthright (25:29–34)
Amid famine and Philistines: Blessing; man and wife (26:1–10)
   Amid famine, the promise of blessing for all (26:1–6)
   Rebekah's beauty: man and wife endangered and saved (26:7–10)
Conclusion: command—Do not touch man or wife (26:11)

Isaac and the outside world: wealth

Introduction: wealth leads to envy, separation (26:12–17)
   Isaac finds a hundredfold, and becomes great (26:12–14a)
   Stopping the father's wells: Philistines: "Go . . ." (26:14b–17)
Reopening the father's wells: Quarrels, peace (26:18–22)
God of Abraham his father: I will bless you (26:23–25)
Abimelech: Let us make a covenant (26:26–30)
Conclusion: peace—oaths; the servants find water (26:31–33)

command and Abram's departure with his wife (12:20–13:1). The first panel as a whole has significant similarities not only with chapters 12–13 but also with 19:30–chapter 20.

The introduction (25:19–26) contains overlapping structures, one time-based (three-part and sequential), the other chiastic, as outlined by Fokkelman (1975, 93).

Comment

Panel One (25:19–26:11)

[25:19–26] Introduction. The beginning of Jacob's life: conception, pregnancy, and birth. The story, which begins as "the generations of Isaac" (25:19), is essentially the story of Jacob. The specific history-related role of Isaac becomes secondary to the more general role of Jacob's primordial biography (see Introduction, Chapter 11). But, at the beginning, Isaac's role is important, and so the emphasis on him is appropriate.

The beginning of the Jacob story is thorough and systematic. It tells first of Jacob's conception (25:19–21), then of the pregnancy (25:22–23), and finally of the birth (25:24–26).

The word "Jacob" is not used until the birth; the story is told with nonattachment, not from the exclusive perspective of someone writing "a life of Jacob" but from the inclusive viewpoint of one who is simply watching all that is happening. In such a view the initial emphasis is on Isaac.

The account therefore contains balance of viewpoints. There is a complex matter-of-fact inclusiveness, which tells things as they happen (life is one thing after another). And there is also a life-of-Jacob viewpoint, which has a specific focus (life is more than the scattered pieces; it has a center).

While guarding the sense of general complexity, the narrative nonetheless gives a systematic account of Jacob's two kinds of origin—human and divine. The words "human" and "divine" are not used, but, in two successive verses, the two aspects are balanced. Jacob's human origin goes back to his parents and grandfathers (26:20). And, insofar as his conception depends on Isaac entreating Yhwh to overcome Rebekah's barrenness, his origin also goes back to God (26:21). From the beginning, therefore, there is more to Jacob than a purely human story.

These verses about origins (26:20–21) also intimate another dimension of Jacob's life—his long sojourn with Laban in Aram (chaps. 28–31). Three times some form of "Aram" is used: Rebekah is the daughter of Bethuel "the *Aramean* of Paddan-*aram*," and sister . . . of Laban "the *Aramean*." The presentation seems casual, almost awkward—needlessly repetitive—but as an introduction to Jacob's life it is eminently suitable.

The pregnancy (26:22–23), with the two children clashing within the womb, is not only an intimation of future conflict; it is also a radical reflection on life.

Rebekah's words, "If it is so, why am I?", raise a question about why she should go on living. The context, where someone is about to be born, gives the question further weight; it implies a question about going ahead with birth, and thus a question about life in general. Why give birth? Why go on living? Such questions are probably best understood in the context of wisdom literature—such literature encompassed ancient Egyptian discussion about suicide (*ANET* 405–407)—and in the context of Jeremiah's curse on the day he was born (Jer. 20: 14; cf. Job 3:3).

When Rebekah consults Yhwh—the wording suggests she went to a sanctuary (for details, see Hamilton, II, 177)—Yhwh not only tells her she has twins, but gives her a special insight about their nature and future: the twins embody two nations; one shall be stronger than the other and, crucially, the elder shall serve the younger. This prediction, set at the beginning of the Jacob story, has a role somewhat similar to Joseph's dreams (37:5–11): at the beginning of a major section of Genesis it foretells how a younger son will achieve predominance.

The birth (25:24–26) also points to struggles to come. The first child, who is reddish (*'admônî*) and hairy (*śē'ār*), signals Israel's traditional enemy—Edom and Edom's mountain, (Mount) Seir. Curiously, the child's name, Esau, seems meaningless. The second child, who grasps his brother's heel (*'āqēb*), is called Heeler or Heel-gripper (Jacob)—an intimation of how he will challenge and supplant his older brother.

But "Jacob" has another meaning: "Jacob (*y'qb*) is a short form of a proper name, *y'qb-'l*, 'may God protect,' which occurs in ancient Near Eastern sources" (Murphy, 2:44). This further meaning, evoking God's protection, touches another aspect of Jacob. His struggle with his brother, however domestic or local it may be, has a wider dimension. It has overtones of the struggle with the serpent (including the heel, chap. 3). The general impression is that while at one level Jacob ("may God protect") may indeed be a grasping upstart, at another his struggle is primordial.

In summary therefore, the introduction to the Jacob story (25:19–26) has three levels. First, it is the systematic account of the beginning of an individual life (conception, pregnancy, and birth). Second, it intimates a larger struggle between nations. And third, it evokes basic questions about life in general—about its origin in God, its radical difficulty, and its struggle against all that the serpent represents.

[25:27–34] **Growing up amid diverse characteristics, divided affections, and sibling intrigue. In hunger, Esau forswears his heritage.** The atmosphere in which Jacob grows up is captured in a deft combination of general contrast and specific incident. The general contrast is between field and tent: Esau was a man "knowing the hunt, a man of the field," but Jacob, a "whole (*tām*) man," was "dwelling in tents." The parents' affections are divided correspondingly (25:28): Isaac's love for Esau is guided by his stomach (his love of game), but Rebekah's love for Jacob is just a gift (as was the kindness with which she once watered the camels).

The specific incident (25:29–34), in which Esau sells his birthright for a gulp of pottage, shows him as crude and as like his father—guided by his stomach. Jacob, in contrast, is alert and tough-minded. Jacob's use of food to achieve his purposes is something he may have learned from watching Esau's relationship to Isaac (Alter, 128).

The overall sense is of a setting with tensions and divisions, and with limited loves. This is not some idyllic holy family.

Again this domestic picture has another dimension. The Esau-Jacob contrast has overtones of a wider conflict. Esau's identification with the field, and the terrible price he pays for food, echo the serpent and the eating in the Garden (3:1–13; cf. 4:7). The emphasis on eating is underlined starkly by "there was game in his mouth," a phrase which, whether it refers to Esau or his father, clarifies the nature of the bond between them. (Esau's concentration on the hunt links him with Nimrod, the mighty hunter, 10:9, a dubious figure, but at least Nimrod's hunting was "before Yhwh," something not said of Esau.)

So when Esau throws away his birthright, something of the original loss of Eden is being reenacted in him. Jacob remains grasping, yet his struggle, however self-centered, may ultimately have a positive dimension.

The characterization of Jacob seems to contain a contradiction. He is *tām*, "wholesome/innocent/blameless/simple," echoing something of Noah (*tāmîm*, 6:9), yet his name, Jacob, has the same root as *'aqob*, "crooked" (Alter, 128) and his conduct is not simple. It is as though at the center of his life, at least initially, there is something unresolved (somewhat like an eastern puzzle or koan). Wholeness may have as much to do with Jacob's eventual development as with his initial state. Jacob's story is that of someone coming to wholeness. His association with tents may have overtones of the sanctuary.

[26:1–6] Amid famine, Isaac holds precariously to the sworn heritage of his father. The story moves from a picture of someone starving—the starved Esau—to a situation of famine. Famine causes Isaac to go to king Abimelech in Gerar, and Yhwh is seen by him and tells him to stay there, not to go to Egypt. The sequence—Esau hungry and Isaac in famine—leads to a contrast. While hunger led Esau to forswear his birthright, the famine does not lead Isaac to abandon the sworn heritage of his father, Abraham.

The memory of Abraham is emphasized both in introducing the famine (26:1), and again when Yhwh speaks to Isaac. While renewing the promise of land and descendants, Yhwh recalls both the giving of the oath to Abraham (26:3) and also Abraham's response, his hearing of Yhwh's voice (26:5). The promise, therefore, is not a disembodied philosophy; it comes from both Yhwh and Isaac's father. As coming from his father, it may be called Isaac's heritage.

Central to this heritage is hearing. Hearing what God says is like living in God's land. Here "land" is used ambiguously; it refers both to "this land," the specific place where Isaac sojourns (26:3), and "the land that I will say to you" (26:2). "The land that I will say to you" is a variation on "the land that I will make you see" (13:1). Taken together, these phrases indicate that the land is a place of God-given seeing and hearing.

It is because of the emphasis on saying and hearing (26:2, 5), rather than simply seeing, that Yhwh concludes by emphasizing things that are said, namely "commandments . . . statutes . . . instructions" (26:6).

Unlike Esau—close to animal existence, showing almost no sensitivity, for-swearing his heritage—Isaac hears. At the end of God's long speech, Isaac obeys; he settles in Gerar (26:6).

[26:7–11] **Rebekah as sister: Isaac's lapse in word.** Just as Abraham, at the beginning of his story, lapsed in dealing with Sarah (in Egypt, 12:10–13:1; cf. chap. 20) so does Isaac in dealing with Rebekah. The Isaac incident happens after an indefinite length of time ("as the days were prolonged," 26:8). Appar-ently Isaac, seeing that Rebekah was not being molested, eventually grew care-less in his dealings with her (Alter, 133), and proceeded to laugh/play with her—the same multifaceted verb used concerning Abraham (17:7), Sarah (21:6), and Ishmael (21:9), but now with a sexual connotation.

Apart from implicitly underlining the prohibition on adultery, the incident lays emphasis on a central issue of the previous episode—on *saying*. Yhwh had emphasized the importance of what is said (26:2–6), but Isaac, under pressure, makes a travesty of the process of saying. Hearing what God says will bring people a blessing (26:4), but listening to Isaac almost brings guilt (26:10; guilt is seen as objective: a sinful act, even if done in ignorance, incurs guilt).

Then, as if to highlight the power of what is said, the power of words and commandments, the conclusion consists of a resounding word of command: a command not to touch the man or his wife (26:11).

Panel Two (26:12–33)

[26:12–17] **Isaac grows great and is sent away.** Suddenly, under God's blessing, Isaac blossoms: the triple use of *gādal*, "grow great" (26:13), forms a crescendo of greatness, and the picture is no longer of a small family but of a teeming household, with "very many servants" (26:14a).

Paradoxically the boom brings loss: the envious Philistines block his father's wells, and Abimelech expels him (26:14b–17). What happens is understandable. Isaac's people had become too numerous for the place. The episode is also like a parable about the ambiguity of riches.

One of the puzzles about the process of moving or expulsion is that from one point of view nothing seems to be lost. Abimelech had told Isaac to go away, in other words, away *from Gerar*, but the result is that "he encamped at the wadi/torrent/valley *of Gerar*" (26:17). In a sense he still is where he was. His grip may be looser; "encamped" suggests a fragile existence in a tent. But his location in the valley suggests a place where, sometimes at least, there is water, thus making it perhaps the best place in Gerar.

[26:18–22] Re-opening the father's wells: quarrelling and moving. The ambiguity of riches is followed by a picture of the apparent ambiguity of the father's wells. Isaac and his servants embark on recovering a central part of the father's earthly heritage—the wells Abraham had dug. Isaac even uses the old names for them. But the finding of water, like the earlier growing in riches, instead of bringing peace, brings quarrelling between the shepherds. The quarrelling stops only when Isaac accepts losses, when he twice moves on.

Apart from echoing the theme of the ambiguity of wealth and the need to accept losses, the episode also touches the difficult issue of trying to recover a father's heritage, especially the earthly heritage. The acceptance of loss—the second move—is followed not by any sense of bitterness, but by thankfulness for what is finally available and by a sense of anticipation about the fruitfulness of the future (26:22).

[26:23–25] In Beer-sheba: recovering another dimension of the father. Curiously, the moment Isaac seems to be finally settled, when he is looking forward to being "fruitful in the land" (26:22), he moves. Without explanation or apparent pressure he goes up to Beer-sheba. There he encounters his father's heritage in another way: Yhwh is seen by him as "the God of Abraham" (26:23). God speaks at night and tells Isaac not to be afraid. The promise is renewed, and when Isaac builds an altar, calls on Yhwh, and pitches his tent, there is a sense of starting over, of coming to a new place. Having found another dimension of his father, his father's God, he or his servants can now dig for a new well.

[26:26–30] Abimelech seeks a covenant and recognizes Isaac as blessed. Abimelech, having seen Isaac's progression, decides that God is with him and so Abimelech asks for a covenant. It is not riches that inspire Abimelech into believing that God is with Isaac. On the contrary, Isaac's earlier riches had caused Abimelech to send Isaac away. But now, after so many losses and quarrels and moves, Isaac's rediscovery of his father's God induces Abimelech, with his counselor and commander, to seek peace. It is now that Isaac is recognized as "blessed" (26:29). And so, in a gesture of solidarity, they all eat and drink.

[26:31–33] Covenant peace, and the finding of water. At the end, on the very day the covenant has been sworn, the story comes back to the digging of a well. The servants, who apparently had begun a process of digging after the apparition at Beer-sheba (26:25), arrive with news: "We have found water." It is like a confirmation of a new beginning.

30 Blessing and Betrothal: Jacob Deceives and Is Deceived (26:34–29:30)

The Deceptive Blessing (26:34–27:45)
The Deceptive Betrothal (27:46–29:30)

Introductory Aspects

The Basic Story Line

Much of the story tells of blessing and betrothal. It begins with Esau's marriages—just one verse (26:34)—and moves quickly to blessing.

The blessing is a long drama. When Isaac's eyes and life are failing, Rebekah helps Jacob to put himself in Esau's place and thus gain Isaac's blessing. Esau, bitter, resolves that when the father dies he will kill the deceitful Jacob.

Rebekah, resourceful as ever, organizes Jacob's flight into exile—to her brother in Haran. The exile will not be easy, but on the journey, in two incidents involving stones, Jacob shows surprising strength. First he uses a stone as a pillow (very macho-heroic) and stands it up to form a pillar (no small feat). Then he removes a huge stone from the mouth of a well. So it is not surprising, when he reaches Laban, that he shows endurance in work. Then the story comes back to the idea with which it started, that of betrothal and marriage.

But the deception surrounding the blessing is not forgotten. When Jacob marries he finds that an elder sister has been put in the bride's place.

Literary Form

The narrative synthesizes a number of literary types or conventions—an itinerary, a last blessing, a betrothal, and a vision-like dream. Two of these types need special attention—the last blessing and the betrothal.

The convention of the *last blessing*, along with that of the last discourse, was generally reserved for someone facing death. Underlying the blessing is a "fixed ritual procedure" (Westermann, II, 435), but, like any literary convention, the account could be adapted to the situation (Speiser, 212). Jacob's death will provide a further example of a last blessing (47:29–chap. 48; cf. chap. 49).

Jacob's *betrothal* does not occur until the end of his journey (29:1–30), yet the whole narrative, including the initial blessing, is framed by images of betrothal/marriage. Both panels begin with references to Esau's Hittite marriages (26:34–35; 27:46), and the second panel, concerning Jacob's journey and betrothal, culminates with his marriages to Rachel and Leah.

Compared to the long betrothal scene (29:1–30), the *vision-like dream* is brief, introductory (28:10–22). In Moses' case the emphasis will be reversed: a brief betrothal scene introduces a long vision account (Exod. 2:11–4:17). What is important, amid the diverse literary types, is the centrality of blessing and betrothal.

Complementarity of Blessing and Betrothal

BLESSING AS BASIC

The combination of blessing and betrothal is not accidental. It means that betrothal, however central it may be, is not isolated. It is linked to something further, to the larger reality of life and love, the larger reality of blessing. Blessing means the passing on of vitality (Westermann, II, 436) and it is rooted in God, in what God gives to the world and its people (Gen. 1:22, 28; 2:3, *pace* Westermann, ibid.). Marriage love, given by one human to another, is often more tangible than blessing, but blessing is the more basic reality. Marriage love depends on creation and on creation's quality of blessing.

The relation between creation's blessing and marriage first emerges, implicitly, in the scene of creation. While the first creation panel culminates with an emphasis on blessing (1:22, 28; 2:3), the second culminates in marriage (2:18–24).

The blessing-betrothal connection is seen more clearly in the betrothal of Rebekah and Isaac. While the entire account (chap. 24) is cast in the framework of a betrothal, the Rebekah-Isaac marriage is secondary to the larger reality, to the betrothal-like blessing of Abraham (chap. 24).

It is likewise with Jacob. His betrothal, important though it is, is part of a drama that is concerned with the larger reality of the world and its people, especially the larger reality of blessing. The whole first panel (essentially chap. 27) is a struggle for blessing, a blessing that, even though it comes through an individual, Isaac, involves the world's peoples (27:27–29). And the second panel (essentially chaps. 28–29), though directed, at one level, toward Rachel and marriage (29:1–30), is overshadowed at another level by the blessing-filled dream, a blessing that is not just for Jacob but for "all the clans of the ground" (28:14). The emphasis on the "ground" (*ʾădāmâ*) strengthens the echo of creation.

The whole diptych scene then (26:34–29:30) is a dramatization, in the down-to-earth situation of Jacob's youth, of blessing and betrothal, two realities which are basic to creation, and which, in another form, culminated Abraham's life.

In this story, blessing is also connected with food; Isaac's meal precedes his blessing. This food-first idea may be "because of the connection between blessing and vitality" (Murphy, 2:46), but it is in contrast with Abraham's servant who postpones food until he has finished recounting Abraham's blessings (24:31–35). Apparently part of the problem with Isaac is that his sense of blessing is unduly dependent on food. Esau also had given undue priority to food.

As Jacob journeys along, midway between blessing and betrothal, alone and vulnerable, there is an intervention. A dream (at Bethel) raises his awareness from blessing to promise (28:10–22). As already indicated (in discussing God's promises to Abraham, 12:1–3), blessings can be counted, but promises, of their nature, have an incalculable aspect; one has to trust. At first the promise's impact on him seems limited—he simply continues his journey—but its overall effect is important, and when he is dying he recalls it (48:3–4; cf. 28:10–22; 35: 6–15).

Leading Elements

The great difference between the Jacob story and creation is that the blessing here is not totally God-given; it may not simply be taken for granted. The first panel (chap. 27) does not flow as harmoniously as the first panel of creation (1: 1–2:4a). Jacob has to struggle for blessing; he has to contend with his brother, has to wrest the blessing from him.

The wresting process appears unseemly. The deceiving of Isaac—the lies, the grief caused to Esau—looks like the pathway not to blessing but to condemnation.

At one level, that is so. There is something about Jacob's deceit that deserves retribution. And so retribution is given. As he did to his brother concerning blessing, substituting in his place, so was done to him at marriage. The older sister was substituted for his beloved Rachel. The issue of deceit, therefore, is addressed by the story.

But the narrative has another level, one in which Esau is seen, not just as an individual brother, but as a representative figure who has an affinity with the serpent. Elements of this affinity were noted earlier—the animal-like hairiness, the closeness to the field, the focus on the superficial quality of food, and the discarding of the birthright (Esau's discarding of his birthright for food echoes the couple's food-related loss of their form of birthright, 25:24–34; 3:1–7). (Esau is also complex in ways that are positive; Spina, 1998.)

Once Esau is seen, at one stage of his life, as representing the serpent, Jacob's wresting of the blessing from him becomes more understandable. The whole drama with the food, the tasty food which misleads Isaac and causes him to give away the blessing, emerges as a reversal of the drama in the Garden, when the attractive-looking food misled the couple and caused them to incur curse, to lose blessing.

Jacob now is like a personification of the struggle of fallen creation. The curse and condemnation in the Garden had spoken of a struggle involving the woman and her offspring, involving head and heel (chap. 3, esp. 3:14–15). In the Garden the woman had been a leader in losing to the serpent, a leader in losing the original blessing. Now, in the person of Rebekah, she leads the recovery. It is Rebekah who provides the leadership Jacob needs—the attentiveness, the energetic ingenuity, and the willingness to take the curse on herself. When all is ready she hands the food to Jacob, as the woman once did to the man, and thus she directs him not to a curse but to a blessing.

When the taking of the blessing causes Esau's murderous hatred, she will again be attentive, sending Jacob away for a while, lest the wresting of blessing lead to greater evil (27:41–45).

But she cares also for betrothal, she in whom blessing and betrothal were first fully integrated (chap. 24). So she speaks to Isaac and instigates a second complementary reason for sending Jacob away, namely that, amid a world of blessing, he might be betrothed (27:46–27:5).

Rebekah emerges then, in this whole scene, as a guiding force for Jacob. She gives his world energy and blessing, and she sets him on his way. She may seem to deal harshly with Esau and Isaac, yet the final result of her work is not to deprive Esau and Isaac but, in subtle ways, to guide them also. As the scene advances, they seem not less attentive to reality but more so. By the time Jacob is about to leave, Isaac appears less mournful, and Esau more aware (28:1–9).

Some modern scholars, reading the story of Rebekah at one level only, have vilified her, but the oldest Jewish commentators regarded her positively, and Christine Garside Allen, having reviewed the opinions and the evidence, concludes: "If we view the complete circumstances . . . Rebekah . . . can stand as a model of profound significance . . ." (1979, 159–172, esp. 171). The context—for instance, how Esau's marriages brought "bitterness of spirit (ruaḥ) for Isaac and Rebekah" (26:34)—"gives information to understand Rebekah's motivation" (Jeansonne, 1990, 66). Bitterness of spirit was not a passing inconvenience. It was a situation of radical ill-health. Furthermore, Rebekah knew, as apparently Isaac did not, what the oracle or voice of God had said before birth about the younger child (25:23). Tamar will have to use deception (chap. 38), and for Rebekah, too, there seems to be no other way.

After this diptych Rebekah fades from the picture, and it is never said that she died, only that her nurse died (35:8). At the end, Jacob's final words recall that Rebekah had been buried ("There they buried Abraham and his wife Sarah. There they buried Isaac and his wife Rebekah," 49:31). The highlighting of Sarah's death (chap. 23) makes the silence about the death of Rebekah all the more remarkable.

Relationship to Preceding Chapters

This three-chapter diptych breaks new ground, yet, as just indicated (see above "Leading Elements"), it has multiple reworkings and echoes of earlier chapters, especially of chapters 1–3 and 24. The images of the heel and the head, for instance, mentioned in kernel form in the struggle of the offspring and the serpent (3:15), may, perhaps, have contributed, in some inverse form, to Jacob's involvement with images of heel and head (heel, 25:26; head, 28:11, 12, 18). There is an echo also of the Cain and Abel story (4:1–16), but thanks to Rebekah, the murderous plot is defused. Like Yhwh, Rebekah is attentive to the (would-be) murderer (4:9–16; 27:41–45).

Structure (Table 30.1)

As elsewhere this diptych contains overlapping structures. One of these structures—apart from the diptych structure itself—is that of seven interlocking dialogues (27:1–28:4, including a sevenfold use of the word "blessing"). Following the conventions of biblical narrative, each of these dialogues has "only two interlocutors . . . (as in Aeschylean tragedy)" (Alter, 137).

Further subdivisions could be added to the table. For instance, Rebekah's conversation with Jacob (27:5–17) could be divided into four (beginning at 27:5, 8, 11, 14), but the more basic division is into two, beginning first with "Rebekah heard . . ." (27:5), and then with "Jacob said to Rebekah . . ." (27:11).

Table 30.1. Blessing and Betrothal (26:34–27:45 //
27:46–29:30)

Blessing: Jacob deceives

Introduction: bitterness and the shadow of death (26:34–27:4)
    Esau's wives bring bitterness
    Isaac: old and, before blessing, needing something tasty
Deception planned: Rebekah to Jacob: hear my voice (27:5–17)
Deception and blessing: Isaac and Jacob: Not hearing (27:18–29)
Aftermath: Esau and Isaac: bitterness, then weeping (27:30–40)
Conclusion. Hatred and a greater shadow of death (27:41–45)
    Esau, deprived of blessing, plans murder
    Rebekah tells Jacob to go—because of blessing-related fury

---

Betrothal: Jacob deceived

Introduction: wives, right and wrong (27:46–28:9)
    Rebekah prompts Isaac to send Jacob for betrothal
    Esau hears and undertakes a corresponding marriage
Jacob's dream: the stone that opens a stairway for all (28:10–22)
Jacob's betrothal: removing the stone for the sheep (29:1–14)
Conclusion: wives, right and wrong (29:15–30)
    Jacob serves for seven years to marry Rachel
    The substitution of Leah for Rachel

Comment

Panel One (26:34–27:45)

[26:34–27:4] Introduction. Amid bitterness and deathly old age: Isaac's dim search for taste and blessing. The first panel (roughly chap. 27) begins with a bleak introduction—first, a brief note that Esau's two marriages to Canaanite women had brought "bitterness of spirit" to Isaac and Rebekah (26:34–35); then, a picture of Isaac as old, virtually unseeing, thinking of old age and death (27:1–4).

In this difficult situation Isaac's consolation seems to be his stomach. When he decides to give his blessing to Esau, the blessing must wait until he eats the tasty food that Esau brings. Given the context of bitterness, the tasty food seems like an antidote.

[27:5–17] Deception planned: Rebekah hears, averts the curse, and works for the blessing. Like Isaac, Rebekah also had been described as enduring bitterness of spirit because of Esau's marriages (26:35), but she does not allow the bitterness to immobilize her. In contrast to Isaac she is attentive and active. Above all, she still hears, and does so in a context where hearing suggests awareness and openness, including openness to the wider world of God's word (cf. 26:2, 5, 6). She "hears" Isaac's instructions, and in her conversation with Jacob there is an emphasis on hearing, commanding, and obeying ("Rebekah heard . . . 'Behold I heard' . . . 'Now my son, hear my voice,' " 27:5, 6, 8, 13, 14). There is also an emphasis on the presence of the divine. Her report of what Isaac had said to Esau links the blessing not, as Isaac had said, to Isaac's own soul (27:4) but to "Yhwh's presence" (27:7).

Jacob does not really plot with her. Apart from making an objection—he mentions the danger of incurring curse rather than blessing—he simply obeys. Jacob's objection fits the scene. Rebekah's sending of him, based as it is on God's word, is like a commissioning, and one of the motifs of a conventional commissioning was an objection.

Rebekah is remarkable not only by her involvement in the world of hearing and obeying, but also by her willingness to take the curse on herself (27:12–13). It is as though evil does not intimidate her; in some way she can absorb it.

And she shows great practical wisdom and resourcefulness. She prepares the right food (not one kid but two!), chooses the right clothes, and organizes an ingenious disguise (27:14–16). Then she gives the food "into the hand of Jacob, her son" (27:17)—shades of Eve giving the fruit.

[27:18–29] Deception: Isaac's failure to hear. Isaac's first question to Jacob, "Who are you?," is incidental at one level—a minor detail in a complex drama—but central at another. As the adult Jacob enters the stage, this question confronts him about his basic identity. It "touches the exposed nerve of identity and moral fitness that gives this ambiguous tale its profundity" (Alter, 139). The first spoken words in the Gospel of John consist of the same question.

Jacob's answer grasps a feature of birth: "I am Esau your first-born" (27:19). Esau, faced with the same question, will do likewise, also identifying himself as the first-born (27:32). The narrative itself has been more reticent; so far it has not applied the term "first-born" to Esau (Alter, 139).

As Isaac repeatedly tests the deception, the scene is "tension-packed" (Murphy, 2:46). Isaac cannot rely on his eyes, but when Jacob arrives with the food, Isaac speaks to him at length and uses all the other four senses—touch, hearing, taste, and smell. Three of these, touch, taste, and smell, indicate the presence of Esau (the smell is conveyed through Jacob's use of Esau's clothes, the result of Rebekah's careful planning). The fourth, hearing, tells the truth: "The voice is the voice of Jacob. . . ." But, unlike Rebekah, Isaac ignores what he hears, and so he is deceived. As a result of not hearing, he eats Jacob's tasty meal and gives away the first-born's blessing, rather as Esau himself had given away his first-born's birthright for a gulp of pottage.

The blessing (27:28–29) is rich. Its invoking of fertility (dew, fat, grain, and wine) reverses an important part of the curse in the Garden (3:17–19). Its granting of priority over brothers recalls how Noah, while cursing Canaan (Ham), blessed Shem (9:25–27). And its establishment of Jacob as a source of cursing and blessing for others ("blessed be those who bless you") echoes the role of Abraham (12:3). According to this blessing, therefore, Jacob is not only blessed; he is to be a form of mediator of blessings for others.

[27:30–40] Aftermath. Trembling and bitter crying: Isaac and Esau realize their loss. Another blessing. When Esau returns he prepares the food, speaks confidently, and asks for the blessing as though he had never sold his birthright.

At the realization of what Jacob has done, Isaac trembles uncontrollably and Esau gives a terrible bitter cry. "The scene . . . could scarcely be surpassed for pathos" (Speiser, 213). The impression is of a powerful sense of loss. For Esau the loss is compounded. He recalls that this is the second time his brother has taken what is his (27:30–36a).

But just when Esau seems to have lost all, when even his appeal to his father for something stored up seems to find no response, his weeping voice, like a lament, somehow reaches Isaac and causes him to answer with another blessing (27:36b–40). Blessing was not something magic or autonomous; it followed convention, and convention, while not allowing recall, did allow modification (Fretheim, 538). This second blessing calls for struggle and service but it allows Esau the same blessings of earth and heavens, and it promises that in the end there will be freedom (27:40): "When you rebel, you shall throw off his yoke from your neck."

[27:41–45] Conclusion. Amid hatred and the shadow of multiple death: Rebekah's call to save the lives of her sons. Esau's reaction to being deprived by his brother is murderous hatred. He plans that, when his father dies, he will kill Jacob. Thus the bleakness that overshadowed the introduction—bitterness and deathly old age (26:34–27:4)—is now compounded. But

Rebekah is told of the simmering murderousness—an indication that Esau cannot contain himself—and she again intervenes, calling on Jacob to hear her voice and to flee to her brother in Haran.

Rebekah's concern, it now emerges, is not for Jacob only. She is faced with the prospect, scarcely stated, of suddenly losing not only Isaac and Jacob, but also Esau. As a murderer, Esau may be hunted or lost; or the twins may kill one another. Her first love was for Jacob (25:28), and it was never said that she cared for Esau. Nor has Esau suddenly become morally attractive. In fact, the very opposite is true. Esau now carries murder in his heart. Yet precisely at this lowest moment of Esau's life, Rebekah reveals implicitly that she does not want to lose him: "Why should I be bereaved for both of you in one day?"

Thus while Esau is watching the days till death and murder ("They draw near, the days of mourning for my father"), Rebekah is watching the days till death goes away from Esau's heart ("settle . . . some days, until your brother's fury turns away . . . until [his] anger turns . . . and he forgets what you did to him").

The prospects for a change in Esau may not look good. Both Esau and Isaac have seemed so fixed on their stomachs that little else appears to reach them. When Esau first lost his birthright, he had walked away without a thought, without any glimmer of awareness that there was more to life than instant gratification (25:34).

Yet, when Esau lost his blessing, both he and his father had shown another side. The father, though sated with delightful food and wine, became greatly upset. Esau, far from walking away without a thought, cried out in bitterness. Only then did he reveal that he regretted having lost his original birthright (27:37). And as the conversation went on, the crass hunter broke down and wept (27:38).

At one level, the tears did little good. The bitterness and weeping gave way to a murderous heart. But Rebekah, too, has been struggling with bitterness; that was how the episode began (26:34–35). And so she waits for the days when Esau will turn . . . turn . . . and forget, that she may not lose him.

What she does not realize is that at one level she is losing Jacob for good. He will spend twenty years with her brother, not just "some days" (27:44), and there is no account of them ever meeting again. But she has done well for him. She has achieved the blessing and launched him on his life's journey.

Panel Two (27:46–29:30)

[27:46–28:9] Introduction. From loathing toward love: Rebekah moves the men away from Canaanite marriage and toward Abraham-related marriage. The second panel, which tells of Jacob's journey to Haran (roughly chaps. 28–29), begins with Isaac's sending of Jacob to find a suitable wife. The previous panel had also told of the sending of Jacob, not by Isaac but by Rebekah, and for a different reason—to save lives (27:41–45).

The two commands to Jacob—from Rebekah and Isaac—are often seen as independent, even contradictory, but that is not so. Jacob sets out only once (28:5). The two reasons are complementary; and, crucially, both originate with Rebekah.

Rebekah has been involved in two types of bitterness—her own bitterness at Esau's marriages (26:34–35), and Esau's murderous bitterness at losing the blessing (27:34, 41–45). The two are connected, not only in the text (by balancing one another, within the panel, as introduction and conclusion), and not only in Rebekah, but inherently: the loss of deep-seated marriage love is akin to the loss of divine blessing. Stated positively, there is a kinship between deep-seated marriage love and the experience of divine blessing (see above, "Introductory Aspects"). The blessing-betrothal connection was illustrated at length in the original betrothal of Rebekah (chap. 24): the blessing of Abraham was portrayed through the drama of a betrothal. Blessing, when received with awareness, has a kinship with betrothal.

For Esau, both betrothal and blessing are lost. He goes from bad marriages to losing his blessing. And the bitterness of both losses pours out on Rebekah. She knows therefore, and implicitly has known ever since her own betrothal, how these two losses are inherently connected.

When she first commands Jacob to go (27:41–45), she is waiting for Esau to recover from the loss of his blessing ("Esau bore resentment against Jacob because of the blessing . . . ," 27:41). And when, at Rebekah's prompting, Isaac also sends Jacob, he does so to avoid a wrong betrothal (27:46–28:9). The two commands, therefore, originating in Rebekah, are complementary and, in her experience, are bound together. The present text is coherent (Alter, 147).

When Rebekah prompts Isaac indirectly to send Jacob away she says nothing of Esau's bitterness about the blessing, but she complains her own bitterness, her loathing, lest there be a wrong betrothal or marriage (27:46). In doing this she is not only moving the emphasis from blessing to betrothal. She is also involving Isaac in the whole process. This has an immediate superficial advantage—it provides an explanation, within the family, for Jacob's departure. There is no need then to disclose that the original reason for leaving had to do with the loss of the blessing.

But the advantage is not only diplomatic. Isaac's involvement is real. This is the first time Rebekah is shown as speaking to him. And he listens. Furthermore, Esau also becomes involved in the larger process of listening (28:6–9). "Esau saw that . . . Jacob had heard his father and his mother," and, in light of that, Esau took a further wife, Mahalath—a woman descended from Abraham.

The entire introduction (27:46–28:9), therefore—Rebekah's complaint, Isaac's sending of Jacob, and Esau's taking of an Abrahamite wife—takes its impetus from Rebekah and from her voice. It is a voice which not only sends Jacob on his way, but which also brings increased life to Isaac and Esau.

[28:10–22] The stone that opens a stairway to blessing: Jacob sleeps and dreams of God and of blessing for all. The picture of Jacob journeying implies a form of beauty—the simplicity of coming to an undefined "place," of spending the night "for the sun had gone," of taking a stone, putting it at his head, lying down, dreaming. Yet the scene is not simple. It has a ring of antiquity, especially because it includes an etiology of the name "Bethel" (28:19). The history of the scene's interpretation is complex (Steinmetz, 1986).

In the dream, the beauty gives way to a stairway of messengers ("angels"). The image of the stairway or ramp probably reflects the ramp of Mesopotamian ziggurats, but this scene involves far more than a ziggurat. The ziggurat serves as a foil for something greater: Yhwh's words, including a promise of great blessing. Already, at departure, Isaac had blessed Jacob (28:1–4), and now that blessing is intensified by Yhwh: "You shall spread to the west and to the east and to the north and to the south" (28:14).

Yet despite the vastness of the blessing, much of God's attention is toward Jacob himself, and toward being with him on his journey (28:15). Jacob in turn acknowledges Yhwh's awesome presence (28:16–17), and in the morning turns the stone into a pillar or monument. This was no small task. Stone pillars were usually several feet high (Alter, 150) and so setting it up would have required great strength. Then Jacob vows, "if God will be with" him, to accept Yhwh and to turn the stone into a house of God. Again there is a certain simple beauty: "If God will be with me, and will guard me on this way . . . and give me bread . . . and clothes . . . and I come back in peace to my father's house. . . ."

The scene repeats certain words: place, stone, head. The repetition of "place" indicates that the location or scene is important and something significant is happening. "Head" and "stone," especially when combined with Jacob's removal of the large stone (29:10), may perhaps be evocative of some kind of struggle—as though the head were pitted against the stone (stones do not make comfortable pillows and never have). The primordial Eden scene had spoken of a struggle involving head and heel (Gen. 3:15). Having already used the heel motif in the struggle at Jacob's birth ("grasping Esau's heel," 25:26), the narrative now speaks of the head and does so as if it involved the integration or mastery of the weight of the stone. Alter (150) connects Jacob's tough attitude at the end of this scene, his bargaining with God (*"If* God will be with me . . . ," 28:20), with his tough character as a wrestler, a heel-grabber. There is indeed continuity in Jacob but there is also a change.

In any case, the whole scene suggests some form of breakthrough. The stairway or ramp, with its implication of a Mesopotamian ziggurat, suggests that Jacob is moving into new territory; "Jacob in general is represented as a border crosser, a man of liminal experiences" (Alter, 149).

The basic effect of the dream is to reestablish some of the sense of connectedness with God, which had been lost earlier, especially in the primordial sins (Gen. 3:1–4:16). Already blessing had been won, won *back* as it were, from

Isaac (chap. 27). Now this reestablishment of connectedness strengthens that sense of blessing. Jacob's subsequent action, in setting up a pillar (28:18), is an indication of a future sanctuary or temple (Westermann, II, 459). In the sanctuary the sense of blessing and connectedness will find a down-to-earth means of expression.

[29:1–14] **The stone that leads to betrothal: Jacob's removal of the stone opens the way for the shepherdess (Rachel) and for the sheep.** The narrative moves from one stone to another, as it were, from the stone that leads to Jacob's dream of blessing to the stone that leads to Jacob's betrothal. Here, too, Jacob comes to a place where there is a remarkable sight. Three flocks of sheep are near a well but, because of the great stone on the well, they cannot drink. Removal of the stone waits on the gathering of all the shepherds, in the evening. Associated with these three flocks, known to their shepherds, is a further (fourth) flock, that of Laban, shepherded by Rachel.

Jacob, seeing the sheep waiting, first suggests that they be brought out to pasture. In this simple spontaneous suggestion he shows a key characteristic, his care as a shepherd.

When Jacob sees Rachel and the sheep, he does what otherwise one person could not do—remove the stone. This opens the way both for the sheep to drink and for his own kissing of the shepherdess. "There is a pun between 'he watered' (wayashq) and 'he kissed' (wayishaq)" (Alter, 152). This meeting with Rachel at the well has all the marks of a betrothal, and Laban's subsequent words ("you are my bone and flesh," echoing 2:23) confirms the ethos of betrothal or marriage.

In both these episodes—the dream, and the well—Jacob's handling of the stone opens a way. In the first, it leads to the dream of the stairway to heaven, a sign of access to heaven for people from all directions. In the second episode, Jacob's removal of the stone opens the way for the (four) flocks of sheep and for betrothal to the shepherdess.

The impression, again, is that the blessing and the betrothal are related. The blessing, renewed while Jacob is on his journey, provides a basis for his betrothal. And while both blessing and betrothal are given to particular people—to Jacob and Rachel—there is a strong communitarian aspect. The stairway with its blessing has implications for many people. And the kiss at the well is associated with many flocks coming to drink. The implication: Jacob's dream and betrothal will lead many people to God.

[29:15–30] **The marriage and the deception.** By the time his wedding festivities are over Jacob finds himself with two wives and two concubines. However, his original purpose was to marry just one woman, Rachel. The other three were given, unasked, by Laban. The implied contrast, between wanting one woman and receiving four, seems to reflect some ambiguity in Genesis concerning polygamy. Polygamy is not advocated, but it is sometimes tolerated. (A similar ambiguity occasionally exists today among some Christians in Africa.) The seven years, which seemed but a few days "in his eyes" (29:20), emphasize the romantic aspect of the story. The deception was possible because the bride wore a veil.

Laban's deception toward Jacob seems cruel: he substitutes the older sister, Leah, for the much-loved Rachel. Yet, given Jacob's deception of Esau—substituting himself for his older brother—the deception has a certain appropriateness. "With strong poetic irony, he was forced to acknowledge the rights of the first-born child" (Armstrong, 1996, 85). Now he has some idea how Esau felt.

In other ways, too, Jacob seems to have felt like Esau. His desire for Rachel ("Come! My wife! . . . ," 29:21) has something of the urgent desire of Esau when he was starving for food (25:29–34). And, like Isaac when the tasty food was brought to him, Jacob in his marriage bed apparently was not intent on the sound of the (woman's) voice (for details from rabbinic midrash, see Alter, 155). In the dark he was like blind Isaac—relying on touch.

---

31   Jacob's Children and Flocks (29:31–Chap. 30)

The Generating of Children (29:31–30:24)
The Generating of Flocks (30:25–43)

Introductory Aspects

The Basic Story Line

The story is about how Jacob went from being a lone figure to being someone with a great family and great flocks. The family includes eleven sons and the hope of a twelfth.

Jacob's path to prosperity is not easy. The story of the birth of the children is dominated by the story of the tension and rivalry between his two wives—two sisters, matching the earlier rivalries between brothers. When the despised Leah gives birth to four sons, the young and beautiful Rachel becomes desperate and finally chooses surrogate motherhood. She gives her slave woman to Jacob as wife, thus acquiring two sons and some sense of pride in relation to her fertile sister.

Leah decides to play the same game. Though cut off from childbearing—and also apparently from Jacob's bed—she, too, gives her slave woman to Jacob and so she also acquires two sons by surrogate motherhood. Then in a lucky break, through her eldest son's discovery of (aphrodisiac) mandrakes, she drives a bargain with the barren Rachel, thus returning to sleeping with Jacob, and so she begets two further sons, giving her a total of six, and a daughter, Dinah.

Finally God remembers Rachel. She gives birth to Joseph, and she even hopes for a further son. Though this final son is not yet born, the total of children, including Dinah, is already twelve. Thus at one level the picture has a completeness.

The account of the birth of the children is brief, but some of its aspects, especially the naming the children, evoke a huge background drama concerning the relationships between Jacob and the rival sisters.

The second part, the birth of the flocks (30:25–43), occurs in the context of a further rivalry, namely between Jacob and Laban. Jacob drives a simple but deceptive bargain with the tough Laban: he, Jacob, will acquire all the animals with unusual coloring. Laban agrees, and he also takes steps to prevent the development of such coloring. But Jacob, using an old form of genetic engineering, outwits Laban. The result: Jacob has twelve children and great flocks.

Literary Form

The literary form of the first panel, concerning the children, is "like a genealogy" (Westermann, II, 471). The second panel, concerning the flocks, corresponds at least in part to the form of a dialogue contract (Westermann, II, 480), but it also contains an aspect which, if not genealogical, is generational—connected to the process of generating.

Complementarity and Leading Elements

The two panels have an obvious complementarity. One tells of the generating of Jacob's children (29:31–30:24), the other, of the generating of Jacob's flocks (30:25–43).

While recounting the growth of the family and herds, the texts weave in other dramas. The birth of the children is framed by the rivalry between two women—Rachel and Leah. The development of the herds occurs in the framework of the rivalry between two men—Jacob and Laban.

The complementarity between the two panels is heightened by a further factor: to some degree both the children and the flocks are representative of the future people. This is clear in the case of the children. They carry the names of the future tribes. But the flocks, too, are linked to the people. In particular, they are linked to Jacob and his original betrothal at the well. The betrothal, though centered around Jacob and Rachel, involves flocks. These flocks are cared for within the context of the betrothal and impending marriage (29:1–14). Thus the marriage, source of the children, involves the flocks also.

The link between the flocks and the marriage emerges strikingly in one peculiar detail. The dramatic opening of the mouth of the well, allowing the flocks a flow of water, is tied with the dramatic kissing of Rachel (presumably on the mouth), and a flow of tears (29:10–11). Many other biblical texts—Ezekiel 34, for instance—link the images of people and flock.

The two panels, therefore, one of children, the other of flocks, have a deep-seated complementarity. The children are still few and small, but Jacob's success in caring for his flocks, in bringing them to numbers and strength, is an indicator of the future fate of Jacob's children, ultimately of the children of Israel.

Relationship to Preceding Chapters

Within the context of Genesis as a whole, these two pictures of generating may be described, partly, as a variation on the paired genealogies—such as the paired genealogies in Genesis 4:17–chapter 5 (those of Cain, 4:17–26; and Adam, chap. 5). Furthermore, their position within the second half of Genesis—they form the third diptych—corresponds to that of the paired genealogies (Cain-Adam, 4:17–chap. 5) within the first half of the book.

Structure (Table 31.1)

The first panel, concerning the children (29:31–30:24), seems easy to discern. The structure is governed by the contrast between Leah and Rachel. Leah

Table 31.1. Jacob's Children and Flocks (29:31–30:24 // 30:25–43)

Jacob's children

Introduction: God gives Leah children. Rachel: barren (29:31)
Leah and Bilhah (Rachel's maid) (29:32–30:8)
    Leah: four children: Reuben, Simeon, Levi, and Judah (29:32–35)
    Rachel's maid, Bilhah: Dan and Naphthali (30:1–8)
Zilpah (Leah's maid) and Leah (30:9–21)
    Leah's maid, Zilpah: Gad and Asher (30:9–13)
    Rachel tries mandrakes; Leah again: Issacher, Zebulun; Dinah (30:14–21)
Conclusion: God remembers Rachel: Joseph; hope for another son (30:22–24)

Jacob's flocks

Introduction: Jacob to Laban: Let me go; you know my service (30:25–26)
Proposal, and reply (a verbal manoeuvre) (30:27–30)
    Laban: Stay, and decide your own pay (30:27–28)
    Jacob: You know my service. Now I must do for myself (30:29–30)
Proposal, and reply (a physical maneuver) (30:31–36)
    Jacob: proposal to take only colored animals (30:31–34)
    Laban removes colored animals (30:35–36)
Jacob turns the remnant into a strong flock (30:37–42)
    Jacob uses shoots to generate colored flocks (30:37–40a)
    Jacob builds separate flocks and strengthens them (30:40b–42)
Conclusion: Jacob expands, and his flock becomes many (30:43)

achieves priority—she is the first to bear children—but, in the end, attention comes back to Rachel.

The second panel, concerning the flocks (30:25–43), is more difficult. The conclusion (30:43) presents no problem—it stands apart—but the introduction is not as clear-cut. However, it seems best to limit the introduction to Jacob's opening statement about wanting to go (30:25–26). Such an introduction, though brief, sets the scene for what follows; and it also provides the kind of repetition that often indicates division: its concluding phrase, "you know (how) . . . I have served you" (30:26), recurs in the concluding statement of the first part (30:29).

The remainder of the text (30:31–42) tells how Jacob multiplied his flocks—first his proposal to do it (30:31–36), then the actual doing (30:37–42). Within each of these latter stages (proposal and doing) there is a moment when, for their own individual purposes, Laban and Jacob separate some of the flock (Laban, 30:35; Jacob, 30:40b). These moments of separation seem to indicate further, minor, divisions. The division within 30:40 is tentative.

Comment

Panel One (29:31–30:24)

[29:31–30:8] **Leah and Rachel, hated and loved: a drama of reversal and of changing fortunes.** As often in biblical stories, the situations of the protagonists are reversed. God favors the hated Leah, while Rachel, though loved, remains barren. "Hated" expresses choice rather than emotion; while it may have an emotional aspect, it is also "a technical legal term for the unfavored co-wife" (Alter, 155).

Life is not easy for either woman. Leah begins to bear children, but at first she feels frustrated. As her comment about her first child reveals ("now my husband will love me"), she wants to gain her husband's affection. But as time goes on her viewpoint fluctuates. The name of her third child ("My Wrestling") implies that her relationship with her sister is one of wrestling or struggling, like the relationship between Jacob and Esau. However, when the fourth child is born, she speaks not about her husband but about praising Yhwh.

This fourth child will become the leader of a people, and so his name—Praise/Sing-praise (Judah)—is of great significance. It suggests, for the people of Judah/Judea, and for those who learn from them, that, whatever life's suffering, their ultimate heritage is something positive or praiseworthy, something that evokes thanksgiving.

But if life is improving for Leah, it is becoming worse for Rachel. Her first two spoken sentences (30:1, 3) have echoes respectively of the first anguished words of Esau (at death's door, 25:30) and of Sarah (frustrated by childlessness and giving her slave woman, 16:2). She is envious and desperate, forgetting that her fate in childbearing depends on God. Her description of the slave woman Bilhah as bearing "on my knees" (30:3) may refer to a mode of delivery—the children are delivered on to Rachel's knees (de Vaux, 1965, 42)—or to an adoption rite (ibid., 51; Rachel adopts her slave woman's children). The birth of Bilhah's two children gives her a sense of God's justice, and seems to bring her some form of peace.

[30:9–24] **The drama resumed.** The form of peace that was first achieved by Leah and Rachel proves temporary. Leah decides to do what Rachel had done—give her maid (Zilpah) to Jacob. The resulting two children, Fortunate and Happy (Gad and Asher), suggest an improving situation.

But when Leah's eldest, Reuben, finds mandrakes—tomato-shaped wild fruit used as aphrodisiacs—and brings them to his mother, the episode takes a fresh turn. Rachel reveals that, whatever God's role, she will try using the mandrakes. And Leah, though she had apparently come to think she would have no more children, bargains for the right to sleep with Jacob. The result for Leah: three more children; for Rachel: still nothing.

It was not the mandrakes that had given more children to Leah, but God, who heard her. At the end, Leah seems grateful for what she has received from God, and concerning her husband, she sounds, as ever, hopeful (30:17–21).

Finally, "God remembered Rachel" (30:22), as God had once remembered Noah (8:1) and Abraham (19:29). Joseph is born, and Rachel, too, sounds grateful and hopeful—hopeful for another child, but unaware of what the birth of that child will do to her.

Panel Two (30:25–43)

[30:25–30] **Jacob moves Laban toward accepting his terms.** The second panel brings a change of emphasis concerning the process of generation. In the first panel, dealing with children, the emphasis had been placed on the role of God (29:31: 30:2, 22–24). But now, in breeding animals, the emphasis falls on the human factor, on Jacob's ingenuity. This variation, from divine to human, is one aspect of the texts' complementarity.

The account of the birth of the children, especially of Joseph, flows into the account of the increase of the flocks (30:25). The drama of increasing the flock begins when Jacob, having done his service, asks Laban to go.

In the subtle struggle between the two men, it is not clear whether Jacob has read his adversary, whether he has guessed in advance that Laban, ever anxious to delay and extract more, will ask him to stay.

Certainly, when Laban does ask him to stay, and tells him he can decide his own wages, Jacob shows no surprise. But, instead of grabbing the apparently generous offer, Jacob makes Laban wait. He repeats his initial demand, but does so with emphasis on his selfless service to date—how much he has gained for Laban, how little for himself (30:29–30). This leaves Laban at a disadvantage: as he waits, he is unsure whether his generous offer is good enough; and, insofar as he is capable of it, he is feeling guilty. Thus before responding to the offer, Jacob is already in a strong position. Almost any proposal he makes will seem acceptable. Formerly, in the first wage-discussion (29:15–30), "Laban was the helmsman of the conversation, coming directly to the crucial point. . . . Now the positions are reversed" (Fokkelman, 1975, 149).

[30:31–43] **Building the remainder into strong flocks.** Jacob's proposal, when it comes, seems in fact to be very acceptable: he will continue pasturing Laban's flocks provided he is allowed to keep whatever animals have unusual color.

Commentators are uncertain about the details of this proposal, both about what exactly is agreed (in 30:32–33), and about Jacob's procedure in achieving his purpose (30:37–39; translations are tentative). But the essential story seems clear. Normally, goats are dark, and sheep light; so Jacob asks that he keep the exceptions—dark sheep and light goats (light meaning speckled or spotted).

At first it seems that Jacob has little chance of gaining many animals. Laban cheats: he immediately gives animals of unusual color to his sons, and removes these animals and himself from Jacob by three days. Jacob's situation is challenging indeed. Laban's taking of the animals is rapacious. Furthermore, the sudden appearance of Laban's sons, here mentioned for the first time, gives pause. And the three day distance from colored animals is daunting. The combination—rapaciousness, sons, and distance—could be overpowering. Jacob is left to care for the remainder (literally, for those who "remain," *yātar*).

Jacob, however, does not believe that the development of the flocks is decide . purely by biological factors. He had regarded the development of his own family as coming ultimately not from biology but from God (29:31–30:24, esp. 30:2). Likewise now, when biological factors seem discouraging, when he must begin with a lack of the kinds of animals he wants, he relies on another factor—on external visual stimulus. It was believed in parts of the ancient world that a stimulus to the eyes affected birth, so Jacob uses tree shoots, pared down, to stimulate the coloring of the animals, and, having thus begun with these pared tree shoots, he rebuilds the flock. Some of this imagery—of stripping tree shoots as a way of rebuilding a remainder—is akin to the language of Isaiah about rebuilding the remnant of the people (Isa. 1:8–9; 6:11–13).

32   The Long Journey Homeward (Chaps. 31–33)

The Fear in Meeting Laban (31:1–32:2)
The Greater Fear in Meeting Esau (32:3–Chap. 33)

Introductory Aspects

The Basic Story Line

After many years in Haran, Jacob realized something had changed and so he decided to take all he had and go home. Having reached a position of unprecedented power and wealth, he embarked on a major transition.

But the journey was not easy, for it meant facing the two most intimidating people in his life—his powerful uncle and his murderous brother. In diverse ways he tried to escape them. He fled in secret from his uncle, and thought of taking a gamble to save half his family from Esau. But his uncle came after him with power and overtook him; and Jacob also realized he would have to face Esau.

The story (chaps. 31–33), then, is about this longing for home and about the facing of danger and death.

The pace of the journey varies, first fast and furious, then measured and slow. When Laban overtakes him, Jacob at first is careful and deferential. But finally, in an angry apologia, he confronts his exploiting uncle, and later the two make peace.

The meeting with Esau affects Jacob even more deeply. As never before he passes through the dark valley of the fear of death.

The homecoming never really happens, at least not as foreseen. Unlike Homer's Odysseus, Jacob does not return to the old house, to the way things used to be. Instead, in a brief puzzling account, Jacob experiences homecoming of another kind.

Literary Form

The primary literary type, encompassing all of chapters 31–33, is that of an itinerary or travel narrative, particularly travel narratives related to death. A somewhat comparable phenomenon will occur in Luke's travel narrative, when, as death beckons faintly in the distance, Jesus sets his face to Jerusalem (Luke 9:51). Jacob, too, sets his face—toward the mountain (31:21). In Luke the turn in the narrative is sharp—the face is set immediately (Luke 9:51)—whereas in Genesis the development is more gradual; the setting of the face is late and enigmatic. Aspects of such a gradual enigmatic journey occur in other Gospels (for instance, in the departure for Galilee, John 4:1–6), but, within the Gospels, Luke probably remains the clearest illustration of the death-related itinerary in the Gospels. Jacob's struggle on the other side of the river (32:23–33) contains some echoes of a very specific genre of travel narrative, namely travels in the Netherworld (Margalit, 2001).

Within this framework—the itinerary—several other literary types have been incorporated. Two passages are particularly important, the night struggle (32:22–32) and Jacob's greeting of Esau (33:1–11).

The night struggle (32:22–32), while echoing travels in the Netherworld, also combines and reverses two standard scenes. At one level it is a variation on an initiatory struggle (Kuntzmann, 2001), and as such it continues the former struggles (25:22–23, 27–34; 26:34–27:45). It is also a radical reversal of a betrothal scene. The meeting is not with a woman (as in meeting Rachel, 29:1–30) but with God, and what results is not betrothal but blessing. Aspects of such a variation were already seen in the case of Abraham's old age: the primary emphasis at the well was not on the woman and betrothal but on an encounter with God and blessing (24:1–49). And in Jacob's original journey, away from home (26:34–29:30), blessing and betrothal were interwoven.

In the night struggle there are several details that mirror or reverse the idea of betrothal: the strange or foreign location; the scene-setting reference to wives and children; the river (instead of a well); the togetherness all through the night; the reference to the thigh ("the hollow of the thigh," 31:25, 31–32; cf. Abraham's thigh, 24:2, 9); and the final reference, typical of betrothal scenes, to eating (32:32).

The idea of reversal bears repeating: the night struggle is not a betrothal; it is a radical changing of what betrothal means. The reference to eating is negative: "the sons of Israel do not eat. . . ."

Yet the key concept of betrothal is important. Jacob's night of struggling, of confronting death, may indeed involve letting go of all that he holds dear. In that sense all his normal ties, his usual bonds of betrothal, are reversed, broken. Yet in that breaking there is another form of betrothal—an intimacy with God that gives blessing and enables him to emerge into the sunlight, ready for what is coming.

Jacob's subsequent greeting of Esau (33:1–11) follows a "well-known court ceremonial" (Westermann, II, 524). Jacob "greets Esau as a vassal greets his patron with a ceremonial which had its origin in the royal court; there is a display of solemnity as becomes rank, the sevenfold obeisance, the submissive address, the presentation of gifts of homage" (ibid.). While Jacob approaches like a vassal, Esau's conduct is more like that of a brother.

Apart from this vassal-brother dimension, Jacob's meeting with Esau (33:1–11) contains echoes of his betrothal. Following the scene-setting reference to the wives and children (33:1–2), the actual meeting—the kissing and weeping—recalls Jacob's original meeting with Rachel (29:11). Seeing Esau's face is like seeing the face of God (33:10); and with Esau, as with God, there is a blessing (33:11).

As the unusual Abraham-related betrothal scene was followed by the betrothal of Isaac and Rebekah (chap. 24), so here, but with more radical variation, the night betrothal has an impact on the subsequent meeting with Esau. The essence of Jacob's meeting with Esau is that by accepting Esau (and his implicit threat of death), Jacob confirms his betrothal-like encounter with God. Meeting Esau is the practical working-out of the more decisive meeting in the night; having met God and made peace with God in the night, he could now meet Esau. Esau, instead of being seen as a destroyer, could be accepted as the continuation of the face of God.

Complementarity and Leading Aspects

In this journey, the most difficult in Jacob's life, both panels are long: the meeting with Laban, fifty-seven verses; and the meeting with Esau, fifty.

The initial link between the two panels is reasonably clear. Laban and Esau had been the two most threatening or powerful people in Jacob's life. Now, in successive episodes, he has to confront them. This alone, this confronting of powerful threats, is enough to bind these two panels together.

Another obvious link is the journey. The entire scene, including both confrontations, is the account of a single journey—the move from his northern location to Succoth and Shechem.

This journey is not easy; to a large extent it is a flight, governed by fear. The Laban episode begins with flight (31:17–21); and when Jacob realizes that Esau is coming with four hundred men his first thought is to get away (32:7–9). He redistributes his people so that at least some will escape.

Central to the whole two-panel scene is Jacob's fear of death. In the Laban panel, this fear is not clear, yet from the beginning, when Jacob first "heard" and "saw" a change in Laban's sons and Laban's face (31:1–2), shades of fear hover over Jacob's life. Real harm does not happen, but it comes close and has to be prevented, first by dream (31:24, 29; cf. 31:7), then by covenant (31:52). The prevention, though effective, heightens awareness of the danger. When Jacob is pressed by Laban, his fear becomes explicit: "I was afraid" (31:31). In the case of Esau, who once planned to kill Jacob and who now approaches with four hundred men, the fear is expressed sooner, and it is stronger: "Jacob was very afraid and he was distressed" (32:7). Thus both panels tell of fearful flight, but the second panel is more intense.

Despite this tendency to flee, Jacob finally confronts his fear. In the Laban panel the confrontation happens slowly and somewhat indirectly, with some repetition. All Jacob wants is to get away, but when Laban overtakes him, he has to talk, and eventually, not by decision but by provocation, he confronts Laban (31:36–42).

In the Esau panel, even though Jacob's first thought is flight, he begins, slowly, to address the source of his great fear. First he prays (31:9–12). Then he sends a huge offering to Esau, to Esau's face (31:13–21). And finally, after a lonely night struggle with a shadowy person, with the face of God (in a sense with himself), he emerges, limping in sunshine, and ready to meet Esau (31: 22–32).

Within the diptych as a whole, therefore, the night struggle (21:22–32) is the climactic moment. This is the point when, having let go of everything, Jacob is alone with the darkness and with God. In some ways it appears to be the most frightening passage, but because he is no longer trying to flee, Jacob turns it into a moment of blessing: ". . . 'Bless me'. . . . And he blessed him" (32:26, 29).

At one level then the whole two-panel scene is a portrayal of the encroaching fear of death, of the flight from that fear, and of the complex process of confronting it.

Other complementarities include the following:

Jacob's journey to the mountain—rising, taking his family, crossing the river, and setting his face (31:17–18, 21)—is echoed and varied in his embarking on the night struggle (32:22–24).

The allusions to far-reaching searches—the confusion of Laban's heart (31: 26–30) and the vain search for the household gods (a search carried out largely in the tents of the women, especially that of Rachel as she sits during her monthly period, 32:32–35)—seem to provide a foil for Jacob's intimate encounter with God (32:24–32).

The Jacob-Laban relationship, which ends in a covenant (31:45–32:2), forms a preparation for the Jacob-Esau relationship with its overtones of a betrothal (33:1–11). Laban's kisses are for his daughters, Jacob's wives, but Esau's are for Jacob himself. At the end, both Laban and Esau go away peacefully.

Relationship to Preceding Chapters

The whole long scene (31:1–33:20) breaks much new ground, but it also has multiple affinities with preceding chapters. Some echoes of the betrothal scenes (chaps. 24 and 29) have been noted. The reconciliation of Esau and Jacob contains echoes and reversals of the Cain and Abel story (for instance, offering and its acceptance; the face being lifted up; the need to master a strange adversary; 4:3–7; 32:20, 28).

There is continuity between the night struggle (32:22–32) and the night dream at Bethel (28:10–22):

Just as God encountered Jacob when he fled the promised land because of his brother's anger, so also God now encounters him at the point of reentry, with his brother's anger once again focusing his energies. In both cases, Jacob appears deeply vulnerable and alone, in need of divine care. This time, however, God approaches him in a much more ambiguous manner. (Fretheim, 565)

Jacob's long journey has a particular affinity, at one level, with the flood story. Within the initial Jacob drama (25:19–37:1) this whole difficult diptych (31:1–33:20) is comparable, in its length and its sense of crisis, to the role of the flood within Genesis 1–11. There are links, too, in crucial details. In particular, the flood story's opening picture of corrupt hearts and some form of false worship—or false relationship to gods ("sons of god/God;" 6:1–2, 5)—finds an echo in Laban's preoccupation with heart and household gods (31:19–20, 26–35). In contrast, Noah is just (6:8–9), and so is Jacob (31:36–42). There is affinity, too, in the making of the covenants (9:9–17; 31:45–32:2).

Structure (Table 32.1)

The structure assumed here allots fifty-five verses to chapter 31. This follows the Greek and many English translations (the Hebrew starts a new chapter after fifty-four verses [Greek 31:55 = Hebrew 32:1] so the verse numbers in Hebrew are one higher than in this commentary and outline). Ideally, if it were ever possible to redraw the chapter divisions, chapter 31 would have fifty-seven verses—as far as 32:2.

PANEL ONE (31:1–32:2)

This panel contains three main parts of roughly equal length—somewhat like the first panel of the flood story.

PANEL TWO (32:3–CHAP. 33)

Panel two, however, which has just two main parts, contains one that is unusually long—the account of Jacob's wrestling at night (32:7–32). The length of this part corresponds broadly with some other lengthy texts, for example, the relaunching of humankind after the flood (8:15–9:7), and Judah's climactic speech (44:18–34).

Comment

Panel One (31:1–32:2)

[31:1–16] Introduction. Threat and alienation: confirmed by (the angel of) God. The whole two-panel account (chaps. 31–33) occupies the same kind of pivotal role as the deluge (6:1–9:17) within chapters 1–11; and this intro-

Table 32.1. The Long Journey Homeward (31:1–32:2 // 32:3–33:20)

Journeying in fear, Jacob meets Laban

Introduction: Threat and alienation: God/angel speaks (31:1–16)
   Initial threat: Jacob hears/sees Laban's change; Yhwh says "Go back" (1–3)
   Initial threat developed: the women; angel says "Go back" (4–13)
   Women, alienated, confirm the divide and say "Do as God says" (14–16)
Jacob on the defensive: he departs and Laban overtakes him (31:17–25)
   Jacob steals away . . . to Mount Gilead (17–21)
   Laban pursues, is warned, and overtakes at Mount Gilead (22–25)
Jacob on the defensive: Laban's complaint and Jacob's answer (31:26–35)
   Laban's complaint: you stole, stole away (26–30)
   Jacob's answer: I was afraid; search for what is stolen (31–35)
Jacob's *apologia* (31:36–44)
   Jacob's complaint: All I've done for you (36–42)
   Laban's answer: All are mine; let us make a covenant (43–44)
Conclusion: reassurance, peace; covenant bears witness (31:45–32:2)
   Initial reassurance: The covenant mound; meal (45–47)
   Initial reassurance developed; mound, monument: The women; meal (48–54)
   Women's peace as Laban kisses good-bye (unlike Lot) (31:55–32:2)

Journeying in greater fear, Jacob meets Esau

Introduction: the messengers (32:3–6)
   Messengers are sent (3–5)
   Messengers return (6)
Jacob sends gifts (32:7–22)
   Jacob, afraid (7–12)
   Jacob sends droves ahead as a gift (13–21)
   Jacob's wrestles with God (22–32)
The meeting with Esau (33:1–11)
   They meet and weep (1–4)
   Women and children come and bow down (5–7)
   Esau accepts gifts (8–11)
Conclusion: journeying on to Succoth and Shechem (33:12–20)
   As Jacob goes slowly, Esau journeys to Seir (12–16)
   Jacob journeys to Succoth and Shechem (17–20)

duction (31:1–16) is comparable in its difficulty to the introduction to the deluge (6:1–8).

In contrast to the preceding picture of advancing strength and prosperity—a picture of being able to outmaneuver Laban—Jacob now begins to show a certain vulnerability. He seems unnerved by what he both hears and sees: he hears Laban's sons, their troubling words; and he sees Laban's own changed face.

The realization of the change comes suddenly—there was little previous indication of it—yet it is significant. Laban's relative wealth seems to shrink.

And Laban's attitude (his "face") changes from what it had been "yesterday or three days ago" (an indefinite period).

Along with the realization of change, there comes the word of the Lord, telling him to go back: "I will be with you" (31:3), a phrase that echoes God's promise at Bethel (28:15). It is as though, just when his world becomes fragile, God sends him back to something, and reassures him about being with him. The overall implication is that Jacob is facing an important turning point.

The impression of a turning point is confirmed in the following perplexing section (31:4–13) when Jacob calls both his wives (now seen in unison) and talks to them at length—nine uninterrupted verses (31:5–13). He recounts how he received first a message (about the flocks) and then the identification of the speaker—God (31:10–13). The perplexity comes from the peculiar sequence: among other things "it is unusual that the message . . . be delivered before the identification" (Maly, 2:115). Accordingly, some commentators rearrange the text (cf. Westermann, II, 491).

The presence sequence, however, has its own coherence:

"I lifted up my eyes and saw in a *dream*. . . ."

"The *messenger of God* said to me in the dream . . . 'Lift up your eyes. . . . ' "

". . . I am the *God* of Bethel.' "

The essence of the sequence is a progression: a dream; a messenger/angel of God in a dream; and finally, God's own self. Thus the overall progression that occurs in this whole pivotal diptych (chaps. 31–33) is already signaled in the introduction. There is an increasing clarity about God's presence.

As Jacob talks, he goes back over his history with Laban. It now emerges that this history is more troubled than was previously indicated. In particular, Laban had often changed the rules about payment through the breeding of flocks. But as well as being more troubled, the history is also richer—as seen especially in the progression from the dream to the angel to God.

God's awareness of the problems of Jacob and his flock (31:12–13) is somewhat like God's later awareness of the sufferings of the Israelites in Egypt (Exod. 3:1–2, 7). On both occasions, God directs the leader (Jacob/Moses), who is caring for his flock, to leave the place of servitude. Ultimately, both accounts of God's care for the threatened flock constitute echoes of God's care for threatened humanity at the time of the deluge. As God directed Noah to build the ark, so God directed Jacob and Moses—through dream and vision respectively—to bring the people to a new place. This emphasis on the people helps explain the emphasis on the wives. In some sense Jacob's wives, like the flocks, represent aspects of the people.

This more troubled account of Jacob's history is not a contradiction of the earlier version (the successful account in 30:25–43). Rather, the whole narrative has shifted to a further level, and to a later viewpoint, that of someone who is generally more aware of Laban's attitude.

As well as being more aware of Laban, Jacob at some level is also more aware of God: "Jacob wants to make it vividly clear to his wives at this tense juncture that God . . . [is] with him. It serves his purpose to explain his spectacular prosperity . . . as the revelation of an angel of God. It thus makes narrative sense that he should omit all mention of the elaborate stratagem of the peeled rods in the troughs" (Alter, 167).

Through talking to his wives, whose apparent mutual reconciliation seems to intimate the forthcoming Jacob-Laban reconciliation, Jacob spells out some of his initial sense of unease with Laban, and, when they reply, they in turn spell out further aspects of trouble, aspects of their own alienation from Laban, especially because of his focus on possessions (31:14–16). Apparently Laban, instead of following the frequent custom of returning much of the bride-price (*mōhar*) to the bride, had simply kept it all (all the wages of Jacob's fourteen years), thus effectively making money from his daughters—selling them. It is no accident that this picture of selling his daughters is followed by the image of shearing his sheep. (Judah's later shearing has a similar negative connotation; it is implicitly contrasted with Joseph's shepherding; cf. 37:13 and 38:12.)

In the introduction to the deluge, the primary problem was related not so much to possessions as to the disordered taking of wives. Here, on the contrary, the wives are involved in the decision to move. They encourage him: "Now, all God has said to you, do it."

There is therefore a triple indication to go back—from Yhwh (31:3), from the recollection of the angel of God in the dream (31:11–13), and from the two wives as they tell him to do as God says. At one level, the whole threefold process is like a portrayal of someone going through a searching process of discernment.

[31:17–25] **The shadow of harm: as Jacob steals away and sets his face toward the mountain, Laban pursues.** Jacob's departure evokes both wealth and fear. The wealth is suggested by the camels and by words that are possessions-related (31:17–18). The fear is suggested by other factors: the departure takes place, surprisingly, in Laban's absence; and the picture of Laban as shearing is faintly disturbing (31:19). Furthermore, Jacob's journey suggests a path that is not easy—crossing the river, and setting his face toward the mountain.

The link between the mountain and danger becomes clearer when Laban, taking with him "his brothers" (his kinsmen, presumably including the resentful sons), pursues Jacob and catches up with him on the mountain. The pace of the flight and pursuit seem to have been hectic; in "seven days" Laban covered a huge distance—from trans-Euphrates to trans-Jordanian Gilead (later, Jacob uses slowness rather than speed to stay clear of Esau, 33:13). "The mountain" identified as Gilead seems to have an echo of the unnamed mountain where Abraham, in offering Isaac (chap. 22), faced another form of death.

In a dream, God now warns Laban not to do Jacob any "harm" (literally, to say nothing to him, good or bad). The warning is simultaneously reassuring and disturbing; it ensures Jacob's safely, but it confirms the reality of the danger. The sudden reference to Laban as "the Aramean" introduces an international aspect that seems to add further tension.

Central to the outwitting of Laban is the process of stealing (*gānab*). The primary stealing is by Rachel, who steals the household gods, and by Jacob who steals away; literally, he "steals the heart" of Laban, thus outwitting him. Generally speaking, household gods were images of the gods that cared for a household. In this case they may have had a more specific function: they were "human-shaped images of gods that were symbols of Laban's authority over his household, perhaps tokens of inheritance" (Fretheim, 557). The double action of stealing, as led by Rachel, involves a radical challenge to Laban and to whatever he represents, a challenge to his gods and his heart! (On sons of god, and reference to the heart, cf. Gen. 6:2, 5). For Rachel, challenging Laban is no small matter. Laban is the father who once governed much of her life, including her wedding night.

[31:26–35] **On the mountain. Laban's complaint and Jacob's answer: the search for the heart and the gods.** Laban is armed; he reminds Jacob that he has "the power to do harm" (31:29), and he accuses Jacob of acting as if he were leading a warring party (31:26). The situation therefore is highly dangerous.

Laban's complaint is about his heart and his gods. He speaks first of the heart, and though his complaint is specific—concerning Jacob's secret flight with his daughters—Laban's brief speech manages to use images that touch a wide range of the human heart's experiences and feelings: the agony of women who are driven as prisoners of war ("of the sword"); the celebration of music and song; the sweet sorrow of kissing good-bye; the deep longing for home. In brief: war and song; kissing and longing.

Then, in the same breath, he goes from the heart to the gods: ". . . and why did you steal my gods?" In Jacob's reply the issues of heart and gods are likewise interwoven. Jacob says he had been afraid, but the fear is the fear of losing the daughters, his wives, and so the fear includes a form of love (31:31). Or, to turn it around, the love involves fear. As for the gods, they are associated ironically with death ("Whoever you find with your gods shall not live"). In the subsequent search, the gods are associated not so much with death as with frustration (Laban, searching, goes around in circles, apparently trying Leah's tent twice). The gods also endure ridicule (being sat on by Rachel—and during her period, thus adding legal impurity). Thus the portrait of some of the extreme experiences of the heart is followed by a picture of the difficulty of dealing with the gods.

[31:36–44] **Jacob's complaint/rebuke and Laban's answer. Reliance not on heart and gods but on justice and God.** In contrast to Laban, who seems preoccupied by the emotions of the heart and by gods, Jacob speaks of justice and God—the just way he has lived for twenty years (31:36–41), and the God of Abraham, who gives attention and judgment (31:42).

The contrast between these two worlds—one of stolen heart and frustrating gods, the other of steadfast endurance and God—suggests that Laban's position is weaker. And his reply confirms that impression. He emphasizes touchingly that the daughters and (grand)children are his, but then he confesses that he can do nothing for them (31:43). And so, apparently recognizing the reality of the situation, recognizing Jacob's character and God, he proposes a covenant.

The obscure reference to Isaac ("the God of Abraham and the Dread of Isaac," 31:42) strengthens the impression that on this mountain there is indeed an echo of how Abraham, in bringing Isaac to a mountain and thus facing a form of death, showed his fear of God.

[31:45–32:2] Conclusion. Reassurance and peace—confirmed by covenant. The introduction and conclusion balance one another in many subtle ways (see above, "Structure"). Having begun with varying repetitive images of threat and alienation (31:1–16), the Laban panel concludes with varying images of reassurance and peace (31:45–32:2). The threat was confirmed by (the messenger/ angel of) God, and now, in the conclusion, the sense of reassurance is confirmed by a covenant and by the signs of the covenant—a single stone (a monument) and a multiplicity of stones (a mound). The image of the stone(s) takes up the introduction's allusion to the earlier (stone) monument (31:13; cf. 28:18).

The initial assurance (the stone monument, 31:45–47), like the initial threat (31:1–3), is brief, but it establishes the idea of a stable relationship between Jacob (Israel) and Laban (Aram). The setting up of the single-stone monument, reminiscent of the stone on which Jacob dreamed, provides a unifying point of reference (31:45). The mound of gathered stones is more evocative of diverse people being brought together, and in fact, when describing it, Laban and Jacob use different languages (one Aramaic, the other Hebrew, a reminder of the inter-nation dimension), but in both languages the meaning is the same— mound of witness. The inter-nation aspect indicates that, at one level, this text is referring to the establishment of a border between two nations.

Then the assurance is spelled out (31:48–54). The mound of stones will be both a mound-of-witness (gal-'ēd) and a watch (miṣpah), for, as Laban says, the Lord will watch over himself and Jacob, and will witness. The account of this watching and witnessing is repetitious (31:49–52), as is the corresponding part of the introduction, when God kept an eye on the devious proceedings with the flocks (31:6–12). In this final case, the repetitiveness is part of a larger rhetorical flourish, which accompanies the making of the treaty (cf. Alter, 175).

It is necessary to take the two texts together, the introductory account of seeing the devious juggling of the flocks (31:6–12), and the concluding account of watching over the fate of the daughters (31:50). As indicated by the balance between the two panels of the preceding diptych (29:31–chap. 30)—one about the daughters and their children (29:31–30:24), the other about flocks (30:25– 43)—the images of flocks and daughters are connected. The connection probably comes from mutual affinity with the idea of the people. (In biblical imagery the people are sometimes visualized as a flock or a woman.)

This background—the people-related images of flocks and daughters—helps to explain the covenant promise to do no harm (31:52). The avoidance of harm is not something negative and narrow, not a kind of local nonagression pact. Rather the avoidance of harm is part of a mutual care for the people. These people may be diverse, but whatever their distinctions, there is a basic unity, a positive quality. The daughters have real links with both Jacob and Laban.

Jacob's allusion to God as "the Dread of my father Isaac" is a reminder that for Jacob the entire drama (chaps. 31–33) involves an element of fear and awe.

"Bread," eaten during the night ceremonial on the mountain, means more than just bread; it refers to an entire meal (Alter, 176). Combined with sacrifice the implication is of an extraordinary night.

At the end (31:55–32:2), Laban leaves his two daughters with a kiss and a blessing—signs of positive peace (contrast Lot's final dealings with his two daughters, 19:30–38). Another detail about Laban is positive. His early rising puts him in the company of Abraham (19:27; 21:14; 22:3) and the honest Abimelech (20:8). Though Laban leaves the story, the final implication is that, wherever he is, he remains significant. For, when Jacob moves on and meets the angels, he may indeed see only one encampment of God, yet it is twofold: "He called the name of that place Two Camps." Given the context—the Laban-Jacob covenant—Laban is part of that twofold vision.

Panel Two (32:3–33:20)

[32:3–6] Introduction. Announcing Jacob's life: the messengers (mal-'ākîm), sent to Esau, announce Jacob's past and a frightening prospect in the future. When Jacob sends messengers to Esau to tell of his impending return, the mood surrounding the mission is ambiguous. On the one hand, Jacob is announcing his life's achievement, telling how his time with Laban has earned him great wealth. On the other hand, Esau had once planned to kill him; and the messengers' announcement on their return—Esau is coming with four hundred men!—seems to renew the threat of death. Jacob's achievements, therefore, however great, suddenly look fragile. He is at a crossroads. Whatever his success, however much the stolen blessing promised that he would rule over his serving brother, he now addresses his brother as "Lord," and describes himself as a servant.

The messengers, too (mal'ākîm), are surrounded by ambiguity. They may be ordinary at one level but (mal'ākîm) also means angels—angels of God—and was so used in the preceding verses (32:1–2). The ambiguity may not be of much encouragement to Jacob, but for the reader it adds a touch of color to what is otherwise a very ominous situation. The threat of death is not as negative as it may look.

Curiously, a combination of elements found here—"field" and "four hundred" (the field of Edom, and Esau's four hundred men, 32:3, 6)—occurred also in the buying of a burial place (the field of Ephron, and the four hundred shekels paid to Ephron, 23:13–15). In 1 and 2 Samuel "four hundred is a standard number for a regiment or raiding party" (Alter, 178).

[32:7–32] Jacob's prayer, offering, and night struggle: from great fear to the shining sun. The account of how Jacob dealt with his deathly fear— fear of Esau and his four hundred—is spread over three interwoven episodes.

First (32:7–12), he seeks some form of escape. By redistributing his people into two camps he hopes that one will escape. Then he turns from organizing escape to asking God for it: he prays for deliverance. As he prays (32:9–12) his words express an increasing sense of all God has done and of God's promise of goodness. When he has finished, there is no further talk of escape. The prayer was real; it changed him.

Second (32:13–21), having apparently left aside ideas of escape, he begins to address the problem directly. He turns his attention to the oncoming Esau. This is difficult; it takes place at night, and there is an implication that facing Esau is like facing the darkness.

His action is to give an offering to Esau. The offering is massive—more than five hundred animals, ranging from goats to bulls to camels—and it seems to involve a real letting go. The animals are transferred "from what had come to his hand . . . into the hand of his servants" (32:13, 16).

Despite the size of the offering Jacob is still being careful, still hesitant about going forward. The animals are in separate herds, with space between them, and the servant in charge of each herd is to say that Jacob is coming. So he is, but he is "behind," always "behind" (32:16, 18, 20). His hope is that the offering may appease Esau's face and thus lead Esau to lift his, Jacob's, face, in other words, to forgive him. (In the Cain-Abel tension, the thought of sin and/or death involves a face that is cast down; 4:4–5.)

The diverse herds of animals are "designed to assuage Esau with waves of generosity at three distinct intervals" (Murphy, 2:53). Thus the idea of an advancing process, already suggested in Jacob's dream concerning the flock (31: 10–13), is now applied to Esau.

Third (32:22–32, the night wrestling), he addresses the oncoming threat in a way that is yet more direct—as it exists within himself.

Before doing so, however, before concentrating on being alone, he has to deal with those closest to him. Having already separated himself from more than five hundred animals, he now places an enigmatic distance between himself and his family. He makes them pass over the Jabbok (32:22–23). The repetition in the account of the crossing suggests intensification—the Jabbok (a trans-Jordanian tributary of the Jordan) is expressly described as a *nāḥal*, "stream/ torrent/wadi" (32:24), and he eventually puts across everything. There is an evoking therefore of a complete letting go or a complete separation from every-one and everything.

"That night . . . Jacob was left alone. And a man wrestled with him until the rising of the dawn." The wrestling is a high point in a series of wrestlings or struggles that have characterized Jacob's life, beginning at birth (25:26).

Jacob's opponent is first described from Jacob's perspective simply as a man. But this mysterious figure appears to have three dimensions—human, divine, and demonic. Human, because that is the initial impression and description ("a man"); divine, because Jacob is described as having wrestled or contended with God; and also apparently demonic. The demonic is indicated partly by the text and the context. In the text there are allusions to passing over a river and to danger from river-spirits (spirit/numen/demon; Murphy, 2:54; Sarna, 403). And in the context—the echoes of Cain and Abel—there is a variation on the struggle that Cain should have undertaken (against the deathly crouching animal, 4:7, a variation on the struggle with the serpent, 3:15).

However, even if some of the background to this account involved river-spirits, the present version does not. "Jacob knows nothing of any river-spirit. . . . Folk tales provided the literary model for this biblical narrative. But a careful and radical purging of all elements offensive to the monotheism of Israel has taken place" (Sarna, 403).

Many ancient Jewish writers held that Jacob's opponent was an angel (Miller, 1984, 114), an idea that is quite compatible with Israel's monotheism. Philo, for instance, variously regards the opponent as a good angel or a divine word (ibid., 122). For Gregory the Great, Jacob's wrestling illustrates the struggle of the contemplative life, and "the angel represents God" (ibid., 132).

The essence of the struggle is the human struggle surrounding sin and death. The one with whom one wrestles is human—to some degree it is oneself—but it involves aspects of both the divine and demonic, for within the human there is both the original divine blessing and also demonic deviation, beginning with the desire to be a god.

Jacob is left limping, a variation apparently on the wounded heel (3:15), but he also struggles his way to a blessing. Thus he has entered into the fundamental mystery of human existence. He has absorbed its negative weight. But that negativity, that seemingly demonic inheritance, is not a distinct god. Even the wound comes ultimately from the person who blesses. Thus the wound is contained, as it were, in a greater world of blessing. The opponent in the struggle is divine-human, but containing, integrating, the negative. By going through the night with this person, Jacob also achieves an integration. When the struggle is over, he may indeed be limping, but he is blessed, and the sun is shining on him.

Obviously the struggle is linked to the approach to Esau, and the adversary is "in some sense a doubling of Esau . . . but he is also a doubling of all with whom Jacob has had to contend, and he may equally be an externalization of all that Jacob has to wrestle with within himself. . . . Jacob whose name can be construed as 'he who acts crookedly,' is bent, permanently lamed, by his nameless adversary in order to be made straight before his reunion with Esau" (Alter, 181).

The centrality of Jacob's struggle, its radical nature, is reflected in its threefold etiological influence: it explains the name of the people ("Israel"); a place name that recalls the closeness to God (God's face, "Penuel"); and an eating taboo that is felt "to this day" in the lives of the sons of Israel.

[33:1–11] **The meeting with Esau: from fear of death to seeing the face of God.** When Jacob sees Esau coming he again redistributes his people, but not as previously (31:7). He no longer makes a division that is aimed at escape, nor does he place himself at the back. Instead, having arranged all his wives and children, he directs them toward Esau, and he himself walks before them (33:1–3). Making himself even more humble and vulnerable, he bows to the ground ritually as he comes close to his brother—an ancient sevenfold bowing such as was done when approaching a king.

The result is not injury but embrace (33:4).

Then, in a kind of relaxed denouement (33:5–7), the women and children also come and bow down.

And finally (33:8–11), in a culmination of reconciliation, Esau accepts Jacob's offering, his "blessing" (33:11). Jacob's gifts to Esau are a form of restitution for the stolen blessing (Westermann, II, 530). Jacob "does not give the blessing 'back' to Esau, but the blessing that he has received has been so bountiful that it can flow through him to Esau as well" (Fretheim, 572).

At the end, when Esau has already received him favorably, Jacob still insists on giving him the great gift. The motivation now is not to placate, but something much more positive—gratitude ("because God has been gracious to me").

Esau, who at one point had represented the dreaded approach of death, has become, in reconciliation, the face of God (33:10). The negative is the gateway to the positive. At some initial level Jacob has made peace with the face of death.

[33:12–20] **Leaving Esau, slowing down, and finding shelter.** Despite the reconciliation, Jacob does not go with Esau to Seir. In urging Esau to go ahead while he follows at a gentler pace, he evokes both an unwillingness to join Esau immediately and a general slowing down.

His destination is puzzling. Despite a twenty-year absence there is no reference to going home to Isaac and Rebekah. (This is in stark contrast to Homer's dramatic return after twenty years to his own house.) The crossing of the Jordan, fabled and evocative, is unmentioned. And the destination to which he does go is curiously twofold: first he builds a house in Succoth, and then he buys land in Shechem.

The house in Succoth is associated with something temporary, livestock shelters (*sukkôt*)—huts made from boughs. The land at Shechem, in contrast, has a suggestion, at least at one level, of something much more permanent. Its purchase (33:19) has echoes of the purchase of the field of Ephron (chap. 23).

This combination, of a temporary house and permanent land, while perplexing as a linear account, helps to evoke Jacob's larger destiny. Any house he dwells in is temporary; and ultimately he will be brought to the field of Ephron (49:30; 50:13).

However, the immediate focus in Shechem touches another level of his life—the idea of arriving in peace (33:18). In Shechem he pitches his tent and "stations" (*nāṣab*) an altar.

The first time Jacob had seen something "stationed" was in his youthful dream. The stairway, though stationed upon earth, touched the heavens (28:12). On that day in Bethel he had said that if he came back to the house of his father, Yhwh would be his God (28:21). In one sense it did not work out as he envisaged. He does not come back to his father's house. Much has changed, even his own name, "Israel." Yet God has not left him, even though God, too, seems changed, renamed. But the renaming of God corresponds to the change in himself: the God to whom he "stations" or builds the altar is "El, the God of Israel." Now more than ever God is his God. The dream still lives.

33   From Paralysis to Pilgrimage (34:1–35:20)

Dinah: Paralysis at Shechem (Chap. 34)
Deborah: Pilgrimage through Bethel (35:1–20)

Introductory Aspects

The Basic Story Line

If Jacob thought he had reached a place of easy peace he soon loses that illusion. No sooner is he settled down than disaster occurs—his only daughter is raped. As Jacob watches, his angry sons escalate the violence, luring the Shechemites into a bogus covenant, including a betrothal, and then attacking them savagely, leaving Jacob apparently helpless. The problems are no longer with outside figures, with Laban and Esau, but within his own house (Jacob, 235).

However, Jacob undergoes a basic transition. He moves from the experience of being overwhelmed by a world of rape, deceit, and murderous violence to a fresh sense of energy and hope. In face of the rape and defilement, he lays defilement aside and he takes to the road, ready to cope even with death.

Literary Form

The two primary literary forms are those of betrothal (chap. 34) and itinerary (the journey through Bethel, 35:1–20). The rape scene is also a story of crime and punishment (Sternberg, 1985, 445; Noble, 1996, 203).

To some degree the connection of the Dinah episode with betrothal is obvious. Most of the chapter is about arranging a marriage, a marriage of two individuals (Dinah and the man who raped her, Shechem), and also of two peoples (the text is two-dimensional—family and tribal). Adaptation of the betrothal convention is common in biblical writing (Alter, 1981, 51–62), but in this case the convention is almost twisted out of recognition. There is no well or water, an indication that the whole process is empty, an emptiness that accompanies the absence of God. However, the other standard elements of a betrothal scene are present: a man-woman encounter in a strange land; a rush home (by Dinah's brothers) at the news of the stranger's arrival; and the arrangement of a betrothal. But the encounter is destructive; the rush home is angry; and the arrangement is murderously deceitful. The only eating is by "the mouth of the sword" (34:26). Chapter 34, therefore, is a betrothal scene, but contorted.

The itinerary, on the other hand, the journey beyond Bethel (35:1–20), is full and hopeful. From first verse to last, from the reminder of fleeing the murderous Esau (35:1) to the burial of Deborah and Rachel (35:8, 20), it is shadowed by death, yet its overall tone is strong.

Complementarity of the Two Panels

The two panels form a sharp contrast, a kind of antithetical parallelism. The first, Shechem's rape of Dinah (chap. 34), shows Jacob as virtually paralyzed. He never moves, and when he finally speaks, his words are fearful and useless. In the second panel, however, during the complex journey to Bethel and beyond (35:1–20), he moves with energy, and, despite problems, his words are decisive and hopeful.

A basic difference between these two panels, between the paralysis and the pilgrimage, is that God is absent from the first, but takes a leading role in the second. The rape of Dinah (chap. 34), in fact, is one of the few panels in all of Genesis that makes no mention whatever of God. But in the pilgrimage (35:1–20) God intervenes immediately: "God said to Jacob, 'Arise, go up . . . '" (35:1). And midway through the panel, God's initiative is renewed: "God was seen again by Jacob . . . and he blessed him" (35:9).

The two-panel account, therefore, is like one in which a paralyzed man is told "Arise and go . . . ," and when that happens the scene is transformed.

The links between chapters 34 and 35 are "indirect but important" (Fretheim, 584). In fact, the panels have significant complementarities. For instance—a minor point—one features Dinah, the other, Benjamin, the last children respectively of Leah and Rachel. Most of the complementarities are sharp contrasts. The first begins with foreign rape and defilement (34:2–5), the second with the removal of foreign gods, purification, and the changing of clothing (35:2). In one, land and progeny (intermarriage) come from a foreign alliance

(34:9–10, 21), in the other, from God (35:11–12). In Shechem, the time of pain (following circumcision) leads to killing (34:25–26), but on the Bethel-Bethlehem road the time of pain leads to childbearing (35:9).

Both panels use aspects of the covenant of circumcision (chap. 17). The first exploits it to bring Shechem to circumcision and thereby to death (cf. 17:10). The second, however, recalls the covenant as a source of life and courage (35:9–13; cf. 17:1, 5–8, 22).

Relationship to Preceding Chapters

One of the features of Jacob's pilgrimage (35:1–20), and one of the reasons for its complexity, is that it echoes some of the events of his youth, especially his first journey away from home—his journey from Esau, through Bethel, to Rachel (27:41–29:30). But in a special way, it echoes aspects of the journey of Abraham—from his call to his burial of Sarah (chaps. 12–23). Some of these Abraham-related aspects are as follows:

The altar at or near Bethel (35:1, 3; cf. 12:8; 13:3–4).

A sense of divine protection against surrounding nations and death (35:5–8; cf. chaps. 14–15).

The renewal of the promise (35:9–13; chap. 17).

The surprising birth, the ambiguity of death, and the burial (35:16–20; chaps. 21 and 23).

The sharp transition, from paralysis to pilgrimage, which in this case occurs between the two panels of a single diptych (at 35:1), finds a partial precedent in 12:1, in the transition between the diptychs surrounding the call of Abraham. In that case the narrative goes from increasing fading and immobility (chap. 11, esp. the godless genealogy, vv. 10–32) to God's energizing word (chaps. 12–13).

Leading Elements

SECURITY

Jacob's paralysis in the Dinah episode seems to be linked to a desire for security. By meeting Laban and Esau (chaps. 31–33) Jacob had taken a major step in the process of confronting danger and death. Yet his acceptance of Esau had not been total. Esau embraced him, but it was not said that he embraced Esau (33:4). Esau had suggested they walk together, but Jacob held back (33:14); and having allowed Esau to go ahead, Jacob turned aside to the apparent safety of Succoth and Shechem (33:17–20). There, after his years of work and a difficult journey of confrontation, his primary interest seems to have been security.

LOVE AND DEATH

Of the various complementarities, one of the most basic concerns love and death. The Dinah episode brings out some of the ambiguity of sexual love; and the Bethel journey brings out some of the ambiguity of death.

In the Dinah story sex and sexual love constitute a driving force strong enough not only to ravage Dinah but also to push Shechem—both the individual rapist and the town—toward embracing Jacob's family and his sign of the covenant. In itself sexual love is positive, but here it becomes very negative. The effect of the story is to indicate that in this case such love brings a harvest of fear, rage, deception, and death.

This is the second time that Genesis has questioned human love. Already, through Abraham's offering of the beloved Isaac, God was placed above parental love. Parental love, despite its goodness, is not absolute, not an idol. Now, despite an intervening depiction of the positive side of love in the Rebekah story (24:67), Genesis uses the Dinah story to portray the negative side of erotic love.

The journey through Bethel, in contrast, shows the ambiguity of death. Death is not altogether negative. The first death is indeed accepted as tearful: Deborah's burial under the "Oak of Tears" not only suggests weeping but also recalls the preceding reference to a tree, the oak tree of Shechem, which was a burial place of the false gods (34:4, 8). Thus the tears surrounding Deborah's death evoke Shechem-related gods or idolatry. In chapter 34 Shechem is associated with disordered love. Tears, too, can be disordered, even idolatrous.

The second death, however, that of the beloved Rachel, instead of being far more lugubrious, as one might have expected, involves a startling reversal. Jacob renames the child—not Son of My Sorrow but Son of the Right Hand, in other words, Son of Fortune (35:18). And instead of burying Rachel under a tree of tears, Jacob "raised a monument" on her tomb, as he had done shortly before at Bethel in renewing the life-giving covenant (35:9–14, 20). Thus, Rachel's monument, toward Bethlehem, is not an isolated place. It is in the shadow of the covenant monument at Bethel.

The result of these two burials is to give two interpretations of death: it can be an occasion for tears (possibly idolatrous); or death can be an occasion to renew the memory of the life-giving covenant, the memory of the God who heard in distress and who promised life and continuity (34:3, 9–15).

Structure (Table 33.1)

PANEL ONE (CHAP. 34)

Within the Dinah story there is a balance between the introductory rape (34: 1–5) and the deathly conclusion, a conclusion which is like the rape of a whole

Table 33.1. Dinah and Bethel: From Paralysis to Pilgrimage
(chap. 34 // 35:1–20)

Rape and paralysis

Introduction: the rape (34:1–5)
  The rape itself (1–2)
  Afterward: take her for me as wife (3–4)
  Jacob's mute reaction (5)
Discussion: Hamor and Shechem propose (inter)marriage (34:6–12)
Discussion: Jacob's sons set a condition: circumcision (34:13–17)
Action: Hamor and Shechem carry out the circumcision (34: 18–24)
Conclusion: the killing (34:25–31)
  The killing by the sword (25–26)
  Afterward: the pillaging, and the taking of the wives (27–29)
  Jacob's ineffectual reaction (30–31)

Purification and pilgrimage

Introduction: God said: Go to Bethel (35:1–4)
  Worship of the God who heard Jacob's distress on the road (1–2)
  Burial of false gods under a tree (3–4)
In Bethel (35:5–8)
  Worship/altar for the God who came to Jacob in flight (5–7)
  Burial of Deborah under a tree; tears (8)
On return from Paddan-Aram: God was seen . . . (35:9–15)
  Renewal of the covenant of life [cf. Genesis 17] (9–13)
  Jacob raises a monument to the covenant (14–15)
Conclusion: going from Bethel towards Bethlehem (35:16–20)
  Amid Rachel's pains, a name that reverses fortune (16–18)
  Jacob raises a monument to Rachel, on the road (19–20)

---

people (34:25–31). Between these balancing horrors there are three brief episodes of negotiation.

PANEL TWO (35:1–20)

Panel two, concerning the journey to Bethel and beyond, may seem, at first sight, to lack unity. The impression of disconnection is due especially to the accounts of the deaths of Deborah and Rachel (35:16–20). But the deaths are integral to the text.

The two deaths blend in with other aspects of the journey. Deborah's burial, under an oak, echoes the burial of the false gods. But Rachel's death echoes the true God and covenant. Her terrible pain, on the Bethlehem road, recalls the distress of Jacob on the road. And the monument on her grave is like a variation of the monument raised to the covenant.

The variety of place names, including the reference to returning from Paddan-aram, builds a momentum, a sense of movement or pilgrimage. Jacob has rediscovered the God who helped him when he was fleeing and in distress, and so he is willing to journey onward.

Within the pilgrimage panel the elements are diverse. But they all fit; they all form a single coherent pattern. Their diversity is a sign not of confusion but of the diversity of life. One of the effects of the diversity is that a relatively short passage—twenty verses (35:1–20)—manages to suggest a fairly long process of journeying.

Comment

Panel One (Chap. 34)

[34:1–5] Introduction. Shechem's rape of Dinah: compulsion toward the woman . . . and pressure on the two fathers. The story begins with a young man's double compulsion—first to rape; and then, when he falls in love with Dinah, to marry. His soul/life-breath clings to her.

The second compulsion has a positive aspect. By offering to marry the raped woman, Shechem does what tradition required (Exod. 22:15; Deut. 22:29). The alternative for Dinah was a disgraced life in her father's house. Marriage can salvage her honor. The relationship between compulsion and respect remains unclear.

The compulsiveness or pressure is not only of the young man against a woman but also, in a more subtle way, of a young man against a father. After the rape the young man pushes his father into negotiating a marriage. And the other father, Jacob, seems even more subject to his sons: he says nothing until they come.

Thus there are two issues—young men's abuse of a woman, and, more subtly, young men's pressure on their fathers. Jacob apparently is beginning to get old. The portrait of abusing the woman is accompanied by suggestions of bullying the elderly. The woman never speaks. When Jacob speaks his words are dismissed (34:30–31).

A further dimension is the representative role of the characters. The opening, Dinah's attempt to see the women of the land ("daughter . . . to . . . daughters"), is a first intimation of the larger attempted merging of two peoples. The person who rapes Dinah is likewise representative of a people. "Shechem" is the name both of the town and of the man. His father, Hamor the Hivite, is representative in another way; he is the chieftain of the land.

[34:6–12] Discussing the marriage: the young men move in. The discussion of the marriage is introduced as a meeting between the two fathers: "Hamor, father of Shechem, went out to Jacob to speak with him." But before they have a chance to speak together, the young men muscle their way into the conversation. The result is a dialogue that is somewhat disrupted and repetitive.

Initially the listening is to be done by Jacob (34:6), but by the time the discussion begins, the angry sons overshadow Jacob (34:7). Hamor, the other father, does speak, offering intermarriage, but his first words are "Shechem, my son" and when he is finished, he in turn is overshadowed by his son. Shechem, without introduction, interjects—repetitive, brief, brash, money-no-object. His focus is clear: whatever the money, just "give me the girl/young woman."

His sudden intrusion into the discussion, instead of being a sign of another source, is a literary reflection of his character, of his crass intrusiveness, with no sense of limits.

[34:13–17] The reply—not by Jacob, but by his deceitful sons. Originally (34:5) Jacob did not speak because his sons were out; he needs them. But when they are present he still does not speak. It is the sons who reply, and though they speak to Shechem's father, Hamor, the order of the names is such that their words are addressed first to Shechem, the son: "The sons of Jacob answered Shechem and Hamor his father."

Their strategy is simple. By exploiting Shechem's desire, they demand circumcision: "Be circumcised [or] we will take our daughter." Shechem had already reduced marriage, and now, with equal crassness, they reduce the sign of the covenant (marriage and covenant were connected as early as the flood story; see comments on 6:1–9:17). Shechem uses marriage for lust, and they will use the sign of the covenant for violent revenge. Circumcision is "also the infliction of pain on what is in this case the offending organ" (Alter, 192). They make no mention of the deeper meaning of circumcision, involving God, an omission that fits both with their frame of mind and with the absence of God from this chapter. Ironically, in defending their sister, as they see it, from prostitution, Jacob's sons embark on a course of action that involves prostituting the sign of the covenant.

[34:18–24] Circumcision, for love and money—led by Shechem. The reply of Jacob's sons seems good to both the father and son, but it is the son who takes action about getting circumcised; and his action is decisive: "he carried the most weight in all his father's house."

Both father and son (Hamor and Shechem) go to address the men of the city. Priority goes to the name of Hamor, the father (34:20, 24), but given that the son has already made the decision and is the most influential person in the household, the implication again is that the father is being manipulated by the son. Shechem's motivation was delight in Dinah, but when he and his father addressed the men of the city, the pivotal motivation was adapted: not just lust or love but possessions (34:23): "Their livestock . . . will they not be ours?"

[34:25–31] Conclusion. The rape of a whole people . . . and the dismissal of a father. The revenge takes place in two waves. First, just two of the sons, full brothers of Dinah, come with their swords and they kill all the men. To some degree, this attack with the swords on the city is like the original rape, at least in its brutal surprising of the physically weak. As with Ehud (Judg. 3:16–23; Alter, 1981, 39) the sword may have a sexual overtone. The description of the dead as "pierced" (*ḥālāl;* cf. *ḥālal,* "to pierce/bore") adds further to an overtone of sexual violation.

But just as the original rape soon involved the rest of Jacob's sons, so the revenge goes into a second stage, one that involves the other sons: they capture what has been left from the first attack. The double attack—first the killing with the sword, and then the capturing—corresponds broadly with the original attack on Dinah: first she was raped, and then, as the conclusion suddenly reveals (34:26), she had been taken away.

At the end, Jacob finally speaks—a complaint based on his apparent weakness. The sons dismiss him.

Panel Two (35:1–20)

[35:1–4] Introduction. Embarking on a new journey. Suddenly, just when Jacob seems intent on staying in Succoth, God tells him to arise and go. This new command has overtones both of Yhwh's original command to Abraham (12:1) and more explicitly of Jacob's first departure from home, when he fled from Esau and traveled, through Bethel, to Laban and Rachel (27:46–29:30).

The basic command is simple: Go up to Bethel, settle, and make an altar there. The "going up" suggests a kind of pilgrimage, and the making of an altar recalls how when Abraham first journeyed near Bethel, he built an altar (12:8; 13:3–4).

But the reference to fleeing from Esau adds a reminder of mortality. This journey may be new and relatively simple, but Jacob's God now is associated with flight from Esau. In making the altar to this God he will have an awareness of being saved from death.

Apart from carrying an echo of mortality, his journey must also deal with a complex household and with all it has accumulated. Before moving there must be a cleaning out and renewal: "Remove the foreign gods . . . purify yourselves . . . change your garments" (35:2). The three elements—gods, purification, garments—suggest a renewal that is thorough, extending from mind and heart to externals. While chapter 34 portrayed defilement, this episode begins with purification (Alter, 196). Then, following the mention of God's answering, there is a reference also to giving up earrings. Earrings were often idol-related (figurines of gods or goddesses), and therefore subject to censure. Furthermore, in the context of communicating with God (God's answering), the context of hearing, they have an added dimension: giving up such earrings is effectively a call to renew hearing—hearing God.

To get rid of the gods and earrings Jacob buries them under a tree (terebinth; Septuagint, oak). The tree becomes a repository of idolatry.

[35:5–8] Traveling in the shadow of death, toward the house of God.
The journey to Bethel is shadowed by multiple reminders of death. The departure has to be protected lest the surrounding cities attack. There is another reference to fleeing from Esau. And then, most explicitly, there is a sudden death, sudden in the sense that it intrudes, unannounced, in the narrative. It is the death of Deborah, the nurse of Rebekah. Its intrusiveness in the narrative does not mean that it does not belong there. Rather it illustrates vividly one of the narrative's key concerns—the shadow of death, and the unpredictability of the way death strikes. Deborah apparently is the kind of person who is scarcely noticed till she dies.

Yet, despite the emphasis on death, the journey as a whole is positive. The only terror is the one which God uses to defend the travelers. The place to which they go, Luz, is a further reminder of God—they turn it into Bethel, "the house of God." And when Jacob builds an altar, there is indeed a reminder of fleeing from Esau, but there are also clear echoes of the fresh journeying of Abraham (12:8, 13:34).

As for Deborah, she is buried under an oak tree, which they called the Oak of Weeping (or Oak of Tears, 35:4, 8). Her tearful burial, under the tree, forms a precise literary continuity with the burial of the foreign gods under a tree (35:4, 8). The apparent suggestion, is that, while tears have their place—they are prominent in the *Odyssey*—they can also be foreign gods, idols, and it is right at a certain point to bury them, to put them away.

The overall effect at the end of this journey to Bethel is a delicate balance between the shadow of tearful death and the sense of being within God's protection, within God's house.

[35:9–15] Journeying with yet more encouragement. After the burial of Deborah, the Bethel narrative makes a fresh start: "God was seen by Jacob again, when he came from Paddan-aram, and he blessed him" (35:9). The blessing sets a new positive tone. The preceding part of the narrative (35:1–8) had been largely about basic renewal, about putting away false gods, and surviving amid shadows of death. But now, instead of mere survival, there is blessedness.

In this situation one of the signs of blessedness is naming. Jacob is called Israel, God becomes El Shaddai, and the place is called Bethel (35:10, 11, 15). None of these names is new; the newness, such as it is, seems to be in Jacob, at some level of awareness. A related ethos occurs in the renewal of the covenant with Abraham (Gen. 17), when God is El Shaddai, and there are new names for Abram and Sarai (17:1, 5, 15). For Jacob, too, as with Abraham (17:4–6), there is a renewal of the promise (35:11): "Be fruitful and multiply. A nation, and an assembly of nations shall come from you. . . ." In fact, the promises to Abraham and Isaac of progeny and land are explicitly recalled (35:12). Having finished speaking, "God went up from him" (35:13)—as in chapter 17 (17:22).

In fact, Jacob's two scenes of name-change, the night wrestling and the appearance of El Shaddai (32:22–31; 35:11–13), correspond partly to Abraham's two scenes of covenant-making—the night-related scene, and the appearance of El Shaddai (chaps. 15 and 17). The emergence of "Israel" echoes the emergence of the covenant.

Then Jacob did what he once had done when, on his way to marry, he was young and filled with a dream. He set up a monument or pillar and poured oil on it; and he called the place Bethel (35:14–15; cf. 28:18–19). Curiously, however, now that he is older, he also pours out a libation or drink-offering. More is poured out, therefore, yet at some level, the dream still continues.

[35:16–20] Conclusion. **Journeying on amid death and blessedness: Rachel dies and Benjamin is born.** In the conclusion, as the journey goes on, the elements of the preceding episodes come together in sharper form. In particular, the shadow of death now strikes as never before—in the death of Rachel. And blessing, instead of being merely a promise, turns into a surprising new reality—a new child, Benjamin.

The sadness is highlighted not only in Rachel's dying but in the name she first gives to the child—Ben-oni, "Son of My Sorrow." But Jacob, however great his own sorrow must have been, has learned enough about God's protection on the road and about God's promise of blessedness to give the child a positive name—Ben-jamin, "Son-of-the-Right-Hand," or "Son of [Good] Fortune."

Jacob's understanding therefore even of this death, death of the beloved, has a positive aspect. Rachel's burial is so placed in the narrative that it echoes that of Deborah; but it also contrasts with it. The mood here is not that of tears (and perhaps of false gods), but of building a monument, something Jacob had done when he was young and hopeful.

---

34   Genealogies: Jacob Declines and Esau Prospers (35:21–37:1)

The Shrunken Genealogy of Jacob (35:21–29)
The Expansive Genealogy of Esau (Chap. 36)

Introductory Aspects

The Basic Story Line

Jacob may have learned to cope with the raping of Dinah and its attendant violence, but now his world receives new blows. His eldest son commits incest. And his father dies.

Suddenly he seems very small. The first part of the story contains a list of his twelve sons—surely a source of great pride—yet the narrative is extremely short and it is sandwiched between accounts of the incest and death.

The death itself has a positive quality, a reminder of Isaac's full years, but at some level, such a death is a reminder of mortality, of limitation. The only person who really blossoms in this story is his old rival Esau. Esau attends the burial and is listed before Jacob. Then, through a long genealogy, the world of Esau seems to expand into a glorious future. The list of Jacob's sons is not only surrounded by incest and death; it is overshadowed by a list that is far greater.

Jacob seems to be going nowhere.

Literary Form and Complementarity

Each panel is a kind of genealogy, and each suggests something about the life of its subject. The first, the short one about Jacob (35:21–29), indicates that at this time Jacob's life seems diminished. In some way, he is fading. The second genealogy (36:1–37:1), whatever its full agenda (see Hoekveld-Meijer, 1996), has an immediate impact: its long text shows Esau as flourishing.

The complementarity is antithetical, like opposite sides of the same coin. The picture of Esau as flourishing sharpens the sense of Jacob as fading. He has grown small, left behind by his strong brother.

Relationship to Preceding Genealogies

Insofar as the two panels constitute a pairing of genealogies, there is a precedent for them in the paired genealogies of Cain (4:17–26) and Adam (chap. 5).

Concerning the specific form of the Jacob genealogy, a partial precedent occurs in the genealogy of Abraham (25:1–18), a text which consists essentially of two elements—descendants and death. In the Abraham genealogy both these elements are found twice, first for Abraham himself (25:1–11) and then for his son Ishmael (25:12–18). In the Jacob genealogy, however, they occur only once, and briefly—first the descendants (35:23–26), then the death (of Isaac, 35:27–29).

Unlike the Abraham text, the Jacob genealogy has a third element—the opening reference to the incest of Reuben, Jacob's first-born (35:21–22). It is appropriate that a first-born son and his sexual union with a woman should be at the beginning of a genealogy, but when the union is incestuous it casts a shadow over the genealogy. So it is here. Reuben, instead of inaugurating the genealogy with grace and strength, brings shame. This apparently is part of the reason that the genealogy as a whole is shrunken.

Concerning the specific form of the Esau genealogy (36:1–37:1), aspects of a precedent occur in the genealogy of Shem (11:10–32). The most obvious connection is the double use of "These are the generations of . . ." (11:10, 27; 36:1, 9). Furthermore, both the Shem and Esau genealogies change as they advance, but in opposite ways. The Shem genealogy shrinks (numbers fall; life

Table 34.1. Contrasting Genealogies (35:21–29 // 36:1–37:1)

The shrunken genealogy of Jacob

Jacob's eldest son, Reuben, commits incest (35:21–22)
Jacob's twelve sons (35:23–26)
Jacob's father, Isaac, dies (35:27–29)

The expansive genealogy of Esau

Introduction: Esau's sons; Esau leaves Canaan (36:1–8)
Esau's sons . . . and the chieftains (36:9–19)
Seir's sons . . . and the kings (36:20–39)
Conclusion: Esau's chieftains; Jacob stays in Canaan (36:40–37:1)

becomes fragile, barren); the Esau genealogy expands (concluding with kings, 36:31–39).

Structure (Table 34.1)

PANEL ONE (35:21–29)

The structure of the Jacob genealogy is defective. It has three parts but no introduction or conclusion.

PANEL TWO (36:1–37:1)

In panel two, however, the account of Esau, is long and full. Apart from a twofold introduction and conclusion (36:1–8; 36:40–37:1), there are two large central parts. The mention of "Canaan . . . Jacob" in the second part of the introduction (36:6–8) is balanced by the mention of "Jacob . . . Canaan" in the second part of the conclusion (37:1).

Within the Esau genealogy the rank intensifies. There is a progression from sons to chieftains (compare the introduction and conclusion; and see the first central part, 36:9–19). And, within the two central sections there is a further progression—from chieftains to kings.

Comment

Panel One (35:21–29)

[35:21–22] **Reuben: incest in the chosen family.** Jacob's family has largely grown up, but Jacob himself, instead of being settled, is in transition. He is pictured as moving on, in a tent, and as going to some obscure place—Migdal Eder ("tower of the flock"), location unknown (but perhaps near Jerusalem; Fretheim, 585).

While he is there, his eldest son Reuben sleeps with Bilhah, mother of two of his children. This action, taking over one of the father's women, may have included an assertion of power, a bid for leadership (cf. 2 Sam. 16:20–22).

"And Jacob heard" about the incest, but not another word is said. With consummate artistry the narrative evokes the dread reality of incest, a whispered secret about which, so often, nothing is said.

The silence does not mean that the incest has no effect on Jacob. He will recall it, and its sorrow, on his death-bed (49:3–4). Coming so soon after his daughter's rape and his sons' violence (chap. 34), its sorrow is compounded.

[35:23–29] **Descendants (twelve sons) and the father's death.** The listing of Jacob's twelve sons could have been an occasion for colorful details and literary flourishes. These twelve, after all, are nothing less than the founders of the twelve tribes of Israel! But the first son is Reuben, and, partly for that reason, the list is minimal and matter-of-fact.

Jacob's arrival home is also curiously subdued. His mother Rebekah is not mentioned and though he comes to his father, the account moves quickly to his father's death. The sense of the father's death is positive—180 years, old and full of days, and with faint geographical reminders (Mamre, Kiriath-Arba, Hebron) of the haunting burial-place of Sarah (35:27; cf. 23:2).

In the Abraham genealogy (25:1–18) the primary death that was recounted was the ideal death of Abraham himself, and the result for Isaac was blessing (25:11). Here Jacob is not the one who dies. He is an observer, and there is no mention of a blessing.

"They buried him, Esau and Jacob his sons." The narrative may be about Jacob, but Esau has come back. His sudden appearance at the burial is appropriate and even reassuring. But again, as at birth, he is first. The scene is set for the next genealogy.

Panel Two (36:1–37:1)

[36:1–37:1] **The genealogy of the older brother.** At first the introduction seems negative; it gives a reminder of Esau's controversial marriage to Canaanite women (36:1–5). But then, when there is a further case where excessive riches cause problems (cf. 13:5–9; 26:15–22), it is Esau not Jacob who, echoing the generous precedent of Abraham and Isaac, removes himself, and, for that reason, goes away to Mount Seir, in Edom (36:6–8).

The two main parts of the genealogy (36:9–19, and 36:20–36) form a spiraling crescendo. First, the listing of sons (36:9–14) gives way to the listing of chieftains (36:15–19). Then, a more elaborate listing of children and chieftains (36:20–30) gives way to a climactic list of kings, kings who reigned before there was any king in Israel (36:31–39). The second list of children (36:20–30), apart from being more elaborate, is enlivened further by the presence of a sister and daughter, and by a startling reference (36:24) to the discovery—while pasturing donkeys—of water in the wilderness. (The word for water is obscure. Westermann, II, 560, opts for "hot springs," but Speiser, 279–280, invoking transposed letters, makes a better case for "water.")

Many of the names are unknown or at odds with other data. Historically the list is not plausible. The list of kings "is strongly reminiscent . . . of king lists . . . from Sumer, Babylon, and Assyria. . . . The list conveys the impression of . . . consecutive monarchs. . . . This conclusion raises serious problems. . . . [Historically] there is not the slightest suggestion of a settled kingdom of Edom in this period" (Sarna, 409).

But artistically the list has its purpose. It has the effect of portraying Esau's line in a way that is positive, even regal.

Following on the flourish of springs and kings, the conclusion is brief (36: 40–37:1)—first a summary glance back to Edom's chieftains (36:40–43), and then a forward glance, to Jacob, still in Canaan (37:1). Thus the scene is set for the next and major development.

PART SEVEN

THE STORY OF JOSEPH

Genesis 37:2–50:26

The story of Joseph, recounted in seven diptych scenes, overlaps with the later part of the Jacob drama. Joseph's survival is like a protective mantle cast over Jacob's old age.

Old age is not easy, at least not for Jacob. The first scene leaves him in sackcloth, mourning the loss of Joseph (37:1–chap. 38), and even though Joseph is still alive in Egypt (scene two, chaps. 39–40), the subsequent account shows Jacob as sunk even lower, white-haired, mourning further loss (chaps. 41–42).

Yet all the while the tide has been slowly turning. When Joseph's brothers return to Egypt they finally reach a stage where they are ready to turn away fully from their former crime against him (chaps. 43–44). As a result Joseph is revealed, he embraced his brothers, and, against all apparent odds, the aged Jacob embarks on a remarkable journey into the arms of his beloved son (45:1–47:11). Even when famine and death come close there is life-saving action and blessing (47:12–chap. 48). And in the last scene of all, when Jacob dies and goes to burial, the sense of blessing is even greater (chaps. 49–50).

Prophecy and Conversion (37:2–Chap. 38)

Joseph, the Prophetic Dreamer, Is Sold (37:2–36)
Judah's Whoring and Conversion (Chap. 38)

Introductory Aspects

The Basic Story Line

Much of the Joseph narrative is about two sons—a young dreamy shepherd and an older tougher sheepshearer. The dreamy shepherd was so favored by his old father that his brothers thought of killing him, but the tough-minded sheepshearer had a more profitable idea—selling him as a slave. And, having done that, the sheepshearer, Judah, turned aside and embarked on his own self-centered career. Many years later, with their old father's fate hanging in the balance, the two sons met in a foreign land and went back in memory to the moment of selling. After a further lapse of many years, the dying old man singled out the two of them for special blessing.

The story begins (chap. 37) with the selling of the young shepherd. The complex figure of Joseph has several levels—pampered, prophetic, providential—but the only thing his brothers see is pampering and pretentiousness and so, despite the pain to their father, they eliminate him, and even make a profit out of it. The prophetic dreamer is stilled.

It is then that Judah, the one who thought of selling him, embarks on a career in which there is no shadow of dream or prophecy (chap. 38). He marries and deals in marriage, moving the pieces as he likes, including his daughter-in-law, Tamar. But Tamar rattled his cage, and the experience was sufficiently disturbing to make him reconsider his life.

Aspects of the Larger Joseph Story

The Joseph story is not a special pearl, different from the rest of Genesis. Rather it is of a piece with the book as a whole. It is Genesis breaking into full bloom, a blossoming that builds on all that precedes. In particular, it is "the second half of the Jacob story" (Wenham, II, xxvi). It is also part of the unity whereby Genesis moves gradually from being episodic to being clearly sequential (see Introduction, Chapter 2, "Spiraling Structures").

The relationship of the Joseph story to history is not essentially different from that of the rest of Genesis. The Joseph narrative shows knowledge of Egyptian life and customs, but "such evidence . . . could also be found in a work of fiction" (Murphy, 2:60), and, while the essential account is historically possible—world history, including that of Egypt, often tells of foreigners doing well (cf. de Vaux, 1978, 298; Wenham, II, xxv; note the story of Sinuhe)—the Joseph narrative is generally described not as history but as a story (Murphy, 2:60). Some commentators try to be more specific, identifying the Joseph story as a novella/short story (Gunkel, 397; von Rad, 433; Humphreys, 1988), or didactic tale (de Vaux, 1978, 295), but such categories, even if partly true, do not obscure the more basic truth that the Joseph story is fully integrated into the larger unity of Genesis.

The Joseph story breaks the pattern of the history of Abraham, Isaac, and Jacob. Along with others features, it shows that Genesis is governed primarily not by the portrayal of the specific events of history but by the portrayal of the more general pattern of human life (see Introduction, Chapter 11). The way the Joseph story breaks patterns fits with a further feature—its role as a model of reconciliation (Fischer, 2001). Reconciliation means breaking patterns. (In discussing the deluge, it was indicated that reconciliation/forgiveness means breaking human calculations.)

Furthermore, the Joseph story indicates that history is not just history; it contains a whole other dimension—God's providence. The Joseph story is also the story of God: "God, not human heroes, provides the unity in the story" (Fretheim, 594). God never appears to Joseph, but God is with him, and Joseph's role is often close to the role of God. As God once created the earth, so Joseph now has a role in caring for God's creation, for the whole earth.

Part of that providence involves the land. The land of Egypt, which is acquired by Joseph and the best of which is granted to Jacob and his family (45:18–20; 47:11, 18–20), has a deep ambiguity. On the one hand, it has a great richness, and, coming at the end of the book, is almost like a paradise regained. (In Lot's view of things, Egypt is on a par with the pre-catastrophe Jordan valley and with the Garden of Yhwh, 13:10.) On the other hand—just as the Garden and pre-catastrophe Jordan were lost through sin (2:25–4:16; 18:1–19:29)—so the land of Egypt would turn out to be a trying place. The land of promise would prove to be elsewhere.

Within that providence—within the Joseph story—is the story of Judah. Among Joseph's brothers, Judah emerges clearly (37:26–27; chap. 38; 43:8–10; 44:14–34; 46:28; 49:8–12). The story involving Judah and Tamar (chap. 38), far from being a digression, is essentially a capsule form of the story of the conversion of Judah, and the development of that conversion (43:3–10; 44:14–34) eventually sees Judah being effectively appointed as leader (49:8–12). Thus the Joseph story opens the way for the future history of Judah.

Literary Form

As the Joseph story begins, Genesis's pattern of increasing complexity reaches a new level. The two opening episodes—the selling of Joseph (37:2–36) and the whoring of Judah (chap. 38)—involve a synthesizing of diverse literary types and an echoing of several earlier chapters.

The first panel, the selling of Joseph (37:2–36), is a variation on the conventional account of a prophetic vision or call. The call here is that of Joseph.

Normally prophetic visions begin with a dramatic encounter by God, and then there are usually certain set features—introductory word, commission, objection, reassurance, and sign (Habel, 1975; cf. Exod. 3:1–4:17, Isaiah 6, Jeremiah 1, Ezek. 1:1–3:21).

For this call of Joseph, however, there is no dramatic appearance by God. In fact, God is not mentioned (37:2–36), even though Joseph will later say that God was at work in sending him to Egypt (45:8).

Apparently what has happened is that the convention of the prophetic call has been adapted to the language of wisdom, language which was particularly strong in Egypt. God is at work, but the way of speaking of God's activity is different; God is visualized as working through day-to-day people and events.

Once allowance is made for such adaptations the main elements of the prophetic call begin to emerge:

The initial sense of a God-related message: the dreams. Genesis's other references to dreams (those of Jacob, the prisoners, and Pharaoh [28:10–22; 40:8; 41:25–32]) all involve a sense of God's presence or of God speaking. Dreams indicated revelation (Wenham, II, 352, 359). "The dreams anticipate reality" (Murphy, 2:61).

Commission: Jacob sends Joseph to his brothers to shepherd the flock, a flock otherwise ill-treated (37:2–3, 12–13). Here, as in the call of Moses (Exod. 2:23–4:17), the prophetic call is associated with looking after sheep. Joseph's "Here I am" is reminiscent of Isaiah when called (37:13; Isa. 6:9).

Sign: the concluding sign is the blood-stained coat (misunderstood by Jacob). In prophetic calls the sign is sometimes ominous—a boiling pot in Jeremiah (1:13–16), a felled tree in Isaiah (6:11–13). The coat itself is enigmatic but may well be a variation on the general idea of a prophetic mantle (cf. 1 Kings 19:19; 2 Kings 2:8; "many-colored" is based on the Greek translation, not on the Hebrew). As prophetic it would indeed be his dreamcoat—his coat of prophetic dreams.

Genesis does not have the usual pattern of objection and reassurance, but perhaps this feature is partly reflected in practical action: as Joseph sets out he wanders until an unknown man tells him where to go (37:15–17). Objection and reassurance seem to be replaced by confusion and redirection.

The phenomenon of doubling within the Joseph story (e.g., pairs of dreams, of journeys) should probably be taken in conjunction with the binary divisions in the Jacob story (Alter, 178, 184, 210) and in the context of Genesis's larger phenomenon of diptychs (see Introduction, Chapters 2–3).

The second panel—Judah and Tamar—is complex. In the framework (38:1–11, 24–30) there are elements of a genealogy (Westermann, III, 49), but the ge-

nealogy turns into a birth story (esp. 38:27–30). At the center, the "businesslike
. . . dialogue" (Alter, 1981, 8) between the disguised Tamar and Judah (38:15–18)
contains aspects of a dialogue contract (as in Abraham's buying of the field, chap.
23, and Jacob's negotiating with Laban concerning the flocks, 30:25–36).

The primary literary type, however, for the episode of Judah and Tamar is
that of a conversion story. Part of the process of conversion involves recognition—Judah explicitly recognizes the items that identify him (38:25–26)—and
so this episode may also be described as a recognition story, akin to Homeric
recognition stories (e.g., *Odyssey* 19:250, 390). Yet, conversion, with its sense
of inner change, is more far-reaching than recognition, and the general idea of
conversion is more biblical than Greek. Conversion is central to the prophets.
In the Gospels, conversion stories are particularly explicit (e.g., the prodigal
son, Luke 15:11–32). But long before the Gospels, the Old Testament depicts
conversion, and the story of Judah (Genesis 38) is one example.

An intimation of Judah's conversion occurs in the selling of Joseph: instead
of killing Joseph—something initially accepted by all (37:18–20)—Judah suggests merely selling him (37:26–27). Judah's motivation in saving Joseph should
not be overestimated. Selling is more profitable.

In chapter 38, however, the picture of sinfulness, of deviation, is drawn at
far greater length. Judah's first move is indicative: "Judah turned aside from
his brothers" (38:1), a precise contrast to the first thing said of Joseph: "Joseph
was shepherding the flock with his brothers" (37:2). Nor does Judah shepherd
any flock. As the story goes on it emerges that his interest in sheep is not in
caring for them but in shearing them (38:12).

The more pervasive contrast, however, concerns Judah's role as a father.
Unlike the Jacob-Joseph ethos of love and solidarity for the whole family, Judah
goes his own deviant way. He turns aside to link up with some Adullamite
man; then he marries a Canaanite woman. In family matters he becomes increasingly irresponsible (38:1–5), especially concerning Tamar (38:6–12). Finally, in an event that crystallizes his behavior, he loses his identifying signs
for the sake of a brief moment with a whore (38:15–23). As a final mark of
moral confusion and inner unawareness, he maintains a powerful and brutal
veneer of moral indignation ("Bring her out and burn her," 38:24).

When he recognizes his identifying signs there comes the moment of truth—
his explicit admission that the whore is more just than himself, and an indication
that he did not resort to her any more (38:24–26). The added information—that
he did not resort to her any more—may seem redundant but it emphasizes the
broader idea that Judah's whoring is over. The result, in the birth of the twins, is
an exuberant sense of life—of breakthrough and dawn (38:27–30).

Complementarity of the Two Panels

The essence of the two episodes is straightforward. Joseph the dreamer is a
prophetic figure; "the narrator saw these dreams as prophetic" (Wenham, II,

359); and the rejection of Joseph is ultimately a rejection of prophecy—a sinful rejection of prophetic vision (37:2–36). "One is reminded of the various responses to the visions of the prophets" (Fretheim, 601).

The second episode (chap. 38) takes Judah, one of the characters highlighted in the rejection of Joseph, and focuses on him more closely, first on his sinfulness, especially his whoring with the disguised Tamar, then on his conversion.

The overall effect of the diptych—the two episodes—is to place the focus on Judah and on Judah's conversion. As the Joseph story progresses (43:8–10; and especially 44:14–34), Judah's conversion will become pivotal to the larger account of recognition and reconciliation. Thus the way is prepared for one of the Joseph story's key scenes—the death-bed blessing, which establishes Judah as leader among the sons of Jacob (49:8–12).

Insofar as Genesis is a prologue to the history of the land of Judah and its capital, the diptych of Judah's sinfulness and conversion is central. In these two episodes (chaps. 37–38) the narrative expresses graphically much of what the great prophets say both about the sinfulness of Judah, a sinfulness often described as whoring, and about the call to conversion.

Sinfulness notwithstanding, the final impact of the two-part scene is positive. The first panel, despite its treachery and Jacob's mourning over Joseph, ends with Joseph arriving, still alive, in a prestigious place (37:36). And the second, despite all its seediness, ends with a birth scene full of vitality (38:27–30).

The complementarity between the two panels, especially between the two climactic moments of recognition, involves several details (Alter,1981, 10; Hamilton II, 431).

Relationship to Preceding Chapters

There is a broad relationship with the beginning of the Abraham story (chaps. 12–13). Against a background of ebbing life (chap. 11), Abraham set off for a new land, a land which God would make him see. Likewise here, as Jacob leaves behind a sense of the limitedness of his life (35:21–chap. 36), and as he enters old age, the story of Joseph constitutes a new land as it were, a new space in which to live.

There are some other echoes of preceding chapters. The birth of the twins, for instance, with its sense of reversal (38:27–30), contains aspects of the birth and development of Esau and Jacob (25:24–34). Tamar's energetic action in disguising her identity so as to secure posterity for Judah (38:15–19) has echoes of Rebekah's energetic action in disguising Jacob's identity so as to secure the final blessing for him (27:14–27; Alter, 1981, 8).

Leading Elements

At the level of linear narrative—of historiography—the Judah-Tamar episode interrupts the story of Joseph. At that level it scarcely belongs.

But it is not an interpolation. This account of Judah among the Canaanites is somewhat similar in function to the story of Isaac among the Philistines (much of chap. 26; Wenham, 363), and as such it forms an early interlude in the developing story.

Furthermore, once the overall Joseph account is seen not just as a colorful story but as a particular form of prophetic narrative, the inclusion of the Judah story is altogether appropriate. Judah's response to prophetic Joseph is a narrative portrayal of the later Judah's conduct in the time of the prophets. This story is "the crown of the book of Genesis and Tamar one of the most admirable women" (Jacob, 261). In insisting on the law of levirate, Tamar is more aware than Judah of the significance of Judah's own family: "the hero of the following story is Joseph, but salvation will come from Judah (ibid., 262–263).

The Joseph story, of course, has a much broader interest than the history of Judah—its vision ranges across much of human life—but the Judah dimension is important.

Structure (Table 35.1)

PANEL ONE (37:2–36)

The introduction (37:2–11) and conclusion (37:31–36) are primarily two-part, but one of these parts is double: there is a double picture of dreaming (37:5–11) and a double picture of mourning (37:31–35).

Concerning the panel's two main parts (37:12–22 and 37:23–30), the division between them is governed largely by the distinction between Joseph's being sent, and his being abused. This division is marked by references to movement, especially the indication of the moment of Joseph's arrival (37:23, "Joseph came . . .").

PANEL TWO (CHAP. 38)

Here there are three main parts; the divisions are signaled largely by designations of time (see the beginning of 38:1, 6, 12, 24, 27). In the second dividing point ("Judah took a wife for Er his first-born," 38:6) the passage of time is merely implied—the passage of Er from birth to the age of marriage.

The most perplexing structural feature in chapter 38 is the size of the second main part, Tamar's bold action in securing posterity for Judah (38:12–23). As well as being out of proportion with the two other main parts, it is itself three-fold.

To some degree this arresting threefold expansion is understandable: by dramatizing Judah's crucial failure to recognize someone who has been wronged, it prepares for the later encounters with the unrecognized Joseph. In particular, its threefold pattern-breaking structure prepares for later threefold pattern-breaking structures—the recognition-inducing speech of Judah (44:18–34), and

Table 35.1. Joseph and Judah: Prophecy and Conversion
(37:2–36 // chap. 38)

Prophecy spurned: the selling of Joseph

Introduction: Joseph, loved and dreaming (37:2–11)
    Joseph, the shepherd with a coat, loved and resented (2–4)
    The dream of the sheaves (5–8)
    The dream of the sun, moon and stars (9–11)
The sending of Joseph to his brothers; they plot (37:12–22)
    Jacob sends Joseph to shepherd the flock (12–14)
    A man redirects Joseph (15–17)
    The brothers: Kill the dreamer; Reuben's protest (18–22)
Joseph abused: stripped, put in a pit, and sold (37:23–30)
    The brothers throw Joseph into the pit (23–25a)
    The brothers see the Ishmaelites; Judah: sell him (25b–27)
    The Midianites intervene; Reuben's confusion (28–30)
Conclusion: Joseph, lost and mourned (37:31–36)
    Mourning: Jacob recognizes Joseph's coat and mourns (31–34)
    Mourning intensified: Jacob refuses to be comforted (35)
    Joseph, sold in Egypt (36)

Tamar: Judah's whoring and conversion

Introduction: Judah leaves his brothers and turns aside (38:1–5)
Judah neglects Tamar and responsibility (38:6–11)
Tamar acts to induce responsibility and recognition (38:12–23)
    Tamar disguises herself to encounter Judah (12–14)
    Judah encounters Tamar, giving her his seal (15–19)
    Subsequent failure to locate the woman (20–23)
Judah recognizes and acknowledges his lack of justice (38:24–26)
Conclusion: aftermath; birth and vitality (38:27–30)

---

then Joseph's recognition speech (45:4–16). Both here and in chapters 44–45, the breaking of the pattern is a literary way of expressing what the narrative is about—breaking set expectations.

Genesis 38 may also be divided in a chiastic-related way, with an emphasis on Judah as descending and ascending (Lambe, 1998).

Comment

Panel One (37:2–36)

[37:2–11] **Joseph, the young shepherd, sees (in dreams).** Like Moses and David, Joseph is introduced as a shepherd. The wording is strained so as to tie this shepherding with his brothers: "Joseph . . . was shepherding with his brothers the flock" (37:2a). Already there is an intimation that his brothers are identified with the flock, and that he will shepherd them. Ultimately shepherding is focused on human beings.

Shepherds, however, are not always good. After the picture of Joseph as shepherding with his brothers there is a contrast: Joseph sends a negative report about some of his brothers (37:2b). The implication is that some of the shepherds are bad.

This evil is compounded by the brothers' attitude toward Joseph. When they see that he is especially loved—the son of Jacob's old age, clad in the ample coat—they respond with resentment. The brothers then are in the shadow of Cain and Abel.

To some degree the roots of the Cain-Abel type of relationship are clearer here than in the original Cain and Abel story. What Joseph has above all is love, that of his father, a love that is gratuitous, as was God's regard for the offering of Abel (4:4). And it is the deprivation of this love, or at least the sense of being thus deprived, which then turns into hatred.

Joseph is "a boy" (*na'ar*), meaning both a youth and an apprentice shepherd. Jacob's love for Joseph contrasts with Abraham's love for Isaac, also described as a (*na'ar*) (22:5). Abraham's love was serene, clear. The atmosphere surrounding the Jacob-Joseph relationship, however, is not only loving. It is also confused, in some way disordered. Benjamin, rather than Joseph, had the claim to being the son of Joseph's old age; and Jacob's response to the loss of Joseph is not just sadness but also a clinging to sadness.

The brothers' hatred is compounded by the dreams that suggest that he will in some way rule over his family (37:5–10). The first dream is down-to-earth, set in the fields. The second, however, moves attention upward, toward the sun, moon, and (eleven) stars. At the end of the chapter, in the counterbalancing images, not of dreaming but of mourning (37:31–35), the movement is downward, toward Sheol.

In interpreting the image of the sun, moon, and eleven stars, Jacob says "I and your mother and your brothers," apparently assuming that "Rachel is still alive" (Alter, 211). But Rachel had died on the road (35:19). Yet the sun-moon-stars image has its purposes. By alluding to the dead Rachel as if she were still alive, the narrative prepares for the explicit "still alive" motif of the Joseph story (43:7, 27–28; 45:3, 25, 28; 46:30), a motif linked to Genesis's larger engagement with the question of death. Furthermore, the sun-moon-stars image has another aspect: it evokes nature. "In Egypt, Joseph, to a large extent, was able to rule over the famine; and if he rules over famine, he rules over nature, and the sun and the moon do bow down to him" (Sacks, 308). This emphasis on nature accords with the larger balance between the Joseph story and Genesis 1–11, especially the creation texts.

Given Joseph's prophet-like role, as shepherd and dreamer, the special coat has a double function. On the one hand, it is a sign of being pampered; apparently the coat is ornamented, "ancient *haute couture*" (Alter, 209; cf. Speiser, 289–290). On the other hand, it seems to be a variation on the idea of the prophetic mantle or cloak such as Elijah bestowed on Elisha (1 Kings 19:19; 2 Kings 2:8, 14).

Joseph's dreams, about his brothers, his people, are a form of seeing, a variation on the experience of Abraham ("Go . . . to the land that I will make you see . . . and I will make you a great nation," 12:1–2). The dreams also echo Jacob, whose dream leads into watering the sheep and generating his twelve sons (28:10–30:24). Later, the shepherding of Moses becomes the occasion for his vision about the people (Exod. 3:1–7). The dreams then are a form of revelation; they are like a word; "His father kept the word in mind" (37:11). But the dreams also have a narrow aspect; they may express "the hidden desires and self-perception of the dreamer" (Alter, 209).

Overall then Joseph contains a deep tension. He is the favorite child, a pampered tattletale who dreams grandiosely and interprets naively. But he is also the keen apprentice shepherd, bearing the prophetic cloak and envisioning the future.

As well as suggesting a pampered boy and a shepherd prophet, the figure of Joseph evokes yet a third level, that of God. In general, God is rarely mentioned in the Joseph narrative, but God is present in other ways including, partly, in the figure of Joseph. This God-related aspect of Joseph helps explain why the second dream—the sun, moon, and stars bowing before Joseph—"teeters on the brink of blasphemy" (Alter, 211). The reason it is not blasphemous is that ultimately the bowing is before God.

[37:12–14] **The sending of Joseph.** Jacob's sending of Joseph to his brothers, to shepherd the flock, is like the sending of a prophet. But the world of this prophetic mission is enigmatic, at least geographically. On the one hand, the geography is slightly ominous. Shechem, Joseph's destination, "has already been linked with disasters" (Alter, 211). When Abram was making a fresh start, he seemed to avoid Shechem (see comment on 13: 2–4). On the other hand, there is a kind of freedom in dealing with geography. Joseph seems undaunted by the long distance: he has to travel all the way from Hebron up to Shechem. And, in a further overturning of the difficulties of geography, Hebron, an elevated area, is described as "a valley" (38:14). The attitude to geography seem akin to that of Isaiah 40, where hills are laid low (Isa. 40:4).

[37:15–22] **Wandering toward murderous brothers.** The picture of Joseph wandering toward his murderous brothers (37:15–17) has multiple echoes of Cain's wandering, following the murder of his brother (4:1–16, esp. 4:8–14). The precise Hebrew verb for "wander" varies from one text to another yet the scenes have many connections, including:

favoritism for one brother leads to resentment, to(ward) murder;

the murderous scene involves going into a field;

asking questions about the whereabouts of (a) brother(s);

wandering, and finding.

However, the Joseph story echoes the Cain scene not to repeat it but to reverse it. Joseph, instead of wandering away from his brothers goes toward them, and eventually he will lead them in a direction that is the very opposite of murder, toward wholehearted reconciliation.

To some degree Joseph himself is lost; he has his own pampered problems. Yet the ones who seem even more lost are his brothers—he finally locates them in Dothan, an extra twenty miles to the north—and his wandering search for them seems to be a reflection of how lost they are. They are now in the situation Cain was in after the murder. They have not only moved farther away but have turned their hatred toward murder (37:20). And ironically they associate their intended murder with an animal: "Let us kill him and throw him in one of the pits, and we shall say a harmful animal has eaten him. . . ." For Cain, the urge to murder was like a crouching beast (4:7). The brothers' intention is particularly callous: not only to kill Joseph but to leave his body exposed in a pit. Lack of burial was regarded as a horror.

Suddenly, the eldest, Reuben, tries to exercise his leadership. Formerly known only for finding aphrodisiacs (mandrakes) and for incest (30:14; 35:21–22), he now proposes that, rather than strike Joseph and shed blood, they simply throw Joseph into "this pit . . . in the wilderness." But Reuben's leadership seems to have a shadow of weakness. He has to repeat his suggestion in varied form, and a lapse occurs before there is any indication that his brothers respond to him (37:21–22).

[37:23–30] The abusing of the dream. Two leaders and two agencies. Only when Joseph has arrived is it indicated that the brothers will follow Reuben's suggestion. They strip Joseph of the coat, throw him in the pit, and cold-bloodedly sit down to eat. But when Judah makes a proposal to sell Joseph to the passing Ishmaelites, a proposal which in various ways ignores that of Reuben, his brothers' response is noted immediately: "his brothers heard him" (37: 27). The resulting narrative may look repetitious and confused, but as an artistic portrayal of two leaderships, that of the first-born and that of Judah, it is clear. As a leader, Reuben is faltering and ineffectual. The man of destiny is Judah. When he speaks, he can effectively ignore Reuben, and his brothers listen.

When the Ishmaelites and Midianites enter their roles overlap, yet in the context of the larger story, this overlapping makes sense. Together they indicate that, as Joseph will later explain (45:8), the selling of Joseph involved two agencies—one human, the other divine (see Introduction, Chapter 1).

The Ishmaelites are very human—ordinary and observable. The reference to them is anachronistic. Ishmael was too close and recent a character to be able to speak of Ishmaelites as though they were some distant group; "the only 'Ishmaelites' would be their first cousins" (Alter, 213). This closeness of the Ishmaelites corresponds to the depiction of them as particularly visible and calculable: they are seen as they approach and their journey is explained in detail. They are traveling from Gilead to Egypt, camels laden with gum, balm, and myrrh.

The Midianites, on the other hand, seem to come from nowhere and for no specific purpose. All that is known of them is the minimum required to bring Joseph to Egypt: they buy and sell. Like the divine intervention, "as on the day of Midian" (Isa. 9:4), they appear as a bolt from the blue.

As a result of the Midianites' intervention Judah's leadership is acknowledged, and there is an indication, perplexing but real, that, in Joseph's fate, there is a further unexplained hand. Much later Joseph will explain: "It was not you who sent me here, but God" (45:8). Judah's role, therefore, however important, is not ultimate. The ambiguity surrounding the roles of the Ishmaelites and the Midianites reflects the ambiguity of the forces at work in Joseph's fate. The Ishmaelites indicate that, at one level, the process is quite earthbound and understandable. The Midianites, however, indicate a presence that is unexplained.

As for Reuben, his leadership goes nowhere (37:29–30). He is pictured as coming back to the pit, tearing his clothes because Joseph is not there, and then lamenting helplessly before his brothers: "And I, where shall I go?" As part of a linear sequence of events, this picture is confusing. But as art, as a portrayal of Reuben's bankrupt leadership, it is clear and strong.

As for Judah, he will need further attention (chap. 38).

[37:31–36] Conclusion. **The recognition that leads to mourning.** Given the brothers' mood, it cannot have been a problem for them to wantonly kill one of the herd, a kid goat. The kid's blood on the long coat presented Jacob with a parent's nightmare: "Recognize, please, if it is your son's robe or not." In former days Jacob had seemed masterful in such situations. He had once used clothing and the killing of two kids to deceive his old father (27:8–23). He had also been able apparently to make a fine piece of clothing (37:3). And he seemed to know everything about goats; he had used them in a form of genetic engineering (30:31–43).

Jacob is shattered. His exclamations are of "great psychological truth and shocking effect. The first is not even a complete sentence as if language failed him. He could only repeat the words of the others. The next shows his mind at work and draws the worst conclusion. They are exactly the words of the sons. . . . With the third exclamation the unhappy man collapsed . . ." (Jacob, 256).

Jacob's tearing of his clothes is like a sign of his world coming apart. The sackcloth on his loins is like the quenching of his fire. And he mourns "many days," an unspecified time that has no clear limit.

The mourning is in two intensifying stages: first when he mourns (37:31–34); then when he refuses to be comforted (37:35). The impetus is downward, toward Sheol, the shadowy place of the dead. And the final picture is of tears: "And his father wept for him." The general impression is of a process of mourning that is unhealthy. The prophetic dreams at the beginning had tended upward, moving from the field to the skies, but this downward movement seems to lack any glimmer of prophecy, of seeing.

Meanwhile, if only Jacob knew it, "the Midianites sold [Joseph] in Egypt to Potiphar" (37:36). Again the Midianites, and again out of the blue. The two phrases, concerning his father's weeping and the Midianites' selling, follow one another immediately. And the appearance of the Midianites is all the more startling because they were already said to have sold Joseph—to the Ishmaelites (37:28).

Again, as a linear sequence the account seems muddled. But here, too, as art, the narrative is coherent. At one level, it may indeed be the Ishmaelites, so observable and earthbound, who will sell Joseph. But given that there have been dreams of something incalculable and that there is another hand at work, it is appropriate to speak again of the elusive Midianites.

And Potiphar ("Gift of Re"), however distant, is not a road to nowhere. He is the chief steward of Pharaoh.

Panel Two (Chap. 38)

[38:1–5] Judah turns aside: a picture of growing abandonment and irresponsibility. Unlike chapter 37, with its dreams and puzzles, chapter 38 is straightforward.

Chapter 37 had opened three main story lines—Jacob, Joseph, and the sons. The first two, concerning Jacob and Joseph, were set in motion—Jacob into mourning, and Joseph into Egypt. And so the main story, which awaits development, is that of the sons or brothers.

Among the brothers the de facto leader is Judah, fourth child of Leah, and fourth also among the twelve, after Reuben, Simeon, and Levi (29:31–35). Reuben, the first-born, he of the mandrakes and incest, had tried to exercise leadership in the betrayal of Joseph, but his effort had faltered, been ignored, and become pitiful. For Simeon and Levi the most effective mouth is that of the sword: they have never spoken except "with the mouth of the sword" and in retorting to their father (34:25–31). But Judah spoke, and when he did, his brothers listened ("his brothers heard him," 37:27); they sold Joseph.

After that, however, when the crime is done, communication among the brothers apparently breaks down. When Reuben laments the loss of Joseph, there is no reply. The next time they are seen together, they are simply looking at each other (42:1).

It is within the context of this crisis among the guilty brothers that the story focuses on their leader, Judah (chap. 38). Spread over many years, it is a story of isolation and deviance, ultimately a story of sin and conversion. By showing sin and repentance in Judah, the narrative prepares for the time when all the brothers, led by Judah, will repent.

The story begins with a brusque desertion: "Judah went down from his brothers and turned aside . . ." (38:1)—a contrast with Joseph, who was first introduced as "with his brothers" (37:2). Judah's turning aside leads to strangers and to a Canaanite wife. But even with her he is not responsible. Apparently he was involved in the naming of the first child, Er, but not in that of the second, Onan; it is left to the mother to name him. As for the third, Shelah, he was not even present at the time of birth (38:5); he was away in Chezib, a placename that is difficult to identify (Achzib? Josh. 15:44; Mic. 1:14; Westermann, III, 51). The unknownness of the place seems to say something: Judah is out of reach.

Judah's problem is not minor. "If [Genesis] has . . . made one thing clear it is that one is one's brother's keeper—which generally means that one is here to take care of others. . . . One must guard and keep one's little brothers and one's children. In this critical respect Judah fails miserably" (Ajzenstat, 2000, 6). Judah's wrongdoing therefore may now seem banal—he is not doing anything dramatic, just drifting through the years—but in fact he is lost.

[38:6–11] Judah's abandoning of his daughter-in-law, Tamar. The story moves quickly. The rapid-fire children are scarcely born when it is time for the eldest to get married. "Judah took a wife for Er . . . and her name was Tamar" (38:6). But Er was wicked, and Yhwh put him to death. No explanation is given of Er's wickedness, but his punishment thickens the shadow over Judah. Even if one turns aside to some Canaanite place, wickedness still receives punishment.

Following the law of levirate (cf. Deut. 25:5–10) Judah told his second son Onan to raise children for his brother. But Onan did not want children who legally would not be his, and so he always frustrated sexual intercourse, spilling the semen on the ground. For this irresponsibility toward his dead brother and Tamar—and not for the physical act of frustrating intercourse—God put him also to death.

Punishment for sin of any kind was ominous for Judah, but punishment for irresponsibility toward a brother was doubly unnerving. He wanted to have no more to do with Tamar, and despite the obligation to ask the remaining brother, Shelah, to have children by her, he used Shelah's young age as an excuse to send her home to her father. Apparently there was more parental responsibility in Tamar's father than in Judah.

[38:12–23] Tamar induces Judah toward recognition and responsibility. Again the story moves quickly. Judah's wife dies—an untold story in itself—and Judah, quickly comforted (so unlike Jacob), goes up to Timnah for the sheepshearing (so unlike Joseph; Joseph tended but Judah shears). Here also, as at the beginning when he first "turned aside," he is with his strange friend, Hirah the Adullamite (38:12; cf. 38:1). And when he sees a harlot he "turns aside" to her. Thus Judah's original turning from his brothers is now expressed by this turning to harlotry. The scene is set in Enaim, apparently meaning "Twin Wells," and forming a brusque variation on a betrothal scene (Alter, 220). As payment, he promises the woman a kid goat, and as a pledge of payment he effectively leaves his signs of responsibility and identification, his staff and corded seal (the cord was attached to the seal, making the seal easier to carry). (In icons these items are associated with royal power; Beach, 1997, 294–305.)

Tamar, having conceived, returns dutifully to her widow's state. Judah, however, is a picture of confusion. He is reduced to having his friend search for the woman, diplomatically changing her designation from that of whore to cult-prostitute, and soon giving up the search, lest he become an object of scorn. Tamar knows who she is, but Judah is lost, searching in vain.

[38:24–26] Judah's first moment of recognition. When pregnant Tamar is accused of harlotry, Judah's condemnation is swift and deadly: "Bring her out and burn her." However, when faced with his own signs of identification, his seal, cord, and staff, Judah recognizes them and comes to self-awareness: "She is more just than I, for indeed I did not give her Shelah, my son." His response is "magnanimous . . . beyond what would have been necessary. . . . The text is not . . . pessimistic regarding changes that can take place within individuals. . . . Judah does change . . ." (Fretheim, 606–607). Furthermore, though he has moved away from home, the recognition has echoes of his father's recognition of the death of Joseph—young Joseph. Judah had been trying to protect Shelah—young Shelah.

[38:27–30] The birth of Breakthrough and Dawning. The pregnancy results in twins, and the final episode, describing their birth, is one of vitality, a contrast both with the birth of Judah's earlier sons (two of them ill-fated, 38:3–10), and with the final episode, which told of Joseph's death and Jacob's mourning (37:34–34). Given the treachery and irresponsibility of the whole two-chapter diptych, the birth brings a sense of a new beginning, a beginning highlighted by the names, Perez and Zerah—Breakthrough and Dawning. The first recognition led to a sense of death and mourning (37:33–35), but the later recognition leads to a surprising sense of life (38:27–30).

Judah is no longer mentioned at the birth. But he has had a moment of recognition, and the vitality of his new-born twins is like a portent of fresh life.

---

36   Joseph: The Initiatory Trials (Chaps. 39–40)

The Moral Trial (Chap. 39)
The Interpretation Trial (Chap. 40)

Introductory Aspects

The Basic Story Line

The story takes up a great motif—the adventure of a young man in a foreign land. Joseph was a slave, but Egypt was a prestigious society, and the man who bought him was a courtier of Pharaoh himself. Joseph had landed near the pinnacle of the known world.

In his work as a slave God was with him so that his master placed him in charge of his house. Following his refusal of sexual advances, he was accused and imprisoned, thus moving from the pinnacle to the pit.

The story tells especially of how in diverse ways Joseph was tested, not only how his master's wife tried to seduce him (chap. 39), but also how two high-ranking prisoners with dreams tested his powers of interpreting (chap. 40). Yet despite his competence, his integrity, and his ability to interpret, Joseph eventually has to face a grim reality: he is not only in prison; he is forgotten.

Literary Form and Complementarity

The narrative involves a mixing of literary types. Its framework is "the story of advancement" (Westermann, III, 60); Joseph moves to positions of increasing responsibility (39:1–6a, 19–23; 40:1–4, 20–23). Within that framework, the main part of the text (39:6b–18; 40:5–19) follows the literary convention of the initiatory trial, a type-scene, which, like the temptations of Jesus in the synoptic Gospels, is generally set near the beginning of a narrative. The purpose is to test character, usually the character of the main actor.

The two tests show that Joseph has the necessary character, moral and intellectual (intellectual in a broad sense). The story of advancement indicates not only that he is coming closer to the center of responsibility, but that, apart from moral and intellectual qualities, he also has a practical, administrative, wisdom. The wisdom in administration emerges in the way he looks after two institutions, first his master's house (39:4–6a), and then the prison (39:22–23; 40:4).

Joseph emerges as someone of positive qualities. The first panel, when he is twice placed in charge of everything, shows him as caring and competent, as somehow profoundly good. The second panel, when he interprets the dreams, depicts him as wise. Taken together, the two panels suggest a kind of pairing, like goodness and truth, or goodness and wisdom.

Relationship to Primordial Sin (3:1–4:16)

Joseph's story, particularly concerning Potiphar's wife, has some resemblance to Egyptian literature (to *The Tale of Two Brothers*, Fretheim, 609), but it also echoes earlier sections of Genesis itself.

The full extent of Joseph's goodness becomes clearer when these two panels are compared with the accounts of the two primordial sins, those involving the couple (2:25–chap. 3) and Cain and Abel (4:1–16).

Like the couple in the Garden, Joseph has complete freedom, but unlike the story in Genesis 3, he does not yield to the woman. And when faced by the two characters in jail, both angry and downcast, as Cain had been, he is able, in some way at least, to help them to do what Cain could not do—raise up their heads.

There are other connections between the jail scenes and Genesis 3–4. First, there are some details, varying in clarity: the complete sense of freedom and responsibility; the one forbidden thing (the fruit of the tree; the wife); the debate before the (attempted) sin; Joseph's attractiveness, like that of the fruit; the flight after the event; the clothing/tunic; the condemnation for what has been done; the idea of keeping (*šāmar*) Abel/the two men (4:9; 40:3); the rage; the faces; and, apart from the raising of the heads, the reminder of being driven/taken away from the land.

As well as such small details, there is the position of both diptychs within their respective dramas. Both occur in second place, after the creation diptych (chaps. 1–2), and after the opening diptych of the Joseph story (37:2–chap. 38).

The essential factor, however, is that, through Joseph, God's goodness and truth are finding expression in a way that rises above the sins of the past

Structure (Table 36.1)

Panel one (chap. 39) contains some difficulties. The description of Joseph's attractiveness (39:6b) may be placed with the introduction or with the subsequent story of the attempted seduction. It seems best to place it with the attempted seduction (39:6b–18). Concerning the active response of Joseph's master—the anger (39:19)—this seems to belong to the conclusion, thus balancing the role of the master in the introduction.

Comment

Panel One (Chap. 39)

[39:1–6a] Joseph: down to Egypt, but Yhwh is with him. When Joseph comes back on stage, there is a reminder of his status—a slave, bought by Potiphar. This reference to the name "Potiphar" is often seen as a harmonizing gloss, to bring the text into line with the reference to the Potiphar who bought Joseph in the final verse of chapter 37. But, precisely on the question of names, these two verses (37:36; 39:1) show a glaring lack of such superficial harmonization: the names of the sellers vary from Midianites (37:36) to Ishmaelites (39:1). It does not make sense to claim that an editor harmonized the buyers but not the sellers. Such a claim is another example of invoking an editorial process, which initially seems plausible but which, when looked at closely, emerges as incoherent, self-contradictory. It implies a nonharmonizing harmonizer.

Rather than reduce part of the text to a gloss it is better to try to understand its purpose, admittedly perplexing. In this case the overloading of the name of the buyer ("Potiphar, a eunuch of Pharaoh, the chief steward, an Egyptian"),

Table 36.1. Joseph: The Initiatory Trials (chap. 39 // chap. 40)

Potiphar's wife: the moral trial

Introduction: Joseph in Egypt, as servant (39:1–6a)
  Joseph brought down, down to Egypt (1)
  Yhwh with Joseph; his lord places Joseph in charge of all (2–4)
  Yhwh blesses Joseph; his lord does not need not to worry (5–6a)
The attempted seduction, and Joseph's refusal (39:6b–10)
  Joseph's attractiveness (6b)
  Attempted seduction and Joseph's lengthy refusal (7–9)
  Joseph's continued refusal (10)
Wife, again failing to seduce, accuses Joseph (39:11–18)
  Facing seduction, Joseph, leaving his tunic, flees (11–12)
  The woman's accusation (13–15)
  The woman's accusation repeated to the lord (16–18)
Conclusion: Joseph in prison, in charge (39:19–23)
  Joseph placed in prison (19–20)
  Yhwh's kindness with Joseph; Joseph in charge of all (21–22)
  Yhwh makes Joseph prosper. The governor need not see to things (23)

Joseph in prison: the interpretation trial

Introduction: the jailing of the butler and baker (40:1–4)
  Pharaoh jails the two offenders (1–3)
  The governor places Joseph in charge of them (4)
Dreams which lead to being angry and downcast (40:5–8)
  Both prisoners dream (5)
  The dreams cause disturbance (6–8)
Joseph interprets the butler's dream (40:9–15)
  The butler's dream recounted (9–11)
  Interpretation: his head will be lifted by restoration (12–15)
Joseph interprets the baker's dream (40:16–19)
  The baker's dream recounted (16–17)
  Interpretation: his head will be lifted by hanging (18–19)
Conclusion: the releasing of the butler and baker (40:20–23)
  Pharaoh lifts the two heads, restoring and hanging (20–22)
  The butler forgets Joseph (23)

following the reference to being brought down to Egypt, has the practical effect of overshadowing Joseph: like a list of titles or degrees it suggests that at some level Joseph is in the presence of someone or something far greater than himself. Such a presence is ambiguous; it can be taken as either supportive or intimidating.

But about another presence there is no ambiguity: "Yhwh was with Joseph . . ." (39:2). Potiphar is now designated "lord," and if Yhwh was read at some level as "Lord" then there is a wordplay involving Lord/lord, which interweaves God with Joseph's master, and which further suggests God's interwovenness with Joseph's daily life and fate, even when things apparently go wrong. (A somewhat similar Lord/lord wordplay occurs in 24:12, 14, 27, 35–49). At one level, or at least in some people, God is in Egypt. Joseph is given charge of "all" that belongs to the lord. It is an intimation of Joseph's later coming to yet greater responsibility.

The account of God's presence is followed by a reference to God's blessing (39:5–6a), a blessing that extends to house and field. The result for the Egyptian is a great sense of ease: all he need attend to is the bread he eats, an apparent reference to distinctive Egyptian eating habits connected with "religious or dietary reasons" (Murphy, 2:63; cf. 43:32). This situation, where the master is attending only to his food, also helps to set up the following event, where apparently he is not attending to his wife.

[39:6b–18] **The attempted seduction.** Joseph is now described as attractive in both form and figure, as Rachel had been (29:17), "the only two people in the OT to be awarded this double accolade" (Wenham, 354). The narrative is both sensuous and instructive. It is sensuous because, having established a setting of great ease and freedom (the all-prospering Joseph and his carefree lord, 39:1–6a), it then introduces both Joseph's attractiveness and the woman's ongoing desire. There is a special note of sensuousness, somewhat touching, in her handling of Joseph's clothing after he has fled: "she rested his garment beside her."

The instructiveness is both in the picture of resistance—Joseph's actual resistance (flight) and the woman's allusion to how she should have resisted (by calling out)—and also in the depiction of the evil of adultery (a "great harm," 39:9; cf. 20:3; 26:10). There is instruction, too, about the nature of passionate desire, the way in which it can turn into forms that are lying and destructive. The desire is also mixed with anger. In accusing Joseph, the wife suggests that some of the blame lies with the husband: "He came to me, the Hebrew slave whom *you* have brought us. . . ." The word "Hebrew" was often derogatory, suggesting a slave or a coward (Sacks, 342). In part, the husband may in fact have been to blame; and his guilt may have contributed to his harsh condemnation of Joseph, without trial.

The contrast between the woman and Joseph is heightened by their conversation (39:7–9): she, in her desire, is brief; he, in his search for a way out, speaks at length.

[39:19–23] **Joseph in prison—but Yhwh is with him.** The panel ends with a variation on how it began, by handing Joseph over, in this case to "the round house," the prison for the prisoners of the king.

"But Yhwh was with Joseph . . . ," as when he was first brought down to Egypt. In fact, God seems even closer: "Yhwh . . . stretched out kindness (*ḥesed*) to him." And Joseph's role of responsibility in the prison seems even greater than in the house of Potiphar. Potiphar at least had seen to his own food, but the chief of the round house "did not see to anything at all." Ironically, imprisonment involves a form of promotion, greater responsibility. It also brings Joseph closer to the king, at least insofar as he is among the king's prisoners. At one level, therefore, chapter 39 portrays a descent, down to Egypt, and further down into prison. At another level, it involves positive development, greater closeness to God and greater responsibility on behalf of humans.

Panel Two (Chap. 40)

[40:1–4] Introduction. Pharaoh jails the butler and baker. The "anger" of a "lord," which first brought Joseph into prison (39:19–20), now brings Pharaoh's butler and baker to the same place (40:1–2). But whereas Joseph was there because he had refused to "sin (ḥāṭâ') against God" (39:9), they were there because they had indeed "sinned (ḥātâ') against their lord" (40:1). Morally, therefore, Joseph is in a different category; and correspondingly, within the prison, he is also at a different level: he is appointed to oversee the two prestigious prisoners. To some degree, as far as these two are concerned, Joseph has assumed some of the overlordship previously held by Pharaoh.

[40:5–19] Joseph as interpreter. Triple vine and three baskets: two dreams about the lifting up of the head—in diverse ways. Dreams were regarded as important in the ancient world, particularly in Egypt, where dream interpretation was a developed art. Joseph, too, treats dreams as important, but he is circumspect about their interpretation: "Are interpretations not from God?" For Joseph, dreams have a dimension that may surpass purely psychological human analysis.

The dreams of the butler and baker, involving respectively three vine branches and three breadbaskets, center around basic elements—wine and bread. The complementarity between the two heightens the eventual sense of contrast, and so does the wordplay concerning the lifting up of the head. One head will be lifted up through restoration, the other through hanging.

The contrast emphasizes Joseph's powers of discernment. He is neither a charlatan compelled to say all is positive and peaceful, nor is he a prophet of doom, seeing only what is ominous. Rather, he discerns wisely.

Something else also begins to emerge. He talks about his own life and begins to develop a true sense of his own history and role (40:14–15). Within the context of the positive interpretation, he makes a plea for himself: "Remember me. . . . Make Pharaoh remember me. . . . For I was stolen, stolen from the land of the Hebrews, and . . . have not done anything that they should put me in the pit." And he carries no guilt for the attempted seduction—a clarity of mind which, for many people in such situations, is rare and enviable.

[40:20–23] Conclusion. The interpretations fulfilled. Joseph forgotten. The sense of Pharaoh as supreme, already intimated by the introductory "sinned against their lord" (40:1), is reinforced in the conclusion. Pharaoh arbitrates life and death. His "lifting up of the head" means restoration for one and hanging for another. Insofar as he has a certain power over life and death Pharaoh acts like God.

The process of Joseph's promotion (in 39:1–6a, 19–23; 40:1–4) now reaches a tense balance. On the one hand, he achieves a higher status than ever before. As in the case of Pharaoh, there is even a touch of God about him. He had said interpretations belong to God (40:8), yet he himself had given interpretations (40:9–19), and now (40:20–22) these interpretations prove to be true. On the other hand, this new status seems useless. The butler did not remember him. The kindness (*ḥesed*), which had been present formerly (from God, 39:21) and which had been requested by Joseph from the restored butler (40:14), is no longer mentioned. Joseph is just one more forgotten prisoner.

---

37 | **Remembering Joseph: His Rise and the Brothers' Conversion (Chaps. 41–42)**

Joseph Becomes the Wise Ruler of Egypt (Chap. 41)
The Anatomy of the Brothers' Conversion (Chap. 42)

Introductory Aspects

The Basic Story Line

Moving away from the narrow pit of Joseph's prison, the story opens out two years later on another scene, on two dreams of Pharaoh himself (chap. 42). The setting in the first dream was appropriately majestic and reassuring—the banks of the Nile—but the content was horrific: two of the most innocuous and supportive elements of life, cows and ears of grain, turned destructive. And for the disturbed Pharaoh all the wise men of Egypt could do nothing.

Then the butler remembered.

When Joseph is rushed to the scene, freshly shaved and changed, he is very calm and he puts the interpretation of the dream in the hands of God. Then, having listened to Pharaoh, he announces the approach of a great famine.

Again he is calm, and his advice is so clear that he is appointed governor of Egypt. He sets to work, making the best of the years of plenty, founding a family, and forgetting his painful history and his father's house. Then the famine arrives, gripping the earth.

Meanwhile, back at his father's house (chap. 42), old Jacob seems sullen. But he takes action: while keeping Benjamin with him, he sends his ten sons to Egypt to buy provisions. Cross-examined by a harsh governor, they find themselves forced to talk about their family.

Then they start to remember.

As the remembering develops, Joseph loses some of his calm and has to turn aside. But he maintains his resolve. He keeps one of the brothers in prison and sends the others home in a way that stirs the family memory even more.

Literary Form

Joseph's promotion to wise ruler (chap. 41) involves a synthesis of two literary forms, partly that of the dream that turns into reality, and especially that of the success of the wise courtier (Westermann, III, 85).

The second panel, describing the brothers' journey to Egypt and back (chap. 42), may be described partly as a travel report (Westermann, III, 103), but its more essential nature is that of a conversion account. The kernel of a conversion account had already been used concerning the change in Judah (chap. 38), but this chapter goes further: it gives not only a conversion's kernel, but, as it were, its basic anatomy.

The process of conversion is seen most clearly in chapter 42, in the contrast between diverse stages (42:1, 28). At the beginning there is no communication between the brothers. All they do is look at each other with unspoken guilt (42: 1). In fact, in the biblical narrative they have not spoken to one another since the day they sold Joseph. But later, after they have gone through a process of learning to communicate, remember, and reflect, they open not only their mouths but their hearts ("Their hearts went out, and they trembled each toward his brother . . . ," 42:28).

Complementarity of the Two Panels

While this two-panel scene emphasizes food, it attaches even more importance to wisdom, to the way Joseph's God-given wisdom suddenly blossoms before Egypt, indeed before the world; and to the way this wise Joseph deals with his guilty brothers, using a mixture of tough realism and deep compassion to move them slowly toward conversion.

Joseph may be described as wise insofar as he does what all the magicians and wise men of Egypt itself cannot do (41:8, 24)—Egypt's wisdom was famous throughout the world (Jacob, 281)—and insofar as he meets his own requirements of being wise (42:32). But his wisdom is not abstract or even predictable. In fact, Joseph's location is startling—running from a pit, unshaven, and dirty (41:14). And he is rooted in God (42:18; cf. 42:38, "in whom is the spirit of God"). While the brothers had simply wanted to buy grain, Joseph gradually awakens them to their other need, to have their sin judged and forgiven.

The issue of sin and judgment is not reserved to the second panel. Pharaoh's attention is first drawn to Joseph in the context of someone recalling sin and judgment (42:9–13). "My sins I remember today," says the chief butler, and then he recalls the diverse fates of two offenders, one restored, the other condemned to death. This contrast concerning the fate of offenders or sinners is recounted just before Joseph comes on stage, and it sets the scene not only for his entry before Pharaoh (chap. 41) but also for his dealing with his sinful brothers (chap. 42). At one level, it sets a scene of judgment.

Relationship to Preceding Chapters

The image of a worldwide famine contains echoes of the worldwide flood (6:1–9: 17) and of the flood's remaking of creation (8:1–9:17; cf. 1:1–2:4a).

Just as the flood was inextricably linked to the human heart, to its sinfulness (6:5; 8:21) and to God's own heart (6:6), so the picture of the famine is linked in this scene with sin, especially the sin of the brothers (41:9; 42:21–28). Their hearts are involved (42:28) and so, implicitly, is that of Joseph. He weeps (42: 24).

Some other echoes may be mentioned:

Famine, Egypt, and Pharaoh (Abraham and Sarah, 12:10, 18; cf. 26:2).

Two periods of seven years (Jacob with Laban, 29:20, 30).

The morning after a dream (Jacob at Bethel, 28:18; butler, baker, 40:6).

Interpreting dreams (Joseph with the butler and baker, 40:9–23).

God reveals a coming catastrophe (41:25, 28; Abraham, regards Sodom, 18:17).

Total obedience to the word (41:40, 55; creation, chap. 1; Noah, 6:22; 7:4).

Leading Elements

Joseph's way of dealing with his brothers may at first appear harsh or manipulative. But if he had revealed himself immediately and offered forgiveness they would probably never again have been at ease either with themselves or with him. They would have died wondering how real was the forgiveness, or carrying a sense of moral inferiority. Instead, through a form of "tough love," he gave them a unique opportunity: to return, in slow motion, to the situation of their crime, an opportunity to do things differently, and to prove to themselves and to him that they had another side. As a result, when Joseph's self-revelation finally came, the way is open to a reconciliation that is full and peaceful.

For the moment, however, the situation is not easy. "Nearly all the actors are trapped by their past. The brothers cannot escape the power of their past guilt by being honest now either to Joseph or their father. . . . Jacob . . . is even more paranoic. . . . Even . . . Joseph . . . is overtaken by emotion . . ." (Wenham, II, 412). So far, Joseph is the only one who has remembered the dreams (42:9). Remembering is central, both in the Joseph story as a whole (see Green, 1996) and especially in this diptych.

Structure (Table 37.1)

PANEL ONE (CHAP. 41)

The introduction (41:1–13) apparently includes not only the two dreams (41:1–7) but also the morning after, when there is no interpreter, and the butler "remembers [his] sins," remembers the interpreter in prison (41:8–13). This sets the stage for the entry of Joseph. Joseph's name, not used in the introduction, is reserved for the next main part, the summons from prison and the recounting of the dreams (41:14–24).

Table 37.1. Remembering Joseph (chap. 41//chap. 42)

Remembered sins lead to Joseph's rise in Egypt

Introduction: Pharaoh dreams and the butler remembers (41:1–13)
    The dream of the seven cows (1–4)
    The dream of the seven ears of grain (5–7)
    Remembering sins and Joseph (the butler, 8–13)
Dreams recounted: Pharaoh summons Joseph (41:14–24)
    Sending for Joseph (14–16)
    Pharaoh recounts the dreams (17–24)
Dreams interpreted: Joseph interprets and recommends (41:25–37)
    The interpretation: years of plenty, years of famine (25–32)
    Joseph recommends: appoint a wise administrator (33–37)
Authority and action: Joseph given responsibility (41:38–49)
    Joseph appointed governor of Egypt (38–45)
    Joseph at thirty and the seven years of plenty (46–49)
Conclusion: Joseph amid affliction and fruitfulness (41:50–58)
    Forget, Double Fruit (Manasseh, Ephraim): two sons (50–52)
    From seven years of plenty, to seven of famine for all (53–57)

Joseph causes his brothers to remember their sins

Introduction (Canaan): paralysis, and survival action (42:1–5)
    As sons look at each other, Jacob hears and acts (1–2)
    Ten go to Egypt, but Jacob holds on to Benjamin (3–5)
Joseph moves the ten towards facing reality (42:6–17)
    The first meeting and minimal exchange (6–7)
    Joseph, accusing falsely, begins to unearth the truth (8–13)
    Proposal for a brother-related test, and imprisonment (14–17)
The sons remember their lost brother . . . and God (42:18–28)
    Days later: intensifying the brother-related test (18–20)
    The ten begin to talk to each other about their sin (21–24)
    The ten open their hearts to each other . . . and about God (25–28)
Conclusion (Canaan): the developing feelings intensify (42:29–38)
    The brothers, seeing money in all sacks, become afraid (29–35)
    Jacob becomes even more mournful (36–38)

The birth of the two sons, with its sharp variation in time and content, marks the conclusion (41:50; compare with the beginning of the introduction, 41:1).

PANEL TWO (CHAP. 42)

The introduction (42:1–5) apparently extends to the mention of "the land of Canaan" (42:5). Thus the introduction, though focused toward Egypt, retains an initial emphasis on Canaan as the starting point. The same emphasis, "the land of Canaan," marks the conclusion (42:29).

Within the first main part (42:6–17), the subdivisions begin with "Joseph" (42:6, 8, 14), and virtually conclude, in two cases, with "the land of Canaan" (42:7, 13).

In the second main part (42:18–28), it seems better that the subdivision on the sons' remembering of Joseph should include not only Joseph's weeping but also his coming back to them (42:21–24). At a certain level, his coming back to them mirrors and completes their remembering of him.

The dividing of the conclusion (42:29–38) into two parts is indicated not only by content but also by the repetition of "Jacob their father" (42:29, 36).

Comment

Panel One (Chap. 41)

[41:1–13] Introduction. Pharaoh dreams, and the chief butler remembers his sins and Joseph. The scene begins with a major shift, not only to a new time ("At the end of two years . . ."), but also right into Pharaoh's world: ". . . Pharaoh dreamed."

The opening moment of the dream has a classic simplicity: "Behold, he was standing by the Nile." The scene seems set for a painter. But the central elements of the dreams—the Nile, cows, and grain—are all prime symbols of the food supply, and the dream endings are ominous.

Pharaoh's consultation of Egypt's finest minds would have been a lengthy process—it involved "all the magicians of Egypt and all its wise men"—but it is recounted in less than a verse (41:8). In contrast, the butler's recollection about a Hebrew prisoner is recounted at length (41:9–13), thus eclipsing, even by its quantity, the wisdom of Egypt. Something greater is at hand.

[41:14–24] Dreams recounted. Pharaoh sends for Joseph and tells him his dream. Joseph's emergence is not from a prestigious wisdom-school, but from "the pit." He is sent for and made to run. Then he shaves and changes. (Unlike other Near Eastern peoples, the Egyptians were clean shaven). As far as Pharaoh is concerned, he is from another world. And indeed, when Pharaoh begins by mentioning Joseph's reputation as an interpreter, Joseph immediately says, "Not I. God. . . ." Yet Joseph's reference to God, *Elohim*, is sufficiently general (unlike "Yhwh") not to be strange or offensive to Pharaoh. The interpretation, suggests Joseph, will lead to well-being: "God will answer for Pharaoh's peace."

When Pharaoh recounts his frightening dreams they lose nothing in the telling. Despite his closeness to the original account, he adds details that make the dreams yet more disturbing. Their ominous character, instead of fading, becomes starker. In speaking of the second set of cows, Pharaoh inserts a further sentence, which highlights the threat: "I have not seen their like for evil in all the land of Egypt."

Pharaoh is not just exaggerating; at some level he knows that his dream intimates something really terrible. Now it is Joseph's turn to speak.

[41:25–37] **Dreams interpreted: Joseph interprets and recommends. The famine, and the good word.** From one viewpoint, Joseph's interpretation is strongly negative (41:26–27). After apparently circling vaguely and repetitively concerning something involving seven years, he suddenly drops the news: famine, "seven years of famine!" "Famine" is mentioned before "plenty," and is repeated more often.

Yet the overall impact of Joseph's message is positive. The news of the famine, as well as being followed by the news of plenty, is encased in a twofold framework of providence and planning. Providence is the preface: Joseph begins by saying that what he is going to talk about is coming from God ("God has told Pharaoh what he is about to do," 41:25, 28). And planning is the epilogue. Without being asked, Joseph adds, as part of his interpretation, a plan of practical action, beginning with the appointment of someone "discerning and wise." Providence does not lessen human responsibility. Even in the wording the providence and planning are related:

41:25: "God has told Pharaoh what he is about to do."

41:33: "And now, let Pharaoh see. . . . Let Pharaoh do. . . ."

Joseph's emphasis on providence and planning is such that, despite his message of famine, when he finishes, "the word was good" (*dābār yāṭab*) in the eyes of Pharaoh and his servants.

The most practical measure is the laying aside of one fifth of the grain ("a double tithe," Jacob, 277). Later, as a permanent arrangement, Joseph will ask the people to continue paying a fifth (47:24).

[41:38–49] **Authority and action: Joseph, with the Spirit of God, receives Pharaoh-like authority to command; then he goes out, to work.** Pharaoh is not glib about finding someone wise. He has realized, apparently from dealing with his own wise men and Joseph, that wisdom is not easily found; and so he asks: "Shall we find such a man as this, in whom is the Spirit of God?"

The result is that he appoints Joseph. Joseph's credentials are twofold, divine and human. Pharaoh, acknowledging that Joseph already has the divine dimension, goes on to invest him, to an extraordinary degree, with the human dimension, with all the signs of office (41:40–45). The call that preceded Joseph's chariot, *'Abrēk*, is Egyptian apparently, meaning perhaps "Attention!" or "Make way!"

Then Joseph "went out" and turned the commands into reality. He passes through the land, and heaps up grain "like the sand of the sea." This image implies something limitless, and what follows is even more explicit: "he stopped counting it, for it was countless." These images of sand and countlessness echo Genesis's earlier promises of progeny (like the dust, and like the stars, 13:16; 15:6). The picture of Joseph also evokes God's word or wisdom going out into the world and accomplishing something of divine dimension, something touching the whole world.

Joseph's Egyptian name and Egyptian wife underline further his relationship to God and the world. His new name, Zaphenath-paneah, means "God speaks and lives/makes live." And Asenath, his wife's name, means "She who belongs to the goddess." Asenath's father was a priest of On (seven miles from modern Cairo), renamed famously by the Greeks as Heliopolis, "the city of the sun," because it was a center of sun worship. The connotations of these various names, especially that given to Joseph himself, are basic and far-reaching.

[41:50–58] Conclusion. Joseph amid affliction and fruitfulness: forgetting the past and bearing fruit in the present. At the end of a chapter in which Joseph has moved from the pit to the peak, the birth of his two children crystallizes his journey. The first, called Forget (Manasseh), leaves the past behind, including his father's house The second, Double Fruit (Ephraim), looks to what is to be done in the land of his affliction.

The full extent of what needs to be done becomes apparent when the famine strikes, and the word is "Go to Joseph." Joseph does not give the grain away; he sells it. Now the worldwide dimension is no longer simply evoked. Rather, it is said explicitly that "the famine had become severe in all the earth."

Panel Two (Chap. 42)

[42:1–5] Introduction (in Canaan). Paralysis and initial movement. While the sons look at each other, Jacob sees and hears and cautiously seeks life—grain in Egypt. Jacob was last seen as death-centered, weeping inconsolably (37:31–35), and he has been eclipsed by his children, especially by Judah and Joseph. Now, about twenty years later, one might expect that he would have become lifeless and bitter.

When he reenters there is indeed an edge to his words, a hint of bitterness: "Why are you looking at one another?" But he is alert: "Jacob saw. . . . And he said, '*I hear* that there are provisions. . . . ' " This hearing is somewhat like that of Sarah, listening even when all seemed lost (18:10). Whatever his anguish, Jacob has not given up, has not stopped listening to what life has to offer. More than his children, he is receptive, aware. And he seeks life, "that we may live and not die."

But he is cautious, and he keeps with him the precious Benjamin, Joseph's brother, "Lest a disaster befall him." The earlier disaster, involving Joseph, still weighs on him and he will not let go of it.

Virtually lost behind this picture of the struggling Jacob is any sense of the sons. They say nothing. Ironically, it is they, rather than Jacob, who are half-dead. They look at one another—a small world indeed—the faces hiding the brothers' betrayal. Their only focus, insofar as they have one, is the one given them by their father, "to buy grain . . . to buy . . . for the famine was in the land." The initial account of their journey does not even say, as their father did, "that we may live" (42:3). Their mission, governed by buying and famine, seems to lack positive motivation of their own.

[42:6–17] Joseph, recognizing the brothers, moves them toward reality and talking. Joseph may seem vindictive and manipulative in dealing with his brothers. Despite recognizing them as they bow to him, he withholds recognition, and, instead, speaks as a stranger, and harshly.

But, as already suggested, his reticence has a positive purpose. Given the circumstances, immediate mutual recognition would have been a debacle, with emotions so tangled, so blocked and conflicting and confused, that it would have been virtually impossible afterward to unravel these emotions and to restore trust.

Since the day the sons got rid of Joseph, it is not only Joseph who is out of contact. They are out of contact with each other. Judah is shown as leaving them (38:1). When they reappear, in this chapter (42:1–5), there is not a word between them.

Joseph's position is better insofar as for him the past is simply forgotten, not suppressed in the same way. But even he needs some time to recognize the situation fully, to remember the dreams. And so his process of recognition is stated twice (42:7, 8).

His strategy, in dealing with his brothers, is to shake them slowly out of their paralysis, to bring them back step by step to an awareness of the meaning of brotherhood, of human solidarity. Then, and only then, will they be ready for recognition.

The first thing is to get them to talk. And so Joseph starts with a question: "Where do you come from?" This is simple, yet, if pushed, it is loaded. They are coming not only from a specific location, but also from a dark past.

Then Joseph accuses them of being spies (spies are said to look on the land's "nakedness," in other words, they see what is not supposed to be seen, at least not by them). The accusation is completely untrue, but to deal with it they have to start saying who they really are, and thus to start talking about themselves.

In their original departure for Egypt (42:3, 5) it was said simply that they came: "to buy grain . . .", "to buy amidst those who came, for the famine was in the land of Canaan." Now, as Joseph presses them, all they will do at first is repeat the idea of buying grain. But slowly their answers begin to expand, and to go back (42:7, 10–11, 13):

"From the land of Canaan, to buy food."

"No, my lord. Your servants came to buy food. We are all sons of one man. We are honest. . . . [We] are not spies."

"Your twelve servants are twelve brothers, the sons of one man in the land of Canaan. Behold, the youngest is with our father this day, and one is no more."

At last: "and one is no more." However obliquely, they have managed to say it. They still have not spoken to each other.

Then Joseph puts them in prison for three days and apparently places them together: "he gathered them in under guard" (42:17). "Guarding/keeping" can be translated loosely as "placing in custody," but "guarding" has a connotation that in some way he is taking care of them, as, for instance, one keeps a flock. He has become his brothers' keeper. And he leaves them with a testing proposal, that one of them go home to bring back the eleventh brother.

Elsewhere, too, Genesis speaks of three days: Abraham's three-day walk to Moriah (22:4); the three-day walk from Laban's flock to Jacob's (30:36; 31:22); the prisoners' three-day wait between dream-interpretation and fulfillment (40: 12) (Sacks, 366).

[42:18–28] The sons remember: from talking to each other to trembling toward each other. Only on the third day of imprisonment is there a first reference to God. "Do this and you will live," says Joseph, "for I fear God." He does not lecture them about God, but in a moment of being merciful, he lets them know implicitly that his mercy comes from God. He lets them go and gives them food. But he holds Simeon—till Benjamin comes.

Since their selling of Joseph, receiving this food is their first recorded experience of mercy. But the loss of Simeon sharpens the memory of losing Joseph, and, coming after the questioning and the imprisonment together, its effect is considerable: "They said to each other, 'Truly we are guilty for our brother.' " And so they begin to talk to each other.

They review the crime, especially their refusal to hear: "And we did not hear him." Reuben, in reminding them of his own failed intervention, reinforces the point: "And you did not hear." It is Reuben also who spells out the extent of their plight: "Now comes a reckoning for his blood." The full horror, the full extent of their guilt, is finally surfacing: "his blood."

It is at this stage, at a high point of their guilt and alienation, that Joseph, unknown to them, weeps for them (42:24, the first of three times; cf. 43:30, and climactically, 45:2; cf. 50:17). And Joseph's next move—"he came back to them and spoke to them"—is like an intimation of ultimate reconciliation.

Yet reconciliation is not to be rushed. Joseph's imprisonment of Simeon happens before their eyes. This may seem harsh, but it helps them further in reliving their original loss of a brother. Now, watching Simeon, they can see more clearly what they did. Finally, Joseph commands that their money, silver, be put back in their sacks. Silver was what they once received for selling Joseph.

When just one of them opens his sack on the way home, in the relative isolation of a night camp, they are shaken, thus bringing them, as never before, into an awareness of one another and of God: "Their hearts went out. They trembled each toward his brother, saying, 'What is this that God has done to us?' "

It is not God who has done it to them but Joseph, or rather God through Joseph; "we are invited to think of . . . Joseph . . . as God's instrument. . . . Thus a double system of causation, human and divine, is brought to the fore" (Alter, 249).

[42:29–38] Conclusion (in Canaan). The developing feelings intensify: fear and bereavement. When the sons return they give their father, Jacob, a carefully edited account of events. In contrast to the crass way they once sent Joseph's bloodied coat to their father, thus punishing him for his favoritism (37:32), they now want to spare him. They tell of the need for the youngest to go down to Egypt, but make no mention of their being in prison. Even Simeon is just resting! They make no mention either of a discussion about blood-guilt, or of money in one of the sacks. And, in an apparent bid to distract Jacob, they invent a little promise by the man in Egypt: "And you shall travel about in the land," an activity often associated with trading.

Not a bad story, until they all open their sacks. "They saw . . . they and their father. . . ." And "they were afraid." So had Sarah been afraid, after she heard at the tent entrance (18:15).

This opening of the sacks by all does not contradict the earlier opening, at the camp, by just one (42:27). The apparent presumption, in the camp, was that the presence of the silver, though disturbing, was an isolated case. Now it emerges that the problem is deeper.

As for Jacob, he is undone. The brothers' hope of not mentioning Joseph is dashed as the father apparently sinks lower than ever, lamenting Joseph, Simeon, and now Benjamin. "Me you have bereaved!" he says, not realizing the full truth of his words, and of its impact on them. And he concludes with "It's on me it all comes!" He is not only sad; he is wallowing in it.

Reuben tries again, again vainly, to save the situation (42:37). He offers his own two sons as guarantee that he will bring Benjamin back. But Jacob is beyond reassurance: "My son shall not go down with you, for his brother is dead, and he alone remains," and he reverts to where he was before they went down to Egypt, to the fear that a disaster will happen to Benjamin (42:38; cf. 42:4). In fact, he almost reverts to where he had been when he first lost Joseph. He talks of going down "with sorrow to Sheol." And now as he goes down his head is white.

38   Back to Egypt: The Generosity That Brings Conversion (Chaps. 43–44)

An Initial Turning and Joseph's Generous Meal (Chap. 43)
The Final Turning Back, Led by Judah (Chap. 44)

Introductory Aspects

The Basic Story Line

The scene begins with the painful decision to go back to Joseph, even though it means bringing Benjamin. It is painful for Jacob, because he has to let go, and painful for the sons because they have to take responsibility for their young brother, a sensitive point for them. But their visit, though a little nervous, becomes very positive. Joseph offers splendid hospitality, especially a wonderful meal (chap. 43).

Then on the way home, just when all seems well, the discovery of Joseph's silver cup in Benjamin's bag causes a crisis, a radical test of the brothers' responsibility with regard to their youngest brother and their father (chap. 44). In effect, they have to relive the crisis concerning the youngest, and they do so in the presence of Joseph.

Literary Form

The literary type in chapter 43 is partly that of a travel account (the journey down to Egypt; Westermann, III, 118). However, this journey to Egypt contains another major emphasis, namely food. The chapter begins with the lack of food ("famine . . . eating . . . food," 43:1–2), and later mentions it repeatedly:

> Jacob's surprising generosity in sending scarce food to "the man" (Joseph, 43:11).

> In Egypt, the preparations, ordered by Joseph, for a meal (43:16, 24).

> Finally, the splendid meal (43:32–34).

It seems best therefore that Joseph's reception of his brothers (chap. 43) be classified as some kind of meal episode.

A partial precedent for such a meal occurs before the destruction of Sodom. Abraham's generous meal (18:1–8), itself linked to the generosity of God, sets the stage for the subsequent display of God's justice in Sodom and for Sodom's fateful decision, its refusal to repent (the sons-in-law treated the idea as a joke, 19:14). Likewise here, but more elaborately: Joseph's splendid meal sets the stage for the crucial moment of decision, for reliving the crisis concerning the youngest and the father.

The literary type in chapter 44, when the discovery of Joseph's cup in Benjamin's sack forces the radical crisis, is partly that of a travel narrative, and partly that of a traditional Egyptian episode (treasure in the sack; Irvin, 1977, 190–191).

However, the primary literary category is biblical, namely that of a conversion story. This is the third picture of the process of conversion. The first, the conversion of Judah (chap. 38), had been seen, so to speak, through a long-distance lens; the actual conversion was just one small pivotal part in a larger picture. The second picture, during the brothers' initial journey to Egypt (chap. 42), had given a fuller portrayal; it had revealed more clearly the basic anatomy of conversion. Now, however, as conversion reaches its radical stage, the camera closes in as it were on the brothers, especially on Judah.

Complementarity of the Two Panels

The process of conversion, so strong in the second panel (chap. 44), is already present in the first (chap. 43), especially in the gradually changing attitude of Jacob and Judah (43:3–15).

The meal boosts the process. It does not make the conversion easy, but it takes away any impression that conversion is a humiliation. The meal's generosity and splendor make conversion possible and even attractive. The food is like goodness calling to Jacob's sons, reminding them of generosity (chap. 43). And in the second panel (chap. 44) they respond.

While chapter 43 lays the emphasis on giving gifts, chapter 44 tells of a complementary dynamic, uncovering guilt, in other words, revealing sin and accepting one's sinfulness. As already seen, in discussing Sodom, Genesis sees justice as flowing not from weighing-scale precision, as among the Greeks, but from great generosity. Mercy is not measured or strained. It flows toward the sinner like a great stream; guilt is surrounded by gift. This guilt–gift balance emerges most clearly concerning the silver money in the sacks. In chapter 43 the nervous brothers are told that the silver in their sacks is a gift from God: "Your God . . . has given you treasure in your sacks. Your silver came to me" (43:23). But in chapter 44 the discovery of the silver cup in Benjamin's sack leads Judah to declare: "God has found out your servants' guilt" (44:16).

The various journeys, especially the first two, give a kind of historiographical unity to the larger surrounding text (chaps. 42:1–47:11, esp. chap. 42–45; cf. Westermann, III, 118), but, within the artistry of the diptych structure (43–44), the deeper unifying factor is the theology-related balance between generosity and conversion. There is balance, too, between the first, long, introduction (43:1–15) and the final, long, conclusion (44:18–34), a balance of structure and also of content, particularly concerning the conversion of Judah. A further unifying factor in these two chapters is their unique degree of emphasis on Benjamin.

Relationship to Preceding Chapters

This diptych occupies the same position (fourth) within the Joseph story as does the flood within Genesis 1–11. As the flood story echoed creation, so this diptych has some echoes of the beginning of the Joseph story (chaps. 37–38), especially of the selling of Joseph (chap. 37).

Joseph's call (37:2–11).	*Judah's call (43:1–15).*
Joseph approaches (37:12–22).	Approaching Joseph's house (43:16–23).
Joseph comes (37:23–30).	Joseph comes (43:24–31).
Recognizing horror (37:31–36).	Looking in amazement (43:32–34).

Radical conversion, such as occurs here, especially in Judah, involves major upheaval of a positive kind. This upheaval is in line with the three other central upheavals in Genesis, the flood (6:1–9:17), the fire (18:1–19:29), and the confrontation of fear (chaps. 31–33). In diverse ways, all four upheavals probe into the heart both of humankind and of God.

There are various continuities between chapters 43–44 and the three other central diptychs concerning flood, fire, and fear. For instance, the first chapter (chap. 43), with its emphasis on food, suggests a spirit of generosity, of sheer gift, which echoes both the grace/favor accorded to Noah (6:8) and the generous meal offered by Abraham (18:1–8). And there seems to be continuity also concerning the images of the tent or house, with its entrance (18:9–15; 19:6–11; cf. 43:16–23; 44:14).

Furthermore, the sons' journey back to Egypt to face their powerful brother Joseph has several echoes of the homeward journey in which Jacob faced the powerful Laban and Esau (chaps. 31–33). There are discussions about undertaking the journey (31:1–16; 43:1–14), a sense of fear (at the first encounter, 31:31; 43:18), then a meal to establish a form of peace (31:53; 43:30–34), and finally a renewed sense of crisis (concerning the approach of Esau, 32:3–12; concerning the need to face Joseph after the cup incident, 44:1–12). This renewed crisis is resolved in diverse ways: whereas Jacob wrestled at night (prior to meeting his welcoming brother, 32:32–33:11), Judah surrenders himself to slavery (prior to the revelation of his brother, 44:18–45:14).

Leading Elements

In depicting this radical conversion there is no massive flood or fire. What is present, however, is a world-wide famine, and it is precisely with an emphasis on the severity of the famine that the account begins: "The famine was heavy on the ʿereṣ ('earth, land') . . ." (43:1). The famine account is not as concise or confined as those concerning the flood and the fire. Like the related idea of conversion it is spread out over several episodes; it is dispersed or continuous rather than episodic (see Introduction, Chapter 2). The same combination, famine-conversion, occurred in the previous diptych (chaps. 41–42). Now, however, it is present in a more intense form; the famine becomes severe, "heavy" (kābēd). The overall impression is that the most frightening things in life— flood, fire, enemies, famine—can be occasions not for despair but for conversion, for a more positive awareness of God.

Structure (Table 38.1)

PANEL ONE (CHAP. 43)

The structure of the long introduction (43:1–15), the first part of the travel narrative (cf. Westermann, III, 123), is like that of a whole panel: three parts, the third being twofold. It even has its own introduction (43:1) and conclusion (43:15).

PANEL TWO (CHAP. 44)

The long conclusion in panel two (44:18–34) is similarly complex.

Comment

Panel One (Chap. 43)

[43:1–15] **Return to Egypt. The sending of Judah.** The setting is unsettling: "The famine was heavy on the land/earth. . . ." Yet this unsettling introduction is also like the setting for prophetic calls: the fifth year of the king's exile (Ezek. 1:2); the year the king died (Isa. 6:1); two years before the earthquake (Amos 1:1). In this case it is the background for the second departure for Egypt.

Unlike the brothers' first departure, brief and taciturn (42:1–5), the second is expansive and communicative, a real commissioning. Again, as with the initial departure, it is the father who takes the initiative. Without explanation, his tone has lightened: "Go back. Buy us a little food." The lack of explanation seems significant. The central issue in this whole text (chaps. 43–44) is conversion, something that breaks the patterns of logic and expectation. Like grace in the flood story (6:8), there is a sense of surprise.

Even more different is the attitude among the sons, especially in Judah, who, as in the selling of Joseph (37:27–27), now assumes leadership. The essence of his message is that there is a connection between "the brother" and "the face" (43:3), between bringing their brother Benjamin and seeing the man's face. This

Table 38.1. Benjamin: Generosity and Changing Dispositions
(chap. 43//chap. 44)

Benjamin and Judah's disposition

Introduction: sending Benjamin; Judah's pledge (43:1–15)
    Introduction: The heavy famine (1)
    1st exchange: Judah to Jacob: You need to send the youngest (2–5)
    2d: "They" to Jacob: We did not know what the man would ask (6–7)
    3d: Judah: I will be responsible. Send the lad with me (8–10)
        Jacob: Take gifts. And take your brother (11–14)
    Conclusion: they took the gift and arose and went (15)
Inside Joseph's house: a sense of fear (43:16–23).
    Benjamin seen; meal quietly ordered. Brought into the house (16–17)
    Fear of being inside the house . . . because of the money (18)
    Reconciliation at the entrance; Simeon is brought out (19–23)
Inside Joseph's house: a sense of acceptance (43:24–31).
    Brought into Joseph's house—this time at their ease (24–25)
    Peaceful meeting between Joseph and the brothers (26–28)
    Emotional meeting with Benjamin. The meal begins (29–31)
Conclusion: the festive meal (43:32–34)
    Places, distinct; arrangement, orderly, but communicative (32–33)
    His serving of many portions—especially for Benjamin (34)

Benjamin in peril and Judah's full conversion

Introduction: the command to place the cup in the sack (44:1–2)
    The command about placing the cup in Benjamin's sack (1–2a)
    The doing according to the commanding word (2b)
The departure, and the command to overtake and confront (44:3–6)
    Joseph gives the command to overtake and confront (3–5)
    The overtaking and confronting—as commanded (6)
The search for the cup (44:7–13)
    The agreement about punishment for stealing the cup (7–10)
    Finding the cup, all return (more than was agreed, 11–13)
Judah and all fall before Joseph, back in the house (44:14–17)
    Joseph's searching question: what have you done? (14–15)
    Judah's general admission of guilt. (16–17)
Conclusion: saving Benjamin; Judah's speech (44:18–34)
    Introduction: Judah approaches the unrecognized Joseph (18)
    Part 1: On Joseph's initial request to see the youngest (19–23)
    Part 2: On the father's fearful reaction (24–29)
    Part 3: The dilemma (30–31)
        The solution: Judah offers himself for Benjamin (32–33)
    Conclusion: I cannot go to my father without my brother (34)

connection has a larger connotation: relationship to one's brother or sister is tied in with relationship to the lord/Lord.

The issue of brother awareness surfaces in Jacob's questioning of his sons: "Why did you . . . tell . . . the man you had another brother?" (43:6). They reply that he had asked them, but in fact he had not, at least not directly. Rather, they had spontaneously told him or blurted it out (42:13). It is as though brother awareness, even if relegated to the back of one's mind, remains important and, at some level, needs expression.

Judah implicitly challenges both the sons and Jacob—the sons, that they should take the young brother to Egypt (a change from selling Joseph), and Jacob, that he should let go of the beloved son (shades of Abraham).

At first Judah's leadership is repetitive (43:3–5), and it is also somewhat tentative or general: "Send our brother with us." But, after a reminder both of his father's hurt and of Joseph's concern about his father and brother (43:6–7), Judah bites the bullet: "Send the lad with me."

And then (43:8–10) he speaks like a man breaking free: "We will arise and go. We will live and not die, both we and you and also our little ones. And I will pledge myself for him . . ." (unlike Reuben, who pledged his two children, 42:37). The last time Judah pledged anything, it was for faceless prostitution (38:18). Now, his pledge means the unflinching confronting of sin: "If I do not bring him back to you and set him before you, I shall be guilty of sin before you for all days." There is no more turning aside, no more avoidance. At some level he has come home to himself, especially concerning his relation to others.

The result of this commitment is a not a sense of sadness or confinement. On the contrary, the commitment seems to complete the process of breaking free. "If we had not delayed," he adds, with a touch of exuberance, "we would now be back twice."

The mood is catching: "And Israel their father said to them, 'If so, then do this . . . ,' " and he tells them, encouragingly, to bring something. At first (43:11–12), he speaks at length of simple but delightful things: "Bring . . . as tribute a little balm . . . honey . . . pistachio nuts . . . silver," goods which partly recall those of the Ishmaelites (37:25). But nothing is said about whether the brothers see the resemblance. The overall context of the present two chapters suggests not that these gifts are of little use to Jacob but that he is rising to a surprising generosity. Yet his gift to the powerful man in Egypt is but a faint shadow, almost pathetic, of the gift, the great tribute (over five hundred animals), he once sent to Esau (32:14–15).

Then he, too, bites the bullet: "And take your brother."

Having said that, he also is like a man breaking free: "Arise, go again to the man. And may El Shaddai give you mercy. . . ." And he makes a further leap: "As for me, if I am bereaved, I am bereaved."

[43:16–34] The generous noon meal—in Joseph's house. The visit to Egypt (nineteen verses) is described as if it were essentially an invitation to a wonderful meal. The meal is described in three stages of advancing togetherness.

The first stage (43:16–23), in Joseph's house, is one of fear. Joseph, unseen, notes that Benjamin has arrived and he instructs his householder to invite them all in for a meal. The invitation to Joseph's house is more than the brothers can accept. Their position, at the entrance, reflects their uncertainty. Guilt comes to the surface, and they need the words of reassurance: "Peace (šalom) be to you. Do not be afraid. Your God and the God of your father has given you treasure in your bags." The sudden release of Simeon (43:23b) embodies the reassurance.

The idea of God putting treasure in their sacks has a touch of the fantastic, but they need that kind of idea, something that will help them move beyond the normal patterns of human calculation and into the logic-surpassing world of forgiveness. Even the reference to the donkeys (43:18, 24; cf. 44:3), insofar as it has a comic touch, helps to move the story out of the rut of set human patterns.

The second stage (43:24–31), which takes place within Joseph's house, begins and ends with washing—the brothers' washing of their feet, and Joseph's washing of his weeping face. They give themselves to him. They offer both themselves, by bowing down, and what they have, their gift. And he, by private weeping, shows that on his side, too, there is a form of giving or outpouring. Joseph, then, is not some kind of dispassionate observer; he is fully involved. Heart responds to heart, as God's did at the deluge though in a different way (6:5–6; 8:21). God bestowed grace on Noah, and, through Joseph, God is gracious (ḥāhan, 43:29; cf. Noah, 6:8) to Benjamin. The closeness to God is highlighted by the "bowing down:" elsewhere in the Pentateuch this verb (qādad) is used only toward God.

The third stage (43:32–34) is the meal (or "bread," an expression for the whole meal). The meal is a time of union. Yet, at one level, the union is not full. There are no details of a conversation with Joseph. He is apart, as are the Egyptians. The apartness of the Egyptians is explained as an Egyptian problem (due perhaps to an Egyptian prohibition against eating lamb; cf. Alter, 258), but the larger implication is that, despite the togetherness, something remains unresolved. So it is, until the conversion is full.

The emphasis, for the moment, however, is not on what is unresolved, but on what is positive, on the degree of unity that has already been achieved, and especially on Joseph's attentiveness, his sharing of his portions with them, and his surprising knowledge of them. He arranges them by age. How could he know? Yet, by giving special portions to Benjamin, he subverts attention to age. This favoritism for Benjamin is also an implicit test: will they resent it as once they resented the favoritism given to young Joseph? as Cain once resented Abel? They have reached a turning point, and have done so in a setting that is positive, amid treasure, and washing, and now, great conviviality.

This convivial drinking, however, with its implication of cups or goblets, sets the scene for focusing on a special cup, the silver cup of Joseph.

Panel Two (Chap. 44)

[44:1–13] **The silver cup and the search for the doer of harm.** This next panel begins, it seems, with more of Joseph's generosity: the grain bags are filled to the maximum, and the silver is put back with the grain. But, in a final touch, Joseph's own silver cup is included in Benjamin's bag.

To some degree the role of the silver is perplexing. The silver cup will play an important role in the subsequent story but not the silver in the other sacks. However, this emphasis on the silver is understandable. On the one hand the silver is the symbol of the still-unresolved betrayal (Joseph had been sold for twenty silver pieces, 37:28). Ever since, the silver seems to stick to them. Like Lady Macbeth, unable to get the blood of the murdered king off her hands, they cannot get away from the bloody silver.

But the silver is not only negative. To some degree it is like grace, the symbol of the gift of God: "Your God and the God of your fathers has given you treasure in your bags" (43:23). The silver then embodies the transition from betrayal to God's treasure. (Somewhat similarly, in the Gospel of John, the charcoal fire embodies both betrayal and reconciliation, 18:18; 21:9). The betrayal in the past is not something to be buried away; rather it is brought to the forefront of consciousness and turned into something else, turned into a basis for conversion, ultimately into well-being and thanksgiving. Even if the silver in the sacks does not figure explicitly in the subsequent story, it sets the scene in chapter 44: it is a reminder to the reader that the silver-related issue of betrayal and grace is about to be confronted.

At first the episode looks wonderful and easy. The brothers, with Simeon restored, have been feted and replenished, and now they set off into the sunrise, into "morning light," they "and their donkeys"—the precious donkeys about which they had fretted so much.

Suddenly the glow is shattered. Joseph's servant overtakes them and, referring to the cup, confronts them. For the reader, the mood is not lightened by the episode's echoes of Laban overtaking Jacob, looking for his household gods. Joseph's man accuses them of repaying harm for good.

As if for the first time the full reality of evil dawns on the brothers. Joseph's generosity has heightened their awareness. And in their indignation they are ready to punish, even to punish themselves: whoever has the cup, "let him die. And besides, we will become my lord's servants." The "let him die" echoes what Jacob had said about whoever stole Laban's household gods (31:32).

But in their enthusiasm they have gone too far, and they are told, effectively, that punishment is for the offender alone. There are echoes here of Abraham's debate about punishing Sodom, about ensuring that the just are not punished with the unjust (18:16–33). Those who do not have the cup "shall be free of blame." Yet their offer to become servants, effectively slaves, shows their overall disposition to make restitution.

The search points to Benjamin, he who was young and favored.

At one stage in their lives the brothers had abandoned the young favored Joseph, thus inducing their father to rend his garments. Now, though they are acquitted as blameless, they themselves rend their garments. And they turn back to accompany Benjamin to the city. Their disposition has come almost full circle. And it is about to be completed—in Judah.

[44:14–34] Let me stay as a servant: Judah's fulfillment of his pledge. The Judah who once left his brothers and turned aside (38:1) now comes not only with them but as their leader in reconciliation and in generosity. The phrasing gives him a unique position: "Judah came and his brothers to Joseph's house. . . ."

Joseph's question is one that rings throughout Genesis: "What is this deed that you have done?" Then Joseph mentions the cup, yet the emphasis is not on the cup but on what it implies about Joseph himself—that he divines. Divination within Israel was forbidden (Lev. 19:31; Deut. 18:10–11), but its practice by Egyptians is apparently taken for granted. The diviner read the cup's contents, its final traces and drops of wine (as one might read tea leaves in a cup). It was a difficult art, unless one had Joseph's gifts of insight. The focus on the cup suggests that the truth is about to be divined, uncovered.

Judah's reply, though alluding to the cup, is applicable to the larger reality of human sinfulness: "What shall we say to my lord? What shall we speak? And by what shall we justify ourselves?"

Then Judah goes further, recognizing this painful moment as the positive work of God: "God has found out your servants' guilt. Behold, we are my lord's servants, both we and also he in whose hand the cup was found." While innocent of the immediate accusation about the cup Judah was aware of other guilt, especially concerning Joseph, and now it all comes to the surface. After twenty years, the truth is out.

Yet amid the guilt there is solidarity, a readiness to accept a share in the guilt of Benjamin. Joseph rejects this principle of collective punishment, this punishing of the just, and tells them that with one exception, they may go: "And you, go up in peace to your father."

Peace! Without the youngest/smallest brother! For Judah this is the final challenge.

Judah now comes close to the unrecognized Joseph (44:18), a move that echoes his approach to the unrecognized Tamar (38:15). The encounter with Tamar was a culmination of infidelity to brothers and family.

Judah's extraordinary speech (44:18–34), the longest in Genesis apart from the servant's speech at Rebekah's betrothal (24:34–49), deals with three moments—Joseph's initial request to see the youngest (44:19–23); the father's fearful reaction (44:24–29); and the present dilemma (both the dilemma itself

[44:30–31], and his solution, namely to give himself in place of his brother [44:32–34]).

The repetitiveness of the speech forms a kind of downward spiral, at least in its increasingly sad picture of the father: he will die (44:22); he will go down "in harm to Sheol" (44:29); and he will go down "in sorrow to Sheol" (44:31). But, at the end, Judah's offer of himself reverses the downward motion. This is the first time that Joseph hears how his father responded to his apparent death.

The speech is a plea equally for both the father and the smallest brother. The central focus is on the father, but the implications concerning the father's attitude—his life and love and death are bound up with the smallest brother (44:20, 22, 30)—involve a highlighting of the existence and importance of the smallest. It also means that Judah now accepts what he once rejected, his father's favoritism for the youngest son.

39   ## Joseph Revealed: Vision-Led Recovery of Relationship and Land (45:1–47:11)

Joseph Revealed: Reconciliation and Sending (Chap. 45)
Jacob's Journey to Pharaoh: Reconciliation and Land (46:1–47:11)

Introductory Aspects

The Basic Story Line

Amid all his splendor, the great calm Joseph finally breaks down before his brothers and reveals his identity: "I am Joseph. Is my father still alive? . . . Come close . . . I am Joseph, your brother."

This double focus, on his brothers and his father, governs this part of the story. First, Joseph speaks at length to his brothers (chap. 45), explaining God's role in the troubled history, and also in effect directing their attention away from the past to the future.

Then (chap. 46) the focus switches to the father. Having heard of Joseph, the old man sets off on an extraordinary journey. Carried on a wagon and surrounded by his great family, he goes to meet his long-lost son in an encounter where Joseph again weeps and weeps.

Finally, the brothers (some of them) and the father have further separate meetings, with Pharaoh. The last scene therefore is of the old patriarch, after all his years of wandering, entering into the greatest court on earth.

Then he goes out and dwells on the best of the land.

Literary Form

The primary literary form is that of a vision or theophany, a form that emphasizes the role of God. Joseph's self-revelation to his stunned brothers is recounted along the lines of a divine revelation or vision (chap. 45). And Jacob's journey to Egypt (46:1–47:11) is explicitly described as beginning with visions of the night (46:2). Between the beginnings of these two chapters, these visions, there are "formal parallels" (Fretheim, 644). As usual in the literary convention of the vision, the vision itself is accompanied by various aspects of divine confrontation, introductory word, commission, objection, reassurance, and some kind of sign (Habel, 1975).

Joseph, in revealing himself, reveals God also: "God sent me before you. . . . God . . . has set me as . . . lord of all . . . Egypt" (45:5, 9). Like Ezekiel, Isaiah, or Jeremiah when called and sent by God (Ezek. 1:1–3:21; Isa. 6; Jer. 6), the brothers are initially overcome, and, as is usual in visionary calls, it takes some time before they respond positively and accept their mission.

In this case, the mission is to go and bring the revelatory word to their father. The father in turn is overcome (45:25–28), but when he has absorbed "the words" and the sight (the wagons; 45:27) he agrees to go ("the words" and the wagons are like other aspects of the vision—word and sign). For Jacob the visions in the night are a form of reassurance (46:2). Thus, the shades of a prophet-like call, which had been building slowly through several passages, here become clear.

The journey to Egypt, so hazardous for the entire family, involves aspects of other literary conventions, especially promise, itinerary, and genealogy (Westermann, III, 154).

Complementarity of the Two Panels

The panels of this diptych, the fifth in the Joseph story, contain a change of style. Joseph's climactic self-revelation (chap. 45) gives way to Jacob's journey (46:1–47:11). Yet the two are connected. The revealing of Joseph has the practical effect of relaunching Jacob, of giving him fresh life. "Chap. 45 . . . must be seen as closely coordinate with chap. 46" (Fretheim, 643).

Within the fifth diptych of the Jacob story (chaps. 34–35) there was a somewhat similar change of style. The apparent trauma of Dinah's rape (chap. 34) gave way to the account of Jacob's journey to Bethel and beyond (35:1–20).

The self-revelation of Joseph results in two emotional meetings, first with his brothers (45:1–16), and, later, with his father (46:28–30). Both moments are intense, accompanied by seeing, falling on the neck, weeping, and speaking (45: 14–15; 46:29–30). Full explicit forgiveness will not be reached till the end (50: 15–21).

Apart from the complementarity between these two intense moments when Joseph meets his brothers and meets his father, there is a larger complementarity between the whole episode of Joseph's self-revelation to his brothers (chap. 45) and Jacob's subsequent journey to Egypt to meet Joseph (46:1–47:11). Essential to the two meetings is reconciliation, the brothers' reconciliation with each other, and Jacob's reconciliation with death. Jacob's first words to Joseph are, "Now I can die . . ." (or, "I can die this time . . . ," 46:30). The reconciliation therefore is of two kinds, horizontal, with brothers, and vertical, with the God-given limitations of human existence, limitations epitomized by death. Jacob's embracing of Joseph is like an embracing of the embodiment of God's creation and providence, including death.

This multifaceted reconciliation is associated with land, the land of Goshen, the best land in Egypt (literally, "the good of the land"). First, as the brothers are reconciled, the land is promised (45:10, 18–21). Later, when Jacob and all his progeny journey from Canaan back to Goshen, the land is given over (46:34; 47:4–6, 11): "Joseph settled his father and his brothers . . . in the land ('ereṣ) . . . in the good of the land, in the land . . ." (47:11).

Relationship to Preceding Chapters

Insofar as this diptych (45:1–47:11) is an account of achieving reconciliation in the good land it is like a down-to-earth reversal of the loss of the Garden of Eden. The disruption at Eden, likewise narrated in two complementary panels (2:25–chap. 3; and 4:1–16), was centered on alienation and loss of the land. The alienation was double, vertical, from God, and horizontal, between brothers, Cain and Abel; and it led also to alienation from the land (the land became cursed, and Cain was driven from the land, 3:17; 4:11).

Thus as Genesis approaches its conclusion, there is not only a general sense that Joseph's wise administration somehow balances or redeems the sinfulness of the early history (Gen. 1–11; Dahlberg, 1982). There is also a specific balance between the alienation in Eden and the reconciliation in Egypt. The loss of Eden ended with a troubled departure (Cain, 4:17); the reconciliation in Egypt ends with an orderly arrival (47:11).

Jacob's journey also involves a final trial, akin in some ways to the final trial in which Abraham was asked to sacrifice Isaac. Abraham was asked to go on a journey to offer his son. Jacob is asked to give himself to the journey—to meet his son. Many of the affinities between the two episodes (chap. 22; and 46:1–47:11) are fairly obvious:

Beer-sheba; offering sacrifice; Isaac; "Jacob, Jacob . . . Here I am;"

"Go down . . . and up again" (cf. 22:5, going and returning);

putting his hand; arose from/to Beer-sheba; a genealogy;

a blessing (46:1–5, 8–27; 47:7, 10; cf. 22:1–2, 5, 11–12, 17–24).

What is important, however, rather than the details, is the larger pattern. As Abraham embraced one aspect of God's death-related providence, so Jacob embraces another. While Abraham was tested in his old age and was required to undertake a journey that brought him and his son face to face with death (chap. 22), so Jacob and his sons set off not only for the journey to meet Joseph (46:1–30), but also to answer the trial-like questions of Pharaoh (46:31–47:10).

Structure (Table 39.1)

PANEL ONE (CHAP. 45)

The major part of Joseph's self-revelation (45:4–16) follows the somewhat unusual triple arrangement found in Judah's earlier statement (45:5–16; cf. 44:19–34; within the triple arrangement the third section is twofold).

Aspects of the narrative are double. Joseph is revealed first to the sons (45:1–16), and then, indirectly, to their father, Jacob (45:25–28).

PANEL TWO (CHAP. 46)

This panel also contains a double focus: the journey to Egypt, which involves both Jacob and his family ("his sons"), focuses first on meeting Joseph (46:1–30), and then on meeting Pharaoh (46:31–47:10).

Comment

Panel One (Chap. 45)

[45:1–3] Joseph's initial self-revelation. The culmination of Judah's repentance leads to a corresponding culmination in Joseph's pent-up emotion. The emotion, going out of control, bursts into expression—in his voice, his weeping, and his self-revelation: "I am Joseph."

The revelation has two levels or dimensions, human and divine. The human level is the drama of suddenly being faced by a long-lost brother. The divine dimension is the aspect that corresponds to something more. Joseph at this point evokes God. As if he were almost divine, his authority is supreme ("Have everyone go out from me"); he is apart from people ("there did not a man stand with him"); his voice seems to carry all over Egypt ("Egypt/the Egyptians heard"). And above all, when he pronounces, "I am Joseph . . ." his self-revelation is overpowering: "they were overcome/disturbed in his presence."

Yet he is supremely vulnerable. There is nothing here of the atmosphere of "Dr. Livingstone, I presume." Joseph is emotional. Now that all have left him except his brothers, his words are no longer in Egyptian, through an interpreter, but in his brothers' native tongue. As he says later (45:12), it is his own mouth that speaks to them.

Table 39.1. Joseph Revealed: Embraces and Journeys
(chap. 45 // 46:1–47:11)

Brothers embrace Joseph and journey home

Introduction: Joseph's initial self-revelation (45:1–3)
  Joseph, overcome and alone (1–2)
  Joseph's self-revelation causes disturbance (3)
Joseph's fuller self-revelation (45:4–16)
  Introduction: Come close (4)
    God sent Joseph (5–7)
    Joseph sends his brothers (8–11)
    Recognition: Your eyes see . . . my mouth (12–13)
      Kissing and weeping (14–15)
  Conclusion: The voice was heard in Pharaoh's house (16)
Pharaoh to Joseph: come to the land (45:17–20).
  Tell your brothers . . . father to come to me . . . to the land (17–18)
  And you, command them also—to take wagons (19–20)
Joseph gives provisions (45:21–24)
  Provisions for the road: Wagons, clothing and silver (21–22)
  Provisions for his father on the road, especially food (23–24)
Conclusion: The revelation to Jacob (45:25–28)
  Jacob, when told of Joseph, does not believe (25–26)
  Jacob, hearing the words and seeing the wagon, revives (27–28)

Jacob journeys to Egypt and embraces Joseph

Introduction: Jacob's Abrahamlike call to go (46:1–4)
  While journeying: sacrifice to the God of Isaac (1)
  Night visions: Do not be afraid to go to Egypt . . . to Joseph (2–4)
Journeying in wagons to Joseph in his chariot (46:5–30)
  Jacob's wagons go to Egypt (5–7)
  Jacob's seventy sons (8–27)
  Meeting Joseph in his chariot (28–30)
The trial-like meeting with Pharaoh (46:31–47:6)
  Joseph prepares his brothers for Pharaoh's questions (46:31–34)
  Pharaoh's questions (47:1–4)
  Pharaoh grants the land (47:5–6)
Conclusion: Jacob meets Pharaoh: harm and blessing (47:7–11)
  Jacob meets Pharaoh, and, amid complaints, blesses him (47:7–10)
  Joseph settles his father and brothers in the land (47:11)

Joseph, recalling the brothers' actions, speaks of God ("It was not you who sent me here but God," 45:8), yet the agency of one does not exclude the other. It is better to accept the effectiveness of both; "both can influence and be influenced, resist and be resisted" (Fretheim, 646). As already seen, this idea of two active agencies is corroborated by the perplexingly interwoven roles of the Ishmaelites and Midianites (37:25–28).

[45:4–16] Joseph's fuller self-revelation. When Joseph speaks further (45: 5), the divine dimension of his fate becomes explicit: "I am Joseph . . . whom you sold. . . . Do not be grieved . . . because, to preserve life, God sent me before you."

Joseph's self-revelation is repetitive, and so has been used as an indication of diverse sources, but as commentators increasingly recognize, the circumstances warrant repetition (Westermann, III, 142).

He immediately mentions their selling of him into Egypt, but he brings it to the surface only to lay it aside, so that they not be sad or angry with themselves ("do not let anger be in your eyes").

The three-part structure of Joseph's speech is indeed like that of Judah (in 44:18–34), but despite much continuity between the two speeches, there is also contrast. Judah's speech spiraled downward, but Joseph's revelation is a call to action. While the downward movement in Judah's speech led to an image of sorrow, the sorrow of death and mourning ("bring the white head of . . . our father in sorrow to Sheol"), Joseph's speech begins with a form of sorrow, and leads away from it (the sorrow of sin: "And now, do not be grieved . . .").

In the first stage of Joseph's speech (45:5–7) the emphasis is on survival and initial growth, moving out of grief and anger, preserving life, surviving another five years of famine, developing from a remnant (*šĕʾērît*) toward a great deliverance. Through his suffering, however harrowing, God has preserved his people.

The second stage (45:8–11) is one of greater strength and action: Joseph is father of Pharaoh; he is lord; and it is time to move: "Hurry. . . . Go up. . . . Come down. . . . Do not stand still. . . . You shall settle in the land of Goshen, and you shall be near me." Goshen is the part of the rich Nile Delta that is closest to the Sinai peninsula.

The latter idea, of being near Joseph ("Come down to me"), dominates most of the third stage (45:12–15; part 3a). Nearness is not just a proposal; it is a reality: the brothers embrace and weep (45:14), Joseph's third time of weeping (cf. 42:24; 43:30).

As in Judah's speech, the conclusion (45:16) adds a fresh aspect: the arrival of Joseph's brothers becomes good news for Pharaoh and his servants.

[45:17–20] Pharaoh to Joseph: Come to the land. Joseph's commission to the brothers, to go up and bring their father down to Egypt, now takes increasingly concrete form. Pharaoh becomes involved, like a symbol of some other dimension of the commissioning of the brothers, and he is very practical. He speaks to Joseph about Jacob coming "to the land of Canaan" and then coming "to me." Pharaoh's words about the journey have echoes of the original call of Abraham (12:1–5), but he is more down-to-earth; he refers to the best of the land (literally, "the good of the land") and "the fat of the land." And he is even more down-to-earth about transport. "Load your animals," he says at first; and later, "Take . . . wagons," the first such reference in Genesis. The wagons are "for your little ones and your wives, and you shall carry your father."

[45:21–24] **Joseph gives provisions.** The provisions for the journey become even more detailed—food, new clothes, with extra for the youngest. Coats and silver, so negative in the selling of Joseph (chap. 37), are now heaped on Benjamin. He receives five changes of tunic and three hundred pieces of silver. They are like an abundance of reversal and restitution, leading not to rancor but to a sense of festivity. Instead of receiving clothing, Joseph gives it; he reverses the pattern (Matthews, 1995).

There is even more provision for the father. In place of the meager precious gifts Jacob had sent to Egypt ("a little balm . . . pistachio nuts," 43:11), Joseph now sends an abundance of provisions, twenty donkeys loaded.

At the end of the commission the emphasis on what is down-to-earth becomes more specific, literally, close to the road: the provisions are "for his father on the road;" and he tells them not to be apprehensive "on the road."

[45:25–28] **Spirit coming alive: the revival of Jacob/Israel.** When the sons tell their father, he is stunned: "His heart went cold, for he did not believe them." One may even say that his heart stopped: "The Hebrew verb plainly means to stop, or more precisely, to intermit" (Alter, 271). Two factors, however, bring about a change in him, the words and the wagons. He hears the words, and he sees the wagons, and, in a process evocative of recovery from death, his spirit comes alive.

Rab, he says, "Enough/abundant," a word that echoes so many promises about abundance. His revival is not for himself only; as well as being Jacob he is also called Israel (the two names occur in immediate succession, 45:27–28).

Panel Two (46:1–47:11)

[46:1–4] **Jacob's Abraham-like call to go: Beer-sheba, sacrifices, and words of reassurance.** As Jacob sets out, several factors combine to make this journey daunting—his age, the distance, and the unknownness of Egypt. Small wonder, as he offers sacrifices to God, that his reply to God, "Here I am," echoes that of Abraham when he was sent to sacrifice his son on an unknown mountain (chap. 22). Small wonder, too, that he receives multiple reassurance about not being afraid—about being accompanied, about coming up again from Egypt; about Joseph's hand on his eyes, to close them, at death. As with Abraham's journey to the unknown, the issues behind the journey are those of love and death. For Abraham the emphasis was on love; for Jacob it is on death.

[46:5–30] **Journeying in wagons to Joseph in his chariot.** The first part of the journey is made easier by the fact that its focus is not so much on Egypt as simply on Joseph, in Goshen.

In fact the journey, far from seeming arduous or distressing, turns into a form of procession. First, because Jacob and many others travel in the wagons, and there is a rich accompaniment (46:5–7). Further, because, despite discrepancies, the names of the seventy, spelled out with rhythmic solemnity, add to the impression of a serene parade (46:8–27). And also, because when Joseph comes to meet them, he comes in a chariot (46:28–29).

This first part of the journey, far from being stressful, ends in a long embrace and, explicitly, in a readiness to die.

The account of the journey (46:5–30) is so structured that there is a balance between the opening reference to the wagons (46:5) and the closing reference to the chariot (46:29). This raises the question of whether the wagons, apart from their role as practical transport, have something of the connotation of a chariot, either as symbols of the transcendence of God (Ezekiel 1) or as vehicles that transcend death (as in Elijah's ascent, 2 Kings 1). The whole vision-like diptych has a general affinity with Ezekiel 1, and Jacob's calm journey toward death is somewhat akin, in its calm tone, to the final journey of Elijah (2 Kings 1). The subsequent incidents, undergoing Pharaoh's life-probing questions and settling in the land (46:31–47:11), may be read as having a death-related dimension.

Joseph, when he comes to meet Jacob, is said to "appear" before him, or "be seen by him," "a slightly odd phrase . . . more typically used for the appearance of God" (Alter, 277). Once again Joseph has a dimension of the divine. Yet despite this divine dimension, it is Joseph, not Jacob, who weeps.

Judah has the role of leading the way to Joseph. Such a role is hardly necessary, but, in the context of the larger story, it has its place: it maintains the sense of Judah as a leader.

[46:31–47:6] **The journey goes further: the visit to Pharaoh.** The second part of the journey consists of a visit to Pharaoh by five of the sons. The reason for five is not clear, but it may, perhaps, be related to other references to five: Benjamin's five extra handfuls (43:34), the five remaining years of famine (45:7, 11), five new garments (45:22), the giving of a fifth to Pharaoh (47:26–26).

Visiting Pharaoh could be intimidating. For the chief butler and chief baker, going to Pharaoh's feast was an occasion for radical judgment (40:20–21). And in this episode, Pharaoh is questioning: to the sons, he asks, "What do you do/make/work?" and to Jacob he will ask, "Like what [*or*, how many] are the days of your life?" (47:3, 8).

Yet, as with the journey, the pervading mood is one of reassurance. Joseph prepares his brothers for Pharaoh's question, and, whereas he once gave a bad report about some of the sons' shepherding (37:2), he now tells them that they may answer that they are shepherds. In this way, Pharaoh will send them away to Egypt's Goshen territory. (Apparently the Egyptians, though they kept flocks, looked down on shepherds and were glad to keep them at arm's length, for instance, in Goshen, on the eastern border.)

So it happens: Pharaoh sends them to Goshen. Yet aspects of the encounter are enigmatic. In particular, despite the Egyptian aversion to shepherds, Pharaoh seems so impressed that he asks Joseph to send men of worth as chief of his (Pharaoh's) own livestock (46:31–47:6).

Pharaoh's response to the five chosen brothers—rather than replying directly, he speaks to Joseph—is perplexing. Perhaps part of the response's function is to set up a contrast for the following scene, when he does respond to the old man. The last time there was a discussion about inviting Jacob's family into new land (in chap. 34, esp. 34:21) it was the sons who commanded the discussion, and Jacob was sidetracked. Not any more. The old man is back at center stage.

[47:7–11] Conclusion. Jacob meets Pharaoh: complaints and blessing. This is an extraordinary moment, worthy of a great painter or film director. The aged patriarch, after so much wandering and waiting, enters the splendor of the world's greatest court.

Jacob gives a strangely negative summary of his years ("few and full of harm" or "few and evil/bad"), but the negative summary is surrounded by blessing: Jacob blesses Pharaoh twice, both in greeting him and in saying farewell to him.

The result is that the brief scene has wide implications. First, in the literary structure of the scene, the negativity of Jacob's life is sandwiched between blessings (47:7–10). Given the primordial role of Jacob's biography, this suggests a statement about life: it is indeed short and difficult, yet it is bound around by blessing.

Furthermore, blessing is not limited to a chosen few. As Westermann indicates, it is for all: "the blessing of Pharaoh by Jacob [is] a sign that the blessing bestowed on the patriarchs and passed along from the fathers to the children . . . reaches beyond the succession of the patriarchs and is a blessing intended for humanity" (1996, 102).

Blessing, therefore, belongs both to life and to humankind, or more simply, to human life. Jacob may indeed be special; he is chosen. Yet his role is for a purpose greater than himself; it is for humankind at large. His role is like that of a religious institution: it has a chosen role, but only to serve humankind, to facilitate blessing.

Later (47:11), when Joseph has brought his brothers and father through the meeting with Pharaoh, he, Joseph, settles them in the best of the land. The designation of the land as that of Rameses (47:11) is faintly disquieting. The name "Rameses," apart from belonging to a later Pharaoh, is associated with the Israelites' slave labor (Exod. 1:11). Yet within Genesis the sense of the land is positive. The giving of the land depends on the command of Pharaoh, the higher power. The effect of recalling Pharaoh's command is to surround the granting of the land with a sense of legality and security.

40   Amid Famine and Death: Life and Blessing (47:12–Chap. 48)

Amid Famine, Life (47:12–28)
Amid Death: Blessing (47:29–Chap. 48)

Introductory Aspects

The Basic Story Line

The scene's two panels are like two storms, both of which have been gathering for a long time—the famine, and the dying of Jacob. Famine and Jacob's death have their roots as far back as chapter 37, in the grain-related dream of Joseph (37:5–8) and in Jacob's mournful talk about going down to Sheol (37:34–35). The same two themes returned in chapters 41–42, beginning with the grain-related dreams of Pharaoh (41:1–7) and with Jacob's further talk of going down to Sheol (42:38).

However, though the actual famine began in chapter 41 (41:53–57), only now do its ravages emerge fully. It is so bad that, in a startling development, Joseph takes over Egypt; the people give him everything—money, livestock, lifeless bodies, and ground—and they become servants of Pharaoh (47:12–28). Likewise, only now does Jacob's death-knell strike fully: "Israel's days to die drew near . . ." (47:29). The whole second panel (47:29–chap. 48) takes place around his death-bed.

In one sense, therefore, the two-panel scene is profoundly death-like. The collapse of the earth (*ʾereṣ*) is followed by the collapse of Jacob.

Yet the overall impact of the scene is not negative. Joseph's takeover of the famine-struck land, however harsh at first sight, becomes a basis for a form of renewal (47:23–25), and this renewal is set within the framework of Joseph providing for the life of his family, including a fresh lease on life for Jacob (47: 12–13, 27–28; Jacob reaches 147 years). Furthermore, the scene at Jacob's death-bed is dominated not so much by death but by blessing. In the two-part scene as a whole therefore the pervading mood is not of doom, but of renewed life and blessing.

Literary Form

The primary literary category for the account of acquiring the land (47:12–28) is the same as for the account of acquiring the field (chap. 23)—a contract dialogue. Most of the text (esp. 47:15–25) is a dialogue between Joseph and the people.

The primary literary category for the second panel, concerning the approach of Jacob's death (47:29–chap. 48), is that of a last blessing, a variation on the scene of Isaac's last blessing (Gen. 27).

Joseph's acquisition of the land contains an etiological aspect: it gives the impression of explaining aspects of the origin of the Egyptian agrarian and tax system (Westermann, III, 173–174), including Pharaoh's ownership of all the land of Egypt, the origin of the need to pay one fifth in tax, and the priests' exemption from tax.

This etiological aspect, with its focus on history, has sometimes dominated the interpretation of Genesis 47. To some degree this emphasis on history is warranted. There is independent evidence that, nominally, Pharaoh was considered the sole owner of the land of Egypt and that the temple, with its priests, were exempt from tax (Westermann, III, 173–174).

Yet, there are problems with the accuracy of this account of Joseph taking over the land. Pharaoh's ownership goes back to the first dynasty, almost 3000 BCE. It need not be accounted for through a second-millenium minister such as Joseph (Westermann, III, 173).

The crucial issue, however, is not whether the Joseph story of acquiring the land is true historically, but whether it has another aspect or level. Closer examination indicates that, in fact, the etiological factor is not the full explanation (*pace* Westermann, III, 177). While the author did indeed have access to some genuine information about the agrarian situation in Egypt, that information has been adapted to express a more general idea.

The concept of land is central to Genesis, and Joseph's acquisition of the land is part of a much larger pattern about possessing the land and serving it. The idea of serving (*ʿābad*) the ground (*ădāmâ*) or land first appears in Genesis as something very positive, in the Garden of Eden (Gen. 2:5, 15). So when Joseph acquires the ground (*ădāmâ*) and induces the people into being servants (*ʿebed;* 47:19, 21), his action has two levels of meaning. At one level it is a subjection to servitude. At another, it is a recovery of an aspect of the primordial human relationship to the ground. At the beginning, the inert human became a living soul (*nepeš ḥayyâ*, 2:7). In a sense, Joseph, too, gives life; the people say he has kept them alive (causative of *ḥāyāh*, "to live," 47:25).

To serve Pharaoh is not necessarily bad. The figure of Pharaoh does not yet have the negative connotation it will acquire in the book of Exodus. In the Joseph story, Pharaoh is almost a divine figure, like a divine judge; and besides, the people's immediate relationship is to Joseph.

Complementarity of the Two Panels

The basic combination of elements in this diptych (47:12–chap. 48)—famine and death—is not unique in the Bible. As already seen, aspects of this diptych reflect elements of Genesis 1–2. Furthermore, the combination of upheaval in

nature (famine on earth) along with upheaval in human fortune (Jacob's dying)
has some biblical analogues. The death of David, for instance, is preceded by
chapters which, whatever their origin, include upheavals in nature—famine and
pestilence (2 Sam. 21–24, esp. 21:1–14; 24:10–17).

A rough equivalent to this kind of scene will occur also in the synoptic
Gospels when a picture of the collapse of the universe (an eschatological discourse) is followed by the first stage in the death of Jesus (see, for instance, the
sequence between Mark 13 and Mark 14:1–31). (Unlike Jesus, who will give
his parting blessing or speech at a supper, Jacob gives it in bed, 48:2.)

Relationship to Preceding Chapters

As Genesis draws toward its close it begins to gather up many threads and
weave them together, thus leading to a synthesis of unusual complexity (cf.
Westermann, III, 211–214). This complexity involves resonating many texts.

In particular, the two panels, about the *land* and the *end-blessing* (or death-
blessing; 47:12–28; and 47:29–chap. 48), have multiple echoes of the *begin-
ning-blessing* (1:1–2:4a) and the *Garden* (2:4b–24). The forces that once led to
creation (Genesis 1–2) are now continued in another form, even through famine and death (47:12–chap. 48). In a sense, death is a further form of creation.

Already the move to the best land in Egypt (45:1–47:11) was seen as containing a reversal of some of the early chapters of Genesis, a form of recovery
of the loss of Eden (2:25–4:16; see previous diptych). Now, as famine and
death descend, the process of engaging the beginning of Genesis continues.

There is an engagement, too, with the end of the Abraham story. As already
seen, Jacob's journey to Egypt (46:1–47:11) echoes the sacrifice-related journey
of Abraham (chap. 22). And Joseph's subsequent acquisition of the ground,
including fields (47:20), echoes Abraham's subsequent acquisition of the field
(chap. 23), an immensely positive development. Both acquisitions occur near
the end of their respective halves of the book.

The hand under the thigh and the insistence on going to the right place (48:
29–31) echo the oath to Abraham (24:1–9). The conclusion, concerning the bow
(48:21–22), may, perhaps, be related to the shoulder and bow of the Ishmael
story (21:14, 16, 20).

Structure (Table 40.1)

The limits of panel one (47:12–28) are set by the balancing references first to
Joseph providing for his father and family (47:12–13) and then to Israel settling
in Egypt, and Jacob living in Egypt (47:27–28). As Murphy notes (45:70) "the
conclusion to [the] notice [essentially in v. 12] is to be found in vv. 27–28."
What 47:12 begins is concluded in 47:28.

Table 40.1. Famine and the Approach of Death
(47:12–28 // 47:29–48:22)

Amid famine, life

Introduction: Joseph provides for his father (47:12–13)
 Bread for the family, but famine on the earth (12–13a)
 Famine exhausts the lands of Egypt and Canaan (13b)
Joseph gathers all money and livestock (47:14–17)
 The money (14–15)
 The livestock (16–17)
The second year: Joseph acquires people and ground (47:18–22)
 The people ask to become servants (18–19)
 The people become servants (20–22)
Joseph gives seed and keeps people alive (47:23–26).
 The seed which keeps people alive (23–25)
 The tax (except for priests): a fifth for Pharoah (26)
Conclusion: Israel settled in Egypt (47:27–28)
 Israel in the land of Egypt, increasing and multiplying (27)
 Jacob in the land of Egypt, many years (28)

Amid death, blessing

Introduction: as death approaches, Israel prepares (47:29–48:2)
 Israel exacts an oath and sinks down (47:29–31)
 Israel is told of Joseph's sons and sits up (48:1–2)
Blessing—with a deathly shadow (48:3–7)
 Jacob recalls everlasting blessing (3–4)
 Jacob incorporates two Egyptian-born sons (5–6)
 The death of Rachel (7)
Blessing—with a surprise, and doubled (48:8–20)
 Israel as weak, but kissing, embracing (8–10)
 The surprising boys are blessed surprisingly (11–16)
 The blessing is explained (17–20)
Conclusion: Jacob's final promise to Joseph (48:21–22)
 The promise of return to the land "of your fathers" (21)
 The enigma of the shoulder, sword and bow (22)

Comment

Panel One (47:12–28)

[47:12–13] Bread for Joseph's family in the context of bread for the earth. The introduction speaks of bread being needed by two bodies of people (immediate *family* and the people of the *earth*/land), and of the famine exhausting two lands (*Egypt* and *Canaan*). Part of the effect of the introduction is to interweave the fate of the family with Egypt, Canaan, and the larger world. It is not clear whether there is some kind of correspondence between the two pairs, between family-earth and Egypt-Canaan.

[47:14–17] In exchange for bread, Joseph gathers all the money and livestock of Egypt and Canaan. The lack of bread leads Joseph to gather in all the silver (money) of Egypt and Canaan, and all the livestock of Egypt. The account may be understood as an example of normal tough commerce—food in exchange for money and animals. But the transaction has connotations of something more. The introduction established a context involving the whole earth. The emphasis on all—"all" money and livestock—suggests a power that is supreme. And the " 'Come' . . . 'Come' " (" 'Come! Bread' . . . 'Come! Your livestock' ") has an echo of the drama at the tower of Babel, when God asserted authority over human pretentiousness (11:3–7). Joseph's gathering, therefore, of all the money and livestock, has an echo of the action and power of God.

[47:18–22] Joseph acquires bodies and ground. The connotation of God-like power becomes even greater when the people, in their need of bread, give their lifeless bodies ("carcasses") and their ground. Again there is a suggestion of submitting to some form of total power: "We will not conceal. . . . Nothing remains for my lord except our carcasses and our ground." The earlier gathering of "all" (47:14, 17) is now balanced and completed by the "nothing" that remains (47:18). And the word "lord" (47:18) increases the connotation of divinity. What Joseph offers is nothing less than averting death.

In this deathly situation, there is one exception: the priests' special statute or law, a ruling that allows them to eat, to have their own source of food.

[47:23–26] Joseph gives seed and keeps people alive as servants of the ground (Pharaoh's ground). Given how power tends to corrupt, and given later oppression in Egypt, one could imagine that Joseph's increasing power would cause growing fear and resentment. But the opposite happens. In this third phase, when Joseph distributes seed and establishes the grain tax—a fifth—the people's mood changes from one of clamoring to one of gratitude. Before this they had led the discussion, but now Joseph leads, and their response does not seem to be based on compulsion: "You have kept us alive. May we find favor in the eyes of my lord, and let us be servants to Pharaoh." It is no accident that the share they give to Pharaoh, a fifth, is the same as was put aside by Joseph during the good years as a way of surviving the famine (41:34). In face of death, Joseph has given them fresh life.

[47:27–28] Conclusion. Israel settles in the land of Egypt, with property, increasing and multiplying. The positive mood of those who sowed seed and stayed alive seems to be continued among the people of Israel: "Israel settled in the land of Egypt. . . . And they acquired property . . . and they were fruitful and multiplied much." The impression of the introduction is reinforced: the fate of the two—Egypt and Israel—is interwoven.

Tied to that interweaving is the fate of Jacob. It suddenly emerges (47:28) that he has a new lease of life, seventeen years in Egypt. This lifts the story of both himself and Egypt beyond the famine. The sense of moving to a new time frame is reinforced by the reference to his full age, 147 years. The two sevens (17 and 147) may perhaps recall the famine, but, if so, they also echo a much larger pattern of repeated sevens, beginning with creation (2:2–3) and including the 17 years of Joseph's youth.

Taken as a whole, the first panel (47:12–28) shows how, even though all must serve Joseph's Pharaoh, one group stays free—Israel. Israel, first and last, has a special position (47:12, 27–28). This special position has some kinship with the special position of the priests.

Panel Two (47:29–chap. 48)

[47:29–48:2] **Introduction. As death approaches, Israel prepares.** The introduction to the second panel records two moments that are quite common in the death of old people, first the general sense of approaching death (47:29–31) and, later, the specific moment when death is imminent (48:1–2). The two are so described that they form a unity.

At one level, the introduction suggests a man who is sinking; Jacob goes from being assertive to being weak and passive. On the first occasion, when his time is simply drawing near, he seems assertive. He calls Joseph and has him swear, hand under his thigh, not to bury him in Egypt (47:29–31). The echoing of the Abraham incident of the thigh (24:1–9) strengthens that sense of assertiveness.

On the second occasion (48:1–2), however, Jacob is passive. He neither calls Joseph nor sees him coming. Rather, Joseph is informed, with an explicit reference to his father becoming weak, and Jacob in turn is informed that Joseph has come. The presence of Joseph's two sons adds to the sense of a decisive moment. Jacob is ebbing.

Yet, at another level, something further is happening; Jacob is not just sinking. The final phrases are curious:

47:31, "Israel bowed down upon the head of the bed."

48:2, "Israel summoned his strength and sat up upon the bed."

These two phrases may be taken as distinct details, and as such they are important, evocative of being confined to bed. But when taken together they form a pattern, obscure but real, of descent and ascent: "down . . . up." The implication is that, while Jacob is indeed sinking in these final chapters, the full reality of what is happening to him is more complex. The only other time that Jacob was described as lying down, during his dream (28:10–22), there was another image, involving angels, of going up and going down.

The two main parts, which now follow, have a corresponding ambiguity. Both tell of blessing, but with a basic variation.

[48:3–7] **Blessing, with a deathly shadow.** This first main part (48:3–7) is framed by two references to youth and to death: the youthful moment at Luz when, as he journeyed, he dreamt (28:10–22); and a later moment, when, on another journey, having come back from "Paddan"—a reference to Paddan-Aram—his beloved wife Rachel died on the road to Ephrath (35:14–20). These two moments are like landmarks in his life, or at least in one level of his life, the external level of a journey that sinks from dreams into death. It is with this level, therefore, that the first main part (48:3–7) is primarily concerned.

As he speaks, the first thing on the mind of the dying Jacob is the great tradition of blessing and promise (48:3–4). It is a tradition that gave energy to his own life—"at Luz [Bethel] . . . He blessed me . . ." (cf. 28:10–22)—and that, as he describes it, resonates with both the memory of his ancestors and the original blessing of creation ("I will make you fruitful and multiply you"). It is a tradition for the past and also for the future, for hope. Jacob recalls that the promise tells of a land that is "an everlasting property" (48:4). Thus he invokes a promise that goes from creation to eternity.

With regard to this future, Jacob then becomes more specific (48:5–6): "And now, your two sons, born . . . in Egypt . . . shall be mine." They may be Egyptian-born of an Egyptian mother, but Jacob wants as it were to graft them on to his own inheritance, to adopt them, and through them to transmit the inheritance to possible future children. This adoption is "a legal act with parallels in the ancient Near East" (Fretheim, 659). The implication is of an inheritance that spreads not only across time, from creation to eternity, but also across space, to those born in Egypt (48:5–6).

Yet, when Jacob looks again to his earlier days, those related to Luz [Bethel], after he had come from Paddan, he remembers the other reality, the death and burial of the beloved Rachel (48:7). The grief still lingers.

Thus the memories of his journey, from Luz to Paddan to Ephrath, are primarily those of blessing and promise, but they also include death and burial. The blessing seems to peter out.

[48:8–20] Blessing, with a surprise, and doubled. In this second main part (48:8–20), the blessing, instead of petering out, seems to develop and surprise. While the first encounter with Joseph and the sons started powerfully and ended with a recalling of death, the second encounter tends in the opposite direction. At first Jacob appears weak: he has to ask who the sons are (48:8); his eyes are heavy with age, not able to see (48:10); and Joseph thinks he does not know his right hand from his left (second childhood, 48:17).

Yet, as the episode develops, the overall effect, amid this picture of loss, is of great blessing. The word "bless" is used five times. Even the quantity of the text is much greater than in the previous part. God is referred to in three ways (48:15–16; cf. 31:10–13, the dream, the angel, God).

The first incident (48:8–10) is one of embracing—kissing and embracing children.

The second (48:11–16) tells of surprising birth. Jacob had not expected to see Joseph yet now he sees both Joseph and his descendants (48:11). The phrasing is curious: "He made them go out from between his knees" (the knees of someone in bed). To place a child on someone's knees was a formula of adoption (Alter, 287). In this case the adoption formula is phrased as if it had some further dimension.

There is also a suggestion of Jacob's authority over Joseph. Joseph bows before him (48:12b, reversing the dream of 37:10), and Jacob, crossing his hands, reverses Joseph's arrangement about which son gets the primary blessing (48:13–14).

The God of Jacob's blessing is the God not of creation (as in 48:3–4) but of personal history, the God who is related to his fathers, to the course of his own life, and to redeeming him from harm (48:15–16a). But the blessing, while thus rooted in the family history, then turns outward to become a form of blessing for the earth; the family will be "a multitude in the midst of the earth" (48:16b).

When Joseph (48:17–20) objects to the reversal, to giving priority to the younger, Jacob answers calmly. Then, in variant form, he repeats the process. He blesses the boys again, and this time he reverses the order of the names ("he put Ephraim before Manasseh"). The focus in this second blessing is not on the whole earth, but simply on Israel. Thus the two blessings complement one another.

Jacob's procedure, both in adopting the two boys into the ranks of his own sons, and in reversing seniority among the two, is a major instance of "the great Genesis theme of the reversal of primogeniture" (Alter, 287). Here the reversal is compounded: the mother of the two adopted boys is Egyptian.

The concluding repetition of the name "Ephraim" (48:20) seems to echo the concluding repetition of the name "Ephrath" (48:7). "Ephraim" means doubly fruitful (cf. 41:52); "Ephrath" also means fruitful, but, in its context (48:7), is associated with death. The overall suggestion is that death is in some way fruitful.

[48:21–22] Conclusion. Jacob's final promise to Joseph. Jacob's authority, already established during the blessing, continues, and now reaches a new high point. Jacob is no longer asking God; Jacob is telling Joseph what God will do for him (Joseph). And, in tandem with what God will do for him, he tells what he, Jacob, will also do for him. (The tone at the end of Jesus' last discourse will be similarly authoritative [John 17:24–26]).

Jacob's concluding phrase to Joseph, concerning a shoulder and bow (48:22), is notoriously obscure. Alter (291) lessens the problem: in place of "one shoulder/Shechem" he translates "with single intent" (cf. Zeph. 3:9). But a puzzle remains, the phrase ". . . which I took . . . with my sword and . . . bow." The details, whatever their significance (cf. chap. 21?), seem so deliberately obscure as to suggest a reality that is itself enigmatic, something that surpasses language.

41   Jacob's Death and Burial (Chaps. 49–50)

Jacob's Final Blessings and Death (Chap. 49)
Jacob's Burial (with Mourning and Aftermath) (Chap. 50)

Introductory Aspects

The Basic Story Line

The two final chapters tell of two closely-related episodes—death and burial: Jacob dies at the end of chapter 49 and is buried in chapter 50.

A death-and-burial story can seem empty. But not here. The death (chap. 49) is primarily a scene of blessing. Jacob calls his sons, and instead of moaning about all that is lost and gone—his moaning phase is over—he directs them toward the future. He recalls the past only insofar as it helps him to indicate a future leader (the past helps to disqualify the three eldest sons).

The burial (chap. 50) is a scene of haunting splendor. Jacob receives the fullest Egyptian ritual, literally the best in the world. But then, in an extraordinary counter move, he is given something that the larger world cannot give—a journey that breaks normal geographical patterns and that brings him to the God-related site at Mamre, the site first bought for Sarah. This enigmatic journey involves a great gathering beyond the Jordan—of family, nation, and distant onlookers—for seven days. And when the burial is over, the effect is not to dissolve or lessen the relationship between the brothers but to bring them together as never before in explicit forgiveness.

At the very end (50:26) the burial of Joseph is brief and down-to-earth, forming a prosaic counterpoint to the events surrounding Jacob. Taken together the two burials provide two accounts of death, one ending with a rumor of transcendence, the other in a coffin. The implications of the difference between the two—one surrounded by chariots and horses, the other in a box—will become clearer in the contrast between Elijah, taken up to heaven (2 Kings 2:11), and Elisha, reduced to bones (2 Kings 13:20).

Literary Form

Jacob's words to his twelve sons (chap. 49) have been described as a last will and testament (Westermann, III, 181–182), or as the Testament of Jacob (Speiser, 370). The genre question, however, is not simple (Sarna, 331). Chapter 49 involves a synthesis of three literary types: the death-bed blessing (cf. Isaac's blessing of Jacob and Esau, chap. 27); the farewell address or last discourse (cf.

Joshua's farewell, Josh. 23–24); and the tribal poem (cf. the Song of Moses, Deut. 32). Accordingly, Jacob's words involve diverse elements, including rebukes (especially to the three senior sons, 49:3–7).

Yet, as the chapter develops, the sayings tend, overall, to become more positive, and at the end the author refers to them as blessings (49:28). Three positive aspects stand out—the long positive statement to Judah (49:8–12), the pithy mid-point saying about waiting on Yhwh's salvation (49:18), and the penultimate blessing-filled statement to Joseph (49:22–26).

If chapter 49 is defined by its beginning then it is simply a testament, and it consists of sayings. But if it is defined by what it becomes then it is best seen as Jacob's blessings. It appears appropriate, amid the complexity, to accept the author's own designation (49:28): Jacob's words are primarily blessings.

As well as shifting from negative to positive, the sayings also involve a shift from individual sons to tribes ("All these are the tribes . . . and . . . their father . . . blessed them . . . ," 49:28). The immediate effect of this change is to move the focus toward the future, toward the days when the sons will have developed into tribes. In accordance with this shift toward the future, I-you language soon fades and gives way to the third person. The larger effect is that the approach of death, instead of seeming to be negative and focused on the past, appears increasingly positive and hopeful.

The turning point in this positive development is the little saying about waiting on salvation (49:18). This saying is intrusive, but precisely for that reason it helps to mark a change, a shift to a more positive perception.

Concerning chapter 50, particularly its literary form, Westermann speaks of "a report shaped into narrative form which follows step by step the procedures proper to the death of a family member" (III, 197). Consequently chapter 50 is probably best described simply as a burial narrative. But the burial is of someone who is far more than a family member; in Jacob's death, the mourning is far-reaching.

As often in burials, the ceremony is followed by a shift in focus from the one who has died to the surviving family. It is likewise here: the later part of chapter 50 switches the focus back to the sons, especially to the relationship between them (50:14–25).

Complementarity of the Two Panels

The most basic complementarity between chapters 49 and 50 is very obvious: death and burial are almost like two parts of a single process.

Furthermore, unlike many cases of death and burial, the atmosphere surrounding both these events is primarily positive and future-oriented. Jacob's dying words to his sons, despite some initial negativity about the past, become increasingly positive, more like general blessings for the future (chap. 49). And after the burial, the conversation between the sons, some of it purportedly quoting the dying Jacob, likewise becomes increasingly positive. The fear about evil deeds of the past gives way to forgiveness and to practical assurances about the future (50:15–21).

Relationship to the Whole Book of Genesis

Jacob's final poem is fully integrated into the finished book. The prominence, for instance, of Judah and Joseph in these sayings fits most plausibly not with some tentative historical reconstruction[1] but with their verifiable prominence in the Joseph story itself, in the completed text of Genesis. This suggests that the origin of Genesis 49 is as late as the completed book.

It is not unique to find that a seemingly old poetic composition is in fact quite late. It is generally accepted, for instance, that the ancient-sounding Song of the Sea (Exod. 15:1–21) was written long after the date assigned to the

---

1. The various sayings of chapter 49 are sometimes seen as emerging neither from Jacob himself, as Genesis indicates, nor from the author of Genesis, but from any of several historical settings (see esp. de Hoop, 1999, 26–62). Speiser (371), for instance, sets Jacob's poem much later than Jacob himself, but before the first millennium. De Hoop (1999, 451–631, esp. 628–630) gives distinct but early dates to two layers in the text.

In general, the fragmenting of Genesis 49—breaking it from the rest of Genesis, and then breaking it internally into isolated sayings—comes more from the presuppositions of the romantic era than from literary criticism; "the isolation of Genesis 49 from its literary context is mainly based on a form-critical classification instead of on literary critical arguments" (de Hoop, 1999, 79).

The difficulty of attributing a distinct date to one of the sayings may be seen, for instance, from the case of Levi. It is easy to imagine a connection between the picture of Levi—deprived of inheritance and with no hint of cultic privileges (49:6–7)-and a distant time of conquest (Alter, 292). But the easiness of imagining something, even something plausible, does not make it true. A Levi-conquest link is completely unverifiable. What is verifiable is the literary continuity between the picture of Levi as a killer (49:6–7) and the preceding account of Levi avenging Dinah (chap. 34).

There is further literary continuity between the picture of Levi as a killer (49:6–7) and the subsequent account of Moses, from the tribe of Levi, killing (hārag, the same verb in Gen. 49:6 and Exod. 2:14). This picture of Moses, as a disinherited Levite killer with no link to cult, is not used to link the composition of Exod. 2:11–15 to the time of the conquest. And the same applies to the picture of Levi in Genesis 49. The absence of Levi's clear link with cult is not a reliable indication that the text is ancient, that it goes back to the conquest. Very often in a long narrative things develop slowly. Within Genesis the transition from episodic text to continuous text is slow, and in the Primary History as a whole, the transition, for instance, from Enoch to Elijah is slow. In presenting the first Levites-Levi himself and Moses-it is not necessary to include everything-not even cult. The cult aspect will be incorporated later (Moses soon meets Aaron, Exod. 4; and Moses' blessing will reinforce the link between Levi and the cult, Deut. 33:8–11). The initial distance between Levi and cult is a reflection not of an ancient date but of a long narrative, which has ample time-as far as 2 Kings-to bring things together.

For the moment, in Genesis 49, it is enough that the Levi saying of Jacob be a ringing condemnation of angry violence. This condemnation complements the adjacent condemnation of sexual abuse (the incest of Reuben, 49:3–4). Negatively, the two condemnations-concerning sex and violence-form a programmatic pair. They are relevant for all times and their archaic formulation does not require that they be set in distant ages. With a little research most good writers can compose archaic formulations.

Exodus, and there has even been a serious proposal that it was composed during or after the rebuilding of the walls of Jerusalem, in the later half of the fifth century (Brenner, 1991, 177).

Be that as it may, Genesis 49 involves a convergence of the four main streams of Genesis. Sarna (331) mentions three—those flowing from the stories of Abraham, Jacob, and Joseph—and, as will be seen, there is also a stream that reflects creation.

Within the blessings, the arrangement of the tribes is unique but reflects "careful design" (Sarna, 331). The sons of Leah and Rachel form a frame for the sons of the maids; and among the sons of the maids, those of Rachel's maid, Bilhah, frame those of Leah's maid, Zilpah. The result (Sarna, 331) is "a deliberate chiastic arrangement: LEAH, Bilhah-Zilpah, Zilpah-Bilhah, RACHEL."

Some of the continuity between this diptych (chaps. 49–50) and earlier chapters is reasonably clear. The accounts of the deaths and burials of Jacob and Joseph draws several narrative threads to a close. The emphasis on the place of burial, the cave in the field at Machpelah, facing Mamre (49:29–32; 50:12–13) culminates a steady pattern. The concluding reconciliation between the brothers (50:14–21) acts as a final reminder of an idea that, since the story of Cain and Abel, has been one of the main ideas of Genesis and especially of the Joseph story—the need for mutual brotherly acceptance.

The role of the various sons within the final sayings of Jacob (49:3–27) corresponds in diverse ways to their roles in the larger Jacob-Joseph narrative:

The opening rebukes to Reuben, Simeon, and Levi (49:3–6) recall specific incidents in Jacob's life (34:25–31; 35:21–22; see Fleishman, 2001).

The prominence of Judah and Joseph among the sayings accords with their prominence in the Joseph story.

The reducing of six of the sons into a cluster (two adjacent compact groups of three, 49:13–21) corresponds to the way they have appeared earlier in Genesis: they have never appeared except within a cluster (in some form of genealogy, 29:31–30:24; 35:23–26; 46:8–27).

The isolating of Benjamin, at the end of the sayings (49:27), corresponds to the late but important role of Benjamin in the Genesis account (35:18; 42:36–45:22).

Overall, therefore, the roles played by the sons in Genesis explain aspects of Jacob's final sayings. But only some; other aspects require further explanation. One element of chapter 49 is that, along with chapter 50, it echoes or counterbalances Genesis's beginning, thus forming a kind of *inclusio* or bridge in the book as a whole.

The sayings begin, for instance, as does Genesis 1, with the ideas of a beginning (*rēšît*, "first-fruit of . . . ," 49:3; cf. 1:1) and of uncontrolled water (49:4; cf. 1:2; on turbulent character as like the troubled sea, cf. Isa. 57:20; Sarna,

333). Furthermore, the emphasis on words, on the implicit power of Jacob's words to foretell or shape the future (49:1–2), is like a distant variant of the creative power of God's words. And much of the imagery in chapter 49—the animals, seashore, heavens, deep—corresponds, broadly, with the imagery of creation.

The role of Judah, as ruling (49:8–12), corresponds broadly to that of humankind in creation (humankind will master, dominate, 1:28). Likewise, Judah's hand on the neck of his enemies (ʾoyēb 49:8) echoes humankind's enmity (ʾêbâ, 3:15) with the serpent and the serpent's head (3:15). There are references, too, to judgment, and to strife between a serpent and heels (49:16–17; cf. 3:14–15).

The sayings' late emphasis on blessing (49:25–26) corresponds broadly with the place of blessing in Genesis 1 (1:22, 28). Even the conclusion, with its sense of a certain finality (49:28–33), has some resonance of the conclusion of creation (2:1–4a).

As for chapter 50, its implicit contrast between the two burials, one touching transcendence, the other earthbound, brings out a motif that has hovered over many passages of Genesis, including for instance, the taking away of Enoch (5:24) and the enigmatic death of Sarah (chap. 23). There may also be continuity between the evoking of the whole earth (esp. 50:7–13) and aspects of the beginning of Genesis (esp. of chap. 2).

Whatever the details, what is essential is the general principle: before attempting to connect the conclusion of Genesis with fragile reconstructions of centuries of history, it is necessary to check its connection with the rest of the book.

Structure (Table 41.1)

PANEL ONE (CHAP. 49)

The distinctness of the introduction and the conclusion seems reasonably clear. As for the body of the text, the sayings that extend from Reuben to Benjamin (49:3–27), a dividing line is formed by the intrusive verse on hoping for salvation (49:18). Whatever its origin, it effectively forms two parts, one dealing with seven sons/tribes (49:3–17), the other with five (49:18–27).

Within each main part (within the seven and the five respectively), the focus, both in quantity and quality, is on the *centers*—on Judah and Joseph. (In the two main parts of the first creation panel [1:1–2:4a], the focus was not on the centers but on the *ends*—on days 3 and 6. Now, in chapter 49, there is a complementary phenomenon: emphasis on the centers).

PANEL TWO (CHAP. 50)

The most difficult question here is whether to make a division after "mourning for . . . seven days" (50:10).

Table 41.1. Jacob's Death and Burial (chap. 49 // chap. 50)

Amid blessings: Jacob's death

Introduction: Superscription; gather, and hear (49:1–2)
Sayings to seven sons, centered on Judah (49:3–17)
    Reuben, Simeon, Levi (3–7)
    Judah (8–12)
    Zebulun, Issachar, Dan (13–17)
Sayings to five sons, centered on Joseph (49:18–27)
    Gad, Asher, Naphthali (18–21)
    Joseph (22–26)
    Benjamin (27)
Conclusion: the blessed completion (49:28–33)
    These are the tribes . . . and blessings (28)
    Final words: the burial-place: the location, facing Mamre (29–30)
                 the burial-place: the people buried there (31–32)
    Commands completed, Jacob is gathered to his people (33)

Amid glory and peace: Jacob's burial

Introduction: mourning—Egyptian and Israelite (50:1–6)
    Embalming—following Egyptian practice (1–3)
    Burial—to follow Jacob's covenantlike instructions (4–6)
The great burial journey (50:7–10)
    The great attendance . . . Egyptians . . . chariots . . . horsemen (7–9)
    Morning on the treshing floor beyond the Jordan (10)
The Canaanites and Canaan (50:11–13)
    The Canaanites watch (11)
    Burial in Canaan: in the cave in the field (12–13)
Aftermath: reconciliation (50:14–21)
    Indirect approach: first explicit plea for forgiveness (14–17)
    Direct approach: Joseph speaks to their hearts (18–21)
Conclusion: The death of Joseph (50:22–26)
    Joseph's life and greatgrandchildren (22–23)
    Final words: God will bring you . . . as sworn (24)
                 Swear you will bring my bones (25)
    Death and embalming (26)

Comment

Panel One (Chap. 49)

[49:1–2] **Introduction. Jacob calls his sons to hear.** The introduction begins
with a superscription: "Gather, and I will tell you . . . [of] the after-days," a
reference not so much to the end-time as simply to a time that is later, somewhere in the future. In part, of course, this poetry looks to the past, to what
the sons have done and become, but its basic orientation is to the future. Jacob
now refers to himself as both "Jacob" and "Israel," an ambiguity that catches

the dimensions of the poetry: it is about the individual sons of Jacob, but, as becomes clear, it is also about the future tribes of Israel.

[49:3–17] The blessing of seven sons, especially Judah. The first half of the blessings deals with Leah's six sons, and Dan (son of Rachel's maid, Bilhah). Leah's sons are listed in order of birth, except for the reversal, at the end, of Issachar and Zebulun.

The three eldest sons, Reuben, Simeon, and Levi, are dealt with quickly (49:3–7). No leadership is accorded to them, basically because of incidents related to sex and violence. Reuben was preeminent, first-born, but, breaking a long silence, Jacob now speaks of Reuben's incest (35:22), and this incest seems to have been a genuine reflection of character ("uncontrolled/turbulent/boiling like water"). Reuben's efforts at leadership had been correspondingly ineffective (37:21–30; 42:22, 37). The image of ineffectiveness, particularly clear in the selling of Joseph (37:21–30), is echoed later in the song of Deborah (Judg. 5: 15–16: amid much heart-searching, the tribe of Reuben does nothing).

Simeon and Levi had shown extreme violence in avenging Shechem's violation of Dinah (34:25–31), and so Jacob, instead of blessing them, curses them, or at least curses their anger: "Cursed be their anger so fierce. . . . I will divide them . . . scatter them." The scattering took such a form that the tribes of Simeon and Levi did not hold distinct territories of their own. Simeon was absorbed into southern Judah; and Levi's priestly status, achieved later, was nonterritorial (Deut. 33:8–11). (Perhaps it is not an accident that even within the space of the poem, Levi in a sense is nonterritorial: grouped with Simeon, it receives no special saying. Thus the number of sayings in the poem, like the number of tribes on the ground, is one short. Later, however, in the sayings of Moses, Levi receives ample space, Deut. 33:8–11.)

Judah (49:8–12) stands out in both quantity—five verses—and content. He had stood out also at his birth, fourth though he was, by his mother's unusually positive mood ("Praise Yhwh") and by his correspondingly positive name: "Praised" (Judah, 29:35). Since then, despite sinfulness, he had shown both repentance and leadership (37:26–27; chap. 38; 43:8–10; 44:14–34; 46:28). It is not surprising, therefore, that the praise comes not from his mother but from his brothers: "Judah (are) you, your brothers praise you."

But the praising of Judah, as given here, goes beyond the Judah-related incidents of Genesis 29–48. He is set apart:

powerful (in relation to both enemies and brothers); lion-like;

retaining power (scepter, staff) until a future enigmatic figure receives the obedience of the nations;

with paradisal prosperity (and apparently, beauty in eyes and teeth).

The powerful well-being of Judah is often connected with some portrait of David, either David as reconstructed historically, or David as described in the biblical text. Judah's well-being may also be connected with the well-being of humankind at the beginning of Genesis, a well-being which was to survive the enmity of the serpent (3:14–15; cf. the crouching beast, 4:7). These two points of reference, David and humankind, are inherently related: the David narrative is so written that it elaborates and develops the Genesis account of the struggle of humankind (Brueggemann, 1968, 1971, 1972).

The broad correspondence between the words concerning Judah (49:8–12) and the later picture of David does not reveal reliably the date of the origin of these words. Such correspondence indicates primarily that the Primary History (Genesis–Kings), in its own artistic way, was well planned.

Zebulun, Issachar, and Dan (49:13–17) are dealt with quickly. Apart from genealogies (35:23–26; 46:8–27) they had not been mentioned by name since their births (30:6, 17–20). All three tribes were toward the north, especially Dan, which finally settled near Mount Hermon (cf. Josh. 19:40–48; Judg. 18). Zebulun's maritime status, as given here, is otherwise unknown. Apparently it was an inland tribe. Issachar seems, implicitly, to be reproached: though strong, he chose ease and became a serf. Dan shall judge (*dîn*) his people, meaning achieve justice for them; and the way Dan does this is connected enigmatically with the serpent—able, despite its low stature, to bring down a horseman, by biting the horse's heels. The attack on the heel "may be a reminiscence of [what] . . . is addressed to the serpent in the Garden" (Alter, 297).

[49:18–27] **The blessing of five sons, especially Joseph.** The saying about waiting for "salvation" (or deliverance, 49:18) marks both a mid-point and the beginning of a further shift to a more positive emphasis. The essential role of this salvation saying depends on the larger context, the deaths and burials of both Jacob and Joseph. In diverse ways, both Jacob and Joseph, in dying, waited on something more, on being brought to the land of promise (49:29–32; 50:4–6, 24–25). In the two panels, therefore, there is a form of balance. In the first (chap. 49) the explicit idea of waiting for salvation is placed at the *center* (49:18); and in the second (chap. 50) an enigmatic form of waiting for delivery forms a *framework* (at the beginning and close of the panel, 50:4–6, 24–25). Together the three references (49:18; 50:4–6, 24–25) complete each other.

The sayings concerning Gad, Asher, and Naphtali are of a summary kind (49:19–21). All three sons, along with Dan, were sons of slave-women (rather than of Leah and Rachel) and, like Zebulun, Issachar, and Dan, had not been not mentioned since their births (30:7–13), except in genealogies (35:23–26; 46:8–27).

Gad (49:19), in vulnerable Transjordan, will suffer raids but will also raid in return. The heel imagery ("but he will raid at their heels") echoes that of Dan ("biting the horse's heels").

Asher's rich food (49:20) suits the fertility of its later location, on the coast north of Mount Carmel. Naphtali, compared to a graceful animal ("a swift hind, giving lovely fawns," 49:21), is also north of Mount Carmel, but inland.

Joseph (49:22–26) stands out, as did Judah, in both quantity and praise. There is no explicit reference to the details of Joseph's history, but Joseph was the father of the two central northern tribes, Manasseh and the great tribe of Ephraim.

Joseph (in 49:22) is *bēn pōārt*, meaning literally either the son of a wild ass or *the son of a fruit-bearer*, a poetic expression for whatever bears fruit—a tree or branch. The context—wordplay, the role of Ephraim ("double fruit"), the apparent continuity (in 48:7, 20) between Ephraim and Ephrath (close to *pōrāt*), and the subsequent evoking of fertility (49:24–25)—suggests the latter meaning: Joseph is a fruitful tree/branch. (Alter, 298, argues for "fruitful son.")

The picture, after that, is of the tree being attacked and resisting successfully, with divine help. This divine element is described in terms related to nature (49:24–25a); and the blessings also (49:25b–26) are nature-related, involving both creation and woman's body ("heavens . . . deep"/ "breasts . . . womb").

Benjamin (49:27), at the end, "is a ravenous wolf . . . eat[ing] the prey," an image that corresponds to some of Benjamin's later war-like history (cf. Judges 19–20). Coincidentally or not, the image of the devouring wolf eating prey forms a stark contrast with Naphtali: "Naphtali is a swift hind, giving lovely fawns."

[49:28–33] **Conclusion. Jacob's death.** The conclusion is somewhat chiastic (like 2:1–4a). In its middle (49:29–32) is a brief speech.

First, there is a look back at the sayings, and a designation of them as blessings. There is an echo here of the completing of creation, including its emphasis on blessing (2:1, 3–4a). There are verbal echoes, but with reversals ("completed," "these are the . . . ," 49:28, 33; cf. 2:1, 4a).

The short speech, about the place of burial, is powerful, not because it adds much that is new, although it does tell of Leah's burial, but because it echoes and re-echoes with central memories.

Finally, with a great sense of appropriate completion, echoing faintly the completion of creation, "Jacob . . . gathered up his feet into the bed, and he expired and was gathered to his people."

Panel Two (Chap. 50)

[50:1–6] **Introduction. Caring for Jacob's body and burial.** When Jacob dies there is great affection and reverence for his body: Joseph weeps and kisses him; the Egyptians embalm or mummify him, requiring forty days; and the Egyptians weep, for seventy days. (Joseph's weeping here, 50:1, is part of a larger pattern; cf. 42:24; 43:30; 45:1–2, 14–15; 46:29; 50:17. He weeps more than anyone else in Genesis.)

When Joseph is addressing Pharaoh's household, his reference to Jacob's burial place is puzzling. Jacob had designated the place clearly—Abraham's field with the cave (at Machpelah, facing Mamre, 49:30; cf. 50:13)—but Joseph makes no reference to Abraham and instead quotes Jacob as saying he had cut his own tomb ("my grave which I cut for myself in the land of Canaan," 50:5). Apparently Joseph is adapting the description of the burial place to suit Egyptian expectations, in other words, to suit "the emphasis an Egyptian would place on his own burial place" (Hamilton, II, 693). In the same way, Joseph omits his father's words: "Do not bury me in Egypt" (47:29). There is no point in giving offence. As with the embalming, at this stage the mourning for Jacob conforms to Egyptian custom.

Pharaoh's reply is gracious, but, by repeating the reference to the oath (". . . Bury your father, as he made you swear/promise on oath"), he evokes an oath-based covenant, which goes beyond Egyptian custom and expectations.

The indirectness of Joseph's approach to Pharaoh (he speaks through intermediaries, 50:4) may be an intimation of what is to come in the book of Exodus, a situation where a new Pharaoh does not know Joseph (Exod. 1:8). Later, Joseph alludes clearly to the Exodus (50:24).

[50:7–10] Journeying to burial: the great attendance ("camp") at the threshing floor beyond the Jordan. The funeral procession out of Egypt is no small event. The attendance of "all the servants of Pharaoh" is doubly significant, since, following Joseph's buying up of Egypt (47:20–21), "Pharaoh's servants" effectively means the whole population. The emphasis on elders adds weight to the implied numbers. So there is a great attendance, great prestige, plus two households (those of Joseph and his father). The final details—the absence of children and animals, and the presence of chariots and horsemen—add further contrast and color. The description, "a very heavy camp," implies a very great funeral, a form of glory.

But some aspects of the journey suggest that it is evoking something more. To some degree, especially because of the horsemen and chariots, it is like some form of rehearsal for the Exodus. The seven-day mourning at the threshing-floor of Atad seems to have some special significance—especially in view of the decisive role, near the end of David's life, of the threshing-floor of Araunah (2 Sam. 24:15–25). And the location "beyond the Jordan," geographically inexplicable, suggests that the Jordan designates more than geography. When Jacob, after meeting Esau, moved to Shechem (33:16–18), there was no reference to crossing the Jordan, but now that he is dead the Jordan is introduced. The Exodus would lead to the Jordan; Moses would die across the Jordan (Deut. 34). There is a particular continuity between Jacob's journey and that of Elijah, who crossed the Jordan and departed in a chariot (2 Kings 2:7–11).

Apart from two references to the Jordan plain (13:10–11, Lot sees the plain and chooses it), the Jordan river is mentioned only twice in Genesis: first when Jacob, faced by the threat of death, recalls crossing the Jordan with his staff (32:10–11); and here, on the way to Jacob's burial (50:10). Both contexts involve aspects of death.

[50:11–13] The Canaanites watch; burial facing Mamre. The final picture is one of haunting beauty. The Canaanites watched the mourning, and they did so with great earnestness, sufficient to designate the mourning as great or glorious (literally, heavy) and to change the name of the place. The haunting quality is partly in their mixture of knowing and unknowing: they observe so earnestly, yet they know so little; they think the whole event is Egyptian. (This ambiguity—what looks Egyptian really is not so—is part of a larger pattern: geographically Genesis seems to move toward Egypt, but there is a contrary focus toward Mamre [see Introduction, Chapter 11, "Space"].) And there is a haunting quality, too, in their identity—"those who inhabited the land/earth"— a designation that accords with the idea that, at some level, the Canaanites represent the nations, the people of the earth. It is as though, in some way, the whole earth is engaged with the mourning for Jacob.

Then, again evoking the breaking of normal geographical expectations, the account adds, "It is across the Jordan."

The burial, when it comes, is not some kind of sudden lifeless thud. The recounting of the location, "the land of Canaan . . . in the cave of the field of Machpelah . . . facing Mamre," has by now become a kind of soulful chant. And the closing word, "Mamre," recalls the presence of a God who, at Mamre, surpassed human calculations (18:1–5).

[50:14–21] **The brothers' final reconciliation.** While the burial may have been splendid as a testimony to Jacob, there remains a question of what his death will do to those left behind. A happy death does not necessarily mean a happy aftermath. And so the focus switches from the dead to the survivors, specifically to the relationships between the brothers.

The effect is positive. The death and burial of Jacob, instead of unleashing an old grudge, becomes a moment for reaching a deeper reconciliation, repeating and varying some of the earlier drama of reconciliation (44:16; 45:1–9). Using an indirect approach to Joseph, and quoting their father, the brothers make their first explicit request for forgiveness (50:16–17). The effect is that Joseph weeps, probably in part because the request is like the voice of his father from beyond the grave. Here, as in the flood story (6:1–9:17), reconciliation occurs in a context that surpasses normal human calculations.

Later, when they speak to him directly, Joseph reemphasizes the role of God, and then, as never before, "he comforted them and spoke to their hearts." And so, as never before, there is full reconciliation. Joseph's speech lifts them above their guilt and brings them to "a fresh way of understanding what has happened" (Brueggemann, 373).

Joseph's question, "Am I in the place of God?" (50:18), implies a negative answer, but it has an ambiguity, a reminder that in various ways God has been with Joseph; Joseph has been a form of divine presence. The result is not to overpower his brothers but to set them free from fear: "Do not be afraid . . . ," are his last words to them until he is about to die. Thus he seeks to lay to rest the specter of fear which, beginning with Eden and Cain, seemed to underlie so much of human existence.

[50:22–26] **The death of Joseph.** Joseph's death at a 110 brings the story to a fitting close. For Egypt, 110 was an ideal life span (Murphy, 2:73), and the mention of Joseph's grandchildren adds a note of vitality to that old age. To say these grandchildren were "born on Joseph's knees" indicates adoption

(Murphy, 2:73). His closing statement speaks of an oath to "Abraham, Isaac, and Jacob," the first such threefold reference in Genesis.

Joseph's final words echo those of his dying father, but they also look forward to the Exodus. So do other aspects of the conclusion. Joseph's burial is in a coffin/sarcophagus, 'ărôn—a word also used of the *ark* of the covenant (Deut. 10:8; 31:9,25; Jos. 3:6, 8; 4:9; 6:5). And the last words in the book, "in Egypt," while they have a sense of finality, the culmination of a movement that began in the east (2:8), also set the scene for the great struggle that follows.

APPENDICES

TRACING SOURCES: TOWARD CLARIFYING
THE CRITERIA FOR DETECTING SOURCES

As a general literary principle, it is not possible to take a finished text and reconstruct diverse sources that otherwise have never been seen—sources that are hypothetical. Those who discuss source criticism in literature at large (Morize, 1922, 82–131; Saunders, 1952, 162–191; Wellek and Warren, 1962, 257–258; Altick and Fenstermaker, 1993, 106–119; cf. Bateson, 1972, 192) never envisage the feasibility of reinventing lost sources.

What is possible, though it is often difficult (see the above-mentioned authors), is to identify a known text as one of the sources of another known text. It is possible, for instance, to demonstrate that Virgil used Homer, that Chronicles used Genesis-Kings, and, for most scholars, that Matthew used Mark.

Consequently the invoking of unknown documents—such as JEDP for the Pentateuch—is, at best, a last resort, to be undertaken only if there is no connection with known documents and if there are special indications that the hypothesis is working coherently and successfully.

The brittleness of hypotheses invoking unseen documents is illustrated in the nineteenth-century effort to distinguish sources in the *Epic of Gilgamesh:* the only success depended not on an internal analysis of the *Epic* but on comparison with other, known, texts (Berlin, 1983, 132–134; cf. Tigay, 1982; Moran, 1995).

The primary purpose of this appendix is to clarify the criteria for claiming that one known text depends on another.

In the case of Genesis the situation may seem discouraging. For a long time the book looked unique—unrelated to other literature—and so there was no question of trying to trace its dependence on known writings. But now, research has connected Genesis with several kinds of literature, especially with historiography, epic, and prophecy, and so there is the prospect of finding specific texts used by the author of Genesis.

However, before embarking on this task, it is useful to stand back and look at the larger picture of using sources. The discussion is threefold:

Writing as rewriting: ancient writing as a culture of preserving and rewriting.

The present gradual recognition of diverse categories of rewriting.

The clarifying of criteria for recognizing sources.

Writing as Rewriting: Ancient Writing as a Culture of Preservation—of Imitating and Emulating

Almost the entire history of writing has been accompanied by a huge instinct for preservation. Whatever was written well was respected and, in some way, guarded. The Jewish care for used manuscripts—preserving them in a *geniza*—was but one symptom of a larger protective attitude.

The full reasons for this attitude are not clear. Apparently the whole apparatus of writing was regarded as rare and fragile. The craft was specialized, the manuscripts precious.

Later, however, the attitude changed. Soon after the printing press arrived, and especially after the mass production of encyclopedias, the emphasis on preservation began to wane (Ong, 1971, 277–279). The essential fact is this: until the eighteenth century—when the encyclopedias were multiplied—it was of the essence of writing that one engaged the work of previous writers. The Akkadians and Babylonians reshaped the work of the Sumerians, the early Greeks borrowed from Mesopotamia, the later Greeks rewrote the earlier Greeks, the Romans rewrote the Greeks, and the Renaissance reshaped the whole classical heritage (Burkert, 1992; Brodie, 1984, 17–19; Highet, 1949). In the Greco-Roman tradition the process of rewriting and reshaping was refined by the doctrine and practice of imitation (*mimēsis, imitatio;* Abrams, 1953, 8–14, 30–47; Boyd, 1968; Brodie, 1984, 19–32).

In the eighteenth century, however, as the dawning of the romantic era glorified personal experience, the emphasis on imitation gave way to the promotion of originality. The change was articulated in 1759, in Edward Young's "Conjectures on Original Composition" (Kaplan, 1975, 220–250; Abrams, 1953, 198–203). In 1762, Rousseau attacked imitation in painting; artists should copy only nature (Webb, 1981,157). The centrality of the old writings began to fade (Boyd, 1968, 98–117). Then, toward the end of the twentieth century there was a further development: the old writings were not only allowed to fade; they were often explicitly condemned. They began to be seen, at least by some, not as classic but as oppressive.

What counts here is the basic fact of changing attitudes. The present freedom concerning former writings is not typical of ancient times. On the contrary, whatever was written well was preserved, in some form. The trouble is, the form varied, almost endlessly.

This phenomenon—limitless variation—is the heart of the problem. There was no one set form for preserving what was already written. Nor was there a set of forms—a set of, say, three or four basic ways of reshaping a text. Morize (1922, 96–127), discussing French literature, lists seven kinds of sources but emphasizes (p. 127) "the impossibility of predicting every type of case that may arise." On the contrary, there were no limits. At one extreme, one could rewrite the subtext (the original) almost word for word; at the other extreme, one could distill it to its essence and stand it on its head, mingling it with other sources. Thus at times it was easy to recognize the source(s); at other times, extremely difficult.

The Lack of Well-Developed Criteria

One would imagine, given the central difficulty in recognizing sources, and given the modern deluge of dissertations and publications, that there would be numerous systematic studies for dealing with the problem, numerous guides setting out comprehensive criteria for establishing literary dependence.

Apparently there is none. At least, the present writer, despite prolonged searching in good libraries, has failed to locate one. Part of the search involved a telephone conversation with George Steiner (December 21st, 1979). Steiner said that when writing *After Babel* he looked for some such comprehensive survey but could not find one. Morize (1922, 128) envisaged a book of basic criteria and even gave the hypothetical book a title—*Practical Handbook for the Investigation of Sources*—but he was ambiguous toward the project: he dismissed the very idea, yet proceeded to give an inadequate substitute for it (1922, 128–130). Homeric scholar Dennis R. McDonald, speaking at the SBL (New Orleans, Nov. 25, 1996), said he had worked out five criteria for judging literary dependence, but he indicated, cautiously, that these five needed refinement.

To some degree the lack of a basic guide is understandable. Tracking literary dependence is like detective work; it needs instinct, and instinct cannot be learned, at least not in an organized way.

However, like detective work, literary tracking needs much more than instinct; it needs a huge proportion of methodical plodding. (Jonathan Z. Smith, in discussing the larger question of comparing religions, speaks of drudgery: *Drudgery Divine: On the Comparison of Early Christianities and the Religions of Late Antiquity*, 1990). Unlike instinct, drudgery can be organized. Detectives can learn the rules for methodical plodding. Yet when one looks for general guides to methodical plodding in tracing literary sources, there are none. There are indeed numerous specialized studies, usually about the most obvious cases— Babylon and Sumer; Chronicles and Kings; Matthew and Mark; Virgil and Homer; Seneca and Euripides; Racine and Seneca. There are books about writing in general, and about vast literary traditions, and about the whole phenomenon of literature, but there is no book that tries in a systematic way to identify both the dynamics between the texts and the criteria for identifying them.

The reason for this omission seems to lie in the modern antipathy to imitation—not only to practicing it but even to studying it. Until 1996 the *Oxford Classical Dictionary* had no entry for it, though it was foundational for the classics, and the *Princeton Encyclopedia of Poetry and Poetics* (1975, ed. Preminger, 378–380) begins its discussion of imitation by noting that it is only now that the term is coming back after its banishment in the nineteenth century.

Also coming into use now is the term "intertextuality." This can be misleading: the term refers primarily not to a text's dependence on another specific text but to its larger dependence on a whole cultural context (on the history and meaning of the term "intertextuality," see Culler, 1981, 100–118; on Julia Kristeva, originator of the term, see Roudiez, 1980, 1–20; Lechte, 1994, 141–144). Intertextuality "has nothing to do with matters of influence by one writer on another, or with the sources of a literary work; it does, on the other hand, involve the components of a *textual system* such as the novel, for instance. It is defined . . . as the transposition of one or more *systems* of signs upon another, accompanied by a new articulation of the enunciative and denotative position" (Roudiez, 1980, 15). In discussing literary dependence therefore it is generally better not to use this broad term—to do so is like hitting a tack with a sledgehammer—but the term has been useful insofar as it has helped to alert researchers to a specific practice which, in ancient composition, was central.

In the case of Genesis, therefore, the situation is difficult. There is an emerging relationship to world literature and to the prophetic books, but in the tracing of possible dependence there are no agreed procedures or criteria.

The Tyranny of the Verbatim Criterion

The difficulty caused by the absence of wide-ranging criteria is compounded by the obvious presence of one simple criterion: verbatim similarity. When modern studies neglected rewriting as a whole, verbatim similarity was sometimes so glaring that it could not be ignored, and so it led to the recognition of literary dependence. Chronicles was recognized as using Kings, Matthew as using Mark. Then, imperceptibly, the criterion of verbatim similarity became exclusive; in effect, it established a kind of tyranny. Other criteria were often not considered. "Literary dependence" became equated with just one model. The Matthew-Mark model, standing at the entrance to the New Testament, sometimes sets the tone, even for scholars of the Old Testament.

The difficulty is illustrated in gospel studies: two of the inter-gospel connections (Matthew-Mark and Luke-Mark) are so obvious that they make the third (John-Mark) look strange. And so some scholars reject the third; implicitly using the obvious Matthew-Mark model as a criterion of what is meant by literary dependence, they reject the idea of literary dependence between John and Mark. In a sense they are right; there is no literary dependence *of the Matthew-Mark kind*. But there is another more complex form of literary dependence—a form for which there is abundant evidence (Brodie, 1993a).

The John-Mark difficulty is a salutary warning. If biblical scholarship cannot bridge the short gap between John and Mark there is little chance that it will ever bridge the gap between Genesis and its extant sources.

The Present Gradual Recognition of Diverse Categories of Rewriting: Transition from the Tyranny of the Verbatim Model

Since about 1950 there has been a gradual discovery of diverse categories of rewriting. To some degree these categories were already known, especially to Jewish and classical scholars, but now they have come closer to the forefront of research. Such discoveries have the implicit effect of moving the discussion of rewriting beyond the level of verbatim similarity. The process of discovery is still incomplete, but its existence and its gradual expansion establish a context that is conducive to discovering the categories possibly involved in composing Genesis.

The following categories of rewriting are particularly noteworthy.

Midrash

"Midrash" means literally the "searching" of a text—searching its meaning and applicability to a new situation. In general, the searching or application of a text can be either explicit or implicit (overt or covert, quoted or merely implied), and there is a debate about whether the technical term "midrash" should be used of both forms (Le Déaut, 1971; Porton, 1979). But whatever the terminology, the reality remains essentially the same: in traditional Judaism, and within the biblical books themselves, there was a massive phenomenon of adapting existing texts. Despite its centrality this widespread practice remained largely unexplored (*"domaine encore à peu près complètement inexploré"*—Bloch, 1957). The exploration is still continuing (e.g., Porton, 1985; Hartman and Budick, 1986).

Synthesis and Transformation

Among recent studies of the inner-biblical reworking of texts, Fishbane's work (1985) deserves special mention. Under the general heading of "inner-biblical hermeneutics" he has emphasized the ideas of synthesis and transformation, and has linked prophetic texts with texts from the Pentateuch. Thus, in principle, his work opens the road to bridging the gap between Genesis and the prophetical books. But Fishbane's work, though it constitutes a breakthrough, leaves the breakthrough undeveloped. The emphasis is on a limited range of texts, and in particular there is no general discussion concerning the direction of the flow of influence.

Rewritten Bible

The term "rewritten Bible" has been used to describe the way early noncanonical books—such as *Jubilees, Assumption of Moses*, Pseudo-Philo's *Biblical An-*

tiquities—rewrite the biblical texts, especially narrative texts. The process involves "a free rewriting of part . . . of Israel's sacred history" (Harrington, 1986, 242). This process is late (around the turn of the era) and emphasizes narrative (rather than prophecy), but its underlying concept—rewriting the sacred, freely—provides a further sense of the possibilities in reworking the sacred text.

Rewritten Prophecy: The Pesharim

Fifteen Qumran texts consist of pesharim, "interpretations"—systematic adaptations of prophetic texts. They quote the prophets explicitly—quite unlike the Pentateuch—but the freedom with which they adapt the text suggests possibilities for how the Pentateuch may have done so. The prophet's words about the Babylonians, for instance, are interpreted as referring to the Romans—a leap across time, space, culture, and diverse circumstances. The implied hermeneutical principles are diverse; Brownlee (1951, 60–62) counts thirteen, but Horgan (1979, 244–245) reduces them to four.

Rewritten Epic

The Homeric epics, from the time of their completion in writing (ca. 700 BCE), were copied and variously adapted. Such adaptations of Homer, begun apparently in his younger contemporary Hesiod (O'Brien and Major, 1982, 51), flourished in fifth-century drama, and remained a central feature of much writing in Greece and beyond. The *Odyssey*, in particular, was adapted repeatedly in multiple ways and places (Stanford, 1963)—including the early church (MacDonald, 1994, 17–34) and Joyce's *Ulysses*. Significantly, Homeric epic underlay the development of historiography (Lesky, 1966, 218–221).

Imitation (mimēsis), Including Literary Imitation/Emulation

In contrast to the modern search for originality, the ethos of much of the ancient world emphasized imitation. Nature itself was an imitation of a higher world (Plato, *Timaeus* 29); and all art—including literature—imitated nature (Aristotle, e.g., *Physics*, II, 2.194a22; II, 8.199a15–17). Literature, therefore, may be described as *mimēsis*, as mirroring the external world (cf. Auerbach, 1953). In Trible's words : "The most ancient and persistent [literary] approach holds that literature mirrors a world external to itself. The Greek word *mimesis* (imitation) denotes the concept" (1994, 10).

Literary *mimēsis*, however, was not limited to imitating nature; it also imitated other literature. Other literature provided a key to nature, an initial insight. There was no need, as with the romantics of the eighteenth and nineteenth centuries, to reinvent nature or the world every time one took up a pen.

The ancient writer worked with what other writers had already captured and expressed.

Imitation, however, was not slavish; verbatim imitation was unusual; the challenge was to combine imitation with emulation (*zēlos*)—in other words, simultaneously to absorb and surpass previous writers (Brodie, 1984, 19–26). This process of combining imitation and emulation applied also to historiography (ibid., 26–32).

The overall impression, from these emerging categories, is of a vast field of possibilities. As Steiner said in a broader context: "The [writer] need not cite [the] source-text . . . [but] can treat it in a limitless variety of perspectives . . . from interlinear translation . . . to the faintest most arcane of allusions. . . . It is up to us to recognize and reconstruct the particular force of relation" (1975, 424–425).

That is the problem: it is up to us. If that is so, if we are to undertake this task, then it is first necessary to establish criteria.

Amid the Emerging Categories of Rewriting: Toward Establishing Criteria for Judging Literary Dependence

Most researchers, no matter how open-minded, are not in the habit of dealing with complicated claims to literary dependence; and without long practice, it is difficult to judge such claims. It is particularly difficult to do so at speed—for instance, when reviewing books. It is tempting, very often, to reject such dependence or simply ignore it.

The burden for establishing criteria lies with the one making the claim. If that person does not indicate the criteria—often the case—there is little room for complaint when readers or reviewers do not engage the evidence.

To a limited degree other researchers have already suggested brief summaries of procedures and/or criteria (Morize, 1922, 87–96, 128–130; Saunders, 1952, 167–172; Altick and Fenstermaker, 1993, 108–118; Wellek and Warren, 1962, 258; Feldman, 1996, 14). The purpose here is to develop these suggestions.

The task is not easy—one is dealing with art not science, and at times the criteria or the ways of applying them are inadequate. But a beginning can be made.

Criteria are of two kinds—positive (positive indications) and negative (explanations that mislead).

Positive Criteria

There are three main kinds of indications that one text depends on another—external plausibility, internal similarities, and the intelligibility of the differences.

There is no point in trying to show that Genesis depends on Ovid's epic poem *Metamorphoses* (completed in exile, at Tomis, on the Black Sea). It is true that the Black Sea borders Asia Minor, and so the text would probably have been physically accessible. But without even glancing at Ovid's work it can be ruled out on the basis of an external factor—date (composed ca. 10 CE). Dependence can be invoked only if external factors make such dependence plausible. The *Epic of Gilgamesh*, in contrast, would not only have been accessible—versions have been found both in Asia Minor (in the Hittite capital, Hattusha) and in Babylonia—but would also have been old enough; those versions date from the second millenium (*ANET* 72–73).

Another external factor—already mentioned—is the pervading attitude toward previous writings. If the general attitude to preceding writings was one of independence or even hostility, then dependence would be implausible. If, for instance, the Gilgamesh epic, originally Akkadian, had been banned or ignored by others—by the Hittites, Hurrians, Assyrians, and Babylonians—then the idea of its use in Genesis would be correspondingly implausible. But the opposite was the case; the *Epic of Gilgamesh* was popular and accessible (Feldmman, 1996, 13).

SIMILARITIES

Similarities are of diverse kinds, ranging from vague, isolated, or insignificant to crucial and decisive.

> *Similarity of theme.* Similarity of theme can be an initial clue to dependence between writings. For instance, some of Shakespeare's tragic themes—such as the power of evil forces over life—can trigger awareness of his possible use of Seneca's tragic dramas. In the case of Gilgamesh and Genesis there is a shared emphasis on the theme of journeying. Such sharing of themes usually proves nothing—themes tend to be too general for drawing conclusions—but it can set the stage for a more probing investigation.

> *Pivotal leads or clues.* Even if the relationship between two texts is complex or obscure the author may give some key indication of a link between the two. When Luke, for instance, uses the Elijah-Elisha narrative, he provides initial clues to what he is doing: he invokes the example of Elijah and/or Elisha in two leading texts—the opening scene (Luke 1:5–25; see 1:17) and the inaugural speech (Luke 4:16–27). To some degree, the same thing happens in Genesis: whether intended or not, some episodes, especially the flood story, are so strikingly similar to well-known epics that they act as a leading indication that perhaps Genesis as a whole is using further epic material.

Action/plot. Similarity of action can be a strong clue to literary dependence. The clearest example here is the Atrahasis story, which "displays the same basic plot as Gen. 2–9" (Clifford, 2:2; for more detail, see Tsumura, 1994a, 46–47). In the case of the Gilgamesh epic and the *Enuma Elish* the evidence is not as easy, but it is significant.

Completeness. If similarities are confined to an isolated passage, or if only some passages from a possible source appear to be reflected in the finished writing, then a problem arises about the nature of the relationship between the texts. Why should some be missing? And does this absence cast doubt on the relationship to the text as a whole? (A classic problem is the impression, at first sight, that Luke omits almost two chapters of Mark.) But if all the passages of the possible source are reflected in some form in the final text then the case for direct dependence is greatly strengthened.

Order. When random elements occur in two documents in the same order the similarity requires explanation. Similarity of order does not occur easily. If two people, independently of each other, arrange the numbers 1 to 5 at random, the chance that they will arrange them in the same order is less than one in a hundred. If the numbers are 1 to 10 the chance is less than one in a million.

Telltale details (linguistic or otherwise). The link between two texts is sometimes given away by a small detail. If the detail remains isolated, it generally proves nothing; but if a series of details emerge then they become more significant—especially if clustered together or in the same order.

Complex coherence. The relationship between some texts is so complex and coherent that the only plausible explanation is literary dependence. There is a degree of complexity which oral tradition cannot handle. As Ong says in a related context, "closer plotting requires writing" (1977, 254).

THE INTELLIGIBILITY OF THE DIFFERENCES

In judging possible questions of dependence, the issue is not whether there are differences but whether the differences are intelligible. If two people, one black and one white, have a child, the child will be different from both. The differences may be great, but they do not exclude dependence; in the circumstance, they are intelligible.

Likewise with two texts. For instance, Jesus' refusal to call down destructive fire from heaven (Luke 9:54–55) is in direct contrast to Elijah's killing of more than one hundred soldiers (2 Kings 1), but the difference fits with Luke's wider portrayal of Jesus. Likewise with the other war-like incidents in the Old Testament: they have been transformed to accord with a different strategy—a focus not on a specific land but on the kingdom of God. What counts, then, is not difference, but intelligibility. Genesis is massively different from Herodotus, and even more so from the prophets and the *Odyssey*. But differences, *no matter how great,* do not clinch the issue. Some writers want to contradict an earlier text at every level. What counts is whether the similarities are significant and whether the differences are intelligible.

Negative Criteria: Principles That Can Mislead

In assessing evidence about literary dependence there are a number of factors that sometimes mislead or cause confusion.

SOME CONNECTIONS ARE WEAK

Total analysis is virtually impossible, and so in almost every comparative analysis of two texts there are points where the comparison is uncertain, where the connections are weak—obscure, questionable, apparently nonexistent. If the discussion focuses on these weak elements, then confusion follows—like judging the strength of a country's defenses by its babies. Insistence on what is weak, whether by the one presenting the comparison or by someone questioning it, obscures the decisive issue: are there arguments that are strong? One is dealing not with a single chain where the overall strength depends on the weakest link, but with a whole series of chains. That some are weak does not matter as long as there are enough that are strong.

Weaknesses occur in an analysis not only because total analysis is almost impossible, but also because the analyst makes mistakes or is inexperienced. Again, however, the issue is not whether there are mistakes but whether there is enough that is true to make the overall connection credible, or at least to make it worthy of further study. As in detective work, what the investigator needs is the ability to sift through evidence that is weak or misleading and to see whether there are a few good leads, or at least one.

THE DIFFERENCES ARE TOO GREAT

This question has been mentioned already but it bears repeating for it is a matter of great confusion. The differences between texts may be misleading; they may give the false impression that one text cannot possibly depend on the other. But differences do not decide the issue. The purpose of writing—as distinct from copying—is to say something that is in some way different. Difference, therefore, is of the essence of writing.

There is no limit on how different a writer may be from predecessors. Even the most sacred text can be rewritten or reversed: "It was said to you of old. . . . But I say. . . ." As already mentioned, the books called "the rewritten Bible" contain "a free rewriting of [a] part . . . of Israel's sacred history" (Harrington, 1986, 242).

The issue, therefore, when comparing texts is not whether there are differences, but whether, as already indicated, the differences are intelligible. In comparing Ezekiel with John 10, for instance, Bultmann (1971, 367) points to the dissimilarities, and then decides against dependence. But for Brown these dissimilarities are not decisive; the issue rather is "whether there is sufficient similarity to suggest that the OT supplied the raw material for . . . [a] creative reinterpretation" (1966, 397).

Creative reinterpretation—that is central to the discussion. It is creative reinterpretation that first causes the differences and it is the concept of creative reinterpretation that subsequently makes them intelligible.

THE DIFFERENCES PRECLUDE DEPENDENCE AND POINT
RATHER TO A SHARED TRADITION

There are times when, even if two writings show clear similarity and difference, direct dependence may not in fact be the explanation. Perhaps, instead of borrowing directly, both writings used a shared source—and interpreted it differently.

This is possible, and cannot be directly disproved. But very often it is a gratuitous claim and cannot be proved. And since it bears the burden of proof— it claims documents that no one has ever seen or sources that are unverifiable— it is in the weaker position.

One of the results of this claim to a third entity is that it avoids the phenomenon of direct dependence and thereby avoids dealing directly with the problem—the difference between the two documents. At a superficial level it makes the problem easier. The difference, with all its difficulty and richness, disappears under the cover of a third unproven element. The moment in which the difference occurred is pushed into an inaccessible background.

This removal of the difficulty can create the illusion that the difficulty has been solved. But it has not. To avoid saying A changed B, this theory says A and B both used C (A changed C, and possibly B changed C as well). But why should these hypothetical changes be more plausible than that of A changing B? The problem will not go away: at some stage someone changed a source significantly. If that change is accepted in principle—in fact it is unavoidable— then why not accept it immediately? The simplest hypothesis that accounts for the data is to say A changed B. The old adage applies: "Things should not be multiplied without necessity."

THE SIMILARITY MAY BE DUE TO GENERAL FAMILIARITY
RATHER THAN DIRECT LITERARY DEPENDENCE

If someone absorbs the works of, say, Pascal or Dickens, it is likely that at a later stage the thoughts and phrases of these authors will reappear in the person's speech and writing. Much of the process is unconscious and it is not a question of direct literary dependence. It may seem therefore to follow that identifying direct literary dependence is almost impossible.

The conclusion that follows, however, is not that identifying literary dependence is impossible but that the researcher needs to be doubly careful. The positive criteria, given above, need to be applied rigorously, checking not only for broad similarities, for style and for occasional phrases and details, but for the whole range of factors that might indicate direct dependence—from external plausibility to a sequence of details.

A SOURCE IS ALREADY PRESENT, THEREFORE A SECOND ONE CANNOT BE ADMITTED

Having established the use of a major source there may be a tendency to deny the presence of other sources. But a text may be a complex synthesis; "a poem or a page of prose is often a sort of mosaic" (Morize, 1922, 107). "Text" is derived from *texere*, "to weave" and so is at home with interweaving. The presence of one source does not exclude another.

Conclusion

The ancient method of composing was unlike the modern. Today's writer, in using sources, often has a basic choice—acknowledge or ignore. In this modern view, knowledge and writing are like personal property. But for the ancient writer, what was written was not personal property; it was so to speak, out there, and was not to be ignored. One built on previous writings and did so without acknowledgement. The issue therefore concerning the use of previous writings was not whether but how—how to take what was best in existing writings and how to reshape them to one's own vision.

There were no limits on the how—on the ways of reshaping an older document. Consequently, the ways in which some sources were used will probably forever escape detection, even when those source documents are extant. This is especially so in the case of minor sources.

But other sources have played a greater role, and, even if radically rethought and reshaped, can be detected. The criteria outlined above are not complete but, in this search for sources, they provide an initial orientation. The task is difficult, but not out of reach. At least it is possible, building on the work of others, to give a partial framework.

SOURCES: GENESIS'S USE OF THE PROPHETS

The idea that Genesis used the prophets may seem unlikely or impossible. Genesis is a form of history; it is at the beginning of the Bible; and its story is set in a time long before the prophets existed.

Yet the division between Genesis and the prophets is not so clear. Genesis is ambiguous. Such was the perception in tradition, and such is the perception in modern research.

In tradition, Genesis, along with Exodus-Kings, has been regarded in two diverse ways. At times it has been treated as history, but in other ways it has been regarded as in some way prophetic, written by the great prophet Moses.

Modern research maintains the ambiguity, but with greater precision. On the one hand, Genesis-Kings has been seen to adopt the genre or literary form of ancient history (van Seters, 1983, 1992). On the other hand, evidence is emerging that Genesis shows awareness of the prophets.

Such awareness of the prophets is inherently likely. It is generally recognized that Genesis, despite its ancient setting, was not composed, or at least not completed, until after the time of the great prophets (Isaiah, Jeremiah, Ezekiel). It is difficult to reconstruct a scenario within the Jewish community whereby the writers of history were unaware of the great prophetic writers. This is particularly so because the Jewish people had just a few main centers (ultimately only one, Jerusalem), because the number of those involved in writing would have been small, and because the custom of ancient writers was to incorporate the work of previous writers.

Besides, as a general principle in literary development, prose follows poetry: "Continuous prose, though often regarded . . . as the language of ordinary speech, is a late and far from "natural" stylistic development, and is much less direct and primitive than verse, which invariably precedes it in the history of literature" (Frye, 1981, 8; cf. Lesky, 1966, 219, 221). It is plausible then that the prose of Genesis-Kings follows the more poetic work of the prophets.

The general priority of poetry over prose does not necessarily mean that this specific poetry (the great prophets) was prior to this specific prose (Genesis). Perhaps both the prophets and Genesis were but a small part of a huge literature, now mostly lost, within which they were not related to each other. But the hypothesis of a huge lost literature is itself a fragile claim. At the least, the general priority of poetry lends a certain plausibility to the relative lateness of Genesis.

In a broad way this sense of the priority of poetry has been recognized by diverse Scripture scholars. As Albright commented approvingly : "Gunkel saw that the narratives of Genesis were a prose form of earlier poetic traditions" (1964, viii). But both Gunkel and Albright consigned this poetry-to-prose transition to an unverifiable realm of oral tradition.

The breakthrough from this general link to a specific dependence came from Hans H. Schmid, when he established that certain sections of the Pentateuch presuppose written prophecy. Schmid (1976, 19–22) indicated that the call of Moses (Exod. 2:23–4:17), for instance, follows the same literary pattern as Isaiah 6, Jeremiah 16, and Ezekiel 1:1–3:17, and that the Exodus text is so written that it appears to build on the prophetic accounts. Schmid (1976, 119–153) maintained that something similar is true of Genesis's patriarchal promises: they presuppose prophetic writings.

A specific case of dependence on the prophetic literature has been highlighted by Ha's analysis of Genesis 15. He concludes:

> Gen.15 . . . the work of a single author . . . commands a broad familiarity . . . with the prophetic literature. In addition to the prophetic flavour of his work, he seems to betray his special liking for, if not his rooting in, this literature. . . . He makes particular use of Is. 7:1–17 to present the theologoumenon of faith supported by sign. . . . [And] Jer. 34:18–20 provides him the rite by which to express YHWH's self-obligation to free Abraham's descendants and give them the land. (1989, 215)

More recently the relationship of Genesis 15 to the prophets has been developed, in a general way, by Hagelia (1994, 198–199). Links of some kind between the Primary History and the prophets have also been suggested by Gosse (1997, 90–133).

The leadership in this discerning of prophetic roots has now passed to van Seters (1992, 1994, 1994a). Van Seters has indicated areas of Genesis, such as the Eden account, which depend not on hypothetical documents but on the prophets and their writings (1992, 119–22; cf. 231–235, 238–241). He also shows that the Pentateuchal account of Moses depends on the prophets (1994a). For instance, in Moses' lament (Exod. 5:22–23), "Moses is made to resemble Jeremiah" (1994a, 75); furthermore, it is "most probable that the plague narrative is heavily dependent upon the prophetic tradition in its exilic literary form" (p. 86); and the author of Exodus "has decided to read this triumphal departure [from Second Isaiah] back into the exodus event . . . (Ex. 14:8)" (1994a, 147–148).

The purpose of this appendix is to complement the work of van Seters. While he establishes many specific links, the aim here is to provide something more general—an overall map or outline of Genesis's relationship to the major prophets (Isaiah, Jeremiah, Ezekiel). As van Seters implies, Genesis's use of the prophets is intricate—the author often weaves several diverse threads into a new synthesis—but the basis for this intricate procedure is orderly: Genesis uses the three great prophets schematically, as a clear foundation, and then, using the kind of interweavings implied by van Seters, it proceeds to build a complex text. Thus, the focus here is on mapping the orderly foundation—one component.

Note: The Direction of Dependence

Before tracing Genesis's orderly relationship to the leading prophets it is first necessary to ask who depended on whom—the prophetic books on Genesis-Kings, or Genesis-Kings on the prophetic books? Generally, neither quotes the other directly, at least not explicitly.

A discussion of dates is normally not helpful. Genesis, for instance, tends to be associated with the second millenium BCE, long before the prophets. But the actual writing of the book, particularly its finalizing, is usually associated with a later time, well after the main prophets.

The evidence indicates that the dependence is of Genesis-2 Kings on the prophets; the prophets have priority. There are three main reasons: general literary development; absence of direct quotations; and practical testing.

First consider general literary development. As mentioned above, it is a general principle, in the development of literature, that poetry precedes prose (Frye, 1981, 8). Such, for instance, is the case in Greek literature (Lesky, 1966, 218–221). This general principle proves nothing about the specific case in question but, other things being equal, it tilts the probability of priority toward the more poetic text—toward the prophets.

The second issue concerns the absence of direct quotations. The absence of direct quotations is more understandable if the prophets came first.

On the one hand, if Genesis, or some version of Genesis, had been first, the prophets would almost certainly have quoted it; it would have lent authority to their preaching. But they do not; despite their intense calls to conversion, they do not recall clearly the great events of Genesis; their calls are to a past that— though powerfully evocative, especially concerning the desert—is largely undefined. It is as though they had never seen or heard any written form of Genesis.

Some details may suggest otherwise. Isaiah sometimes refers to people or places who appear in Genesis, and so it may seem that there is some dependence in the other direction—that part of Isaiah depends somehow on Genesis (cf. van Seters, 1992, 241). There are references to Noah (54:9), Abraham (29:22; 41:8; 51:2; 63:16), Sarah (51:2), and especially Jacob (about thirty times; see, for instance, 9:8; 10:21; 41:8, 14, 21; 42:24; 43:1, 22, 28; 44:1, 2, 5, 21, 23; 65:9).

And there is an allusion to the sinfulness and fall of Sodom and Gomorrah (1:7–10; 3:9; 13:19; cf. Gen. 19).

But Isaiah's references to Sodom and Gomorrah do not appear to depend on the text of Genesis. In particular, there are no connecting details. Rather, they apparently draw on some other rather general source (or tradition). Likewise with Abraham and Sarah; Isaiah's references are general, showing no reflection of the detail of Genesis. The reference to Noah (54:9) is closest to Genesis but this reference is very brief, and its distinctive phrases ("swore;" "the waters of Noah") do not occur in the Genesis text; so again the impression is of reliance on some other general source. The references to Jacob are mostly to Jacob as representative of Israel, with no apparent reflection of the story of Jacob as recounted in Genesis. Ezekiel, too, refers back to Abraham (33:24), but again the reference is brief and does not appear to depend on Genesis.

On the other hand, the failure of Genesis to quote the prophets is understandable. Genesis's literary form—ancient historiography—precluded direct quoting from the prophets. Unlike the Gospels, which proclaim that they fulfil the prophets, Genesis sets out to describe the world before the prophets. Genesis, therefore, can be inspired by the prophets, but it cannot quote them. It must translate them into a radically different idiom—from exile-related prophetic poetry into ancient-sounding prose. Von Rad (1962, I, 146), for instance, can say, concerning the likeness of God and humanity, that "Ezek. 1:26 is the theological prelude . . . to Gen. 1:26." The implication is that Ezekiel is first. The further implication is that Ezekiel's theological insight has been cast into the idiom of Genesis 1, a chapter which is so written that it echoes and emulates aspects of the second-millenium *Enuma Elish*. Thus, while Ezekiel may be central to Genesis's reshaping of the *Enuma Elish*—and of other ancient writings behind Genesis 1–11—Ezekiel's own idiom has been transformed, and the complexity of that transformation is not easy to unravel. Abraham could be portrayed by the author in a way that exemplifies the kind of faith that was later preached by Isaiah; but, given his ancient setting, Abraham could not be seen to quote Isaiah.

The third issues involves practical testing. In testing the two hypotheses—the prophets used Genesis, and Genesis used the prophets—it is the second that works best: Genesis used the prophets. This is the hypothesis which again and again best explains the detailed relationship between the texts.

In future research, this third argument will be crucial. It is only on the basis of repeated testing, repeated trial and error, that the question of the relationship between the texts will be settled.

Outline of Genesis's Use of Ezekiel, Jeremiah, and Isaiah: General Comment

Taken together, the three prophets (Ezekiel, Isaiah, and Jeremiah) are several times longer than Genesis. In becoming components of Genesis they are greatly

compressed or distilled. The image of a great fall, for example, is not limited
to Ezekiel 28; it pervades and unites the surrounding chapters (Ezek. 26–32);
and these chapters have been distilled so that their essence becomes just one
component of Genesis 2–3.

In adapting the prophets, one of the most basic changes concerns a central
factor—the word. Genesis introduces a new perspective: the word of prophecy
has become the word of promise. To some degree the element of promise was
already present in prophecy, but the form of historiography brings that promise
further down to earth.

Ezekiel and Jeremiah are particularly basic; they are like the foundations
respectively of the two halves of Genesis. Ezekiel, with its almost-primitive
imagery, underlies much of Genesis 1:1–25:18; and the story of Jeremiah underlies that of Jacob (Gen. 25:19–chap. 50). But Isaiah also is important. Its
strong faith pervades Genesis, particularly the accounts of Abraham and Joseph.

The relationship between the texts is summarized in Table A.1. The outline
is exploratory, and, even when accurate, deals only with components or aspects.

The Outline: Specific Comments

The following comments are introductory. They are a minimum indication of
aspects of continuity between the major prophets and Genesis. Closer analysis
is left to further research. Question marks (??) indicate tentativeness.

1. *The human likeness (Ezek. 1:26; Gen. 1:26).* Genesis 1, apart from using
Ezekiel's idea of the likeness—(Ezek. 1:26; cf. von Rad, 1962, I, 146: Ezek. 1:
26 is a prelude to Gen.1:26)—may also have drawn on other aspects of Ezekiel's
opening vision (1:1–3:21), especially its sense of awesome creation-related grandeur (Ezek. 1:1–25) and of challenging mission (Ezek. 2:1–3:15; cf. Gen. 1:28).

2. *The loss of communication, and the reduction of the people (Ezek. 3:22–chap.
5; Gen. 11).* The breakdown of language at the brick-built city of Babel
(Gen.11:1–9) reflects Ezekiel's sudden inability to communicate: he is struck
dumb, and has to scratch a city on a brick (Ezek. 3:22–4:3). In both cases the
breakdown is connected with sin (Ezek. 4:4–8) and dispersal (Ezek. 4:13). The
subsequent punishment, namely the reduction and dispersal of the people
(Ezek. 5:11–17), helps to account for an aspect of the subsequent genealogy
(Gen.11:10–32)—for the way its numbers fade and its survivors move away.

3. *Sin, punishment, and a new covenant (Ezek. 6–11; Gen. 6:1–9:17, the flood).*
The story of the flood—with its sin, punishment, and new creation, including
a covenant (Gen. 9:8–17)—draws on Ezekiel's long description, first of sin and
punishment (6:1–11:13) and then, implicitly, of a new covenant (11:11–14, esp.
11:20). Ezekiel's emphasis on dates, for instance—on "the day" of punishment

Table A.1. Ezekiel, Isaiah, and Jeremiah as Components of Genesis

An Exploratory Outline

Ezekiel	Genesis (mostly 1–14)
1. The likeness of a human (1:26)	Human likeness of God (1:26)
2. Language loss; diminishment (3:22–ch 5)	Babel; diminishing genealogy (11)
3. Sin, punishment, new covenant (6–11)	The flood (6:1–9: 17)
4. Sin, perfect in Eden, a fall (12–22, 25–33)	Eden and sin (2:2b–4:16)
5. Whoring in Egypt; loss of a wife (23–24)	Abram/Sarai in Egypt (12:10–13:1)
6. The shepherds of Israel (34)	Jacob as shepherd (30:25–43)??
7. Destruction; dry bones (35–37)	Dry body (Sarah's); Sodom (18–19)
8. Invasion, resistance, restoration (38–39)	Four kings defeated (14)
9. Altar-focused temple and land (40–48)	Land and altars (12–13)

Isaiah 1–39	Genesis (mostly 15–21)
10. A whole people sick (1–2)	Sodom (18:1—19:29)
11. The vineyard and misconduct (3–5)	Noah's vine; misconduct (9:18–29)
12. Isaiah's vision; a child promised (6–7)	Abram's vision (15)
13. Conception, birth, wandering (8–12)	Hagar and Ishmael; Isaac (16,20–21)
14. The nations and God's anger/plan (13–27)	The nations—under God (10)??
15. Babbling lips; threatened life (28–39)	Babel; fading life/genealogy (11)

Jeremiah 1–31,46–51	Genesis (mostly Jacob)
16. Birth, conflict, a pot (1)	Birth, conflict, pottage (25:19–34)
17. Recall to spousal love (2:1–4:4)	Spousal love endangered (26:1–14)
18. War threats (4:5–ch 6; wells, 2:13)	Tension about wells (26:15–33)??
19. God's anger will inflict exile (21)	Esau's anger exiles Jacob (27:42)
20. Shepherds, bad and good (23)	Jacob waters the sheep (29:1–10)
21. Vision: Exiles will return (24)	Dream; hope of return (28:10–22)
22. The nations (25:14–38; chaps. 46–51)	Cf. Genesis 10??
23. Israel: 70 years in exile (25–29)	Jacob: 20 years with Laban (29–31)
24. Restored exiles will return (30–31)	The return of Jacob (32:3–chap. 33)

Jeremiah 32–45,52	Genesis (Abraham, Joseph)
25. Jeremiah buys a field (32)	Abraham buys a field (23)
26. Death, recovery, an heir (33)	Isaac almost sacrificed (22)??
27. Die in peace; freedom (34)	Freedom; die in peace (15)??
28. Idealistic lifestyle, in tents (35)	Cf. Abraham (esp. 12–13)
29. Prophet mistreated; murder (36–41)	Joseph sold (almost killed, 37)
30. Jeremiah in Egypt (42–45)	Joseph in Egypt (esp. 40–42)
31. The prophecy fulfilled (52)	The word fulfilled (50:17–23,25)

Isaiah 40–66	Genesis (mostly Joseph)
32. Prophetic call: God as shepherd (40)	Joseph: shepherd, prophetic (37)
33. The servant (esp. 41–42,49,50,52–53)	Joseph, servant, savior (39–47)
34. God as creator (42–45)	Creation (1)
35. Blessings; nations see glory (65–66)	Blessings; nations watch (49–50)

and on exact dates (7:7, 10, 12; 8:1)—helps to account for Genesis's preciseness about dates and the exact day (Gen. 7:11–13).

4. *Exile, responsibility, nakedness, and a fall in Eden (Ezek. 12–22,25–33; Gen. 2:4b–4:16)*. The story of exile from Eden (Gen. 2:4b–4:16), apart from using the image of Eden in Ezekiel 28 (van Seters, 1992, 119–122), draws also on the surrounding descriptions of a fall from strength and beauty (Ezek. 26–32). It also uses earlier elements of Ezekiel, such as the following:

The protective mark (Ezek. 9:4; cf. the sign on Cain, Gen. 4:15).

The divine breath or spirit in humans (Ezek. 11:13–25; Gen. 2:7).

Exile or expulsion (Ezek. 12:1–20; Gen. 3:23; 4:16).

Responsibility (Ezek. 14:12–23; chap. 18; Gen. 3:11–13; 4:9–10).

Nakedness, beauty, temptation, and shame (Ezek. 16; Gen. 2–3).

The flashing sword (Ezek. 21; cf. the sentry, 33:1–9; Gen. 3:24).

No pleasure in the death of the wicked (Ezek. 33:10–20; Gen. 4:15).

5. *Whoring in Egypt, and losing one's wife (Ezek. 23–24; Gen. 12:10–13:1)*. The account of how Abraham effectively gave Sarah over to Pharaoh (12:10–13:1) appears to combine at least two elements from Ezekiel—the whoring in Egypt (Ezek. 23), and Ezekiel's loss of his wife (Ezek. 24:15–27).

6. *The shepherds of Israel (Ezek. 34; Jacob as shepherd: Gen. 29:1–10; 30:25–43; 31:38–39; 33:13–14)*. The consistent portrayal of Jacob as an able caring shepherd corresponds broadly with Ezekiel's ideal of shepherding. Joseph also is a careful shepherd (Gen. 37:2, 12–17)—unlike Judah, who seems more interested in shearing the flock than tending it (Gen. 38:12; cf. the kid goat in 38:16).

7. *Destruction and renewal—including renewal of body or bones (Ezek. 35–37; Gen. 18:1–19:29)*. In rebuilding Israel, God's action is twofold: destruction of sinful enemy cities (Ezek. 35); and renewal of Israel—a process that is like renewing a body (giving it a new heart and spirit, Ezek. 36), or like bringing dry bones to life (Ezek. 37). These contrasting images—of destruction and of reviving a body or bones—have been used in depicting the destruction of Sodom and the revival of Sarah's body (Gen. 18:1–19:29, esp. 18:9–15).

8. *Invasion, resistance, restoration (Ezek. 38–39; Gen. 14)*. Ezekiel's account of a semi-apocalyptic invasion, and of subsequent resistance and restoration, provides part of the background for the account of the invasion by the four great kings (Gen. 14).

9. *Viewing the temple/altar and land (Ezek. 40–48; Gen. 12–13)*. Ezekiel's great final vision (chaps. 40–48) is of the temple, including the temple altar, and the land. This culminating vision is to be the basis of restoration. Genesis takes this vision and uses it not as a culmination, but, in adapted form, as the foundation for the account of Abraham—for the way he goes through the land, traveling and building altars (Gen. 12:1–9; 13:2–18).

10. *A whole people sick (Isa. 1–2; Gen. 18–19)*. One component for the account of Sodom and Gomorrah (Gen. 18–19) has apparently been distilled from the beginning of Isaiah—from the condemnation of a people as completely sinful, like Sodom and Gomorrah (Isa. 1), and from the subsequent intervention of God (Isa. 2). Shared features include the totality of the sinfulness (Isa. 1:6; Gen. 19:4), the divine intervention as brilliant or dazzling (Isa. 2:5, 10, 19, 21; Gen. 19:11), and the need to take refuge in a cavern or cave (Isa. 2:10, 19, 21; Gen. 19:30).

11. *The vine/yard, the nakedness, and the cursing (Isa. 3–5; Gen. 9:18–29)*. Noah's planting of a vine, and the subsequent incident involving his nakedness and his sons (Gen. 9:18–29) has apparently drawn on Isaiah 3–5, especially on the account of how the planting of a vineyard turned out badly (Isa. 5:1–7). Shared features include:

Planting a vine/yard; a surprising result (Isa. 5:1–4; Gen. 9:20–21).

The insolence of youth (Isa. 3:5–6; Noah's son, Gen. 9:22).

The uncovering of nakedness (Isa. 3:17; Gen. 9:21).

A protective canopy or covering (Isa. 4:4–6; Gen. 9:23).

Subsequent curses or woes (Isa. 5:8–24; Gen. 9:25).

12. *The overpowering vision: reassurance and a sense of the people's future (Isa. 6–7; Gen. 15)*. Genesis 15, apart from having "close affinities" with Isaiah 7 (Schmid, 1976, 58), has further affinities with Isaiah 6—the vision, the sense of God's presence as overpowering, the association of the overpowering presence with forms of fire, the reassuring word, the positive response (Isaiah's readiness; Abram's trust), a sense of the people's difficult future (Isaiah: desolation and exile; Genesis: exile and captivity), and the people's eventual renewal or return.

13. *Conception, birth, wandering (Isa. 7–12; Gen. 16, 20–21)*. The Genesis account of the conception and birth of Ishmael and Isaac appears to draw considerably on Isaiah's prophecies concerning various interconnected children (chaps. 7–12). Some shared aspects include:

The woman will call the child Immanuel/Ishmael (Isa. 7:14; Gen. 16:11).

Going to a woman who conceives and gives birth (Isa. 8:3–4;
Gen. 16:4, 15).

The distressed wandering (Isa. 8:21–23; by Hagar, Gen. 16:7; 21:15–16).

Divine intervention, and a child (Isa. 9:1–7; Gen. 16:7–10; 21:17–22).

In both books these births are interwoven with the fate of various foreigners or foreign nations.

14. *The many nations—all under God (Isa. 13–27; Gen. 10)??* If the list of nations in Genesis 10 depends on the prophets, then it is likely that it depends partly on Isaiah 13–27. The essence of both texts is not only to list nations but also to indicate that such nations are under the power of God (see commentary on Genesis 10). Furthermore, both lists are set in a context that depicts God's power as total: Isaiah's oracles are framed by the fall of Babylon (chap. 13) and an apocalypse (chaps. 24–27); Genesis's list is framed by references to the flood (Gen. 10:1, 32).

15. *Babbling lips, and the threat of death (Isa. 28–39; Gen. 11).* Isaiah 28–39 has two main parts—first (chaps. 28–35), a series of oracles, which begin with images of the failure of language (babbling, strange lips, foreign tongues, 28:7–13; lies, 28:14–18; lip service, 29:13); second (chaps. 36–39), a double death threat from invasion and sickness. This second part, in describing the invaders' conversation with Jewish representatives, also depicts language as a source not only of communication but also of incomprehension (36:11–13).

These two parts (language problems and death threats) have probably been used as components in Genesis 11—first, at Babel (11:1–9), and second, in shaping the genealogy, which fades in numbers and ends under the shadow of death (11:10–32).

Isaiah 28–39 also contains a positive dimension but this does not appear to have been used in Genesis 11.

16. *The conflicted births—Jeremiah and Jacob (Jer. 1; Gen. 25:19–34).* Jeremiah is born to conflict—an idea that is re-expressed graphically in the struggle that surrounds the birth of Jacob.

17. *Recall to spousal love (Jer. 2:1–4:4; Gen. 26:1–14).* Rebekah's brush with the Philistines, while Isaac is at Gerar (Gen. 26:1–14), seems to be colored partly by Jeremiah's oracles on Israel's spousal love—on its loss and on the need to come back to it.

18. *Wells and war-like threats (Jer. 4:5–chap. 6; wells, 2:13; Gen. 26:15–33)??* It is not clear (at least to the present writer) whether or how Genesis used a

large section of Jeremiah—most of chapters 4–20. However, the portrayal of a threatening invasion (Jer. 4:5–chap. 6) may have seen used to depict the tense relationship between Isaac and the Philistines (Gen. 26:15–33). The crucial image of the well or spring (Gen. 26:15–21, 25, 32–33) is probably related to Jeremiah's idea of God as a fountain of living waters (Jer. 2:13).

19. *Anger will inflict exile (Jer. 21:1–10; Gen. 27:41–45).* Genesis's picture of the deadly anger of Esau, and of how it drove Jacob into exile (27:41–45) corresponds significantly with Jeremiah's announcement that God's anger will inflict death and drive people into exile (Jer. 21:5–10). Apart from death, both texts include an emphasis on seeking life.

20. *Shepherds, bad and good (Jer. 23:1–4; Gen. 29:1–10).* The picture of Jacob as shepherd (Gen. 29:1–10: 30:25–43; 31:38–39; 33:13–14), apart from any use of Ezekiel 34, makes use also of Jeremiah's text on good and bad shepherds (23:1–4).

21. *Vision/dream: hope of return from exile (Jer. 24; Gen. 28:10–22).* Jacob's dream, assuring him that he will return from exile (Gen. 28:15, 20–21), depends in part on Jeremiah's vision concerning the return of the exiles (Jer. 24:5–7). Both the vision and the dream occur at a holy place (the temple, Jer. 24:1; the house of God, Gen. 28:17, 22). After the return, Yahweh will be the God of the people (Jer. 24:7) and the God of Jacob (28:21).

22. *The nations (Jer. 25:14–38; chaps. 46–51; Genesis 10)??* If Genesis used Jeremiah's oracles concerning the nations, then perhaps, like those of Isaiah 13–27, they have contributed to the picture of the nations in Genesis 10 (see section 14 above).

In the Greek version of Jeremiah, the oracles against the nations are a unit (chaps. 46–51 follow 25:14–38)—an arrangement which "certainly represents an older form of the text" (Couturier, 1990, 18:9). It is useful then, in considering how Genesis may have used the oracles against the nations, to include the possibility that, for the author of Genesis, the contents of chapters 46–51 may have been placed after 25:14–38.

23. *Israel/Jacob: years in exile (Jer. 25:1–13; chaps. 26–29; Gen. 29, 31).* Israel spends years of exile in Babylon (Jeremiah), and Jacob spends years of service with Laban (Genesis). Some shared features include:

My years: as prophet (Jer. 25:1–7); as servant (Gen. 31:36–42).

Years of service: seventy (Jer. 25:11–12); twice seven (Gen. 29:18–30).

No festive rejoicing (Jer. 25:10; Gen. 31:27).

Opposition; consultation of people (Jer. 26), of wives (Gen. 31:1–16)??

Carried off: vessels (Jer. 27:16–28:6); idols (Gen. 31:19, 32–35).

Proposing peace (Jer. 29; Gen. 31:45–32:3).

24. *Exiles return to reconciliation (Jer. 30–31; Gen. 32:3–chap. 33)*. See Brodie, 1981 for an analysis of this factor.

25. *Buying a field (Jer. 32; Gen. 23)*. In difficult circumstances, Jeremiah and Abraham both buy fields.

26. *Death, recovery, an heir (Jer. 33; Gen. 22)??* Jeremiah's hope-filled buying of a field (chap. 32) is paired with another hope-filled episode—concerning recovery from deathly siege, a siege in which death is inflicted by God (Jer. 33, esp. 33:5). In Genesis, the buying of the field is paired (chap. 23) with the near-death of Isaac (chap. 22); and so the question arises whether Genesis 22 has drawn in some way from Jeremiah 33.

The most obvious similarity is in the promises of numerous descendants (Jer. 33:19–22; Gen. 22:15–19).

27. *Die in peace; freedom for slaves (Jer. 34; Gen. 15)??* Jeremiah emphasizes that the king will die in peace (34:5) and that slaves are to be freed (34:8–16). These elements—death in peace, and freedom for the enslaved—may, perhaps, have contributed to Genesis 15 and 17 (cf. 15:12–15; 17:12, 23). The texts share some further features: the covenant (Jer. 34:13, 18; Gen. 15:18; 17:2); passing between the halves of the animals (Jer. 34:18–19; Gen. 15:10, 17); the corpses and preying birds (Jer. 34:20; Gen. 15:11).

28. *Idealistic lifestyle, in tents (Jer. 35; Abraham, esp. Gen. 12–13)*. The idealistic lifestyle of the Rechabites—living in tents—seems to have contributed to the portrayal of Abraham, Isaac, and Jacob, especially to the picture of Abraham in Genesis 12–13.

29. *The mistreating of the prophet (Jer. 36–41; Gen. 37)*. The general mistreatment of Jeremiah has contributed to the portrayal of the mistreatment of Joseph by his brothers. In particular, the burning of the prophetic scroll (Jer. 36) apparently underlies the despising of the prophetic dream (Gen. 37:5–11).

30. *The prophet is brought to Egypt (Jer. 42–44; Joseph, esp. Gen. 40–42)*. In its final stage the Jeremiah story moves to Egypt and includes references to Pharaoh (44:30), Pharaoh's palace (Jer. 43:9) and famine (42:16; 44:12–14, 18)—a setting that corresponds broadly with the setting for the final stage of the Jacob story (Joseph in Egypt). Further shared features include the following:

Removal of the prophetic figure to Egypt (Jer. 43:6; Gen. 37:36).

Assurance regarding kings and interpretation (Jer. 42; Gen. 40–41).

Calling Judah to repent (Jer. 44; Gen. 44:18–34; cf. chap. 38).

The promise of return (Jer. 44:28; Gen. 50:24).

On Jeremiah 46–51, see section 22 above.

31. *The prophetic word fulfilled (Jer. 52; Gen. 50:17–23, 25).* The closing chapter of Jeremiah recounts the fall of Jerusalem to the Babylonians, yet the basic emphasis of the chapter is positive—both because the fall in effect fulfills Jeremiah's prophecy, and also because the final note is one of hope: the king of Judah is pardoned and honored (thus preparing the way for the eventual return to Jerusalem).

This climate of fulfillment, reconciliation, and hope occurs also at the end of Genesis. The brothers recall the word of their father (Gen. 50:17) and Joseph in effect fulfills it—thus bringing a further degree of pardon and reconciliation. At the end, Joseph dies in Egypt, as the king apparently will do in Babylon, yet Joseph's death looks to an eventual return.

32. *The call of the prophet (Isa. 40; Gen. 37).* Both Isaiah 40 and Genesis 37 are variations on the conventional type-scene of the prophetic call. Furthermore, they both share a number of details, essentially in the same order:

The word (in comparable positions: Isa. 40:8; Gen. 37:11).

The towns (Isa. 40:9; Gen. 37:12–17).

Behold . . . who comes (Isa. 40:10; Gen. 37:19).

The shepherd and flock (Isa. 40:11; Gen. 37:2, 12–18).

Water (Isa. 40:12; Gen. 37:25).

Lifting up the eyes (Isa. 40:26; Gen. 37:25).

Calling on Jacob to recognize (Isa. 40:27–28; Gen. 37:32).

33. *The servant savior (Isa. 41–42, 49, 50, 52–53; Joseph, Gen. 39–47).* The portrayal of Joseph—a faithful and wise servant who later saves both his brothers and the multitudes—corresponds significantly with Isaiah's idea of the servant, particularly as described in the four servant songs (Isa. 42:1–9; 49:1–6; 50:4–11; 52:13–53:12).

34. *God as creator (Isa. 42–45; Gen. 1).* Genesis's clear doctrine of God as creator (Gen. 1) corresponds largely to that of Isaiah 42–45. Perhaps Genesis's providence theme also—in the Joseph story—draws on Isaiah 42–45.

35. *Jacob's sons are blessed, and the nations see his glory (Isa. 65–66; Gen. 49–50).* The two final chapters of Genesis—Jacob's blessings (chap. 49) and burial (chap. 50)—depend partly on the two final chapters of Isaiah (chaps. 65–66).

Some sections of Isaiah 65–66 have been used elsewhere—in particular, aspects of the image of a woman as in labor with the birth of a nation (Isa. 66:5–16) have been used in describing Rebekah's labor (Gen. 25:23)—but nonetheless the dependence is significant.

Both texts involve a basic shift—from an initial focus on the sons of Jacob (Isa. 65; Gen. 49) to a wider view which, in some way, includes the whole earth (Isa. 66; Gen. 50). In dealing with the sons of Jacob the emphasis is on future blessing (Isa. 65; Gen. 65). When the view opens to include the nations of the earth, the emphasis is on a witnessing of glory—the glory of God's coming (Isa. 66:1–2, 18–23), and the glory of Jacob's mourning (Gen. 50:7–11).

Some of the similarities may be summarized as follows:

God/Jacob call people to them (Isa. 65:1; Gen. 49:1a)??

The future of the descendants/sons of Jacob (Isa. 65:9; Gen. 49:1b).

"You" statements, bad and good (Isa. 65:11–14; cf. Gen. 49:2–27).

Repetition of blessing (Isa. 65:8, 15–25; Gen. 49:28).

Nations witness his glory/glorious mourning (Isa. 66:18; Gen. 50:9–11).

All . . . the brothers, the horses, the chariots (Isa. 66:20; Gen. 50:7–9).

Assessing the Evidence

The preceding analysis is preliminary, and so the assessment, too, must be preliminary. Yet the indications of Genesis's dependence on the three prophets are strong.

To start, there is the external plausibility. It is hard to imagine that the person who composed Genesis was not aware of the heritage of Ezekiel, Jeremiah, and Isaiah. And being aware, it would have been appropriate to use that heritage. Such usage would not only acknowledge Israel's heritage of prophecy but would also accord with the ancient practice of incorporating the work of previous writers.

Furthermore, there are the similarities:

First and obviously, the shared themes such as creation, sin, redemption, covenant, the word of promise, and faith.

Second, some broad similarity of plot, such as occurs in the accounts of Jeremiah and Jacob (the conflict-filled birth; the years of exile; the description of return; the descent into Egypt).

Third, the persistent similarities of detail.

Fourth, some significant similarity of order.

Fifth, a certain form of completion: Genesis contains a reflection of virtually every major area of the three prophetic books.

The similarity of themes could be seen as coincidence, as could some similarities of plot and detail. But eventually the accumulation of similarities involving plot and detail surpasses the probability of coincidence. And the final aspects—concerning order and completion—also surpass coincidence.

Finally, there is the intelligibility of the differences. The decision to follow the literary form of historiography meant that the poetic oracles of the prophets had to be rendered into a new idiom. And the history's ancient setting required and permitted further adaptations. The buying of the field, for instance, so clear in Jeremiah's dealing with his cousin (chap. 32), takes on a different dimension when recast as Abraham's dealing with the Hittites (Gen. 23). The distant setting enables the Genesis writer not only to keep a sense of hope—there is a form of hope in Abraham's energy—but also to surround that hope with a gracious ritual.

It is better at this stage not to attempt to reach a definitive conclusion. There is need for a fuller analysis and for a more rigorous application of the criteria for judging dependence. But the idea of Genesis's dependence on the major prophets is no longer quite so sketchy and tentative. Such dependence forms a reasonable working hypothesis.

SOURCES: GENESIS'S USE OF HOMER'S *ODYSSEY*

Genesis's Use of Mesopotamian Epic

The first awareness that some of Genesis's sources may still exist came in December 1872, when George Smith publicized a translation of Assyrian accounts of the flood (*ANET* xiii; Hess and Tsumura, 1994, 5) (see Introduction, Chapter 8). Further research eventually led to a major breakthrough on the source question—the realization that, to a significant degree, Genesis 1–11 as a whole (or at least Genesis 1–9) was modeled on epic poetry, especially on the epic poetry of Mesopotamia. (Genesis 10 is elusive, more akin to genealogy and world maps than epic.)

It is now a commonplace to see Genesis as dependent on works such as the *Epic of Gilgamesh*, the *Atrahasis Epic*, and the *Enuma Elish* (Heidel, 195 O'Brien and Major, 1982; Clifford, 2:2; 1994, 144–150; on the Near East, cf. Hess and Tsumura, 1994, 75–282; on Genesis 1–11 and several other creation stories, see van Wolde, 1997).

All three texts, *Gilgamesh, Atrahasis,* and *Enuma Elish,* help in understanding Genesis. With regard to the *Epic of Gilgamesh,* the task of tracing dependence is complicated by the diversity of versions, but "there are a number of points of possible and probable contact with the OT. Wherever these contacts appear the Hebrew poets and storytellers have transformed the material into a vehicle of their own beliefs" (McKenzie, 1968, 312).

The *Enuma Elish* also has contributed, even if only in Genesis 1–2; there is significant similarity of content and style. But the older text has been adapted thoroughly. For instance, the Genesis idea of the relationship of the divine to creation is "totally different" (O'Brien and Major, 1982, 195–198, esp. 196).

Particularly important was the *Atrahasis Epic.* Along with other Mesopotamian materials it provided a model for Genesis 2–11, especially for the plot of Genesis 2–9 (Clifford, 2:2). Kselman expresses the same general idea:

> The biblical Flood story . . . depend[s] . . . on such Babylonian sources as the Gilgamesh Epic and the Atrahasis myth. This ancient Near Eastern material was consciously reshaped and altered in accord with Israelite theological per-

spective: e.g., Noah, the survivor of the flood, is not immortal; the cause of the flood is ethical (human sin) and not overpopulation, as in some ancient Near Eastern parallels. (91)

Kselman's words express a key feature of composition. The culture of Mesopotamia, however prestigious it may have been, was not swallowed unthinkingly by Genesis. It was consciously reshaped.

Bergant (1997) clarifies briefly a basic aspect of this reshaping: Genesis *demythologized* the narratives of Israel's neighbors, and not just the narratives of Mesopotamia but those of Egypt also. This inclusion of Egypt is far from new. It has long been accepted, for instance, that aspects of the Joseph story reflect an Egyptian background (Humphreys, 1988, 154–175). There is also significant affinity with Ugaritic (Parker, 1989, 225).

What is essential, however, is that Genesis 1–11 uses and adapts Mesopotamian epic. Thus, a precedent for Genesis's use of foreign epic is already established.

Widening the Field of Investigation

In recent decades, scholars of Genesis's origins have begun to examine the Greeks. First, it emerges that there is a partial affinity of genre between the Primary History and Greek historiography (see Introduction, Chapters 6–8). In particular, the Hesiod-related *Catalogue of Women*, with its mixture of genealogy and narrative, provides a partial analogue to Genesis; it was a form of primeval history, the result "not of a gradual accumulation of materials but . . . [of] a systematic plan with careful construction of its various parts. . . . The *Catalogue* was perhaps the original *archaiologia* and the basis for all later attempts at primeval history" (van Seters, 1992, 89–90). Furthermore, Genesis has already been compared to Greek epic—to the work of Hesiod—but without claiming dependence (O'Brien and Major, 1982, 47–65).

To facilitate investigation of this wider field it is useful to start mapping it. Accordingly Appendix 5 provides a preliminary skeletal survey of basic aspects of ancient literature. The usefulness of such a survey has yet to be measured. At the very least it alerts readers to some of the Greek writers' views on women. In this regard, Hesiod was deadly (*Theogony*, 570–620; *Works and Days*, 47–105; see comment on Gen. 2:18–23; and in Appendix 5, see the final comments on Pythagoras and Parmenides). More generally, Appendix 5 gives a sense of the larger literary world surrounding the Primary History.

In the meantime, it is useful to focus on one Greek work, Homer's *Odyssey*.

What is true of Genesis 1–9 is true also, in modified form, of later chapters. Genesis 11–50 made use of the great epic poetry of the time. In particular, it used the journeys of Homer's *Odyssey* as one component—distilled and domesticated—for describing the journeys and lives of the patriarchs.

Antiquity's Greatest Epic of Wandering

The word "component" is important. Homer does not dominate Genesis 11–50. The subtext has been used as just one part of an account that has a vision quite different from that of Homer. The heroics of the *Odyssey* have been distilled and domesticated, often even reversed. As Kselman said about the Mesopotamian epics: the "material was consciously reshaped and altered in accordance with Israelite theological perspectives" (91). The biblical text has affinities with epic, but it may also be described as an anti-epic (Damrosch, 1987, 47–50). The Greek narrative was adjusted to fit into the broad patterns that had already been established in Genesis 1–9. To that extent, more than the Mesopotamian epics, the *Odyssey* is secondary.

Furthermore, the dependence of Genesis 11–50 on Greek epic is not as obvious as the dependence of Genesis 1–9 on Mesopotamian epic, especially on Mesopotamian flood accounts. This variation in obviousness is somewhat akin to the variation within the Gospel of Luke: during the infancy narrative (Luke 1–2) the dependence on another literature (the Old Testament) is obvious; but, as the Gospel goes on, the nature of this indebtedness changes; the obviousness fades. In Genesis, the variation in obviousness seems to be part of a larger pattern of graded stylistic changes.

The presence of Homer's epic entails a dimension of fiction—historiographical fiction, but fiction nonetheless. At one level this seems alien to Genesis, alien to the Pentateuch, to the revered Torah. Yet the idea of the presence of fiction is not new. In Whybray's words, "Fiction is, after all, a major genre in the Old Testament. . . . It is well established that a major proportion of the narratives in the Pentateuch are fiction" (1987, 240). What counts is not whether there is a dimension of fiction, but whether that fiction has been incorporated into a larger world of genuine art. Art, including fictional art, expresses the deepest truths: "The fictional mode is adopted because it presents a unity to the imagination more intense than the documentary materials" (Frye, 1981, 25).

Yet in describing the Bible it is generally better to avoid the word "fiction." "Fiction" may be technically correct, but as plain English it is often misleading; it communicates the idea of something trivial. Genesis is not trivial, neither in itself nor in its sources. The *Odyssey* is not only a great story and a form of biography; it is also a form of wisdom literature, an encyclopedia of ancient knowledge: "Homer is didactic, and . . . the tale is made subservient to the task of accommodating the weight of educational materials which lie within it" (Havelock, 1963, 61–86, esp. 61).

External Plausibility

The idea of Genesis's dependence on Homer may seem strange at first. Genesis is East, and Homer is West, and ne'er the twain could meet. They are worlds apart.

However, as already seen (see Introduction, Chapter 6), this clear East-West division did not exist in ancient times. The Greeks were interwoven with the Persians and with much of the known world. The land of Homer, and the initial Greek intellectual hub, Ionia, were within the Persian empire, within its developed system of transport and exchange.

Greek writers were not cut off from the East—from the world of Mesopotamia and the Bible. Genesis's literary genre finds its closest analogue in Greek historiography (van Seters, 1983, 1992). Greek writing—including that of Hesiod, on the Greek mainland (in Boetia)—was itself heavily influenced by Mesopotamia (Burkert, 1992; Morris, 1992; Feldman, 1996; Marblestone, 1996). Greek historians wrote of the East (Drews, 1973). The *Iliad* has affinity with Iran and India (Baldick, 1994). In particular, the *Odyssey* sometimes echoes the *Epic of Gilgamesh*:

> The plot of the Odyssey has more detailed antecedents than the Iliad in the literatures of the Near East. To recapitulate: the plot, insofar as it is the episodic wanderings of a hero that end in coming home, has marked similarities to the Gilgamesh Epic. Both texts start out with descriptions of the hero who traveled far and wide, gaining great experience. Nor is the resemblance limited to such generalities. The two epics share detailed episodes. (Gordon, 1962, 223)

If Genesis used aspects of the *Epic of Gilgamesh*, it is unlikely to have objected to the epic of Homer. The gap between Genesis and Homer is much greater in modern imagination than in historical reality.

Freedman (1991, 9–10) compares and contrasts the Primary History with the *Iliad* and *Odyssey*, particularly the diverse ways in which the *Iliad* and the Primary History focus on the fall of a great city. Interestingly, too, the way in which the Primary History manages to locate the Commandments at the center of the whole work—largely through a massive process of recalling (Moses' speeches in Deuteronomy recall Sinai; Freedman, 1991, 11)—has a basic affinity with the way Odysseus recalls his journey (*Odyssey*, Bks. 9–12, Odysseus's banquet speech to the assembled Phaeacians).

The *Odyssey* is at least a century or two older than Genesis. Homer's epic, whatever its distant roots, seemingly existed in written form around the year 700 BCE: "There is general agreement that the Homeric epics . . . were composed and written down—essentially in the form in which we have them—in the second half of the 8th century BC, the Odyssey somewhat later than the Iliad" (Crielaard, 1995, 201). Apparently the text was further standardized around 550 BCE, on orders of the Athenian ruler, Peisistratus (Rieu, 1991, xxxiii). Genesis probably was not completed until some time in the Persian Empire (ca. 550–330 BCE). Many of Genesis's roots of course may be older than those of Homer, but in the end Genesis is a single unified book, and most researchers place its completion after 550 BCE.

Like the *Epics of Gilgamesh* and *Atrahasis,* but more so, the Homeric epics were the known world's most famous stories. For many, Homer was almost a form of bible. "Fifth-century authors, such as Herodotus and Thucydides, speak of Homeric epic as the outstanding classical and virtually canonical text of antiquity" (Gordon, 1962, 219). Homer of course was written in another language. But so were the epics of Mesopotamia. And, like the Mesopotamian epics, the Homeric epics would have been accessible. If courier services from Homer's country could reach Susa in nine days (see Introduction, Chapter 6), there should have no problem about reaching the author of Genesis in a century or two. A writer who thought on a world scale and who used epics is unlikely to have ignored such an opportunity.

Homer as Model and Foil: Initial Comparison

With the exception of the Bible, Homer has been the most used text of all time, the most adapted and rewritten—from the first apparent echoes in Hesiod to later echoes in James Joyce. He pervaded Greek education, and partly through Virgil's Romanizing of him, overshadowed Roman education also. Later he was Christianized, but Christians treated him with ambiguity, part model, part foil: "In the Church . . . he was banished and embraced, excoriated and adduced, repudiated and imitated" (MacDonald, 1994, 26; see Lamberton and Keaney, 1992).

Ambiguity toward Homer occurs already in Hesiod. C. M. Bowra, while describing Hesiod in near-biblical terms, points to a critical attitude:

> Tending his sheep under Mount Helicon, [Hesiod] had a vision of the Muses, who said to him . . . "We can . . . reveal in words what the truth is." Then they gave him a staff . . . and breathed into him a divine voice. . . . This vivid revelation made Hesiod a poet without ceasing to be a farmer. That he believed in its authoritative authenticity we cannot doubt, and the result was his *Theogony.* . . . Hesiod . . . claims for himself an authority far greater than Homer claims. . . . He seems to go back to a distant past when poets were prophets. (1966, 61)

Writing perhaps a generation after Homer, Hesiod does indeed pay due homage to the heroic tradition (*Works and Days,* 156–172), but much of his poem is an antithesis to Homer—a call not to heroics but to daily work and honesty. "His view of life is not that of a king or noble, but of a struggling farmer" (Bowra, 1966, 60). Hesiod, then, in part, is like a protest against Homer. Later (ca. 400), Plato's attitude to Homer was one of "passionate opposition" (Griffin, 1980, 1). Genesis's critical attitude to Homer therefore is not unique.

The central plot—in the *Odyssey*—is that of a journey in quest of land and family. Odysseus, after a ten-year war in ancient Troy (ca. 1200 BCE), seeks his homeland, Ithaca; and during his journey, lasting another ten years, he wonders about the fate of his wife, his young son, and his elderly father. Old age threatens the father. And suitors threaten the wife and son; they want to marry her and kill him. Eventually, in disguise, he returns. The finale is like a great drama of judgment—a tense mixture of recognition and revenge (he and his son kill the suitors).

These elements are present in Genesis also, but they are spread over two narratives—those of Abraham (chaps. 12–25) and Jacob (chaps. 25–50)—and they are but part of a larger story. Both Abraham and Jacob spend much time journeying, searching for aspects of land and family. The Abraham account lays the emphasis on the wife and young son, and the Jacob account gives more space to an elderly father and to a drama of climactic recognition.

Genesis involves some radical reversals. Instead of son and father exacting final revenge, Abraham has to let go completely of his son (chap. 22; death in Genesis is not a vengeful punishment or a dread abode but something that in varying ways is accepted; cf. chaps. 22–23 and 48–49). And the finale, in the Joseph story, is not avenging punishment but forgiveness.

To compare the texts more closely it is first necessary to summarize the *Odyssey*.

The Homeric Epic

The *Odyssey* (traditionally divided into twenty-four books)[1] recounts events that cover the entire life of Odysseus—from his father (24:375–382), mother (11: 85), and hunt-loving youth (17:291–317; 19:405–454) to his eventual peaceful death (foretold in 11:134–137). Within that lifetime the primary focus is on the twenty-year period of war and wandering. But even these years are not recounted in sequence. Instead, the action begins near the end, and the sequential narrative fills just about forty days:

1. For a critical edition, see Allen, 1917–1919; for a close English translation, with line numeration, see Lattimore, 1965; Rieu, 1991.

My awareness of the Genesis-Homer link came about as follows. While searching for a single adjective to describe Jacob (February 2, 1996), the word that came was "wily," but this seemed unusable because the same word is often applied to Odysseus, and to use it of Jacob would be confusing and misleading. Still, the coincidence was perplexing, and I mentioned it soon afterward to a philosopher colleague, Philip McShane. He immediately referred to the Jewish philosopher, Emmanuel Levinas, whom he had known while studying in Fribourg, Switzerland. Levinas had explicitly contrasted Jacob and Odysseus. A search through several of Levinas's works yielded nothing except an obscure Abraham-related reference to an unavailable work in Dutch (de Broux, 1972). McShane then said that perhaps the contrast had been made in conversation. Emmanuel Levinas had died on December 25, 1995.

Resuming the study of Jacob, the account of moving the great stone (29:1–10) recalled the *Odyssey*'s story of the Cyclops moving a massive stone (Od. 9:24). On checking the Homeric passage, other connections began to emerge.

The connection with the massive stone would not have been made perhaps but for Oona Ajzenstat of Ontario. In conversation and in a paper to the SBL (Philadelphia, November 18, 1995) she had emphasized the influence of the story of the Cyclops.

six days for the beginning of the journey of young Telemachus (Bks. 1–4);

twenty-five days approximately for Odysseus's raft-building and for his twenty-day voyage from captivity to the hospitality of the Phaeacians (Bk. 5);

three days among the friendly Phaeacians (Bks. 6–12);

and six days back in his native Ithaca (three at his country estate, Bks. 13–16; and three in his own house and in that of his father, 17–24).

During this intense forty-day narrative there are a series of flashbacks and prophecies, which fill out the larger picture of Odysseus's life. Furthermore, the epic as a whole evokes something of the full dimensions of a human life: it begins with a picture of youth (Telemachus, Bks. 1–4), and concludes with pictures of death, mourning, and old age (Bk. 24).

It is useful to divide the *Odyssey* into four main parts:

The departure and journey of young Telemachus (Bks. 1–4);

The journey of Odysseus (Bks. 5–12);

The return to Ithaca (Bks. 13–18);

The judgment: recognition and vengeance (Bks. 19–24).

THE YOUNG TELEMACHUS (BKS. 1–4)

In the tenth year after the fall of Troy, while Odysseus was enduring a seventh year of captivity on the island of the beautiful goddess Calypso, and while his wife Penelope, at home in Ithaca, was beset by greedy suitors, the gods agreed in principle that Odysseus be released. Furthermore, Athena, the daughter of Zeus, directed the young son, Telemachus, who till then had been intimidated by the suitors, to confront them and to embark on his journey. The purpose of this journey was both to find his father and to establish his own name (Bk. 1). The confrontation with the suitors is tense—they tell him to banish his mother—and Telemachus secretly sails away (Bk. 2). His voyage brings him to two old friends of his father, Nestor, king of Pylos (Bk. 3), and Menelaus, king of Sparta (Bk. 4). The first, Nestor, is extremely gracious, and, apart from giving his son Peisistratus as companion, gives some initial information about those who returned from Troy. But it is the second, Menelaus, along with his wife, Helen, who has information about Odysseus—that he is still alive—and who gives the best accounts of the struggle to return home from the war. Meanwhile, back in Ithaca (end of Bk. 4), word of Telemachus's departure spreads. His mother, Penelope, is distressed, and the suitors plan to kill him.

THE JOURNEY (BKS. 5–12)

Odysseus, helped by Athena, finally escapes captivity, and, following an almost-fatal storm, lands on an unknown shore (Bk. 5). Next day he meets the beautiful

Nausicaa and she introduces him to her land, that of the Phaeacians—a friendly people, who receive him with feasting (Bks. 6–7) and contentious games (Bk. 8).

Books 9–12 are a massive flashback. During a Phaeacian banquet Odysseus recounts his years of traveling—including his encounters with the deathly Cyclops (Bk. 9), with dangerous women (when betrothal-like scenes turned nasty, Bk. 10), and with the shades of the dead (Bk. 11). He concludes by telling of the triple peril that led to the destruction of his ship (and to his consequent captivity by Calypso, Bk. 12).

THE RETURN (BKS. 13–18)

The Phaeacians give gifts to Odysseus and bring him, at last, to the shores of his native land, Ithaca (Bk. 13). Athena disguises Odysseus as an old beggar, and the wily traveler cautiously approaches his property. Coming first to the hut of his herdsman, Eumaeus the swineherd, the disguised Odysseus is welcomed, as Eumaeus cares faithfully for the animals and property of his absent master. The old beggar recounts his apparent story, telling of years in Egypt (Bk. 14).

The epic switches to Telemachus: after a complex journey—including a meal, a prophet, and an escape from the suitors' trap—he, too, approaches the herdsman's hut (Bk. 15). Soon afterward, while the herdsman is gone into the city to tell Penelope that Telemachus is back, Odysseus reveals himself to his son (Bk. 16). Finally, following this self-revelation, Telemachus and Odysseus decide to leave the herdsman's hut and go separately down to the city, to Odysseus's manor or palatial home (Bk. 17). Odysseus is still disguised as an old beggar, and soon after arriving at his own house is pushed by the suitors into fighting another beggar—for food. In the suitors' presence, Penelope now appears—seductive, and eliciting gifts (Bk. 18).

THE JUDGMENT (BOOKS 19–24)

As the disguised Odysseus is planning to punish the suitors—by killing them— Penelope questions him mournfully about her long-lost husband. When he describes a tunic he had once seen on the wandering Odysseus, she recognizes from the description that it is the tunic she herself had once made for him. Later she tells him of her dreams. And, unknown to Penelope, there is a further recognition: the old nurse recognizes Odysseus's scar—inflicted long ago by a wild animal (Bk. 19).

The next day brings two events: first, a high feast, with a solemn sacrificial assembly (the assembly includes a new ally, Philoitios, an oxherd and leader; Bk. 20); and second, a fateful test—the stringing of the bow (the suitor who most easily strings Odysseus's old bow is to marry Penelope, Bk. 21).

The only one able to string the bow is the old beggar, and the stringing is the cue for imposing on the household—suitors, officials, and maidservants—a terrible judgment: Odysseus, Telemachus, and two herdsmen kill or hang all those who are judged guilty (Bk. 22).

Penelope is called, yet when she is told that the avenging visitor is her husband, she does not believe it; she simply looks at him, then tests him. Eventually there is a transformation and rapprochement: he undergoes a certain transformation, and together, in bed, husband and wife reach a heartfelt rapprochement (Bk. 23).

At the end, as the shades of the dead suitors arrive in Hades, there is an account from Hades of the extraordinary mourning that once accompanied the death of the great Achilles. Meanwhile, Odysseus discloses his presence to his old father, and, in face of impending trouble from the suitors' relatives, brings about a quick reconciliation (Bk. 24).

Homer and Genesis 11–50: Further General Comparison

BASIC DIFFERENCES

Form. Unlike the *Odyssey*, with its focus on a climactic period of forty days, Genesis, at one level, is like history, a sequential account—one thing after another; there is a strong sense of memory and promise, but there are few flashbacks.

The *Odyssey* is voluminous poetry; Genesis, dense prose. This prose is powerfully poetic, but, unlike Homer, it does not follow a set meter. It has its own distinct history-like rhythm.

Setting. There is a major difference in setting—not so much a contrast between West and East as between sea and land. Homer's world includes Troy, Phoenicia, and Egypt, but it centers on the sea—and Ithaca. The vast world narrative of Genesis centers on the land from Babylonia to Egypt, especially the land of Canaan—and Hebron.

Content. There is a basic difference also in content. The epic is heroic—full of deeds that are extraordinary. Genesis by and large is prosaic, close to the day-to-day reality of historical existence. There are indeed some extraordinary events and people, especially in Genesis 1–11, but, generally speaking, Abraham, Isaac, and Jacob are ordinary people living ordinary lives. They drive donkeys, not flashy chariots.

The gods, too, are different. In the *Odyssey* there is a whole complex pantheon. Apparently it was partly because of this complexity that, shortly after Homer, Hesiod sought, in his *Theogony*, to introduce some order in the portrayal of the gods. In any case, the God of Genesis is one. Within this unity—already clear in the prophets—there is some complexity, some diversity of names, and this complexity may perhaps reflect aspects of Homer's pantheon, but the basic sense of a single God is a major change from Homer.

BASIC SIMILARITIES—AND FURTHER CONTRASTS

The sense of a life. Largely through the figures of Odysseus and Jacob, both books evoke the sense of life as a whole, from origin to death (Od. 19:395–412; 11:119–137; Gen. 25:19–34; 49:29–33), and both lay special emphasis on a central period, away from home, of twenty years (for Odysseus, twenty years of war and wandering; for Jacob, twenty years of working for Laban—and against him).

Jacob's lifestyle is poorer than that of Odysseus (Genesis has fewer chariots, baths, and feasts). Yet the dimensions of Jacob's life are richer: his struggle is set against the background of the faith of Abraham; and his old age is surrounded by the providence that is embodied in Joseph. In a sense, Odysseus can seem one-dimensional: twenty years of youthful strength. But Jacob is three-dimensional: youthful strength; courageous old age; and all founded on the faith that is linked to Abraham. The author of Genesis has taken the *Odyssey* apart and used it to build something which, though simpler, is deeper and more inclusive of old age.

When closely examined the *Odyssey* in fact is not one-dimensional; it has its own human richness and depth. "The heroic ideal finds physical gifts indispensable, but sets hardly less value on gifts of mind and character" (Bowra, 1966, 26). To some degree, Genesis's task has been to unpack that depth. However, as well as unpacking, Genesis has added further factors, thus opening a new vista.

The changes wrought by Genesis may spring partly from sociological factors and from changes that occurred in the Greek literary world between the eighth and seventh centuries BCE:

> In the eighth century the old system of local kings still prevailed in most parts of the Greek world, and it was they who patronized and encouraged the epic. But in the seventh century kings gave place in many districts to small classes of nobles, who divided among themselves the royal powers and privileges. Full of the pride of success, and eager to draw attention to themselves, they turned from the past to the present, from the old heroic ideal to a new sense of personality and individual worth. . . . Poetry was brought down from its majestic detachment to play a fuller part in common life. (Bowra, 1966, 57–58)

Aspects of these changes appear already in Hesiod, and his "performance shows that the emergence of the self in poetry was by no means confined to a few privileged nobles" (Bowra, 166, 66). Literature, in effect, was entering more and more into the flesh-and-blood reality of daily life.

Variation in style. Both the *Odyssey* and Genesis change style toward the end. The Joseph story brings a variation, and there is a variation also in the *Odyssey:* "for every hundred who study the first half of the Odyssey in the Greek, perhaps hardly a dozen carry their study to the end" (Merry, 1899, vi). In the

Odyssey "the action becomes simpler and more concentrated in the later books, as the various threads are brought together towards the dramatic finale" (Bowra, 1966, 25). In particular there is a change from diverse episodes (Od. 1–12; Gen. 12–35) to a flowing narrative, which is more unified (Od. 13–24; Gen. 37–50).

SHARED THEMES

As already mentioned, some themes are reversed (the finale is not revenge but forgiveness; and the attitude to death is more positive). But other themes are quite similar, among them the following:

The wandering (with a special emphasis on twenty years).

The endangered wife (Penelope; Sarah/Rebekah).

The greedy presence (the suitors; Lot).

The friendly foreigners, with whom one sometimes contends (the Phaeacians and their king, Alkinoös; the Philistines and King Abimelech).

Egypt as a place of service and opportunity.

Wondering if the separated one is alive and well (the Joseph story).

Reunion and recognition.

A full comparison of the *Odyssey* and Genesis would require a separate volume—an undertaking that, for the present writer, does not seem advisable. What follows therefore is essentially a preliminary survey.

Genesis and the *Odyssey:* General Outline

The affinity between the *Odyssey* and Genesis is not limited exclusively to Genesis 11–50; Homeric elements occur also in Genesis 1–10. But within Genesis 1–10 such elements are more secondary and apparently less systematic than in Genesis 11–50.

The approximate relationship between the two texts is summarized in the accompanying outline (Table A.2).

Genesis tends to keep the order of the *Odyssey*. Within Books 1–11, only two Books are out of order (4 and 5). Rearrangements, such as they are, seem due partly to internal structures. For instance, the *Odyssey*, has two inherently connected beginnings—concerning Telemachus and Odysseus (Bks. 1 and 5 respectively)—and so Genesis, in telling of Abraham, combines these beginnings: Books 1 and 5 are used in Genesis 12–15.

Genesis, however, has two major stories, two endings—concerning Abraham and Jacob/Joseph. So the prolonged finale of the *Odyssey* (Bks. 12–24) has been divided between the final parts of these two stories—divided between Genesis 18–23 and Genesis 37–47, 50.

Table A.2. The Odyssey and Genesis 11–50. General Outline

Odyssey	Genesis 11–50 (minus genealogies)
The Young Man	
The initial journey is planned (1)	The initial journey of Abraham (11–13)
Telemachus, banish your mother (2)	Banishing Hagar (16)
Nestor: conduct and ritual (3)	Covenant of conduct and ritual (17)
Menelaus's struggle for home (4)	Jacob's struggle to reach home (31–33)
The Journey	
Odysseus's exile ends; storm (5)	Battle; exile will end (14–15)
Meeting Nausicaa (6–7)	Meeting Rebecca (24)
Odysseus contends (8)	Jacob contends with Esau, Abimelech (25–26)
Odysseus outwits the Cyclops (9)	Jacob outwits Isaac (27–29)
Betrothals turn nasty (10)	Dinah (34–35)
The dead speak (11)	Dying Jacob speaks (48–49)
Destruction of the ship (12)	Destruction of Sodom (18–19)
The Return	
At last: the land (Odyssey 13)	At last: the son (Gen. 19:30–chap. 21)
The faithful servant/swineherd (14)	Joseph as faithful servant (39)
Telemachus: journey home (15)	Journey to Egypt and back (43–44)
Odysseus's self revelation (16)	Joseph's self-revelation (45)
Odysseus goes down to the manor (17)	Jacob goes down to Pharaoh (46:1–47:11)
Fighting physically for food (18)	Fighting morally for food (47:12–28)??
The Judgement	
Recognitions and dreams (19)	Joseph dreams; Jacob, Judah recognize (37–38)
The assembly and the test (20–21)	The test and the assembly (22–23)
Judging the suitors, officials (22)	Judging the officials (40)
Transformation and rapprochment (23)	Transformation and rapprochment (41–42)
Mourning Achilles; reconciliation (24)	Mourning Jacob; reconciliation (50)

Apparently the *Odyssey* did not contribute significantly to the genealogical material—to the genealogies and the generating of family and herds (Gen. 25: 1–18; 29:31–chap. 30; 35:21–37:1).

Preliminary Analysis: A Survey

The following exploratory comparison is not meant to be read at speed. It consists mostly of headings—one-line summaries of large passages; and for each book of the *Odyssey* that is summarized the reader will probably need hours—

sometimes longer—to check the dense headings against the relevant sections of the *Odyssey* and Genesis.

In the following comparison, references in brackets [ ] are out of order or do not seem to fit the pattern. The purpose of the occasional marks (*, +, −, =) is to facilitate comparison. Double question marks (??) indicate tentativeness.

Book 1: The Initial Sending (Od. 1; Gen. 11–13)

In Book 1, Athena sends Telemachus away from home, partly to find news of his father, but also to establish his own identity—to make his own renown or reputation (1:94–95). Apart from the invocation (1:1–10), the Book may be divided into three scenes, scenes which—when distilled, domesticated, and Is-raelitized—find echoes in Genesis 11–13:

ODYSSEY, BOOK 1

Invocation: The fall of Troy and the wandering (1–10).

Odysseus's captivity (11–21); his captivity and his aged father (187–199).

The endangered wife and the missions of father and son (22–186, 200–251).

Anger; the mission restated and pondered (252–444).

GENESIS 11–13

The failure of Babel and the scattering (11:1–9).

[Genealogy, 11:10–26;] Abram and his father under the shadow of death (11:27–32).

The mission, with its promise; and the endangered wife (12:1–13:1).

Quarrel; the mission's promise restated and deepened (13:2–18).

The fall of Troy is partly reflected in the failure of Babel. The dilemma of trapped Odysseus and his aged father, Laertes, contribute to the picture of Abram and his father, Terah, as living in the shadow of death (see comment on 11:27–32). The *Odyssey* apparently provides no precedent for the genealogy (11:10–26).

The basic content of *Odyssey* 1:22–444, a divine mission, which is first given, then deepened (1:306–424), finds a significant equivalent in the way Abram is sent (12:1–13:1) and then the promise is deepened (13:2–18). In both cases there is a moment of anger or quarrelling (Od 1:252; Gen. 13:7) between the initial mission and its deepening. Despite affinities, there are perpetual contrasts. Telemachus, for instance, is to make his own name (his reputation or renown, 1:

95). But in Genesis the name is made by God (12:2, unlike the builders at Babel, 11:4). For further comment, see below, "Toward a More Complete Analysis."

Books 2 and 3: Banishing the Mother, but Welcoming the Foreigner and Servant (Od. 2–3; Gen. 16–17)

Books 2 and 3 of the *Odyssey* show Telemachus as undergoing two very diverse experiences. At home, the murderous suitors press him to banish his mother (Bk. 2). But when he sails among strangers (King Nestor and his people), he and his crew are welcomed, welcomed even to a ritual feast—though their status at first is like that of strangers and servants (Bk. 3).

This contrast—between domestic hostility and foreign welcome—has contributed to the contrast between the domestic antagonism of Genesis 16 (Sarah and Hagar) and the welcoming covenant of Genesis 17 (embracing foreigners and servants).

ODYSSEY, BOOK 2

Distressed Telemachus calls, in assembly, for justice (2:1–83).

Scheming Penelope, caught by one of her maids (2:84–110).

Dismiss your mother; get her another husband (2:111–145, 194–223).

[Ominous birds, 2:146–193; cf. carrion birds, Gen. 15:11.]

[Risking sword/sea against great odds, 2:224–56; cf. Gen. 14:13–16.]

On the shore, Athena appears: Go home; he confronts suitors (257–336).

Telemachus's clear plan and awareness of a god (2:337–434, esp. 372).

GENESIS 16

[Sarai, barren; go to the slave girl, 16:1–2; cf. Od. 1:429–433; also 4:10–14, birth by a slave girl, because gods give no more children to Helen.]

Scheming Sarah, outdone by the maid (16:3–4).

Distressed Sarai calls on Abram and Yahweh for justice (16:5).

Dismissal (effectively) of the mother-to-be (Hagar, 16:6).

By the spring, angel: Go back; child will confront brothers (16:7–12).

The maid, with a sense of God, proceeds to bear the child (16:13–16).

ODYSSEY, BOOK 3

Athena to Telemachus : Proceed ahead; prayer (3:1–64).

[Nestor: Where from? Where to? 3:65–74; cf. Gen. 16:8.]

Athena: quest for the father will engage the world (3:75–101).

[How Zeus scattered the Achaians at Troy, 3:102–183; cf. Gen. 11:1–9.]

Impossible for father to return; Athena: No, it is not (3:184–238).

[The day Agamemnon is revenged, Menelaus returns, 3:239–328.]

For strangers, ship boys: kindness, a sacred feast (3:329–370, 464–472).

Prayer for fame/name (*kleos*, 380) for self, wife, children (3:371–403).

[Slaughtering the animal(s), 3:404–463; cf. Gen. 15:7–10.]

[Departure in a chariot, 3:473–497? link with Bk. 4 and/or Joseph?]

GENESIS 17 (VERY TENTATIVE)

Yahweh to Abram: Walk before me . . . Abram fell on his face (17:1–3a).

God: You will be father of nations (17:3b–6).

For foreigners, slaves: inclusion in covenant (17:9–14).

New names for Abram, Sarai (17:5, 15).

Impossible for a child to be born; God: No, it is not (17:16–19).

Book 4: The Struggle to Reach Home (Od. 4; Gen. 31–33)

Book 4 recounts the visit of Telemachus and his companion to the court of Menelaus and his famous wife Helen (now back from Troy). Telemachus is seeking his father Odysseus, and the conversations lead to accounts both of Odysseus's heroics and of Menelaus's own struggle to return home.

The later part of Book 4 turns to the situation back in Telemachus's homeland: Penelope is greatly distressed about whether Telemachus will come home. Then, through a dream, she becomes more reassured.

Both scenes—at Menelaus's court and back home—are concerned with aspects of the difficulty of reaching home—of reaching father and fatherland.

The two scenes provide components for the two panels concerning Jacob's journey home—first his meeting with Laban, and then, nearer home, his distressing journey toward Esau. Despite the distress, Jacob calms down, and he makes plans, which show him as more reassured.

ODYSSEY, BOOK 4

The people and splendid possessions of Menelaus. But . . . (4:1–119).

Helen on her chair (4:120–154).

What Menelaus would have done for Odysseus (4:155–182).

Strong emotion (tears); recalling the heroics of Odysseus (4:183–305).

Getting home: consulting a goddess and the Ancient (4:351–387, 465–485).

    Wrestling with the Ancient (4:306–350, 388–464, esp. 343, 346).

    Homecomings (diverse) (4:486–575).

Reconciliation (with the gods), and a mound (4:576–587a).

    Gift, and letting go of Telemachus (4:587b–624).

Announcement (accidental) of Telemachus's journey (4:625–656).

Announcer goes; plan to intercept with twenty men (4:657–674).

Penelope's great distress and prayers (4:675–786).

Penelope's reassurance (through a dream) (4:787–847).

GENESIS 31–33

Getting home: consulting wives and God (31:1–16).

    [Flight and pursuit, 31:17–25??]

What Laban would have done for Jacob (31:26–30).

Rachel on her cushion (31:31–35).

Strong emotion (anger); Jacob recalls his prosaic heroic record (31:36–42).

The people and possessions of Laban. But . . . (31:43–44).

Reconciliation (human), and a mound (31:45–32:2).

Messengers announce Jacob's journey and return (32:3–5).

Messengers return: Esau is coming with four hundred men (32:6).

Jacob's great distress and prayers (32:7–12).

Jacob becomes more assured (makes plans) (32:13–21).

    Wrestling with the mysterious one (32:22–32).

    Homecoming: Jacob meets Esau (33:1–7).

    Gift, and letting go of Jacob (33:8–17).

Book 5: The Storm/Battle, and the End of the Captivity (Od. 5; Gen. 14–15)

In Book 5 the *Odyssey* leaves the story of Telemachus, and, finally focusing on Odysseus, tells how he was freed from captivity—from the island of the loving nymph, Calypso. This beautiful goddess tried to allure him with the offer of agelessness, but he wanted to rejoin the human race—even though the wife who waited for him would suffer old age and death.

Eventually the gods decree that he may leave this captivity, but his departure is lonely and difficult. The loneliness is seen in the cast of characters: apart from Odysseus they are all gods. And the difficulty is seen in the twenty-day journey: seventeen on a raft, and then three wrenching days, when, amid a terrible storm, he has to trust one of the gods, abandon everything, and swim.

Finally he comes to a new island—virtually dead; and there, like a fresh coal in a bed of dying embers, his sleep prepares him to emerge with new life, new fire (5:456–458, 488–493).

This theme—escaping captivity/servitude—occurs also in Genesis 14–15 (Od. 5:13–15, 112–115, 153; Gen. 14:4, 16; 15:13–14). The captivating powers are diverse—not feminine beauty but imperial force (four great kings, and, implicitly, Pharaoh)—yet there are several points of affinity. If Book 5 is broken into nine sections, each section finds an echo in Genesis 14–15—in a somewhat different order.

ODYSSEY, BOOK 5

* Divine complaint and response: regards home, threatened son (5:1–42).

Diverse gods (Hermes, Calypso) contend for Odysseus (5:43–200).

+ Despite long exile: desire for home, death, old age (5:201–227).

− Goddess sets Odysseus out to sea, steering by the stars (5:228–281).

A swirling storm—north/south/east/west—against freedom (282–332).

= Odysseus effectively trusts Ino—and swims (5:333–375a).

** Athena wills Odysseus back . . . despite more trouble (5:375b–387).

++ Deathly struggle (5:397–450).

− − Odysseus recovers, like fresh fire amid dying embers (451–493).

GENESIS 14–15

A swirling battle—four kings—to enforce servitude (14:1–16).

Diverse kings (of Salem, Sodom) contend for Abram (14:17–24).

* Complaint and divine response: regards house and no heir (15:1–4).

− Yahweh takes Abram outside, to see the stars (15:5).

= Abram trusts Yahweh (15:6).

[15:7–11—the animals, and birds of prey.]

+ Future exile; then home; death, with old age (15:12–15).

** They will come back (15:16).

++ No sun, thick darkness (15:17a).

− − The fire amid the [dead] pieces (15:17b).

[15:18–21, the covenant.]

Two areas of Genesis 14–15—the animals and the covenant (15:7–11, 18–21) seem to find no precedent in Book 5, and even where there is a precedent, it supplies only one aspect. This is clearest in the relationship between the storm and the battle. In Odysseus's experience, storm and battle are two of a kind (5:224), and hence interchangeable, thus making it easy for the author of Genesis to insert a battle in place of the storm. But though Homer's storm text provides an aspect, most of the content for the battle/war (Gen. 14:1–16) comes from other source material.

The ending of the servitude involves both human and divine initiative. In Homer the emphasis falls first on the divine, later on the human (on Odysseus's own role). Genesis, in this case, reverses the emphasis—first the human (chap. 14), then the divine (chap. 15).

These texts (Od. 5; Gen. 15) are the only full scenes in the larger accounts (Odysseus; Abraham-Jacob) in which, apart from a divine presence, the protagonist is alone.

Books 6 and 7: Meeting the Bride-to-Be (Od. 6–7; Gen. 24)

On the day after coming ashore in Scheria, the island of the Phaeacians, Odysseus meets Nausicaa, a beautiful princess who is intent on marriage. This meeting (Bk. 6) and Odysseus's subsequent visit to her home (Bk. 7)—her father, Alkinoös is king of Scheria—has several elements in common with the meeting between Abraham's servant and Rebekah (the betrothal scene, Gen. 24). The subdivisions listed here do not always correspond one on one; they are more like approximate tables of contents:

ODYSSEY, BOOKS 6–7

Setting the scene: sleeping Nausicaa is ready for marriage (6:1–47).

At the river: Nausicaa and maids wash marriage linen (6:1–95).

[Maidens bathe, eat, remove veils, and play, 6:96–109.]

[Odysseus wakes, and wearing an olive branch, approaches, 6:110–138.]

Odysseus, reflecting and seeking kindness, meets Nausicaa (6:139–185).

Nausicaa offers food, drink, bathing—and admiration (6:185–250).

Nausicaa's speedy return to the house (6:251–321).

Odysseus pauses, and prays for love and mercy (6:321–331).

Second meeting: a young girl, with jug, runs, guiding Odysseus (7:1–49a).

[Idyllic woman, palace, beauty, trees, fountains, 7:49b–132.]

Odysseus seeks mercy, blessing, kindness; he waits (7:133–166).

Alkinoös, welcoming Odysseus, arranges for the morning (7:167–229).

Repetition of Odysseus's story (7:230–297).

[Odysseus may arouse jealousy, 7:298–307; cf. envy, Gen. 26:14b.]

Alkinoös offers Odysseus Nausicaa—or help in going home (7:308–328).

Odysseus prays happily to Zeus—to return home (7:329–333).

To bed (7:334–347).

GENESIS 24

Setting the scene: Abraham's servant is to seek a bride (24:1–9).

At the well: reflection, and prayer about kindness (24:10–14).

Rebekah, with water jug, runs, offers drink and kindness (24:15–27).

Rebekah runs home (24:28).

The servant receives welcome, and water to wash (24:29–32).

Servant waits before eating—repeating his story (24:33–49).

Laban offers Jacob Rebekah—to take home (24:50–51).

Servant bows down before Yahweh (24:52).

They eat, drink, and spend the night (24:53–54a).

Morning and departure (24:54b–61).

Second meeting: Rebekah and a younger man, Isaac (24:62–67).

The first three Homeric texts in square brackets (6:96–109; 6:110–138; 7:49b–132) have an idyllic quality, which has some affinity with Genesis 2–3.

Book 8: Contending and Making Amends (Od. 8; Gen. 25: 19–26:33)

The day after the meeting with Nausicaa, the Phaeacians hold games. Young men contend with one another; and finally, angered Odysseus contends. Later there is a song of marital infidelity; and the one who angered Odysseus makes amends.

This picture of contention with the friendly Phaeacians is echoed in the Jacob-Esau contention and in Isaac's strained dealings with the Philistines:

ODYSSEY, BOOK 8

Phaeacians' dawn assembly—to help Odysseus home (8:1–71).

Internal/verbal clash; contention was foretold (song, 8:72–82).

[Odysseus weeps, 8:83–95.]

External/physical contention (games, 8:96–130).

Phaeacians provoke Odysseus to contend (8:131–240).

Marital infidelity—seen from the doorway (song, 8:241–384).

Amends, and a feast proposed (8:385–417a).

Riches: Odysseus receives gifts and clothing (8:417b–457a).

[Nausicaa: poignant farewell, 8:457b–468.]

[Odysseus weeps during the song of battle, 8:469–586.]

GENESIS 25:19–26:33

[Rebekah conceives, 25:19–21.]

Internal clash by twins; contention is foretold (25:22–23).

External/physical contention—the heel and the birthright (25:24–34).

Marital playfulness—seen from a window (26:1–11).

Riches and greatness (26:12–14a).

[Envy toward Isaac, 26:14b; cf. jealousy and Odysseus, 7:298–307.]

Philistines' hostile contention with Isaac—about wells (26:15–21).

[More wells—without quarrelling, 26:22–25.]

Amends and a feast (26:26–30).

Philistines' dawn departure in peace (26:31–33).

Two aspects are particularly puzzling in their own right—the tears (Bk. 8) and the wells (Gen. 26). It is not clear whether or how these aspects connect with anything in the other book.

Book 9: Outwitting the Powerful One Who Does Not See (the Cyclops, Od. 9; Isaac, empowered with blessing, Gen. 26:34–29:30)

When Odysseus, at banquet with the Phaeacians, begins to recount his travels (Bks. 9–12), the first major episode concerns his struggle with the Cyclops— the hungry giant, apparently one-eyed, who trapped him in his cave. To escape from the cave, which was blocked by a huge stone, Odysseus and his companions blinded the Cyclops and then, using the sheep to cover them, made their way to freedom.

This struggle has contributed to the account of how Jacob outwitted Esau and his dim-eyed father, and how, in an adventure involving the sheep (at the well), he then went away to Laban.

Both struggles—Odysseus's against the Cyclops, and Jacob's against Esau and his dim-eyed father, Isaac—are part of larger dramas. The Cyclops is the son of Poseidon—Earthshaker, lord of the sea, and brother of Zeus—and Poseidon is the enemy of Odysseus. The Cyclops therefore is like an incarnation of enmity.

The figure of Isaac is more complex. On the one hand, he has a negative aspect: the struggle of Jacob and Rebekah against Esau and Isaac, has overtones of the primordial enmity with the serpent (see commentary on Genesis 27). On the other hand, Isaac's primary power lies not in enmity but in blessing. Thus while keeping the idea of needing to outwit someone powerful, Genesis has moved the emphasis to what is positive—to blessing.

ODYSSEY, BOOK 9

[Introduction: good food; and deathly adventure, 9:1–78??]

[The lotus—attractive, but not to be eaten, 9:79–104; cf. Gen. 2?]

   [The Cyclopes: giant, lawless, isolated, 9:105–141; cf. Gen. 6:1–12?]

Odysseus's arrival: poor visibility; a hunt for wild food (9:142–165).

* Coming to Cyclops's island; finding confined flocks (9:166–186a).

+ The sleep of the mountain-like man, utterly isolated (9:186b–215).

Elaborate preparing of food—by Cyclops for himself (9:215–249).

Who are you? Odysseus's lies. The meal (9:250–298a).

− Cyclops removes the huge stone to let the sheep out (9:298b–317).

   [The hot pole in the eye, 318–394.]

Crying out at being tricked (9:395–414).

= Blinded Cyclops gropes; the sheep cover Odysseus's escape (9:415–479).

Furious Cyclops tries to sink the departing ship (9:480–499, 522–566).

Truthful self–identifications (9:500–521).

GENESIS 27–29

Isaac: poor vision, and a desire for hunted food (27:1–4).

Elaborate preparing of food—by Rebekah for Isaac (27:5–14).

= As semi-blind Isaac gropes, animal skins cover Jacob (27:16, 21–23).

Who are you? Jacob's lies. The meal (27:18–20, 24–25).

Crying out at being deceived (27:30–40).

Furious Esau plans to kill Jacob, so Jacob departs (27:41–45).

   [Jacob's departure, 27:46–28:9.]

+ The sleep of Jacob, dreaming of heaven, God and home (28:10–22).

* Coming to the land of the east; finding crouching flocks (29:1a).

− Jacob removes the great stone to let the sheep drink (29:2b–10).

[The kiss with tears, 29:11.]

Truthful self-identification (29:12–14).

Among the elements that do not find corresponding elements in the other book, two stand out: the poke in the eye, and the kiss.

Book 10: A Possible Betrothal Scene Turns Violent, and the Subsequent Journey Is Tearful (Od. 10; Gen. 34:1–35:20)

Still speaking at the banquet, Odysseus tells of two islands, which were almost traumatic. First, among the Laistrygonians, an apparently safe harbor and a betrothal-like scene (10:87–111) turned into a scene of violence. Then, having fled to the island of the goddess Circe, Odysseus scarcely saved his companions; he did so amid divine help, loss, tears, and death.

Jacob's safe return from his years of journeying is likewise followed by two difficult episodes—first (chap. 34), the rape of Dinah, mixing betrothal and violence; and then (35:1–20) the difficult journey—amid divine help, loss, tears, and death.

ODYSSEY, BOOK 10

[Sleepless labors, 10:1–86, esp.76–86; cf. Jacob's labors, 31:38–42.]

Safe harbor; exploration: a violent betrothal-like scene (10:87–130).

Flight: a god's guidance . . . and pity on the way—a deer (10:131–209).

Dangerous animals do not attack because of a god's spell (10:210–219).

[Men become pigs, 10:220–243; cf. Jacob made stinking, 35:30??]

The loss (disappearance) of friends causes tears (10:244–260).

On the way, Hermes speaks; an oath is fulfilled (10:261–445).

Journeying; tears, libations; death of the youngest (10:446–574).

GENESIS 34–35

Safe home; Dinah's exploration; violent effort at betrothal (34:1–3).

Flight; God is seen; God answers distress on the road (35:1–4).

Dangerous cities do not pursue because of God's terror (35:5).

The loss (death) of Rebekah's nurse causes weeping (35:8).

On the way, God speaks; the promise is confirmed (35:9–13).

Journeying; libations, death; birth of the youngest (35:14–20).

Book 11: From the Place of Death: A Vision of Coming Home, and a List of Diverse Lives (Od. 11; Gen. 47:29– chap. 49)

Before he could go home, Odysseus first had to visit the place of the dead, particularly to hear Teiresias, the dead blind prophet (*mantis,* "prophet/diviner/soothsayer," 10:493; 11:99). While in the place of the dead, Odysseus also meets the young Elpenor (killed at the end of Bk. 10), his mother, and finally a series of great figures of the past.

Genesis has no visit to the place of the dead, but in the scene of Jacob's death (47:29–chap. 49), Jacob's voice is like that of someone who has already accepted death. The essential characteristics of Teiresias—dead, blind, prophetic—are all echoed in Jacob: dying, unable to see, and foretelling the future, especially about going home.

There are two basic adaptations: the overall sense of death is much more positive in Genesis; and the focus on the past gives way to a focus on an essentially hopeful future (the often-woeful figures of the past are replaced by the generally-blessed figures of the future—the twelve sons/tribes of Jacob).

ODYSSEY, BOOK 11

Coming to the place of the dead (11:1–50).

Elpenor asks for burial; Odysseus promises to do it (11:51–58, 71–83).

Elpenor recalls his death, and what is promised Odysseus (11:59–70).

* Teiresias foretells that Odysseus will come home (11:84–134a).

\+ Teiresias foretells that Odysseus will die peacefully (11:134b–137).

Discussion between mother and son (11:138–224).

Two lists (past-oriented): the dead and their exploits (11:225–640).

GENESIS 47:29–50:13

Coming to die, and bowing down (47:29a, 31b).

Jacob asks for burial at home; Joseph swears to do it (47:29b–31a).

Jacob recalls the promise and Rachel's death (48:3–4, 7).

Discussion between father and son (48:8–20).

* Jacob foretells that Joseph will return home (48:21–22).

A two-part list (future-oriented): the sons/tribes of Israel (49:1–27).

+ Jacob dies peacefully (49:28–33).

The slender relationship between the lists—the mournful list of the *Odyssey* and the largely-blessed list of the sons of Jacob—is a good example of the way in which the *Odyssey* sometimes provides just one component.

Book 12: Danger Foreseen; Destruction (of Ship/Sodom); and Survival (Od. 12; Gen. 18:1–19:29)

Odysseus recounts how before he left the island of the divine Circe, she warned him of a triple danger: listening to the enchanting voices of the Sirens; pausing between towering Skylla and cavernous Charybdis; and harming the cattle of Helios. During the subsequent voyage, he and his crew mastered their hearing; they did not listen obediently to the Sirens. But in the later dangers they suffered considerably, and finally the ship and crew were lost. Only Odysseus, who did no harm, was saved.

Many of the same dynamics occur, in adapted form, in the account leading up to the destruction of Sodom and its people. Here too, the danger is foreseen. But Genesis contains several basic changes. In particular, the test of not listening is turned into an implicit test of listening positively: at a meal, Sarah listens. In outline:

ODYSSEY, BOOK 12

[The burial of Elpenor, 12:1–15; cf. the burial of Jacob, 50:1–13.]

Meal, by Circe, for Odysseus and his companions (12:16–30).

Do not hear/listen to the enchanting voices (Sirens, 12:31–54).

* Keep on moving (Skylla/Charybdis, 12:55–126).

+ Do no harm (Helios's cattle, 12:127–141).

Circe departs (12:142–143).

On the way: communicating the divinations to companions (12:144–164).

Know—by coming to us: an invitation from the Sirens (12:165–200).

− Smoke; the sea is like an overflowing cauldron on a fire (12:201–259).

Not listening to avoidance of harm; Zeus destroys ship (12:260–419).

= Odysseus survives—thanks to the father of gods (12:420–453).

GENESIS 18:1–19:29

Meals, by Abraham and Lot respectively, for visitors (18:1–8; 19:1–3).

Sarah listens and thinks of pleasure (18:9–15).

On the way: communicating divine plans to Abraham (18:16–18).

* Keeping the way (Abraham will keep the way of Yahweh, 18:19–21).

+ Avoiding harming people (Abraham's plea with Yahweh, 18:32).

Yahweh departs (18:33).

Know carnally: a demand from the men of Sodom (19:4–11).

Not listening well to those who save from destruction (19:12–22).

– Fire destroys Sodom and Gomorrah (19:23–28).

= God remembered Abraham (19:29).

Book 13: The Joyful Breakthrough: Reaching the Land (Od. 13), and Having a Son (Gen. 19:30–chap. 21)

In Book 13 Odysseus finally reaches his native land, but he does so in his sleep—borne along by the Phaeacians, who place him, still sleeping, near a cave in Ithaca. When Athena shows him where he is, there is great joy, and he and Athena then begin to lay plans for the future—especially concerning the threatened wife and son.

In Genesis the pivotal breakthrough is the joyful birth of Isaac, an event which within Genesis's diptych structure is connected and contrasted with scenes of sleep (Lot's oblivious sleep, and Abimelech's dream). The picture of a threat to a wife and child, which in the *Odyssey* applies to Penelope and Telemachus, in Genesis is double: in diverse ways there are threats first to Sarah and her child, and then to Hagar and Ishmael. In both books, these threats are addressed.

ODYSSEY, BOOK 13

Morning: royal court: gifts, wives, good wishes (13:1–69).

Sleep—oblivious (Odysseus), near a cave (13:70–124).

[Ship turned to stone, 13:125–164; cf. Lot's wife, 19:26.]

* As foretold, so it is accomplished (negatively) (13:165–187a).

[Joyful discovery, by a devious wanderer; 13:167b–371; cf. Gen. 20:13.]

+ Pact between Odysseus and Athena (13:372–396a).

Threatened wife and son; his journey (13:396b–428).

[The body becomes old (13:429–440; cf. childbirth in old age, Gen. 21:1–7).]

GENESIS 19:30–CHAP. 21

Morning: royal court: gifts, wives, prayer, devious wanderer (20:8–18).

Sleep—oblivious in a cave (Lot), and wakeful (king) (20:1–7).

* As promised, the old couple have a child—joyfully (21:1–7).

Threatened wives (Sarah/Hagar) and sons; the journey (21:8–21).

+ Covenant between Abraham and Abimelech (20:22–34).

The three Homeric texts in square brackets have been combined with other passages. In particular, the long account of joyful discovery and devious wandering seems to have contributed both to the joy at Isaac's birth (21:1–7) and to the picture of Abraham as referring deviously to his wanderings (20:11–13).

Book 14: The Faithful Servant and the Story of Years in Egypt (Od. 14; Gen. 39)

When Odysseus lands in Ithaca and, disguised as an old beggar, sets out to his own property—his country estate—the first human he meets is his swineherd. This swineherd still misses his own original home (14:140–143), but despite that, and despite Odysseus's long absence, he cares faithfully for all Odysseus's house properties. Odysseus, still disguised, gives a version of his own story, and he includes a painful episode about working in Egypt.

Genesis shows Joseph, working in Egypt, as the faithful servant, caring for all Potiphar's properties. Some of the minor elements of the Homeric text—attractiveness and spousal fidelity (14:64, 130, 177)—have been expanded in Genesis into a major event involving Potiphar's wife. The texts with an asterisk have been combined.

ODYSSEY, BOOK 14

The faithful swineherd, caring for Odysseus's household (14:1–39).

* Faithful in master's absence; a wife (14:40–184, esp.64, 130, 177).

Odysseus's story, involving work in Egypt (14:184–350, esp. 245–297).

Again the faithful servant (14:360–456).

* The test of the servant (concerning the mantle, 457–533).

GENESIS 39

Joseph, sold into service in Egypt (39:1).

The faithful servant, caring for Potiphar's household (39:2–6).

* In masters' absence: the test, involving wife, mantle (39:7–20).

Again the faithful servant (39:21–23).

Book 15: During a Dangerous Journey (to Ithaca/Egypt): A Generous Meal, and a Test with Sorrow (Od. 15, Gen. 43–44)

The *Odyssey* now returns to Odysseus's son, Telemachus, and to his need, despite danger, to journey back to Ithaca. The journey is accompanied by gifts and a generous meal, and then by elements of religion—libation from a golden cup, an omen, and a fugitive prophet.

Back in Ithaca, talking to Odysseus, the swineherd is tested and tells of the sorrow of a father and a son (the father is Odysseus's own father, Laertes; the son is himself, the swineherd).

In Genesis, the single journey home has been replaced by a double journey: back to Egypt, and then home again. The members of Jacob's family realize that, despite the danger to Benjamin, they have to go back to Egypt. They bring gifts, and on arrival are treated to a generous meal. But when they attempt the journey home they are caught by religious and ethical elements—the silver cup for divining and the question of doing good and evil.

The scene ends with the climactic testing of Judah and with his emphasis on his father's sorrow. The asterisks indicate combination. (Climactic scenes often involve complex combinations.)

ODYSSEY, BOOK 15

Preparing to go back quickly to Ithaca, despite danger (15:1–47).

Bringing gifts (15:48–85).

The generous meal and discussion of gifts (15:86–142).

Departure; golden cup libation; an omen; continuing (15:143–216).

The prophet—questioning, and confessing (15:217–300).

[A distinguished life abroad, 225–55; cf. Joseph, Genesis 40–41??]

* Testing the swineherd (15:301–345).

* A father's/mother's sorrow (15:346–379).

* A son's sorrow (15:380–495a).

[The Phoenician woman, 417–480, cf. Potiphar's wife, Gen. 39:7–20??]

* Son unknowingly approaches father (15:495b–557).

GENESIS 43–44

Preparing to go back to Egypt, despite danger; quickly! (43:1–10).

Bringing gifts (43:11–14).

In Egypt: discussion of gifted money, and a generous meal (43:15–34).

Departure; silver cup; divining; the need to turn back (44:1–13).

The diviner (Joseph)—questioning, and evoking confession (44:14–17).

* Testing Judah; sorrow of father and son (44:18–34).

Book 16: Emotional Self-Revelation, and Future Plans (Od. 16; Gen. 45)

When Telemachus, back from his journey, returns to the swineherd's hut there are two emotional meetings—first between Telemachus and the swineherd, and later, while the swineherd is absent (announcing the news to the mother), between Telemachus and his long-lost father, Odysseus. Odysseus's self-revelation to his son has provided a partial model for Joseph's self-revelation to his brothers. The asterisks indicate texts that are interwoven.

ODYSSEY, BOOK 16

* Tearful meeting; question about mother (16:1–39).

Clothing and provision for the visitor (16:40–89).

The people are not hostile (16:90–129).

Go quickly, tell the mother the son is well (16:130–155).

* Alone: self-revelation and emotional response (16:156–219).

Future plans—for fighting the suitors (16:220–330).

Announcing to the palace: Telemachus has come (16:321–341).

Palace response: take possessions and kill him (16:342–451).

   [The gods and killing the son, 16:403–406, 447; cf. Gen. 22:2??]

Back on the farm: old Odysseus; word and ship (16:452–481).

GENESIS 45

* Alone: self-revelation, tears, question about father (45:1–8).

The people seem favorable (45:2; cf. 45:16).

Go quickly, tell your father Joseph is well (45:9).

Future plans—about countering the famine (45:10–13).

* Emotional response (45:14–15).

Announcing to the palace: Joseph's brothers have come (45:16a).

Palace response: come, share possessions with us (45:16b–20).

Clothing and provision for the travelers (45:21–24).

Back with old Jacob; the words and seeing the wagons (45:25–28).

The most difficult connection is the last—between the swineherd's return to the old visitor and Telemachus (16:452–481) and the brothers' return to Jacob (45:25–28). The *Odyssey* supplies just one component. The swineherd tells of the word (*epos*, 16:467) and of seeing the ship (16:472); to Jacob they spoke the words and he saw the wagons (45:27).

Book 17: The Old Beggar Goes Down to the Manor (Od. 17) and Old Jacob Goes Down to Pharaoh (Gen. 46:1–47:11)

The *Odyssey* (Bk. 17) now recounts a long-awaited moment: young Telemachus and Odysseus return to the city, to Odysseus's great house or manor. Telemachus goes first and he tearfully meets his mother. Then Odysseus comes, more slowly, looking like an old beggar, accompanied by the herdsman. Down in the city, the herdsman enters, then so does old-looking Odysseus.

Genesis tells of old Jacob and his family going down to Egypt, to Pharaoh. First there is a tearful meeting of father and son, and then they enter Pharaoh's presence—shepherds first, and then old Jacob.

ODYSSEY, BOOK 17

Going down to the city for a tearful son-mother meeting (17:1–165).

Odysseus's journey: sacrifice, guidance, contempt for the old (17:166–243).

The herdsman goes ahead and is received (17:244–335).

[The old hunting dog, 17:290–327; cf. Esau hunting, Gen. 25:27??]

Odysseus enters, blesses, suffers, tells of Egypt (17:336–491).

[The beggar stalls Penelope, 17:492–590.]

Back to the land: the herdsman returns to herding (17:591–606).

GENESIS 46:1–47:11

Jacob's journey: sacrifice, guidance, care for the weak (46:1–7).

[Jacob's family: a form of genealogy, 46:8–27.]

Going down to Egypt for a tearful son-father meeting (46:28–30).

Shepherds/brothers go ahead and are received by Pharaoh (46:31–47:6).

Jacob enters before Pharaoh, blesses, tells of suffering (47:7–10).

Back to the land: Jacob's family settle down on good land (47:11).

When Odysseus finally enters the great house, his first words are a form of blessing on Telemachus, the young man of the house: "Zeus above, make Telemachus happy" (*olbios*, 17:354, "happy, blest," Lat. *beatus*). And when Jacob entered the presence of Pharaoh, "Jacob blessed Pharaoh" (Gen. 47:7).

Book 18: In the Face of Hunger: Fighting for Food and Gifts (Od. 18; Gen. 47:12–28)

Of the various *Odyssey*-Genesis connections mentioned thus far, this is the most slender and questionable.

Book 18 tells essentially of three episodes: a fight for food (18:1–157); a body-display which attracts gifts (18:158–303); and a work-display which is not for food, yet is food-related (18:304–428).

The body-display is by Penelope; inspired by Athena, she no longer conceals herself, but shows herself modestly to the suitors—thus attracting gifts. The fight and the work-display involve Odysseus; he is forced to fight a hungry beggar for food; and when he offers to work—to tend the braziers all night—he is accused of being food-centered, and so he yearns for a working contest (a display of working).

Elements of these episodes appear to have added coloring to the account of how Joseph overcame the famine (47:12–28). The fight for food (18:1–157) seems to be echoed dimly in the adversarial character of the exchange when the people first ask for food (47:14–17, " 'Come' . . . 'Come' "). The people's decision not to conceal but to give their bodies to gain bread (47:18) has some affinity with Penelope's decision not to conceal herself but to show herself, however modestly, to gain gifts (18:158–303). And the concluding emphasis on service and food (47:21–25) corresponds in small part to the concluding emphasis on work and food (18:304–428).

The initial picture of Joseph as providing for his family and the world (Gen. 47:12–13) has similarities to the role once given to Penelope—to be in charge of everything and to care for parents (18:266–67).

While Penelope's emergence (18:158–303) apparently contributed in some small way to Genesis 47, its greater role is in the account of the emergence of Tamar (Gen. 38).

Book 19: Amid Plans of Murder: Dreams and Recognitions (Od. 19; Gen. 37:2–chap. 38)

As Odysseus, disguised in his own house, plans to kill the suitors, Penelope questions him at length—especially about his wanderings, about long-lost Odysseus's clothing, and about her dreams. As the disguised man describes the clothing, she recognizes it as that of Odysseus. And the nurse, unknown to Penelope, recognizes Odysseus's scar—once inflicted by a forest boar. Then Penelope returns to mourning.

Many of the key elements from Book 19 occur at the beginning of the Joseph story (Gen. 37:2–36)—a plan to kill; an account of clothing, dreams, and wandering; and mournful recognition.

The picture of Penelope, left behind by her wandering husband, has contributed to the picture of Tamar, widowed, and abandoned by wandering Judah (Gen. 38). Both these women are faithful and resourceful. Part of the portrayal of Tamar draws on an earlier scene—when Penelope, changed and veiled, appeared before the suitors and, in their hearts, seduced them (18:158–303, esp. 206–210).

ODYSSEY, BOOK 19

Planning to kill the suitors (19:1–52).

Questioning Odysseus about his wanderings (19:53–122).

Abandoned Penelope, grieving, weaving, scheming (19:123–161).

Straying away from home (Odysseus, 19:162–202, esp. 19:169).

Two recognitions (clothing, animal scar, 19:203–243, 249–250, 312–507).

[A companion, Eurybates, 19:244–248; cf. Hirah, 38:1, 12, 20.]

Making the clothing; a promising word (epos, 309) (19:251–311).

[Naming children, 19:399–412; cf. 38:29–30??]

Mourning for Odysseus (19:508–534, 600–604).

Dreams (Penelope's) and their interpretation (19:535–599).

GENESIS 37–38

Making a tunic for Joseph; a promising word (37:3, 11).

Dreams (Joseph's) and their interpretation (37:5–10).

Questioning Joseph and finding him wandering (37:12–17).

Planning to kill Joseph (37:18–20).

[Thrown into a pit, 37:21–25a.]

[Sold into Egypt, 37:25b–30, 36.]

Two recognitions (clothing! an animal!, 37:31–33; 38:25).

Mourning for Joseph (37:34–35).

Straying away from home (Judah, 38:1, 5).

Abandoned Tamar, leaving widow's clothes (38:6–26; cf.18:206–210).

Books 20 and 21: The Test and the Festive/Solemn Assembly (Od. 20–21; Gen. 22–23)

On the night before the bloody finale, Odysseus and Penelope lie awake at different times struggling with anxiety about life. Odysseus trusts the goddess

(20:45–57a), but Penelope wishes for death, and tells of children whose parents the gods killed (20:66–67).

These contrasting images—of trusting the goddess, and of gods killing parents—have contributed something to the account of Abraham trusting the God who told him to kill his son (Gen. 22:1–2). Abraham's climactic act of trust has been described as a test (Gen. 22:1a)—the image that dominates the next book (Bk. 21, the climactic test of stringing the bow).

Next morning there are practical preparations for a sacrificial assembly—for the feast of Apollo (21:122–394). The practical preparations for sacrifice have contributed something to the practical preparations for the sacrifice of Isaac (Gen. 22:3–10), and in some complex way the references to a solemn assembly apparently contributed to the evoking of a solemn assembly in Genesis 23. The details are unusually difficult. And the picture of trying to string the bow (Bk. 21), while it gives the key idea of a test to Genesis 22, appears to have been transformed and/or dispersed.

ODYSSEY, BOOKS 20–21

[Odysseus: inner struggle, 20:1–30a; cf. Abraham: distress, 21:11??]

* Athena: Here is your . . . son; trust me. Odysseus trusted (21:30b–57a).

* Penelope prays: Take my life; gods killed parents (20:57b–90).

[The omen; the portent—thunder, 20:91–121??]

Morning: preparations for the festival; conversation (20:122–64, 172).

Among the Achaians: esteemed by Philoitios (20:165–239).

An eagle signals the end of the plot to kill Telemachus (20:240–246).

Sacrifice—including sheep (20:247–256).

[The assembly—festive, deathly, 20:257–394; cf. Gen. 23:3–18??]

Announcing a test: string the bow (21:1–4, 63–79,101–117).

[The bow reminds, 21:5–100, esp.40; cf. the rainbow, Gen. 9:16??]

[Stringing the bow, 21:118–187, 245–434??]

[Wine causes problems, 21:285–310; cf. Noah, 9:20–22??]

[Revealing, promising, going back, 21:188–244; cf. Gen. 22:15–19??]

GENESIS 22–23

Announcing a test (22:1a).

*God: Take your son, and offer him. Abraham trusts (22:1b–2).

Morning: preparations for the offering; conversation (22:3–10).

An angel calls not to harm Isaac (22:11–12).

Sacrifice—a ram (22:13–14).

[Genealogical conclusion, 22:20–24.]

[Sarah's death, 23:1–2.]

Among the Hittites: esteemed by Ephron (23:3–18).

[Sarah's burial, 23:19–20.]

Book 22: Within the Closed House: The Rendering of Terrible Judgment (Od. 22; Gen. 40)

In Book 22 Odysseus and his three allies impose a terrible judgment: they kill all the suitors and hang twelve maidservants (twelve out of fifty). Three officials—the diviner, the singer, and the herald—plead for mercy. Odysseus beheads the diviner, but spares the others two.

The bloodiness (bloodlust?) of this scene is never matched in Genesis, but elements of it find counterparts in the prison scene (Genesis 42), when Joseph interprets the dreams of Pharaoh's two officials: one will be restored; the other will have his head lifted; he will be hanged. Genesis keeps the basic idea of a discerning judgment, but is very different in two ways: it omits the picture of slaughter; and it surrounds the judgment with a mantle of interpretation—a form of meaning.

Some shared elements include:

Theme: crime/sin and punishment/judgment.

Setting: closed, a round house (22:442, 459, 466; Gen. 39:20–40:5).

Characters: singer, diviner, herald (22:310–380); butler, baker (40:1).

Result: some condemned, some acquitted.

Lifting up a fine cup at the feast (22:8–21; 40:11, 20–21).

"Remember [me]" (22:208; 40:14).

Hanging (22:170–200, 461–472; 40:22).

Removing the head (22:329; 40:19–20).

The animals/birds eat the flesh (22:30, 302–309, 402, 475; 40:19).

Recognizing/remembering (22:501; 40:23).

Book 23: Change in Attitude: From Looking Suspiciously at One Another to Openheartedness (Od. 23; Gen. 42)

Book 23 tells of two central events—a transformation and a rapprochement. The transformation is of Odysseus: he goes from being dirty to being resplendent—like an immortal god (23:117–165). The rapprochement is between husband and wife—Odysseus and Penelope (23:85–116, 166–372). (At first Penelope, looking at Odysseus, had not recognized him; but then she moved slowly from being suspicious of the stranger to openheartedly accepting him as her husband.)

These two events, the transformation and the rapprochement, have been used in Genesis 41 and 42 respectively. The transformation of Odysseus has been used in the portrayal of the transformation of Joseph—his move from prison to power (Gen. 42, esp. 42:14–45). And the rapprochement between husband and wife has been used in portraying the rapprochement between the brothers who go down to Egypt (Gen. 42; initially they just look at each other, but—though Joseph's identity remains hidden—gradually they begin to talk, and eventually they open their hearts to one another).

TRANSFORMING ODYSSEUS (OD. 23:117–165)

Make plans. Reply: Yours are best, Odysseus (23:117–128).

Change clothing and wash (23:119–132).

Interpretation/song: murder sounds like a wedding (23:133–151).

Transformation in clothing and appearance (23:152–165).

TRANSFORMING JOSEPH (GEN. 41:14–45)

Change of clothing and a shave (41:14).

Interpretation of a famine dream is good (41:15–32).

Make plans, Pharaoh. Reply: Yours are best, Joseph (41:14).

Transformation in clothing and power (41:40–45).

The most difficult link here concerns the interpretation—whether the song (making a murder scene sound like a wedding) has had some small role in portraying Joseph's interpretation (making interpretation of a famine dream sound good).

In any case, the account of the transformation of Odysseus has supplied only one component to Genesis 41. Other components may be found, for instance, in aspects of Penelope's dreams (19:535–581), and in aspects of Odysseus's account, told to the faithful servant, about how he gathered power and possessions in Egypt (14:257–287).

THE MARITAL RAPPROCHEMENT (OD. 23:1–116, 166–372)

Sunken in sorrow: mournful Penelope will not listen (23:1–84).

Looking at each other: Odysseus and suspicious Penelope (23:85–103).

From suspicious tests to marital open-heartedness (23:103–116, 166–299).

Telling all that happened; coming to the old father (23:300–372).

THE BROTHERLY RAPPROCHEMENT (GENESIS 42)

Looking at each other: the guilty brothers (42:1–5).

From suspicious tests to brotherly open-heartedness (42:6–28).

Coming to old Jacob; telling all that happened (42:29–35).

Sunken in sorrow: mournful Jacob will not listen (42:36–38).

Book 24: After Death and Great Mourning: Reunion and Reconciliation (Od. 24; Gen. 50)

The final book (24) begins in the place of the dead: Hermes is leading the souls of the suitors to the place of former heroes; and two great former leaders, Achilles and Agamemnon, are in conversation. In particular, Agamemnon describes the mourning for Achilles. This account has contributed partly to the account of the death of Joseph and especially to the account of the mourning for Jacob. Both texts then go on to tell of reunion and reconciliation.

ODYSSEY, BOOK 24

The dead: former heroes; the death of Agamemnon (24:1–34).

The mourning for Achilles (24:35–97).

   [The story summarized, 98–204??]

Another tearful reunion: Odysseus with his old father (24:205–412).

   [Old father faints, revives, 24:345–350; cf. Jacob, Gen. 45:26–27.]

From intending battle to making a sudden truce (24:413–548).

GENESIS 50

The mourning for Jacob (50:1–13).

Another conciliatory reunion: Joseph with his brothers (50:14–17).

From fear of intended harm to reconciliation (50:18–21).

   [Joseph's great/grandson, 22–23; cf. Laertes' grand/son, 24:515??]

The death of Joseph; former great figures (50:24–26).

The connections just indicated—both between *Odyssey* 24 and Genesis 50, and between the *Odyssey* as a whole and Genesis—are just a beginning. Even if all the connections are valid, each needs testing and development.

Toward a More Complete Analysis:
The Case of *Odyssey* 1 and Genesis 11–13

Having surveyed Genesis's overall affinity with the *Odyssey,* it is appropriate to give a sample of how a more complete analysis might develop. The sample is limited to the opening texts—*Odyssey,* Book 1, and Genesis 11–13.

Introduction to the Texts

Both sets of texts constitute beginnings: Book 1 provides a brief background and an opening episode for the wanderings of Odysseus. And as far as the history of the patriarchs is concerned, Genesis 11–13 has a similar function: it provides background and an opening act.

In both texts the central theme is that of a divine mission which, despite negative circumstances, sends people forward with energy and wisdom. In Homer there is a variety of deities, particularly Zeus and Athena, and there are two complementary missions—those of Odysseus and Telemachus. In Genesis there is just one deity, Yhwh, and one mission—that of Abram. Yet the overall sense of divine intervention and mission is significantly the same. Years after Troy, the gods send Odysseus and his son (*Odyssey,* Bk. 1). Years after Babel, Yhwh sends Abram (Gen. 11–13).

(A) *ODYSSEY,* BOOK 1: INVOCATION, PRISON, AND JOURNEYS

Apart from two opening snapshots, the text consists of a long account of how the gods gave missions to Odysseus and especially to his son, Telemachus.

The first snapshot is the invocation—the call on the divine Muse to speak (1:1–10). The story to be told is that of a wandering warrior who plundered Troy and then struggled with a great heart on land and sea to bring his companions home.

The second snapshot is that of Odysseus imprisoned on an island (1:11–21). He had not been able to save his companions, and when all those who fought at Troy had either gone home or died, he was left alone, longing for his native Ithaca, longing for home and wife. He had come to a form of prison: the beautiful goddess Calypso was holding him for herself on her island.

The remainder of Book 1 tells of the divine intervention and its effects (1:22–444). Here the key gods are Zeus, the supreme god (father of all gods and humans), and Athena, his daughter. Zeus, reflecting on humankind, is first to speak, beginning with an expletive (*ō popoi,* "Oh shame/bother/blazes," 1:32). And later, when reflecting on the situation of Telemachus, Athena repeats *ō popoi* (1:253). These expletives seem to coincide with a division of the text in two:

Initial decision and assessment: Zeus speaks and Athena intervenes (1: 22–251).

Strengthening the decision: Athena announces the plan and it sinks in (1: 252–444).

The details of this simple twofold division are quite colorful.

The Initial Decision (1:22–251). The decisive intervention came from Mount Olympus. Here, at a meeting of the gods, Zeus wished to show how many humans' troubles came from themselves rather then from the gods, and so he was recounting a famous case, that of a man who stole a wife and killed her royal husband, thus incurring revenge (Bk. 1:22–43).

But then Athena intervened. She recalled, heartbroken, the damage being done by a goddess to Odysseus—someone who had often offered sacrifices. Did Zeus not care? (Bk. 1:44–62).

When Zeus protested that he had not forgotten Odysseus—though he was concerned that another god, Poseidon, had a grudge against the wanderer—Athena pressed her case: Send the divine messenger, Hermes, to the island, to announce the decision that Odysseus must set out for home in Ithaca. Meanwhile, she herself would go straight to Ithaca, and urge Odysseus's son to set out elsewhere, toward Sparta, to hear (*akouō*) of his apparently-dead father, and to establish his own reputation—his fame (*kleos*) (1:76–95, esp. 1:80–87, 93–95).

Then, spear in hand, the goddess Athena sped to Ithaca. Arriving there, she took the appearance of a family friend, a soldier, and so she blended with the household (1:96–105). But Telemachus noticed the visiting soldier, and Athena, while keeping her disguise, spoke to him at length. She recalled the past, Odysseus's captivity, and particularly Odysseus's father, Laertes, who had become too old and infirm to come to the city (1:187–199).

As she spoke to Telemachus the scene was one of lust and greed. In the absence of the noble Odysseus—presumed dead—enemy suitors had moved into the princely house, seeking to marry his wife, Penelope, and, while waiting to take her, they were devouring Odysseus's wealth—drinking, and feasting on his herds. As for Odysseus's son, Telemachus, they despised him, and were disposed to kill him (cf. 1:106–251).

Strengthening the Decision: Athena Announces the Plan and It Sinks In (1:252–444). The gravity of the situation gives Athena anger and energy. She looks to the future, and gives him hope and a mission: she visualizes the apparently-dead Odysseus returning and scattering his rivals; and, at the same time, she tells Telemachus to leave the land—to sail away, especially to Sparta, that he might hear what had become of his father, and that he might develop the courage to confront the enemy suitors (1:252–318). As Athena left, there was a sense of something divine—in her and then in himself—and his spirit was renewed (1:252–324, esp. 306–324).

Soon, at the feast, Penelope appeared, beautiful but bereft, unable to bear the songs about unreturned heroes. Telemachus, however, spoke calmly to her, and she was amazed at his wisdom (1:325–364). Then, Telemachus also spoke to the rapacious revelers, confronting them—telling them to leave, so that he might rule his own house and possessions and slaves. He kept the secret of his divine visitor (1:365–424).

At night, when they had gone—at least for the moment—Telemachus went up to his bedroom, pondering. The place was unusual: it was a lofty room, which looked out all around—like a periscope (1:425–427; the room is *peri-skeptos*, 1:426, an adjective derived from *peri-skopeō*, "to look around on all sides" or "to consider well"). And the tone of the place was set by the presence of Eurycleia, the faithful old nurse. She had been bought by Odysseus's father, Laertes, as an expensive young slave-girl (the price of twenty oxen), but—for the sake of harmony with his wife—Laertes had never slept with her. She had nursed Telemachus as a baby, loving him, and now she still attended to him—providing light and folding his clothes. Then she went away (1:428–442). And there, all through the night, his heart pondered the journey (*hodos*) Athena had laid before him (1:443–444).

(B) GENESIS 11–13: BABEL, THE SHADOW OF DEATH, AND THE JOURNEY OF ABRAHAM

The Genesis text, before recounting the journey of Abraham (originally "Abram"), gives two brief sketches of human limitation (Gen. 11).

The first sketch recounts the failure to build the towering city, Babel (11:1–9).

The second sketch implies the fading of the genealogy of Abram's father, Terah (11:10–32). It begins with a genealogy that shrinks: in the list from Shem to Terah the life spans decrease, 11:10–26). And the subsequent picture of Terah's family contains several reminders of various forms of death (11:27–32): Terah's youngest son, Haran, dies prematurely; Terah's daughter-in-law, Abram's wife Sarah (originally "Sarai") is barren; and Terah himself, when he attempted to travel with his family to Canaan, failed to reach it. Instead he settled in Haran, a name almost identical to that of the son who died prematurely. Thus Terah's family lives in the shadow of death.

These two sketches—of failure and deathly fading—provide a starkly negative background for the longer, positive text concerning Abraham.

These chapters (Genesis 12–13) contain two major parts:

The initial mission, with its test concerning beauty (the beauty of Sarai; 12:1–13:1).

The fresh start, with its test concerning wealth (the wealth of Lot, 13:2–18).

Abraham does not do well in the initial test. When the Egyptians focus on Sarah, he is undone by the threat to his own life—and by the attraction of wealth. But in the second part, when he seems as it were to begin again, and when he is tested more directly on wealth, he shows fresh vision and courage.

The Texts: A Comparative Outline

For practical purposes of comparison each of the texts may be said to have four basic parts: two brief introductory parts, and then, concerning the mission, two longer narratives.

Genesis has its own agenda, style, structure, and special sources, especially the prophets. But it has also distilled Homer's narrative. In describing the mission of Genesis 12–13 (less than forty verses) it has sifted the long flowery account of the mission of Odysseus and his son (over four hundred lines). Yet Homer supplies just one component. In the outline, Table A.3, brackets [ ] indicate variation of order (texts have been moved to facilitate comparison); double brackets [[ ]] indicate that the material is essentially without parallel.

A Slightly More Detailed Comparison

THE FALL OF THE GREAT CITY (TROY, BABEL) AND THE
SCATTERING (OD. 1:1–10; GEN. 11:1–9)

Homer's invocation not only calls on the divine to tell the story. It also summarizes that story—the fall of the great city of Troy, and the attendant process of wandering and homelessness. These elements—the divine power to grant speech; the fall of a great city; and the attendant process of wandering—are all found, in varied form, in the biblical story of Babel. In outline:

Invocation (Od. 1:1–10)	*Babel (Gen. 11:1–9)*
	Whole earth: one tongue, one speech.
1. Asking the divine Muse to speak.	[The divinity: Let us babble their speech.]
2. There was a man who wandered far . . .	They wandered to the east . . . and settled.
3. . . . after sacking the citadel of Troy.	[So they stopped building the city . . . Babel.
4. Many people's cities . . . many pains . . .	Let us build city . . . tower [One people, one tongue . . .]
5. . . . for his own *life.*	?? Let us make our *name*
6. . . . and comrades' return (folly led to loss);	lest we be scattered.

Table A.3. Odyssey 1 and Genesis 11–13

Odyssey, Bk 1	Genesis 11–13
1. Invocation: The fall of Troy and the wandering (1–10)	The failure of Babel and the scattering (11:1–9)
2. Odysseus' years-long captivity (11–21). [The captivity, and father Laertes' non-coming to the city (187–99)]	[[Genealogy]]. Abram in death's shadow, and . . . father Terah's non-coming to Canaan (11:10–32)
3. Taking a wife, killing the man. Punishment (22–43)	———
Plea for Odysseus, who offered sacrifices (44–75)	———
The blessed gods' plan (82,86; prophecy, 200–205):	Yhwh pronounces a clear purpose with blessings:
Let Odysseus go home; let his son set out	Go forth from land . . . birthplace . . . father's house
to another place to which I'll guide him, to hear . . . and to win his own reputation/fame	to a land that I will make you see . . . I will make your name great . . .
among humankind (76–95, esp. 80–87, 93–95; cf. 1:32)	all . . . the earth will bless themselves by you
———	Abram offers worship at altars (12:1–9)
	They will kill me, let your live. [Plagues]
Ithaca: rapacious men covet attractive Penelope (96–251)	Egypt: coveting beautiful Sarai (12:10–13:1)
4. Anger. Restating the mission: Go . . . fight/kill (252–305)	Restarting the mission. Quarrel (13:1–7)
New strength/courage/wisdom/confrontation (306–424)	Abram: new wisdom: no quarrelling (8–9)
To the high room that looks all round, pondering (425–27)	Lot looks all round, considering (10–13)
The old servant—a former slave-girl (428–42)	[See Genesis 16].
There (the room) all night: pondering the journey (443–44)	Abram looks around: fresh revelation (14–18)

7. the Sun god prevented their return.	The divinity scattered them
8. Again asking the divine Muse to speak.	The divinity babbled their speech.
	. . . and scattered them over the whole earth.

Here, as earlier, brackets [ ] indicate variation of order; the texts have been moved to facilitate comparison.

In both texts:

The divine has power over speech—power to make it speak well (*Od.* 1:1, 10); power to make it babble (Gen. 11:7, 9). The two divine powers— to grant either eloquence or babbling—are like two sides of the same coin.

A great city succumbs: Troy is sacked (*Od.* 1:2); and Babel is abandoned (Gen. 11:8). Within Troy the focus was on its citadel (*ptoliethron*); and within Babel on its tower (*migdāl*, Gen. 11:4, 9).

The mention of the fall of the great city is preceded by an image of wandering, and followed by images of being left homeless or scattered.

Other details are not as clear (especially 4 and 5 in the outline), and it is better, in this brief investigation, not to press them. Furthermore, there is much in the Babel account—such as the emphasis on diversity of language—that is either absent or different from the invocation.

Nonetheless, what is certain is that three key components of Homer's invocation correspond to three key components of the Babel story. And these components include details: power over speech *occurs twice;* the cities' fall focuses on their highest buildings; and the images of wandering and being homeless/scattered constitute a frame over the accounts of the cities' fall.

Overall, then the main elements of the Greek prologue reappear in the Hebrew account, but there are two major kinds of adaptation.

On the one hand, Homer's drama has been restaged, distilled, and synthesized. The stage has been moved largely from sea to land—a move that befits the change from sea-loving Greeks to land-oriented Hebrews. Many colorful details, particularly about heroic fighting and feasting, have been distilled or omitted—a change that befits the move away from heroic epic poetry to the calmer medium of prose historiography. And some aspects have been synthesized. In particular, the power of two diverse gods—that of the Muse over language, and that of the sun god to prevent return—have been combined as aspects of the power of Yhwh—the God of languages and scattering. Furthermore, just as the drama as a whole is restaged from sea to land, so individual elements are moved from character to character—or synthesized into a single character—depending on the requirements of the new account. Thus the various elements, including the characters, are subject to the larger plot.

On the other hand, this particular Greek text (the invocation, *Od.* 1:1–10) supplies just one part of the dense account of the tower of Babel. The Hebrew writer is drawing on other background material—including, for instance, the existence of ancient towers or ziggurats. Homer, therefore, provides just one component.

THE HERO STRANDED, IN A MYTHOLOGICAL CAVE (OD. 1:11–
21), AND IN DEATHLY HISTORY (GEN. 11:10–32)

The link here, if there is one, is minimal—more of function than content.

After the invocation, the *Odyssey* focuses in on the hero's dilemma: he is imprisoned by the beautiful Calypso in a cave (later described as on an island, 1:197–199). He longs for home and wife, but, despite the passing of the years, he cannot reach his own land.

And after Babel, Genesis gradually focuses in on the dilemma of Abram. He is a member of a family line that is going nowhere. His whole genealogy is fading (the life spans are diminishing, 11:10–26), and his father's immediate family, surrounded by reminders of death, is stranded (11:27–32).

In comparison to Odysseus's prison, the next text in Genesis is vastly different. Far from being mythological, its forms—a genealogy and brief travel account (11:10–32)—are thoroughly historiographical. The genealogical form comes not from Homer but from certain strains of historiography (see, for instance, Hellanicus, and Hesiod's *Catalogue of Women*).

Nonetheless, there is a question here for research. Has the mythological picture of Odysseus as imprisoned for years, wife-less and far away, contributed to the history-like picture of Abram as stranded with a barren wife amid a fading family? Clearly, the actual materials in Genesis are not from the *Odyssey*, but the way these materials are presented, the way they show Abram—as stranded in a deathly situation—corresponds broadly to the situation of Odysseus.

One detail is more specific. A *later* reference to Odysseus's captivity describes Odysseus's father, Laertes, as too old and infirm to come to the city (*Od.* 1: 188–199). And Abram's father, Terah, sets out for Canaan but does not reach it, settling instead in a city with a death-related name (Haran, Gen. 11:31–32). In other words, the two fathers, Laertes and Terah, are pictured as essentially unable to travel. The picture of Odysseus's father corresponds to one component of Abram's father. Apparently the picture of Abram as stranded—apart from using history-like materials—is drawing not just on one picture of Odysseus's imprisonment but on a combination of such pictures (1:10–21 and 1:188–199).

THE FOUNDATIONAL DIVINE INTERVENTION: SENDING THE
HERO(ES) TO A NEW LAND (OD. 1:22–251; GEN. 12:1–13:1)

Suddenly both texts introduce dramatic changes of scene. The *Odyssey* switches from Odysseus's prison cave to the halls of Mount Olympus and to the solemn pronouncements of Zeus about the fate of humankind (1:26–34). And Genesis switches from a God-less picture of Abram's deathly family (11:10–32) to an account of Yhwh as suddenly making a solemn pronouncement that has impli-

cations for all humankind: "Go forth. . . . In you all the clans of the earth . . ."
(12:1).

The essence of what follows is that those who lived in various forms of deathly constriction are sent forth to a new land: Odysseus from his prison to his longed-for home; Telemachus from his father's house to a land indicated by Athena; and Abram from his father's house to a land that Yhwh shows him.

There are further significant similarities:

> Two leading elements—Zeus's initial statement about wife-stealing (1:22–43), and the central picture of Odysseus's wife, attractive Penelope, as surrounded by rapacious suitors (see 1:96–251)—correspond closely with the most developed episode in Genesis 12, namely the taking away of Sarah by the Egyptians and Pharaoh (Gen. 12:10–13:1).

> Athena's first argument for letting Odysseus go—for sending him to his home—is a reminder that, on the plains of Troy, he used to offer sacrifices (1:60–62). And when Abram reaches Canaan, he build altars (Gen. 12: 7, 8; cf. 13:18).

> Athena's first proposal for sending Telemachus (1:76–95, esp. 80–87, 93–95) has several elements of affinity with the sending of Abraham (Gen. 12: 1–3): departure from one father's house; the journey is to a land indicated by the divinity; the journey will establish a reputation (*kleos*, 1:95) (*Odyssey*) or name (Genesis). In Genesis (12:2) the name is not self-made (as in 1:95, and at Babel, Gen. 11:4); it is given (Gen. 12:2).

> In particular, Athena's description of the gods as blessed (*machar*, 1:82) and as having a definite plan (*boulē*, 1:86) corresponds significantly to Genesis's picture of Yhwh, who obviously has a clear purpose, which spreads blessing (Gen. 12:1–3).

AMID FRESH ENERGY: A RESTATING/RESTARTING OF THE MISSION (OD. 1:252–444; GEN. 13:2–18)

When Telemachus finishes recounting the danger to Penelope and himself (esp. 1:241–251) there is a shift of tone. Athena gives a burst of emotion—she becomes troubled (*ep-alasteō*, 1:252) (*alasteō*, "to be angry/hateful")—and her purpose reaches a new stage. In effect she now draws Telemachus more closely into the divine purpose. That purpose is extremely robust: she speaks of how Odysseus would fight to kill, and of how Telemachus, having journeyed and learned, can come back and kill (1:252–305). Thus she imparts a form of anger and energy, which give Telemachus new heart—fresh wisdom and courage, and a touch of divinity (1:306–424). And so at night, in the "periscope" bedroom he ponders the future journey (1:425–444).

In Genesis also there is an outburst—a quarrel/dispute (*rîb*) with Lot's party—concerning property; and unlike his behaviour in dealing with Sarai in

Egypt, Abram now shows a new courage and wisdom. But it is not the courage of fighting. Instead, Abram asks that there be no dispute, and he allows Lot to have his choice of property (Gen. 12:5–9).

Without attempting a full analysis, these basic similarities may be summarized:

There is a fresh beginning and anger. Athena expresses her expletive ($\bar{o}$ popoi) (1:253), as did Zeus at first (1:32), and then she encourages a plan to fight and kill (1:253–305). In Genesis Abram makes a fresh start—he goes back to where he had begun (Gen. 13:2–4)—and then there is a quarrel (Gen. 13:5–7).

Next there is a new sense of the hero. In various ways, both in the presence of Athena and in his subsequent words to Penelope and the rapacious suitors, Telemachus shows new strength, courage, wisdom, directness, and even a touch of the divine (1:306–424). And Abram also now shows himself as able to handle a crisis: he avoids quarrelling and graciously gives Lot a clear choice (13:8–9).

At the end of Book 1 there are two references to Telemachus as pondering in a particular room—a high room that was first described as looking out on all sides (*Od.* 1:425–427, and 1:443–444). And at the end of Genesis 13 there are two references—to Lot, and Abram—as looking all around and considering (Gen. 13:10–13, and 13:14–18). (Here, Lot and Abram correspond partly to the rapacious suitors and renewed Telemachus, but it is useful to concentrate on the looking around.)

Conclusion to the Analysis of Odyssey *1 and* Genesis *11–13*

The position of the two texts, at the beginning of two foundational accounts, lends an initial credibility to the possibility of a link between them.

That possibility is greatly strengthened by a series of similarities, from sharing a general theme to sharing such details as opening pictures of doomed city heights and closing pictures of places from which to look all round.

The vast differences between the two texts are generally intelligible. Writers other than the author of Genesis quickly rewrote the *Odyssey* into another form so it is understandable Genesis should do likewise. In addition, a biblical writer would have reason for adapting the epic poetry yet further.

There is significant evidence then that Genesis has used the elements from Homer but has adapted them to suit a new narrative.

Genesis's Affinities with the *Odyssey*:
Assessing the Initial Evidence

There are huge differences between the *Odyssey* and Genesis. But, as already explained, differences, no matter how great, do not decide the issue. Rather, there are three basic kinds of criteria.

1. *External plausibility.* It is plausible that Homer was available to almost every writer in the known world, particularly to those who, like the inhabitants of Homer's homeland, lived within the Persian empire. And it is plausible that such outstanding epic poetry, as well as being available, was actually used in composing Genesis. Whoever used epic poetry to compose Genesis 1–9 was likely to do something comparable in composing Genesis 11–50.

2. *Similarities.* Not only are there broad similarities—some sharing of themes (such as wandering, home/land, and family) and a sharing of aspects of overall plot (such as the move from years of wandering to a climax of emotional reunions and recognitions)—but, more importantly, there are also similarities involving completeness, order, and details.

Completeness refers to the way in which the general relationship of the texts involves their entirety: every book of the *Odyssey* is used in some way; and, apart from genealogy-related material, every chapter of Genesis 11–50 uses the *Odyssey*. The easiest explanation of this relationship is that the author of Genesis had a copy of the *Odyssey*.

There is also some similarity of order. The opening and closing of the *Odyssey* (Bks. 1 and 24) are used respectively for the opening and closing of Genesis 11–50 (chaps. 11–13 and 50); and there is a general tendency, both within Genesis 11–50 as a whole, and within each block or chapter, to follow the order of the original.

Details often correspond. There are several details, for instance, in the dreams and recognitions surrounding the appearance of Odysseus (Bk. 19) that correspond to aspects of the dreams and recognitions at the beginning of the Joseph story (Gen. 37–38). And the more developed analysis of Book 1 and Genesis 11–13 likewise shows significant correspondence of detail.

3. *The intelligibility of the differences.* The differences are great. In fact, there is perhaps more contrast than continuity; while the *Odyssey* is heroic poetry, Genesis is neither poetry nor heroic. But these differences are understandable. Genesis's literary form—historiography—demanded an abandonment of poetry (part of the larger movement from poetry to prose [Lesky, 1966, 218–221]). And several factors—sociological and theological—demanded an abandonment of the heroic model. Genesis's starting point—there is one God and that God is with ordinary people—left little room for the Homeric sense of divine capriciousness and human heroics.

The change from the heroic is associated with other changes, other shifts of emphasis: from the extraordinary and the external (the physical body), to the ordinary and the internal; from women's role as pervasive to women's role as less conspicuous (this de-emphasizing of the presence of women may, perhaps, be connected with de-emphasizing the external, the body).

The relationship between the texts emerges as one of complex coherence—a blend of similarities and differences which shows a consistent pattern, and which, in its complexity, cannot be accounted for by coincidence.

General Conclusion

The investigation of Genesis's relationship to the *Odyssey* will require years of research—detailed analysis and thorough application of the criteria for dependence—and, until such research is developed, it is difficult to draw definitive conclusions.

But, as with the case of Genesis and the prophets, there is already sufficient evidence to propose that Genesis's use of Homer is a reasonable working hypothesis. The author of Genesis used the *Odyssey*, especially in composing chapters 11–50, but also, partly, in chapters 1–10. There is no other explanation that can account for the data. Within chapters 11–50 the use of the *Odyssey* is essentially complete.

The copy of the *Odyssey* that was used was reasonably close—if not almost identical—to the present standard version.

The unified way in which Genesis uses the *Odyssey* indicates that Genesis as a whole reflects a single process of composition. That process of composition, however, was not simple. Two great bodies of poetry—the prophetic and epic— were distilled, synthesized, and then translated into another idiom, that of historiography. Genesis is thoroughly composite.

Corollary: Using Sources; Some Procedures of Composition

A first rule in Genesis's use of the *Odyssey* may be named "one on one": one book of the *Odyssey* provides material for one chapter or section of Genesis. Essentially the same one-on-one pattern occurs within each block. For instance, in the relationship between the initial sending of Telemachus (*Od.* 1) and the initial sending of Abram (Gen. 12–13), each major part of *Odyssey* 1 is used once, and, apart from genealogical material, each major part of Genesis 12–13 reflects some use of the *Odyssey*. The overall picture is of completeness and coherence.

A further starting rule in Genesis's use of the *Odyssey* was to follow the original order. As noted earlier, Genesis tends to echo the order of the *Odyssey*.

However, these two rules—one on one, and keeping the order—are not absolute. They are general guidelines, a broad framework, which, while giving a sense of groundedness and orientation, allows considerable freedom in adapting the source. Such adaptations are of three main kinds—concerning order, form, and content.

Adaptations of order refer especially to various practices of moving, combining, and dividing. The moving means a departure from the order of the original—and can involve anything from a whole Homeric book to a small detail. The combining and dividing mean a departure from the one-on-one rule: two or more events may be combined into one; and one may be divided into two or more. The portrayal of Tamar, for instance, as emerging from her abandonment to seduce the irresponsible Judah (Gen. 38), involves a combining of aspects from two pictures of Penelope—Penelope as effectively left abandoned (19:123–161), and Penelope as emerging to seduce the hearts of the suitors (18: 158–303).

Adaptation also involves compression or synthesis—a change from the voluminous metered poetry to compact prose. The *Odyssey*, though several times longer than Genesis 11–50, is distilled not only to the dimensions of the smaller book, but to just one component within that book. And the metered poetry, so resonant of oral communication, gives way to a prose, which, despite its qualities of poetry and orality, reflects the studied composition of a precise writer.

This is likewise the case with Genesis's use of the prophets. The outline of the relationship between the texts (see Appendix 2) indicates the same two basic rules as in the use of the *Odyssey*—one-on-one, and in the same order. Reflecting this respect for order, Genesis 1 highlights a component from Ezekiel 1; and Genesis 50 combines elements from the last chapters of both Isaiah and Jeremiah.

Again, however, these two rules are not strict; they are simply general guidelines, orientation points from which to branch out in other directions—particularly in the direction of combining, dividing, and synthesizing. Genesis 1, for instance, quite apart from its use of ancient epics, combines aspects of Ezekiel 1 (especially the idea of the likeness) with aspects of Isaiah 42–45 (concerning God as creator).

One of the procedures in composing Genesis-Kings may be described as prophetizing—rewriting great literature in light of the commanding vision of Israelite prophecy. The word "prophetize" is awkward, but perhaps it is the best word available. Alternatively, rather than speak of prophetized history, one could refer to historicized prophecy. Prophetic texts, originally composed as poetry for one occasion, have been transformed into another idiom—into prose with a universal message. In another context van Seters (1992, 25–27), speaks of both the historicization of myth and the mythologizing of history.

This process, of prophetizing foreign culture, has multiple analogues. The Greeks, for instance, "hellenized" Roman culture; Aquinas in turn "baptized" some of the Greeks. Such processes are diverse: they can be blinding and enslaving; or they can be enlightening and liberating.

In the case of Genesis the prophetizing of foreign culture was primarily positive. Human dignity, for instance, which seems neglected in some of the

Mesopotamian stories, received new emphasis in light of the prophets. It is not clear whether the specific dignity of women was also enhanced (if there was an engagement with Hesiod, then it certainly was).

The overall impression concerning the composition of Genesis is that the process was unified but complex. There was one central author—perhaps aided by others—who distilled and reshaped several sources into a new writing. The core of the traditions concerning Abraham and Jacob may have come from texts such as Isa. 51:2 and Hosea 12 respectively (cf. de Pury, 1989, 259–270), but the larger account, as now found in Genesis, came from the reshaping of much broader sources, especially the major prophets and the *Odyssey*.

SOURCES: THE THEORY OF FOUR
HYPOTHETICAL DOCUMENTS (J, E, D, AND P)

By the time extant sources of Genesis began to emerge in 1872 (cf. Appendix 3) several hypothetical sources had already occupied the imagination. The emerging extant sources gradually gained a foothold, but only in a secondary position: they were generally seen as sources not of Genesis but of the hypothetical documents. The hypothetical documents retained their primary place.

Yet as already stated (beginning Appendix 1), it is not possible—as a general literary principle—to take a finished text and reconstruct diverse sources that otherwise have never been seen, sources that are hypothetical. Such a conjectural process is a last resort, to be undertaken only if there is no prospect of identifying sources that are known, and if, through unusual circumstances, the hypothetical documents emerge clearly and withstand prolonged testing.

In the case of Pentateuchal studies this conjectural process was virtually the first resort, thus causing centuries-long confusion. The detailed history of such literary theorizing is rich and complex (for surveys of scholarship see esp. Westermann, 1984, 567–574; 1985, 86; Knight, 1985; Rogerson, 1991; Moberly, 1992; Campbell and O'Brien, 1993, 1–20; Houtman, 1994; Whybray, 1987; 1995, 12–28). What is important, however, in assessing its lasting value is not its rich complexity but its underlying logic, the pivotal dynamics that have enabled it to function. The purpose of this appendix is to summarize leading aspects of that logic.

The Runaway Principle

In 1678, Richard Simon's pioneering study (*Histoire critique du Vieux Testament*) concluded that Moses was not the only author of the Pentateuch. Thus he launched the quest for the Pentateuch's origin, for its sources.

Seventy-five years later an answer came from a French medical doctor working at the court of Louis XIV. Jean Astruc, though he held for Mosaic authorship, saw that Genesis uses two divine names (Elohim; and YHWH), and so he drew a simple conclusion: Moses' Pentateuch is based on two different sources.

Earlier rabbis, who had also noticed the variation, had regarded the different names as expressing different aspects of God (Sandmel, 1978, 329). Astruc did not refute the rabbinic tradition, but his conjecture—his book was called *Conjectures* (1753)—had a double advantage: it is easier to imagine two documents than two aspects of God; and, above all, whether Astruc wanted it or not, the idea of two documents filled the developing vacuum in the theory concerning the sources of the Pentateuch. In commercial terms, the market needed sources, and Astruc's documents, however conjectural, however simplistically conceived, seemed to meet that need. The idea of two documents stayed.

Implicitly, a central literary principle was thereby established: variation in the text may be used as an indication of diversity of sources. There was no litterateur at hand to say that the principle was utterly unreliable, that for several reasons authors may change style and point of view.

Over the next two hundred years, application of the variation principle engendered a proliferation of claims to sources and editors. Every variation or complexity could be seen as evidence of diverse sources. The principle of variation went out of control. Applied to the Pentateuch it tended to divide it into fragments.

History: A Decisive Role

There were essentially two possible ways of bringing equilibrium to the runaway literary principle: (1) genuine literary criticism, a literary appreciation that would set the phenomenon of variation in literary context; or (2) historical criticism, a picturing of Israel's history around a few main lines or events, thus attracting the scattered fragments into a few main clusters.

Of these two possibilities, what was needed was the first. The problem, the runaway principle, was literary, and needed a literary solution. But literary help was scant. Most biblical scholars were preoccupied with theology, history, or apologetics, and another two centuries would pass before full-fledged literary criticism would influence biblical research deeply.

In the interim, the prevention of literary proliferation was carried out by historical criticism. Without really clarifying the literary principles, the historians effectively tied the discussion of sources to a specific historical framework, including the historical hypothesis that Deuteronomy constituted the program for a seventh-century reform by Josiah (2 Kings 22–23). (This hypothesis was formed without engaging the question of the possible literary unity of Genesis-Kings or without considering how well the account of finding the lost Law fits into the Primary History's overall plot.) Wellhausen (1883) provided the linchpin. He linked a plausible reconstruction of the history of Israel to a theory of four hypothetical sources (JEDP). The plausibility of the historical reconstruction lent plausibility and stability to the idea of the four hypothetical sources. JEDP became standard.

The Attraction

The JEDP theory is extremely attractive. It not only provides three sets of answers—concerning history, sources, and variations—but does so with a minimum of difficulty. The essential dynamics are easy to grasp: diverse historical situations produce diverse documents; these diverse documents are assembled into one text; and, almost inevitably, the one resulting text contains tensions or variations.

Within this attractive theory there is still room for great movement. The history may be adapted (for instance, by changing dates); the sources may be redefined, or reduced (say, to three; or, for Genesis, to two); and some of the variations may be explained in some other way. The dating of the hypothetical J provides a good example of variation: estimates range from Solomonic times (von Rad, 1962, I, 55; Wittenberg, 1988) to the exile or later (van Seters, 1975; Schmid, 1976; 167; Blenkinsopp, 1995, 1). Or one may place both J and E in the eighth century (Seebass, I, 34).

This flexibility—this room for movement—makes the theory all the more attractive. The JEDP hypothesis, therefore, forms a congenial place in which to live and work.

Assessment

As already suggested, the JEDP theory has two aspects—historical and literary. It implies a reconstruction of Israel's history; and it also claims to account for a literary text, that of the Pentateuch, including Genesis.

At the historical level, the theory is coherent. This does not make it true. The idea, for instance, that Deuteronomy provided a program for a seventh-century reform has now been countered (McConville and Millar, 1994, 141). Ultimately the historical reliability of the account of finding the Law is akin to the historical reliability of the account of writing it. But at least the theory is not self-contradictory. True or not, it has an advantage: in discussing distant centuries, it fills a void. This is probably its primary strength, the decisive reason it has endured.

At the literary level the JEDP theory is a mixture of insight and confusion. It is insightful insofar as it distinguishes, at least implicitly, between two of the basic stages in the composition of the Pentateuch—an initial stage of writing an overall account (J or JE), and a final stage of composing law (much of D and P) (see Introduction, Chapter 9).

But there is confusion also, particularly because of the principle that variation is a clue to distinction of sources. The problem is twofold.

First, the principle does not work well. The effort to apply it appears, in practice, to result in changes and inconsistencies. As far as Genesis is concerned the theory meant three sources: JEP. Then, under closer scrutiny, some proponents found the distinction between J and E unconvincing (e.g., van Seters, 1992, 4), and so, for these, the theory, as applied to Genesis, now means just two sources: JP. But the criteria for distinguishing J and P show multiple inconsistencies (see esp. Rendtorff, 1990). A so-called pedantic feature of P occurs in a classic J text (Rendtorff, 1990, 149–150); likewise, a verb usage that is supposed to be a mark of P occurs in J (ibid., 151–152); P is distinguished at one stage by being rambling, at another by being brief (ibid., 153). And so on; many of the supports for the theory turn out under inspection to be made of sand (see also Blum, 1984; Radday and Shore, 1985, 8). The confusion is complete when those who hold for the JP distinction disagree on its basic meaning— on whether P supplements J (van Seters, 1992, 4) or J supplements P (Blenkinsopp, 1995, 1) (see also Vervenne, 2001). At times, the disagreement seems based on views of history rather than on literary criticism. Overall, the contradictions in the explanation are greater than the apparent contradictions in the text.

Second, and more importantly, the principle itself is emerging as wrong. Variation in the text need not indicate variation of source. Inch by inch, as literary understanding develops, the variations are emerging as expressions of deliberate art, literary art which is theology-oriented.

Thus the conclusion begins to dawn: like a confusing myth, the JEDP theory has created an unreal world.

It is symptomatic of the unreality of the JEDP world that instead of using the term "editor" it prefers to speak of "redactors." Editors are indeed of various kinds, yet the word "editor" has a reasonably clear meaning, one generally associated with bringing texts into order. The perverse glory of the word "redactor" is that it is essentially meaningless, and so it can be used to fill any gap in any theory. It may be connected with order; or it may just as easily be connected with confusion. It may refer to minimal activity, but then again it may be associated with thorough authorship. Hence Vervenne's question (2001, 65): "What is meant by the terms 'redaction'/'redactor'?"

The distinction between J and P is something like the distinction between East and West, the distinction that excluded the influence of the Greeks; it appeals to a superficial differentiation of people(s). As the East-West distinction appealed to caricatures of Greeks and Asians, as though they had nothing in common, so the JP distinction has appealed implicitly to caricatures of two supposedly distinct authors: one, full of humanity (J), but curiously incapable of handling some basic features of life, including genealogies; the other, a priest (P), competent with genealogies, rituals, and some other features, but lacking humanity.

The problem involves a paralysis of imagination.[1] For complex reasons, historical and psychological, there is difficulty sometimes in imagining a human priest. In this situation, priest, by definition, means a lack of humanity. Humanity, almost by definition, has little to do with the world of priests. The problem is akin to others, such as the difficulty of grasping the unity of the transcendent and the earthly (Gen. 1 and 2), or the difficulty in times past of imagining a woman author. People are boxed within narrow categories.

The truth is the opposite: people who are fully human break all sorts of categories. A woman writer such as Annie Proulx of Wyoming—author of *Close Range* and *The Shipping News*—can enter fully into the reality of masculine life. People who are thoroughly human make the best priests; a true priest is fully human. Priest authors/historians include Berossos of Babylon, Manetho of Egypt, Josephus, numerous chroniclers, and, later, thinkers such as Luther, Copernicus, and Teilhard de Chardin.

This does not necessarily mean that priests were largely responsible for the Pentateuch or Primary History. If the Athenians could commission an outsider, Hellanicus, to write their history, then the Jerusalem authorities could likewise. It simply means that the division between P and J, particularly as applied to Genesis, has more to do with modern constricted categories than with the rich reality of ancient litterateurs. "P," as used in the JEDP theory, is a caricature. Ironically, van Seters and Blenkinsopp are both essentially right. The texts—all the Genesis texts—supplement each other. Or, more simply, they form a unity.

As for who wrote these texts, maybe it was a priest. Or maybe the Jewish authorities put their trust in a great prophetic writer, who, while well acquainted with worship, was able to place worship in the context of a larger world. It may seem unlikely that a prophetic writer would have such knowledge of detail, including detail of worship. But again, greatness of spirit does not exclude gathering sources and attending to detail. Annie Proulx may build primarily on insight; but she takes extraordinary pains to get every detail right.

Dividing the Unity

It can be objected of course that one source (J) has none of the characteristics of the other (P). Therefore the two are distinct. They are indeed distinct, but only because modern scholarship has made them so. If, from some complex

---

1. For Vervenne (2001, 41–42), the P debate sometimes "underestimates creative forces . . . deal[s] with a narrow concept of 'redactors' . . . [uses] clichés . . . tend[s] towards some form of 'ideologization' . . . [and] is fraught with a great deal of emotion." The paralysis of imagination is particularly powerful when the imagined division between a Yahwist and a priest is identified—consciously or unconsciously—with a real division between modern religious groupings. The division becomes a matter of faith.

object I remove all those components that have a specific series of traits, I will effectively divide the object in two—one part with those traits, the other without. I can then claim they are distinct; one part has none of the distinguishing features of the other.

With this kind of reasoning one could conclude that a Mercedes is not one object. Rather it is a combination (a mechanical redaction) of a small house (the outer frame of the car, including windows) with an open-air many-wheeled traveling machine (the lower part). The proof: the house has no wheels. True enough, the top of a Mercedes does not make a wonderful house, but neither do some of the conjectural sources make wonderful narratives. The J source, of course, makes a fairly good narrative. Indeed; and the bottom half of a Mercedes could make a powerful driving machine.

Most complex objects can be divided in two (or three or four). Some of Picasso's paintings, particularly those with overlapping faces, could be taken as reflecting two artists. The human body can be deboned, thus giving two distinct entities—a complete skeleton, and a body that, apart from being boneless, is near complete. Neither has any of the distinctive traits of the other, but that does not prove that they are of diverse origin. One may argue about which supplements which, but in fact they are a living unity; together they come into being, and they live through each other; there is only one body, a body that is greater than the sum of its parts. To treat the skeletal frame as separate—to comment on P as a distinct source—is to treat what is living as if it were dead. And to treat J without P is to create an animal that is spineless.

Further confusion occurs when the alleged diversity of JEDP is compared with the actual diversity between versions of certain ancient epics, such as the *Atrahasis Epic* or the *Epic of Gilgamesh* (see particularly the nuanced presentation of Carr, 1996, esp. 16–40). These epics existed in diverse versions, and therefore, according to this argument, so could the Pentateuch—in J, E, D, and P (Carr concentrates largely on P). The Jesus narratives are another example; there are four versions.

But in the cases of the epics and Jesus the versions are real; the diverse texts or manuscripts exist. For JEDP, however, there is not a shred of evidence, not a fragment of a manuscript of any one of these alleged versions. The comparison with *Atrahasis, Gilgamesh,* and Jesus serves not to confirm JEDP but to disqualify it even more thoroughly, to underline its unreality.

The issue is not whether something can be divided in two (or three or four) but whether it is more intelligible when taken as a unit. When Genesis is taken as a unit it is indeed perplexing, but ultimately it is supremely intelligible—great literary art, with a magnificent vision of the struggle and richness of life and of a transcendent dimension surpassing human calculation. Its variations emerge increasingly as features of literary artistry, including artistry that is diptych-shaped. The text is complex, but it is orderly—a delicate tapestry where essentially every piece fits. Some aspects still await explanation, but their proportion is diminishing.

And all the while, while literary explanations are gradually blurring the distinctions underlying the hypothetical documents, the presence of extant literature is coming closer and closer to the center of the Primary History, closer especially to the center of Genesis. Extant epics, including the *Odyssey,* are no longer the sources of hypothetical sources. Rather, they are among the sources of Genesis itself. Such are the prophetic books, especially Ezekiel, Isaiah, and Jeremiah. The old principle applies: entities are not to be multiplied unnecessarily. JEDP are not only increasingly unfounded; they are also increasingly unnecessary. Rendtorff's judgment (1993, 44) is truer than ever: "I believe that the traditional Documentary Hypothesis has come to an end."

In Kuhn's analysis of scientific revolutions (1970, 144–159, esp. 151), the old paradigm lives on after the basic revolution has happened and even after an alternative theory has achieved essential credibility. It is likely then that some form of the JEDP theory will continue for many years.

LANDMARKS IN THE DEVELOPMENT OF LITERATURE: TOWARD A MAP OF LANGUAGE, WRITING, AND LITERATURE

The literary tradition behind Genesis-Kings is vast—more than twenty centuries of writing, from the beginnings in Sumer and Egypt about 3000 BCE to the voluminous blossoming in Greek. This background has been partly indicated in several publications (especially *ANET*, and the work edited by Hallo and Younger, 1997–2001); and several connections with biblical writing have been established, most notably between Mesopotamian epic and Genesis 1–9.

But there is reason to suspect that the network of connections was far greater, extending into Greece, and that many of these connections can yet be traced. Ancient writers depended heavily on their predecessors. Writing and scripts have a genealogy (Gelb, 1963, x–xi). The Greeks also have a genealogy; they were not vacuum-packed. The roots of Greek art and writing are solidly in the East (Burkert, 1992; Morris, 1992), and, probably more than any other ancient nation, the Greeks traveled (Boardman, 1980).

The purpose of this appendix is to indicate tentatively what a broader map of ancient literature would look like, literature related to Genesis-Kings.

Egypt

Writing's beginnings were weak. There was no Cervantes or Tolstoy, no Jane Austen. Still, in other forms, there were significant developments:

Minimal Biography (2900–2300 BCE): Tomb inscriptions developed into short biographies. These attested to the person's standing, partly to ensure preservation of the person's soul.

Wisdom Literature (2900–2300 BCE): This time apparently also saw the beginning of extensive wisdom literature, including eventually (ca. 1900) a dialogue about life and death, and *The Teaching of Amenemope*.

Prophecy: The Prophecy of Neferti (a legendary wise man of Egypt). Written around 1900 BCE, under the Twelfth Dynasty, this prophecy is set in an earlier period (Fourth Dynasty, ca. 2650 BCE) and describes times to come, including the advent of Amenemhet, founder of the Twelfth Dynasty. The prophecy served to promote the Twelfth Dynasty.

Narratives (from ca. 1900 BCE onward): There are several short accounts of royal proposal-and-fulfillment (a king proposes a plan to the members of a council, and after they have praised the idea, he fulfils it). These brief texts—in modern times grandiosely dubbed royal novellas—are not at all as elaborate as other narratives about lesser figures (van Seters, 1983, 160). Such other narratives include:

> *The Story of Sinuhe* (early Twelfth Dynasty): When King Amenemhet dies, Sinuhe, a courtier of the queen, flees Egypt and spends years traveling and working. Finally he returns, is accepted, and reinstalled.

> *The Tale of the Shipwrecked Sailor* (ca. 1900 BCE) A soldier/sailor, to raise his commander's spirits, tells how he was shipwrecked on an island, alone with a great snake. The snake rescued him and foretold his safe return.

> *The Tale of Two Brothers* (Nineteenth Dynasty): One brother's wife makes advances on the other, younger, brother, and when rebuffed, accuses him of seeking her. Protesting his innocence, the younger brother castrates himself. "The story degenerates into an aetiological tale of the bull-god Bata with significant influence of Canaanite motifs" (Redford, 1995, 2228). Several other stories depict sexual advances (Irvin, 1977).

Narratives (mythological): These accounts contain features of human-interest stories, but they use these features to explore deeper forces.

> *Astarte and the Sea* (Eighteenth Dynasty): An adaptation of a Canaanite myth: ꜥAleyan Baal, helped by Astarte, defeats the monstrous Sea. "There is some evidence . . . that the immediate model of the Egyptian version was Hurrian" (Redford, 1995, 2229).

> *The Contendings of Horus and Seth* (Nineteenth Dynasty): In court, before the gods, young Horus challenges villainous Seth for the office of deceased Osiris. The narrative includes eighteen episodes, including, at the center, several combats.

Mesopotamia

Much of Mesopotamian literature is in two languages, Sumerian, which provides the literary foundation, and Akkadian, a semitic language, which adapted

and developed the Sumerian heritage. The Sumerian literature was as voluminous as the Bible, but, apart from some inscriptions, letters, and codes, was
almost all poetry.

There were four main periods or phases:

Old Sumerian Phase (2500–2200 BCE): This period produced incantations;
hymns; hymnic myths and epics, including stories of Gilgamesh (later developed, in Akkadian, into the *Epic of Gilgamesh*); then or later, the *Paradise Myth of Enki and Ninhursag,* and the story of the Flood.

Neo-Sumerian Phase (2200–1900 BCE): The literature of this era included
hymns on royal lives; letter-prayers; some forms of lament; suffering, lament, and restoration; and, then or later, *Inanna's Descent to the Under-
world.*

Old Babylonian Phase (1900–1600 BCE): This era saw the development of
the *Atrahasis Epic;* the Code of Hammarubi; priest poets; congregational
laments; royal historiographers; dynasties, especially the *Sumerian King
List;* flourishing scribal schools; and literary disputations.

Post-Sumerian Phase (1600 BCE onward): Sumerian texts were catalogued,
copied, and translated or adapted into Akkadian.

The main literary forms were as follows:

Epic poetry: Initially epic poetry was heavily colored by spontaneous storytelling
and local rivalries. Gradually, however, it took more definite form and opened
out to wider horizons.

The Epic of Gilgamesh (probably late third millennium BCE, Sumer): The
invention of writing in Sumer was eventually followed by the emergence of
written stories about a leader called Gilgamesh. In bridging the gap from Sumerian into the neighboring language of Akkadian, some of these stories were
adapted and synthesized into a new form—the Gilgamesh epic. By 1500 BCE,
"Gilgamesh's adventures had come into full vogue in the Near East" (Sasson,
1992, 1025). The two most complete versions are a thousand years apart, one
from Babylonia (ca. 1600 BCE), the other from Assyria (ca. 650 BCE). Akkadian
fragments of the Gilgamesh epic have been found, for instance, in Syria and
Megiddo. In Asia Minor (in the Hittite capital), there have been yet more such
Gilgamesh fragments, and in three languages—Akkadian, Hittite, and Hurrian
(Sasson, 1992, 1024–1027).

The epic tells of an ancient Mesopotamian king, Gilgamesh, who initially
seems inhuman. He is two-thirds god and one-third man, and he is violent and
lustful. Then the gods create Enkidu—very different in character—and, after
an encounter with a woman, Enkidu eventually engages Gilgamesh in friendship, combat, and adventure. When Enkidu dies, Gilgamesh mourns and, in
search of life, decides to journey to Utnapishtim, the survivor of the deluge.

Utnapishtim recounts the story of the deluge and enables Gilgamesh to find the plant of life. But while Gilgamesh is swimming, a serpent steals the plant.

The *Atrahasis Epic* (probably early second millenium BCE, Babylon): In contrast to Gilgamesh, first seen as violent and lustful, Atrahasis emerges as wise ("Atrahasis" means "Exceedingly Wise"). However, in the course of transmission there has been some interaction between the two epics; and, as with the Gilgamesh epic, the two main sources for the *Atrahasis Epic* are from Old Babylonia (ca. 1600 BCE) and Assyria (ca. 650 BCE). These two sources provide just fractions of the full texts, so it is possible to piece together only the outline of most of the story (O'Brien and Major, 1982, 71, 77; *ANET* 104).

The narrative begins at the beginning—among the gods, before humans exist. All is well, but some of the gods find that the burden of work is too much, and so, as a way of shifting that burden, they create humans. The creation process is complex—involving clay and some elements from the gods (blood and spittle)—and results in the birth of fourteen humans.

In the next available piece of the story, the situation has changed greatly: humans have become a problem. They have been multiplying for more than a thousand years, and they cause so much noise that one of the gods, finding it hard to sleep, finally decides to wipe them out with a flood. But one of the humans, King Atrahasis, has a friend among the gods, and having received warning, Atrahasis survives in a boat. The other gods are glad that humans have survived, and one of them makes plans to appease the god who had been hostile. From the sole survivor, creation of human beings starts again, but this time in a way that will limit the rate of population growth.

Enuma Elish (probably ca. 1100 BCE, in Babylon): The scope of the *Enuma Elish* is quite narrow: it tells of the generating of the gods, especially the glorious generating of Babylon's god, Marduk. But while glorifying Marduk, it recounts his acts of creation, first the creation of the sky, earth, and stars, then the creation of humans (O'Brien and Major, 1982, 10, 24–26).

Wisdom literature: A new feature of Akkadian literature—as opposed to Sumerian—was a form of wisdom writing that went "beyond . . . the inherited mythology. . . . [These wisdom writings were] commonly presented as dialogues but occasionally also as monologues" (Bottéro, 1995, 2297). Such writing included essays, reflections, and theological discussions. Among them were *Dialogue of a Man with His God, In Praise of the Lord of Wisdom,* and the *Babylonian Theodicy.*

Prophecies: Akkadian prophecies, written in prose, would first "predict" some past events and, having thus established credibility, would then discuss either the present or future—all in the form of predictions (van Seters, 1983, 96).

Lists and Chronicles of Kings/Rulers: Much writing was not only at the service of kings but about kings. Some accounts of kings were very brief (especially in the *Sumerian King List*), but there were chronicles that dealt with successive kings at greater length. These chronicles "vary in content, sometimes going far back into the past in search of material and sometimes restricting themselves to a well-defined period" (Bottéro, 1995, 2297). Yet despite this variation in content "they often use the same formulaic language in the dating portion of the texts" (van Seters, 1983, 80).

Even apart from formulaic dating, the records of the kings have a terrible sameness, focusing largely on warring and building (see, for instance, Luckenbill's two-volume collection [1926–1927] of the records of Assyria). The wars of Tiglath-Pileser I (ca. 1100 BCE) are typical (Luckenbill, I, 73–75):

> Tiglath-pileser, the mighty king, king of the universe, who is without a rival, king of the four quarters (of the world) . . . shepherd (?), king of kings, the exalted priest . . . whom [the god] Assur has caused to brandish his weapons. . . .
>
>   In the beginning of my reign, twenty thousand men of the land of Mushki and their five kings who for fifty years had held the lands of Alzi and Purukuzzi, which in former times had paid tribute and tax unto Assur . . . they came down and seized the land of Kutmuhi. With the help of Assur, my lord, I gathered my chariots and my troops. I looked not behind me. Mount Kashiari, a difficult region, I traversed. With their twenty thousand warriors and their five kings I fought in the land of Kutmuhi and I defeated them. The corpses of the warriors I hurled down. . . . Their blood I caused to flow in the valleys and on the high places of the mountains. I cut off their heads, and outside their cities, like heaps of grain, I piled them up. Their spoil, their goods, their possession, I brought out. I carried off six thousand (men) . . . who had fled before my weapons. . . .
>
>   At that time also I marched against the land of Kutmuhi . . . which had withheld tribute and tax. . . . Their booty, their goods, and their possessions I brought out. . . . The rest of the people . . . who had fled from before my weapons, crossed over to the city of Shereshe, which is on the further bank of the Tigris. . . . I hewed a way [over the mountain] with pickaxes. . . . I crossed the Tigris and conquered the city. . . . I scattered their warriors . . . and made their blood flow in the Tigris and on the high places of the mountains.
>
>   At that time also I beat down the forces of the Kurtê like a gust of wind(?) . . . The corpses of their warriors I piled up in heaps on the peaks of the mountains, and the river Nâme carried the dead bodies of their fighting men into the Tigris. . . . Their king, my hand captured. . . . His wives, his son . . . his household . . . the choicest of their possessions, I carried away.

Sometimes the building reports are brief. Sargon (724–705 BCE), for instance, states simply: "At that time, hard by the springs at the foot of Musri Mountain above Nineveh, I built a city and named it Dûr-Sharrukîn" (Luckenbill, 1926–1927, II, 93–94).

Amid all the repetitive stories of blood and bricks there are variations. The records of Sennacherib (705–681 BCE), for example, while they begin as do those of Tiglath-Pileser ("king of the universe . . . king of the four quarters . . . shepherd") (Luckenbill, II, 1926–1927, 115), and while they list campaigns repetitively ("In my first campaign . . . my second campaign . . . my third . . . my eighth") (Luckenbill, 1926–1927, II, 116–125), nevertheless, in speaking of his elaborate building projects, they present another aspect (Luckenbill, 1926–1927, II, 173): ". . . Ruler of widespreading nations am I. The . . . goddess of procreation looked upon me with favor (while I was still) in the womb of my mother . . . while Ea provided a spacious womb, and granted me keen understanding."

In the Neo-Babylonian chronicles, collected by Grayson (1975), the emphasis is not on war and building but on the interwoven sequence of kings—kings of Nineveh, Babylon, and Elam. Each is dated, not by an overall scheme, but by immediate circumstances such as the reign of a predecessor or contemporary. The accounts of the reigns are generally very brief; see, for instance, Chronicle 1, lines 1–26 (Grayson, 70–73):

1–5   [The 3d year of Nabu-nasir] king of Babylon, Tiglath-pileser (III) ascended the throne of Assyria. . . . In that year [he] plundered . . . and abducted. . . .

9–10   The 5th year of Nabu-nasir: Humban-nikash ascended the throne of Elam.

11–13 The 14th year Nabu-nasir . . . died. . . . For fourteen years Nabu-nasir [had] ruled Babylon.

23   Tiglath-pileser (III) ascended the throne in Babylon.

24   The 2d year, Tiglath-pileser died. . . .

25–26 For *eighteen* years Tiglath-pileser [had] ruled Akkad and Assyria. For two of these years he ruled in Akkad.

Phoenicia and Canaan (Ugaritic Epic)

The major source of documents for Phoenicia and Canaan is the ancient city of Ugarit, modern Ras Shamra (Ebla, in Syria, has yielded little concerning Canaan). Three texts stand out, all epic poems from ca. 1400 BCE, *Keret, Aqhat,* and *Baal:*

Keret: Keret is a king who, childless, goes to bed weeping. But he dreams of El appearing to him, listening to him, and then sending him to offer sacrifice and lead an army to the city of Udum. Along the way he makes a vow to the goddess, Asherah, promising a gift if all goes well. After besieging Udum and negotiating with its king he marries the king's daughter, and, blessed by El, the couple produce a large family.

Having overcome this crisis concerning children, Keret later faces two other crises—concerning sickness, because he did not fulfil the vow to Asherah, and a threat to his throne by his son. The overall theme seems to be El's power, wisdom, and benevolence (Parker, 1995, 2403).

Aqhat: Aqhat, born to the formerly childless Danil, receives a composite bow and, because of his refusal to surrender the bow to the goddess Anat, he is killed by someone who takes the form of a bird of prey. Danil's daughter, however, puts on weapons under her dress, goes to the killer's camp seeking vengeance, and at the camp she joins him in drinking. There the story breaks off.

Baal: The story of the god Baal—a series ("cycle") of diverse episodes—is extensive and mythological. There are "three successive subjects: the conflict between Baal and Yamm ('Sea'); the building of a palace for Baal; and the conflict between Baal and Mot ('Death')" (Parker, 1995, 2404).

Among second millenium languages and literatures, the heritage of Ugaritic "represents better than any other . . . the antecedents of the language and literature of ancient Israel" (Parker, 1989, 225).

Western Asia (Asia Minor/Anatolia)

The Hittites, the dominant power in Anatolia, received their original literary inspiration from Mesopotamia: "the [Hittite] scribal school absorbed literary models that were curricular because of the prestige of Mesopotamian culture and because Akkadian was the written language of the entire Syrian region" (Archi, 1995, 2367).

This indebtedness to Mesopotamia does not extend to historiography. The Hittites have no king lists or sequential royal chronicles. What they have instead are occasional annals—records of the deeds of individual kings (van Seters, 1983, 100, 105–113).

In other ways, however, the Mesopotamian influence on the Hittites was indeed great. Excavations in the Hittite capital, Khattusha (modern Bogazkoy, Turkey), have revealed several works variously indebted to Mesopotamia—"rituals, auguries, hymns, wisdom texts, and some parts of the Gilgamesh and Atrahasis poems, all in Babylonian, in addition to the legends of Sargon and Naram-Sin, the two great kings of the Akkad dynasty, in Hittite translation" (Archi, 1995, 2367). The impression is that the great Mesopotamian epic tradition became part of the writing culture of Anatolia.

The Founding Greeks (700 BCE): Homer (Western Asia) and Hesiod (Greece)

As writing continued to spread westward, to the Greeks, the Greeks remained heavily indebted to their Eastern neighbors, yet they made significant changes. Thus, in adopting the alphabet, semitic *Aleph, Beth, Gimel, Daleth,* and *He* became *Alpha, Beta, Gamma, Delta,* and *Epsilon.* The Greek names are slavishly imitative of the semitic (the semitic names have inherent meanings; the Greek adaptations do not), but the Greeks adapted the fifth letter, from *He* to *Epsilon* (= e), thus introducing an important development, namely the inclusion in the alphabet of letters that spell out the vowel sounds explicitly (Burkert, 1992, 25–29).

When Greek writing first flourished, in Homer and his younger contemporary Hesiod, ca. 700 BCE, the relationship to Eastern neighbors likewise showed a mixture of dependence and independence. The dependence is significant. Both in genre and content the initial epic poetry follows the most prestigious traditions of Mesopotamia. This is true not only of Homer, in western Asia (Burkert, 1992, 88–100), but also of Hesiod, living across the Aegean, near Athens, in Boetia (Feldman, 1996; 18; O'Brien and Major, 1982, 51). Boetia "had its orientalizing period too; it lies close enough to Euboea, the center of East-West trade in the eight century" (Burkert, 1992, 112–113; on Greece-eastern connections cf. Cook, 1963; Walcot, 1966; Boardman, 1980, 35–110; Vernant, 1982, 15–22; Morris, 1992).

However, as well as dependence, there was also independence. Homer and Hesiod broke new ground. Homer told of a different story, concerning Troy, and did so in a way that, in its tracing of causes and connections, prepared the way for the writing of history (Lesky, 1966, 218). And Hesiod's *Theogony* involved a bold effort to bring some coherence into the various myths concerning the gods.

The two works attributed to Homer are quite diverse in content: the *Iliad*, concerning the abduction of Helen, the Trojan war, and the fall of Troy (ca. 1200 BCE); and the *Odyssey*, concerning the leaving of home, wandering for twenty years, and coming home.

The works associated with Hesiod, a Boetian shepherd called by the Muses to be a poet, are even more diverse:

Theogony: Concerns the gods—a synthesis on origins and relationships.

Works and Days: Focuses on human life—as ordinary, not heroic.

Catalogue of Women (added to *Theogony*, ca. 600–550 BCE): A history, framed by genealogies.

Hesiod, less known, needs further description. *Theogony*, an account of the generating of the gods, is "a creative compendium of the theological traditions of ancient Greece" (Lamberton, 1993, 12); and *Works and Days* tells of honest living and rural life. Hesiod gives a negative picture of the creation of woman (*Theogony*, 570–620; *Works*, 47–105) and implies a myth of decline, a drastic fall (*Works*, 106–201; see O'Brien and Major, 1982, 48–62, 108–118, esp. 112).

The *Catalogue of Women*, attributed to Hesiod, has survived only in fragments, but enjoyed great prestige in antiquity. It "contained comprehensive genealogies covering the whole of the heroic age . . . genealogies which were interspersed with many narrative episodes and annotations. . . ." (West, 1985, 3).

Key Greek Forms (Asia to Italy):
Philosophy, Tragedy, History

Epic poetry, especially that of Homer, contributed to the development of two major Greek genres—history and tragedy (tragic drama). Epic also has some role in the emergence of a new form of wisdom literature—philosophy. The tragedies often elaborated a scene from Homer or history. These dramas, however, despite being rooted in epic, established new forms, especially new conventions of dialogue.

Drama was a specialty of Athens, centered particularly in the annual Dionysiac Festival. Philosophy and history, however, were divided as epic poetry had been: between Asia/Ionia, which generally led the way, and mainland Greece, including Athens, which developed more slowly.

Philosophy: 600–300 BCE (Ionian; later, Athenian)

From Ionia, on the central part of the west coast of Anatolia, came thinkers who were leaders in investigating the nature of the world (Cavendish, 1964; Copleston, 1946, 13–80):

Thales of Miletus (ca. 624–546 BCE).

Anaximander of Miletus (ca. 610–546 BCE).

Anaximenes of Miletus (ca. 585–528 BCE).

Pythagoras of Samos (ca. 571–497 BCE).

Xenophanes of Colophon (ca. 520–450 BCE).

Heraclitus of Ephesus (flourished ca. 500 BCE).

These thinkers did not emerge from a void. Their reflections came ultimately from the rich east-related background that produced the Homeric poems, and they themselves sometimes reflected and engaged Homer. Thales' emphasis on water finds a prelude in Homer's idea of the water-related nature of the world (Onians, 1951, 247–253). Xenophanes attacked the portrayal of the gods in Homer and Hesiod (Kahn, 1996, 1628;). Heraclitus was stronger: "Homer should be turned out of the lists and whipped" (Copleston, 1946, 38).

Some of these Ionians and others may be looked at more closely:

Thales: A philosopher and scientist, who taught but apparently did not write. Dissatisfied with ideas such as those of Hesiod's *Theogony* as an explanation for reality, he attempted a fresh synthesis of knowledge and concluded that the first principle of life was water. His renowned approximate prediction of the solar eclipse of May 585 BCE was apparently based on Chaldean ideas (Lesky, 1966, 162; Flacelière, 1964, 123).

Xenophones: Challenged the anthropomorphic picture of the gods; "he believed in a single god. . . . He avoids highly abstract arguments and . . . technical terms. He was at once theologian, philosopher and scientist" (Bowra, 1966, 161).

Pythagoras: Moved from Ionia to southern Italy where he founded a monastic-type community which, among things, combined mathematics with mystical contemplation. Regarded as a prophet and a son of one of the gods (Apollo or Hermes), he "powerfully advanced the spiritual life of antiquity" (Lesky, 1966, 165). Like the great heroes Heracles and Theseus, he was said to have gone down to hell and come back to earth (Flacelière, 1964, 124). On the sexes he wrote: "The good principle created order, light and men; the evil principle gave birth to chaos, darkness and women" (ibid., 178–179).

Parmenides (ca. 520–450 BCE): Of Elea, southern Italy, Parmenides wrote in epic hexameters and made a sharp distinction between reality and appearance: reality is a single, unchanging unity, but appearance is a mass of contradictions. He learned this he says by going in a chariot to the Gates of Night and Day, where a welcoming goddess made a revelation to him (Bowra, 1966, 161). In Parmenides' own words: "The mares that draw my chariot have brought me . . . along the pathway of the Goddess. . . . The axles grew hot in the wheel's hub, and cried out like the sound of a flute; two pairs of wheels, drawn by the fierce energy of the horses, drew me towards the radiance of the daughters of the Sun . . . and their hands drew back the veils that were upon my eyes. There stand the gates that open the way from Night into Day. A great beam is set above them, and the threshold is made of stone . . ." (Fragment 1, in Flacelière, 1964, 177). For Parmenides, "the two sexes are unequal: On the right, in the fecund womb, boys; on the left, girls. Now, the right side is the side of light; the left, or 'sinister' side, that of darkness" (ibid., 178).

The skilled wisdom teachers ("sophists"): As the emphasis shifted somewhat from (epic) myth to empirical knowledge, and as democracy developed during the rule of Pericles (461–431 BCE), people emerged with diverse skills or techniques, including especially skills in philosophy and in speaking (rhetoric). Such people were judged wise ("sophist"). They traveled from town to town, charged stiff fees (an innovation), and brought a new degree of rational reflection and analysis. This was a philosophical revolution. Later they tended to become carried away by their technique—especially their skill in speaking—and "sophist" took on a negative overtone (Lesky, 1966, 340–360; Cheilik, 1991, 98–99).

Socrates (Athens; 469–399 BCE): A philosopher, a "sophist," but one who refused money. Socrates never wrote; in fact he despised books. He married Xanthippe, who was said to be difficult, but, for the Athenians, Socrates was even more difficult. He often opposed popular views and demands, and he brought wisdom/philosophy into daily life. At seventy, he was condemned to death for changing the gods and corrupting the youth. His huge following included Plato and, indirectly, Aristotle.

Plato (429–347 BCE): Admired Socrates ("I was so disgusted [by his death] that I turned my back on the wretchedness of the times"—*Letter*, 325a). Plato visited southern Italy, Cyrene, and Egypt, then returned to teach in Athens, at the Academy, and wrote thirteen *Letters* and especially forty-two *Dialogues* (all survive, though the authenticity of some is contested). Some *Dialogues* are a form of biography of Socrates. Plato constructed "an imposing conceptual system that has made a lasting impression on the thinkers of every age" (Flacelière, 1964, 274). He records how Socrates viewed reality as having three levels: eternal unchanging Ideas; reflections or imitations of the ideas, in tangible realities; and imitations of the tangible realities in art.

Isocrates (b. Athens, 436–338 BCE): Followed Socrates, and outlived Plato. He ran a school of rhetoric in Athens, with students from all over Greece, and emphasized practical methods of rhetorical imitation (*mimēsis*) (Lesky, 1966, 583–591).

Aristotle (b. Macedonia, 384 BCE): Studied in Athens under Isocrates and Plato, but after Plato's death (347 BCE), moved to Asia Minor, near Lesbos, and helped reform the system of government. Five years later Philip of Macedonia appointed him to tutor fourteen-year-old Alexander. Aristotle married at forty-five, and when bereaved, later married again. Returning to Athens, he set up his own school, the Lyceum, which rivaled Plato's Academy. Later, following tension between Macedonia and Athens, he was accused of impiety, and, to avoid Socrates' fate, fled to Euboea and died there. He wrote about four hundred works, on every topic, including rhetoric (of these forty-seven survive complete, and about one hundred others in fragments). None of his written dialogues has survived. Building on Plato, Aristotle described all of art as an imitation of nature, but "his conception of Ideas differed from Plato's; he regarded them as existing, not outside and above the universe, but within it and by means of it. The philosopher ought not to withdraw from the visible world and lose himself among . . . personified abstractions such as the Good or the Beautiful, but should study every kind of reality patiently and at first hand before claiming to have arrived at its essence" (Flacelière, 1964, 323). Aristotle's dates (384–322 BCE) are also those of Athens' greatest orator, Demosthenes.

Fifth-century Athenian Tragedy (Developed from Epic/History)

The origin of tragic drama is obscure (Lesky, 1966, 223–233). What is essential is that it often showed courage as culminating not in victory but in defeat. The stories which illustrated this were frequently drawn from the epic tradition.

Phrynichos (Athens; flourished ca. 500 BCE): Composed one-actor tragedies, including *The Capture of Miletus,* and *The Phoenician Women.*

Aeschylus (Eleusis, 525–455 BCE): Fought the Persians at Marathon and Salamis. Of his ninety tragedies (some in trilogies), seven survive, including *Prometheus Bound; Persae* (set fairly sympathetically in the Persian court and based partly on Phrynichos's *The Phoenician Women*): and the trilogy (*Orestia*, adapting Homer and including the theme of the sanctity of marriage). "A believer, interested in theology . . . the gods and the fate of humanity . . . [he] wrote in a grave and noble style, difficult and often rather abrupt. . . . He showed traces of archaism" (Flacelière, 1964, 150, 195). He was the main founder of Greek tragedy (two or three actors, each possibly playing multiple parts), and he staged plays in Greece and Sicily.

Sophocles (b. near Athens; 495–406 BCE): Sophocles was a handsome poet, musician, and dancer. When young, he celebrated the battle of Salamis in a choir, and played the part of Nausicaa, the girl who met Odysseus. He was also a part-time official and general. And he was religious: "he held priesthoods in certain cults and received signal religious honors" (Harsh, 1944, 89). Yet his life contained explosive tension: married to an Athenian, he fell in love with a foreign woman. His *Oedipus the King* concludes: "For mortal men, it is their last day that they should think about" (Flacelière, 1964, 194–195). From more than a hundred tragedies, seven survive. These surviving plays are taken from a Homeric background.

Euripides (b. near Athens, on Salamis, around the time of the battle; 480–406 BCE): He studied philosophy with the sophists, and wrote ninety-two plays. Nineteen survive, some of them Homeric. *The Trojan Women* is largely a lament for the fall of Troy. In comparison to Sophocles, Euripides belonged to a younger, more secular generation. He was a towering writer: "In the eyes of the Greek world in general, if not of the Athenians, Euripides was the foremost figure of the times even before his death" (Harsh, 1944, 157). He was unhappily married, twice. He "secularized tragedy, in the sense that his characters are motivated by purely human passions, and not as in Aeschylus, by the will of the gods . . . or . . . religious conviction, as in Sophocles. But since the great majority of the Athenians remained believers, it may well have been that Euripides was anxious to satisfy them and therefore introduced the gods at the beginning and end of his plays" (Flacelière, 1964, 222–223). Euripides' masterpiece is *Medea:* Jason's foreign wife, Medea, has saved his life and is the mother of his two sons, but Jason abandons her for a younger woman and so she is exiled. She sends a garment, which brings death, to the other woman and, to gain revenge on Jason and avoid being a laughingstock, she plans to kill the two sons, but then she is caught in a storm of internal conflict: "Too well I know what horror I intend, but passion overwhelms my mind, worst cause of man's worst ills" (*Medea*, 1078–1080; cf. Flacelière, 1964, 225). His relationship with Athens was tense, and eventually he moved to Macedonia, where he died (de Romilly, 1985, 75–76).

In a summary of the three great tragic writers, Bowra asserts: "Aeschylus, despite his concern with grave and enigmatic issues, is the veteran of Marathon, who believes that in the end most questions can be answered and that the darkest catastrophes have the promise of some comforting light. Sophocles . . . examines . . . the contemporary scene with a more searching insight. Euripides speaks for more troubling forces. . . ." (Bowra, 1966, 121).

Pindar (ca. 520–440 BCE): In conjunction with drama, it is appropriate to mention the lyric poetry of the Boeotian poet Pindar. The intricacy and repetitiveness of his compositions are akin to features of parts of the Pentateuch (Douglas, 1995, 242).

Early Greek Historiography (Asian and Athenian, ca. 550–350 BCE)

(On Hecataeus, Herodotus, and Hellanicus, see also Introduction, Chapter 7.)

Hecataeus (b. Miletus, ca. 565–490 BCE): Hecataeus, a geographer-historian, composed a mythical-legendary history (*Genealogies*, now surviving in thirty-five fragments/quotes), and a *Description of the World*, which included travels, tales, and a map (now surviving in more than three hundred fragments/quotes; Pearson, 1939, 96). He begins his history with his own name ("Hecataeus of Miletus . . . ," a tradition followed by Herodotus and Thucydides (Pearson, 1939, 97), and then continues: "What I write here is the account . . . I consider . . . true. For the [Greeks'] stories . . . are numerous, and in my opinion ridiculous" (Bury, 1909, 13).

Herodotus (b. Halicarnassus, Asia, a place with Ionian culture; ca. 500–425 BCE): Herodotus traveled the known world, whether Persian or Greek, especially Mesopotamia, Egypt, and southern Italy, and found Greek-speakers virtually everywhere (Flacelière, 1964, 167). His famous *Historiae* ("Inquiries/Researches") deals with far more than a narrow recounting of the past. His interests and purpose were universal: "that . . . great deeds . . . not be forgotten . . . whether of Greeks or foreigners, and especially the causes of war between them" (opening of Bk. 1; trans., Burn/Sélincourt, 1972). Continuing Homer's epic tradition, but in prose, he moves from pre-Homeric times across the known world and into the world of the Persian empire. He "was also interested in natural history, as well as cosmography, physical geography and pretty well everything else, but it was to human geography and ethnography that his attention was mainly directed . . . man always occupied the centre of his mind" (Flacelière, 1964, 171).

Hellanicus (b. Mytilene in Lesbos, Ionia, ca. 480–400 BCE): Hellanicus, a well-established writer, produced a millenium-long history of Athens in three parts: 1) The prehistoric/mythical kings (ca. 1600–1200 BCE), especially Theseus (based partly on a free adaptation of the genealogies and episodes in the *Catalogue of Women;* 2) The intermediate period (to the fifth century); 3) The great civil war ("Peloponnesian," end of fifth century). The great work survives in fragments.

Thucydides (Athens, ca. 460–400 BCE): Thucydides was a disciple of the rationalistic philosophers ("the sophists"), and, partly for that reason, was much more careful than Herodotus in his writing of history. He took account, for instance, of economic factors. His interest was in the great civil war that consumed his own generation ("the Pelopennesian War"), but he begins with a brief review of the history of the Greeks (*History*, Bk. 1:1–23)—an account usually known as the *archae-ologia* ("account of beginnings") (Flacelière, 1964, 232; de Romilly, 1985, 99–108). This beginning is much more plausible than the extended beginning or introduction of Herodotus (*Histories*, Bks. 1 to 5:27, esp. Bk. 1). Thucydides' (unfinished) history is about the same length as Herodotus's *Histories* or the biblical Primary History.

Xenophon (Athens, ca. 428–354 BCE): When Xenophon was young, Socrates one day barred his way on the street, questioned him about becoming a good man, and said "Then follow me and I will teach you," and so he became one of Socrates' disciples (Flacelière, 1964, 265). At times he teaches indirectly: his *Cyropaedia* uses the life of Cyrus to communicate a political treatise. At other times, he describes events and people he knew directly or indirectly. Such is the case with his *Anabasis,* on his journey with the Ten Thousand into Asia; and *Memorabilia,* on the life of Socrates. Xenophon's history of Greece in his own day is called *Hellenica.*

Greek-style Historiography of Non-Greek Peoples

History-writing as developed among the Greeks provided a model for writing the history of many surrounding peoples and also contributed to the development of biography. Examples of writers who incorporated the Greek model include:

Berossos: A priest of Marduk at Babylon, Berossos wrote *Chaldaïka,* a three-book "Chaldean History" in Greek, which survives only in fragmentary quotations, especially in Josephus and Eusebius. Berossos lived under and wrote for Antiochus I of (Syrian) Antioch (285–261 BCE). His history covered thirty-six thousand years—from the beginning of humanity to the fall of Babylon (331 BCE, under Alexander).

Manetho: An Egyptian priest at Heliopolis, Manetho wrote *Aegyptica,* "Egyptian History," in Greek, apparently under the reigns of Ptolemy I and II (third century BCE). This history survives only in fragmentary quotations, especially in Josephus, Africanus, and Eusebius. "The works of Manetho and Berossos may be interpreted as an expression of the rivalry of the two kings, Ptolemy and Antiochus, each seeking to proclaim the great antiquity of his land" (Waddell, 1940, x).

Polybius (from Arcadia, Greece; ca. 200–118 BCE): Polybius's *Histories* covered the period of Rome's development into a world power. It is an extensive account.

Dionysius of Halicarnassus (Ionia, ca. 60 BCE–10 CE): His *Roman Antiquities* recorded Roman history from legendary times to the period covered by Polybius. It is a more extensive history even than that of Polybius.

Josephus (ca. 37–100 CE): A Jewish priest and soldier, Josephus modeled his *Jewish War* (covering 66–73 CE, with background) especially on Thucydides. And *The Jewish Antiquities,* concerning Jewish history (creation to 66 CE), while adapting the Bible, was modeled partly on Dionysius of Halicarnassus.

The Greek-style tradition continued into Latin. For instance:

Sallust (b. near Rome; 86–35 BCE): Sallust composed historical monographs: *The Cataline Conspiracy; The Jugurtine War.*

Livy (b. northern Italy; ca. 60 BCE–15 CE): Livy wrote a massive work *From the Founding of the City,* which recounted Roman history, from the origins to 9 BCE.

Tacitus (b. France; ca. 56–120 CE): Tacitus composed *The Histories,* which covered 69–96 CE, and *The Annals,* which covered 14–68 CE.

Suetonius (b. Rome? ca. 70–130 BCE): Suetonius wrote biographies: *Lives of the Caesars;* and *Lives of Illustrious Men.*

Conclusion

Those who wrote great histories of Babylon, Egypt, the Jewish people, and Rome did not confine themselves to methods learned among their own specific cultures. Rather, they adapted the leading historiographic method of the whole Mediterranean area—the Greek-based tradition, which first developed in western Asia, around 500 BCE. It is likewise the case with the Primary History. Despite drawing on indigenous traditions, including prophetic writings, the Genesis-Kings account adapts literature from the larger area of the Mediterranean, including especially Greek historiography. In other words, the Primary History, while distinctive and complex, fits within the broad and rich Ionia-based tradition. It does not fit to the same extent within the largely undeveloped chronicles and annals of the ancient Near East. The Near Eastern texts do not present a suitable precedent for either its character or size. The Greek texts do. And Genesis's link with the *Odyssey* confirms the Greek connection.

THE LANDSCAPE AND THE LION: GENESIS
AND THE GOSPELS

The purpose of this brief appendix is not to solve a problem but simply to promote a discussion. In some ways the discussion is as old as the church: the question of the relationship of Genesis to the Gospels is part of the centuries-long debate about the relationship of the Old Testament to the New. But several factors—especially the dividing of texts according to history, and the specializing of scholars into New Testament and Old (Hebrew Scriptures and Christian Writings)—have pushed this discussion into the background. Roland de Vaux, despite his expertise in Old Testament, joked about how little he knew of the New. And Rudolf Bultmann had little interest in the Old; he spoke of it as a failure (*Scheitern;* 1952, 183).

Yet comparison is instructive—not to show one as better than the other but to clarify both. The two are connected, and in a substantial way. Joseph's announcement to his brothers "serves as a straightforward gospel word" (Fretheim, 646). "Genesis is as much a gospel as John . . . [and] Matthew" (Gage, 1984, xiii). Charles Cochrane's work (1984) is entitled *The Gospel According to Genesis.*

Like the Gospels, the book of Genesis tells good news. While depicting the reality of evil (especially in chaps. 1–11), Genesis shows the greater reality of faith, courage, and providence (especially in Abraham, Rebekah, Jacob, and Joseph). Ultimately, therefore both Genesis and the Gospels may be called positive interpretations of human existence.

Such a minimal description, however, does not do justice to these writings, and it is useful, in order to get a clearer sense of both Genesis and Gospels, to compare them more closely. At first sight the comparison may appear uneven, at least for a Christian. Genesis, after all, may seem obscure and barbarous. The Gospels, in contrast, seem clear and positive.

Yet the relationship is not so simple. Dietrich Bonhoeffer believed that one may not simply choose the Gospels in preference to the Old Testament; one must absorb both: "Who[ever] desires to think and feel in terms of the New Testament too quickly and too directly is in my opinion no Christian" (quoted by Brown, 1968, 71:47). Others find that in some ways the old stories, like the old wine, taste better. As an old nun in South Africa commented at the end of a retreat based on Genesis: "Much better than listening to poverty, chastity, and obedience."

What then is the relationship of Genesis to the Gospels?

From a literary point of view both Genesis and the Gospels involve a blending of genres, especially of history and biography. In Genesis as a whole history is dominant, but in dealing with Jacob (from 25:19 onward) there is a shift toward biography. In the Gospels the emphasis on a form of biography is clearer.

At some level both Genesis and the Gospels are quite episodic. The episodes in the Gospels are generally shorter than those of Genesis, but toward the end, and especially in the final quarter (in Jesus' final week; in the story of Joseph or of Jacob's old age), the narratives become more continuous.

It is likely that the biographical element in Genesis provided part of the inspiration for the shaping of the Gospels. But such inspiration has been filtered through other factors and other accounts, including the prophetic biographies of Elijah-Elisha (Brodie, 1984, 45, n. 133; *Crucial Bridge*, 2000, 79–97). Jacob and Jesus therefore belong to the same literary genealogy, yet they are very different, far from being twins.

Jacob and Jesus both have foundational roles, Jacob with his twelve sons, Jesus with his twelve apostles. Yet the Genesis character who seems closest to Jesus is not Jacob but Joseph. Joseph is the precocious youth who eventually assumes great authority and becomes an expression of God's providence. Among writers of the early church Joseph was seen as a type or forerunner of Jesus: his survival of apparent death foreshadowed the resurrection (Steindl, 1989, 66–132). Jesus, therefore, combines aspects of both Jacob and Joseph.

There are continuities, too, in basic theological content. Gage (1984, 5) identifies five great themes—"the doctrines of God, Man, Sin, Redemption, and Judgement"—not only as belonging to texts such as the Gospels but also as "derived from Genesis 1–7."

There is a richness in Genesis that is not equaled in the Gospels. If, as has sometimes been said, poetry is a lion in the heart, then Genesis is a vast landscape of varied vegetation and animals, including lions. At times the richness of the landscape is too much. One becomes lost in the vegetation, confused by the multiplicity and variety of the animals.

The Gospels, in contrast, are more like a highlighting of the lion. Jesus is the lion, derived from the jungle, reflecting its essence, so strong and clear as to capture the heart. A vibrant lion concentrates the mind.

The two experiences—of the vast landscape and of the one vibrant lion—are not mutually exclusive. Without the landscape there is no lion. Without the one vibrant lion some people see the landscape as lacking clear focus, as having no center, no hearth.

The Gospels then can seem both poorer and richer than Genesis. They have narrowed the focus of the old literary heritage—thus winning and losing. But they have not dismissed that heritage. On the contrary they presuppose it and in varying ways continue to draw life from it.

Much of the impact of these books—Genesis and the Gospels—depends on what the reader brings to them. One of the basic reasons the Gospels are so powerful for so many is that they have invested so much of their faith, of their lives, in Jesus. Comparing the Gospels with another book can be like comparing a spouse whom one loves with a film star. At one level the film star cannot compare. One puts one's faith in Jesus, but not in Abraham. Jesus therefore has an obvious advantage.

But Abraham, too, has an advantage: Abraham's faith is in God, the God who told him to look at the uncountable stars, and for many people such a God is a more appropriate center of faith than any man, even a God-man.

The gap between the two forms of faith is not as wide as may sometimes appear. When St. Paul is looking for a model for Christian faith he takes that model from the book of Genesis—Abraham (Rom. 4). The implication is that, to a significant degree, the faith of the Christian is modeled on Genesis.

What is difficult is to clarify the precise nature of the shift between Genesis and the Gospels. Such a difficulty is not surprising: New Testament scholarship has had serious problems in clarifying the relatively simple shift between the synoptic Gospels and John. To some degree the Gospels are part of a much larger process, found elsewhere in literature, of internalization—of moving attention from what is outside, including outside action, to what is internal (Gusdorf, 1967, 24–33; 1974, 1170–1179, esp. 1171). Aspects of this seem to appear already in the comparison between Genesis and Homer: Auerbach (1953, 6, 11–12) contrasts Homer's attention to external detail with Genesis's attention to something more internal, to thoughts and feelings, which are multilayered.

The discussion of shifts in ancient writing and perception is complicated by the occurrence of shifts in modern times—shifts that affect the way in which diverse generations tend to view all preceding literature. Even within the children of one family the viewpoint of those who grew up before, say, the mid-1950s, may be quite different from that of those who grew up after that time. Among poets there was a significant shift after World War II: clear statements about major topics, especially about the human condition (Yeats, Eliot, Pound, Auden, McNiece), largely gave way to tight-lipped compositions about topics that were domestic, introspective, or preoccupied with self (Fennell, 1993, 166). Historical consciousness and the development of the historical critical method led to a way of using Scripture that was very different from that of St. Paul and the evangelists. In general, the historical critical method moved the emphasis toward an aspect that was external—toward the question of the occurrence (or nonoccurrence) of specific events. The recent emergence of psychology seems likely to lead to yet another shift—back toward the internal.

The overall conclusion—tentative—is that while Genesis and its faith have partly inspired the Gospels, the Gospels moved well away from Genesis; and modern perception in its turn has moved well away from the Gospels.

APPENDIX SEVEN

GENESIS IN THE LECTIONARIES

Like much ancient writing Genesis was composed not only to be read but above all to be heard, to be read aloud. Such reading generally takes place in homes, in schools, and especially in synagogues and churches.

Synagogue practice has varied—for instance between the annual Babylonian cycle and the triennial Palestinian cycle (Perrot, 1988, 137–143; cf. Mann, 1940)—but the general synagogue custom has been to read the entire text ("continuous reading"). This is demanding but it facilitates understanding.

Church practice tends to be selective. For Roman Catholics, for instance, who rely on the triennial cycle of Sunday readings, the offerings are meager and are largely confined to Lent:

Year A:	Lent, 1st. Sun:	2:7–9; 3:1–7:	Creating a human from clay; the Garden; the eating.
	Lent, 2nd. Sun:	12:1–4:	Abraham departs for a new beginning.
Year B:	Lent, 1st Sun:	9:8–15:	The covenant after the flood.
	Lent, 2nd Sun:	22:1–2, 9–13, 15–18:	The offering of the beloved.
	10th Sun:	3:9–15:	God finds the couple, and curses the serpent.
	27th Sun:	2:18–24:	Creation of woman.
Year C:	Lent, 1st. Sun:	15:5–12, 17–18:	Faith in the incalculable leads to a covenant.
	Corpus Christi:	14:18–20:	Melchizedek offers bread and wine.
	16th Sun:	18:1–10:	Mamre: the rejuvenation of Abraham and Sarah.
	17th Sun:	18:20–32:	The grilling plea for justice.

Easter Vigil	1st reading:	1:1–2:2	Creation.
	2nd read-ing:	22:1–18	Offering the beloved.
Pentecost Vigil		11:1–9:	Babel, illusory city.

The Anglican Sunday readings tend toward offering much more.[1] Genesis is to be read not only at the beginning of Lent, but also on several successive Sundays of year A, between May and August, beginning with Trinity Sunday. The texts for these May-August readings are as follows:

1:1–2:4a:	Creation, especially the essential goodness of things and people.
6:9–22; 7:24; 8:14–19:	The flood: people's evil engenders compassion rather than condemnation.
12:1–9:	Amid a fading world (chap. 11), Abram sets out courageously.
18:1–15 (21:1–7):	The rejuvenation of Abraham and Sarah.
21:8–21:	Expelling Hagar: Abraham's child—a fugitive and an Egyptian.
22:1–14:	Offering the beloved.
24:34–38, 42–49, 58–67:	Rebekah and the depth of God's steadfast love for Abraham.
25:19–34:	Jacob's childhood: rooted in a family's tensions and in God.
28:10–19a:	Jacob's dream: a young man awakens to a new dimension of life.
29:15–28:	Jacob's marriage: life's adventure, deserved deception, and tenacious love.
32:22–31:	Jacob's struggle: beginning the engagement with the shadow of death.
37:1–4, 12–28:	Jacob's old age and loss of Joseph: staring death in the face.
45:1–15:	"Is my father still alive?" Amid apparent death, Joseph brings new life.

The challenge in presenting scattered passages is to set each passage in its context and in the context of Genesis's overall progression from creation (chaps.

---

1. See *Lectionaries for Trial Use in the Church of Ireland*. It was produced by an Interprovincial Consultation representing the Church of England, the Church of Ireland, the Church in Wales, and the Scottish Episcopal Church. It was published in Dublin in 1995 by the General Synod of the Church of Ireland.

1–11) to reconciliation (the Joseph story). Here the Anglican plan is helpful; its thirteen successive Sundays contributes toward the building of a sense of continuity.

However, even without such Sunday continuity, church lectionaries or prayer books generally offer readings that provide openings for engaging the full text. The purpose of the rest of this appendix is to review one noncontinuous reading plan—the Roman Catholic use of Genesis *on weekdays*—and to comment *very briefly* on the readings in a way that begins to draw the texts together (details may be found in the commentary). Hopefully, for other churches with non-continuous reading plans, something similar is applicable.

This weekday reading of Genesis occurs in odd-numbered years ("Year I" in a two-year cycle): Genesis 1–11 in February ("Weeks 5 and 6"), and Genesis 12–50 in June/July ("Weeks 12–14") The texts are as follows:

February, "Week 5": Genesis 1–3 (see commentary, 123–152)

Monday, 1:1–19: The First Four Days of Creation

This text is primarily not about the chronological origin of the universe but about its nature and about its present rootedness in God. Despite turmoil and tears, the earth is good, essentially a place that welcomes creatures and gives life. Earth is a wonderful location. There are "sermons in stones, books in the running brooks and good in everything" (Shakespeare, *As You Like It*, II, i).

Tuesday, 1:20–2:4a: Creation, Days 5 to 7

Despite instances of savagery, animals are good—they are blessed—and people are very good. The sense of a welcoming place, already implied on days 1 to 4, now becomes stronger—especially in the picture of God as resting. Central to existence is the positive ability to rest—to do nothing, to appreciate and enjoy.

Wednesday, 2:4a–17 (omitting 10–14): Created from Clay; Human Closeness to the Ground

Having already mentioned human relationship to God ("image"), the readings now touch two further primordial relationships—to the ground (2:4a–17), and, in Thursday's reading, to another person (2:18–25). Both these relationships can bring problems, yet, as their origin shows, they are essentially positive. The earth is kindred and the trees are "good."

Thursday, 2:18–25: Creation of Woman; Human Closeness to Another Person

Unlike some Greek myths, the picture of the woman is immensely positive. Already described, implicitly, as equal (1:27) and "very good" (1:31), she now emerges as a helpful companion. However, the man's enthusiasm for the woman has a shadow of self-centeredness, of failure to appreciate her otherness.

Friday, 3:1–8: Disorder from Within; the Consuming That Rejects Limitation

The shadow of misperception, already found in the man, in his slightly self-centered response to the woman, now appears in the woman herself—in her self-centered desire, which rejects limitations and manipulates the thoughtless man. Their rejection of limitation, instead of bringing peace, brings alienation. Humans were to have mastered animals (1:28; cf. 2:20), but—as seen in the serpent—self-centeredness induces an animal power that masters the humans.

Saturday, 3:9–24: Alienation, Loss, and a Different Sense of God

The aberration, while bringing alienation and a haunting loss, also brings a new sense of God—as close to humans, walking in the Garden, and making clothes for them. The struggle with the serpent may be difficult, but there is a hope.

February, "Week 6": Genesis 4–11 (and Hebrews 11) (see commentary, 142–205)

Monday, 4:1–15, 25: Cain and Abel

The self-centeredness that was seen earlier, first in the man and then in the woman, now reaches stronger form, and sin, previously seen as a serpent, now becomes a crouching animal (4:7). The story presupposes that life is unfair. The question then is not whether life is fair but what to do about it. Cain had a choice between mastering the self-centeredness (the crouching animal) and aggravating the cycle of savagery. Eve, mother of the murderer and the murdered, instead of despairing, manages to begin again, with a new child, Seth (4:25).

Tuesday, 6:5–8; 7:1–5, 10: Corruption, the Flood, and the Ark

The world is so corrupt that it makes God totally disillusioned. Everything is rotten. Yet, there is grace: Noah found grace ("favor") in God's eyes. And so, amid all the corruption, Noah listens to God and starts a long process of building.

Wednesday, 8:6–13, 20–22: The Flood Abates; Corruption and Forgiveness

The picture of the earth emerging from the flood waters recalls how the earth first emerged from primordial chaos. The flood shows that the earth is indeed corrupt, yet the emergence from that flood reveals God's will to give new life. Human weakness, which was previously a motive for condemnation (6:5), now becomes a motive for compassion ("Never again will I . . .", 8:21).

Thursday, 9:1–13: After the Flood; the New Beginning and the Rainbow

Amid the new beginning, so like the original creation, there is a greater awareness of evil—such as the threat of murder. Yet there is also a more explicit sense of God's covenant. The rainbow captures the ambiguity: as rain-related it recalls the flood, with all its attendant corruption, but precisely by being rain-related it becomes something wondrous and related to God's covenant.

Friday, 11:1–9: Babel, the Illusory City

The story of Babel, apart from discussing languages (already mentioned in 10:5, 20, 31), is a symbol of what comes from asking a city, or any great human achievement, to do the impossible—to reach the sky, and implicitly to satisfy every human longing. No city is a place of ultimate abiding.

Saturday, Hebrews 11:1–7: The Faith of Abel, Enoch, and Noah

The famous text from Hebrews spells out one of the implications of Genesis 1–11—the need for openness to what is beyond immediate sense perception.

This theme of faith is taken up in the reading about Abraham—in June/July.

June/July, "Week 12": Abraham; Genesis 12–18 (see commentary, 208–248)

Monday, 12:1–9: Abram's Courageous Departure

Abra(ha)m's previous situation had looked hopeless (Gen. 11). Babel represented the collapse of the world's greatest project (11:1–9); and his own family was being overtaken by the shadow of death (11:10–32). The life spans were shrinking (11:10–26), and the family was being engulfed by premature death [Haran], barrenness, failure to reach a destination, and settlement in Haran— a reminder of premature death (11:27–32). Life looked bleak. But instead of despairing, Abraham follows a call to a new land.

Tuesday, 13:2, 5–18: Seeing Beyond the Wealth

Genesis 12 and 13 highlight two powerful elements—beauty (12:10–13:1) and wealth (13:2–18). In dealing with the first—the crisis Sarai's beauty caused in Egypt—Abram had failed; he had been guided by self-interest. But now, in the dispute concerning wealth, he shows a new maturity. By yielding wealth he gains at another level. The promise is intensified.

Wednesday, 15:1–12, 17–18: Seeing Beyond Death— to the Incalculable

In Genesis 14 Abram had faced war, but now, aware of distant death ("I go . . . ," 15:2, meaning I go toward death), he becomes fearful. God brings him from his fearful place and induces him to make the leap into life's incalculable dimension, symbolized by the stars. The leap is then ratified by a powerful ritual of covenant-making.

Thursday, 16:1–12, 15–16: The Childless Woman Finds Her Voice, and the Slave-girl Finds Her Dignity

Sarai has been on a roller coaster. First introduced as barren (11:30), she goes from being the toast of Egypt, the world's most prestigious society (12:10–16), to being despised by an Egyptian slave (16:4). Her first words are disillusioned and bitter; they just barely acknowledge a God who should judge (12:5). The slave-girl, who despite being with child, feels she must run away, gains a fresh sense of herself—on grounds other than being with child—and so is able to return.

Friday, 17:1, 9–10, 15–22: Laughing at Life

While Sarai had effectively expelled the slave-girl (Gen. 16), God now makes a covenant that includes slaves (Gen. 17). Earlier (15:2), Abram had complained that his life's expectations were not being met. Now (17:15–22), he laughs in incredulity because at another level God is giving him more than he had expected. Here and in Genesis 15 there is a sense of God-given life as going against one's calculation and beyond them.

Saturday, 18:1–15: In Welcoming the Strange Visitor, the Old Find New Life

This is a central passage in the Abraham story. Despite scorching heat, old Abraham is bounding with generosity. And, though once touched by bitterness, Sarah is still able to hear. In a sense they both rediscover a form of youth.

June/July, "Week 13": Abraham, Jacob; Genesis 18–24, 27 (see commentary, 248–310)

Monday, 18:16–23: God's Justice Under Scrutiny

How can a just God allow catastrophes such as the destruction of a city? God is respectfully grilled by Abraham. The answer is oversimplified: only the guilty will suffer. (As ever, the issue of evil is not answered satisfactorily.) Yet God pushes the question (the impetus for the grilling comes from God's own self, 18:17, 33). The person who asks has a high standard (Abraham is generous and just, 18:1–8, 19). And the account as a whole (18:1–19:29) shows another truth: despite the catastrophe there is also a great mercy at work.

Tuesday, 19:15–29: Lot Loved to Choose

Even as God's messengers are trying to save Lot, he insists on choosing—as he had first chosen carefully (13:10–13). He has the illusion that life consists of his choices, unaware that life is far greater than his careful choices. In his effort to control life, he is the antithesis of Abraham.

Wednesday, 21:5, 8–20: Expulsion of the Slave and Her Son

One aspect of the enigmatic expulsion is that, as the desert incident shows, God is with people who differ in ethnic background, status, and way-of-life. In the subsequent account (21:21), Hagar has Ishmael marry an Egyptian—thus returning to her own roots, and also bringing it about that apparent Egyptians will in fact be children of Abraham.

Thursday, 22:1–19: The Offering of the Beloved

From God's point of view there is no question of killing the beloved Isaac; the command is explicitly described as just a test (22:1). And Abraham has become so close to God that at some level he knows that what God is commanding will be all right. This is Genesis's first use of the word "love" (22:2). Part of the account has to do with keeping love in perspective, with preventing anybody, even the unique Isaac, from becoming an idol.

Friday, 23:1–4, 19; 24:1–8, 62–67: Sarah's Death; and the Betrothal

Sarah's death is enigmatic: it leads to initial possession of the promised land (Gen. 23). And Isaac's betrothal is likewise enigmatic: Genesis 24 as a whole is largely about God's care for Abraham, and it covers the account of Abraham's life with the splendid divine-like figure of Rebekah.

Saturday, 27:1–5, 15–29: Jacob Steals the Blessing

The story of Jacob is the Bible's first biography, womb to tomb (25:19–chap. 50). The stealing of the blessing has two levels. First, it is a deception—and as such it is duly punished (as Jacob replaced his brother, so, at marriage, his beloved is replaced by her sister). Second, Rebekah's wresting of the blessing from animal-related Esau has echoes of the primordial effort to recover the blessing that was lost in the beginning (Gen. 1:1–4:17).

June/July, "Week 14": Jacob, Joseph; Genesis 28–50 (see commentary, 310–417)

Monday, 28:10–22: The Journey Out; Jacob's Dream

Emerging from a difficult family background, the young man becomes aware, amid his rough journey, that his life is connected to something far greater than himself. The sense of blessing, already gained in ambiguous circumstances, now strengthens and expands.

Tuesday, 32:23–33: Twenty Years Later, on the Journey Back; Jacob's Struggle

Jacob is no longer so young and his long journey homeward entails an initial confronting of ultimate death. First he faces formidable Laban (31:1–32:2), then terrifying Esau (32:3–chap. 33). The night struggle, culminating this confrontation, is full of the ambiguity of both life and God. At the end Jacob is limping, but he is blessed and the sun is on his face.

Wednesday, 41:55–57; 42:5–7, 17–27: Joseph Stirs Memories Constructively

Since selling Joseph the brothers had not been shown speaking to one another. Judah's departure (chap. 38) is a symptom of their alienation. All they do is look at each other (42:1). They are in a knot of guilt, suppressed memory, and silence. Joseph's strategy, rather than reveal himself immediately—something that would have left them permanently guilty and embarrassed—is to stir their memories constructively. Eventually (Thursday's reading) he leads them to a situation where they get a second chance to make a choice about the fate of the youngest brother and their father (43:8–10; 44:18–34).

Thursday, 44:18–29; 45:1–5: Judah's Speech Undoes the Original Crime

Judah had been the ringleader: it was he who first suggested selling Joseph (37:27); then, when he went away, effectively abandoning his brothers, his acknowledgement of Tamar's innocence intimates his own conversion (38:26); and finally he puts himself on the line to save his father and brother (43:8–10; 44:18–34). Thus, when Joseph reveals himself the meeting is a source not of greater guilt but of joy.

Friday, 46:1–7, 28–30: Jacob's Journey; Facing the Unknown and Death

Jacob, who previously feared the intimation of death (chaps. 31–33) and who, as death approached, mourned and moaned (37:33–34; 42:29–38), now finds new courage to face a strange journey and to face death. Through Joseph he knows that the dream he once had—of a certain providence (28:20–22)—has stayed alive. Now he can die.

Saturday, 49:29–32; 50:15–26: Jacob's Death and Burial

As Jacob is dying the emphasis is not on loss or curse but on blessing (chap. 49). The description of the burial place, repeated in Genesis, is like a haunting melody (23:17–20; 25:10; 35:27–29). Mamre (49:30), for instance, recalls God's visit to Abraham long ago, at Mamre (18:1–15). Jacob's funeral, too, has a haunting beauty: it is watched, half knowingly, by "the inhabitants of the earth/land" (50:11; his dream spoke of people from north/south/east/west, 28:14). The Jordan and the chariots give an intimation of Elijah (2 Kings 2:7–11). The burial's aftermath is not bitterness but forgiveness (50:14–21), the first time that forgiveness becomes explicit.

BIBLIOGRAPHY

Asterisks (*) indicate bibliographies and reviews of research.
Name in **bold**: indicates commentaries, cited by author only. Some authors
have two forms of entry: e.g., Brueggemann and **Brueggemann**.

Abela, A. 2001. "Is Genesis the Introduction of the Primary History?" In *The Book of Genesis*, ed. A. Wénin, 397–406. See Wénin, ed.

Abrams, M. H. 1953. *The Mirror and the Lamp: Romantic Theory and the Critical Tradition*. New York: Oxford University Press.

Adar, Zvi. 1990. *The Book of Genesis: An Introduction to the Biblical World*. Jerusalem: Magnes.

Ajzenstat, Oona. 1995. "Jesus and the New Odysseus: An Analysis of a Literary Source of John 9 and 10." Paper delivered to the SBL, Philadelphia, Nov. 18, 1995.

———. 2000. "Tamar or how the messianic symbol stands for the teaching of ethics." Paper delivered at Thornloe University, March 2000.

Albertz, Rainer. 1992. *Religionsgeschichte Israel in altteestamentlicher Zeit. Vol. I. Von den Anfängen bis zum Ende der Königzeit*. Grundrisse zum Alten Testament; Ergänzungsreihe 8/1. Gottingen: Vandenhoeck & Ruprecht. EngTrans: *A History of Israelite Religion in the Old Testament Period*. I. London: SCM, 1994. [Vol II, *From the Exile to the Maccabees*. Louisville, Westminster/John Knox, 1994].

Albright, William F. 1964. "An Introduction to H. Gunkel's *The Legends of Genesis*." See Gunkel, 1964.

Alexander, T. D. 1992. "Are the Wife/Sister Incidents of Genesis Literary Compositional Variants?" *VT* 42: 145–153.

———. 1997. *Abraham in the Negev: A Source-critical Investigation of Genesis 20: 1–22:19*. Carlisle, England: Paternoster.

Allen, Christine G. 1979. " 'On Me Be the Curse, My Son!' " In *Encounter With the Text: Form and History in the Hebrew Bible*, ed. M. J. Buss. Missoula, Mont.: Scholars; and Philadephia: Fortress, 159–172.

Allen, Thomas W. 1917–1919. *Homeri Opera*. 2d ed. *Tomus III: Odyssae Libros I–XII continens* [1917]. *Tomus IV: XIII–XXIV* [1919]. Oxford: Clarendon.

Alter, Robert. 1981. *The Art of Biblical Narrative*. New York: Basic Books.

————. 1984. "The Decline and Fall of Literary Criticism." *Commentary* 77: 50–56.

————. 1985. *The Art of Biblical Poetry*. New York: Basic Books.

————. 1986. "Sodom as Nexus: The Web of Design in Biblical Narrative." *Tikkun* 1: 30–38.

————. 1992. *The World of Biblical Narrative*. Basic Books. New York: Harper-Collins.

Alter, Robert. 1996. *Genesis: Translation and Commentary*. New York/London: W. W. Norton.

Altick, Richard D., and John J. Fenstermaker. 1993. *The Art of Literary Research*. 4th ed. New York/London: W. W. Norton.

Anderson, Bernard W. 1978. "From Analysis to Synthesis: The Interpretation of Genesis 1–11." *JBL* 97: 23–29.

Arafat, Karin W. 1996. "Theseus." *OCD 3*: 1508–1509.

Archi, Alfonso. 1995. "Hittite and Hurrian Literatures: An Overview." *CANE* IV: 2367–2377.

Armajani, Yahya. 1972. *Iran*. Englewood Cliffs, N.J.: Prentice-Hall.

Armstrong, Karen. 1996. *In the Beginning: A New Interpretation of Genesis*. New York: Alfred A. Knopf.

Assmann, J. 1992. "Egyptian Literature (Survey)." *ABD* II: 378–390.

Astruc, Jean. 1753. *CONJECTURES SUR LA GENESE. Conjectures sur les Memoires Originaux Dont il paroit que Moyse s'est servi pour Componer le Livre de la Genese. Avec des Remarques, qui appuient ou qui éclaircissent ces Conjectures*. A BRUXELLES, Chez Fricx, Imprimeur de Sa Majesté, vis-à-vis l'Eglise de la Madelaine. M. DCC. LIII. Avec Privilege & Approbation.

Auerbach, Erich. 1953. *Mimesis: The Representation of Reality in Western Literature*. Princeton, N.J.: Princeton University.

Auld, Graeme A. 1996. "The Deuteronomists and the Former Prophets." Address to the Deuteronomistic History Section of the SBL, New Orleans, Nov. 23, 1996.

Bailey, Kenneth E. 1996. "Inverted Parallelisms and Encased Parables in Isaiah and Their Significance for Old and New Testament Translation and Interpretation." In *Literary Structure and Rhetorical Strategies in the Hebrew Bible*, ed. L. J. de Regt et al. Assen, the Netherlands: Van Gorcum/Eisenbrauns, 14–30.

Baker, D. W. 1980. "Diversity and Unity in the Literary Structure of Genesis." In *Essays on the Patriarchal Narratives*, ed. A. R. Millard and D. J. Wiseman. Winona Lake, Ind.: Eisenbrauns, 197–215.

Bal, Mieke. 1986. "Sexuality, Sin and Sorrow: The Emergence of Female Character (A Reading of Genesis 1–3)." In *The Female Body in Western Culture: Contemporary Perspectives*, ed. Susan R. Suleiman. Cambridge, Mass.: Harvard University, 317–328.

Baldick, Julian. 1994. *Homer and the Indo-Europeans: Comparing Mythologies*. London/New York: I. B. Tauris.

Barr, James. 1992. *The Garden of Eden and the Hope of Immortality*. London: SCM.

Bateson, F. W. 1972. *The Scholar-Critic. An Introduction to Literary Research*. London: Routledge & Kegan Paul.

Beach, Eleanor Ferris. 1997. "An Iconographic Approach to Genesis 38." In *A Feminist Companion to Reading the Bible: Approaches, Methods and Strategies,* ed. A. Brenner and C. Fontaine. Sheffield, UK: Sheffield Academic, 285–305.

Beck, Astrid B., et al., eds. 1995. *Fortunate the Eyes That See: Essays in Honor of David Noel Freedman in Celebration of His Seventieth Birthday.* Grand Rapids, Mich.: Eerdmans.

Beentjes, Pancratius C. 1996. "Discovering a New Path of Intertextuality: Inverted Quotations and their Dynamics." In *Literary Structure and Rhetorical Strategies in the Hebrew Bible,* ed. L. J. de Regt et al. Assen, the Netherlands: Van Gorcum/Eisenbrauns, 31–50.

Beitzel, Barry, J. 1992. "Roads and Highways." *ABD* V: 776–782.

———. 1992a. "Travel and Communication." *ABD* VI: 644–648.

Benson, F. J. 1981. "Roads and Highways." *Encyclopedia Britannica.* 15th ed. 15: 892–906.

Ben Zvi, Ehud. 1998. "Looking at the Primary (Hi)story and the Prophetic Books as Literary Theological Units within the Frame of the Early Second Temple: Some Considerations." *SJOT* 12: 26–43.

Bergant, Dianne. 1997. "The Medium Is the Message." *TBT* 35: 5–9.

Berlin, Adele. 1983. *Poetics and Interpretation of Biblical Narrative.* Sheffield, UK: Almond.

———. 1996. "A Search for a New Biblical Hermeneutics: Preliminary Observations." In *The Study of the Ancient Near East in the Twenty-First Century.* The William Foxwell Albright Centennial Conference, ed. J. S. Cooper and G. M. Schwartz. Winona Lake, IN: Eisenbrauns, 195–207.

Berquist, Jon L. 1995. *Judaism in Persia's Shadow: A Social and Historical Approach.* Minneapolis: Fortress.

Betchel, L. M. 1995. "Gen 2.4b–3:24: A Myth about Human Maturation." *JSOT* 67: 3–26.

Black J. A., and W. J. Tait. 1995. "Archives and Libraries in the Ancient Near East." *CANE* IV: 2197–2209.

* Blenkinsopp, Joseph. 1992. *The Pentateuch: An Introduction to the First Five Books of the Bible.* ABRL. New York/London: Doubleday, 1–30.

———. 1995. "P and J in Gen 1:1–11:26: An Alternative Hypothesis." In *Fortunate the Eyes that See: Essays in Honor of David Noel Freedman in Celebration of His Seventieth Birthday,* ed. A. B. Beck et al. Grand Rapids, Mich.: Eerdmans, 1–15.

Bloch, R. 1957. "Midrash." *DBS* V: 1263–1281.

Blum, E. 1984. *Die Komposition der Vätergeschichte.* WMANT 57. Neukirchen-Vluyn: Neukirchener.

———. 1990. *Studien zur Komposition des Pentateuch.* BZAW 189. Berlin/New York: De Gruyter.

Boardman, John. 1980. *The Greeks Overseas: Their Early Colonies and Trade.* New York: Thames and Hudson.

Bodelsen, C. A. 1966. *T. S. Eliot's Four Quartets: A Commentary.* 2nd ed. Copenhagen: Rosenkilde & Bagger.

Bolte, M., and C. J. Hogan. 1995. "Conflict over the Age of the Universe." *Nature* (Aug. 3) 376: 399–402.

Bonz, Marrianne Palmer. 2000. *The Past as Legacy. Luke-Acts and Ancient Epic*. Minneapolis: Fortress.

Boorer, Suzanne. 1989. "The Importance of a Diachronic Approach: The Case of Genesis-Kings." *CBQ* 51: 195–208.

———. 1992. *The Promise of the Land as Oath: A Key to the Formation of the Pentateuch*. BZAW 205. Berlin/New York: De Gruyter.

Borowsky, Irvin J., ed. 1992. *Artists Confronting the Inconceivable: Award Winning Glass Sculpture*. Philadelphia: American Interfaith Institute.

Bottéro, Jean. 1995. "Akkadian Literature: An Overview." *CANE* IV: 2293–2303.

Bowra, C. M. 1966. *Landmarks in Greek Literature*. London: Weidenfeld & Nicolson.

Boyd, John D. 1968. *The Function of Mimesis and Its Decline*. Cambridge, Mass.: Harvard University.

Brenner, Martin L. 1991. *The Song of the Sea: Ex 15:1–21*. BZAW 195. Berlin/New York: De Gruyter.

Brentjes, Burchard. 1995. "The History of Elam and Achaemenid Persia: An Overview." *CANE* II: 1001–1013.

Brichto, Herbert Chanan. 1998. *The Names of God: Poetic Readings in Biblical Beginnings*. New York/Oxford: Oxford University Press.

Bright, John. 1981. *A History of Israel*. 3rd ed. London: SCM.

Brodie, Thomas L. 1979. "A New Temple and a New Law: The Unity and Chronicler-based Nature of Luke 1:1–4:22a." *JSNT* 5: 21–45.

———. 1981. "Jacob's Travail (Jer 30:1–13) and Jacob's Struggle (Gen 32:22–32): A Test Case for Measuring the Influence of the Book of Jeremiah on the Present Text of Genesis." *JSOT* 19: 31–60.

———. 1981a. "Jesus as the New Elisha: Cracking the Code [John 9]." *ExpT* 93: 39–42.

———. 1981/87. *Luke the Literary Interpreter: Luke-Acts as a Systematic Rewriting and Updating of the Elijah-Elisha Narrative in 1 and 2 Kings*. Ph.D. diss., Pontifical University of St. Thomas, Rome, 1981. Ann Arbor, Mich.: UMI Dissertation Services, 1987.

———. 1983. "The Accusing and Stoning of Naboth (1 Kgs 21:8–13) as One Component of the Stephen Text (Acts 6:9–14; 7:58a)." *CBQ* 45: 417–432.

———. 1983a. "Luke 7:36–50 as an Internalization of 2 Kings 4, 1–37: A Study in Luke's Use of Rhetorical Imitation." *Bib* 64: 457–485.

———. 1984. "Greco-Roman Imitation of Texts as a Partial Guide to Luke's Use of Sources." In *Luke-Acts: New Perspectives from the Society of Biblical Literature*, ed. C. H. Talbert. New York: Crossroad, 17–46.

———. 1986. "Towards Unravelling Luke's Use of the Old Testament: Luke 7.11–17 as an *Imitatio* of 1 Kings 17.17–24." *NTS* 32: 247–267.

———. 1986a. "Towards Unravelling the Rhetorical Imitation of Sources in Acts: 2 Kgs 5 as One Component of Acts 8,9–40." *Bib* 67: 41–67.

———. 1989. "The Departure for Jerusalem (Luke 9:51–56) as a Rhetorical Imitation of Elijah's Departure for the Jordan (2 Kgs 1,1–2,6)." *Bib* 70: 96–109.

———. 1989a. "Luke 9:57–62: A Systematic Adaptation of the Divine Challenge to Elijah (1 Kings 19)." In *SBL Seminar Papers*, ed. D. J. Lull. Atlanta: Scholars, 236–245.

———. 1990. "Luke-Acts as an Imitation and Emulation of the Elijah-Elisha Narrative." In *Critical Essays on Luke-Acts*, ed. E. Richard. Wilmington: Glazier, 78–85.

———. 1992. "Not Q but Elijah: The Saving of the Centurion's Servant (Luke 7:1–10) as an Internalization of the Saving of the Widow and her Child (1 Kgs 17: 1–16)." *IrBibSt* 14: 54–71.

———. 1992a. "Fish, Temple Tithe, and Remission: The God-based Generosity of Deuteronomy 14–15 as One Component of the Community Discourse (Matt 17:22–18:35)." *RB* 99: 697–718.

———. 1993. *The Gospel According to St. John: A Literary and Theological Commentary*. New York/Oxford: Oxford University Press.

———. 1993a. *The Quest for the Origin of John's Gospel: A Source-Oriented Approach*. New York/Oxford: Oxford University Press.

———. 1993b. "Vivid, Positive, Practical: The Systematic Use of Romans in Matthew 1–7." *PIBA* 16: 36–55.

———. 1994. "Again Not Q: Luke 7:18–35 as an Acts-oriented Transformation of the Vindication of the Prophet Micaiah (I Kings 22:1–38)." *IrBibSt* 16: 2–30.

———. 1995. "Re-opening the Quest for Proto-Luke: The Systematic Use of Judges 6–12 in Luke 16:1–18:8." *Journal of Higher Criticism*, 2: 68–101.

———. 1995a. "Luke's Redesigning of Paul: Corinthian Division and Reconciliation (1 Corinthians 1–5) as One Component of Jerusalem Unity (Acts 1–5)." *IrBibSt* 17: 98–128.

———. 1996. "The Systematic Use of the Pentateuch in 1 Corinthians: An Exploratory Survey." In *The Corinthian Correspondence*, ed. R. Bieringer. BETL 125. Leuven: Leuven University/Peeters, 441–457.

———. 1997. "Intertextuality and Its Use in Tracing Q and Proto-Luke." In *The Scriptures in the Gospels*, ed. C. M. Tuckett. BETL 131. Leuven: Leuven University/Peeters, 469–477.

———. 1999. "The Unity of Proto-Luke." In *The Unity of Luke-Acts*, ed. J. Verheyden. BETL 142. Leuven: Leuven University/Peeters, 627–638.

———. 2000. *The Crucial Bridge: The Elijah-Elisha Narrative as an Interpretive Synthesis of Genesis-Kings and a Literary Model for the Gospels*. Collegeville, Minn.: Liturgical.

Bronner, Leah. 1968. *The Stories of Elijah and Elisha as Polemics against Baal Worship*. Leiden: Brill.

Brown, John Pairman. 1995. *Israel and Hellas*. BZAW 231. Berlin/New York: De Gruyter.

Brown, Raymond E. 1966. *The Gospel According to John (I-XII)*. AB. New York: Doubleday.

———. 1968. "Hermeneutics." *JBC* 71.

Brownlee, W. H. 1951. "Biblical Interpretations among the Sectaries of the Dead Sea Scrolls." *BA* 14: 54–76.

Brueggemann, Walter. 1968. "David and His Theologian." *CBQ* 30: 156–181.

———. 1971. "Kingship and Chaos (A Study in Tenth Century Theology)." *CBQ* 33: 317–332.

———. 1972. "Life and Death in Tenth Century Israel." *JAAR* 40: 96–109.

———. 1972a. "Weariness, Exile and Chaos (A Motif in Royal Theology)." *CBQ* 34: 19–38.

———. 1973. *In Man We Trust: The Neglected Side of Biblical Faith*. Richmond, Va.: John Knox.

———. 1977. *The Land: Overtures to Biblical Theology*. Philadelphia: Fortress.

Brueggemann, Walter. 1982. *Genesis: Interpretation*. Atlanta: John Knox.

———. 1985. "Genesis." *HBD*, 336–338.

Bultmann, Rudolf. 1952. *Glauben und Verstehen: Gesammelte Aufsätze, II*. Tübingen: J. C. B. Mohr (Paul Siebeck).

———. 1971. *The Gospel of John: A Commentary*. Philadelphia: Westminster.

Burke, Mary T., and Judith G. Miranti, eds. 1995. *Counseling: The Spiritual Dimension*. Alexandria, Va.: American Counseling Association.

Burkert, W. 1992. *The Orientalizing Revolution: Near Eastern Influence on Greek Culture in the Early Archaic Age*. Cambridge, Mass.: Harvard University.

Burn, A. R. 1972. *Revision of A. De Sélincourt's translation of* Herodotus The Histories. Harmondsworth, UK: Penguin.

———. 1985. "Persia and the Greeks." In The Cambridge History of Iran, ed., Ilya Gershevitch, 292–391. See Gershevitch, ed.

Bury, J. B. 1909. *The Ancient Greek Historians*. New York: Macmillan.

Bury, J. B., and Russel Meiggs. 1975. *A History of Greece to the Death of Alexander the Great*. 4th ed. London: Macmillan.

Buss, M. J., ed. 1979. *Encounter with the Text: Form and History in the Hebrew Bible*. Philadelphia: Fortress; and Missoula, Mont.: Scholars.

Butler, George. 1883. *The Public Schools Atlas of Ancient Geography in 28 Maps*. New Edition. London: Longmans, Green, & Co.

Calame, Claude. 1990. *Thésée et l'Imaginaire Athénien: Légende et culte en Grèce antique*. Lausanne: Payot.

* Campbell, Anthony F. and Mark O'Brien. 1993. *Sources of the Pentateuch: Texts, Introductions, Annotations*. Minneapolis: Fortress.

Carlson, R. A. 1970. "Élisée—le successeur d'Élie." *VT* 20: 385–405.

Carmichael, Calum. 1974. *The Laws of Deuteronomy*. Ithaca: Cornell University Press.

———. 1979. *Women, Law, and the Genesis Traditions*. Edinburgh: Edinburgh University Press.

———. 1985. *Law and Narrative in the Bible: The Evidence of the Deuteronomic Laws and the Decalogue*. Ithaca: Cornell University Press.

———. 1996. *The Spirit of Biblical Law*. Athens, GA: University of Georgia Press.

Carr, David M. 1996. *Reading the Fractures in Genesis: Historical and Literary Approaches*. Louisville, Ky.: Westminster John Knox.

Carroll, R. P. 1969. "The Elijah-Elisha Sagas: Some Remarks on Prophetic Succession in Ancient Israel." *VT* 19: 400–415.

Cassuto, Umberto. 1961, 1964. *A Commentary on the Book of Genesis*. 2 vols. Vol. I, *From Adam to Noah*. Vol. 2, *From Noah to Abraham*. Jerusalem: Magnes.

————. 1973. [Hebr 1929]. "The Story of Tamar and Judah." *Biblical and Oriental Studies. Vol I: The Bible.* Jerusalem: Magnes, 29–40.

Cavendish, A. P. 1964. "Early Greek Philosphy." In *A Critical History of Western Philosophy,* ed. D. J. O'Connor. NewYork/London: Macmillan, 1–13.

Cheilik, Michael. 1991. *Ancient History.* 2d ed. Harper Collins College Outline. New York: HarperCollins.

Childs, Brevard S. 1960. *Myth and Reality in the Old Testament.* SBT 27. London: SCM.

* Childs, Brevard S. 1977. *Old Testament Books for Pastor and Teacher.* Philadelphia: Westminster.

————. 1979. *Introduction to the Old Testament as Scripture.* Philadephia: Fortress.

————. 1992. *Biblical Theology of the Old and New Testaments: Theological Reflection on the Christian Bible.* Minneapolis: Fortress.

Chouraqui, André. 1975. "Une Traduction de la Bible." *Etudes* 343: 447–462.

Clifford, Richard J. 1990. "Genesis [1:1–25:18]." *NJBC* 2: 1–42.

————. 1994. *Creation Accounts in the Ancient Near East and in the Bible.* CBQMS 26. Washington, D.C.: Catholic Biblical Association.

Clines, David J. A. 1976. *The Theme of the Pentateuch.* Sheffield, UK: JSOT.

————. 1976a. "Theme in Genesis 1–11." *CBQ* 38: 483–507.

————. 1980. "Story and Poem: The Old Testament as Literature and as Scripture." *Int* 34: 115–127.

————. 1990. *What Does Eve Do to Help? and Other Readerly Questions to the Old Testament.* JSOT Sup 94 Sheffield, UK: Sheffield Academic.

Coats, George W. 1976. *From Canaan to Egypt: Structural and Theological Context for the Joseph Story.* CBQMS 4. Washington, D.C.: CBA.

————. 1983. *Genesis with an Introduction to Narrative Literature.* Forms of OT Literature 1. Grand Rapids, Mich.: Eerdmans.

Cochrane, Charles C. 1984. *The Gospel According to Genesis: A Guide to Understanding Genesis 1–11.* Grand Rapids, Mich.: Eerdmans.

Cohen, Norman J. 1995. *Self, Struggle and Change: Family Conflict Stories in Genesis and Their Healing Insights for Our Lives.* Woodstock, Vt.: Jewish Lights.

————. 1996. "The Test:" A Conversation by Cohen *et al.* on Genesis 22. See Moyers, 1996, 219–247.

Cohn, Robert L. 1996. "Narrative Structure and Canonical Perspective in Genesis." In *The Pentateuch: A Sheffield Reader,* ed. John W. Rogerson. Sheffield, UK: Sheffield Academic, 89–102. Reprinted from *JSOT* 25 (1983): 3–16.

Combs, Eugene and Kenneth Post. 1987. *The Foundations of the Political Order in Genesis and the Chāndogya Upanisad.* SCR 1. Lewiston/Queenstown: Edwin Mellen.

Conroy, C. 1996. "Hiel between Ahab and Elijah-Elisha: 1 Kgs 16,34 in Its Immediate Literary Context." *Bib* 77: 210–218.

Cook, J. M. 1963. *The Greeks in Ionia and the East.* New York: Praeger.

————. 1983. *The Persian Empire.* New York: Schocken.

Copleston, Frederick. 1946. *A History of Philosphy. I: Greece and Rome.* London: Search.

Couture, R. A. 1967. "Salmanticenses." *NCE* 12: 987–988.

Couturier, G. P. 1990. "Jeremiah." *NJBC* 18.

Crenshaw, James L. 1998. *Education in Ancient Israel. Across the Deadening Silence.* New York/London: Doubleday.

Crielaard, Jan Paul. 1995. "Homer, History and Archaelogy: Some Remarks on the Date of the Homeric World." In *Homeric Questions: Essays in Philology, Ancient History and Archaeology,* ed. J. P. Crielaard. Includes Conference Papers: The Netherlands Institute at Athens (1993). Amsterdam: J. C. Gieben, 201–288.

Cross, Frank M. 1973. *Canaanite Myth and Hebrew Epic: Essays in the History of the Religion of Israel.* Cambridge, Mass.: Harvard University Press.

———. 1983. "The Epic Traditions of Early Israel: Epic Narrative and the Reconstruction of Early Israelite Institutions." In *The Poet and the Historian,* ed. R. E. Friedman. HSS 26. Chico, CA: Scholars, 13–39.

Crüsemann, Frank. 1989. "Le Pentateuch, une Tora: Prolégomènes à l'interprétation de sa forme finale." In *Le Pentateuch en Question,* ed. Albert de Pury, 339–360. See De Pury, ed.

———. 1996 [Ger 1992]. *The Torah: Theology and Social History of Old Testament Law.* Edinburgh: T & T Clark.

Culler, Jonathan. 1981. *The Pursuit of Signs: Semiotics, Literature, Deconstruction.* Ithaca, N.Y.: Cornell University Press.

Culpepper, Alan. 1975. *The Johannine School.* SBLDS 26. Missoula, MT: Scholars Press.

———. 1983. *Anatomy of the Fourth Gospel.* Philadelphia: Fortress.

Dahl, Nils. 1975. "The Neglected Factor in New Testament." *Reflection* 73: 5–8.

Dahlberg, Bruce T. 1976. "On Recognizing the Unity of Genesis." *ThDig* 24: 360–367.

———. 1982. "The Unity of Genesis." In *Literary Interpretations II,* ed. K. R. R. Gros Louis, 126–133. See Gros Louis, ed, 1982.

Dällenbach, Lucien. 1986. *Mirrors and After: Five Essays on Literary Theory and Criticism.* New York: City University of New York.

———. 1997. *Le Récit Spéculaire: Contribution a l'Étude de la Mise en Abyme.* Paris: Du Seuil.

Damrosch, David. 1987. *The Narrative Covenant: Transformations of Genre in the Growth of Biblical Literature.* Ithaca, N.Y.: Cornell University.

Darr, Katheryn Pfisterer. 1991. *Far More Precious Than Jewels: Perspectives on Biblical Women.* Louisville: Westminster/John Knox.

* Davies, Graham I. 2001. "Genesis and the Early History of Israel." In *The Book of Genesis,* ed. A. Wénin, 105–134. See Wénin, ed.

Davies, Philip R. 1992. *In Search of "Ancient Israel".* JSOTSup 148. Sheffield, UK: JSOT.

———. 1998. "Genesis and the Gendered World." In *The World of Genesis: Persons, Places, Perspectives,* ed. P. R. Davies and David J. A. Clines. JSOTSup 257. Sheffield, UK: Sheffield Academic, 7–15.

Day, John. 1996. "The Development of Belief in Life After Death in Ancient Israel." In *After the Exile,* eds. J. Barton and D. J. Reimer. Fest. Rex Mason. Sheffield, UK: Sheffield Academic, 231–257.

De Broux, J. 1972. *Het denken van de tijd bij Emmanuel Levinas. Een konfrontatie van Abraham en Odysseus* (licence en philosophie et lettres). Louvain: Katholieke Universiteit Leuven.

Deen, Edith. 1978. *Wisdom from Women in the Bible.* New York/London: Harper & Row.

De Hoop, Raymond. 1999. *Genesis 49 in its Literary and Historical Context.* OTS 39. Leiden/New York/Cologne: Brill.

———. 2001. "The Use of the Past to Address the Present: The Date of Genesis Reconsidered." In *The Book of Genesis,* ed. A. Wénin, 359–370. See Wénin, ed.

Dennis, Trevor. 1994. *Sarah Laughed: Women's Voices in the Old Testament.* Nashville: Abingdon.

De Pury, Albert, ed. 1989. *Le Pentateuch en Question: Les origines et la composition des cinq premiers livres de la Bible à la lumière des recheches récentes.* Le Monde de la Bible no. 19. Geneva: Labor et Fides.

———. 1989. "La tradition patriarcale en Genèse 12–35." In *Le Pentateuch,* ed. De Pury. Geneva: Labor et Fides, 259–270.

———. 2001. "Situer le cycle de Jacob. Quelques réflexions, vingt-cinq ans plus tard." In *The Book of Genesis,* ed. A. Wénin, 213–242. See Wénin, ed.

De Pury, Albert, and Thomas Römer, eds. 1996. *Israël construit son histoire: L'historiographie deutéronomiste à la lumière des recherches récentes.* Geneva: Labor et Fides.

De Romilly, Jacqueline. 1985. [Fr 1980]. *A Short History of Greek Literature.* Chicago/London: University of Chicago Press.

Deurloo, K. A. 1997. "Spooren van het boek Jeremia in Genesis 18:14 en 37:35." *ACEBT* 16: 99–106.

De Vaux, Roland. 1961. *Ancient Israel: Its Life and Institutions.* New York: McGraw-Hill.

———. 1965. *Ancient Israel. Its Life and Institutions.* 2d. ed. London: Darton, Longman & Todd.

———. 1978. *The Early History of Israel.* 2 vols. London: Darton, Longman & Todd.

Douglas, Mary. 1993. *"In the Wilderness: The Doctrine of Defilement in the Book of Numbers."* *JSOT* 158. Sheffield: Sheffield Academie.

———. 1995. "Poetic Structure in Leviticus." In *Pomegranates and Golden Bells: Studies in Biblical, Jewish, and Near Eastern Law, and Literature in Honor of Jacob Milgrom,* eds. David P. Wright et al. Winona Lake, Ind.: Eisenbrauns, 239–256.

———. 1999. *Leviticus as Literature.* New York/London: Oxford University Press.

Dreifuss, Gustav and Judith Riemer. 1995 [Hebr 1993]. *Abraham: The Man and the Symbol. A Jungian Interpretation of the Biblical Story.* Wilmette, Ill.: Chiron.

Drewermann, Eugen. 1977–1978. *Strukturen des Bösen: Die jahwistische Urgeschichte in exegetischer, psychoanalytischer und philosophischer Sicht.* Paderborner Theologische Studien. Munchen/Paderborn/Wien: Schöningh. 3 vols.: 1977: *Teil 1. Die jahwistische Urgeschichte in exegetischer Sicht.* 1977: *Teil 2. Die jahwist. Urgeschichte in psychoanalytischer Sicht.* 1978: *Teil 3. Die jahwist. Urgeschichte in philosophischer Sicht.*

————. 1984, 1985. *Tiefenpsychologie und Exegese.* Olten/Freiburg: Walter. 2 vols.: 1984. *1. Die Wahrheit der Formen. Traum, Mythos, Märchen, Sage und Legende.* 1985. *2. Die Wahrheit der Werke und der Worte. Wunder, Vision, Weissagung, Apokalypse, Geschichte, Gleichnis.*

————. 1988. *"An ihren Früchten sollt ihr sie erkennen." Antwort auf Rudolf Peschs and Gerhard Lohfinks "Tiefenpsychologie und keine Exegese."* Olten/Freiburg: Walter.

————. 1991 [Ger 1990]. *Open Heavens: Meditations for Advent and Christmas.* Maryknoll, N.Y.: Orbis.

————. 1993. *Le Cas Drewermann: Les documents.* Introduced and edited by Bernard Laurent. Paris: Cerf.

————. 1994 [Ger 1986]. *Discovering the God Child Within: A Spiritual Psychology of the Infancy of Jesus.* New York: Crossroad.

Drews, Robert. 1973. *The Greek Account of Eastern History.* Washington, D.C.: Center for Hellenic Studies. Distributed: Cambridge, Mass.: Harvard University.

Elgavish, D. 2001. "The Encounter of Abram and Melchizedek: Covenant Establishment." In *The Book of Genesis,* ed. A. Wénin, 495–508. See Wénin, ed.

Eslinger, Lyle M. 1985. *Kingship of God in Crisis: A Close Reading of 1 Samuel 1–12.* Sheffield, UK: Almond.

Exum, J. Cheryl. 1976. *Literary Patterns in the Samson Saga: An investigation of Rhetorical Style in Biblical Prose.* Ph. D. diss., Columbia University, New York.

————. 1980. "Promise and Fulfilment: Narrative Art in Judges 13." *JBL* 99: 43–59.

————. 1981. "Aspects of Symmetry and Balance in the Samson Saga." *JSOT* 19: 3–29.

Feldman, Louis H. 1996. "Homer and the Near East. The Rise of the Greek Genius." *BA* 59: 13–21.

Fennell, Desmond. 1993. *Heresy: The Battle of Ideas in Modern Ireland.* Belfast: Blackstaff.

Fields, Weston W. 1997. *Sodom and Gomorrah: History and Motif in Biblical Narrative.* JSOTSup 231. Sheffield, UK: Sheffield Academic.

Fischer, Georg. 2001. "Die Josefsgeschichte als Modell für Versöhnung." In *The Book of Genesis,* ed. A. Wénin, 243–272. See Wénin, ed.

Fishbane, Michael. 1979. *Text and Texture: Close Readings of Selected Biblical Texts.* New York: Schocken Books.

————. 1985. *Biblical Interpretation in Ancient Israel.* Oxford: Clarendon.

Fitzgerald, Aloysius. 1968. "Hebrew Poetry." *JBC* 13.

————. 1990. "Hebrew Poetry." *JBC* 12.

Flacelière, Robert. 1964 [Fr 1962]. *A Literary History of Greece.* London: Elek Books.

Fleishman, Joseph. 1997–1998. "The Reason for the Expulsion of Ishmael." *DINÉ ISRAEL: An Annual of Jewish Law Past and Present* 19: 75–100.

————. 1999. " 'Should Our Sister Be Treated Like a Whore?' (Jacob Rebuked by His Sons in Genesis 34:31?)." Paper delivered to the Colloquium Biblicum Lovaniense, Leuven, July 1999.

Fohrer, Geeorg. 1968. *Elia.* 2nd ed. AThANT 53. Zürich: Zwingli.

Fokkelman, Jan P. 1975. *Narrative Art in Genesis: Specimens of Stylistic and Structural Analysis.* 2nd ed. Sheffield, UK: JSOT.

———. 1981–1993. *Narrative Art and Poetry in the Books of Samuel: A Full Interpretation Based on Stylistic and Structural Analyses.* 4 vols. Assen: Van Gorcum.

———. 1987. "Genesis." In *Literary Guide to the Bible,* eds. R. Alter and F. Kermode. Cambridge, Mass.: Belknap, 36–55.

Fox, Everett. 1972. "In the Beginning. An English Rendition of the Book of Genesis." *Response* 14:1–159.

———. 1989. "Can Genesis Be Read as a Book?" *Semeia* 46: 31–40.

Frances, Allen, ed. 1994. *Diagnostic and Statistical Manual of Mental Disorders.* Washington, D.C.: American Psychiatric Association.

Freedman, David Noel. 1963. "The Law and the Prophets." In *Congress Volume Bonn 1962.* VTSup 9. Leiden: Brill, 250–265.

———. 1989. "The Nine Commandments: The Secret Progress of Israel's Sins." *BibRev* 5, no. 6: 28–37, 42.

———. 1991. *The Unity of the Hebrew Bible.* Ann Arbor: University of Michigan Press.

———. 1996. "Crazy Eights or the Importance of Being Eight." Paper delivered to the SBL International Meeting, Dublin, July 26, 1996.

Frei, Hans. 1974. *The Eclipse of Biblical Narrative: A Study in Eighteenth and Nineteenth Century Hermeneutics.* New Haven/London: Yale University Press.

Fretheim, Terence E. 1972. "The Jacob Traditions." *Int* 26: 419–436.

Fretheim, Terence E. 1994. "The Book of Genesis: Introduction, Commentary and Reflections." *NIB* 1: 319–381.

Friedman, Richard Elliott. 1995. "The Deuteronomistic School." In *Fortunate the Eyes that See: Essyas in Honor of David Noel Freedman in Celebration of His Seventieth Birthday,* eds. A. B. Beck et al. Grand Rapids, Mich.: Eerdmans, 70–80.

———. 1996. "Some Recent Non-Arguments Concerning the Documentary Hypothesis." In *Texts, Temples, and Traditions: A Tribute to Menachem Haran,* ed. Michael V. Fox et al. Winona Lake, Ind.: Eisenbrauns, 87–101.

———. 1998. *The Hidden Book in the Bible: The Discovery of the First Prose Masterpiece.* San Francisco: HarperSan Francisco.

Frye, Northrop. 1981. *The Great Code: The Bible and Literature.* New York/London: Harcourt Brace Jovanovich.

Frye, Richard N. 1984. *The History of Ancient Iran.* Munich: Beck'sche.

Gabel, John B., Charles B. Wheeler, and Anthony D. York. 1996. *The Bible as Literature: An Introduction.* 3rd ed. New York/Oxford: Oxford University.

Gage, W. A. 1984. *The Gospel of Genesis: Studies in Protology and Eschatology.* Winona Lake, Ind.: Carpenter Books.

Gammie, John G. 1979. "Theological Interpretation by Way of Literary and Tradition Analysis: Genesis 25–36." In *Encounter with the Text,* ed. M. J. Buss, 117–134. See Buss.

Garland, Robert. 1992. *Introducing New Gods: The Politics of Athenian Religion.* Ithaca, N.Y.: Cornell University.

Garraty, J. A., and P. Gay, eds. 1972. *The Columbia History of the World*. New York/London: Harper & Row.

Garsiel, Moshe. 1985 [Heb 1983]. *The First Book of Samuel: A Literary Study of Comparative Structures, Analogies and Parallels*. Ramat-Gan, Israel: Revivim.

Gassmann, Lothar and Johannes Lange. 1993. *Was nun, Herr Drewermann?* Lahr, Germany: Liebenzeller Mission.

Gelb, I. J. 1963. *A Study of Writing*. 2nd ed. Chicago/London: Chicago University Press.

Gellman, Jerome I. 1994. *The Fear, The Trembling, and The Fire: Kierkegaard and Hasidic Masters on the Binding of Isaac*. Landham, Md./New York/London: University Press of America.

Gershevitch, Ilya, ed. 1985. *The Cambridge History of Iran*, Vol. II. London/New York: Cambridge University Press.

Giblin, Charles H. 1985. "Two Complementary Literary Structures in John 1:1–18." *JBL* 104: 87–103.

Gilders, William K. 1997. "The Sin of Sodom: A Jewish Interpretive Tradition from Ezekiel to Nachmanides." Paper delivered to the New England SBL Regional Meeting, March 21, 1997.

Gillmayr-Bucher, Susanne. 1998. "The Woman of Their Dreams: The Image of Rebekah in Genesis 24." In *The World of Genesis: Persons, Places, Perspectives*, ed. P. R. Davies and David J. A. Clines. JSOTSup 257. Sheffield, UK: Sheffield Academic, 90–101.

———. 2001. "Gen 24: Ein Mosaik aus Texten." In *The Book of Genesis*, ed. A. Wénin, 521–532. See Wénin, ed.

Gordon, Cyrus H. 1962. *Before the Bible: The Common Background of Greek and Hebrew Civilizations*. London: Collins.

———. 1963. "The Mediterranean Factor in the Old Testament." In *Congress Volume Bonn 1962*. VTSup 9. Leiden: Brill, 19–31.

———. 1978. "Build-Up and Climax." In *Studies in Bible and the Ancient Near East*, eds. Yitschak Avishur and Joshua Blau. Jerusalem: E. Rubenstein, 29–34.

Gossai, Hemchand. 1995. *Power and Marginality in the Abraham Narrative*. Lanham, Md. /New York/London: University Press of America.

Gosse, Bernard. 1997. *Structuration des grands ensembles bibliques et intertextualité à l'époque perse: De la rédaction sacerdotale du livre d'Isïe à la contestation de la Sagesse*. BZAW 246. Berlin/New York: De Gruyter.

Gowan, Donald J. 1988. *From Eden to Babel: A Commentary on the Book of Genesis 1–11*. ITC. Grand Rapids, Mich.: Eerdmans; and Edinburgh: Handsel.

Grabbe, Lester L. 1994. *Judaism from Cyrus to Hadrian*. London: SCM. (First issued in two vols., Minneapolis: Fortress, 1992).

Graf, David F. 1994. "The Persian Royal Road System." In *Achaemenid History VIII: Continuity and Change*, ed. Heleen Sancisi-Weerdenburg et al. Proceedings of the Last Achaemenid History Workshop. Leiden: Nederlands Instituut voor het Nabije Oosten, 167–189.

Grayson, A. K. 1975. *Assyrian and Babylonian Chronicles*. Locust Valley, N.Y.: J. J. Augustin.

Green, Barbara. 1996. *"What Profit For Us?" Remembering the Story of Joseph.* Lanham, Md.: University Press of America.

Greenberg, Moshe. 1995. "To Whom and for What Should a Bible Commentator Be Responsible?" In *Studies in the Bible and Jewish Thought.* Philadelphia/Jerusalem: Jewish Publication Society, 235–243.

Greenfield, J. C. 1985. "Aramaic in the Achaemenian Empire." In *The Cambridge History of Iran,* ed. I. Gershevitch, 698–713. See Gershevitch.

Greenstein, Edward L. 1982. "An Equivocal Reading of the Sale of Joseph." In *Literary Interpretations, II,* ed. K. R. R. Gros Louis, 114–125. See Gros Louis, ed., 1982.

Griffin, J. 1980. *Homer.* Past Masters. Oxford/New York: Oxford University Press.

Gros Louis, Kenneth R. R., ed. 1974. *Literary Interpretations of Biblical Narratives.* Nashville/New York: Abingdon.

———. 1982. *Literary Interpretations of Biblical Narratives. Vol II.* Nashville: Abingdon.

Gunkel, Hermann. 1901. Revised 1910. *Genesis, übersetzt und erklärt.* Göttingen: Vandenhoek & Ruprecht. (Post 1910 editions unchanged).

———. 1907. *The Legends of Genesis.* A translation of the first edition [1901] of the introduction to Gunkel's commentary on Genesis. Chicago: Open Court.

———. 1964. *The Legends of Genesis. The Biblical Saga and History.* A reissue of the preceding book (Gunkel, 1907), with an introduction by W. F. Albright. New York: Schocken.

———. 1994. *The Stories of Genesis.* A translation of the introduction to the third, expanded edition [1910] of Gunkel's commentary on Genesis. With an added introduction by the translator, J. J. Scullion. Vallejo, Calif.: Bibal.

Gunn, David M., ed. 1991. *Narrative and Novella in Samuel: Studies by Hugo Gressmann and Other Scholars 1906–1923.* JSOTSup 116. Sheffield, UK: Almond.

* Gunneweg, A. H. J. 1985. "Anmerkungen und Anfragen zur neueren Pentateuchforschung." *TRu* 50: 107–131.

Gusdorf, G. 1967. *Les Sciences Humaines et la Pensée Occidentale, II: Les Origines des Sciences Humaines.* Paris: Payot.

———. 1974. "Humanistic Scholarship, History of." *Encyclopedia Britannica*[3,] *Macropaedia,* 8, 1170–1179.

Ha, John. 1989. *Genesis 15: A Theological Compendium of Pentateuchal History.* BZAW 181. Berlin/New York: De Gruyter.

Habel, Norman. 1971. *Literary Criticism of the Old Testament.* Guides to Biblical Scholarship. Philadephia: Fortress.

———. 1975. "The Form and Significance of the Call Narrative." *ZAW* 77: 297–323.

———. 1995. *The Land Is Mine: Six Biblical Land Ideologies.* Overtures to Biblical Theology. Minneapolis: Fortress.

Hagelia, H. 1994. *Numbering the Stars: A Phraseological Analysis of Genesis 15.* CB OT 39. Stockholm: Almqvist & Wiksell International.

Hallo, W. W. 1992. "Sumerian Literature." *ABD* VI: 234–237.

Hallo, W. W., and K. L. Younger, eds. 1997– . *The Context of Scripture*. Vol 1, 1997; vol. 2, 2000; vol. 3, 2001. Leiden/New York/Köln: Brill,.

Halpern, Baruch. 1988. *The First Historians: The Hebrew Bible and History*. San Francisco: Harper & Row.

———. 1995. "What They Don't Know Won't Hurt Them: Genesis 6–9." In *Fortunate the Eyes That See: Essays in Honor of David Noel Freedman in Celebration of His Seventieth Birthday*, ed. A. B. Beck et al. Grand Rapids, Mich.: Eerdmans, 16–34.

Hamilton, Victor P. 1990, 1995. *The Book of Genesis*. 2 vols. 1990: Chaps. 1–17; 1995: Chaps. 18–50. Grand Rapids, Mich.: Eerdmans.

Hanaghan, Jonathan. 1979. *The Beast Factor*. Tansy Books. Enniskerry, Wicklow, Ireland: Egotist.

Harl, Marguerite. 1986. *La Bible D'Alexandrie, LXX. I: La Genèse*. Paris: Du Cerf.

Harrington, Daniel. 1986. "Palestinian Adaptations of Biblical Narratives and Prophecies. 1. The Bible Rewritten (Narratives)." In *Early Judaism and Its Modern Interpreters*, ed. R. A. Kraft and G. W. E. Nickelsburg. Atlanta: Scholars, 239–247.

Harrington, Wilfrid J. 1965. *Record of the Fulfilment: The New Testament*. Chicago: Priory.

Harsh, Philip Whaley. 1944. *A Handbook of Classical Drama*. Stanford, Calif.: Stanford University Press.

Hartman, G. H., and S. Budick, eds. 1986. *Midrash and Literature*. New Haven/London: Yale University Press.

Hauser, Alan J. 1980. "Linguistic and Thematic Links Between Genesis 4:1–16 and Genesis 2–3." *JETS* 23: 297–305.

———. 1982. "Genesis 2–3: The Theme of Intimacy and Alienation." In *Art and Meaning: Rhetoric in Biblical Literature*, ed. D. J. A. Clines et al. JSOTSup 19. Sheffield, UK: JSOT, 20–36. (Reprinted in Hess and Tsumura, eds. 1994, 383–398.)

Havel, Václav. 1997. "The Future of Hope." *Religion and Values in Public Life*, Harvard Divinity School 5 (No. 2/3): 1–3.

Havelock, Eric A. 1963. *Preface to Plato*. Cambridge, Mass./London: Harvard University Press.

Hayes, John H. 1977. "The History of the Study of Israelity and Judean History." In *Israelite and Judean History*, ed. J. H. Hayes and J. M. Miller. Philadelphia: Westminster, 1–70.

Heaton, E. W. 1994. *The School Tradition of the Old Testament: The Bampton Lectures for 1994*. New York/Oxford: Oxford University Press.

Hegel. *See* Wallace.

Heidel, A. 1951. *The Babylonian Genesis. The Story of Creation*. 2nd ed. Chicago/London: University of Chicago Press.

Herion, Gary A. 1995. "Why God Rejected Cain's Offering: The Obvious Answer." In *Fortunate the Eyes that See: Essays in Honor of David Noel Freedman in Celebration of His Seventieth Birthday,*, ed. A. B. Beck et al. Grand Rapids, Mich.: Eerdmans, 52–65.

Heschel, Abraham J. 1962. *The Prophets*. New York/Evanston: Harper & Row.

* Hess, Richard S., and David T. Tsumura, eds. 1994. *"I Studied Inscriptions from before the Flood": Ancient Near Eastern, Literary, and Linguistic Approaches to Genesis 1–11.* Sources for Biblical and Theological Study 4. Winona Lake, Ind.: Eisenbrauns.

* Hess, Richard S. 1994a. "One Hundred Fifty Years of Comparative Studies on Genesis 1–11: An Overview." In *I Studied Inscriptions,* ed. R. S. Hess and D. T. Tsumura, 3–26. See Hess and Tsamura, eds.

* ———. 1994b. "The Genealogies of Genesis 1–11 and Comparative Literature." In *I Studied Inscriptions,* ed. R. S. Hess and D. T. Tsumura, 58–72. See Hess and Tsamura, eds.

Highet, Gilbert. 1949. *The Classical Tradition: Greek and Roman Influences on Western Literature.* New York/London: Oxford University Press.

Hoekveld-Meijer, Gerda. 1996. *Esau. Salvation in Disguise. Genesis 36. A Hidden Polemic Between Our Teacher and the Prophets about Edom's Role in Post-Exilic Israel through Leitwort Names.* Kampen: Pharos.

Hooke, S. H. 1962. "Genesis." *PCB,* 175–207.

Hoop, de. See De Hoop.

Horgan, Maurya P. 1979. *Pesharim: Qumran Interpretations of Biblical Books.* CBQMS 8. Washington, D.C.: Catholic Biblical Association.

* Houtman, C. 1994 (first published 1980). *Der Pentateuch: Die Geschichte seiner Erforschung neben einer Auswertung.* Contributions to Biblical Exegesis and Theology 9. Kampen: Kok Pharos.

Humphreys, W. Lee. 1988. *Joseph and His Family: A Literary Study.* Columbia, S.C.: University of South Carolina Press.

Hurvitz, A. 1988. "Dating the Priestly Source in Light of the Historical Study of Biblical Hebrew a Century After Wellhausen." *ZAW* Supplement 100: 88–100.

———. 1995. "Terms and Epithets Relating to the Jerusalem Temple Compound in the Book of Chronicles: The Linguistic Aspect." In *Pomegranates and Golden Bells: Studies in Biblical, Jewish, and Near Eastern Law, and Literature in Honor of Jacob Milgrom,* eds. David P. Wright et al. Winona Lake, Ind.: Eisenbrauns, 165–183.

———. 1997. "The Historical Quest for 'Ancient Israel' and the Linguistic Evidence of the Hebrew Bible: Some Methodological Observations." *VT* 47: 301–315.

Illich, Ivan. 1973. *Celebration of Awareness. A Call for Institutional Revolution.* Harmondsworth, UK: Penguin.

Irvin, Dorothy. 1977. "The Joseph and Moses Stories as Narrative in the Light of Ancient Near Eastern Narrative." In *Israelite and Judean History,* ed. J. H. Hayes and J. M. Miller. Philadelphia: Westminster, 180–203.

Irving, Clive. 1979. *Crossroads of Civilization: 3000 Years of Persian History.* London: Weidenfeld & Nicolson.

Interprovincial Consultation of the Church of England . . . Ireland . . . Wales . . . Scot[land]. 1995. *Lectionaries for Trial Use in the Church of Ireland.* Dublin: General Synod of the Church of Ireland.

Jacob, Benno. 1974. *The First Book of the Bible.* Abridged, edited, and translated by E. I. Jacob and Walter Jacob. New York: KTAV.

Janzen, J. Gerald. 1993. *Abraham and All the Families of the Earth: A Commentary on the Book of Genesis 12–50.* ITC. Grand Rapids, Mich.: Eerdmans; and Edinburgh: Handsel.

Jeansonne, Sharon Pace. 1990. *The Women of Genesis: From Sarah to Potiphar's Wife.* Minneapolis: Fortress.

Jones, James W. 1996. *Religion and Psychology in Transition: Psychoanalysis, Feminism, and Theology.* New Haven/London: Yale University Press.

Kahn, Charles H. 1996. "Xenophanes." *OCD* 3, 1628.

Kaplan, C. 1975. *Criticism: The Major Statements.* New York: St. Martin's.

Kassel, Maria. 1980. *Biblische Urbilder: Tiefenpsychologische Auslegung nach C. G. Jung.* Munich: Pfeiffer.

Kessler, Martin, 1974. "Rhetorical Criticism of Genesis 7." *Pittsburgh Theological Monograph Series.* 1:1–17.

Kierkegaard, Søren. 1843. *Fear and Trembling.* Published in *Fear and Trembling And The Sickness unto Death.* Translated with Introduction and Notes by Walter Lowrie. Garden City, N.Y.: Doubleday, 1954.

Kikawada, Isaac. M. 1973. "The Unity of Genesis 12:1–9." *PWCJS* 6: 229–235.

———. 1974. "The Shape of Genesis 11:1–9." *Rhetorical Criticism: Essays in Honor of James Muilenberg,* eds. Jared J. Jackson and Martin Kessler. Pittsburg: Pickwick, 18–22.

Kikawada, Isaac M., and A. Quinn. 1985. *Before Abraham Was: The Unity of Genesis 1–11.* Nashville: Abingdon.

Kille, D. Andrew. 1995. "Jacob: A Study in Individuation." In *Jung,* ed. David L. Miller, 40–54. See Miller, David L., ed.

Kim, J. 1993. *The Structure of the Samson Cycle.* Kampen: Pharos.

Kimbrough, Kim. 1982. "Review of Drewermann, *Strukturen des Bösen. Teil 3.*" *JBL* 101: 423–427.

Kissling, Paul J. 1996. *Reliable Characters in the Primary History: Profiles of Moses, Joshua, Elijah and Elisha.* JSOTSup 224. Sheffield, UK: Sheffield Academic.

Kleinig, John W. 1994. "Recent Research in Chronicles." *Currents in Research. Biblical Studies* 2: 43–76.

* Knight, Douglas A. 1985. "The Pentateuch: A Synthesis and Its Dissolution." In *The Hebrew Bible and Its Modern Interpreters,* ed. D. A. Knight and Gene M. Tucker. Philadelphia: Fortress, 263–296.

Knoppers, Gary N. 1997. "The Vanishing Solomon: The Disappearance of the United Monarchy from Recent Histories of Ancient Israel." *JBL* 116: 19–44.

Korsak, M. P. 1993. *At the Start: Genesis Made New. A Translation of the Hebrew Text.* New York/London: Doubleday.

Kristeva, Julia. 1980. *Desire in Language: A Semiotic Approach to Literature and Art.* Translated and introduced by Leon S. Roudiez. New York: Columbia University Press.

Kruger, H. 2001. "Subscripts to Creation Acts: Motifs of Renewal, Reversal, and Moderation. A Few Exegetical Comments on Gen 8,1–9,29." In *The Book of Genesis,* ed. A. Wénin, 429–446. See Wénin, ed..

Kselman, John S. 1988, "Genesis." *HBC,* 85–128.

Kuhn, Thomas S. 1970. *The Structure of Scientific Revolutions.* 2nd ed. Chicago/ London: University of Chicago Press.

Kuhrt, Amélie, and Heleen Sancisi-Weerdenburg. 1991. "Introduction." In *Achaemenid History VI. Asia Minor and Egypt: Old Cultures in a New Empire,* ed. Heleen Sancisi-Weerdenburg et al. Proceedings of the 1988 Achaemenid History Workshop. Leiden: Nederlands Instituut voor het Nabije Oosten, xiii–xviii.

Kuntzmann, R. 1983. *Le symbolisme des Jumeaux au Proche-Orient Ancient: Naissance, fonction, et évolution d'un symbole.* Paris: Cerf.

———. 2001. "Jacob et le thème de la lutte initiatique dans le livre de la Genèse: pertinence et intérêt d'une lecture symboliste." In *The Book of Genesis,* ed. A. Wénin, 533–540. See Wénin, ed.

Lambe, Anthony J. 1998. "Genesis 38: Structure and Literary Design." In *The World of Genesis: Persons, Places, Perspectives,* ed. P. R. Davies and David J. A. Clines. JSOTSup 257. Sheffield, UK: Sheffield Academic, 102–120.

Lamberton, Robert, and John J. Keaney. 1992. *Homer's Ancient Readers: The Hermeneutics of Greek Epic's Earliest Exegetes.* Princeton, N.J.: Princeton University Press.

Lamberton, Robert. 1993. *Hesiod: Works and Days, and Theogony.* Introduction, Notes and Glossary by Robert Lamberton. Indianapolis/Cambridge: Hackett.

Lattimore, Richard. 1965. *The Odyssey of Homer: A Modern Translation.* New York/ San Francisco: Harper & Row.

Leach, Edmund. 1969. *Genesis as Myth and Other Essays.* London: Cape.

Lechte, John. 1994. *Fifty Key Contemporary Thinkers: From structuralism to postmodernity.* London/New York: Routledge.

Le Déaut, Roger. 1971. "Apropos a Definition of Midrash." *Int* 25: 259–282.

Lemaire, André. 1981. *Les Écoles et la Formation de la Bible dans l'Ancient Isra·'* OBO 39. Göttingen: Vandenhoeck & Ruprecht.

———. 1992. "Writing and Writing Materials." *ABD* VI: 999–1008.

Lesky, Albin. 1966. *A History of Greek Literature.* New York: Thomas Y. Crowell.

Letellier, R. I. 1995. *Day in Mamre, Night in Sodom: Abraham and Lot in Genesis 18 and 19.* BIS 10. Leiden/New York/Cologne: Brill.

Levenson, J. D. 1985. *Sinai and Zion: An Entry Into the Jewish Bible.* Minneapolis/ Chicago/New York: Winston.

Levin, S. 1991. "The Abel Syndrome." *JBQ* 20: 111–114.

Levine, Herbert J. 1990. "The Dialogic Discourse of Psalms." In *Mappings of the Biblical Terrain: The Bible as Text,* ed. Vincent L. Tollers and John Maier. Bucknell Review. Lewisburg: Bucknell University Press; London/Toronto: Associated University Press, 268–281.

Levinson, Bernard M. 1990. "Calum M. Carmichael's Approach to the Laws of Deuteronomy." *HTR* 83: 227–257.

———. 1997. *Deuteronomy and the Hermeneutics of Legal Innovation.* New York: Oxford University Press.

Livermore, H. V. 1966. *A New History of Portugal.* Cambridge: Cambridge University Press.

Loewald, H. 1978. *Psychoanalysis and the History of the Individual.* New Haven: Yale University.

Lohfink, Gerhard, and Rudolf Pesch. 1987. *Tiefenpsychologie und keine Exegese: Ein Auseinandersetzung mit Eugen Drewermann.* StBib 129. Stuttgart: Katholisches Bibelwerk GmbH.

Long, Burke. 1973. "2 Kings III and Genres of Prophetic Narrative." *VT* 23: 337–348.

Long, V. Philips. 1989. *The Reign and Rejection of King Saul: A Case for Literary and Theological Coherence.* SBLDS 118. Atlanta: Scholars.

Longacre, Robert E. 1979. "The Discourse of the Flood Narrative." *JAAR* 47: 133.

———. 1985. "Interpreting Biblical Stories." In *Discourse and Literature,* ed. Teun A. Van Dijk. Philadelphia: John Benjamins, 169–185.

———. 1989. *Joseph: A Story of Divine Providence. A Text Theoretical and Textlinguistic Analysis of Genesis 37 and 39–48.* Winona Lake, Ind.: Eisenbrauns.

* Longman III, Tremper. 1995. *Old Testament Commentary Survey.* 2d. ed. Grand Rapids, Mich.: Baker Books, 58–65.

Luckenbill, Daniel David. 1926–1927. *Ancient Records of Assyria and Babylonia.* 2 vols. Chicago: University of Chicago Press.

MacDonald, Ronald. 1994. *Christianizing Homer: The Odyssey, Plato, and the Acts of Andrew.* New York/Oxford: Oxford University Press.

Macqueen, J. G. 1995. "The History of Anatolia and of the Hittite Empire: An Overview." *CANE* II: 1095–1105.

Maher, Michael. 1982. *Genesis.* OT Message. Wilmington: Glazier.

Malamat, Abraham. 1968. "King Lists of the Old Babylonian Period and Biblical Genealogies." *JAOS* 88: 163–173. Reprinted in *I Studied Inscriptions,* ed. R. S. Hess and D. T. Tsumura, 183–199. See Hess and Tsamura, eds.

Mallowan, Max. 1985. "Cyrus the Great (558–529)." In *The Cambridge History of Iran,* ed. Ilya Gershevitch, 420–501. See Gershevitch, ed.

Maly, Eugene H. 1968. "Genesis." *JBC* 2.

Mandela, Nelson. 1994. *Long Walk to Freedom: The Autobiography of Nelson Mandela.* Randburg, South Africa: Macdonald Purnell.

Mann, Jacob. 1940. *The Bible as Read and Preached in the Old Synagogue. Vol. I. The Palestinian Triennial Cycle: Genesis and Exodus.* New York: KTAV. Reprinted 1971.

Mann, Thomas W. 1988. *The Book of the Torah: The Narrative Integrity of the Pentateuch.* Atlanta: John Knox.

Marblestone, H. 1996. "A 'Mediterranean Synthesis': Professor Cyrus H. Gordon's Contributions to the Classics." *BA* 59: 22–30.

Margalit, Baruch. 1999. "Jacob and the Angel (Gen. 32, 23–33) in Light of the Balaam Text from Deir 'Alla (DAPT)." Paper delivered to the Colloquium Biblicum Lovaniense, Leuven, July 1999.

Matthews, Victor H. 1995. "The Anthropology of Clothing in the Joseph Narrative." *JSOT* 65: 23–36.

May, Rollo. 1972. *Love and Will.* Fontana. London: Collins.

McConville, J. G. and J. G. Millar. 1994. *Time and Place in Deuteronomy.* JSOT Sup 179. Sheffield, UK: Sheffield Academic.

McDargh, John. 1993. "Concluding Clinical Postscript: On Developing a Psychotheological Perspective." In *Exploring Sacred Landscapes: Religious and Spiri-*

tual Experiences in Psychotherapy, ed. M. L. Randour. New York: Columbia University Press, 172–193.

McKenzie, John L. 1968. *Dictionary of the Bible*. London: Chapman.

McGuire, Erol. 1981. "The Joseph Story: A Tale of Son and Father." In *Images of Man and God: Old Testament Stories in Literary Focus*, ed. Burke O. Long. BLS 1. Sheffield UK: Almond, 9–25.

Meissner, W. W. 1984. *Psychoanalysis and Religious Experience*. New Haven/London: Yale University Press.

———. 1987. *Life and Faith: Psychological Perspectives on Religious Experience*. Washington, D.C.: Georgetown University Press.

Merry, W. W. 1899. *Homer: Odyssey, Books I–XII*. Oxford: Clarendon.

Merton, Thomas. 1961. *New Seeds of Contemplation*. A New Directions Book. Norfolk, Conn.: James Laughlin.

Meyers, C. L. 1985. "The Tree of Life." *HBD*, 1094.

Millard, A. 1995. "The Knowledge of Writing in Iron Age Palestine." *TynB* 46: 207–217.

Miller, David L., ed. 1995. *Jung and the Interpretation of the Bible*. New York: Continuum.

Miller, J. M. 1966. "The Elisha Cycle and the Accounts of the Omride Wars." *JBL* 85: 441–454.

Miller, Patrick D. 1978. *Genesis 1–11: Studies in Structure and Theme*. Sheffield, UK: JSOT.

Miller, William T. 1984. *Mysterious Encounters at Mamre and Jabbok*. Brown Judaic Studies 50. Chico, Calif.: Scholars.

* Minor, Mark. 1992. *Literary Approaches to the Bible: An Annotated Bibliography*. West Cornwall, Conn.: Locust Hill.

Mitchell, Stephen. 1996. *Genesis: A New Translation of the Classical Biblical Stories*. New York: HarperCollins.

Moberly, R. W. L. 1992. *Genesis 12–50*. OT Guides. Sheffield: Sheffield Academic.

———. 1992a. *The Old Testament of the Old Testament: Patriarchal Narratives and Mosaic Yahwism*. OBT. Minneapolis: Fortress.

Moran, William. 1995. "The Gilgamesh Epic: A Masterpiece from Ancient Mesopotamia." *CANE* IV: 2327–2336.

Morize, André. 1922. *Problems and Methods of Literary History*. Boston: Gill.

Morris, Sarah P. 1992. *Daidalos and the Origins of Greek Art*. Princeton, N.J.: Princeton University Press.

Moyers, Bill. 1996. *Genesis: A Living Conversation*. New York/London: Doubleday.

Müller, Hans-Peter. 1997. "Eine griechische Parallele zu Motiven von Genesis i–ii." *VT* 47: 478–486.

Murphy, Roland E. 1990. "Genesis [25:19–50:26]." *NJBC* 2: 43–73.

———. 1993. Review of Rainer Albertz, *Relegionsgeschichte Israel, Vol 1*. *OTA* 16: 183.

Nagy, Gregory. 1990. *Greek Mythology and Poetics*. Ithaca, N.Y.: Cornell University Press.

Naom, Gil G., and Maryanne Wolf. 1993. "Psychology and Spirituality: Forging a New Relationship." In *Exploring Sacred Landscapes: Religious and Spiritual Ex-*

periences in Psychotherapy, ed. M. L. Randour. New York: Columbia University Press, 194–207.

Negenman, Ian H. 1969. *New Atlas of the Bible*. London: Collins.

Newsom, Carol A. 1996. "Bakhtin, the Bible, and Dialogic Truth." *JR* 76: 290–306.

————. 1996a. "The Book of Job as Polyphonic Text." Paper delivered to the Society for OT Study, Winter meeting, Birmingham, England, January 4,1996.

Niccacci, Alviero. 1994. "Diluvio, Sintassi e Methodo." *Liber Annus Studii Biblici Franciscani* 44: 9–46.

Nicol, George G. 1996. "Jacob as Oedipus: Old Testament as Mythology." *ExpT* 108: 43–44.

Niditch, Susan. 1992. "Genesis." In *The Women Bible's Commentary*, ed. Carol A. Newsom and Sharon H. Ringe. Louisville: Westminster/John Knox, 10–25.

————. 1996. *Oral World and Written Word: Ancient Israelite Literature*. Library of Ancient Israel. Louisville, Ky.: Westminster/John Knox.

Noble, Paul. 1996. "A 'Balanced' Reading of the Rape of Dinah: Some Exegetical and Methodological Observations." *BI* 4: 173–204.

Noth, Martin. 1968. *Numbers: A Commentary*. London: SCM.

O'Brien, J., and W. Major. 1982. *In the Beginning: Creation Myths from Ancient Mesopotamia, Israel and Greece*. Aids for the Study of Religion 11. Chico, CA: Scholars.

Ochs, Carol. 1994. *Song of the Self: Biblical Spirituality and Human Holiness*. Valley Forge, Pa.: Trinity Press International.

Olmstead, A. T. 1948. *History of the Persian Empire*. Chicago: University of Chicago Press.

Ong, Walter. 1971. *Rhetoric, Romance and Technology: Studies in the Interaction of Expression and Culture*. Ithaca, N.Y./London: Cornell University Press.

————. 1977. *Interfaces of the Word: Studies in the Evolution of Consciousness and Culture*. Ithaca/London: Cornell University Press.

————. 1982. *Orality and Literacy: The Technologizing of the Word*. London/New York: Methuen.

Onians, Richard B. 1951. *The Origins of European Thought about the Body, the Mind, the Soul, the World, Time, and Fate: New Interpretations of Greek, Roman and Kindred Evidence Also of Some basic Jewish and Christian Beliefs*: Cambridge: Cambridge University Press.

Overholt, Thomas W. 1996. *Cultural Anthropology and the Old Testament*. Guides to Biblical Scholarship. Minneapolis: Fortress.

Parker, Simon B. 1989. *The Pre-Biblical Narrative Tradition: Essays on the Ugaritic Poems Keret and Aqhat*. SBL Resources for Biblical Study 24. Atlanta, Ga.: Scholars.

————. 1995. "The Literatures of Canaan, Ancient Israel, and Phoenicia: An Overview." *CANE* IV: 2309–2410.

Pearson, Lionel. 1939. *Early Ionian Historians*. Oxford: Clarendon.

————. 1942. *The Local Historians of Attica*. Philological Monographs, XI. Philadephia: American Philological Association.

Peck, Scott M. 1978. *The Road Less Travelled: A New Psychology of Love, Traditional Values and Spiritual Growth.* New York: Simon and Schuster.

Peckham, Brian. 1985. *The Composition of the Deuteronomistic History.* HSM 25. Atlanta: Scholars.

———. 1993. *History and Prophecy: The Development of Late Judean Literary Traditions.* New York/London: Doubleday.

Perrot, Charles. 1988. "The Reading of the Bible in the Ancient Synagogue." In *Mikra: Text, Translation, Reading and Interpretation of the Hebrew Bible in Ancient Judaism and Early Christianity,* ed. Martin J. Mulder. Assen/Maastrict: Van Gorcum; and Philadelphia: Fortress, 137–159.

Pleins, J. David. 1995. "Murderous Fathers, Manipulative Mothers, and Rivalrous Siblings: Rethinking the Architecture of Genesis-Kings." In *Fortunate the Eyes That See: Essays in Honor of David Noel Freedman in Celebration of His Seventieth Birthday,* ed. A. B. Beck et al. Grand Rapids, Mich.: Eerdmans, 121–136.

Polzin, Robert. 1980. *Moses and the Deuteronomist: A Literary Study of the Deuteronomic History, Part 1.* Bloomington/Indianapolis: Indiana University Press.

———. 1989. *Samuel and the Deuteronomist: A Literary Study of the Deuteronomic History, Part 2.* San Francisco: Harper & Row.

———. 1993. *David and the Deuteronomist: A Literary Study of the Deuteronomic History, Part 3.* Bloomington/Indianapolis: Indiana University Press.

Pontifical Biblical Commission. 1994. "The Interpretation of the Bible in the Church." *Catholic International: The Documentary Window on the World* 5 (March): 109–147.

Pope, Marvin H. 1977. *Song of Songs: A New Translation with Introduction and Commentary.* AB. Garden City, N.Y.: Doubleday.

Porton, Gary. 1979. "Midrash, Palestinian Jews and the Hebrew Bible in the Greco-Roman Period." *ANRW* XIX 2. New York/Berlin: De Gruyter, 259–282.

———. 1985. *Understanding Rabbinic Midrash: Texts and Midrash.* Hoboken, N.J.: Ktav.

Powell, Corey S. 1992. "Born Yesterday. A Younger Universe May Spell Trouble for Cosmology." *Scientific American* 266 (May): 28–30.

*Powell, Mark A. 1992. *The Bible and Modern Literary Criticism: A Critical Assessment and Annotated Bibliography.* BIRS 22. New York/Westport, Conn./London: Greenwood.

Preminger, A., ed. 1975. *Princeton Encyclopedia of Poetry and Poetics.* Enlarged edition. Princeton: Princeton University Press.

*Preuss, Horst D. 1993. "Zum deuteronomistischen Geschichtswerk." *TRu* 58: 229–264, 341–395.

Pritchard, J. B., ed. 1950. *Ancient Near Eastern Texts Relating to the Old Testament.* Princeton: Princeton University Press.

———. 1987. *The Times Atlas of the Bible.* London: Times Books.

Puri, Baijnath. 1963. *India in Classical Greek Writings.* Ahmedabad: New Order Book Company.

Radcliffe, Timothy. 1997. "Religious Vocations: Leaving Behind the Usual Signs of Identity." *Religious Life Review* 36: 20–34.

Radday, Y. T., and H. Shore. 1985. *Genesis: An Authorship Study*. AnBib 103. Rome: Biblical Institute.

Redford, Donald, B. 1995. "Ancient Egyptian Literature: An Overview." *CANE* IV: 2223–2241.

Rendsburg, Gary A. 1990. "Redactional Structuring in the Joseph Story: Genesis 37–50." In *Mappings of the Biblical Terrain: The Bible as Text. Bucknell Review*, ed. Vincent L. Tollers and John Maier. Lewisburg: Bucknell University; and London/Toronto: Associated University Press, 215–232.

Rendtorff, Rolf. 1977. *Das überlieferungsgeschichte Problem des Pentateuch*. BZAW 147. Giessen: Berlin.

———. 1990 [Ger 1977]. *The Problem of the Process of Transmission in the Pentateuch*. JSOTSup 89. Sheffield, UK: Sheffield Academic.

———. 1993. "The Paradigm is Changing: Hopes and Fears." *BI* 1: 34–53.

*———. 1997. "Directions in Pentateuchal Studies." *CR: BS* 5: 43–65.

Ricoeur, Paul. 1967. *The Symbolism of Evil*. Boston: Beacon.

Rieu, D. C. H. 1991. *Homer: The Odyssey*. London: Penguin Books.

Robbins, Vernon K. 1996. *The Tapestry of Early Christian Discourse: Rhetoric, Society and Ideology*. London/New York: Routledge.

Robertson, D. 1976. "The Bible as Literature." *IDBSup*, 547–551.

———. 1977. *The Old Testament and the Literary Critic*. Guides to Biblical Scholarship. Philadephia: Fortress.

Rofé, Alexander. 1988 [Hebr 1986]. *The Prophetical Stories. The Narratives about the Prophets in the Hebrew Bible. Their Literary Types and History*. Jerusalem: Magnes.

Rogerson, J. 1991. *Genesis 1–11*. OT Guides. Sheffield, UK: Sheffield Academic.

Rollins, Wayne G. 1995. "Psychology, Hermeneutics and the Bible." In *Jung and the Interpretation of the Bible*, ed. David L. Miller. New York: Continuum, 9–39.

* Römer, Thomas and Albert de Pury. 1996. "L'historiographie deutéronomiste (HD). Histoire de la recherche et enjeu du debat." In *Israël construit son histoire: L'historiographie deutéronomiste à la lumière des recherches récentes*, ed. T. Römer and A. de Pury. Geneva: Labor et Fides, 9–120.

Rosenberg, David, ed. 1996. *Genesis: As It Is Written. Contemporary Writers on Our First Stories*. San Francisco: Harper.

Rosenblatt, Naomi H. 1996. *Wrestling with Angels: What Genesis Teaches Us About Our Spiritual Identity, Sexuality and Personal Relationships*. New York: Delta.

Rothstein, Edward. 1996. "A Beginning Stripped of Awe." *New York Times* (Dec. 1): Section E, 5.

Rottzoll, Dirk U. 1994. *Rabbinischer Kommentar zum Buch Genesis*. Berlin: De Gruyter.

Roudiez, Leon S. 1980. "Introduction" to *Desire in Language: A Semiotic Approach to Literature and Art*, by Julia Kristeva. New York: Columbia University Press, 1–20.

Rudman, Dominic. 2001. "A Little Knowledge Is a Dangerous Thing: Crossing Forbidden Boundaries in Genesis 3–4." In *The Book of Genesis*, ed. A. Wénin, 461–466. See Wénin, ed.

Rulon-Miller, Nina. 1998. "Hagar: A Woman with an Attitude." In *The World of*

Genesis: Persons, Places, Perspectives, ed. P. R. Davies and David J. A. Clines. JSOTSup 257. Sheffield, UK: Sheffield Academic, 60–89.

Ruppert, Lothar. 1979. Review of E. Drewermann, *Strukturen des Bösen, Teil 1. BZ* 23: 116–120.

Rütersworden, Udo. 1993. *Dominium Terrae: Studien zur Genese einer alttestamentliche Stellung.* BZAW 215. Berlin/New York: De Gruyter.

Sacks, Robert D. 1990. *A Commentary on the Book of Genesis.* Ancient Near Eastern Texts and Studies 6. Lewiston, N.Y.: E. Mellen Press.

Sagan, Carl. 1977. *The Dragons of Eden: Speculations on the Evolution of Human Intelligence.* New York: Random House.

Samuelson, N. M. 1992. *The First Seven Days: A Philosophical Commentary on the Creation of Genesis.* South Florida Studies in the History of Judaism 61. Atlanta: Scholars.

Sancisi-Weerdenburg, Heleen. 1995. "Darius I and the Persian Empire." *CANE* II: 1035–1050.

Sancisi-Weerdenburg, Heleen, et al., eds. 1987–1994. *Achaemenid History.* Proceedings of the Achaemenid History Workshop. 8 vols. Leiden: Nederlands Institut voor het Nabije Oosten.

Sandmel, Samuel. 1978. *The Hebrew Scriptures: An Introduction to Their Literature and Religious Ideas.* New York: Oxford University Press.

Sarason, Richard S. 1981. "Towards a New Agendum for the Study of Rabbinic Midrashic Literature." In *Studies in Aggadah, Targum and Jewish Liturgy in Memory of Joseph Heinemann,* ed. E. Fleischer and J. J. Petuchowski. Jerusalem: Magnes, 55–73.

Sarna, Nahum M. 1981. "The Anticipatory Use of Information as a Literary Feature of the Genesis Narratives." In *The Creation of Sacred Literature,* ed. Richard E. Friedman. Berkeley: University of California Press, 76–82.

Sarna, Nahum M. 1989. *The JPS Torah Commentary: Genesis.* Philadelphia/New York/Jerusalem: Jewish Publication Society.

Sasson, Jack M. 1992. "Gilgamesh Epic." *ABD* II: 1024–1027.

Saunders, Chauncey. 1952. *An Introduction to Research in English Literary History.* New York: Macmillan.

Savage, Mary. 1980. "Literary Critical and Biblical Studies: A Rhetorical Analysis of the Joseph Narrative." In *Scripture in Context: Essays on the Comparative Method,* ed. Carl D. Evans et al. Pittsburg: Pickwick, 79–100.

Schatz, Werner. 1972. *Genesis 14: Eine Untersuchung.* EH. Bern: Herbert Lang; Frankfurt: Peter Lang.

Schmid, Hans H. 1976. *Der sogenannte Jahwist: Beobachtungen und Fragen zur Pentateuchforschung.* Zürich: Theologischer.

Schmitt, Hans-Christoph. 1972. *Elisa: Traditionsgeschichtliche Untersuchungen.* Gütersloh: Gerd Mohn.

Schnackenburg, Rudolf. 1982. *The Gospel According to St John.* Vol. III. New York: Crossroad.

Schofield, J. N. 1962. "Judges." *PCB,* 304–315.

Schweizer, Harald. 1974. *Elischa in den Kriegen: Literaturewissenschaftliche Untersuchung von 1 Kön 3; 6,8–23; 6:24–7:20.* SANT 37. Munich: Kösel.

Scullion, John J. 1992. *Genesis: A Commentary for Students, Teachers and Preachers.* Collegeville, Minn.: Liturgical.

Seebass, Horst. 1996. *Genesis I: Urgeschichte (1,1–11,26).* Neukirchen-Vluyn: Neukirchener.

———. 1997. *Genesis II/I: Vätergeschichte (11:27–22:24).* Neukirchen-Vluyn: Neukirchener.

Sheehy, Gail. 1974. *Passages: Predictable Crises of Adult Life.* New York: Dutton.

Sherman, E. J. 1992. "Egyptian Biographies." *ABD* II: 390–393.

Simon, Richard. 1678. *Histoire Critique du Vieux Testament.* 3 vols. Paris.

Ska, Jean-Louis. 1989. "Quelques remarques sur Pg et la dernière rédaction du Pentateuch." In *Le Pentateuch en Question,* ed. A. de Pury, 95–125. See De Pury, ed., 1989.

*———. 1994. "El relato del diluvio: Un relato sacerdotal y algunos fragmentos redaccionales posteriores." *EstBib* 52: 37–62.

*———. 1996. "Le Pentateuch: état de la recherche à partir de quelques récentes 'Introductions'." *Bib* 77: 245–265.

———. 2001. "Essai sur la nature et la signification du cycle d'Abraham (Gn 11,27–25,11)." In *The Book of Genesis,* ed. A. Wénin, 153–178. See Wénin, ed.

Skinner, J. 1910. *A Critical and Exegetical Commentary on Genesis.* ICC. New York: Charles Scribner's Sons.

Smend, Rudolf. 1975. "Der Biblische und der Historische Elia." In *Congress Volume: Edinburgh 1974.* VTSup 28. Leiden: Brill, 167–184.

Smith, Jonathan Z. 1990. *Drudgery Divine: On the Comparison of Early Christianities and the Religions of Late Antiquity.* Chicago: Chicago University Press.

Smith, Stephen G. 1988. *The Concept of the Spiritual: An Essay in First Philosophy.* Philadelphia: Temple University Press.

Soggin, J. Alberto. 1997. "Pison e Gihon: Observationi su due fiumi mitici nell' 'Eden'." In *Deuteronomy and Deuteronomic Literature,* ed. M. Vervenne and J. Lust. Fest. C. H. W. Brekelmans. BETL 133. Leuven: Leuven University/Peeters, 587–598.

Sparks, Allister. 1990. *The Mind of South Africa: The Story of the Rise and Fall of Apartheid.* London: Heinemann.

Speiser, E. A. 1955. "I Know Not the Day of My Death." *JBL* 74: 252–256.

———. 1962. "Ethnic Divisions of Man." *IDB* 3: 235–242.

Speiser, E. A. 1964. *Genesis: Introduction, Translation, Notes.* AB. Garden City, N.Y.: Doubleday.

Spina, Frank Anthony. 1998. "The 'Face of God'; Esau in Canonical Context." In *The quest for Context and Meaning: Studies in Biblical Intertextuality in Honor of James A. Sanders,* eds. C. A. Evans and S. Talmon. Leiden/New York/Köln: Brill, 3–25.

Sprinkle, Joe M. 1994. *"The Book of the Covenant": A Literary Approach.* JSOTSup 174. Sheffield, UK: Sheffield Academic.

Standaert, Benoit. 1978. *L'Evangile selon Marc: Composition et Genre Littéraire.* Brugge: Sint Andriesabdig.

Stanford, W. B. 1963. *The Ulysses Theme: A Study in the Adaptability of a Traditional Hero.* Ann Arbor: University of Michigan Press.

Steinbeck, John. 1939. *The Grapes of Wrath.* Harmondsworth, UK: Penguin.

Steinberg, Naomi. 1993. *Kinship and Marriage in Genesis: A Household Economics Perspective.* Minneapolis: Fortress.

Steindl, Helmut. 1989. *Genugtuung. Biblisches Versöhnungsdenken—eine Quelle für Anselms Satisfakionstheorie?* Studia Friburgensia Neue Folge 71. Freiburg Schweiz: Universitätsverlag.

Steiner, George. 1971. *In Bluebeard's Castle: Some Notes Towards the Definition of Culture.* London/Boston: Faber & Faber, 1971.

———. 1975. *After Babel. Aspects of Language and Translation.* New York/London: Oxford University Press.

Steinmetz, D. 1986. "Luther and the Ascent of Jacob's Ladder." *Church History* 55: 179–192.

Sternberg, Meir. 1985. *The Poetics of Biblical Narrative: Ideological Literature and the Drama of Reading.* Bloomington: Indiana University Press.

Stipp, Hermann-Josef. 1987. *Elischa—Propheten—Gottesmänner.* Münchener Universitätsschriften. St. Ottilien: EOS.

Stock, Augustine. 1982. *Call to Discipleship: A Literary Study of Mark's Gospel.* Wilmington, Del.: Glazier.

———. 1989. *The Method and Message of Mark.* Wilmington, Del.: Glazier.

Stone, Michael E. 1992. *A History of the Literature of Adam and Eve.* SBL: Early Judaism and Its Literature, 3. Atlanta: Scholars.

Taylor, D. J. 1999. "Ready steady write . . ." *The Guardian,* October 29, 1999, 5.

Teugels, Lieve. 1996. " 'A Strong Woman, Who Can Find?' A Study of Characterization in Genesis 24, with Some Perspectives on the General Presentation of Isaac and Rebekah in the Genesis Narratives." In *The Pentateuch: A Sheffield Reader,* ed. John W. Rogerson. Sheffield, UK: Sheffield Academic, 281–295. Reprinted from *JSOT* 63 (1994): 89–104.

Thiel, Winfried. 1991. "Deuteronomistische Redaktionsarbeit in den Elia-Erzälungen." In *Congress Volume Leuven 1989.* VTSup 43. Leiden: Brill, 148–171.

*———. 1994. "Alttestamentliche Forschung in Sammelbänden." *TRu* 58: 1–40.

Thompson, Thomas L. 1974. *The Historicity of the Patriarchal Narratives: The Quest for the Historical Abraham.* Berlin: De Gruyter.

Tigay, Jeffrey H. 1982. *The Evolution of the Gilgamesh Epic.* Philadelphia: University of Pennsylvania Press.

Toynbee, Arnold J. 1950. *Greek Historical Thought: From Homer to the Age of Heraclius.* Introduction and translation by A. J. Toynbee. Boston: Beacon.

Trible, Phyllis. 1978. *God and the Rhetoric of Sexuality.* Philadephia: Fortress.

*———. 1994. *Rhetorical Criticism: Context, Method and the Book of Jonah.* Fortress: Minneapolis.

———. 1995. "Exegesis for Storytellers and Other Strangers." *JBL* 114: 3–19.

———. 1996. "The Test: A Conversation by Trible *et al* on Genesis 22." In *Genesis: A Living Conversation,* ed. Bill Moyers. New York/London: Doubleday, 219–247.

Tsumura, David T. 1989. *The Earth and the Waters in Genesis 1 and 2: A Linguistic Investigation.* JSOTSup 83. Sheffield: Sheffield Academic.

————. 1994. "Genesis and Ancient Near Eastern Stories of Creation and Flood." In *I Studied Inscriptions*, ed. R. Hess and D. T. Tsumura, 27–57. See Hess, R. and D. T. Tsumura, eds. 1994.

————. 1994a. "The Earth in Genesis 1." In *I Studied Inscriptions*, ed. R. Hess and D. T. Tsumura, 310–328. See Hess, R. and D. T. Tsumura, eds. 1994.

Tuplin, C. 1991. "Darius' Suez Canal and Persian Imperialism." In *Achaemenid History VI. Asia Minor and Egypt: Old Cultures in a New Empire*, ed. Heleen Sancisi-Weerdenburg et al. Proceedings of the 1988 Achaemenid History Workshop. Leiden: Nederlands Instituut voor het Nabije Oosten, 237–283.

Tyrrell, William Blake, and Frieda S. Brown. 1991. *Athenians, Myths and Institutions: Words in Action*. New York/Oxford: Oxford University Press.

Van Seters, John. 1975. *Abraham in History and Tradition*. New Haven/London: Yale University Press.

————. 1983. *In Search of History: Historiography in the Ancient World and the Origins of Biblical History*. New Haven/London: Yale University Press.

————. 1992. *Prologue to History: The Yahwist as Historian in Genesis*. Louisville, Ky.: Westminster/John Knox.

————. 1994. "The Theology of the Yahwist: A Preliminary Sketch." In *"Wer ist wie du, HERR, unter den Göttern?" Studien zur Theologie und Religionsgeschichte für Otto Kaiser zum 70. Geburtstag.*, ed. Ingo Kottsieper et al. Göttingen: Vandenhoeck & Ruprecht, 219–228.

————. 1994a. *The Life of Moses: The Yahwist as Historian in Exodus-Numbers*. Kampen: Kok Pharos.

————. 1998. "Some Comments on a Recent Literary 'Discovery': A Response to Richard Eliott Friedman." *RSN* 13 (Nov): 7.

————. 1999. *The Pentateuch. A Social Science Commentary*. Trajectories. Sheffield: Sheffield Academic.

Van Wolde, Ellen. 1994. *Words Become Worlds: Semantic Studies of Genesis 1–11*. BIS 6. Leiden/New York/Cologne: Brill.

————. 1997. *Stories of the Beginning: Genesis 1–11 and Other Creation Stories*. Ridgefield, Conn.: Morehouse.

Vawter, Bruce. 1977. *On Genesis: A New Reading*. Garden City, N.Y.: Doubleday.

Vernant, Jean-Pierre. 1982 [Fr 1962]. *The Origins of Greek Thought*. Ithaca, N.Y.: Cornell University Press.

Vervenne, Marc. 2001. "Genesis 1,1–2,4: The Compositional Nature of the Priestly Overture to the Pentateuch." In *The Book of Genesis*, ed. A. Wénin, 35–70. See Wénin, ed.

Visotzky, Burton L. 1996. *The Genesis of Ethics*. New York: Crown.

Voegelin, Eric. 1956. *Order and History. Vol 1. Israel and Revelation*. Baton Rouge: Louisiana State University Press.

Vogels, Walter. 1997. "The Cultic and Civic Calendars of the Fourth Day of Creation (Gen 1,14b)." *SJOT* 11: 163–180.

Vogelsang, Willem. 1990. "The Achaemenids and India." In *Achaemenid History IV. Centre and Periphery*, ed. Heleen Sancisi-Weerdenburg et al. Proceedings of the 1986 Achaemenid History Workshop. Leiden: Nederlands Instituut voor het Nabije Oosten, 93–110.

Von Balthasar, Hans Urs. 1986. *The Glory of the Lord: A Theological Aesthetics. Vol. III. Studies in Theological Style: Lay Styles.* Edinburgh: T & T Clark.

———. 1992. *Theo-drama: Theological Dramatic Theory. Vol. III. The Dramatis Personae: The Person in Christ.* San Francisco: Ignatius.

Von Rad, Gerhard. 1962. *Old Testament Theology.* 2 vols. New York: Harper & Row.

Von Rad, Gerhard. 1972. *Genesis: A Commentary.* Philadelphia: Westminster.

Waddell, W. G. 1940. *Manetho. With an English Translation.* Loeb Classical Library. Cambridge, Mass.: Harvard University Press; London: Heinemann.

Wahl, Harald Martin. 1997. *Die Jacoberzählungen. Studien zu ihren mündlichen Über-lieferung, Verschriftung, und Historität.* BZAW 258. Berlin/New York: De Gruyter.

Walcot, Peter. 1966. *Hesiod and the Near East.* Cardiff: University of Wales.

Walker, Henry J. 1995. *Theseus and Athens.* New York/Oxford: Oxford University Press.

Wallace, W., trans. 1892. *The Logic of Hegel.* Translated from *The Encyclopedia of Philosophical Sciences.* 2nd ed. London: Oxford University Press.

Walsh, Jerome T. 1977. "Genesis 2:4b–3:24: A Synchronic Approach." *JBL* 96: 161–177.

———. 1982. *The Elijah Cycle: A Synchronic Approach.* Ph.D. diss., University of Michigan.

———. 1996. *I Kings.* Berit Olam. Collegeville, Minn.: Liturgical.

* Watson, Duane F., and Alan J. Hauser. 1994. *Rhetorical Criticism of the Bible: A Comprehensive Bibliography with Notes on History and Method.* BIS 4. Leiden/ New York/Cologne: Brill.

Watt, Trevor. 1995. "Joseph's Dreams." In *Jung and the Interpretation of the Bible,* ed. David L. Miller. New York: Continuum, 55–70.

Webb, B. G. 1987. *The Book of Judges: An Integrated Reading.* JSOTSup 46. Sheffield, UK: JSOT.

Webb, Eugene. 1981. *Eric Voegelin: Philosopher of History.* Seattle/London: University of Washington Press.

*Weippert, Helga. 1985. "Das deuteronomistische Geschichtswerk: Sein Ziel und Ende in der nereren Forschung." *TRu* 50: 213–249.

Wellek, R., and A. Warren. 1962. *Theory of Literature.* 3rd ed. New York/London: Harcourt Brace Jovanovich.

Wellhausen, Julius. 1883. *Prologomena zur Geschichte Israels.* Reprinted 1927: Berlin/Leipzig: De Gruyter. Eng. trans. reprinted 1957: *Prologomena to the History of Ancient Israel.* Meridian Books. Cleveland/New York: World Publishing Company.

———. 1899. *Die Composition des Hexateuchs und der historischen Bücher des Alten Testaments.* 3d ed. (First published in article form, 1876–1878). Reprinted as 4th ed. Berlin: De Gruyter, 1963.

Wenham, Gordon. J. 1978. "The Coherence of the Flood Narrative." *VT* 28: 336–348.

———. 1990. "Contemporary Bible Commentary: The Primacy of Exegesis and the Religious Dimension." In *Proceedings of the Tenth World Congress of Jewish*

Studies. Jerusalem, August 16–24, 1989, ed. David Assaf. Jerusalem: World Union of Jewish Studies/Magnes, 1–12.

———. 1994 [Reprint from 1986]. "Sanctuary Symbolism in the Garden of Eden Story." In *I Studied Inscriptions*, ed. R. Hess and D. T. Tsumura, 399–404. See Hess R. and D. T. Tsumura, eds. 1994.

*———. 1996. "Pentateuchal Studies Today." *Them* 22: 3–13.

Wenham, Gordon J. 1987. Vol. I: *Genesis 1–15*. Word Bible Commentary. Waco, Tex.: Word Books.

———. 1994. Vol. II: *Genesis 16–50*. Word Bible Commentary. Waco, Tex.: Word Books.

Wénin, André. 1998. "Abram et Saraï en Égypte (Gn 12,10–20) ou la place de Saraï dans l'élection." *Revue théologique de Louvain* 29: 433–456.

———. 1998a. "Eve: quand la femme se laisse dire . . ." *Chemins de femmes. Les Cahiers de Paraboles* 4: 7–23.

———. 1999. "Adam et Eve: la jalousie de Caïn, 'semence' de serpent: Un aspect du récit mythique de Genèse 1–4." *Revue des sciences réligieuses* 73: 3–16.

———. 2001. "La question de l'humain et l'unité du livre de la Genèse." In *The Book of Genesis*, ed. Wénin, 3–34. See Wénin, ed.

———. ed. 2001. *The Book of Genesis*. BETL. Leuven: Leuven University/Peeters, forthcoming.

West, M. L. 1985. *The Hesiodic Catalogue of Women: Its Nature, Structure and Origins*. Oxford: Clarendon.

*Westermann, Claus. 1984/1985/1987. *Genesis: A Commentary*. 3 vols. London: SPCK. Bibliographies: 1984/1985/1987, passim. Reviews of research: 1984, 567–574; 1985, 86.

Westermann, Claus. 1974. *Creation*. Philadephia: Fortress.

———. 1980. *The Promises to the Fathers: Studies on the Patriarchal Narratives*. Philadelphia: Fortress.

———. 1996 [Ger 1990]. *Joseph: Eleven Bible Studies on Genesis*. Minneapolis: Fortress.

White, H. C. 1991. *Narration and Discourse in the Book of Genesis*. Cambridge/New York: Cambridge University Press.

*Whybray, R. N. 1987. *The Making of the Pentateuch: A Methodological Study*. JSOT Sup 53. Sheffield, UK: Sheffield.

———. 1995. *Introduction to the Pentateuch*. Grand Rapids, Mich.: Eerdmans.

———. 1996. "What Do We Know About Ancient Israel?" *ExpT* 108: 71–74.

Wilford, John Noble. 1996. "2.3-Million-Year-Old Jaw Extends Human Family." *New York Times* (Nov. 19): 1, and Section C, 5.

Wilson, Robert R. 1975. "The Old Testament Genealogies in Recent Research." *JBL* 94: 169–189.

———. 1977. *Genealogy and History in the Biblical World*. New Haven: Yale University Press.

———. 1984. *Sociological Approaches to the Old Testament*. Guides to Biblical Scholarship. Philadelphia: Fortress.

Wittenberg, Gunther H. 1988. *King Solomon and the Theologians*. Pietermaritzburg: University of Natal.

Yamauchi, Edwin M. 1996. *Persia and the Bible.* Grand Rapids, Mich.: Baker.

Young, T. C. et al. 1981. "History of Iran." *Encyclopedia Britannica* 9: 529–562.

Younger, K. Lawson, Jr. 1990. *Ancient Conquest Accounts: A Study in Ancient Near Eastern and Biblical History Writing.* JSOTSup 98. Sheffield, UK: Sheffield Academic.

Zornberg, A. G. 1995. *Genesis: The Beginning of Desire.* Philadelphia/Jerusalem: Jewish Publication Society.

INDEX TO MODERN AUTHORS

SUBJECT INDEX